FOOD IN
THE ANCIENT WORLD
FROM A TO Z

THE ANCIENT WORLD FROM A TO Z

What were the ancient fashions in men's shoes? How did you cook a tunny or spice a dormouse? What was the daily wage of a Syracusan builder? What did Romans use for contraception?

This new Routledge series will provide the answers to such questions, which are often overlooked by standard reference works. Volumes will cover key topics in ancient culture and society – from food, sex and sport to money, dress and domestic life.

Each author will be an acknowledged expert in their field, offering readers vivid, immediate and academically sound insights into the fascinating details of daily life in antiquity. The main focus will be on Greece and Rome, though some volumes will also encompass Egypt and the Near East.

The series will be suitable both as background for those studying classical subjects and as enjoyable reading for anyone with an interest in the ancient world.

Already published:

Food in the Ancient World from A to Z
Andrew Dalby

Forthcoming titles:

Sex in the Ancient World from A to Z
John Younger

Sport in the Ancient World from A to Z
Mark Golden

Birds in the Ancient World from A to Z
Geoffrey Arnott

Money in the Ancient World from A to Z
Andrew Meadows

Domestic Life in the Ancient World from A to Z
Ruth Westgate and Kate Gilliver

Dress in the Ancient World from A to Z
Lloyd Llewellyn Jones *et al.*

FOOD IN THE ANCIENT WORLD FROM A TO Z

Andrew Dalby

Routledge
Taylor & Francis Group

LONDON AND NEW YORK

First published 2003
by Routledge
11 New Fetter Lane, London EC4P 4EE

Simultaneously published in the USA and Canada
by Routledge
29 West 35th Street, New York, NY 10001

Routledge is an imprint of the Taylor & Francis Group

© 2003 Andrew Dalby

Typeset in Sabon by Taylor & Francis Books
Printed and bound in Great Britain by TJ International Ltd,
Padstow, Cornwall

British Library Cataloguing in Publication Data
A catalogue record for this book is available from the British Library

Library of Congress Cataloging in Publication Data
Dalby, Andrew, 1947–
Food in the ancient world, A–Z / Andrew Dalby.
p.cm.
Includes bibliographical references and index.
ISBN 0–415–23259–7
1. Food habits–Greece–History. 2. Food habits–Rome–History. 3. Drinking
customs–Greece–History. 4. Drinking customs–Rome–History.
5. Greece–Social life and customs. 6. Rome–Social life and customs.
7. Civilization, Classical. I. Title.
GT2853.G8 D35 20003
394.1′2′0938–dc21

ISBN 0–415–23259–7

Contents

Illustrations

Figures

Maps

Postscript

Not long ago Erika Simon asked me why I follow the traditional practice of Latinising the spelling of Greek proper names. I answered that I did it, and I considered it justifiable, only because it was the current practice of all major reference books in English (see p. xiv). This is about to change: the forthcoming Cambridge Guide to Classical Civilization will adopt spellings that are transliterated directly from Greek. In future books I will follow that system, and I urge others who write about ancient Greece in English to do the same.

When drawing the pictures and verifying the scientific names I used two books not listed in the bibliography (Lars Jonsson, Birds of Europe [London: Christopher Helm, 1992]; Peter S. Maitland, Guide to Freshwater Fish of Britain and Europe [London: Hamlyn, 2000. 2nd ed.]). My thanks also to the websites that I consulted at that stage, notably www.fishbase.org, www.itis.usda.gov and www.scs.leeds.ac.uk/pfaf.

I want to thank Richard Stoneman and his colleagues at Routledge for their enthusiastic support throughout this project – and Richard himself for the original idea. For me, this book is a stage in a long journey through adjacent regions of classics, historical linguistics, food history and bibliography. Many people have helped me to cross the frontiers between these territories. I can't acknowledge them all, so I limit myself to thanking John Wilkins and Alan Davidson for help of various kinds over many years.

79120 Saint-Coutant, France

20 March 2003

Introduction

The subject

In this book you will find entries for significant foods, drinks and aromas of archaic and classical Greece, of the Hellenistic Greek states and of the Roman Empire. You will find entries for authors who wrote works in classical Greek and Latin bearing directly on food, wine, dining and drinking, whether or not their writings survive. You will find entries for aspects of the Greek and Roman world that are relevant to food and dining.

The focus is firmly on the classical Mediterranean. This is an excellent unit of study, since the cultures of classical Greece and Rome influenced one another over many centuries, and both have influenced our own. But you cannot ignore what lay beyond, both in time and space. So there is some information here on food and drink in the ancient Near East – the cultures of Egypt, the east end of the Mediterranean and Mesopotamia. There is some information also on food of the prehistoric Mediterranean. On topics such as these that are on the edge of the main subject of this book, you will find relatively less information given directly in the entries; you will need to make more use of the bibliographical references.

Not everyone is familiar with the traditional designations for periods of classical history. Here they are as I use them in this book.

- 'Prehistory' means simply 'before history': that is, before written historical records begin in each region. In Greece, prehistory may be said to end in the eighth century BC.
- By the 'classical period', when speaking of the Mediterranean as a whole, I mean the seventh century BC to the fifth century AD.
- Mycenaean Greece – fourteenth and thirteenth centuries BC.
- Archaic Greece – seventh and sixth centuries BC.
- Classical Greece – fifth and fourth centuries BC.
- Ancient Near East – to fourth century BC.
- Pre-dynastic Egypt – to late fourth millennium BC.
- Pharaonic Egypt – late fourth millennium to fourth century BC.
- Hellenistic Greece and Near East – third, second and first centuries BC.

- Ptolemaic Egypt – third, second and first centuries BC.
- Republican Rome – sixth to first centuries BC.
- Roman Empire – first to fifth centuries AD.
- Late antiquity – fourth to sixth centuries AD.
- Byzantine Empire – sixth to fifteenth centuries AD.

The coverage of this book ends at around AD 500. The latest specialised authors who are regularly cited are Anthimus (writing in northern Gaul about 520) and Aetius, a Byzantine court physician of the early sixth century. Later Byzantine and medieval European sources are very rarely cited here, and only if they provide some evidence about the classical period.

This book and beyond

The principal aims of this book are to identify and define relevant terms in English and to guide you to study materials in English. Serious study requires you to look beyond this book and beyond English. Some specific points:

- One of the reasons underlying the selection of bibliographical references in this book is that these works themselves often contain good bibliographies. Be aware of this opportunity to pursue further insights.
- An ever-growing quantity of information is available on the Web. Don't overlook it – but be critical of it. Web pages often lack source references. Often they have not undergone revision and peer-review processes, while published academic books and articles usually have.
- If you can read German you should as a matter of course consult relevant articles in the great classical encyclopaedia known as 'Pauly–Wissowa' (*RE* 1893–1972) and, when relevant, other big German encyclopaedias listed in the first part of the general bibliography. You can make some use of them even if you don't read German well, because often these articles give extremely comprehensive references to ancient texts and fairly complete guidance (up to the date of compilation) to modern scholarship also. Articles in the one-volume *Oxford Classical Dictionary* (*OCD* 1996) are more up to date and have good bibliographies.
- When pursuing references to Hippocrates, Theophrastus, Cato, Columella, Pliny, Palladius, Porphyry – and many others too, but these seven examples are especially important in the food context – if you can read French you should look at the good annotated editions of these authors in the Budé series (*CUF* in the second part of the general bibliography).

Using classical sources

At the end of nearly every article in this book, classical sources are cited in rough chronological order. This leaves you, the reader, to judge the nature of each source and, on that basis, its reliability in providing the evidence that you need. If it is important as a source of information to you, use the guidance on these topics offered by recent scholars who have worked on the author: it may help to start from the introduction to a recent edition, commentary or translation, or from an entry in OCD 1996.

Although English translations exist for most of the Greek and Latin texts cited here, you should read classical sources in Latin and Greek if you can. Translators take different views over all sorts of questions; sometimes they take a demonstrably wrong view. You have to try to be independent of them.

I have very occasionally said that an ancient text is 'confused'. This means that the author is describing something at second hand and has made serious errors; it doesn't mean that all other sources are free of confusion.

It is often necessary to consider whether an ancient author may be making fun of the reader (which means us). The following example is suggested by Frank Frost's useful paper 'Sausage and meat preservation in antiquity' in *Greek, Roman and Byzantine Studies* vol. 40 (1999) pp. 241–52. In his 'lexicon of sausage terminology' (p. 249) Frost says of *physkai*: 'At Sparta they were nailed to the walls for old men to eat, according to a comedy by Cratinus (Athenaeus 138e).' Follow up the reference, as Frost gives you the means to do. You will find that Cratinus's speaker is not making a statement but asking a question: 'Is it true, as people say, that all comers are well feasted at Spartan dinners, and that in their public-houses sausages hang from nails for their old men to snap at with their teeth?' You are free to conclude that the reply, not quoted by Athenaeus, was 'Yes and no.'

This book guides you to many ancient recipes, and to some modern interpretations of them (see RECIPES). Nothing in this book guarantees the safety in modern nutrition of the things the Greeks and Romans used to eat, or of their methods of preparation. When dealing with ancient recipes and menus the modern cook must rethink them with food safety in mind. Romans liked the sweet flavour imparted by lead channels to water and by lead vessels to sauces, but you would do best not to follow their example. Fish sauces, made the way the Greeks and Romans used to make them, probably contain carcinogens: this is one reason why you would do best not to imitate the ancient method but to buy southeast Asian fish sauce (vegetarians, for whom a similar sauce was made from pears in ancient times, may wish to substitute soy sauce).

Using modern scholarship

When working on a cross-disciplinary subject such as food history, you need to know where an author is coming from. A scientist? Scientists can't be assumed to understand how to handle historical evidence critically. A food writer? Some food writers and journalists treat history as padding, and keep their fingers crossed behind their backs when making historical statements. A linguist? An archaeologist? These two disciplines sometimes appear not to be on speaking terms. A historian? Some historians are able to focus on a narrow band of evidence, and to follow a traditional interpretation of it, sometimes to the exclusion of common sense. All these generalisations of mine are (of course) tendentious, unfair and prejudiced.

Common sense, if you feel the lack of it, can be restored by a judicious use of comparative evidence. All the above disciplines use comparative evidence, though they may disapprove of its use by others. The following example is suggested by Heleen Sancisi-Weerdenburg's paper, 'Persian food: stereotypes and political identity' in *Food in Antiquity* ed. John Wilkins and others (Exeter: Exeter University Press, 1995) pp. 286–302.

Did the young Persians eat 'turpentine wood'? It appears so from B. Perrin's translation of Plutarch's *Life of Artoxerxes* section 3.2 (Plutarch, *Parallel Lives* tr. B. Perrin, vol. 11 [*LCL*, 1926]. You might say, 'We don't eat turpentine wood, therefore the Persians didn't.' This is an invalid argument: if you used the same argument to decide whether Greeks ate cicadas your conclusion would be wrong. But you might, after investigation, say, 'No humans anywhere can be shown to eat turpentine wood, therefore the Persians probably didn't.' This is a valid use of comparative evidence. It is not conclusive but it should impel you to look hard at the source of the dubious information.

This is where you gain if you can be independent of translators (see above). Does the error (if that is what it is) lie with Plutarch or with his translator? You won't know until you look at the Greek words. You will then find that the word *terminthos* means not exclusively the wood but also the fruit or nut of the tree (which is more often called terebinth than turpentine, incidentally) and that people in the Near East do indeed gather and eat its tiny oil-rich fruits; if you have travelled in the region you may well have seen them on sale at street stalls. Common sense assists you to the conclusion that Perrin has indeed made an error and that the young Persians ate terebinth fruits, not terebinth wood (other sources concur with Plutarch; see PERSIANS for a further twist to the argument).

Does it matter? It would be wrong to dismiss this as an antiquarian detail. You may be working on the history of nutrition and intending to judge the food value of the adolescent Persian diet; you may be working on social history and hoping to estimate the unlucky youngsters' need to hunt meat to enliven their rations; you may be a structural anthropologist, semanticising the diets of ephebes and gerontocrats. Whichever you are, you need to know whether this, claimed to be one of two major items in the diet of an age cohort of Persians, is a worthless 'non-food' (to borrow the convenient terminology of Peter Garnsey in *Food and Society in Classical Antiquity* [Cambridge: Cambridge University Press, 1999]) or whether it is a nutritious, oil-rich staple.

And, by the way, there are hardly any statistics in this book, nutritional or otherwise. This is because in ancient history there are practically no statistical data sufficiently reliable and representative to stand in a reference book. You will find useful collections of information on the Roman period in R.P. Duncan-Jones, *The Economy of the Roman Empire: Quantitative Studies* (Cambridge, 1982). For attempts to quantify ancient nutritional matters see the works listed under NUTRITION. The nutritional qualities of individual foodstuffs, as determined by modern research, can easily be found on the Internet: see for example the USDA

Nutrient Database, http://www.nal.usda.gov/fnic/cgi-bin/nut_search.pl. Such information is not included in the entries in this book because its applicability to ancient nutrition is not a simple question. Varieties differ from those farmed two thousand years ago; climates and farming methods differ; preparation and conserving methods differ. Access to food supplies varied with age, sex, class and geographical location, and we cannot be precise about the variation. Consider these problems when using quantitative data on nutrition: they will seriously affect the results.

How to use this book

References to classical sources

Whenever an ancient source is referred to briefly in the text of an article, a complete reference will be found at the end of that article.

Whenever an ancient book title is abridged to one or two upper-case letters (thus: Dioscorides *MM* 2.167) you will find a corresponding entry in this dictionary under the author's name: that entry will explain the abbreviated title and will give some information on editions and translations. In such entries, *LCL* refers to a text and English translation in the *Loeb Classical Library*, now published by Harvard University Press, Cambridge, Mass. *CUF* refers to a text and French translation in the *Collection des universités de France* ('Budé series'), published by Les Belles Lettres, Paris. *BT* refers to a Greek or Latin text (without translation) in the *Bibliotheca Teubneriana*, formerly published by B.G. Teubner, Leipzig and Stuttgart, now published by K.G. Saur, Munich.

Such entries have only been made for texts that are directly concerned with food and wine, dining and drinking. Other ancient texts can be tracked down through library catalogues and reference sources. Especially useful are the *Oxford Classical Dictionary* (see *OCD* 1996 in the first part of the general bibliography) and the 'Canon of Greek authors and works' to be found on the CD-ROM of the *Thesaurus Linguae Graecae*.

A reference thus: Athenaeus *E* 38f–39b citing Alcman 42 Davies, means that there is other information in Athenaeus in addition to the Alcman fragment. A reference thus: Alcman 42 Davies [Athenaeus *E* 38f–39b], means that there is no other information in Athenaeus, but some readers may find the passage easier to consult in an edition of Athenaeus than among the fragments of Alcman.

The abbreviation '*al.*' (*et alibi*, also elsewhere) means that a selection has been made among several equally relevant references in a particular author's works.

The abbreviation '*s.v.l.*' (*si vera lectio*, if the reading is correct) is intended as a warning that there is doubt over a manuscript text, or a usually accepted emendation, which provides important evidence.

References to specific editions

Wherever possible, references to ancient sources adopt standard section numbering as found in most current editions and translations. If confusion is likely because section numbering varies between editions, an editor's name is added.

The abbreviation '*ad l.*' (*ad locum*, on this passage) with an editor's name, means that, in conjunction with the ancient text just cited, there is useful guidance in the named editor's footnote or commentary on the text.

In these two cases, editions are referred to by the surname of the first-named editor alone. If the work concerned is a collection of fragmentary Greek or Latin texts, you will find full details of it in the third part of the general bibliography. If the name is not there, you will be able to find the edition concerned in a library catalogue under the name of the relevant ancient author. More recent editions than the one cited will usually either follow the same numbering or provide a concordance.

References to modern scholarship

Further details of modern works listed in the text of an article by the author's surname alone (thus: Grant p. 28) will be found in the references at the end of that article. Details of works listed by author and date (thus: Casson 1989 p. 32) will be found in the final part of the general bibliography.

The abbreviation *ib.* means 'in the same volume just cited'.

Cross-references

Notice the cross-references between articles, which are in small capitals. If you want to check on any details linked to a cross-reference, you will need to follow up the cross-reference and look at the citations there of ancient sources and modern scholarship.

For an example see the article ACCULTURATION, which mentions 'the symposia of ALEXANDER THE GREAT'. If you want to find out more about these symposia, you must consult the article ALEXANDER THE GREAT. Relevant citations will be found at the end of that article.

Greek and Latin terms

Greek proper names are generally given in the Latinised forms which are traditional in English scholarship. This is done to help readers who do not know Greek and may need to go from this book to other reference books and catalogues in English: most of these use the same system.

All Greek words except proper names appear in the articles in their Greek form, but in Roman script.

These two conventions will not inconvenience those who know Greek. Both for proper names and for other words you can verify the true Greek form in the Greek index.

Classical names for foods and food species are given selectively. These are the names that were in general use, as demonstrated by ancient written usage (and, where relevant, by medieval descendants of the ancient words). You can find additional and alternative terms by consulting the lexica (ancient and modern) and the texts of ancient authors who are interested in terminology, notably Dioscorides, Pliny, Galen and Athenaeus.

Certain technical terms in Greek and Latin – including the names of many fish, wild plants, and foods – had no standard spelling. I have usually not attempted to show the full extent of the variation, but have chosen a single representative form. If you wish to explore linguistic forms further you will need to use editions of Greek and Latin texts with a good 'apparatus' (footnotes showing manuscript variation) ... where such editions exist.

Identification of foods

Entries for plants and animals which are the sources of foodstuffs are, wherever possible, under English names.

I have occasionally commented on misleading translations and misused terms, and perhaps it is worth pointing out here that there are a lot of them about. Translators of Greek and Latin texts use terms such as 'pumpkin', 'marrow', 'squash', 'kidney bean', 'French bean', 'costmary', though the accepted opinion is that these species were unknown in the classical world. Archaeologists carelessly describe terebinth fruits from the prehistoric Mediterranean as 'pistachio', thus confusing the history of the *Pistacia* genus, a history that is well recorded and, when properly interpreted, helps to explain their archaeological finds. Historians sometimes say 'cardamon' or 'cardamum' for Greek *kardamon*, for which the accurate translation is 'cress'. Other misleading translations such as 'ripe cucumber' (for *sikyos pepon*, 'melon'), once enshrined in a standard reference book, seem to live on for ever. Those who care about real history want to get these little things right; I have tried to do so here, which means that I will be really grateful to those who point out my errors.

Some problems of identification are really difficult (see also the entry NAMES AND IDENTIFICATIONS). Pending a fortunate archaeological find we cannot be sure of the source of ancient cinnamon, or of the species represented by Latin *amomum*, because the ancient written evidence in both cases is contradictory and inconclusive. There is a real problem, which archaeobotany has not yet been able to solve, about when cucumber became known in the ancient Mediterranean; there are similar problems about chicken and about sesame. Other perceived difficulties are in fact easily solved. On Greek *bolboi*, Latin *bulbi*, J. Jouanna wrote: 'Les érudits discutent encore sur l'identification de ce bulbe' (on Hippocrates, *Epidemics* 7.101 [p. 253 n. 7]). C. Hünemörder, who undertook to write the article on *bolbos* in *Der neue Pauly* (Stuttgart: Metzler, 1996–)

fulfilled his task without ever becoming aware that *bolbos* is the name of a specific plant. Hünemörder, along with Jouanna's *érudits*, must never have visited Greece, where *volví* (the bulbs of grape-hyacinth, *Muscari comosum*) are still grown for food, are sold at food markets and are served as an appetiser or meze: see Aglaia Kremezi, *The Foods of the Greek Islands* (New York: Houghton Mifflin, 2000) p. 18. As observed by Mark Grant in *Roman Cookery: Ancient Recipes for Modern Kitchens* (London: Serif, 1999), in southern Italy the same species is familiar as *lampascioni* and has not quite lost its ancient reputation as an aphrodisiac.

There is no magical way of making identifications certain. If ancient sources offer just a few mentions, and no full description, identification may begin with a process of elimination and fizzle out in guesswork. Therefore, uncertainty should be read into all such identifications given below.

Scientific Latin names

A short paragraph at the end of nearly all main entries on plant and animal foods supplies botanical and zoological names and classical Latin and Greek names (see above).

The scientific names given in the entries are, I hope, those currently in most favour among taxonomists and archaeobiologists. When two or more species from the same genus are listed in sequence, the first element of the name is given once in full and thereafter, in accordance with the usual convention, abbreviated. There is a separate index of scientific names: in this index I have added the standard abbreviated names of authorities and also some cross-references from commonly encountered 'synonyms'. For a full explanation of the conventions adopted in botanical names see *International Code of Botanical Nomenclature (Saint Louis Code)* ed. W. Greuter and others (Königstein: Koeltz Scientific, 2000). It is usual to give the second element, the specific epithet, a lower-case initial. In this book, because the origins of the binomial names will be of interest to some readers, I have adopted (following the example of Liberty Hyde Bailey and Ethel Zoe Bailey, *Hortus Third: A Concise Dictionary of Plants Cultivated in the United States and Canada* [New York: Macmillan, 1976]) the alternative convention of giving an initial capital to the specific epithet when it is a noun – which means that it will normally have an origin independent of the generic name, and, often, a classical origin. For an explanation of the formation of words in botanical Latin and other details of this special language see William T. Stearn, *Botanical Latin* (London: Nelson, 1966).

A

Abate wine (Greek *Abates*) from vine-yards in Cilicia. Abate wine is said by Galen to be at once austere and sweet, 'thick' and black. Pliny lists *Cilicium* as the second finest type of PASSUM or raisin wine.

Pliny *NH* 14.81; Galen *VA* 99, *ST* 6.337, *SF* 11.648 (read *Abates*); Athenaeus *E* 33b.

Abstinence *see* FASTING; ASCETICISM

Acculturation, the more optimistic view of the phenomenon also described as 'culture clash'. Ancient descriptions of food behaviour often give evidence of misunderstandings and disputes caused by culture clash, whether the focus of the narrative is on boorish foreign visitors or on barbaric foreign hosts. A few topics relevant to Greek–Roman culture clash are hinted at by Plutarch, who remarks, for example, on the social difficulties of 'knowing' and inviting Romans to dinner:

> More recently, in entertaining foreigners, especially men of the leading class [i.e. Roman administrators], it became unavoidable – since one did not even know their followers and their favourites – to leave it to the guest to name [i.e. invite] them, merely specifying a number ... When it comes to relations with leaders and foreigners, there can be no naming, no selection: we simply must receive those who come along with them.

Historical texts give us some salient incidents, described more or less objectively depending on the author: the Persian ambassadors in Macedonia (fifth century BC); Xenophon in Thrace (400); the symposia of ALEXANDER THE GREAT (330–323); Verres at Lampsacus (mid first century BC). Literary evidence must be set beside archaeological. In its most obvious forms, archaeological evidence of acculturation consists of finds of (a) imported products and imported foods, (b) local products that imitate foreign styles and newly naturalised foods. In the period studied here, the cultures that most obviously influenced their neighbours were Phoenician (including Carthaginian), Persian, Greek and Roman.

Herodotus 5.18–5.20; Xenophon, *Anabasis* 7.3, *al.*; Cicero, *Against Verres* 2.1.66; Plutarch *QC* 1.3, 7.6, *al.*

G.G. Dannell, 'Eating and drinking in pre-conquest Britain: the evidence of amphora and Samian trading, and the effect of the invasion of Claudius' in *Invasion and Response* ed. B.C. Burnham and H.B. Burnham (Oxford: BAR, 1979) pp. 177–84; Louise Bruit and Pauline Schmitt-Pantel, 'Citer, classer, penser: à propos des repas des Grecs et des repas des autres dans le livre IV des *Deipnosophistes* d'Athénée' in *Aion* vol. 8 (1986) pp. 203–21; Karen Meadows, 'You are what you eat: diet, identity and Romanisation' in *Proceedings of the Fourth*

Annual Theoretical Roman Archaeology Conference ed. S. Cottam and others (Oxford: Oxbow, 1994) pp. 133–40; Mario Lombardo, 'Food and frontier in the Greek colonies of south Italy' in *Food in Antiquity* ed. John Wilkins and others (Exeter: Exeter University Press, 1995) pp. 256–72.

Acorn, fruit of the oak tree. Some species are bitter and inedible. Others, though typically regarded as food for pigs (as in the *Odyssey* and by Cato), are nutritious for humans when ground into flour and cooked to a mash. They served as winter food in Lusitania and in Asia Minor and as famine food no doubt elsewhere: see Strabo, Galen and Appian. Before the invention of agriculture, according to the myth of the GOLDEN AGE, acorns were among man's first foods. They were linked in cliché with the rustic lifestyle of ARCADIA: this region was inhabited by *balanephagoi andres* 'acorn-eaters' according to a Delphic oracle quoted by Herodotus.

Balanos in Greek, *glans* in Latin are the names for acorns in general, particularly those of the oak *Quercus Robur*; the Latin and Greek words have the same Indo-European origin. In Greek *akylos* is the acorn of the holm-oak, *Q. Ilex*, and *phegos* is the acorn of the Valonia oak, *Q. macrolepis*. All three of these trees are usually *drys* in Greek; in Latin they are *quercus*, *ilex* and *robur* respectively.

Homer, *Odyssey* 10.242 with Eustathius *ad l.*, 13.409; Hesiod *OD* 233 with West *ad l.*; Herodotus 1.66; Hippocrates *R* 55; Theophrastus *HP* 3.8; Lycophron, *Alexandra* 479–83; Cato *DA* 54.1, cf. 1.7; Lucretius 5.939; Strabo 3.3.7, 15.3.18; Ovid, *Fasti* 4.395–402; Dioscorides *MM* 1.106; Pliny *NH* 16.1–25; Pausanias 8.1.6 with Levi *ad l.*; Plutarch *EC* 993f; Galen *AF* 6.620–1, *BM* 6.777–8; Appian, *Civil War* 1.50; Athenaeus *E* 53d–54d.

Buck 1949 pp. 528–32; Zohary and Hopf 1993 pp. 195–6; Sarah Mason, 'Acornutopia?' in *Food in Antiquity* ed. John Wilkins and others (Exeter: Exeter University Press, 1995) pp. 12–24.

- Beech-mast, the comparable fruit of the beech, is discussed by Pliny. According to him it was once used as famine food in

Chios. It really can be used as food. But Pliny sometimes confuses Latin *fagus* 'beech' with Greek *phegos* 'Valonia oak', owing to the obvious relationship between the two words, and he may have done so in this case. The beech tree, *Fagus sylvatica* and *F. orientalis*, is *oxye* in Greek, *fagus* in Latin.

Pliny *NH* 16.16.

Acraephia, small city in Boeotia, origin of a fragmentary inscription of the second century BC listing about fifty sea fish and their market prices. Prices are generally given in *oboloi* (and fractions) per *mna*, roughly 0.75 kg.

François Salviat and C. Vatin, *Inscriptions de Grèce centrale* (Paris, 1971) pp. 95–109; D.M. Schaps, 'Small change in Boeotia' in *Zeitschrift für Papyrologie und Epigraphik* vol. 69 (1987) pp. 293–6.

Adonis, in Greek mythology the lover of Aphrodite and child of Smyrna (who had been turned into a myrrh tree). This and alternative genealogies linked Adonis with the Near East, and he was already in ancient times identified with the Sumerian and Akkadian god of shepherds and farmers, Dumuzi (Tammuz). Myths surrounding these deities reflected the annual decay and rebirth of vegetation. A sketch by Theocritus narrates a festival of Adonis at Alexandria: the god was offered fruits, little artificial gardens, perfumes, and cakes made with wheat flour, honey and olive oil. Festivals of Adonis were held also at Byblos in Phoenicia and at other cult centres.

Aristophanes, *Lysistrata* 389 with Henderson *ad l.*; Theocritus 15 with Gow *ad l.*

Marcel Detienne, *Le Jardin d'Adonis: la mythologie des aromates en Grèce* (Paris, 1972); translation: *The Gardens of Adonis: spices in Greek mythology* (Hassocks: Harvester Press, 1977); review by John Scarborough in *Classical Journal* vol. 76 (1981) pp. 175–8.

Africa, source of wheat and of other foods more or less exotic. The northwest African provinces of the Roman Empire (see also EGYPT and CYRENAICA) had previously been dominated by CARTHAGE. Their well-developed farms, many now the estates of rich Romans, still produced good food, including cattle and sheep, raisins, figs, olives and pomegranates. The pomegranate was *malum punicum*, Punic or Carthaginian apple, in Latin. Sweet wine and olive oil were exported from Africa to Italy and elsewhere. Wheat did so well here that Africa was counted as one of Rome's three 'granaries', so listed by Cicero and Aristides. North African snails were unrivalled in size and succulence.

Some exotic luxuries, but no foods, came to the classical Mediterranean from Africa south of the Sahara in the course of trade. But several domesticated food species familiar in the classical world had come originally from there, notably the melon and the guinea fowl.

Cicero, *De Lege Manilia* 34; Pliny *NH* 14.16, 14.15.74–5; Statius, *Silvae* 4.9.10; Aristides, *Roman Oration* 10–12.

Frank 1933–40 vol. 4 pp. 1–120; R. Lequément, 'Le vin africain à l'époque impériale' in *Antiquités africaines* vol. 16 (1980) pp. 185–93; D.J. Mattingly, 'The olive boom: oil surpluses, wealth and power in Roman Tripolitania' in *Libyan Studies* vol. 19 (1988) pp. 21–41; D.P. Kehoe, *The Economics of Agriculture on Roman Imperial Estates in North Africa* (Göttingen: Vandenhoeck & Ruprecht, 1988); *OCD* 1996 *s.v.* Africa; Dalby 2000a pp. 107–11, 178–81.

Agape, the communal meal shared by early Christians. This is referred to in the Acts of the Apostles simply as the 'breaking of bread'; the Greek term *agape* occurs in two New Testament letters and in other Christian sources. The *agape* was still practised in the fourth century.

Luke Acts 2.42–6, *al.*; II *Peter* 2.13; *Jude* 12; Clement of Alexandria, *Paidagogos* 2.1.3–7; Tertullian, *Apologeticus* 39.

Grimm 1996 pp. 77–82, 100–1, 118–22, *al.*; Michael Symons, 'From agape to eucharist: Jesus meals and the early church' in *Food and Foodways* vol. 8 (1999–2000) pp. 33–54.

Akrotiri, town on the Greek island of Thera, buried in the eruption of the volcano of Thera in the mid second millennium BC. Akrotiri is now being excavated. There are wall paintings in Minoan style. They depict, among other subjects, women picking SAFFRON and a nude man carrying DOLPHIN-FISH. An earthenware beehive found at Akrotiri has served as the oldest evidence of the domestication of bees.

Thera and the Aegean World. Papers Presented at the Second International Scientific Congress, Santorini, August 1978 ed. C. Doumas (London: 1978–80), review by Emily Vermeule in *American Journal of Archaeology* vol. 85 (1981) pp. 93–4; C. Doumas, *Thera: Pompeii of the Ancient Aegean. Excavations at Akrotiri 1967–79* (London: Thames and Hudson, 1983); N. Marinatos, 'The function and interpretation of the Theran frescoes' in *L'Iconographie minoenne: actes de la table ronde d'Athènes, 21–22 avril 1983* ed. P. Darcque and J.-C. Poursat (Athens, 1985); E. Panagiotakopulu and P.C. Buckland, 'Insect pests of stored products from late Bronze Age Santorini, Greece' in *Journal of Stored Product Research* vol. 27 (1991) pp. 179–84.

Alban wine (Latin *Albanum*; Greek *Albanos*), from the slopes near Alba Longa in Latium. It was said that the Gauls, in their invasion of Italy in the fourth century BC, sated themselves on the wines of the Alban hills. Alban is listed equal third, with Surrentine, in the classification of the supreme wines of Italy in the time of Augustus. *Eugenia* was among the varieties grown here. There was a very sweet style and an austere style; the *Epitome of Athenaeus*, calling them *glykazon* and *omphakias*, says that both were best after fifteen years, but Galen knew an Alban that was light enough to be drunk young.

There is little archaeological evidence of amphorae in the Alban region: Tchernia suggests most Alban wine was transported in skins (see CULLEUS) to Rome, and 'bottled' and matured there. If the production was indeed mostly marketed in Rome, this could explain why Alban is not listed among the fine wines commanding a special high price in *Diocletian's Price Edict* at the end of the third century.

Dionysius of Halicarnassus, *History* 1.37.2, 14.8.12; Horace, *Odes* 4.11.2, *Satires* 2.8.16; Dioscorides *MM* 5.6.6–7; Columella *DA* 3.8.5; Pliny *NH* 14.64; Martial 13.109; Juvenal 5.33–5; Galen *ST* 6.275, 6.334, *BM* 6.806, *On Therapeutic Method* 10.485, 10.833, *DA* 14.15–16; Athenaeus *E* 26d, 27a, 33a.

Tchernia 1986 esp. pp. 108, 208; Dalby 2000a p. 34.

Alcoholic drinks familiar in antiquity were WINE, MEAD and BEER. Wine was by far the most important of the three. Although the techniques for distilling alcohol were available by Roman imperial times, resulting liquids were not drunk: spirits and liqueurs (hard liquor) were therefore unknown. The maximum alcohol level that can be attained in fermentation of wine and mead is about 16 per cent; the usual level in modern winemaking is 12 per cent to 13 per cent, and there is no reason to suppose the usual ancient level to be very different from this. No technique practised in ancient times made it possible to increase the alcohol level of wine above what was attained in fermentation.

The power of alcoholic drinks to intoxicate was familiar enough, but the presence in them of alcohol and the nature of alcoholic fermentation were not understood; hence Plutarch's puzzled discussion of why *gleukos*, must or fresh grape juice, is not intoxicating.

Alcoholism, a pathological dependence on alcohol, has not been identified in ancient sources unless perhaps in observations by Aristotle and Plutarch, but chronic DRUNKENNESS and its effects on health were recognised. It was widely accepted that unrestricted drinking of neat wine would cause madness and death.

Aristotle, *Problems* 871a1–878a27; Pliny *NH* 14.137–49; Plutarch *QC* 3.7–8.

Constructive Drinking: perspectives on drink

from anthropology ed. Mary Douglas (Cambridge, 1987); Milano 1994.

Alexander the Great, king of Macedonia (reigned 336–323 BC) and conqueror of the Persian Empire. As a result of his Persian expedition ASAFOETIDA became known to the Mediterranean world, and several edible plants previously unknown in Europe were recorded for the first time in the *History of Plants* compiled by THEOPHRASTUS, successor to Aristotle, who had been Alexander's teacher. At his court Macedonian, Greek and Persian customs – or vices, as Quintus Curtius prefers to put it – were intermixed. His symposia formed the setting for several of the romantic and tragic incidents so prominent in his biography, notably the dispute over *proskynesis* or kowtowing, the disgrace of Callisthenes, the burning of Persepolis, the killing of Cleitus. There was competitive drinking of wine at his symposia, all the more dangerous since Macedonians, unlike Greeks, drank wine unmixed with water, while Greeks, unlike Macedonians, drank through the night. The game caused deaths and may – some believed – have precipitated Alexander's own death. In the course of his expedition large-scale feasts and symposia, probably including the mass Macedonian–Persian wedding feast, were held in Alexander's famous hundred-couch tent. This travelled with him from Macedonia and was, apparently, swept away in a flash flood during his return from India.

Several of the newly discovered foods (including CITRON, PISTACHIO and PEACH) were destined to be transplanted westwards in the centuries that followed Alexander's conquest. Meanwhile, under the Ptolemies of EGYPT and the Seleucids of SYRIA, successors to parts of Alexander's empire, Greek plant foods were transplanted eastwards. Greek gastronomy of the Hellenistic (post-Alexander) period, combining traditions, products and recipes from the eastern Mediterranean and southwestern Asia, was very different from that of earlier Greece.

For Alexander's use of pits to conserve snow see SNOW.

Diodorus Siculus 17.16.4; Quintus Curtius 9.7.15, *al.*; Plutarch, *Alexander* 22–3, 50–5, 76, *QC* 1.6; Arrian, *Anabasis* 4.8, 7.24–6, *al.*; Aelian, *Varia Historia* 8.7; Athenaeus D 155d, 434a–435a, 537d–540a.

J.M. O'Brien, 'Alexander and Dionysus: the invisible enemy' in *Annals of Scholarship* vol. 1 (1980) pp. 83–105; J.M. O'Brien, 'The enigma of Alexander: the alcohol factor' in *Annals of Scholarship* vol. 1 (1980) pp. 31–46; Eugene N. Borza, 'The symposium at Alexander's court' in *Arkhea Makedhonia = Ancient Macedonia III* (Thessalonica, 1983) pp. 45–55; N.G.L. Hammond, 'Alexander: a drinker or a drunkard?' in his *Alexander the Great* (Bristol, 1989, 2nd edn) pp. 278–80; Andrew Dalby, 'Alexander's culinary legacy' in *Cooks and Other People: Proceedings of the Oxford Symposium on Food and Cookery 1995* ed. Harlan Walker (Totnes: Prospect Books, 1996) pp. 81–93.

Alexanders, a root vegetable now seldom grown. Its aromatic juice was likened in ancient times to myrrh. Full instructions for harvesting and use are given by Columella; there is also a recipe in *Apicius*.

Alexanders (*Smyrnium Olusatrum*) is Greek *hipposelinon* or *smyrnion*, Latin *holusatrum*.

Theophrastus *HP* 7.6.3, 9.1.3–4; Nicander *F* 71 Schneider; *Moretum* 71 (*holus*); Columella *DA* 12.58; Pliny *NH* 19.163, 20.117, 27.133–6; *Apicius* 3.15.1, 4.2.19.

Alexandria in Egypt, greatest of the new cities founded by Alexander the Great. This became a place where many pleasures, gastronomic and other, could be purchased. Alexandria was the seaport from which imperial Rome was supplied with Eastern spices transshipped from the Red Sea ports. From here, also, came the big grain ships carrying much of Rome's wheat supply, as well as perfumed oils and other luxuries manufactured in EGYPT.

Luke, *Acts* 27.6–28.14; Lucian, *The Ship*; Athenaeus D 541a.

P.M. Fraser, *Ptolemaic Alexandria* (Oxford: Clarendon Press, 1972), 3 vols.

Alexis, comedy playwright born at Thurii, active at Athens in the later fourth century BC. No complete play by him survives, but Alexis is very frequently quoted by ATHENAEUS. Through these quotations he is a particularly important source for Athenian food behaviour of his period. He appears to have popularised, indeed in a sense to have created, the stock character of the PARASITOS.

Alexis F: fragments. Commentary: W.G. Arnott, *Alexis: the fragments. A commentary* (Cambridge: Cambridge University Press, 1996). Critical text: in *PCG: Poetae comici Graeci* ed. R. Kassel and C. Austin (Berlin: De Gruyter, 1983–). English translation: in *The Fragments of Attic Comedy* ed. J.M. Edmonds (Leiden, 1957–61). References elsewhere in the present book are to the fragment numbering established by Kassel and Austin and adopted by Arnott.

Alkanet, medicinal herb related to, and resembling, borage. Like borage leaves in modern punch, alkanet leaves were added to wine at ancient drinking parties 'to contribute to the cheerfulness and the enjoyment of the participants', as Plutarch puts it.

Alkanet (*Anchusa officinalis*) is Greek *bouglosson* and Latin *lingua bubula*, both names meaning literally 'ox tongue' from the appearance of the leaf.

Dioscorides *MM* 4.127; Pliny *NH* 17.112, 25.81; Plutarch *QC* 1.1; Pseudo-Apuleius, *Herbarius* 41.

Allec, a fermented paste made from shad, anchovy and other fish. Sometimes the solid residue from the manufacture of GARUM was used as *allec*. The legendary gourmet APICIUS (2) invented a recipe for *allec* made entirely from red mullet livers. The Latin word *allec* appears to be connected etymologically with the name of the SHAD, Latin *alecula*, *alausa*.

The substance had a powerful taste and odour and served as a flavouring in Roman cuisine. Nothing like it is now made in Europe: it must have resembled modern Malay *blachan*.

Horace, *Satires* 2.4.74; Columella *DA* 8.17.12; Pliny *NH* 9.66, 31.95–6 (*alex*); Martial 3.77; *Geoponica* 20.46 (*alix*).

Almond, kernel of the fruit of *Prunus dulcis*. The fruit resembles a meagre peach, but is inedible. The kernel is used, sliced or ground, in cooking. Some trees produce bitter almonds; these have to be roasted before eating to eliminate their poisonous prussic acid.

Almonds were being collected from the wild by the inhabitants of Franchthi Cave by 10,000 BC, and in Turkey, Syria and Palestine by that time or soon afterwards. Cultivation was probably under way by the third millennium BC: earliest evidence comes from Jordan. The almond was among the earliest of the domesticated fruit trees of the eastern Mediterranean, since, unlike some others, it can be propagated from seed.

In classical Greece almonds were typical of Thasos and perhaps of the north shore of the Aegean generally. At Greek banquets they were a frequent constituent of dessert (see TRAGEMATA); in Roman cuisine they sometimes served as a flavouring, as in the dish *apothermum*, a kind of frumenty, for which *Apicius* gives a recipe. Bitter almonds were placed in *sacci*, bouquets, to impart their flavour and medicinal properties to wine as it was served. These properties were widely reputed to include the prevention of drunkenness, enabling participants to prolong a drinking bout.

Sweet almonds produce a mild-flavoured oil that was used at the Persian King's Dinner (see PERSIANS); Xenophon encountered bitter almond oil in Persia. Both kinds of almonds, and their oils, were important medicinally.

In Greek the almond is *amygdalon*, the cultivated sweet almond also *karyon Thasion* 'Thasian nut', the bitter almond *karyon pikron*; oil of bitter almond is

netopon, *niopon*. In Latin the almond is *amygdalum*.

Hermippus 63 Kassel; Philoxenus *D* e.21 Page; Hippocrates *R* 55, *Epidemics* 5.66 (*netopon*) with Jouanna *ad l.*; Xenophon, *Anabasis* 4.4.13; Aristotle, *On Marvellous Things Heard* 832a1–5; Theophrastus *HP* 2.2, *al.*; Cato *DA* 8, 133 (*nux Graeca*); Dioscorides *MM* 1.33, 1.123, cf. 4.188; Erotian, *Hippocratic Glosses* s.v. *niopon*; Pliny *NH* 15.26, 15.89–90, 20.185, 23.85, 23.144–6; Plutarch *QC* 1.6; Galen *AF* 6.611, *SF* 11.827, *al.*; Athenaeus *E* 52a–54d; Polyaenus 4.3.32; Macrobius *S* 3.18.8; Gargilius Martialis *DH* 3; Palladius *OA* 2.15.6–13; *Apicius* 2.2.10, *al.*; Anthimus *OC* 90 with Grant *ad l.*; *Geoponica* 10.57–62.

Darby and others 1977 pp. 751–2; Zohary and Hopf 1993 pp. 173–7.

Aloes, bitter sap of an aromatic plant native to southern Arabia, Socotra and Somalia. For long-distance transport the product is boiled until it solidifies. Extremely bitter to the taste, it was (and is) an ingredient in medicines and cosmetics. In particular it acted as a purge, whether taken in water or honey-water or as an ingredient in a medicinal wine; the latter was manufactured in southern Gaul.

Aloes (*Aloe Perryi*) is *aloe* in Greek and Latin.

Psalms 45.8; *Proverbs* 7.17; *Song of Songs* 4.14; Celsus *DM* 1.3.25; Dioscorides *MM* 1.21; Pliny *NH* 14.68, 27.14–20; John, *Gospel* 19.39; Pseudo-Galen, *On Substitutes* 19.731; Aetius, *Medicine* 1.131.

Laufer 1919 pp. 480–1; J.A.C. Greppin, 'The various aloes in ancient times' in *Journal of Indo-European Studies* vol. 16 (1988) pp. 33–48; Casson 1989 pp. 164–5.

- Aloeswood is an entirely different product, the aromatic wood of a tree native to southeast Asia. It is mentioned several times in the Hebrew Bible and also in later Greek sources. Aloeswood, eaglewood or gharuwood (*Aquilaria malaccensis* [*Aloexylon Agallochum*]) is Greek *aloth*, *agalokhon*, *xylaloe*, Latin *agallochon*. Dioscorides's remark, 'aloes comes also from India' is a sign that at this point he or his source has confused aloes and aloeswood owing to the similarity in their trade names.

Dioscorides *MM* 3.22, cf. Galen *SF* 11.821–2.

- Greek *aloe Gallike* 'Gaulish aloes' is a name for gentian (*Gentiana lutea*), Latin *gentiana*, a medicinal herb used occasionally in flavoured wines (and used much more frequently in medieval times).

Dioscorides *MM* 3.3; Pseudo-Apuleius, *Herbarius* 16.

Alphita *see* BARLEY

Ambivius, M(arcus), Latin author on food or wine, mentioned by Columella but otherwise unknown.

Columella *DA* 12.4.2.

Ambracia, coastal city in western Greece, important as a stage on the sea route to Italy and for its food specialities. These consisted mainly of seafood, and included shrimps at one end of the scale and, at the other, the very large *khromis* or ombrine, which the cook may treat like a sea-bass. Bass itself was said to be very good at Ambracia; it may be relevant that it was also known as *akarnax*, Acarnania lying immediately to the south. Ambracian specialities additionally included the freshwater *kapros* (see SHEATFISH) from the River Achelous, which you might also buy at nearby Amphilochian Argos. The wine of Ambracia, *Ambraciotes*, is among the wines recommended to a King Ptolemy by APOLLODORUS, possibly in the third century BC.

Archestratus *H* 15, 25, 30, 45, 54, 56 Brandt with Olson and Sens *ad l.*; Philemon 82 Kassel; Aristotle *HA* 535b16–18; Pliny *NH* 14.76 citing Apollodorus.

Dalby 1995; Olson and Sens 2000 p. 79.

Ambrosia and nectar, food, drink and other supplies of the gods. In the *Iliad* the gods use *ambrosia* as soap and perfume, and feed their horses with *ambrosion eidar* 'ambrosial (or perhaps immortal) food'. It is by means of *nektar* and 'desired *ambrosia*', distilled into his breast, that Achilles is protected from exhaustion by Athene, at Zeus's urging. It is with *ambrosia* and red *nektar* that Patroclus' and Achilles' bodies are preserved from decay after their death. According to Hesiod the gods eat *nektar* and *ambrosia*. Sappho tells of the gods' mixing-bowl, *krater*, filled with *ambrosia* to drink. Other early poets, too, seem to regard *ambrosia* as the liquid or *nektar* as the solid or simply do not specify.

However, in the *Odyssey* the god Hermes eats *ambrosia* and drinks red *nektar*, mixed for him by Calypso (mixed with what? Aristotle asks sharply). Later in the same episode, when Calypso dines with Odysseus, she, as an immortal, also partakes of the *ambrosia* and *nektar*, but what she serves to her lover Odysseus is food and wine appropriate to mortals. Eventually, swayed by this memorable scene among others, Greeks came to accept that *ambrosia* was the food of the gods and of their horses, and *nektar* was their drink, and that it was precisely this nourishment that guaranteed their immortality and set them apart from human beings.

To liken fine wine to nectar has been correct poetically ever since the Cyclops Polyphemus did exactly this in the *Odyssey* and the wine-god Dionysus did the same in a lost play by Hermippus: 'There is a sacred odour through all the high-roofed hall, at once ambrosia and nectar. This is the nectar.' By later poets, then, wine was often metaphorically called *nektar*; by Nicander, for example. Some specific wines were dignified with this name *nektar*, either for what would now be called marketing reasons, or simply as poetic licence, in the latter case especially if it was a good wine such as Lesbian. Callimachus does precisely this. Archestratus exaggerates slightly in describing the *kapros* fish at Ambracia as *nektaros anthos*, the flower of nectar. There is similar exaggeration, possibly, in a proverb quoted by Chrysippus of Soli regarding *bolbophake*: 'Bulb and lentil soup is like ambrosia when the cold weather bites!'

Hesiod, *Theogony* 640 with West *ad l.*; Homer, *Iliad* 5.369, 5.777, 14.170, 16.670, 19.38,

19.347–53, *Odyssey* 4.445, 5.93–5, 5.199, 9.359; Pindar, *Olympians* 1.62, *Pythians* 9.63; Hermippus 77 Kassel; Aristophanes, *Peace* 724, 854; Plato, *Phaedrus* 247e; Archestratus *H* 15 Brandt; Alexis *F* 124 Kassel with Arnott *ad l.*; Eubulus *F* 121 Kassel; Aristotle, *Metaphysics* 1000a12; Chrysippus of Soli [Athenaeus *D* 158a]; Theocritus 7.153 with Gow *ad l.*; Nicander *A* 44; Callimachus fragment 399 Pfeiffer; Lucian, *Dialogues of the Gods* 4; Athenaeus *E* 38f–39b citing Alcman 42 Davies, Sappho 141 Lobel, Ibycus 325 Davies, Anaxandrides 58 Kassel; *Scholia on Odyssey* 5.93 citing Aristotle fragment 170 Rose.

• *Ambrosia* was the name of several wild plants, and of a variety of table grape.

   Nicander *F* 126–7 Schneider; Dioscorides *MM* 3.114, 4.88; Pliny *NH* 14.40, 27.29.

Aminnian wine, apparently a varietal wine based on the *aminnia* group of GRAPE VARIETIES, which originated in Sicily or Italy. The price of Aminnian wine was regulated by censorial decree at Rome in 89 BC. Aminnian wine was being traded in southern Egypt, far from its source, in the first century AD. In the second and third centuries AD 'Aminnian wine' was a type produced in several localities. It is one of the seven named wines that are allowed a special high price (nearly four times that of table wine) in *Diocletian's Price Edict*; and it is the only varietal wine among the seven. Aminnian wine is often named in Galen's medical prescriptions; he sometimes specifies separately Sicilian Aminnian, Neapolitan Aminnian, Tuscan Aminnian and Bithynian Aminnian (see under BITHYNIAN WINE; MAMERTINE WINE; NEAPOLITAN WINES; TUSCAN WINE). Such recommendations, along with the price differential, explain the urge to imitate 'Aminnian wine': Didymus offers a recipe for doing so. Both the fruit and the resulting wine are described by Galen as 'austere' in flavour.

Pliny *NH* 14.95; *Greek Ostraca in the Bodleian Library* vol. 1 P224, P240; Galen *ST* 6.335, *DA* 14.16, *al.*; *Diocletian's Price Edict* 2.4 (*Aminneum*); *Geoponica* 8.22 quoting Didymus.

Frank 1933–40 vol. 1 pp. 284–5; Casson 1989 p. 113.

Ammi *see* CUMIN

Amomum, an aromatic described in ancient sources as originating in Pontus, Armenia, Commagene, Assyria or Media. The spice known in Latin as *amomum*, in Greek as *amomon*, resembled a tiny bunch of grapes with leaves around. It is usually identified with Nepaul cardamom or greater cardamom, *Amomum subulatum*: native to the southern Himalaya, this commodity would have passed through the regions listed if it came to the Roman Empire by an inland trade route. *Amomum* was a constituent of hair oil and other perfumes, and was sufficiently profitable for a King Seleucus, perhaps Seleucus I of Syria, to have tried unsuccessfully to transplant it from its native habitat to Arabia. See also CARDAMOM.

Theophrastus *HP* 9.7.2, *O* 32; Strabo 16.1.24; Dioscorides *MM* 1.6; Pliny *NH* 12.48–9, 16.135; John, *Revelation* 18.13 (translated 'odours' in *AV*, 'spice' in *NEB*).

Laufer 1919 pp. 481–2; Miller 1969 pp. 37–8, 67–9; Dalby 2000a p. 197.

Amphidromia, a family festival at Athens, held five, seven or ten days after a baby's birth. The *Amphidromia* is thought to be distinct from the ceremonial naming of the child which took place at around the same time. A comedy passage, variously attributed to Eubulus and Ephippus, seems to provide a menu:

> Well, then, why is there no wreath in front of the door? Why does no smell of cooking strike the tip of my exploring nose, if it's their *Amphidromia*? The custom then is to bake slices of Chersonese cheese, to fry cabbage gleaming with oil, to stew some fat mutton chops, to pluck wood-pigeons and thrushes along with chaffinches, to nibble little cuttlefish along with squids, to swing and beat many an

octopus tentacle, and to drink many a warming cup.

Athenaeus *D* 370c quoting Ephippus 3 Kassel (= Eubulus *F* 148 Kassel), also 668c–d quoting Eubulus *F* 1–2 Kassel (see Hunter *ad l.*); *Suda s.v. Amphidromia.*

Amphorae, earthenware vessels manufactured in large quantities and used in the distribution and storage of wine, olive oil and GARUM. The typical amphora (Greek *amphiphoreus, amphoreus*; Latin *amphora*) had an elongated, bulbous shape, two handles and a pointed bottom. The capacity was eventually standard: in liquid volume a Roman *amphora* equalled 48 *sextarii* (pints) or 26 litres. A standard older Greek *amphoreus* was 1½ times this, but shapes varied, making the *amphoreus* somewhat ambiguous as a measure: *khion* and *hemikhion*, 'Chian amphora' and 'half Chian amphora' are used as measures in Ptolemaic papyri. However, the variation of shape aided identification of the city of origin or the wine style. Some Greek coins depicted the local amphora shape, confirming such identifications. Amphorae were often stamped and inscribed, identifying a potter, a wine- or oil-maker or a merchant; they were also regularly re-used and when necessary re-labelled.

When the sample is large enough amphora studies can provide copious information on patterns of trade, as exemplified by Tchernia on the wines of Italy. Amphorae gradually fell out of use for wine distribution during the second and third centuries AD, supplanted by wooden barrels (see CUPA). Since the barrels hardly ever survive, our knowledge of the later Roman wine trade is correspondingly more patchy.

The name 'amphora' is also given to certain types of large painted Greek vases, of similar shape, but usually with a flat bottom.

D.P.S. Peacock, 'Amphorae and the Baetican fish industry' in *Antiquaries' Journal* vol. 54 (1974) pp. 232–43; Jeremy Paterson, 'Salvation from the sea: amphorae and trade in the Roman West' in *Journal of Roman Studies* vol. 72 (1982) pp. 146–57; Tchernia 1986; *Recherches sur les amphores grecques* ed. Jean-Yves Empereur and Yvon Garlan (Athens, 1986) (*Bulletin de correspondance hellénique* suppl. 13); D.P.S. Peacock and D.F. Williams,

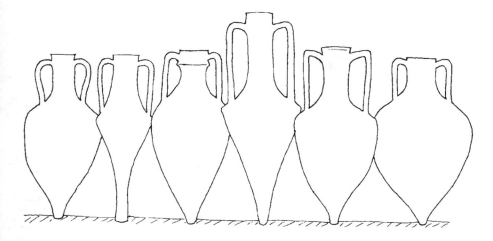

Figure 1 Amphora shapes of the fourth and third centuries BC, based on examples from the Athenian Agora excavations. Left to right: Lesbian, Chian (older and newer styles), Rhodian, Coan.

Figure 2 Amphora shapes of the first centuries BC and AD, based on examples from the Athenian Agora excavations. Left to right: Roman (two styles), Punic, Chian, Coan, Rhodian, imitation Coan.

Amphorae and the Roman Economy: an introductory guide (London: Longman, 1986); Robert I. Curtis, 'Product identification and advertising in Roman commercial amphorae' in *Ancient Society* vol. 15/17 (1984/6); *Amphores romaines et histoire économique. Dix ans de recherche. Actes du colloque de Sienne* (Rome, 1989) (*Collection de l'Ecole Française de Rome*, 114); A.J. Parker, *Ancient Shipwrecks of the Mediterranean and Roman Provinces* (Oxford: Tempus Reparatum, 1992) (*BAR International Series*, 580); *The Inscribed Economy: production and distribution in the Roman Empire in the light of instrumentum domesticum* ed. W.V. Harris (Ann Arbor: University of Michigan, 1993) (*Journal of Roman Archaeology. Supplementary series*, 6); Christian Vandermersch, *Vins et amphores de Grande Grèce et de Sicile, IVe–IIIe s. avant J.-C.* (Naples, 1994) (Centre Jean Bérard, *Etudes*, 1); Albert Leonard, ' "Canaanite jars" and the late Bronze Age Aegeo-Levantine wine trade' in *The Origins and Ancient History of Wine* ed. Patrick E. McGovern, Stuart J. Fleming and Solomon H. Katz (London: Gordon and Breach, 1995) pp. 233–54; Carolyn G. Koehler, 'Wine amphoras in ancient Greek trade' *ib.* pp. 323–37; *OCD* 1996 *s.vv.* Amphorae and amphora stamps, Greek; Amphorae and amphora stamps, Roman.

Amylos *see* WHEAT

Anacreon, Greek lyric poet of the sixth century BC. Anacreon, native of Teos, was regarded in later times as the typical poet of the symposium (see for example Critias 8 Diehl [Athenaeus *D* 600d]). Relatively little of his genuine work survives. Convivial poems now known as the *Anacreontea*, attributed to Anacreon by ancient readers but actually composed after his time, were often recited at dinners. One such occasion is described by Aulus Gellius (19.9).

R. Prestagostini, 'Anacr. 33 Gent. = 356 P.: due modalità simposiali a confronto' in *Quaderni Urbinati* vol. 10 (1982) pp. 47–55.

Anatolia, a region roughly corresponding with modern Turkey. Anatolia is the location of very early Neolithic settlements, such as the excavated sites of Hacilar and Catal Hüyük, dated before 6000 BC. Through much of the second millennium BC Anatolia was dominated by the HITTITES. The region was later (*c.*547–333) to be subject to the PERSIANS as a result of their conquest of LYDIA. After various political vicissitudes in the centuries that followed Alexander's conquests, Anatolia was gradually (133 BC to AD 43) wholly incorporated in the Roman Empire.

Anatolia is important in food history as the origin from which several species of fruit and nut trees gradually spread southwards towards the Near East and westwards towards Greece. There is no written evidence of this movement or of the extent to which it was planned or encouraged by humans; the only evidence comes from archaeobotany, from pollen analysis and from botanical studies of species origins. In classical Greece, however, Anatolia was certainly celebrated as the exporter of dried fruits and nuts among many other products (see Hermippus). Several of these were named for their Anatolian origins. 'Sardian nuts' were chestnuts, 'Pontic nuts' were hazelnuts, 'Heracleotic nuts' were hazelnuts or filberts. The Greek colony of Cerasus, modern Giresun, on the Black Sea coast, was apparently named for the cherries (Greek *kerasos*) that grew in its neighbourhood. Cherries – of some variety or other – were transplanted from this district to Italy, according to Pliny, by the general Lucullus, who campaigned here against Mithradates of Pontus. Fruit trees were also transplanted from Cilicia to Italy. Dried figs were *carica* in Latin, a reminder of how many of them came to Rome from Caria.

It is said by Livy that cooks and music-girls first reached Rome in the baggage train of a victorious Roman army after a campaign in Galatia, in central Anatolia, in 189 BC. Not long afterwards the independent kingdom of Pergamum was to become the Roman province of Asia, noted for its wealth and luxuries and for its contribution to Roman income. According to Galen, a native of Pergamum, some of the finest wines of the second century AD came from western Anatolia. This continued to be the case under the Byzantine Empire. Anatolia was also the source of important spices and aromatics, including saffron and storax.

For regions of Anatolia with their own gastronomic character see CAPPADOCIA; CARIA; CILICIA; EPHESUS; LYCIA; LYDIA; MILETUS. For fine Anatolian wines see ABATE WINE; ASIAN WINES; BITHYNIAN WINE; CNIDIAN WINE; EPHESIAN WINES; HIPPODAMANTIAN WINE; MYSIAN WINE; SCYBELITE WINE.

Hermippus 63 Kassel; Livy 39.6; Cicero, *De Lege Manilia* 14; Pliny *NH* 15.102; Statius, *Silvae* 1.6; Galen, *On Therapeutic Method* 10.830–3, *al.*

Frank 1933–40 vol. 4 pp. 499–918; Ronald L. Gorny, 'Viticulture and ancient Anatolia' in *The Origins and Ancient History of Wine* ed. Patrick E. McGovern, Stuart J. Fleming and Solomon H. Katz (London: Gordon and Breach, 1995) pp. 133–74; Dalby 1996 pp. 128–9; Dalby 2000a pp. 11–12, 133–8, 161–8.

Anchovy *see* APHYE

Anconitan wine (Greek *Ankonitanos*) from the slopes of northern Picenum in Italy. In 218 BC Hannibal already found 'plenty of old wine' in this region: his army used it to rub down their horses. Three centuries later the wine of Ancona was described as 'good, oily' in a brief characterisation in the *Epitome of Athenaeus*.

Polybius 3.88; Strabo 5.4.2; Pliny *NH* 14.67; Athenaeus *E* 26f.

Andron, 'men's room'. In private houses in classical Athens and other Greek cities, a room set aside for dining and entertainment, easily recognised archaeologically by its shape and size. There was room for five, seven or more couches around the walls, and there was a door off-centre on one wall. Sometimes floor markings are found in *androns*, indicating the intended placement of couches and tables. The couches, each accommodating one diner (or two or three at a pinch) are illustrated in vase paintings. The centre of the room (*eis meson, en mesoi*) was public space.

B. Bergquist. 'Sympotic space: a functional aspect of Greek dining-rooms' in *Sympotica: a symposium on the symposion* ed. Oswyn Murray (Oxford: Oxford University Press, 1990) pp. 37–65.

Angler-fish, a large creature that lurks on the sea bottom. Its huge, fearsome-looking head attracts attention, but its long tail – *gastrion*, belly, according to Archestratus – makes good food.

The angler-fish (*Lophius Piscatorius* and the smaller *L. Budegassa*) was known in Greek as *batrakhos* and *halieus*, in Latin as *rana marina* and *rana piscatrix*. The term 'fishing-frog' has been used in English translations.

Archestratus *H* 47 Brandt; Aristotle *HA* 620b13–19, *al.*; *Acraephia Price List*; Oppian *H* 2.86–106 with Mair *ad l.*; Athenaeus *D* 286b–e.

Thompson 1947 pp. 28–9; Davidson 1981 pp. 165–8.

Anise, a plant resembling dill but grown mainly for its sweet and aromatic seeds. The species originated in western Asia and perhaps the Greek islands. Theophrastus, native of Lesbos, lists it among aromatics that did not come from Europe. Dioscorides regarded Cretan anise as the best, followed by Egyptian; it is now a typical product of Lesbos. Anise was and is regarded as warming and digestive; it was aphrodisiac, according to Dioscorides and others. It was included in CONDITUM at appropriate seasons, and was the chief added ingredient in the medicinal wine *annesaton*, now supplanted by ouzo: Oribasius supplies a recipe. Anise seeds were placed in *sacci*, bouquets, according to Pliny, to impart their flavour and medicinal properties to wine as it was served.

Anise (*Pimpinella Anisum*) was *anneson* in Greek, *anisum* in Latin: spellings vary. Ancient authors always distinguish anise from DILL, but translators sometimes confuse them.

Herodotus 4.71; Theophrastus *HP* 1.12.1 (*anneson*), 9.7.3 (*annetos*); Nicander *T* 650; Dioscorides *MM* 3.56, *E* 2.101 (*anesson*); Pliny *NH* 20.185–95; Oribasius *CM* 5.33; Pseudo-Apuleius, *Herbarius* 122.

Darby and others 1977 p. 796; Dalby 1996 pp. 85, 236.

- Star anise (*Illicium verum*), a spice of Chinese origin, has replaced anise in modern commercial products, including mass market brands of pastis and ouzo.

Antelope *see* DEER

Anthimus, author of a manual of dietary advice in Latin. The book takes the form of a letter addressed to the Merovingian king Theuderic (reigned 511–34), who ruled northeastern Gaul from his capital at Metz. Its author is thought to be the same Anthimus who was exiled by the Byzantine emperor Zeno in 478 for treasonable correspondence.

The grammar is so erratic that the book can hardly have been written by a native speaker of Latin, but it still provides interesting evidence of the colloquial Latin of its period, including the earliest record of some important food words. Among these are *mussirio* and *tufera* (*OC* 38), whose modern reflexes include regional French *mousseron* and English *mushroom*, French *truffe* and English *truffle*; also *nauprida* or *lamprida* (*OC* 47), represented by modern French *lamproie* and English *lamprey*.

Anthimus's book is both the last culinary text from the Roman Empire and 'the first French cookery book' (Grant p. 28).

Malchus fragment 15 Blockley.

Nardus Groen, *Lexicon Anthimeum* (Amsterdam: H.J. Paris, 1926); Guy Serbat, 'Quelques traits d'oralité chez Anthime, De observatione ciborum' in *Les Structures de l'oralité en latin: colloque du Centre Alfred Ernout, juin 1994* ed. Jacqueline Dangel and Claude Moussy (Paris, 1996) pp. 85–91.

Anthimus OC: *De Observatione Ciborum*. Text, translation and commentary: Anthimus, *De Observatione Ciborum* = *On the Observance of Foods* ed. Mark Grant (Totnes: Prospect Books, 1996). Critical text and German translation: *Anthimi De observatione ciborum ad Theodoricum regem Francorum epistula* ed. E. Liechtenhan (Berlin: Akademie-

Verlag, 1963) (*Corpus medicorum Latinorum*, 8.1).

Anthosmias, a style of wine in which a proportion of sea water was added to the must before fermentation. This contributed a distinct flavour and aroma, and, probably more important, helped to prevent spoilage of the wine during transport. The method was used for COAN WINE and other cheap wines from the eastern Aegean, especially, perhaps, those intended for export. The Greek term *anthosmias*, literally 'flower-scented', is used by Phaenias of Eresus, who gives brief instructions for making the product; an alternative and more honest name was *oinos tethalassomenos*, brined wine.

Aristophanes, *Frogs* 1150, *Wealth* 807; Xenophon, *Hellenica* 6.2.6; Dioscorides *MM* 5.19; Athenaeus *E* 31f quoting Phaenias of Eresus.

Tchernia 1986 p. 105 and note 188.

- Paraphrases of the word *anthosmias* in archaic Greek texts probably do not refer to wine of this type, but are to be taken literally as 'flower-scented'. The question was discussed by Athenaeus in book 1 of the *Deipnosophists* (to judge by quotations surviving in the *Epitome*), but the discussion does not survive.

Athenaeus *E* 31c–32e citing Alcman 92 Davies; Eustathius, *Commentary on Iliad* 1449.12, 1633.3–51 citing Xenophanes 1 West.

Andrew Dalby, 'The vineyards of Laconia' in *Classica* (Sao Paulo) vol. 11/12 (1998–9) pp. 281–8.

Anthropology (more precisely, social anthropology), the study of human social behaviour. Like other sciences, anthropology progresses when the anthropologist is receptive both to observation and to theory. Observation means fieldwork, often guided by native informants.

If ancient sources of information (textual, iconographical, archaeological) are treated as native informants, an anthropologist can work on ancient societies as on modern ones. The crucial differences are that the 'native informants' cannot be

questioned and that the behaviour they discuss cannot be independently observed. As if that were not enough, a further difficulty, often ignored, is that when information is conflated from sources of very different dates it may not be true that 'the same behaviour' and 'the same society' are being described. When the sources offer conflicting or inadequate information, the anthropologist can use comparative studies (of modern, observable, societies) to suggest a conclusion, but it may be difficult to demonstrate its validity.

Structural anthropology is associated with the name of Claude Lévi-Strauss, who worked on modern cultures, and with Marcel Detienne, Jean-Pierre Vernant and others who have worked on the ancient world. Its aim is to explain social behaviour by hypothesising recurrent patterns of human thinking.

J. Soler, 'Sémiotique de la nourriture dans la Bible' in *Annales: économies, sociétés, civilisations* vol. 28 (1973) pp. 943–55, English translation as 'The semiotics of food in the Bible' in *Food and Drink in History* ed. R. Forster and O. Ranum (Baltimore, 1979) pp. 126–38; *La Cuisine du sacrifice en pays grec* ed. Marcel Detienne and Jean-Pierre Vernant (Paris: Gallimard, 1979), translation *The Cuisine of Sacrifice among the Greeks* (Chicago: Chicago University Press, 1989); P. Farb and G. Armelagos, *Consuming Passions* (Boston, 1980); *Nutritional Anthropology: contemporary approaches to diet and culture* ed. N.W. Jerome, Randy F. Kandel and Gretel H. Pelto (Pleasantville, New York: Redgrave, 1980); J. Goody, *Cooking, Cuisine and Class* (Cambridge: Cambridge University Press, 1982), review by Jean-Louis Flandrin in *Annales* (1987) no. 2 pp. 645–52, and reviews in *Food and Foodways* vol. 3 (1988–9) pp. 177–221; E.A. Smith, 'Anthropological applications of optimal foraging theory: a critical review' in *Current Anthropology* vol. 24 (1983) pp. 625–51; *The Sociology of Food and Eating* ed. A. Murcott (Aldershot, 1983); Helen King, 'Food as symbol in classical Greece' in *History Today* (September 1986) pp. 35–9; P. Stoller, *The Taste of Ethnographic Things* (Philadelphia, 1989); Helen King in *OCD* 1996 *s.v.* Anthropology and the classics; Garnsey 1999 pp. 4–11.

Aphrodisiacs, foods aiding sexual arousal. Greeks and Romans had a long list of these, most of them regarded as clinically ineffective by modern pharmacologists. Some appear to be in the list because their shape resembles the sexual organs (e.g. grape-hyacinth bulbs, SATYRION, CARROT, LEEK, ARUM, maybe even TARO roots) or because the viscosity of their juices resembles that of semen. Examples of this kind are SHELLFISH (especially OYSTERS), SNAILS and EGGS (Heracleides of Tarentum gives that explanation for the use of these three as aphrodisiacs), and perhaps also TEREBINTH fruits, since they are so rich in oil. Others have a physical effect on the urinary system (wild CHERVIL, ROCKET leaves and seed, NETTLE seed, PEPPER) or a general psychological effect (e.g. WINE because it removed inhibitions, MYRRH since its aroma suggested festivity). Some of the ancient aphrodisiacs, notably satyrion and bulbs, retain their reputation in parts of Greece and Italy today.

Apicius provides several recipes for bulbs and includes an extract from a lost work by Varro asserting their aphrodisiac effect (see quotation at BULBS).

Aphrodisiac medicines, as prescribed by ancient physicians to combat frigidity or impotence, sometimes took the form of simple preparations that incorporated two or three of the accepted aphrodisiac foods. For examples see the references below from book 20 of Pliny's *Natural History* and from the *Herbal* ascribed to Apuleius. As a further example, the 'strengthening foods' prescribed for a case of impotence in Petronius's *Satyricon* are 'bulbs, snails served without sauce, and a little unmixed wine'. Sometimes, by contrast, physicians prepared extremely complicated compound drugs that included many exotic ingredients: an example of costly remedies of this kind is provided by Aetius.

Ritual observances were sometimes required in the course of gathering aphrodisiac herbs or preparing aphrodisiac medicines. This is an obvious point of resemblance between aphrodisiacs, on the one hand, and, on the other, those *pharmaka* (magical potions and spells) whose purpose was to attract or retain the sexual attentions of a particular person.

Several foods were regarded as having an antaphrodisiac effect. These included CANNABIS seed, the seed of the CHASTE-TREE, RUE, CRESS and LETTUCE. It is because of this property that at ordinary meals lettuce was customarily served with rocket, which was believed to neutralise it. Red mullet, as daughter of the virgin goddess Artemis, was believed to be antaphrodisiac, according to a comic gastronomic poem by Plato Comicus which also mentions several of the better-known aphrodisiacs. In confirmation of this, a lost work by Terpsicles *Peri Aphrodision*, 'On Sex', listed wine in which a red mullet had drowned as antaphrodisiac and contraceptive. Terpsicles also listed sparrows as an aphrodisiac food, because sparrows breed readily.

Plato Comicus *F* 189 Kassel [Athenaeus *E* 5b–d]; Alexis *F* 175, 281 Kassel, with Arnott *ad ll.*; Theophrastus *HP* 9.18 (for the text see *Theophrasti Eresii opera* ed. F. Wimmer [Paris: Didot, 1866] p. 159; for a translation and notes see Andrew Dalby in *Petits Propos culinaires* no. 64 [2000] pp. 9–15); Ovid, *Art of Love* 2.415–24; Pliny *NH* 10.182, 19.154, 20.57, 20.126, 26.94–9; Athenaeus *E* 63e–64b citing Heracleides of Tarentum; Athenaeus *D* 316c citing Diocles, 325d, 391f citing Terpsicles; Alciphron 4.13; *Apicius* 7.12 Milham quoting Varro (for translation see BULBS); Pseudo-Apuleius, *Herbarius* 15.3; Aetius, *Medicine* 11.35.

H.S. Denninger, 'A history of substances known as aphrodisiacs' in *Annals of Medical History* vol. 2 (1930) pp. 383–93; C.A. Faraone, *Ancient Greek Love Magic* (Cambridge, Mass., 1995).

- The aphrodisiac effect of the *cantharis* (blister beetle, Spanish fly: *Cantharis vesicatoria*) was already known in Roman times.

  Scribonius Largus 189; Pliny *NH* 29.76, cf. 22.78.

Aphye in Greek, *apua* in Latin, a word roughly equivalent to English 'whitebait'.

This was a dish of small fry, fish so small that they could be tossed into a hot skillet (*teganon*) whole in large numbers; they sizzled at once, needed frying for less than a minute, and were eaten whole, crunching the tiny bones along with the flesh. Young gobies, anchovies, sprats and pilchards were typical constituents. This delicacy gave rise to the proverb 'The *aphye* saw the fire' (Clearchus), meaning, roughly, the cat's among the pigeons. *Aphye* was also called *aphros*, *aphritis* 'foam' and *gonos* 'sperm' in its seaborne state, and also *hepsetos* 'fried' with a view to its eventual fate; this last term might also include baby squid and cuttlefish, which could all be fried with the rest.

Aphye was said to be at its finest at the Athenian harbour Phalerum, though also said to be not highly valued by the Athenians themselves; it was good at Rhodes, too, according to Lynceus, while Aristophanes and Cleitarchus together seem to show that it was popular in Boeotia. The dish was best of all, so Archestratus advises, if the small fry were fried together with sea-anemone tentacles; another combination, sketched in a comedy by Eubulus, was with squid and sheep's entrails. *Apicius* gives no fewer than four recipes for *apua sine apua*, whitebait without whitebait, one of those SURPRISE DISHES in which the main expected ingredient is not present.

The small fish that were most likely to be fried together in *aphye* are listed below. Aristotle regarded some of them as successive forms of a single species. A version of this list is given by Dorion, supplemented by numerous other sources quoted by Athenaeus. Romans showed limited enthusiasm for these small fish, at least in literature: hence most of the species names below are Greek.

Aristophanes, *Acharnians* 640, 901, *Birds* 76, *Knights* 642–5 with scholia; Aristotle *HA* 569b9–570a2; Machon *C* 5.35–6 [Athenaeus *D* 244c]; *Acraephia Price List* (*epseitos*); Pliny *NH* 31.95; Oppian *H* 1.762–97 with scholia; Athenaeus *D* 108a–d quoting Eubulus *F* 75

Kassel, also 284f–285f citing Archestratus *H* 9 (see Olson and Sens *ad l.*), Lynceus *F* 8 and Clearchus of Soli 81 Wehrli, also 300f–301c quoting Dorion, also 328c–329b, also 347d, also 357e quoting Mnesitheus; *Apicius* 4.2.12, 9.10.10–12 (*apua*); *Suda s.vv. aphya es pyr, Aphyai*.

Thompson 1947 pp. 21–3, 269 and *s.vv.*; Olson and Sens 2000 p. 238.

- When *aphye* is the name of a particular species, it is the tiny fish sometimes called 'transparent goby' in English, *kobidion* in Greek (*Aphya minuta*); small fry of this kind, pale-coloured, very thin and 'foam-like', could be called *aphye kobitis*. Two sisters who were HETAIRAI at Athens at the time of the orator Hypereides were nicknamed 'the *Aphyai*' because – like these transparent gobies – they were pale and thin, with big eyes. *Apicius* gives a recipe for a *patina de apua* which may be compared with the modern Maltese *fritturi talmakku* described by Alan Davidson. *Aphye* means literally 'unborn', as does the modern Italian name for this same fish, *nonnati*.

Athenaeus *D* 148e citing Cleitarchus, also 284f–285b citing Aristotle fragment 309 Rose and Hicesius, also 586a–b citing Hypereides and Apollodorus; *Apicius* 4.2.11.

Davidson 1981 p. 136.

- Greek *atherine* is the sand-smelt (*Atherina Hepsetus*), 'an elegant little fish' (according to Thompson [above]) which goes in shoals, close inshore, and is early to spawn; its fry therefore also appears early in the year, sometimes in huge numbers, and was caught for *aphye*.

Aristotle *HA* 570b15, *al.*; Oppian *H* 1.108 with Mair *ad l.*; Athenaeus *D* 285a and 300f citing Dorion, also 329a citing Callimachus.

Davidson 1981 p. 139.

- Greek *bembras* or *membras* is a young sprat (*Sprattus Sprattus*) or similar small and cheap fish. A typical ingredient in *aphye*, it was said by Aristotle to be the next stage of growth after the small fry of Phalerum, succeeded in turn by *trikhis*.

Aristophanes, *Wasps* 493–4; Aristotle *HA* 569b25; Machon *C* 5.35–6 (*membras*); *Acraephia Price List*; Athenaeus *D* 287b–f and 300f citing Dorion, also 357e citing Mnesitheus.

Davidson 1981 p. 44.

- Greek *enkrasikholos*, *engraulis* is the anchovy (*Engraulis Encrasicolus*). This small fish was and is typically salted whole and used as flavouring or relish. Anchovy was also a common constituent of GARUM and ALLEC. Fresh anchovies were the usual small fry of the Piraeus, and as such a typical constituent of *aphye*.

  Aristotle *HA* 569b27; Pliny *NH* 31.95; Aelian, *Nature of Animals* 8.18; Oppian *H* 4.468–503; Athenaeus *D* 148e citing Cleitarchus, also 300f citing Dorion, also 329a citing Callimachus.

  Davidson 1981 p. 48.

- Greek *khalkis* is probably the 'sardinelle' of the eastern Mediterranean, *Sardinella aurita*, and perhaps in particular the young of this species. It closely resembles the pilchard or sardine (Greek *sardine*: see under SARDINIA); not surprisingly they are identified by some ancient authors including Epaenetus, while others treat them as separate.

  Athenaeus *D* 328c–329b quoting Epaenetus, also 355f citing Diphilus of Siphnos.

  Davidson 1981 p. 43.

- Greek *trikhis*, *trikhias*, is perhaps the full-grown sprat (*Sprattus Sprattus*); at any rate these two related names are said by Aristotle to belong to the successively more developed stages of *membras* (for which the diminutive *trikhidion* would then be an alternative term). Another possibility is that *trikhis* and *trikhias* are full-grown 'sardinelles' (*Sardinella aurita*), a more developed stage of *khalkis*, which is what Callimachus may intend to say in the reference below. At any rate the *trikhis* was still small enough to be among the typical ingredients in *aphye*. It was common and cheap at Athens; it was a bony fish, but you ate it bones and all, and maybe coughed all night.

  Aristophanes, *Acharnians* 551, *Knights* 662, *Assemblywomen* 55; Aristotle *HA* 569b25; Athenaeus *D* 328c–329b quoting Callimachus, also 357e citing Mnesitheus.

  Davidson 1981 p. 44.

- Young SHAD (Greek *thrissa*) are frequently listed in this group. Young RED MULLET (Greek *trigle*) made a good fry-up which could be called *triglitis* in Greek. Greek *eritimos*, *iktar*, *iops* are names of unidentified fish belonging to this group.

  Acraephia Price List (*wiops*); Athenaeus *D* 300f citing Dorion, also 328c–329b quoting

Nicander *F* 18 Schneider and Callimachus, also 355f citing Diphilus of Siphnos.

Apicius (1). Name of a Roman lover of luxury of the 90s BC. As Tertullian observes, he gave his name to a series of later gourmets and cooks. At this same date or earlier, according to the *Suda*, 'Apicius' was cook to King Nicomedes of Bithynia, but this is an error arising from a misreading of Athenaeus.

Athenaeus *D* 168d citing Poseidonius *F* 27 Jacoby (see Kidd *ad l.*); Tertullian, *Apologeticus* 3.6; *Suda* s.v. *aphya es pyr*, cf. Athenaeus *E* 7d–e.

Apicius (2), M. Gavius. Roman gourmet contemporary with the emperors Augustus and Tiberius. Stories gathered around him. He prescribed (according to Pliny) that red mullet, in order to achieve the highest gastronomic quality, should be drowned in *garum sociorum*; he invented a recipe for making ALLEC entirely from red mullet livers. He lived at Minturnae in Campania, where very large shrimps were found; hearing that even larger ones were to be had in Libya he sailed there through stormy weather, tasted those brought to him by a boat offshore, and, unimpressed, sailed back without touching land: this story from Athenaeus. He committed suicide after calculating that his assets had fallen to ten million *sestertii*, inadequate to sustain his luxurious way of life: so says Seneca. According to Tacitus, he had been the lover of the young Sejanus who later became infamous as the emperor Tiberius's minister. He no doubt gained his cognomen Apicius because, as a man who spent lavishly on luxury, he resembled his predecessor APICIUS (1).

The emperor Elagabalus is said to have admired and emulated Apicius. It seems likely that M. Gavius Apicius, rather than either of his known namesakes, is the person intended.

The *Historia Augusta* says, if correctly emended, that the failed emperor Lucius Verus had 'what others wrote about

Apicius' as bedside reading. This might be a reference to a book *On the Luxury of Apicius* which, according to Athenaeus, was written by the grammarian Apion. At any rate, it cannot refer to the cookbook (APICIUS (4)) as known to us.

Seneca, *Consolation to Helvia* 10.8–10, *Letters* 95.42; Pliny *NH* 9.30, 9.66, 10.133, 19.137; Tacitus, *Annals* 4.1.2; Martial 3.22; Juvenal 4.23; Dio Cassius 57.19.5; Aelian, *On Divine Manifestations* 110–11 Hercher; Athenaeus *D* 294f; *Historia Augusta, Aelius Verus* 5.9 [*s.v.l.*], *Heliogabalus* 18–24; *Suda s.vv. Apikios, Apikios Markos.*

- Several recipes are named 'Apician'; the intention presumably is to attribute them to this or another Apicius. Pliny's *Natural History* refers to an 'Apician method' of keeping cabbage green during cooking.

  Pliny *NH* 19.143; Athenaeus *D* 647c citing Chrysippus of Tyana, also *E* 7a; *Apicius* 4.1.2, 4.2.14, 4.3.3, 5.4.2, 6.7, 7.4.2, 8.7.6.

Apicius (3). According to the *Epitome* of Athenaeus, the name of a cook who found a way of packing fresh oysters to send to the emperor Trajan, while he was on campaign in Mesopotamia around AD 115. It is interesting that the cookbook APICIUS (4) gives instructions for preserving oysters.

Athenaeus *E* 7d; *Apicius* 1.12.

Apicius (4). The surviving Roman cookery book. It evidently borrowed its title from the gourmets of that name, particularly APICIUS (2).

The book is of great linguistic interest. It is written in so-called Vulgar Latin (i.e. colloquial Latin) and contains a very high proportion of Greek loanwords. Both features suggest its origin and use among literate but not fully educated people, perhaps kitchen staff in wealthy households. It may be compared with fragmentary Greek recipe books (see for example CHRYSIPPUS OF TYANA; PAXAMUS): their Greek is non-standard, with more Latin loanwords than usual; however, their style is much fuller. Scarcely any recipes in *Apicius* specify quantities. Methods, if stated at all, are stated with extreme brevity.

Apicius provides the first record in written Latin of some colloquial and technical words that evidently belonged to the spoken language and were to be inherited in modern languages, such as *baiana* 'variety of broad bean' (5.6.4). It also contains familiar Latin words in non-classical, evidently colloquial, forms which are ancestral to those of the Romance languages, such as *amindala* 'almond', *gingiber* 'ginger'.

The book as a whole is difficult to date, because in recipe books each recipe may have its own history and some may be much older than others. A benchmark is suggested by the recipe for preserving oysters (1.12) and the attribution by Athenaeus of just such a recipe to an 'Apicius' of about AD 115 (see APICIUS (3)): some of the collection was perhaps in existence by that date. A second benchmark is provided by Jerome, with the words: 'Paxamus and Apicius are always to hand.' Writing about 400, he is surely naming two current cookbooks. Alongside this goes the fact that no details in *Apicius* suggest Christianity – for example, there are no dishes for fast days, such as were needed and developed under the Byzantine Empire. Since Christianity, already widespread, had become the imperial religion by the mid fourth century, it is a reasonable supposition that *Apicius* as we know it was completed before then, and therefore that ours was approximately the *Apicius* known to Jerome. The two early manuscripts, in the Vatican and the New York Academy of Medicine, are both of the ninth century.

The historical importance of *Apicius* is as a clue to the nature of elaborate cuisine in the Roman Empire. In this it often corroborates other sources. It supplies, for example, recipes for certain dishes mentioned in historical texts. *Apicius* confirms the importance of meat and meat sauces in expensive Roman cuisine, and the use of a range of exotic and costly spices in such dishes. It provides some evidence of the vogue for SURPRISE DISHES. Apart from fish sauce (see GARUM) the most commonly used ingredients are pepper, lovage, cumin, concentrated MUST, rue, coriander, honey, vinegar and olive oil.

A somewhat later text, the *Outline Apicius* by VINIDARIUS, has no close connection with *Apicius* as we know it.

Athenaeus E 7d; Jerome, *Letters* 33.3.

E. Brandt, *Untersuchungen zum römischen Kochbuche* (Leipzig, 1927) (*Philologus. Supplementband*, 19 no. 3); Mary Ella Milham, *A Glossarial Index to De Re Coquinaria of Apicius* (Madison, 1952); Mary Ella Milham, 'A preface to Apicius' in *Helikon* vol. 7 (1967) pp. 195–204; E. Alföldi-Rosenbaum, '*Apicius de re coquinaria* and the *Vita Heliogabali*' and 'Notes on some birds and fishes of luxury in the *Historia Augusta*' in *Bonner Historia-Augusta-Colloquium 1970* ed. J. Straub (Bonn, 1972) pp. 5–18; J. Solomon, 'The Apician sauce: ius Apicianum' in *Food in Antiquity* ed. John Wilkins and others (Exeter: Exeter University Press, 1995) pp. 115–31; Carol Déry, 'The art of Apicius' in *Cooks and Other People: proceedings of the Oxford Symposium on Food and Cookery 1995* ed. Harlan Walker (Totnes: Prospect Books, 1996) pp. 111–17.

Modern interpretations of some of the recipes in *Apicius* are given in Flower and Rosenbaum (below) and in the following books: John Edwards, *The Roman Cookery of Apicius* (London: Hutchinson, 1985); Nico Valerio, *La tavola degli antichi* (Milan: Mondadori, 1989); I.G. Giacosa, *A Taste of Ancient Rome* (Chicago: Chicago University Press, 1992); Eugenia Salza Prina Ricotti, *Dining as a Roman Emperor: how to cook ancient Roman recipes today* (Rome: L'Erma di Bretschneider, 1995); Dalby and Grainger 1996; Junkelmann 1997.

Apicius. Text and translation: *Apicius* tr. Sally Grainger and Chris Grocock (Totnes: Prospect Books, forthcoming). Text and translation: Apicius, *The Roman Cookery Book* tr. B. Flower and E. Rosenbaum (London: Harrap, 1961). Critical text: *Apicii decem libri qui dicuntur De re coquinaria* ed. M.E. Milham (Leipzig, 1969, *BT*). Text, French translation and commentary: Apicius, *L'Art culinaire* ed. Jacques André (Paris: Les Belles Lettres, 1974), 2nd edn. References elsewhere in the present book are to Milham's section numbers, which differ slightly from Flower's.

Apollodorus, physician to one of the Ptolemies of Egypt. As dietician Apollodorus is known only for his recommendation of the most health-giving wines of his time. They were Naspercenite (from the Pontus), Oretic, Oeneate, Ambraciot, LEUCADIAN WINE and, best of all, PEPARETHAN WINE, the latter requiring to be kept for at least six years before drinking. It is likely enough that this Apollodorus is identical with Apollodorus of Alexandria, who wrote works on toxicology in the early third century BC.

Pliny *NH* 14.76.

OCD 1996 *s.v.* Apollodorus (4).

Apophoreta, presents for guests to take away from dinner parties. The custom is well in evidence for Rome in the first century AD. At that period, such gifts might be either valuable or risible, and might be announced by a written message, to be read out to the company, describing the gift more or less obliquely. The SATURNALIA festivities were a normal occasion for this gift-giving. The idea was not originally Greek; it could have reached Rome by way of Hellenistic banquets, inherited in turn from earlier Macedonian and Thracian customs. Martial wrote a whole book of verse couplets suitable for accompanying *apophoreta* presented at the Saturnalia, and another for similar gifts (*xenia*) made on other occasions.

Hippolochus D; Petronius S 56.8, 60.4; Martial 4.46, also book 13 ('*Xenia*') and book 14 ('*Apophoreta*'); Suetonius, *Augustus* 75, *Caligula* 55, *Vespasian* 19; Pliny the Younger, *Letters* 6.31.14.

A. Mau, 'Apophoreta' in *RE* 1893–1972; Martial, *Book XIV: the Apophoreta* ed. and tr. T.J. Leary (London: Duckworth, 1996).

Appellations *see* LOCAL SPECIALITIES; WINE REGIONS

Apple, tree fruit important in ancient food and religion. Wild apples (crab-apples) of the European wild species gradually spread from northern Anatolia after the last ice age. Apples were in due course transplanted, or grown from seed, far to the south of their native habitat, in Mesopotamia in particular, where strings of sliced dried apples are described in literary sources and have been found by archaeologists. In the Near East in the third and second millennia BC the apple was important in cookery, in medicine and also in love charms. There is no evidence that grafting was known at that period, and it is not known at what date cultivated apple varieties of modern type spread westwards from Central Asia, where they originate.

In Greece the apple was a typical orchard fruit, at least from the *Odyssey* (*c*.700 BC) onwards. Early dietary writings such as the Hippocratic *Regimen* discourage the eating of fresh apples, although the juice of cooked apples (*ta apo melou*) is prescribed in *Epidemics VII*. Apples were stored for winter use, Aristophanes suggests, but possibly in dried rather than fresh form, just as in earlier Mesopotamia. In Greek sources such as Archestratus apples are included among TRAGEMATA, that is, alongside dried fruits and nuts. These facts may suggest that sweet varieties – comparable to so many modern kinds – were not yet widespread in classical Greece, and that small, relatively acid and bitter apples, still closely resembling crab-apples, were more familiar, often eaten in dried form. Even in 600 BC, however, there was already one sweet variety, *glykymelon* 'sweet apple', mentioned by Sappho and after her, in poetic tradition, by Callimachus and Meleager.

By the time of Theophrastus (*c*.310 BC) grafting was certainly familiar and many cultivated kinds of apples were known. Alexander the Great found the best apples growing in Babylonia, so Chares says. Romans, three centuries later, undoubtedly had eating apples. Whether the tradition that they followed was Greek, Hellenistic or Carthaginian is not clear, but Roman growers were active in the development of new varieties, several of which could be stored over the winter. Among the numerous variety names of Roman times are *matiana* (see below); *orbiculata*, Greek *epeirotika*; *melimela*, the last identified by Dioscorides with Sappho's *glykymela*. Thus in the mid second century Galen explains, implying the existence of a big range of varieties, that 'some apples have sour juice, some acid, some sweet' and some combine all three flavours. He is able to set aside the older dietary tradition and to recommend sweet apples, well ripened on the tree, to be eaten fresh as part of a healthy diet; other kinds, however, are to be baked rather than eaten fresh. *Diocletian's Price Edict* prices *matiana* apples at four denarii for ten, four times the price of 'smaller' apples, a sign both of the high quality of the best Roman varieties such as this, and of the ubiquity of poorer and less palatable apples on Roman markets.

The history outlined above is in part conjectural and is difficult to trace and confirm, not least because of confusion over names. Greek *melon* in its narrowest sense meant 'apple and/or quince'. In a wider sense it included all round fleshy tree fruits, such as pomegranates and in due course peaches and citrons. Latin *malum* meant 'apple', but poets gave it the same broader senses as its Greek equivalent. Thus incidental references to Latin *malum*, Greek *melon*, might intend any or all of these fruits and do not necessarily point to apples. In particular, the *mela* 'apples' of classical myth – the golden apples of the Hesperides, the apple that distracted Atalanta in her race against matrimony, and others variously symbolic of love and health – might be pomegranates, quinces, or various other types, as the interpreter or sculptor preferred, just as well as apples.

The cultivated apple (*Malus pumila*) is Greek *melon*, Latin *malum*.

Homer, *Odyssey* 7.112–21; Sappho 105a Lobel; Hippocrates *R* 55; Aristophanes, *Wasps* 1055–7; Archestratus *H* 62 Brandt with Olson and Sens *ad l.*; Theophrastus *HP* 2.5.3, 3.11.5, 4.13.2, *al.*; Theocritus 5.95 (*oromalides*) with Gow *ad l.*; Callimachus, *Hymn to Demeter* 28; Meleager 1.27 Gow [*Anthologia Palatina* 4.1.27]; Dioscorides *MM* 1.115; Columella *DA* 5.10.19, 12.47.5–6; Pliny *NH* 15.49–52, 23.104; Plutarch *QC* 5.8; Galen *AF* 6.594–8; Athenaeus *D* 80e–82e, 277a citing Chares; *Diocletian's Price Edict* 6.65–7; Palladius *OA* 3.25.13–19; Anthimus *OC* 84 with Grant *ad l.*; *Geoponica* 10.18–21.

F. Olck, 'Apfel' in *RE* 1893–1972; Erich Ebeling, 'Apfel' in *RA* 1928– ; Buck 1949 pp. 375–6; A.R. Littlewood, 'The symbolism of the apple in Greek and Roman literature' in *Harvard Studies in Classical Philology* vol. 72 (1967) pp. 147–81; Zohary and Hopf 1993 pp. 162–6; Joan Morgan and Alison Richards, *The Book of Apples* (London: Ebury Press, 1993).

- The variety called *matiana* in Greek and Latin is one of the most frequently mentioned in classical sources. Domitian had Matian apples as a light lunch. They were said to originate in the mountains north of Aquileia in northeastern Italy. *Apicius* gives a recipe for a *minutal matianum*, for which apples of this variety are among the ingredients. This variety name, in the form *manzana*, is applied to the whole species in modern Spanish.

  Columella *DA* 5.10.19, 12.47.5; Suetonius, *Domitian* 21; Athenaeus *D* 82c; *Apicius* 4.3.4.

- Greek *hamamelis* may be a name for the European wild apple or crab-apple (*Malus sylvestris*). This is sometimes called *melon agrion* in Greek; in Latin it is *malum silvestre*.

  Dioscorides *MM* 1.115.4; Celsus, *DM* 4.26.5; Pliny *NH* 18.34; Galen, *Hippocratic Glossary* 19.44.

- The development of cider (Latin *vinum ex melis*) awaited the availability of juicy and relatively sweet apples. Both cider and cider vinegar are discussed by Palladius (fifth century AD); cider had previously been mentioned in asides by Pliny and Plutarch. A recipe for a strong cider or apple wine, Greek *hydromelon*, is given in the Byzantine *Geoponica*.

  Pliny *NH* 14.103; Plutarch *QC* 3.2 (*melites*); Palladius *OA* 3.25.19; *Geoponica* 8.27.

Apricot, soft-fleshed fruit resembling a small peach. The species originates in Tibet and western China, and was being cultivated in northwest India by about 2000 BC. The apricot was apparently known in ancient Mesopotamia, but did not become familiar further west until after Alexander's expedition.

The earliest Greek term for apricot (*Armeniaca vulgaris*) was *melon armeniakon*, literally 'Armenian apple'; it also occurs in Latin as *Armeniacum*. This name betrays a confusion: the fruit did not come from Armenia. The later Greek name *brekokkion*, *prekokkion* is borrowed from Latin *praecocium*, meaning 'the early fruit'.

Dioscorides *MM* 1.115.5; Pliny *NH* 15.41, 16.103; Galen *AF* 6.593–4, *SF* 12.76; Palladius *OA* 12.7.1–8; *Apicius* 4.5.4.

Laufer 1919 pp. 539–41; M.A. Powell, 'Classical sources and the problem of the apricot' in *Bulletin on Sumerian Agriculture* no. 3 (1987) pp. 153–6; J. Diethart and E. Kislinger, 'Aprikosen und Pflaumen' in *Jahrbuch der österreichischer Byzantinistik* vol. 42 (1992) pp. 75–8; Zohary and Hopf 1993 p. 172.

Apulia, arid but fertile region of southeastern Italy. There was considerable production of wine in Apulia, as is evident from literary sources and confirmed by archaeology; but Apulian wine is not mentioned in texts concerned with gastronomy or luxury. Brundisium was the centre of this trade, as also of the commerce in Apulian olive oil and wheat.

Varro *RR* 1.8.2, 2.6.5.

Tchernia 1986 pp. 110, 166, 336; Dalby 2000a p. 64.

Arabia, desert region marking the southern limit of early Mesopotamian kingdoms, and eventually the southeastern limit of the Roman Empire. In southern Arabia, well beyond the usual reach of these northerly powers, lay the wealthy kingdom of Sabaea and its neighbours. The region was both a source of aromatics – FRANKINCENSE, MYRRH and BALSAM – and an entrepot for the spices that had crossed the Indian Ocean. Some of these were transshipped at Arabia Eudaemon (modern Aden) or other neighbouring harbours, to continue by sea towards Egypt. Others were transferred here to camel caravan, on routes that reached as far as Mediterranean ports such as Gaza.

G.W. Bowersock, *Roman Arabia* (Cambridge, Mass.: Harvard University Press, 1983); Fergus Millar, 'Caravan cities: the Roman Near East and long distance trade by land' in *Modus Operandi: essays in honour of Geoffrey Rickman* ed. Michel Austin, Jill Harries and Christopher Smith (London: Institute of Classical Studies, 1998); Dalby 2000a pp. 182–4.

Arbutus or tree-strawberry, a small edible wild fruit. The arbutus fruit is *mimaikylon* in Greek; the tree (*Arbutus Unedo*) is *komaros*. Its Latin names are *arbutus* and *unedo*. Pliny explains the latter as 'I eat only one'; it is true that humans seldom eat arbutus fruits unless compelled by famine (the seeds get between your teeth), but birds love them.

Aristophanes, *Birds* 240, 620; Theophrastus *HP* 1.9.3, 3.16.4–5; Pliny *NH* 13.120–1, 15.98–9; Galen *AF* 6.619–20, *SF* 12.34.

Arcadia, mountainous district of the central Peloponnese. To Greeks, and to Roman poets in the Greek tradition, Arcadians typified an old-fashioned pastoral way of life. One feature shared between Arcadians and the people of the GOLDEN AGE, it was said, was a diet of ACORNS; Arcadians are characterised as *balanephagoi andres*, acorn-eating men, in a Delphic oracle quoted by Herodotus. In a description by Harmodius of Lepreum of the meals offered to the choral performers at Phigaleia in Arcadia, probably Hellenistic in date, acorns do not figure.

> The Phigaleian who was appointed *sitarkhos*, victualler, would bring each day three *khoai* [about 8 litres] of wine, one *medimnos* [about 50 litres] of barley meal, five *mnai* [about 3 kg] of cheese, and what would be needed to season the sacrifices. The city provided each of the two choruses with three sheep, a

cook, a rack for water-jars, tables, benches and all such furniture. The *khoregos*, choir-leader, provided the cook's equipment. The meal consisted of cheese and a *physte maza*, light barley cake, served on bronze platters ... With the cake and cheese came a *splankhnon*, offal, and salt as relish. When they had blessed this food, each man might drink a little from an earthenware vessel, and the server would say: '*Eudeipnias*, Dine well!' Then the soup and the crackling were served to the party, and two pieces of meat to each man individually ... For the youngsters who ate heartily more soup was poured, and more barley cakes and wheat loaves were given. Such a young man was thought to be noble and manly: hearty eating was a matter of admiration and fame among them.

Herodotus 1.66; Harmodius of Lepreum [Athenaeus D 148f–149d].

Archaeobiology *see* NUTRITION

Archaeobotany, the study of archaeological plant remains. Depending on the conditions of preservation, archaeologists may find charred or fossilised plant remains associated with storage or cooking, they may find mummified bodies whose stomachs contain plant remains, they may find coprolites (human excrement) containing plant seeds or fibres, and they may find root cavities showing the former presence of a crop. All such remains can be investigated with the aim of determining species and variety, whether the crop was wild or domesticated, whether the plant or seed had been attacked by pests, in what state it was harvested and how it had been treated or cooked.

Ironically, this potential source of information is much better exploited for prehistoric Greece, and for the outlying provinces of the Roman Empire, than it is for classical Greece or classical Rome, because, in classical archaeology, architecture and artifacts have until fairly recently monopolised the archaeologist's attention. It is notable that some foods scarcely ever spoken of in literature appear significant when archaeological sites are investigated: this partiality constitutes a weakness of literary texts when considered as a source for social history. The converse is also true: there are foods so perishable that they are never likely to appear in archaeobotanical or archaeozoological finds and will only ever be known from literature.

Palaeoethnobotany is not the same thing as archaeobotany: it is the study of plant knowledge and use in early cultures (ethnobotany being the comparative study of plant knowledge and plant uses). Archaeobotany is one of the major sources of information for the palaeoethnobotanist, who will also use textual sources when available, archaeological finds (such as millstones, cooking utensils) and comparative information from modern cultures.

Renfrew 1973; *Plants and Ancient Man: studies in palaeoethnobotany. Proceedings of the sixth symposium of the International Work Group for Palaeoethnobotany, Groningen, 30 May–3 June 1983* ed. W. van Zeist and W.A. Casparie (Rotterdam: Balkema, 1984); J.M. Hansen, 'Palaeoethnobotany in Greece: past, present and future' in *Contributions to Aegean Archaeology. Studies in honor of W.A. McDonald* (Minneapolis, 1985) pp. 171–82; *Progress in Old World Palaeoethnobotany* ed. W. van Zeist, K. Wasylikowa, K.-E. Behre (Rotterdam: Balkema, 1991); *New Light on Early Farming: recent developments in palaeoethnobotany* ed. Jane M. Renfrew, Edinburgh: Edinburgh University Press, 1991; J.M. Hansen, 'Beyond subsistence: behavioural reconstruction from palaeoethnobotany' in *Archaeological Review from Cambridge* vol. 10 (1991) pp. 53–9; Jane Renfrew, 'Palaeoethnobotany and the origins of wine' in *The Oxford Companion to Wine* ed. Jancis Robinson (Oxford: Oxford University Press, 1994) pp. 702–4; H. Kroll, 'Literature on archaeological remains of cultivated plants' in *Vegetation History and Archaeobotany* vol. 4– (1995–); Jane M. Renfrew, 'Palaeoethnobotanical finds of Vitis from Greece' in *The Origins and Ancient History of Wine* ed. Patrick E. McGovern, Stuart J. Fleming and Solomon H. Katz (London: Gordon and Breach, 1995) pp. 255–67; Mary Harlow and

Wendy Smith, 'Between feasting and fasting: the literary and archaeobotanical evidence for monastic diet in late antique Egypt' in *Antiquity* vol. 75 (2001) pp. 758–68; Philippe Marinval and Marie-Christine Marinval-Vigne, 'L'archéologie des odeurs' in *Archeologia* no. 387 (March 2002) pp. 40–4.

Archaeochemistry, the chemical analysis of archaeological finds. Chemical analysis can be applied to AMPHORAE and other containers – and their residual contents if any – to determine what was stored in them. It has also been successfully applied to drinking vessels.

Organic Contents of Ancient Vessels: materials analysis and archaeological investigation ed. W.R. Biers and P.E. McGovern (Philadelphia, 1990) (*MASCA Research Papers in Science and Archaeology*, 7); McGovern and others 1995; Patrick E. McGovern, 'Wine for eternity' in *Archaeology* vol. 51 no. 4 (1998) pp. 28–34.

Archaeology, the exploration and study of ancient settlements and sites of human activity. Classical archaeology was often – for good or bad – seen as a separate discipline, distinct from the archaeology of other times and places. That kind of classical archaeology, focusing as it did on public buildings, tombs, inscriptions and works of art, offered relatively little to the present subject, although food and dining were frequently the subject of inscriptions and iconography and some buildings were designed partly or wholly for feasting (see ARCHITECTURE; ANDRON).

Nowadays new archaeological sites, even those of classical Greece and Italy, tend to be explored with greater attention to the decipherment of human activity. It becomes possible to identify the uses of space and the patterns of behaviour, including eating and drinking. Field survey, a relatively new branch of archaeology, asks the same questions of much larger spaces and can provide information on farming and food production.

In the archaeological study of ancient society two sites are of exceptional importance because of their completeness. AKROTIRI suffered a catastrophic volcanic eruption in the mid second millennium BC. Discovered in the 1960s, it exemplifies a small town of the Aegean in Minoan times. The second site is POMPEII (with Herculaneum and neighbouring villas), a prosperous seaside town of Roman Campania, obliterated by the eruption of Vesuvius in AD 79, rediscovered in the late eighteenth century and gradually excavated since that time. A third example might be the inland district near NOLA obliterated by an earlier eruption of Vesuvius, about 1500 BC; here, however, only scattered houses, and no large settlements, have so far been found.

The Archaeology of Household Activities ed. Penelope M. Allison (London: Routledge, 1999).

Archaeozoology, the study of archaeological remains of animals. Most of the relevant finds are of fossilised or charred bones, except where unusual climatic conditions have allowed the preservation of other body parts. As with ARCHAEOBOTANY, the typical aims of investigation are to determine species and variety, whether the animal was wild or domesticated, its age and health when killed, and how it had been butchered and cooked.

S. Bökönyi, 'Archaeological problems and methods of recognizing animal domestication' in *The Domestication and Exploitation of Plants and Animals* ed. P.J. Ucko and G.W. Dimbleby (London, 1969) pp. 219–29; S. Payne, 'On the interpretation of bone samples from archaeological sites' in *Papers in Economic Prehistory* ed. E.S. Higgs (Cambridge, 1972); R. Casteel, *Fish Remains in Archaeology and Paleo-environmental Studies* (London, 1976); G. Caughley, *Analysis of Vertebrate Populations* (Chichester: Wiley, 1977); Rosemary-Margaret Luff, *A Zooarchaeological Study of the Roman North-western Provinces* (Oxford: BAR, 1982); S. Payne, 'Zoo-archaeology in Greece: a reader's guide' in *Contributions to Aegean Archaeology: studies in honor of William A. McDonald* ed. N.C. Wilkie and W.D.E. Coulson (Minneapolis, 1985) pp. 211–44; Paul Stokes, 'Debris from Roman butchery: a new interpretation' in *Petits Propos culinaires* no. 52 (1995) pp. 38–47, with note in no. 54 (1996) p. 67; Terry O'Connor, *The Archaeology of Animal Bones* (Stroud: Sutton, 1996); Martine Leguilloux, 'L'alimentation carnée au

1er millénaire avant J.-C. en Grèce continentale et dans les Cyclades: premiers résultats archéozoologiques' in *Paysage et alimentation dans le monde grec* ed. Jean-Marc Luce (Toulouse, 2000) pp. 69–95.

- A special field of archaeozoology is the study of insect pests that attacked plants and stored foods. They are studied by means of the damage they leave as well as their own remains.

M.E. Kislev, 'Archaeobotany and storage archaeoentomology' in *New Light on Early Farming: Recent Developments in Palaeoethnobotany* ed. Jane M. Renfrew (Edinburgh: Edinburgh University Press, 1991) pp. 121–36; E. Panagiotakopulu and P.C. Buckland, 'Insect pests of stored products from Bronze Age Santorini, Greece' in *Journal of Stored Product Research* vol. 27 (1991) pp. 179–84; E. Panagiotakopulu, 'New records for ancient pests: archaeoentomology in Egypt' in *Journal of Archaeological Science* vol. 28 (2001) pp. 1235–46; Petra Dark and Henry Gent, 'Pests and diseases of prehistoric crops: a yield "honeymoon" for early grain crops in Europe?' in *Oxford Journal of Archaeology* vol. 20 (2001) pp. 59–78.

Archestratus, a Sicilian Greek, author of a Greek gastronomic poem of *c*.350 BC. The work was written in rough hexameter verse. It now survives only in fragments quoted by ATHENAEUS in the *Deipnosophists*. Its subject was the selection of fine food, especially fish, at Mediterranean coastal cities; as such it reads like a traveller's guide rather than a household cookbook. Its pithy and amusing style destined it to be learnt by heart and quoted on suitable occasions, whether at market or at dinner, as shown by Chrysippus and Lynceus. If the author had any other aim for his poem than this, it remains hidden. Its title is uncertain, as is Archestratus's native city: the possibilities are set out in the following extract from the *Epitome of Athenaeus*.

Archestratus of Syracuse (or Gela) composed the work that Chrysippus entitles *Gastronomy*, while Lynceus and Callimachus call it *The Life of Pleasure*, and Clearchus *The Art of Dining*, and others again *Cookery*: it is a hexameter poem, beginning with the line 'Making an exposition of my research for all of Greece …' Archestratus writes: 'All to dine at one hospitable table: let there be three or four altogether, or at most five, or you will have a tentful of plundering mercenaries.'

Of these alternative titles the most likely to be authentic is *Hedypatheia*, *The Life of Pleasure*. It is clear that Archestratus had really travelled widely, because he knew what he was talking about. The local gastronomic opinions that he retails are sometimes paralleled and scarcely ever contradicted in other surviving sources, but in most cases he appears to have been the first to write them down. The poem's general attitude to its subject, often and trenchantly reiterated, is that one should choose fresh food of the highest quality, wherever and whenever it will be at its best, whether it is cheap or expensive, and cook it rapidly, with very sparing use of extraneous flavours. On this basis one should eat and drink simply, with few and well-chosen guests – see the quotation above.

The poem was known to some in the fourth and third centuries BC. Its hedonism aroused the disapproval of philosophers, some of whom, perhaps unfairly, confused its subject matter with that of the sex manual of Philaenis. The last surviving sign of its popularity is that ENNIUS wrote a Latin adaptation or imitation *c.*175 BC.

Athenaeus *E* 4d, *D* 278d, also 313f citing Lynceus *F* 20, also 335d.

Dalby 1995; Wilkins 2000 pp. 357–9, *al.*

Archestratus H: *Hedypatheia*. Critical text, translation and commentary: S. Douglas Olson and Alexander Sens, *Archestratos of Gela; Greek culture and cuisine in the fourth century BCE* (Oxford: Oxford University Press, 2000). Translation and commentary: Archestratus, *The Life of Luxury* tr. John Wilkins and Shaun Hill (Totnes: Prospect Books, 1994). Text: *Corpusculum poesis epicae Graecae ludibundae* ed. P. Brandt, vol. 1 (1888, *BT*). References elsewhere in the present book are to the fragment numbering established by Brandt: this numbering is adopted by Wilkins and Hill and is recorded by Olson and Sens, whose new numbering differs.

Architecture of dining spaces is naturally linked with the forms of conviviality typical of the ancient world. Communal dining was important occasionally in all Greek city states; in some, particularly in Sparta and Cretan cities, it was the regular rule. At Lyttos in Crete, we are told, there was an *andreion*, men's house, a building in which men ate communally and visitors were entertained. Dining customs there are described in some detail (see Athenaeus). Other buildings, focuses for communal dining elsewhere, have been identified archaeologically and linked with the Greek word *prytaneion* (see below). In most such buildings diners apparently sat rather than reclined.

Typical private houses in classical Greek cities, when sufficiently large and elaborate, were likely to include a dining room, identified with the Greek word ANDRON. This room was planned to accommodate a certain number of couches for reclining diners. Roman houses, when sufficiently large, included a room of similar function, often with built-in stone couches, called TRICLINIUM.

Dining often took place as part of a religious observance whose central feature, from the god's point of view, was the SACRIFICE of a domesticated animal. At some Greek shrines, eventually, a purpose-built structure housed this festivity: the building is called *hestiatorion*, and it contained one or several dining rooms. Each room was planned to accommodate couches in the same way as the *andron* in a private house, but often the number of couches was larger and their intended arrangement more complex.

Athenaeus *D* 143a–f citing Dosiadas and Pyrgion.

E. McCartney, 'The couch as a unit of measurement' in *Classical Philology* vol. 29 (1934) pp. 30–5; E. Will, 'Banquets et salles de banquet dans les cultes de la Grèce et de l'Empire Romain' in *Mélanges d'histoire ancienne et d'archéologie offerts à Paul Collart* ed. P. Ducrey (Lausanne, 1976) pp. 353–62; C. Börker, *Festbankett und griechische Architektur* (Constance, 1983) (*Xenia*, 4); B. Bergquist, 'Sympotic space: a functional aspect of Greek dining-rooms' in *Sympotica: a symposium on the symposion* ed. Oswyn Murray (Oxford: Oxford University Press, 1990) pp. 37–65; R.A. Tomlinson, 'The chronology of the Perachora hestiatorion and its significance' *ib.* pp. 95–101; J. Rossiter, 'Convivium and villa in late antiquity' in *Dining in a Classical Context* ed. W.J. Slater (Ann Arbor: University of Michigan Press, 1991) pp. 199–214; N. Bookidis, J. Hansen, L. Snyder and P. Goldberg, 'Dining in the sanctuary of Demeter and Kore at Corinth' in *Hesperia* vol. 68 (1999) pp. 1–54.

• *Prytaneion* is sometimes translated 'town hall'. Many Greek cities in the sixth and fifth centuries BC built a *prytaneion*; its main use, to judge by available sources, was as a building in which to offer entertainment to honoured guests and to deserving citizens, the latter on some particular occasion or for a longer period. Socrates, facing a death sentence for impiety, makes the skittish counter-suggestion that he be awarded dinners for life at the *prytaneion*. LUCULLUS's house is said by Plutarch to have resembled a *prytaneion* for cultured Greek visitors to Rome. At Athens a completely different kind of communal dining took place in an unusual round building, the *Tholos*, where the city's *prytaneis* or 'presidents' ate and slept during their month of duty.

Aristophanes, *Knights* 1404, *Peace* 1084; Plato, *Apology* 36d; Demosthenes, *Against Aristocrates* 130, *Against Polycles* 13; Plutarch, *QS* 4.4 [667d], *Life of Lucullus* 42.

S.G. Miller, *The Prytaneion: its function and architectural form* (Berkeley, 1978); Pauline Schmitt-Pantel, 'Les repas au prytanée et à la tholos dans l'Athènes classique: sitesis, trophé, misthos: réflexions sur le mode de nourriture démocratique' in *Aion* vol. 2 (1980) pp. 55–68; A.S. Henry, 'Invitations to the prytaneion at Athens' in *Antichthon* vol. 15 (1981) pp. 100–10; M.J. Osborne, 'Entertainment in the prytaneion at Athens' in *Zeitschrift für Papyrologie und Epigraphik* vol. 41 (1981) pp. 153–70; F. Cooper and S. Morris, 'Dining in round buildings' in *Sympotica: a symposium on the symposion* ed. Oswyn Murray (Oxford: Oxford University Press, 1990) pp. 66–85.

Argun palm (*Medemia Argun*), fruit tree of Nubia also grown in upper Egypt. This species is possibly described by Theophrastus and, following him, Pliny.

Theophrastus *HP* 2.6.10 (read *kykas*); Pliny *NH* 13.47 (*coecas?*).

Darby and others 1977 pp. 722–3; Brewer and others (1995 ?) p. 51.

Aristippus, Greek philosopher (born *c*.435 at Cyrene, died after 366 BC). A student of Socrates who afterwards lived at the court of Dionysius of Syracuse, Aristippus is of interest in the food context for his insistence on present pleasure as the sole criterion of the good; he went so far as to exclude past and possible future pleasures from the calculation. His views led him to the single-minded enjoyment of luxury and gourmandise and thus to a way of life productive of amusing anecdotes. The philosophical lineage of Aristippus, beginning with his daughter Arete, is conventionally termed the 'Cyrenaic school'.

Diogenes Laertius 2.65–104; Athenaeus *D* 544a–f quoting Alexis *F* 37 Kassel (see Arnott *ad l.*).

Aristophanes (*c*.450–*c*.386 BC), Athenian comedy playwright. Aristophanes was the greatest figure of the 'Old Comedy' tradition, which was already moribund by the time of his death. He is also the only writer of this tradition whose works can now be read in complete form: eleven of his forty plays survive. From his lost plays, as from some of the works of his contemporaries, quotations relevant to food and dining appear in the *Deipnosophists* of Athenaeus. Aristophanes is generally supposed by modern critics to have held conservative political views. There is a fictionalised portrait of him in Plato's *Symposium*.

Old Comedy plots, though fantastic, are deeply rooted in contemporary Athenian social life, because a principal purpose of the genre was to satirise and ridicule prominent men, politicians and others. Owing to their social setting, and their humour which continually turns on food and sex, these eleven plays are indispensable sources for food and festivity in fifth-century BC Athens. They are often cited in the present book.

The following extended passages are particularly relevant to the subject of food. In *Acharnians* 719–1234 a market attracting starving traders from Megara and Boeotia is followed by a feast celebrating peace; the Peloponnesian War, in progress when *Acharnians* was produced in 425, had in fact been disastrous to the trade of Athens's neighbours. In *Knights*, produced in 424, the hero is the *Allantopoles*, sausage-seller, and we learn a good deal of his trade. In *Wasps* 1122–537, produced in 422, Philocleon is taught by his son correct behaviour at a *symposion*, and attends one, with riotous results. *Peace*, produced in 421, opens with two slaves making *mazai* (barley cakes, but in this case they are dung cakes) to feed a giant beetle; the same play ends with an extended feast scene, celebrating both harvest and peace, a scene which may fairly be described as Rabelaisian. Although the birds in *Birds*, produced in 414, are not eaten, there is plenty of incidental information about birds as food. In *Thesmophoriazusae* 277–764, produced in 411, the women's festival *Thesmophoria* is invaded by the poet Euripides's uncle, disguised as a woman. *Assemblywomen*, produced c.392, set in an Athens run by women, ends with a public dinner. The wealth that is allotted to Athens in *Wealth*, produced in 388, is visible largely in food and wine, whether consumed by humans or sacrificed to the gods. In all these scenes the playwright's ebullient and satirical humour makes the task of the straight-faced social historian a fairly complicated one.

The *Scholia on Aristophanes*, sometimes cited in the present book, are running commentaries on the eleven plays. They were compiled by Greek scholars in Hellenistic, Roman and Byzantine times

and include a good deal of information on details of classical social life, much of it probably true. They are not available in translation.

Plato, *Symposium* 185c–193e.

M. Vetta, 'Un capitolo di storia di poesia simposiale: per l'esegese di Aristofane, *Vespe* 1222–1248' in *Poesia e simposio nella Grecia antica: guida storica e critica* ed. M. Vetta (Rome, 1983); John Wilkins, 'Eating in Greek comedy' in *Food in European Literature* ed. John Wilkins (Exeter: Intellect, 1996) pp. 46–56; N. Dunbar, 'Aristophane, ornithophile et ornithophage' in *Aristophane: la langue, la scène, la cité* ed. P. Thiercy and M. Menu (Bari, 1997) pp. 113–29.

Aristotle (384–322 BC), philosopher, born at Stageira in Chalcidice. Aristotle studied under Plato and remained a member of Plato's Academy at Athens for twenty years. He spent some time at Atarneus in Asia Minor, and then on Lesbos, where he did some zoological research. For several years after 343 he served Philip of Macedon as tutor to Philip's son ALEXANDER THE GREAT. In 335 Aristotle returned to Athens and founded his own school, the Lyceum. Here he and some of his students pursued an ambitious series of researches focusing on natural history and several other subject areas. His zoological works, notably the observant and penetrating *History of Animals*, are often cited in the present book for their information on animals that were used for food. Aristotle had many eminent pupils, among them his eventual successor THEOPHRASTUS.

Aristotle HA: *History of Animals*. Translation and commentary: Aristotle, *Historia Animalium* tr. D'Arcy Wentworth Thompson (Oxford: Clarendon Press, 1910) (*The Works of Aristotle Translated into English*, 4).

—— S: *Symposium* or *On Drunkenness*. Text of fragments in *Aristotelis qui ferebantur librorum fragmenta* ed. Valentinus Rose (1886, BT) pp. 97–104.

Army food, a concern of soldiers and, in some states, of their commanders. The armies of the Persian Empire – and perhaps of earlier Near Eastern states –

had their own travelling markets. Pritchett gathers the evidence for the food of classical Greek armies: see also Dalby pp. 23–30 (references below). As a general rule soldiers were given an allowance (*siteresion*) in coin or booty and the facility to exchange it for food, essentially *sitos* 'cereal food'. What they got to eat with their bread, *opson* 'relish', was not the army's concern. Cities which lay on an army's route might arrange markets outside their walls. Soldiers cooked for themselves in mess groups, or kept slaves to cook for them.

The Roman army under the Empire, a relatively large standing army with long-established legionary fortresses and other bases, made much fuller arrangements for soldiers' food. Déry (below) gives a useful outline. The supply of cereal food to the legions (normally wheat) was a responsibility of the *procurator* of each province. Supplies might be requisitioned but were generally purchased; prices were eventually fixed, and DIOCLETIAN'S PRICE EDICT is an elaborate example of a fixed price list for army supplies. On campaign the necessary wheat was where possible transported in wagons (thanks to Roman road-building), but soldiers might on occasion have to carry several days' food supply, as well as their cooking equipment; again, they themselves did the cooking. Excavations of forts and camps have yielded food remains and also documents listing food supplies. In a typical legionary fortress there were hearths in each room and domed bread ovens at the end of each barrack block, showing that even in these permanent bases cooking and baking were not organised centrally.

Vindolanda Tablets 1.4=2.190, 1.5=2.191, 2.180, 2.182, *al.*

R.W. Davies, 'The Roman military diet' in *Britannia* vol. 2 (1971) pp. 122–42, reprinted in his *Service in the Roman Army* (Edinburgh: Edinburgh University Press, 1989) pp. 187–206; W.K. Pritchett, *Ancient Greek Military Practices*, afterwards re-titled *The Greek State at War* (Berkeley: University of California Press, 1971–) esp. vol. 1; J.H. Dickson, 'Exotic food and drink in ancient Scotland' in *Glasgow Naturalist* vol. 19 (1979) pp. 437–42; Tchernia 1986 pp. 11–19; P. Crawford, 'Food for a Roman legion' in *British Archaeological Reports* vol. 340 part 1 (1987) p. 692 ff.; C. Dickson and J. Dickson, 'The diet of the Roman army in deforested central Scotland' in *Plants Today* (July/August 1988) pp. 121–6; C. Dickson, 'The Roman army diet in Britain and Germany' in *Dissertationes Botanicae* vol. 133 (1989) pp. 135–54; W. Groenman-van Waateringe, 'Food for soldiers, food for thought' in *Barbarians and Romans in North-west Europe from the later Republic to late antiquity* ed. John C. Barrett, Andrew P. Fitzpatrick and Lesley Macinnes (Oxford: BAR, 1989) pp. 96–107; Andrew Dalby, 'Greeks abroad: social organization and food among the Ten Thousand' in *Journal of Hellenic Studies* vol. 112 (1992) pp. 16–30; Junkelmann 1997; Carol A. Déry, 'Food and the Roman army: travel, transport and transmission' in *Food on the Move: proceedings of the Oxford Symposium on Food and Cookery 1996* ed. H. Walker (Totnes: Prospect Books, 1997) pp. 84–96; P.P.M. Erdkamp, *Hunger and the Sword. Warfare and food supply in Roman republican wars (264–30 BC)* (Amsterdam, 1998).

Aromatics, vegetable and other products whose major use is to provide flavour and aroma. Aromatics were significant in ancient dining for their contribution to the flavouring of food and drink (see SPICES; HERBS), to the perfumes worn by those who were dining, to the wreaths that they wore while dining (see WREATHS) and to the incenses and oils that were burned in the dining room. In all these uses, if correctly chosen, they were believed to contribute to the health and mood of the participants; Helen in Homer's *Odyssey*, according to an argument retailed by Plutarch, was a forerunner in using aromatics in this way.

Oils were the usual vehicles for perfumes in antiquity. The making of perfumed oils, both to wear and to burn, was already an industry in Minoan and Mycenaean Greece and in Pharaonic Egypt. The Greek islands and Egypt continued to be centres of this industry in classical times.

Homer, *Odyssey* 4.220; Archestratus *H* 62 Brandt with Olson and Sens *ad l.*; Theophrastus

CP 6.14; Pliny *NH* 13.1–26; Plutarch *QC* 1.1, *EC* 999a, *Animals are Rational* 990a–c; Athenaeus *D* 553a–554b, also 686c–692f with medical sources quoted there.

Marcel Detienne, *Le Jardin d'Adonis: la mythologie des aromates en Grèce* (Paris, 1972), translation: *The Gardens of Adonis: spices in Greek mythology* (Hassocks: Harvester Press, 1977), review by John Scarborough in *Classical Journal* vol. 76 (1981) pp. 175–8; H. Georgiou, 'Aromatics in antiquity and in Minoan Crete: a review and reassessment' in *Kritika khronika* vol. 25 (1973) pp. 441–56 and plates 18–19; E.D. Foster, 'An administrative department at Pylos dealing with perfumery and offerings' in *Minos* vol. 16 (1975) pp. 19–51; C.W. Shelmerdine, *The Perfume Industry of Mycenaean Pylos* (Göteborg, 1985); P. Faure, *Parfums et aromates de l'antiquité* (Paris: Fayard, 1987); D. Brent Sandy, *The Production and Use of Vegetable Oils in Ptolemaic Egypt* (Atlanta: Scholars Press, 1989) (*Bulletin of the American Society of Papyrologists*, supplement 6); Nigel Groom, *The New Perfume Handbook* (London: Blackie Professional, 1995); Catherine Connors, 'Scents and sensibility in Plautus' *Casina*' in *Classical Quarterly* vol. 47 (1997) pp. 305–9; Jacqueline Vons, 'Il est des parfums sauvages comme l'odeur du désert: étude du vocabulaire des parfums chez Pline l'Ancien' in *Latomus* vol. 58 (1999) pp. 820–38.

Artemidorus of Tarsus, 'the Pseudaristophanean', Greek author of a *Dictionary of Cookery* and of other works less relevant to food. He is cited eight times by Athenaeus, once merely because he himself had cited EPAENETUS, several times on lexical points, once at length for a detailed recipe for a MATTYE.

Athenaeus *D* 171b, 387d, 663d–e, *E* 5b.

Artichoke, cultivated plant species originating from the cardoon. The latter is a garden plant with long jagged-edged edible leaves. Cardoons are linked with Sicily in ancient Greek sources, with Spain in Roman sources. It is likely to have been in Sicily that gardeners developed the artichoke, a variety of cardoon grown for its large edible flower.

The date at which the artichoke was developed is controversial: it is often said to have emerged in late medieval times.

However, a cardoon with an edible flower was already known to Theophrastus, who describes the flower-bottom, accurately, as 'resembling palm hearts'. 'They are conserved in honey-vinegar with silphium and cumin, so that they may be eaten every day of the year,' writes Pliny. The inedible choke was used as a rennet in cheese-making, as explained by Berytius.

The cardoon (*Cynara Cardunculus*) and artichoke (*C. Scolymus*) are Greek *kaktos, kinara*, Latin *carduus*.

Theophrastus *HP* 6.4.10–11; Pliny *NH* 19.152–3; Athenaeus *E* 70a–71c; Palladius *OA* 11.11.1; *Geoponica* 18.19 quoting Berytius.

Arum, plant genus including English cuckoo-pint or lords-and-ladies and related to TARO. The fleshy root is poisonous until thoroughly slaked. It can then be useful food, and was known as such in classical Greece though scarcely mentioned in general literature. It was regarded by Dioscorides and Aetius as an aphrodisiac. It was also eaten by bears (says Aristotle) as their first food after hibernation. *Arum Dioscoridis* was the species grown and gathered from the wild in Palestine. It was probably *Arum italicum* (Aaron's rod or Italian arum) that saved Caesar's troops from famine when besieging Pompey at Dyrrachium in 48 BC.

> There is also a kind of root, soon discovered by those on potherb duty, which is called *chara*: mixed with milk it considerably relieved the shortage of food. They made it into a kind of bread. There was a lot of it: when Pompey's soldiers were talking to mine and teased them with being hungry, they used to throw these loaves at them in reply. It made them less cocky.

Arum is Greek and Latin *aron*, also late Latin *veta leporina* 'hare's prick'. The name *chara*, given by Caesar in the above quotation, is presumably local, being neither Greek nor Latin. When they sang of this incident at Caesar's triumph, the

soldiers called their emergency food *lapsana* 'charlock' (Pliny *NH* 19.144: see
RADISH) but that is not likely to be the
real identification.

Aristotle *HA* 600b11; Theophrastus *HP* 1.6.10,
7.12.2; Nicander *F* 71 Schneider; Caesar, *Civil
War* 3.48; Dioscorides *MM* 2.167, *E* 2.101;
Pliny *NH* 24.142–8; *Mishnah* Shabbath 18.1;
Aetius, *Medicine* 11.35.

Arval Brothers, Roman religious society.
Its communal meals and other observances
were described in a regularly updated
inscription whose latest entry is for AD
241. The brotherhood had a membership
of twelve, and claimed that its original
members were Romulus, whose wet-nurse
was Acca Larentia, and her eleven sons.
The insignia of the brotherhood was a
garland of wheat-ears.

Aulus Gellius 7.7 quoting Masurius Sabinus.

Werner Eisenhut in *KP* 1975 *s.v. Arvales
fratres*; J. Scheid, *Romulus et ses frères: le
collège des Frères Arvales* (Rome, 1990).

Asafoetida or hing, strong-smelling resin
from a large fennel-like plant that grows
wild in Iran and Afghanistan. Asafoetida
is an important culinary spice and medicinal drug in India, and was evidently
valued in the ancient Near East: it is
mentioned in Akkadian texts and was
required for the Persian King's Dinner
(see PERSIANS). In 328/7 BC the soldiers
of Alexander found it growing in Afghanistan, identified it with SILPHIUM, and
used it as a digestive to help them with
their raw horsemeat. Silphium was probably in fact a different species, now
extinct, but its resin had similar digestive
properties. This event marks the entry of
asafoetida into Greek and Roman use. As
the supply of African silphium disappeared, asafoetida necessarily took its
place in Roman cuisine. It is called for
very frequently in the recipes of *Apicius*.
Its contribution to Roman cuisine may be
compared with that of onion to English
cooking.

Asafoetida (*Ferula Assa-foetida*) is
Greek *silphion* (*Medikon*) 'Median silphium', Latin *silfi, laser, laserpitium*. The
identification of these ancient terms with
modern asafoetida was made by García
de Orta in 1563, although the actual
plant source of asafoetida was unknown
until described by the scientific explorer
Engelbert Kaempfer in the early eighteenth century.

Dioscorides *MM* 3.80; Arrian, *Anabasis* 3.28
citing Aristobulus, cf. Strabo 15.2.10; Galen *SF*
12.123; Polyaenus 4.3.32; *Apicius* 4.4.2, *al.*

García de Orta, *Colloquios dos simples e
drogas he cousas medicinaes da India* (Goa,
1563) ch. 7; Engelbert Kaempfer, *Amoenitatum
exoticarum fasciculi 5* (Lemgoviae, 1712); Yule
and Burnell 1903 pp. 418–19; Laufer 1919 pp.
353–62; H.A. Hoffner, *Alimenta Hethaeorum*
(New Haven, 1974), p. 110; Dalby 2000b pp.
110–12 and plate 14.

• Two other aromatics used in the classical
world belong to the same botanical genus.
Galbanum (Greek *khalbane*, Latin *galbanum*), the resin of *Ferula galbaniflua*, came
from Syria and Persia and was used in
medicines and perfumes.

Dioscorides *MM* 3.83; Pliny *NH* 12.126.

Laufer 1919 pp. 363–6; Miller 1969 pp.
99–100; Dalby 2000a p. 170.

• Sagapenum (Greek *sagapenon*, Latin *sagapenum, sacopenium, serapinum*), the resin of
Ferula persica, was an adulterant in ancient
supplies of asafoetida and a medicinal ingredient in its own right.

Dioscorides *MM* 3.95; Pliny *NH* 20.197;
Galen *SF* 12.117.

Asceticism, the practice of abstinence
from luxuries and pleasures. Various patterns of belief may require the avoidance
of certain specific foods (among those
often avoided are SALT, BEAN, GARLIC,
WINE) or of all foods and drinks except
the minimum needed for survival.

Asceticism in various forms was practised in several ancient schools of philosophy; it is therefore no surprise that the
religious ascetics of ancient India were
identified by Greek observers as 'philosophers'. In the Roman Empire, in due

course, Christian belief provided a new motivation for a continuing and perhaps a more extreme practice of asceticism. Biographies of the Christian hermits of Syria and Egypt are important sources of information both on ascetic lifestyles and on the more usual food behaviour of the period.

Philo, *On the Contemplative Life*; Athanasius, *Life of Saint Antony*; *Historia Monachorum in Aegypto* [for translation see *The Lives of the Desert Fathers* tr. Norman Russell (London: Mowbray, 1981)]; Palladius, *Lausiac History*; *Apophthegmata Patrum* [for translation see *The Sayings of the Desert Fathers* tr. Benedicta Ward (London: Mowbray, 1975)]; John Cassian, *Institutes, Conferences*.

A. Vööbus, *A History of Asceticism in the Syrian Orient* (Louvain, 1958–60), 2 vols; Derwas J. Chitty, *The Desert a City* (Oxford, 1966); Benedicta Ward, *Harlots of the Desert: a study of repentance in early monastic sources* (Oxford, 1987); *Ascetic Behavior in Greco-Roman Antiquity: a sourcebook* ed. Vincent L. Wimbush (Minneapolis: Fortress Press, 1990); F. Thelamon, 'Ascèse et sociabilité: les conduites alimentaires des moines d'Egypte au IVe siècle' in *Revue des études augustiniennes* vol. 38 (1992) pp. 295–321; James E. Goehring, 'Through a glass darkly: diverse images of the *apotaktikoi(ai)* of early Egyptian monasticism' in *Semeia* vol. 58 (1992) pp. 25–45; Susanna Elm, *Virgins of God: the making of asceticism in late Antiquity* (Oxford: Clarendon Press, 1994); Grimm 1996; Garnsey 1999 pp. 85–99; Mary Harlow and Wendy Smith, 'Between feasting and fasting: the literary and archaeobotanical evidence for monastic diet in late antique Egypt' in *Antiquity* vol. 75 (2001) pp. 758–68.

Asian wines, a collective designation for those of the Roman province of Asia. Galen includes in this designation both the big island wines, CHIAN WINE and LESBIAN WINE, and those of the mainland vineyards around Pergamum and along the coast, Homer's 'grape-growing Phrygia'. Wines of this mainland region are dealt with here. For the wine region that lay immediately to the south see EPHESIAN WINES.

Although less ubiquitous in literature than the great wine districts of Latium and Campania, some of the Asian vineyards produced wine that was agreed to rival the best Italian wines in quality. Galen is not the only author to place Tmolite on a level with Falernian and others. Other districts listed here produced light and quickly maturing wines of good quality but without the ability to travel. They are known only because the garrulous Galen describes their products: as he adds with obvious truth, there were such wines in many provinces, and you would only get to know them if you lived there.

Homer, *Iliad* 3.184; Varro *RR* 1.7.6; Galen *ST* 6.275–6; Themison, *Diagnosis of Acute and Chronic Diseases* 10 Fuchs.

Ronald L. Gorny, 'Viticulture and ancient Anatolia' in *The Origins and Ancient History of Wine* ed. Patrick E. McGovern, Stuart J. Fleming and Solomon H. Katz (London: Gordon and Breach, 1995) pp. 133–74; Dalby 2000a pp. 136–7.

- Aegeate wine (Greek *Aigeates*) from Aegae in Aeolis, black, 'thick' and astringent according to Galen.

  Galen *ST* 6.337, *BM* 6.800, *On Therapeutic Method* 10.833.

- Arsyene wine (Greek *Arsyenos*), likened by Galen to Sabine: both are light, white, 'watery' and have little astringency. Arsyene tended to sharpness when young, to bitterness when aged.

  Galen *ST* 6.276, *BM* 6.806, *DA* 14.16, *On Therapeutic Method* 10.483, 10.833, *To Glaucon on Therapeutic Method* 11.87, *On Compounding* 12.517.

- Catacecaumenite wine (Latin *Catacecaumenites*), from a treeless and highly volcanic district of Maeonia, in inland Lydia. *Katakekaumene* means literally 'burnt-up'. Catacecaumenite was counted among the best wines of the Empire in Strabo's view; in the third rank of Transmarine wines according to Pliny. Galen does not mention Catacecaumenite wine by name: instead he occasionally recommends two sweet, black Maeonian wines, 'those called by local people *Karyinos* and *Therinos*', which represent subdivisions of the Catacecaumenite region. This same region was later the source of an expensive grape syrup, *caroenum Maeonium*, according to *Diocletian's Price Edict*.

Strabo 13.4.11, 14.1.15; Vitruvius 8.3.12; Pliny *NH* 14.75; Galen *VA* 99, *ST* 6.338 (read *Therinos … Karyinos*), *BM* 6.801, *On Taking the Pulse* 8.774, *On Compounding* 13.11 (read *Therinon*), *Commentary on Hippocrates RA* 15.632; *Diocletian's Price Edict* 2.13.

Dalby 2000a pp. 136–7.

- Clazomenian wine (Greek *Klazomenios*, Latin *Clazomenius*), from Clazomenae on the mainland coast of Asia Minor. Like Coan, this had an admixture of seawater: it had become all the more wholesome, according to Pliny, because the quantity of seawater had recently been reduced. Galen recommends no wines with seawater added, and does not mention this one.

Dioscorides *MM* 5.6.9; Pliny *NH* 14.73.

- Perperine wine (Greek *Perperinios*), from the coastal slopes of Perperene near Smyrna, where Varro said the vines cropped twice each year. Perperine, a favourite of Galen's, is said by him to be rather 'thick' and astringent. Originally 'black', it would become red, then tawny, then blonde as it aged. This may be the wine of Smyrna that had already been rated highly by Strabo. A 'PRAMNIAN WINE', so called in reminiscence of the epic adjective *Pramnios*, was produced (according to Pliny) in the district of Smyrna next to the shrine of the Mother.

Strabo 14.1.15; Pliny *NH* 14.54, cf. 16.115; Galen *ST* 6.337, *BM* 6.800, 6.805.

- Tibene wine (Greek *Tibenos*), from a place named Tibas. It is described by Galen as 'watery', and tending to sharpness when young, to bitterness when aged.

Galen *BM* 6.806–807, *DA* 14.16, *On Therapeutic Method* 10.833.

- Titacazene wine (Greek *Titakazenos*), described by Galen as 'watery', and tending to sharpness when young, to bitterness when aged.

Galen *ST* 6.276, *BM* 6.806, *DA* 14.16, *On Therapeutic Method* 10.833, *On Compounding* 12.517.

- Tmolite wine (Greek *Tmolites*), from the mountain of Tmolus, south of Sardis in LYDIA. Tmolite wine was familiar to Roman poets around the time of Augustus. A sweet Tmolite and an 'austere' Tmolite are frequently mentioned by Galen in the mid second century, and likened to Falernian in their nature and quality. Both were tawny in colour, very light and translucent; the former

moderately sweet and very aromatic, the latter somewhat astringent, not sweet and not aromatic. Both were hot (in terms of humoral theory) and therefore headachy.

Vergil, *Georgics* 2.98; Ovid, *Fasti* 2.313, *Metamorphoses* 6.15, 6.86; Vitruvius 8.3.12; Pliny *NH* 14.74; Silius Italicus 7.210; Seneca, *Phoenissae* 602; Galen *ST* 6.335, *BM* 6.803, *SF* 11.604, *DA* 14.28–9, *On Therapeutic Method* 10.830, 10.836, *On Compounding* 13.405.

Asparagus, a garden vegetable planted as crowns in raised beds: the immature shoots growing from the crowns are gathered and cooked. Several species of genus *Asparagus* grow in Mediterranean lands and their young shoots are traditionally gathered for food. They are smaller and less succulent, but more tasty, than cultivated plants: 'the finest are not the ones that are planted', according to the *Epitome of Athenaeus*.

There is no evidence that asparagus was cultivated in classical Greece. The earliest description of how asparagus was grown is found in an appendix to Cato's textbook *On Farming*. Whether the plant was domesticated in Italy, or whether the skill was learnt from the Carthaginians, is unknown, but it is stated as a fact that very large cultivated asparagus was to be found in north Africa.

Asparagus is to be eaten with salt and oil, says Anthimus wisely (see Grant 1999 p. 142 for a modern interpretation of Anthimus's recipe). It was known to ancient dieticians as a diuretic.

Cultivated asparagus (*Asparagus officinalis*) is Latin *asparagus*. The wild asparagus of Italy (*A. acutifolius* and other species) is sometimes called *corruda* in Latin. The Greek term is *aspharagos*, *asparagos*.

Hippocrates *R* 54; Theophrastus *HP* 6.4.1–2; Cato *DA* 161; Dioscorides *MM* 2.125, cf. 3.151, 4.144; Columella *DA* 11.3.43–6; Pliny *NH* 19.145–51, 20.108–11; Lucian, *True History* 1.16; Galen *AF* 6.641–4, *SF* 11.841; Athenaeus *E* 62d–63a; Palladius *OA* 3.24.8, 4.9.10–12; Anthimus *OC* 54 with Grant *ad l.*

Darby and others 1977 pp. 668–9.

- Other young wild plants were used in the same way, including the early shoots of butcher's broom (*Ruscus aculeatus*), Greek *myakanthos*, *bryon*, Latin *ruscum*, a most rebarbative plant when mature; young shoots of black bryony (*Tamus communis*), Latin *tamnus*, though the berries and roots are poisonous; young shoots of the white bryony genus (*Bryonia dioica*, *B. cretica* and *B. alba*), Greek *bryonia*, *ampelos leuke*, *ampelos agria*, *ampelos melaina*, Latin *cucurbita erratica*, *vitis alba* and other names, these also poisonous in part; and young shoots of hop (*Humulus Lupulus*), Latin *lupus salictarius* 'wolf in the willows'.

Dioscorides *MM* 4.181–3; Columella *DA* 12.7.1; Pliny *NH* 21.86; Galen *VA* 23; *Diocletian's Price Edict* 6.36; Pseudo-Apuleius, *Herbarius* 67, 85.

Asphodel, a tall wild flower whose bulb was known as a food to early Greeks. 'There is much nourishment in mallow and asphodel,' Hesiod asserts. The legendary sage EPIMENIDES claimed asphodel as one of his two dietary staples. Theophrastus lists thus the edible parts of the plant: 'the stem, seared; the seed, roasted; and most of all the root, chopped, with figs'. Galen observed the use of asphodel as food in times of famine in Asia Minor, and adds that the bulb is poisonous unless repeatedly boiled. The seed-case was sometimes prescribed medicinally.

Asphodel was also good to lie on at open-air feasts, since it repelled venomous creatures (see OPEN-AIR DINING). A Homeric formula, *es asphodelou leimonas*, assures us that asphodel grew in the meadows of the underworld.

Asphodel (*Asphodelus ramosus*) is Greek *asphodelos*, Latin *asphodelus*, *albucium*.

Hesiod *OD* 41 with West *ad l.*; Homer, *Odyssey* 11.539, *al.*; Theophrastus *HP* 7.12.1, 7.13.1–3; Crateuas *F* 5 Wellmann; Dioscorides *MM* 2.169; Pliny *NH* 21.108–10, 22.67–72; Galen *AF* 6.651, *SF* 11.842.

J.-M. Verpoorten, 'Les noms grecs et romains de l'asphodèle' in *Antiquité classique* vol. 31

(1962) pp. 111–29; Michèle Biraud, 'Usages de l'asphodèle et étymologies d'asphodelos' in *Actes du colloque international 'Les phytonymes grecs et latins' tenu à Nice les 14–16 mai 1992* (Nice: Université de Nice-Sophia Antipolis [1993?]) pp. 35–46.

Ass, animal native to the Near East (and domesticated there in prehistoric times). The wild asses of southwestern Asia were well worth eating, according to Varro, Galen and others; the best came from Pessinus in Phrygia, says Varro. As late as the tenth century the Byzantine emperors kept a herd of wild asses for their gastronomic quality.

The wild ass (*Equus Asinus*) is Greek *onagros*, Latin *onager*.

Hippocrates *R* 46; Aristotle *HA* 491a1–4; Galen *AF* 6.664; Oppian, *Cynegetica* 3.183–250; Aulus Gellius 6.16.1–5 citing Varro, *Menippean Satires* 403 Bücheler; Liutprand of Cremona, *Embassy* 38.

- The domesticated ass or donkey is Greek *onos*, Latin *asinus*. Domestic asses were not good to eat (so Galen insists), though some ate them, and there is said to have been a section of the Athens market, *Memnoneia*, where this meat could be bought.

Galen *AF* 6.664; Pollux *O* 9.48; Apuleius, *Metamorphoses* 7.22.

F. Olck, 'Esel' in *RE* 1893–1972; Buck 1949 pp. 142–3; Toynbee 1996.

Assyria *see* MESOPOTAMIA

Athena, Greek goddess, patron of Athens. It was Athena who revealed to mankind the use of the olive tree, an indispensable provider of food to Mediterranean peoples and a source of stored wealth to Greece in particular. According to the myth, she and Poseidon quarrelled over Athens: to assert possession she planted an olive tree on the Acropolis. The sacred tree survived burning by the Persians in 479 BC and was still shown in the second century AD. For an alternative myth see HERACLES.

Herodotus 8.55; Apollodorus, *Library* 3.14.1; Pausanias 1.24 with Frazer *ad l.*

Athenaeus, of Naucratis in Egypt, author of the *Deipnosophists*, an extended dialogue in Greek on food, dining and related subjects. The *Deipnosophists*, a work in fifteen books, takes the form of a series of fictional dinner discussions set in Rome. These discussions are reported, in a frame conversation, by 'Athenaeus' to 'Timocrates'. The dramatic date of the first of the discussions is before the death of Galen in AD 199, since Galen takes part in it; another speaker, 'Magnus', says that as a young man he had known Aristomenes of Athens, a freedman of the emperor Hadrian (*D* 115b). The dramatic date of the last discussion is just before the death of Ulpian about AD 223: Ulpian is a major figure throughout. Both these datings assume that the speaker in question is to be identified with the well-known real person of the same name, Galen the imperial physician, Ulpian the jurist; but that is far from certain. The dramatic date of the frame conversation would be a little later still, when the discussions are supposed to have become famous (*E* 2a) and Ulpian is dead (*D* 686c). 'Athenaeus', the narrator, speaks to 'Timocrates' as if they had both lived under the emperor Commodus (*D* 537f). Putting all this together, it is likely that Athenaeus wrote the work around AD 220–30 at the very latest; perhaps two decades earlier, if the identification with the real Ulpian is rejected.

The dialogue and the speakers are fictional, although they have points of contact with the real world. The speakers – scholars always ready with quotations on any given topic – include doctors, cynics, the pedant Ulpian, the host Larensius, and others less clearly differentiated (*E* 1b–e). They interrupt themselves and others; in asides they question the texts and attributions of their own quotations and throw similar doubt on the quotations of others. The linking subjects are the food, drink and entertainment of the Greeks and their neighbours in the

first millennium BC. Their sources of information are almost exclusively written: partly literary (comedies, memoirs, epics), partly scientific, partly lexicographical.

There is a sequence of topics, a sequence that at times is almost lost in continual digressions. Book 1 dealt with the literature of food, food and drink in Homer, and wine; books 2–3 hors d'oeuvres, bread; book 4 the organisation of meals, music; book 5 lavish display and luxury; book 6 parasites, flattery; books 7–8 fish; book 9 meat, poultry; book 10 gluttony and more wine; book 11 cups; book 12 social behaviour; book 13 love, women; book 14 more music, desserts; book 15 wreaths and perfumes. There is a good selective index in vol. 7 of Gulick's edition (1927–41). Fuller Greek indexes will be found in the older editions by Meineke (1856–65) and Kaibel (1887–90).

Over a thousand authors are quoted in the *Deipnosophists*. References are normally scrupulously accurate, giving author, title and book number. Quotations are fairly accurate when they can be checked, though it has been shown that Athenaeus is not above adjusting quotations to suit a line of argument. Many of his briefer quotations are taken from intermediate sources (such as glossaries and commentaries), but it is hard to dispute that he read and excerpted a great range of works himself. Attributed quotations make up a very high proportion of the whole text. In Kaibel's edition there is a handy separate index of authors quoted.

The dialogue format allowed Athenaeus to incorporate material and to lay down opinions (as narrator or in the mouths of his characters) which would have had to be excluded or toned down if he had been writing plain history. Real conversation is desultory and repetitive, and so are Athenaeus's speakers; but no one reads this book for the sake of the dialogue, rather for the information embedded in it.

One of his favourite categories of sources was certainly the Athenian comedy of the fifth to third centuries BC: of these plays, mostly lost now, we would know little if it were not for Athenaeus. He quotes them briefly, for incidental mentions of foodstuffs or other details of social history: extensively, for boastful speeches by cooks and for menus of dinner parties. Other classical and Hellenistic poetry is also quoted: Sicilian comedy and mime; hexameters of the fourth to second centuries BC; less frequently, archaic lyric, archaic elegy and classical tragedy. Coming to prose, there are long extracts from dietetic writings of Hellenistic times, and also from popular and anecdotal history books of that period. Much is drawn from philological works such as lexica, dialect glossaries and commentaries. Athenaeus is notable for the way he treats historical and literary controversy. He and his speakers take sides in controversies, but if it is a question of a debate between scholars, both sides of the debate are quoted; if it is a question of interpretation, or of morality, the dubious text is put before the reader.

The *Deipnosophists*, like any historical source, must be used circumspectly. Remember that quotations, attributions and interpretations are given on the authority of the speakers, not of the author. Athenaeus vouches for very few facts; his speakers make many assertions of fact, but some of these are challenged in the dialogue, and others deserve to have been challenged.

To some scholars the *Deipnosophists* is a mine of quotations of some author or authors. To others, it is a collection of materials bearing on a particular topic: it is for this purpose that the *Deipnosophists* is usually cited in the present book. But before using any of Athenaeus's materials the reader must ask questions. Where and when did the quoted author write? Is the text authentic? Was it fact or fiction? Is the

the crucial statement intended literally, ironically or in some special context? Is the text being quoted accurately? The speakers will occasionally comment on these questions: whether they do or not, the reader must always have them in mind, though they cannot always be answered.

Many quotations are of passages of dramatic dialogue. It is often doubtful who says what within these extracts, and the answer may affect one's view of what may be fact, what may be irony, and what may be a lie. In the case of prose, there may be no way of distinguishing verbatim quotation from rewriting or abridgement: the punctuation in modern editions and translations may be no more than guesswork. In particular it can be hard to know where a quotation stops. Athenaeus liked to interweave quotations, so that sometimes a speaker will take one authority and repeatedly revert to it, interspersing short quotations from other authors.

In spite of its difficulties, the *Deipnosophists* is consulted by all who work seriously on the food history and social history of the ancient world, and some who begin to read it never end.

The text of the *Deipnosophists* survives in one tenth-century manuscript now in Venice. This copy lacks books 1–2 and a few other pages, totalling perhaps a fifth of the whole work. These sections can only be read in the form of the *Epitome* or abridgement of the *Deipnosophists*, which was made in late Byzantine times. The *Epitome* survives complete. Comparing it with the full text in books 3 to 15 shows that the *Epitome* omits most of the conversational exchanges, retaining a good selection of the quotations. The full text cites author, title and book number of nearly every source used; the *Epitome* does not, and the quotations themselves are often cut down.

M. Henry, 'The edible woman: Athenaeus' concept of the pornographic' in *Pornography and Representation in Greece and Rome* ed. A. Richlin (New York: Oxford University Press,

1992) pp. 250–68; Wilkins and others 1995; Dalby 1996 pp. 168–79; Braund and Wilkins 2000; David Braund, 'Athenaeus' in *Encyclopedia of Greece and the Hellenic Tradition* ed. Graham Speake (London: Fitzroy Dearborn, 2000).

Athenaeus D: *Deipnosophistae*. Text and translation: Athenaeus, *The Deipnosophists* ed. and tr. C.B. Gulick, 7 vols (1927–41, *LCL*). Text: *Athenaei Naucratitae Deipnosophistarum libros XV* ed. G. Kaibel, 3 vols (Leipzig 1887–90, *BT*). References elsewhere in the present book are to the standard text divisions, the page numbers of Casaubon's 1597 edition, which are indicated in both of these current editions. Unluckily these text divisions are not marked in the Greek text on the *TLG* CD-ROM (see www.tlg.uci.edu). In all current editions of the *Deipnosophists*, extracts from the *Epitome*, interpolated from other sources where thought relevant, are printed in the gaps left by the missing sections of the complete text. These gaps are at 1a–73e; 781b–784d (inserted at 466d); an unnumbered passage inserted at 502b; and 701a–702c.

——— **E**: the Byzantine *Epitome*. The sections normally consulted, and cited in the present book, are those for which the full text does not survive. These are included in Gulick's edition and translation and in Kaibel's edition (see above). For books 1 and 2 see also: Athénée de Naucratis, *Les Deipnosophistes. Livres I et II* ed. and French tr. A.M. Desrousseaux (1956, *CUF*). The only edition of the remainder of the *Epitome* is: *Athenaei Dipnosophistarum epitome* ex recensione S.P. Peppinki (Leiden, 1937–9).

Athens, city of mainland Greece. Its land territory consisted of the whole peninsula of Attica.

Athens was politically dominant in the fifth and early fourth centuries BC and became a very large and wealthy city during that period. It continued to be a cultural metropolis throughout ancient times. The city was the source and subject of a large proportion of classical Greek literature, and probably an even larger proportion of the literature that survives. The result of this fact is that we know far more about social life in classical Athens than in any other contemporary city. Like it or not, modern descriptions of classical Greek dinners and symposia are nearly always necessarily descriptions of Athenian dinners and symposia.

For that reason, no full list will be given here of ancient narratives of meals set in Athens. A selective list must include the feasts and sacrifices that occur in ARISTOPHANES's plays (especially *Thesmophoriazusae, Assemblywomen, Peace*). In a play by Menander (*Dyscolus*) a family sacrifice and picnic is to be imagined taking place just off stage. Among narratives of symposia there are several in which Socrates takes a major role; there is also the Aristophanic scene in which Philocleon is taught correct behaviour at a symposium (Plato, *Symposium*, and other dialogues; Xenophon, *Symposium*; Aristophanes, *Wasps* 1122–537). Some materials specifically on Athenian dining are gathered by Athenaeus (*D* 131f–138b quoting Matron and others): in addition to this passage Athenaeus quotes throughout his work a great many dining and drinking scenes set in Athens, taking them from Athenian comedies and from memoirs and anecdotes by LYNCEUS, MACHON and others.

The Athenian *agora* or market-place was, according to the comedy fragments in particular, a source of food which was often excellent and often expensive. There appears to have been special pride in the bread which was industrially baked for sale on the market, as introduced or popularised by THEARION (Plato, *Gorgias* 518b; Athenaeus *D* 111e–112e quoting Archestratus *H* 4 Brandt (see Olson and Sens *ad l.*)). Thyme was locally thought the typical Athenian herb and was among the wild greens sold at street stalls. The hero of Aristophanes's *Knights* is an *Allantopoles*, sausage-seller, and we learn a good deal of his trade in the course of the play. More than about any other kind of food, comedy cooks and gourmets speak of the fish that was sold in the sections of the market called *eis tous ikhthyas* 'at the fish' and *eis toupsa* 'at the relishes': for sources on these and the Athenian market in general see Wycherley.

James Davidson has demonstrated the deep political significance of fish prices and fish gastronomy, not to mention courtesans, to fourth-century Athenians.

Owing to the rapid growth of Athens in the fifth century, its markets attracted traders from several neighbouring cities, whose economies must to some extent have come to depend on this trade. In Aristophanes's *Acharnians* (719–1234) an imagined market, breaching wartime embargoes (*Acharnians* was produced in 425), attracts starving traders from Megara and Boeotia. Whether Megara had slipped into real economic dependence, and whether its exclusion mattered enough to be a major cause of the Peloponnesian War, are controversial. The *Acharnians* and other sources make it clear that BOEOTIA exported to Athens herbs, small birds of many kinds, ducks, geese, and most notably the eels from Lake Copais; MEGARA offered sucking-pigs, garlic and bulbs; fishermen from Hermione and Eleusis supplied fish, especially the *psetta* (Athenaeus D 329e–330b quoting Archestratus H 32 Brandt and Lynceus F 8; IG II.2.1103); Plataea sold cheese, and Plataeans congregated at the monthly green cheese market (Lysias 23.6); Tanagra sold wine (Heracleides Criticus P 1.8); EUBOEA, particularly the neighbour cities Eretria and Chalcis, supplied the seafood of the Euripus as well as fruits and nuts. Radishes came from Boeotia, Corinth and Cleonae (see RADISH. It is relevant to these local specialisms that Aegina, trading city and island south of Athens, was said to be particularly good as a source of the *kestreus* grey mullet (Archestratus H 43 Brandt), while *aphyai* or small fry were said to be at their best at the Athenian harbour Phalerum, though they were also said not to be highly valued by the Athenians themselves (Aristotle HA 569b10–14; Athenaeus D 284f–285f citing Archestratus H 9 Brandt (see Olson and Sens *ad l.*) and others). Athenians of the fifth and fourth centuries BC were proud of the fact that produce from far across the Mediterranean was to be found on the Athenian market: the list given by Hermippus is one of many. They were also proud that (as asserted here by a god in the lost play *The Seasons* by Aristophanes) foods could be bought at Athens even when they were out of their normal season:

'In the middle of winter you will see chate melons, grapes, fresh fruit, wreaths of violets ... in a blinding cloud. The same man sells thrushes, pears, honeycombs, olives, beestings, white puddings [*khoria*], swallows, cicadas, sucking-pigs. You can see snow-covered baskets of myrtle-berries and of figs on display together. They sow melons and turnips together. No one knows any longer what time of year it is ... a good thing if they get whatever they want all year round.'

'A very bad thing, I say. If they couldn't, they wouldn't want the things or spend money on them. What I would do is to supply them for a short season and then take them away.'

'Exactly what I do for other cities, but not for Athens. They are allowed to have all this because they revere the gods.'

'Revering you people has done them very little good, then.'

'Meaning what?'

'You've turned their city into Egypt instead of Athens.'

Olive oil was a source of wealth to Athens. Barley was the reliable local cereal but Athens became an importer of wheat, from the Black Sea shores and from north Africa, ensuring not only the supply of bread on the market but also the alternation of wheat loaves with barley cakes at typical Athenian dinners. The interruption of the city's wheat supply resulted in famine. The wine of Attica was of local interest only; the dried figs were widely known. The honey of Mount HYMETTUS lent its sweetness to Attic

Map 1 Food specialities of the neighbourhood of Athens

cakes, and remained famous in Roman times.

Hermippus 63 Kassel; Thucydides 2.38.2; Aristophanes fragment 581 Kassel; Antiphanes 177 Kassel; Eubulus *F* 74 Kassel.

L. Gernet, *L'Approvisionnement d'Athènes en blé au Ve et au IVe siècle* (Paris, 1909); R.E. Wycherley, *The Athenian Agora, vol. 3: literary and epigraphical testimonia* (Princeton: Princeton University Press, 1957); E.F. Bloedow, 'Corn supply and Athenian imperialism' in *Antiquité classique* vol. 44 (1975) pp. 20–9; L.

Gallo, 'Alimentazione urbana e alimentazione contadina nell' Atene classica' in *Homo edens: regime, rite e pratiche dell' alimentazione nella civiltà del Mediterraneo* ed. Oddone Longo and P. Scarpi (Milan, 1989) pp. 213–30; James Davidson, 'Fish, sex and revolution at Athens' in *Classical Quarterly* vol. 43 (1993) pp. 53–66; James Davidson, 'Opsophagia: revolutionary eating at Athens' in *Food in Antiquity* ed. John Wilkins and others (Exeter: Exeter University Press, 1995) pp. 204–13; Davidson 1997; Dwora Gilula, 'Hermippus and his catalogue of goods (fr. 63)' in *The Rivals of*

Aristophanes: studies in Athenian Old Comedy ed. David Harvey and John Wilkins (London: Duckworth, 2000) pp. 75–90.

Athera *see* EMMER

Athletes, in ancient as in modern times, took diet seriously. Already in classical Greece athletes were advised to eat much more meat than their contemporaries: it was said (see Diogenes Laertius) that this diet was first prescribed 'by Pythagoras', the philosopher or another, but Pausanias gives a different view. Whatever the truth of that, the general impression obtained from literary sources both Greek and Roman is of athletes eating large quantities of meat; they were not recommended to limit their food intake, rather the opposite, if one may judge by many tales gathered by Athenaeus of enormous meals taken by athletes. At symposia, however, they spent their time on KOTTABOS, avoiding dessert and definitely avoiding sex, which was well known to sap the strength: Cleitomachus the pancratiast, it was said, would get up and leave a party if anyone even mentioned sex. The fullest discussion of the diet of athletes is in Philostratus's *Gymnastics*.

Athletes in classical Greece, regarded as having represented and honoured their home cities, might benefit in old age from a grant of free meals at public cost.

The Hippocratic text *Regimen*, cited below, is relevant although it does not concern athletes specifically: it discusses athletic and other exercises in relation to the diet and the individual constitution.

Hippocrates *RS* 7, *R* 61–6, *Ancient Medicine* 4, *Aphorisms* 1.3; Plato, *Republic* 410b, *Laws* 839e; Aristotle, *Nicomachean Ethics* 2.6.7; Diogenes Laertius 8.12 citing Favorinus; Epictetus, *Discourses* 15.2–5; Plutarch *QC* 3.6 [654a], 7.7 [710d], *EC* 995e, *Intelligence of Animals* 970b; Pausanias 6.7.10; Galen *VA* 103, *Exercise with the Small Ball* 5.899–910; Aelian, *Nature of Animals* 6.1; Philostratus, *Gymnastics* 43–51; Athenaeus *D* 412d–414d, 417a–b.

Jane M. Renfrew, 'Food for athletes and gods: a classical diet' in *The Archaeology of the Olympics* ed. W. J. Raschke (Madison, Wis., 1988) pp. 174–81; Louis E. Grivetti and Elizabeth A. Applegate, 'From Olympia to Atlanta: a cultural-historical perspective on diet and athletic training' in *Journal of Nutrition* vol. 127 (1997) pp. 860S–68S.

Attalus Philometor, last king of Pergamum (ruled 138–133 BC). Attalus wrote a book on farming, and one of NICANDER's works is dedicated to him. Attalus is said to have taken a special interest in poisonous plants, to have grown them in his palace garden, and to have included them in dishes that he sent to his friends.

Diodorus Siculus 34.3; Varro *RR* 1.1.8; Columella *DA* 1.1.8; Pliny *NH* 1.18, 18.22; Plutarch, *Life of Demetrius* 20.2–3; Justin, *Epitome of Trogus* 36.4.3; *Suda s.v. Nikandros*.

Atticus, Julius (first century AD), author of a Latin work on vines and wine. His work is lost except for borrowings by later authors, notably COLUMELLA, who cites him twenty-five times.

Augustus (63 BC–AD 14), first Roman emperor. As *princeps*, first citizen, Augustus by his own lifestyle tended to set the Roman fashion. Suetonius's biography devotes some space to his food and dining habits. The dinners that he hosted were modest and not extravagant, with entertainment by street and circus performers. For his choice of food Suetonius is able to quote the emperor's private correspondence:

> As regards food Augustus was very sparing, almost plebeian, with a liking for brown bread, whitebait, soft, spongy hand-pressed cheese, and green figs from a twice-bearing tree. Sometimes he would eat before dinner time, whenever and wherever he felt hungry. Here are his own words, quoted from his letters: 'I had a snack of bread and dates while out in my carriage to-day . . .' and: 'As I came home from the

Regia in my litter I ate a bit of bread and a few *duracina* grapes.'

Suetonius, *Augustus* 74–78, *al.*

Dalby 2001.

Aurochs *see* OX

Avoidance of foods. Greeks and Romans seldom wrote about foods that they avoided, and it is correspondingly difficult to be precise about their beliefs and practices. To these peoples, strange food choices and avoidances were a fact to be noted concerning foreigners rather than themselves. The people of EGYPT, for example, would not eat pork, but they would eat grubs and snakes, so Galen assures his readers. He does not mention in this context that the CICADA provided food for many Greeks (others, incidentally, regarded cicadas as sacred and would not eat them).

It was well known that JEWS followed strict dietary rules, which are discussed by Strabo, Plutarch and other classical authors though usually without full understanding. Also within the ambience of Graeco-Roman culture, worshippers of Cybele were required to abstain from pork, fish and numerous other foods, according to Julian. PYTHAGORAS appears to have issued some quite unusual dietary instructions to his disciples, including, some said, the avoidance of fish.

To Greeks and Romans certain sea creatures were regarded as sacred, notably the dolphin, called by Greeks *delphis* and by Romans *delphinus* (*Delphinus Delphis* and other species) and the pilot-fish, called *pompilos* and *hegemon* in Greek, *pompilus* in Latin (*Naucrates Ductor*). Both of these kept company with ships and appeared to act as guides to mariners. To hunt the dolphin was *apotropos* 'taboo' for most Greeks, according to Oppian. Anyone who broke this rule polluted his household. Thracians and Byzantians, however, hunted the dolphin

eagerly. The pilot-fish was a *hieros ikhthys* 'holy fish', sacred to Poseidon and to the gods of Samothrace, born from the blood of Uranus just as Aphrodite had been. It is not specifically said to be taboo as food, but there is no textual mention of its being eaten. However, those who avoided shark and other carnivorous fish on the grounds that one might indirectly be eating human flesh were surely in a minority and are ridiculed for their views by Archestratus.

Certain birds, also, were not eaten. Herons (Greek *eroidios*, Latin *ardea*) were not eaten, though in medieval Europe they were a prized food. Some species that were not eaten were killed for use in medicine (e.g. vulture) or in magic (e.g. wryneck); some were not killed at all. Birds which were not killed include owls, sacred to Athena, and hoopoes, which were also sacred in Egypt. The ibis, though it too was sacred in Egypt, is said by classical authors including Aelian to feed on poison and to be avoided as food only for that reason. See Thompson 1936 for further examples and references on birds.

The tortoise and turtle, although never stated by ancient sources to be forbidden food, appear nonetheless to have been avoided almost totally, as were reptiles in general. Their only significant use was in certain medicines whose logic was magical rather than scientific (see TORTOISE for references). The dietary qualities of the meat of dogs and puppies, and similarly those of horsemeat, are listed alongside those of other animals in Hippocratic texts, as if they were normal food choices; they are, however, never mentioned in contemporary discussions of food in other genres (see DOG and HORSE for references). Human meat (see CANNIBALISM) was not eaten except in dire famine. Animal BRAINS were regarded as acceptable and sometimes desirable food, except by those who followed the precepts of Pythagoras.

Archestratus *H* 23 Brandt with Olson and Sens
ad l.; Oppian *H* 1.186–211 and 5.67–102 on
the pilot-fish, 5.416–588 on the dolphin;
Strabo 16.2.37–8; Plutarch *QC* 4.5, 8.8; Galen
AF 6.669; Aelian, *Nature of Animals* 2.15,
10.29, 15.23; Athenaeus *D* 282e–283c on the
dolphin, 282e–284d on the pilot-fish; Julian,
Hymn to the Mother 14–18.

Thompson 1936 *passim*; Thompson 1947 pp.
52–6, 208–9; Waldemar Deonna and Marcel
Renard, *Croyances et superstitions de table
dans la Rome antique* (Brussels: Latomus,
1961); Simoons 1994; N. Purcell, 'Eating fish:
the paradoxes of seafood' in *Food in Antiquity*
ed. John Wilkins and others (Exeter: Exeter
University Press, 1995) pp. 132–49; Simoons
1998; Garnsey 1999 pp. 82–99; Louis E.
Grivetti, 'Food prejudices and taboos' in
CWHF 2000 vol. 1 pp. 1496–530.

Azarole *see* MEDLAR

B

Babbian wine, from somewhere in deep southern Italy. Babbian was a very 'austere' wine, 'continually improving' in the mid first century AD but not heard of later.

Pliny *NH* 14.69; Athenaeus *E* 27b (mss. *Barbinos*).

Babies. Mother's milk was the natural and probably the usual source of food for babies in the ancient Mediterranean world, particularly among poorer people: see for example Heliodorus (a fictionalised observation concerning a sub-culture in Egypt). Upper-class babies were the least likely to get mother's milk, as is shown by the need for Favorinus (in the Roman elite of the second century) to argue that this source of food was the best. Varro had observed that slave babies were healthiest if reared on their own mothers' milk, a recommendation perhaps more likely to be observed than that of Favorinus. Similarly Xenophon had said that puppies should be reared by their own mothers, whose milk was best suited to them.

For mothers who could afford it the alternative to giving their own milk was to employ a wet-nurse. The commonness of this choice, at least among those who could read and write, is demonstrated by at least two pieces of evidence: the very detailed instructions given by Soranus for how to choose a wet-nurse, and the existence on papyrus of numerous contracts for wet-nursing from Hellenistic and Roman Egypt. These contracts carefully prescribe details of the wet-nurse's lifestyle during her employment, with the evident aim of ensuring that her milk, and any less tangible influence imparted with the milk, will be wholesome.

Weaning was often not begun until the baby was two years old, according to Soranus.

Xenophon, *Hunting* 7.3; Heliodorus, *Ethiopian Story* 1.5; Varro *RR* 2.10.8; Soranus, *Gynaecology* 2.11–21; Aulus Gellius 12.1 citing Favorinus.

K.R. Bradley, 'Wet-nursing at Rome: a study in social relations' in *The Family in Ancient Rome* ed. B.M. Rawson (Ithaca, 1986) pp. 201–29; S. Dixon, *The Roman Mother* (London, 1988); R.S.J. Garland, *The Greek Way of Life* (London: Duckworth, 1990); D. Gourevitch, 'Biberons romains: formes et noms' in *Le Latin médical: la constitution d'un langage scientifique. Réalités et langage de la médecine dans le monde romain* ed. G. Sabbah (Saint-Étienne, 1991) pp. 117–33 with plates; E.G. Clark in *OCD* 1996 *s.v.* Breast-feeding; Amal Aboul Aly, 'Testing women's milk' in *Sciences exactes et sciences appliquées à Alexandrie* ed. Gilbert Argoud and Jean-Yves Guillaumin (Saint-Étienne, 1998) pp. 207–15; Garnsey 1999 pp. 47–53, 106–7, *al*; Antoinette Fauve-Chamoux, 'Breast milk and artificial infant feeding' in *CWHF* 2000 vol. 1 pp. 626–35.

Babylonia *see* MESOPOTAMIA

Bacchus *see* DIONYSUS

Bactria and Sogdiana, centres of domestication and of urban culture in inner Asia. Corresponding roughly with northern Afghanistan and Tajikistan, Bactria and Sogdiana had a long prehistory before being incorporated into the Persian Empire in the sixth century BC. They were under Macedonian or Greek rule from the late fourth to the second centuries. At the end of that period, in 125 BC, the Silk Road was opened, passing through both these regions en route from northern China to the Parthian and Roman Empires. From this period onwards Bactria and Sogdiana formed part of a succession of central Asian kingdoms, but were heavily influenced by the culture and religion of the Near East, both Parthian and Roman.

Archaeobotanical evidence, e.g. from Shortughai in the Oxus flood plain, demonstrates very early agriculture in Bactria and Sogdiana. This was a centre of variation of several major cultivated plants including durum wheat. Finds of PISTACHIO date to the third millennium BC. Grape cultivation in Bactria began in the early second millennium; it was from here that the grape was introduced to China in the late second century BC. The pistachio and the PEACH spread westwards from central Asia soon after Alexander the Great's conquest. It was at that time, also, that Greeks became aware of the ASAFOETIDA that grew in the mountains of southern Bactria. Both asafoetida and pistachio were noticed (initially identified as *silphion*, silphium, and *terminthos*, terebinth) by the troops on Alexander's expedition. Asafoetida was to be the principal food export from this region to the Mediterranean in Hellenistic and Roman times.

Theophrastus *HP* 4.4.7; Sima Qian, *Records of the Grand Historian* 123; *Periplus Maris Erythraei* 64; Arrian, *Anabasis* 3.28 citing Aristobulus, cf. Strabo 15.2.10.

G. Willcox in Renfrew 1991 pp. 139–53; Nicolas Savvonidi, 'The wine production in ancient Sogdiana' in *La Production du vin et*

de l'huile en Méditerranée ed. M.-C. Amouretti and J.-P. Brun (Athens: Ecole Française d'Athènes, 1993) pp. 237–46; Dalby 2000a pp. 189–200.

Baiae, Campanian seaside resort fashionable under the Roman Empire. The more active holidaymakers could enjoy the pleasures of sea-fishing by walking out along the harbour moles, lined with fish farms. All could spend money on the finest or most admired seafood of the Empire. To east and west of Baiae were places with their own seafood specialities. Misenum, to the west, was a source of sea urchins. *Apicius* tells us of a local seafood dish, *Embractum Baianum*, a lavish way to use these sea urchins.

> Baian casserole: minced oysters, mussels, sea urchins. Put in the saucepan chopped toasted pine kernels, rue, celery, pepper, coriander, cumin, raisin wine, fish sauce, *caryota* dates, oil.

The Lucrine lake, close at hand to the east, was renowned for its SHELLFISH. There were excellent oysters, their reputation perhaps established by Sergius ORATA. A second great speciality of the Lucrine lake was *peloris* (probably carpet-shell, *Tapes decussatus*), which in a poem by Martial is compared to its advantage with an ordinary *aquosa peloris* from the open sea (probably *V. aurea*). Horace and Xenocrates add supporting detail.

More prosaically, Baiae has given its name to the bean in modern English (and German, *Bohne* by way of a variety of broad bean, *baiana*, which must have been well known under the later Empire, though among surviving sources it is mentioned only in *Apicius*.

Cicero, *For Caelius* 47; Horace, *Satires* 2.4.30–4; Martial 6.10; Xenocrates *T* 97; *Apicius* 5.6.4, 9.11 Milham.

D'Arms 1970 pp. 42–3 and *passim*; S.E. Ostrow, 'The topography of Puteoli and Baiae on the eight glass flasks' in *Puteoli* vol. 3 (1979) pp. 77–140; Griffin 1985 pp. 90–7;

Dalby 2000a pp. 52–4.

Bakers *see* BREAD

Balkan provinces of the Roman Empire, lying between Thrace and Macedonia to the south and the Danube to the north. They offered very little to the gastronomy of the Empire, beyond the olive oil (and later wine) of Histria, at the head of the Adriatic, and the wild boars of Pannonia, modern Hungary. The poet Ovid has nothing to say of the food he enjoyed in exile at Tomis, on the Black Sea coast, though something must have come to market in the vast creaking ox-carts of the Getae of which he complains. The Danube itself was the source of several fine fish (see DANUBE FISH). See also BYZANTIUM.

Martial 12.63; Nemesianus, *Cynegetica* 227–30; Cassiodorus, *Variae* 12.4, 12.22.

M. Johnson, 'North Balkan food, past and present' in *Oxford Symposium 1981: national and regional styles of cookery. Proceedings* (London: Prospect Books, 1981) pp. 122–33; E.M. Davis, 'Palaeoecological studies at Stobi' in *Studies in the Antiquities of Stobi* vol. 3, ed. B. Aleksova and J. Wiseman (Belgrade, 1981) pp. 87–94; Dalby 2000a pp. 93–4, 201–2.

Balsam, apparently the aromatic known now as 'balsam of Mecca'. The identification was made by Prosper Alpinus; some scholars, notably Groom, doubt it.

Many ancient authors (e.g. Theophrastus and Justin) believed the tree to be native to Palestine or Syria. It actually originated in southern Arabia and was transplanted to Jerusalem and Jericho in very ancient times. The seedlings were said to have been brought by the Queen of Sheba on her visit to Solomon. The Jews, as they faced defeat by Roman troops in AD 70, tried to destroy these valuable trees. Balsam trees were paraded in Rome at the subsequent triumph of Vespasian and Titus and were assiduously grown as a cash crop in later Roman Palestine. Southern Arabia is the only source of the aromatic today.

Opobalsamum is the name for the pure resin, the most expensive form of balsam. This, the choicest and most expensive of all gums and 'very sweet in taste', was an ingredient in the hair unguents that were used by Roman men. It was also employed in costly medicines. The seed, the seed husk and also the wood of the balsam tree, *xylobalsamum*, were sold for their aromatic qualities, even the wood fetching six denarii a pound in Pliny's time.

Balsam trees were later transplanted to Egypt (whence came the medieval 'balsam of Mathara'), but neither the Palestinian nor the Egyptian plantations survive today. The southern Arabian trees exist, but their resin is hard to come by.

Balsam of Mecca (resin of the tree *Commiphora Opobalsamum*) is Greek *balsamon*, Latin *balsamum*.

Theophrastus *HP* 9.6.1–4, *al.*, *O* 32; Strabo 16.2.41, 16.4.19, 17.1.15; Dioscorides *MM* 1.19; Josephus, *Jewish Antiquities* 14.54, *al.*, *Jewish War* 4.469; Pliny *NH* 12.111–23, *al.*; Tacitus, *Histories* 5.6; Martial 14.59, *al.*; Galen *SF* 11.846, *On Compounding* 12.554, *DA* 14.62; Justin, *Epitome of Trogus* 36.3.1–4.

Prosper Alpinus, *Dialogus de balsamo* (Venice, 1591); Krauss 1910–12 vol. 1 pp. 234–6; Laufer 1919 pp. 429–34; Nigel Groom, *The New Perfume Handbook* (London: Blackie Professional, 1995).

- Balsam ought to be in the Bible, but it has not been identified there with certainty. Traditional interpretations adduce balm or balsam among the merchandise of the caravan from Gilead that took Joseph to Egypt. The relevant Hebrew word *sorī* also occurs in Jeremiah, and there too it is linked with Gilead. That, incidentally, is the excuse for the existence of an English term 'balm of Gilead'; however, in the modern aromatics trade this term is applied, unhistorically, to a resin originating in North America. The biblical *sorī* was an aromatic of some kind, but it is hard to be more precise: the Septuagint and Vulgate translators plumped for *retine* 'resin'. Another Hebrew word, *bešem*, the one from which the Greek is derived, occurs in the *Song of Songs*.

Genesis 37.25; *Ezekiel* 27.17; *Jeremiah* 8.22, 46.11; *Song of Songs* 5.1, 6.2.

Banana (*Musa* cultivars), fruit of a palm domesticated in New Guinea before 2000 BC and well known in India by the time of Alexander's expedition, as a result of which Theophrastus (*HP* 4.4.5) is able to give a brief description. Bananas were never seen in the classical Mediterranean.

Edmond De Langhe and Pierre de Maret, 'Tracking the banana: its significance in early agriculture' in *The Prehistory of Food: appetites for change* ed. Chris Gosden and Jon Hather (London: Routledge, 1999) pp. 377–96.

Barbarians (Greek *barbaroi*; Latin *barbari*). To classical Greeks, 'barbarians' were peoples other than themselves; to Hellenistic Greeks and to Romans, barbarians were peoples other than themselves and their subjects. In either case, you could easily identify a barbarian. They spoke strange languages, dressed strangely, followed strange customs and ate strange foods. Note the definition given in a Pompeiian graffito: *at quem non ceno, barbarus ille mihi est*, 'To me a barbarian is the person with whom I do not dine.'

The identifying of barbarians by their foods begins (as far as literature is concerned) with the *Odyssey*, in which this characteristic marks off not only the *Lotophagoi* or 'Lotus-eaters' (a north African people) but also the cannibal Laestrygonians and the milk-, cheese- and raw meat-eating CYCLOPS who is driven mad by his first taste of wine. The same viewpoint is evident in Herodotus's *Histories*: he explains Persian and Egyptian food habits in detail, but also categorises by their foods the wilder tribes of north Africa (including the duly identified *Lotophagoi*) and of the Scythian steppes; the more distant from Greek lands, the more outlandish the food choices.

Later geographers, though with wider horizons, continue this approach. The *Ichthyophagoi* or 'Fish-eaters' were encountered by Alexander the Great in southeastern Iran and their name remains standard in later sources. And relatively well-known peoples, though they are allowed to have their own names, are still commonly characterised by one or two special foods: the Indians by their rice and sweet reeds (sugar cane), the Carmanians of Baluchistan by their dates, the peoples of Scythia by their millet, the Persians by their cress and terebinth fruit. In a sequence more elaborate than those of Herodotus, Strabo lists the peoples of northeastern Africa, southwards from Egypt, by their foods: there are *Ichthyophagoi* here too, along with *Rizophagoi* 'root-eaters', *Kreophagoi* 'meat-eaters', *Kynamolgoi* 'dog-milkers', *Elephantophagoi* 'elephant-eaters', *Strouthophagoi* 'ostrich-eaters', and, most distant of all, the *Akridophagoi* 'locust-eaters'. It is also from Strabo that we hear of the mouthless people from near the sources of the Ganges, who (of course) did not eat at all but lived on the smells of roast meat, fruits and flowers.

Ancient descriptions of 'barbarians' and their diet are not neutral or objective. Herodotus, in his Egyptian and Persian sections in particular, intends his audience to reflect on the differences between these peoples and themselves in a sophisticated way, while the gradation from ordinary food to wholly outlandish food helps to prove both the civilised status of those at the centre of the world and the savagery of those near its edge. Xenophon describes the young Persians' sparing diet as a kind of model. To Tacitus the way of life of the noble and savage Germans presents a refreshing contrast to civilised and luxurious Rome.

Herodotus 1.192–3, 2.35–48, 2.77–8, 4.16–29, 4.168–99; Xenophon, *Cyropaedia* 1.2.8–11; Strabo 15.1.57, 16.4.7–14, cf. Diodorus Siculus 3.18–31; E. Diehl, *Pompeianische Wandinschriften und Verwandtes* (1910) p. 641; Tacitus, *Germania* 23; Aelian, *Varia Historia* 3.39; Athenaeus *D* book 4.

B.D. Shaw, 'Eaters of flesh, drinkers of milk: the ancient Mediterranean ideology of the pastoral nomad' in *Ancient Society* vol. 13/14 (1982/3 [1985]) pp. 5–31; Louise Bruit and Pauline Schmitt-Pantel, 'Citer, classer, penser: à propos des repas des Grecs et des repas des autres dans le livre IV des *Deipnosophistes* d'Athénée' in *Aion* vol. 8 (1986) pp. 203–21; F. Hartog, *The Mirror of Herodotus: the representation of the other in the writing of history* (Berkeley: University of California Press, 1988) (*The New Historicism*, 5); Edith Hall, *Inventing the Barbarian: Greek self-definition through tragedy* (Oxford: Clarendon Press, 1989); Garnsey 1999 pp. 62–72; *Gegenwelten zu den Kulturen Griechenlands und Roms in der Antike* ed. Tonio Hölscher (Munich: Saur, 2000); Rosalind Thomas, *Herodotus in Context: ethnography, science and the art of persuasion* (Cambridge: Cambridge University Press, 2000).

Barbary nut, a wild iris whose root was sometimes eaten in ancient Greece. The Barbary nut (*Gynandriris Sisyrinchium*) is known in Greek as *sisyrinkhion*.

Theophrastus *HP* 7.13.9; Pliny *NH* 19.95.

Barbier, French term for a small Mediterranean fish (*Anthias Anthias*) which has no English name. The barbier, with its brightly coloured scales and long dorsal spine, is unmistakeable and should be easily identifiable in ancient texts. Not so, unless it is the mysterious *anthias*. This was regarded as a sacred fish by sponge-fishers according to Aristotle, because no dangerous creatures would be found where an *anthias* was. For this reason it was seldom eaten. Seldom but not never: an early Greek poet, Ananius, recommends it in winter; not much later, a character in a comedy by the Sicilian Greek playwright Epicharmus quotes Ananius on the subject with approval. The culinary author Hicesius considered its flesh 'gritty, with good humours, easily excreted, not nourishing'.

However, the *anthias*, according to some descriptions, was a much larger fish than the barbier. In these cases it might be a name for the related mérou (*Epinephelus Guaza*: see under GROUPER). Both identifications are quite uncertain.

Anthias was no longer a current word in later Greek, except among poets. Learned authors disputed whether this name had the same meaning as various others, all of which are now uncertain or wholly unidentified. Dorion stated, if accurately cited by Athenaeus, that *anthias*, *elops*, *kallikhthys* and *kallionymos* were synonymous sometimes, but were also the names of four different species. The *anthias* is identified with the *aulopias* by Aristotle, with the *aulopos* by Oppian, with the *lykos* by Hicesius. For the *elops* see STURGEON; for the *aulopias* see TUNNY; for the *kallionymos* see under WEEVER.

Aristotle *HA* 570b19, 620b33–5; Athenaeus *D* 282a–e quoting Ananius 5 West, Epicharmus 58 Kaibel, Hicesius and Dorion; Plutarch *QC* 4.4, *Intelligence of Animals* 977c.

Thompson 1947 pp. 14–16.

Barley, one of the two major cereal staples of ancient societies. Wild barley is now found growing wild over a range extending from the eastern Aegean, Crete and Cyrenaica eastwards to Tibet. Wild barley was being collected at Franchthi Cave in southern Greece by 11,000 BC and in Palestine before 15,000 BC.

Archaeobotanists distinguish between two subspecies of cultivated barley, two-rowed and six-rowed, based on the arrangement of the seeds. It was two-rowed barley that was cultivated by about 9000 BC at Jericho in Palestine; it was mainly six-rowed barley that was cultivated throughout the Pharaonic period in Egypt. Both subspecies had spread in cultivation as far east as Baluchistan by about 6000 BC, and both were present in the Indus Valley (Harappan) culture before 2000. In the opposite direction, six-rowed barley had spread in cultivation as far west as eastern Spain by 5800 BC. Thus, by classical times, barley was familiar throughout the Mediterranean region, and the six-rowed variety had become predominant over the two-rowed, though nowadays the opposite is the case.

In classical Greece, according to literary texts, barley and wheat were appraised equally as staples, wheat preferably baked into bread, barley preferably as the kneaded (not baked) product *maza*. The difference between them, emerging more clearly when documents as well as literature are considered, is that in central and southern Greece and most of the islands wheat was largely imported, while barley was a home-grown staple. Many grew it themselves; for others it was easily available at a steady price, except in famine.

In Roman Italy it was different. Both barley and wheat were grown, but as a staple for human consumption barley was of distinctly lower status than wheat. To Roman soldiers a diet of barley rather than wheat meant punishment rations. The difference between Greek and later Roman views may well come from the fact that light, leavened bread from bread wheat had meanwhile become more widespread and popular: barley cannot be successfully used to make bread of this kind.

Barley was not in fact very commonly used to make bread (Greek *artos krithinos* 'barley bread') in the classical world. Some better-known barley products are listed below: to this list must be added the barley BISCUIT called *paxamas* and, of course, BEER: this can be made from other grains, but its usual starting point is malted barley (apparently Latin *braces*, though Pliny defines this word as a Gaulish term for spelt).

The two subspecies of cultivated barley are *Hordeum vulgare* subsp. *distichum*, two-rowed barley, and *H. vulgare* subsp. *vulgare*, six-rowed barley: Theophrastus discusses the varieties. Barley is *krithe* in Greek, *hordeum* in Latin. Naked barley, a variety which does not need the initial roasting (see below), was relatively unfamiliar, but was grown in Cappadocia: it is *krithe gymne* in Greek.

Homer, *Iliad* 11.69, *Odyssey* 9.110; Aristophanes, *Knights* 1101; Theophrastus *HP* 8.4.1–2; Pliny *NH* 18.62, 18.71–80, 22.134–5; Galen *AF* 6.501–10, 6.520, *SF* 12.44.

Buck 1949 p. 516; Zohary and Hopf 1993 pp.

54–64; Brewer and others (1995 ?) pp. 23–8; Joy McCorriston, 'Barley' in *CWHF* 2000 vol. 1 pp. 81–9; M.A. Murray, 'Cereal production and processing' in *Ancient Egyptian Materials and Technology* ed. P.T. Nicholson and I. Shaw (Cambridge: Cambridge University Press, 2000) pp. 505–36.

- Greek *kakhrys* was the name for barley grains which had been roasted to hull them, the usual first stage in the process of putting them to food use. The next stage was to grind the hulled grains into meal, a heavy task for the women of an ancient household which was lightened, perhaps, by the singing of working songs such as: 'Grind, mill, grind; even Pittacus grinds, king of great Mytilene.' Greek *erikis* denotes cracked or pounded barley not fully reduced to meal; Greek *kyrebia* denotes the bran removed from the grain.

  Thucydides 6.22; Aristophanes, *Knights* 254 with scholia, *Clouds* 1356–7 with scholia; Pherecrates 10 Kassel; Hippocrates, *Epidemics* 4.41; Plutarch, *Banquet of the Seven Sages* 14 quoting 'Carmina popularia' 23 Page; Oribasius *CM* 4.7 citing Dieuches.

- Greek *alphita* is barley meal. A heap of *alphita* was required at Greek sacrifices to scatter over the animal's head and over the roasting meat. *Alphita* might also be sprinkled on wine, to make a drink or broth much more nourishing than wine alone; other ingredients might be added (see KYKEON). Palladius gives instructions for preparing *alfita* with salt – from half-ripe barley, roasted – to be 'served', he does not say on what occasion. The precise Latin equivalent for *alphita* is *hordei farina*.

  Homer, *Iliad* 11.640, 18.560, *al.*, *Odyssey* 14.77, 14.429, *al.*; Hippocrates *RA* 10–27, *Epidemics* 5.10, *al.*; Archestratus *H* 4 Brandt; Pliny *NH* 22.122; Galen *AF* 6.506; Athenaeus *D* 432b–d, also 263b quoting Pherecrates; Palladius *OA* 7.12; Oribasius *CM* 4.6 citing Dieuches.

- *Alphita* was used to make an important medicinal drink, barley gruel, known in Greek as *ptisane*, in Latin as *tisana*. Grant (1999 p. 70) suggests a modern recipe for this 'barley soup'. Physicians prescribed the addition of a range of herbs and spices to it depending on individual needs.

  Pliny *NH* 22.136; Galen *DP*; Oribasius *CM* 4.1.16–18 citing Galen; *Apicius* 4.4.1–2, cf. 5.5.1.

  E. Darmstaedter, 'Ptisana: ein Beitrag zur

Kenntnis der antiken Diaetetik' in *Archeion* vol. 15 (1933) pp. 181–201.

• Diocles describes a travellers' soup consisting of *alphita* with water and a moderate amount of salt. This is certainly a predecessor of the later standby *tragos*, now known as *trakhanas* (see EMMER).

Diocles of Carystus *RV.*

• Pliny explains that *polenta* differs from *hordei farina* in that it is roasted. In this sense, *polenta* may serve likewise as a translation of *alphita*: thus in Ovid's *Metamorphoses* it is *polenta*, equivalent of *alphita*, that is mixed with wine to make a *kykeon* for the goddess Ceres to drink. Later, Anthimus explicitly equates *polenta* with *alphita* (and with Gothic *fenea*), and this *polenta*, likewise, is to be mixed with hot wine.

Ovid *Metamorphoses* 5.450; Pliny *NH* 22.126; Anthimus *OC* 64.

• Pliny provides a recipe (see Junkelmann 1997 p. 194 and Grant 1999 pp. 41–2 for modern interpretations) for a *polenta* that takes a different and much more solid final form, serving as a food and not a drink: when Apuleius writes of a 'big piece of cheesy polenta', *polenta caseata*, it is this polenta that he means. In literature this *polenta* of the second kind has the character of a staple food, but one for the very poor or the very traditional, and sometimes also a means of feeding and fattening animals: Palladius often calls for *polenta* for various farming purposes; Psyche is advised to take two pieces of *polenta* (mixed with *mulsum*, honeyed wine) to distract Cerberus on her visit to the underworld. The Latin word *polenta* survives in several Romance languages as a name for soups and mashes, but barley is no longer the principal ingredient in these.

Plautus, *Asinaria* 33; Celsus *DM* 4.18.3; Seneca, *Letters* 45.10; Pliny *NH* 18.72; Apuleius, *Metamorphoses* 1.4, 6.18–19; Palladius *OA passim.*

• Greek *maza* appears, in parallel with wheat bread, as the staple at classical Greek dinners. The preparation of *maza* is most fully described in terms of the making of dung-cakes for the giant beetle in Aristophanes's *Peace* – though details must be handled with suspicion. It was not a baked product: the verb applied to its making is *masso* 'knead'. Arnott compares *maza* with Tibetan tsampa. Pollux lists several names of special types of *maza*, some of which are treated as

kinds of bread or cake by other sources. Grant 1999 pp. 63–4 gives a suggested modern recipe.

Hesiod *OD* 590 with West *ad l.*; Archilochus 2 West; Hippocrates *R* 40, *RA* 37; Aristophanes, *Peace* 1–37; Alexis *F* 145 Kassel with Arnott *ad l.*; Pollux *O* 6.76–7; Oribasius *CM* 1.12.2 with Grant *ad l.*

Amouretti 1986 pp. 123–5; T. Braun, 'Barley cakes and emmer bread' in *Food in Antiquity* ed. John Wilkins and others (Exeter: Exeter University Press, 1995) pp. 25–37.

• Greek *physte* was a light *maza*, perhaps aerated in some way, served with cheese.

Aristophanes, *Wasps* 610; Philoxenus *D* b.19 [*s.v.l.*]; Athenaeus 114f, 137e, 149a.

Barracuda, sea fish related to the freshwater PIKE. It is seldom named in ancient sources, but was certainly eaten. It was a commonplace of comedy that what other Greeks called *sphyraina* 'hammer', the Athenians (and some others) called *kestra* 'bolt'.

The fish in question (*Sphyraena Sphyraena*) may be called barracuda in English though, to be precise, that is the name of its Atlantic big sister. Its French name is *spet*. The Latin equivalent to Greek *sphyraina* and *kestra* was (apparently) *sudis*.

Aristophanes, *Clouds* 339; Aristotle *HA* 610b5; Pliny *NH* 32.154; Oppian *H* 1.172; Athenaeus *D* 323a–c.

Thompson 1947 p. 256; Davidson 1981 p. 138.

Barrel *see* CUPA

Basil, aromatic plant. Basil was already being eaten by slugs in ancient Greek gardens, but why it was grown there is uncertain. In the modern Near East basil is grown for its aroma but not traditionally used in food. In the ancient world it was controversial whether basil should be taken as food, though according to Galen some ate it as a salad, dressed with olive oil and *garum*. Its medicinal qualities are recorded from the Hippocratic *Regimen* onwards.

The basil of the Mediterranean is *Ocimum americanum*. The ancient name was *okimon* in Greek, *ocimum* in Latin; the now-familiar name *basilikon* appears first in early medieval texts, and the two are equated in Byzantine sources such as the manuscripts of Simeon Seth's dietary manual, but some scholars, including Laufer, have doubted that ancient *okimon* is really basil.

Hippocrates *R* 54; Theophrastus *HP* 7.2–3; Dioscorides *MM* 2.141; Pliny *NH* 20.119, *al.*; Galen *AF* 6.640, *SF* 12.158; Simeon Seth p. 29 Langkavel.

Laufer 1919 pp. 586–90; Simoons 1998 pp. 7–40.

Bass, fine fish related to the GROUPER and COMBER. The bass was to be found around the mouths of rivers and in lagoons beside the sea, where it spawned and where it was observed to feed voraciously; *labrakes Milesioi* 'Milesian sea-bass' was a proverbial description of greedy people. According to Archestratus bass was good at Calydon and Ambracia, and also in Lake Bolbe in Macedonia; and all these locations were geographically suited to it. But the Milesian bass was best of all:

> These, comrade, are of wonderful virtue. Leave them unscaled, bake them gently, whole, and serve without any oily brine. Let no Syracusan and no Greek of Italy come near you when you make this dish: they do not know how to prepare good fish, but wickedly spoil it by putting cheese over everything and dousing it with watery vinegar and pickled silphium.

Archestratus here concurs with Archippus, likewise quoted by Athenaeus, in urging that the fish should be cooked whole, neither scaled nor gutted. The head of the bass was a special delicacy: Lucilius (or a character in his satire) offered guests 'the abdomen of the tunny and the head of an *acarna*'.

Since the bass did so well in river mouths not far from big cities, it is no surprise in Roman sources to find the *lupus* at its best in the River Tiber at Rome, 'between the bridges' according to the gastronomes mocked by Horace. Which bridges these were is doubtful, but Rome's great sewer, the *Cloaca Maxima*, opened close at hand. A sewer under Subura, said Juvenal, was the real lair of Rome's favourite bass, *vernula riparum* 'home-born slave of the Tiber banks', fattened on the excrement of Rome.

Bass (*Dicentrarchus Labrax*) is Greek *labrax*, Latin *lupus*. It was also known in regional Greek as *akarnax*, perhaps 'the Acarnanian fish', and *akherna*, and in regional Latin *acarna*, *acernia*.

Aristophanes, *Knights* 361 with scholia; Aristotle *HA* 543b3; Ennius *H* 10; Horace, *Satires* 2.2.31–3; Pliny *NH* 9.61, 9.169, *al.*; Juvenal 5.104–6; Xenocrates *T*9, 15 (*akharne*); Oppian *H* 2.128–40, 3.121–5, *al.*; Aulus Gellius 10.20.4 quoting Lucilius 50 Marx; Athenaeus *D* 310e–311e quoting Archestratus *H* 45 Brandt (see Olson and Sens *ad l.*), also 356b quoting Diphilus of Siphnos; Macrobius *S* 3.16.11–18 quoting Lucilius 1176 Marx; Cassiodorus, *Variae* 12.4 (*acernia*).

Thompson 1947 pp. 6, 140; Davidson 1981 pp. 67–9; Higginbotham 1997 pp. 47–8; Dalby 2000a p. 217.

Bay, evergreen aromatic shrub. In classical times bay was more important ceremonially than in the kitchen. The two contexts are, however, not totally divorced, since wreaths evoked an intended mood by their symbolism and aroma. Wreaths worn by victors, whether athletic or military, were typically of bay. Sacred to Apollo, bay leaves were chewed by the Delphic priestess of Apollo in her prophetic trance.

Bay, native to Mediterranean lands, was already in Theophrastus's time known to grow abundantly in lowland Latium, especially around Circeii (see ROME). It is one of the crops that Cato recommends for a farm near Rome (to supply the demand at city markets) and one of the crops whose spread, at the expense of more obviously useful species, is deprecated by Horace.

In cooking, bay leaves are now typically incorporated in a meat stew or sauce (hence the French name of the plant, *laurier sauce*). The evidence for this usage in ancient times is weak. The *folium* or leaf that is sometimes prescribed among sauce ingredients in ancient recipes was, ideally, the related, more exotic and more obviously aromatic tejpat leaf (see CINNAMON). Bay probably substituted. Bay leaves were placed under *mustacea*, must-cakes, when baking; this practice gave its name to a variety called *mustax*. Olive oil aromatised with bay had its uses: instructions for making it are given by Palladius (*OA* 2.19).

Bay (also called laurel in English: *Laurus nobilis*) is Greek *daphne*, Latin *laurus*.

Theophrastus *HP* 1.14.4, 5.8.3; Cato *DA* 8, 121; Horace, *Odes* 2.15; Pliny *NH* 12.3, 15.26, 15.127–38, 23.152–8; Palladius *OA* 12.22.

Bdellium *see* MYRRH

Bean, a major pulse crop of the Old World, but not one of the primary group of domesticated plants of the Near East. The earliest archaeobotanical finds of remains of cultivated beans are from Spain, southern Italy and Thessaly, all three widely separated locations in the fourth millennium BC. Later, apparently, bean cultivation spread to southern France and also to Palestine; later again, in the second millennium BC, to central Europe. It is conceivable that beans were domesticated in Spain, where they were an especially prominent crop in later prehistoric times. The crop ripens in late June in the Mediterranean region. Varieties of the cultivated plant are not prominent in ancient sources. One variety, however, the *baiana*, mentioned in a single source – the *Apicius* cookbook – and presumably named after BAIAE in

Campania, was prominent enough in everyday speech to give its name to the bean in modern English and German.

Beans were eaten raw, boiled and roasted; they were often eaten, roasted, among TRAGEMATA (Archestratus). Anthimus recommends them to his royal patron cooked in stock or in oil and eaten with salt.

As a historic, traditional and homely food of Greece and Italy, beans were offered to the gods in the course of certain rituals. For *puls fabacia*, a Roman sacrificial bean porridge, see PULS. Superstitious beliefs connected with beans (and there were many such beliefs, listed by Pliny and others) may or may not have been the reason why PYTHAGORAS, famously, was said to have forbidden beans to his followers.

The bean (broad bean or fava bean: *Vicia Faba*) is Greek *kyamos*, Latin *faba*.

Archestratus *H* 62 Brandt with Olson and Sens *ad l.*; Plato, *Republic* 372c; Alexis *F* 167 Kassel with Arnott *ad l.*; Theophrastus *HP* 8.5.1, *al.*; Dioscorides *MM* 2.105; Seneca, *Letters* 86.16; Pliny *NH* 18.117–21, 22.140–1; Galen *AF* 6.529–32, *SF* 12.49–50; Athenaeus *D* 406b–408b; Palladius *OA* 12.1; Anthimus *OC* 65 with Grant *ad l.*; Apicius 5.6.4.

Buck 1949 pp. 370–1; Darby and others 1977 pp. 682–5; Ramon Buxó i Capdevila in Renfrew 1991 pp. 237–45; Zohary and Hopf 1993 pp. 106–10; A.C. Andrews, 'The bean and Indo-European totemism' in *American Anthropologist* vol. 51 (1949) pp. 274–92; Corbier 1996; Simoons 1998 pp. 192–266.

- Beans have edible but tough skins; they fetched a better price if skinned and split (Latin *faba fresa*, *faba fracta*), ready to be boiled for bean soup or *etnos*. Beanmeal, Greek *aleuron eregminon*, Latin *lomentum*, was mixed with flour to increase the weight of shop-sold bread.

  Varro *RR* 2.4.17; Dioscorides *MM* 3.80; Pliny *NH* 18.117, 19.40; *Vindolanda Tablets* 2.302 (*faba frensa*); *Diocletian's Price Edict* 1.9–10 (*faba fressa*).

- *Etnos* is the name for a pulse soup, and, unless otherwise specified, one that was made of beans. Oribasius discusses it and its medicinal uses in some detail: a modern recipe is suggested by Grant 1999 p. 68. In *double entendre* in comedy texts the word suggests the female sexual secretion.

Aristophanes, *Acharnians* 245–6, *Assembly-women* 845, *Lysistrata* 1061–2, *Frogs* 62, 506; Plato, *Hippias Major* 290d; Galen *VA* 53; Oribasius *CM* 4.8.7–18.

Henderson 1991 p. 181.

Bear. This should be boiled twice before eating, said Galen fastidiously. The brown bear (*Ursus Arctos*) was not unknown to hunters in the mountains of southern Europe: it is Greek *arktos*, Latin *ursus*.

Petronius *S* 66; Galen *AF* 6.664; Oppian, *Cynegetica* 3.139–82; Apuleius, *Metamorphoses* 14.13–21.

Toynbee 1996.

Beccafico, group of small songbirds traditionally taken for food in Mediterranean lands. They are at their best in autumn, and were regarded as a luxury in classical times, highly priced at forty denarii for ten in DIOCLETIAN'S PRICE EDICT. They could be roasted and served simply, to be eaten whole. They were also a typical ingredient in the surprise dish THRYMMATIS.

Warblers or fig-peckers (zoological family *Sylviidae*) are *sykalis* in Greek, *ficedula* in Latin. The Italian name beccafico is sometimes used in English.

Hippolochus *D* [Athenaeus *D* 129b]; Petronius *S* 33 (see quotation at SURPRISE DISHES); Martial 13.49; Aulus Gellius 15.8.2; Athenaeus *E* 65b–d; *Diocletian's Price Edict* 4.36; Anthimus *OC* 31 with Grant *ad l.*

Beef *see* OX

Bee-keeping *see* HONEY

Beer, alcoholic drink produced from the fermentation of malted cereals, in ancient times usually barley, also millet, rye and wheat (Athenaeus). Beer was an important element of the diet in Pharaonic Egypt. In Sumer and in other civilisations of ancient Mesopotamia, from the third millennium BC, beer was a beverage whose name carried significance. In the *Atrahasis* epic the mother goddess Nintu is described as 'sated with grief; she longed in vain for beer'. Siduri the alewife or tavern-woman is a figure in the Gilgamesh story, advising the hero on his visit to the underworld. Several varieties and qualities of beer are recorded in Sumerian and Akkadian texts.

Beer was little known and generally disliked in Greece and Rome; however, it was the usual beverage in central and western Europe, made locally in various ways and therefore known under various borrowed names in Latin and Greek, as observed by Pliny and as specified below. Beer was important to the Roman army. In *Diocletian's Price Edict zythus* (beer of Egyptian type) is rated at half the price of *cervesia, camum* (beer of Gaulish and Dalmatian type); this again fetches half the price per pint allowed for table wine.

Modern beer can be kept in airtight containers under pressure: the beer of the ancient world was usually drunk when freshly made (although Spanish beer would keep, says Pliny). New beer still contained surface residue and sediment, and was therefore typically drunk with a straw. The practice, depicted on Near Eastern reliefs, is likened by Archilochus to fellatio, and was observed by Xenophon at first hand in Armenia:

> The grains of barley floated on top of the bowls, level with the brim; there were straws in the bowls, some longer, some shorter, unjointed. When thirsty one took a straw into one's mouth and sucked. It was at full strength, unless one added water, and was very pleasant when one was used to it.

Beer is *šikāru* in Akkadian (there are other specialised terms) and *shekar* in Hebrew. Terms used in Greek are *pinon*, also *sikera* for Levantine beer, *zythos* Egyptian beer, *bryton* Thracian beer, *parabias* Paeonian millet beer, *kamon* Dalmatian beer, *kerbesia, kourmi, korma*

Gaulish barley and wheat beers. Terms used in Latin are *sicera* Levantine beer, *zythus* Egyptian beer, *camum, sabaia* Dalmatian beers, *cervisia, cervesa, corma* Gaulish beers, *caelia, cerea* Spanish beers.

Atrahasis tablet 3; *Gilgamesh* [Standard Babylonian version] tablet 10; Isaiah 24.9 (translated 'liquor' in *AV*, 'strong drink' in *NEB*); Isaiah 19.10 [Septuagint version] with commentaries by Eusebius, Theodoret, Cyril and Jerome; Herodotus 2.77 and Xenophon, *Anabasis* 4.5.26–7 (*oinos ek kritheon, oinos krithinos* 'barley wine'); Antiphanes 47 Kassel; Theophrastus *CP* 6.11.2; Diodorus Siculus 1.34.10; Dioscorides *MM* 2.87–8; Pliny *NH* 14.149, 22.164; Luke, *Gospel* 1.15; *Vindolanda Tablets* 1.4=2.190, 2.182, *al.*; Galen *SF* 11.882; Julius Africanus, *Cesti* 1.19.21; Athenaeus *D* 152c citing Poseidonius *F* 15 Jacoby, also 447a–d citing Archilochus 42 West and Aristotle fragment 106 Rose; *Diocletian's Price Edict* 2.11–12; Ammianus 26.8.2; Marcellus, *On Medicaments* 16.33.

H.F. Lutz, *Viticulture and Brewing in the Ancient Orient* (Leipzig, 1922); J. Bottéro, 'Getränke' ['Les boissons': the article is in French] in *RA* 1928– vol. 3 pp. 302–6; Buck 1949 pp. 390–1; L.F. Hartman and A.L. Oppenheim, *On Beer and Brewing Techniques in Ancient Mesopotamia* (Baltimore: American Oriental Society, 1950); M. Civil, 'A hymn to the beer goddess and a drinking song' in *Studies Presented to A. Leo Oppenheim* (Chicago, 1964) pp. 67–89; M. Hopf, 'Bier' in *RGA* 1973– ; G.K. Sams, 'Beer in the city of Midas' in *Archaeology* vol. 30 (1977) pp. 108–15; J. Gelber, 'Bread and beer in fourth millennium Egypt' in *Food and Foodways* vol. 5 no. 3 (1993) p. 255 ff.; Milano 1994; Jeremy Black, 'Mesopotamia' in *The Oxford Companion to Wine* ed. Jancis Robinson (Oxford: Oxford University Press, 1994) pp. 618–19; Brewer and others (1995 ?) pp. 28–9; Alexander H. Joffe, 'Alcohol and social complexity in ancient western Asia' in *Current Anthropology* vol. 39 (1998) pp. 297–322; Delwen Samuel, 'Brewing and baking' in *Ancient Egyptian Materials and Technology* ed. P.T. Nicholson and I. Shaw (Cambridge: Cambridge University Press, 2000) pp. 537–76.

Beet, a field crop of which some varieties, known as chard or Swiss chard, are now grown for their leaves, edible after cooking; others are grown for their swollen red roots, familiar as beetroot. Chard leaves were familiar in Greek and Roman cui-

sine. They were used as wrapping in a classic Greek recipe for eel, as shown by Aristophanes and Eubulus. They were combined with lentils in the soup *teutlophake* (Galen *AF* 6.477) for which Grant (1999 pp. 139–40) suggests a modern recipe. They frequently served as a potherb; Pliny suggests dressing the cooked leaves with mustard. They were also required medicinally, as in the preparation *to en toi seutloi* whose use is described in the Hippocratic text *Epidemics*.

The roots had already been tasted in classical Greece (they were 'rather laxative' according to the Hippocratic *Regimen*) but Pliny's description of them as less fleshy than those of the saffron crocus indicates how small they were compared with the modern root varieties. They were not a part of the everyday diet.

Chard or beet (*Beta vulgaris*) is Greek *teutlon*, Latin *beta*.

Aristophanes, *Peace* 1005–14; Hippocrates *R* 54, *Epidemics* 5.91; Theophrastus *HP* 7.2.5–6, 7.4.4; *Moretum* 71; Pliny *NH* 19.98, 19.132–5, 20.69–72; Athenaeus *D* 371a–b, also 300b citing Eubulus *F* 34, 36 Kassel.

Laufer 1919 pp. 399–400; Zohary and Hopf 1993 p. 187.

Behaviour *see* COMPORTMENT

Bibline wine (Greek *Biblinos oinos*), the kind that came to HESIOD's mind in describing a picnic in the hot June sun. Later writers used the name in suitable epic contexts without any clear idea of its meaning. Conjectures are reported by Athenaeus and in later glossaries.

Hesiod *OD* 589 with West *ad l.*; Euripides, *Ion* 1195; Theocritus 14.15 with Gow *ad l.*; Athenaeus *E* 31a–b; Stephanus of Byzantium, *Gazetteer s.v. Bibline*; *Etymologicum Magnum s.v. Biblinos oinos*.

Birds, both domesticated and wild, were significant sources of food in the ancient world. So were their EGGS.

The domesticated species of the ancient world were CHICKEN, DUCK, GOOSE, PI-

GEON and (less important) GUINEA FOWL and PEAFOWL. Several other species were trapped and kept in aviaries, fated to be killed for food, but were not normally bred in captivity: see BECCAFICO; CRANE; QUAIL; THRUSH and the list below. Although they were observed, described and separately named (see Aristophanes' play *Birds* among other sources) the smaller edible species were not always distinguished by gastronomes, who might, like Archestratus, simply enjoy 'whatever small birds are in season'. Several different ones are among the ingredients of an imaginary miscellaneous dish described in Aristophanes's *Assemblywomen*. In typical Greek cuisine they could be roasted on small spits, their flavour enhanced with a sprinkling of cheese, oil and silphium, and finally served with a sweet sauce, *katakhysma*. A number of species of larger wild birds were hunted. For example, several kinds were brought from Boeotia to Athens to market, if the list in Aristophanes's *Acharnians* is to be taken literally. Separate entries will be found in this book for GROUSE, FRANCOLIN, PARTRIDGE and WOODCOCK.

Some birds were not eaten, for various reasons: see also AVOIDANCE OF FOODS. Songbirds, even those that were sometimes eaten, were also bought and sold to be kept in captivity. It should be remembered that not all birds that are described in sources as having been caught or killed or sold were necessarily intended as human food.

Aristophanes, *Acharnians* 873–6, *Assemblywomen* 1169, *Birds passim*; Archestratus *H* 62 Brandt; Varro *RR* 3.4–11; Columella *DA* 8.1–15; Athenaeus *E* 64f–65e quoting Eubulus *F* 120 Kassel and Antiphanes 295 Kassel.

Thompson 1936; André 1967; A. Salonen, *Vögel und Vogelfang im alten Mesopotamien* (Helsinki, 1973) (*Annales Academiae Scientiarum Fennicae B*, 180); J. Pollard, *Birds in Greek Life and Myth* (London: Thames and Hudson, 1977); Filippo Caponi, *Ornithologia latina* (Genoa: Istituto di Filologia Classica e Medievale, 1979); P.F. Houlihan, *The Birds of Ancient Egypt* (Warminster: Aris and Phillips,

1986); M.E. Kislev, 'Hunting songbirds as a branch of the economy' [article in Hebrew] in *New Discoveries in Ancient Agriculture and Economy: the 12th congress* ed. S. Dar (Ramat Gan, 1992) pp. 52–9; Aristophanes, *Birds* ed. Nan Dunbar (Oxford: Clarendon Press, 1995); Nan Dunbar, 'Aristophane, ornithophile et ornithophage' in *Aristophane: la langue, la scène, la cité* ed. P. Thiercy and M. Menu (Bari, 1997) pp. 113–29; *Volatilia: animali dell'aria nella storia della scienza da Aristotele ai nostri giorni* ed. Oddone Longo (Naples: Procaccini, 1999).

- Greek *aedon*, Latin *luscinia* is the nightingale (*Luscinia megarhyncha*). It was not apparently eaten by Greeks; some Romans considered it a delicacy, while the emperor Elagabalus (according to the *Historia Augusta*) ate nightingales' tongues, believing them to be a prophylactic against disease.

  Horace, *Satires* 2.3.245; *Historia Augusta, Heliogabalus* 20.

  Toynbee 1996.

- Greek *akanthyllis* is the siskin (*Carduelis Spinus*) and serin (*Serinus Serinus*).

  Eubulus *F* 120 Kassel [*s.v.l.*].

  Thompson 1936 pp. 31–2.

- Greek *kepphos* is an unidentified sea bird which was good to eat when fat. *Hydrobates pelagicus*, the stormy petrel, has been doubtfully suggested.

  Aristotle *HA* 620a13; Nicander *A* 165–9.

  Thompson 1936 p. 137.

- Greek *khlorion*, Latin *galbula* is the golden oriole (*Oriolus Oriolus*).

  Aristotle *HA* 616b11, 617a28; Pliny *NH* 10.87 (*chlorion*), 30.28 (*galgulus*); Martial 13.68.

  Thompson 1936 pp. 275, 332.

- Greek *khloris* is probably the greenfinch (*Carduelis Chloris*). It was fattest and best in autumn.

  Oribasius *CM* 1.3.4 with Grant *ad l.*

- Greek *kinklos* is a wagtail (*Motacilla* spp.).

  Aristophanes, *Assemblywomen* 1169.

  Thompson 1936 p. 140.

- Greek *kissa, kitta*, Latin *pica, gaia*, is the jay (*Garrulus Glandarius*).

  Aristophanes, *Birds* 302; Antiphanes 295 Kassel.

Thompson 1936 p. 146.

- Greek *koloios*, Latin *graculus* is the jackdaw (*Corvus Monedula*).

  Aristophanes, *Acharnians* 875; Antiphanes 295 Kassel; Aristotle *HA* 617b16–19.

  Thompson 1936 p. 155.

- Greek *kolymbis* is the grebe (*Podiceps* species), a water bird which was caught at night with net and lantern.

  Aristophanes, *Acharnians* 876, *Birds* 304; Dionysius, *On Bird-Catching* 2.12, 3.24.

  Thompson 1936 p. 158.

- Greek *korydos*, *korydalos* is the lark (*Galerida cristata*). It was caught with the help of birdlime, kept as a songbird and also eaten.

  Aristotle *HA* 617b19–23; Dioscorides *MM* 2.54; Galen *SF* 12.360; Dionysius, *On Bird-Catching* 3.2, cf. 3.17.

  Thompson 1936 p. 164; Dalby 1996 p. 63.

- Greek *melankoryphos* is probably the tit (*Parus* spp.). Like the greenfinch, it was fattest and best in autumn.

  Oribasius *CM* 1.3.4.

- Latin *miliaria* is sometimes identified with the ortolan (*Emberiza Hortulana*) but modern forms of the word denote a sparrow species (*Passer montanus*). Whatever it was, the *miliaria* was kept in pens and fattened for the table.

  Varro *RR* 3.5.2, *On the Latin Language* 5.76.

  W. Meyer-Lübke, *Romanisches etymologisches Wörterbuch* (Heidelberg: Winter, 1930–5) *s.v. miliaria*; Thompson 1936 *s.v. kenkhris*.

- Greek and Latin *phalaris* is the coot (*Fulica atra*).

  Aristophanes, *Acharnians* 875, *Birds* 565; Varro *RR* 3.11.4; Athenaeus *D* 395e.

- Greek *porphyrion* is probably the moorhen (*Gallinula chloropus*). The alternative identification with purple gallinule (*Porphyrio Porphyrio*) is more doubtful since that species does not now occur in Greece. Greek *porphyris* (Aristophanes, *Birds* 304), not identical with *porphyrion*, is unidentified and was perhaps not eaten.

  Aelian, *Nature of Animals* 3.42; Athenaeus *D* 388b–e.

  Thompson 1936 p. 252; Toynbee 1996.

- Greek *psar*, Latin *sturnus* is the starling (*Sturnus vulgaris*). They are priced at twenty denarii for ten in *Diocletian's Price Edict*.

  Antiphanes 295 Kassel; *Diocletian's Price Edict* 4.42.

  Thompson 1936 p. 334.

- Greek *psittakos*, Latin *psittacus* is the ring-necked parakeet (*Psittacus Krameri*) and other similar species. All were native to southern Asia and points east, and were rare treasures in the Roman Mediterranean, prized for their colourful plumage and their imitation of human speech. Nonetheless, Apicius suggests a recipe.

  Apicius 6.6.1.

  Dalby 2000a p. 193.

- Greek *spinos*, *spinidion*, Latin *fringilla* is the chaffinch (*Fringilla coelebs*).

  Aristophanes, *Birds* 1079; Eubulus *F* 120 [*s.v.l.*], 148 Kassel = Ephippus 3 Kassel (see quotation at AMPHIDROMIA).

  Thompson 1936 p. 267.

- Greek *strouthos*, *stroutharion*, later *pyrgites*, Latin *passer*, is the sparrow (*Passer* spp.), sometimes counted among APHRODISIACS. They are priced at sixteen denarii for ten in *Diocletian's Price Edict*.

  Galen *ST* 6.435; Athenaeus *E D* 391e–392a citing Terpsicles and others; *Diocletian's Price Edict* 4.37; Anthimus *OC* 30 with Grant *ad l.*

  Thompson 1936 p. 268.

- Greek *trokhilos*, *troglodytis*, *troglites* is the wren (*Troglodytes Troglodytes*).

  Aristophanes, *Acharnians* 876; Paul of Aegina, *Medicine* 3.45.2.

Biscuit, a cereal product that has been baked twice. The result is relatively light (because little water remains), easy to store and transport (therefore a useful food for travellers and soldiers), sometimes hard to eat without adding water or olive oil.

- The obvious verbal equivalent for English 'biscuit' is Greek *dipyrites* or *dipyros* (*artos*), Latin *dipyrus*. Dipyros 'twice-baked', in a play by Menander, was the name of a courtesan who had two lovers; Martial makes a similar, but clean, joke about the mythological figure Phaethon. In later

Greek, *dipyros artos* served as a classicising equivalent for the un-classical terms *paxamas* and *boukellaton* (below), but no recipe or description indicates whether the earlier *dipyros* was actually identical with either of these types of biscuit. The Latin equivalent term (*panis*) *biscoctus* first appears in medieval texts.

Hippocrates, *Internal Diseases* 25; Alcaeus Comicus 2 Kassel = Eubulus *F* 17 Kassel; Alexis *F* 178 Kassel; Aristotle, *Problems* 928a11; Martial 4.47; Oribasius *CM* 1.9.2 (quoting Athenaeus Medicus) with Grant *ad l.*; Procopius, *Secret History* 6.3; Photius, *Lexicon s.v. dipyros.*

• Greek *paxamas* or *paximadion*, Latin *paximadium* (variously spelt) is the classic biscuit of late antiquity, made by giving a second baking to slices of barley bread. As *paximadi* it is still popular in Greece. The term was borrowed into many languages of the medieval Mediterranean. It has been conjectured that the name, and so perhaps the recipe, originated with the cookery author PAXAMUS. The *nauticus panis* or 'ship's bread' of Pliny is something similar, if not identical.

Pliny *NH* 22.138; Palladius, *Lausiac History* 22.6–7; Pseudo-Galen, *Handy Remedies* 14.554; Pseudo-Macarius, *Apophthegms* [*PG* 34.256]; Gildas, *Preface on Penance* 1; Zonaras, *Lexicon s.vv. dipyros artos, paxamas.*

H. Kahane, R. Kahane and A. Tietze, *The Lingua Franca in the Levant* (Urbana, 1958) *s.v.*; Aglaia Kremezi, 'Paximadia' in *Food on the Move: proceedings of the Oxford Symposium on Food and Cookery 1996* ed. Harlan Walker (Totnes: Prospect Books, 1997) pp. 208–11.

• Latin *buccellatum*, Greek *boukellaton* is a specifically military item, a ring-shaped biscuit made from wheat flour. By the end of the fourth century it had become such a typical army food that soldiers in private armies were called *buccellarii.*

Paulinus of Nola, *Letters* 7.3; Aetius, *Medicine* 3.101; Photius, *Library* 80 citing Olympiodorus.

Bison, wild animal of southeastern Europe. Seldom encountered by inhabitants of Italy or Greece, it was hunted for food by the people of Paeonia in the southern Balkans: Pausanias, in an aside on a bronze bison head dedicated at Delphi, describes how the animal was trapped.

The bison (*Bos Bonasus*) is Greek *bonasos, bison*, Latin *bison, vison.*

Aristotle *HA* 630a18 (*bonasos*); Pliny *NH* 8.38 (*bison*); Martial, *Spectacles* 22 (*vison*); Pausanias 10.13.1–2 (*bison*) with Frazer *ad l.*; Oppian, *Cynegetica* 2.159–75 (*bison*).

Toynbee 1996.

Bithynian wine, from northwestern Asia Minor. The planting and tending of vines here are discussed by Florentinus. He names as examples the *Tarsena* and *Boana* wine districts, where vines were trained on trees. Galen specifies separately the wine from Nicomedia, capital of Bithynia. Pliny adds the name of *Apamenum*, a wine from the coastal city of Apameia on the south coast of the Sea of Marmara. Florentinus names several grape varieties grown in the region.

Pliny *NH* 14.75; Galen, *On Therapeutic Method* 10.834; *Geoponica* 4.1.3 and 5.17 both quoting Florentinus.

• Originating in Sicily, the *aminnia* grape was found to do well here. Bithynian white wine made from this variety is specified by the dietary authors Galen and Oribasius.

Galen *ST* 6.337, *BM* 6.805; Oribasius *CM* 5.6.33; *Geoponica* 5.17 quoting Florentinus.

Black broth *see* MELAS ZOMOS

Blackberry, wild and garden fruit. Blackberries are not prominent in classical literature, but they were certainly eaten by some; blackberry seeds have been found in latrine deposits, for example at Cologne in Roman Germany. Medicinally, Galen prescribes a decoction of blackberries, while Palladius (*OA* 10.16) gives a recipe for *diamoron*, blackberry syrup, made with two parts juice to one part honey. Anthimus recommends blackberry equally in health and sickness.

The blackberry (*Rubus fruticosus* and related species) is not consistently distinguished in Greek from the MULBERRY, a

Figure 3 Top: the wild ox or aurochs (*Bos Taurus*), Latin *urus*. Bottom: the European bison (*Bos Bonasus*), Greek *bonasos*, Greek and Latin *bison*.

superficially similar fruit. Greek *moron* covers both; *batinon* is a later term for the blackberry alone, so named since it grows on the *batos*, bramble. In Latin the black-berry is *morum silvaticum*, literally 'forest mulberry', or *rubus*, while the bramble is *sentix*.

Theophrastus *HP* 3.18.4; Dioscorides *MM*

4.37; Pliny *NH* 15.97, 24.117–120; Galen *On Compounding* 12.920 (*batina*); Anthimus *OC* 86 with Grant *ad l.*

Zohary and Hopf 1993 pp. 199–200.

- Tender spring shoots of bramble are edible as a kind of wild asparagus; they were gathered and pickled in vinegar in Roman Italy. Taken with wine, they were good for the gums and lips. Greek *batis*, Latin *batis* (*hortensis*) is the name for these shoots; some called them *asparagus Gallicus*, Gaulish asparagus, according to Pliny.

  Columella *DA* 12.7; Pliny *NH* 21.86; Pseudo-Apuleius, *Herbarius* 88.

- The raspberry (*Rubus idaeus*) is described by Dioscorides and Pliny but is otherwise generally not distinguished from the blackberry by classical authors. It is Greek *batos Idaia*, Latin *rubus Idaeus*, so named because it grew on Mount Ida in northwestern Asia Minor.

  Dioscorides *MM* 4.38; Pliny *NH* 24.123.

Black-eyed pea, one of the early domesticated pulses of the Near East. You can eat the ripe seeds (dried for storage, then soaked and boiled); you can also eat the immature pods whole. A bean soup or *etnos* was made from black-eyed peas (Oribasius gives details). The fresh tender peas were served as dessert at Sparta, according to Polemon.

Black-eyed pea or cowpea or calavance (*Vigna unguiculata*) is Greek *phaselos, phasiolos*, Latin *passiolus, fasiolus*.

Theophrastus *HP* 8.3.2; Pliny *NH* 18.125; Galen *AF* 6.538–42, *al.*; Athenaeus *E* 56a quoting Epicharmus 151 Kaibel, also *D* 139a quoting Polemon; *Diocletian's Price Edict* 1.21, 6.33; Oribasius *CM* 4.8.7–18; Anthimus *OC* 69.

Darby and others 1977 p. 692.

- Names descended from Latin *fasiolus* (such as French *flageolet*, Italian *fagiolo*) are now applied to a different species (*Phaseolus vulgaris*), known in English as kidney bean, haricot bean, French bean, snap bean, flageolet bean and other names. This species is used in the same ways as black-eyed pea and, most people think, tastes better. Unknown in the classical world, it reached Europe from South America in the late sixteenth century.

Dalby 1996 p. 90 and note 216 with references.

Blessed thistle (*Cnicus benedictus*), potherb and medicinal plant. A probable identification for Greek *leukakantha*, which is listed as a potherb by Galen (*AF* 6.623, 6.636).

Blite, potherb and dye plant. The fruits of blite contain a red juice which has been used as food colouring. This use is implied by Antiphanes, but is otherwise seldom mentioned in ancient sources. The leaves are edible, though bland, when prepared like spinach. The seeds have been found in latrine deposits, for example at Cologne in Roman Germany.

Blite (*Amaranthus Blitum*) is Greek *bliton*, Latin *blitum*.

Antiphanes 274 Kassel; Hippocrates *R* 54, 75, *On Affections* 55; Dioscorides *MM* 2.117; Pliny *NH* 20.252; Galen *AF* 6.633; Athenaeus *D* 649b quoting Theopompus Comicus 63 Kassel; Palladius *OA* 4.9.17.

Blood, spilt on the altar as part of the ceremony of sacrifice, was sometimes incorporated in food in Greek and Roman cuisines. It was, however, forbidden to Jews by their written law. Christians were enjoined to follow the same rule.

Pig's blood was used in cooking as a constituent of black puddings. Hare's blood is incorporated in jugged hare and is looked for in Archestratus's recipe for roast hare at supper, 'hot, simply sprinkled with salt, taken from the spit while still a little rare. Do not worry if you see the *ichor* seeping from the meat, but eat greedily' (*ichor* is the blood of the gods). Bull's blood was widely regarded (by Nicander, for example) as a poison (see POISONS).

Leviticus 3.17; Archestratus *H* 57 Brandt; Nicander *A* 312–34; Luke, *Acts* 15.29; Tertullian, *Apologeticus* 9.13.

Bluefish (*Pomatomus Saltator*), deep sea fish of the Mediterranean. I have proposed to identify Greek *glaukos*, Latin *glaucus* with the bluefish. Its name is that of a colour, grey or grey-blue, and it is usually described as living in the open sea. However, in many details the descriptions of the *glaukos* contradict one another, and they could not possibly all apply to the same species: thus no satisfactory identification is possible. Some references may be to the blue shark (*Prionace glauca*).

Whatever the identification, the *glaukos* was a prized delicacy, and was good to eat throughout the year; the meat from the head is often separately specified. Ennius thought the *glaucus* was good at Cumae in Campania. A recipe is suggested by the comic author Sotades: see the modern version by Grant 1999 pp. 129–30. In translations of classical texts *glaukos* is usually rendered by the invented term 'greyfish'.

The sea-god Glaucus, often linked with the fish in poetry and puns, was said to have come from Anthedon in Boeotia.

Aristotle *HA* 508b13–25, 607b27; Sotades Comicus 1 Kassel (see translation at FISH); *Acraephia Price List*; Ennius *H* 6; Ovid, *Halieutica* 94, 117; Athenaeus *D* 295b–297c quoting Archestratus *H* 20 Brandt (see Olson and Sens *ad l.*), Antiphanes 221 Kassel and others.

Thompson 1947 p. 48; Davidson 1981 p. 100; Dalby 1996 p. 68 and note 73.

- Greek *glaukiskos*, diminutive of *glaukos*, is the name of a different fish, wholly unidentified.

  Philemon 82 Kassel; Damoxenus 2 Kassel; Baton 5 Kassel; Pliny *NH* 32.129.

Boar, European wild relative of the domestic pig. This fierce animal was coveted for its excellent meat in Greece, Italy and elsewhere in the ancient world, and it was hunted – by hunting parties with dogs and nets – using methods that are hinted at by Archestratus in his joky reference to the homonymous *kapros* or 'boar-fish' (see SHEATFISH).

The huge Calydonian boar, famous in Greek myth and illustrated in vase paintings, provided a measure with which to compare any impressively large boar at a real banquet. In the neighbourhood of Rome wild boars were hunted in the Laurentian marshes, though gastronomes might say that these, fattened on sedge and reeds, were not the best. Wild boars also came to Roman markets from Umbria. As now, however, wild boars bought at market might be less than truly wild: Varro explains how to fatten both captured wild specimens and their progeny.

The wild boar (*Sus Scrofa*) is Greek *kapros*, Latin *aper*.

Archestratus *H* 15 Brandt; Varro *RR* 3.13.1–3; Horace, *Satires* 2.4.42; Vergil, *Aeneid* 10.707–10; Martial 9.48, 10.45; Oppian, *Cynegetica* 3.363–90; Athenaeus *D* 401b–402b.

Gamkrelidze and Ivanov 1995 pp. 434–6; Toynbee 1996.

Boeotia, region of central Greece, immediately west of Attica. Lake Copais (now drained) was surrounded by a fertile plain, in turn surrounded by hills and mountains. The chief city, Thebes, was 'the Cadmeian city teeming with fruit' in an epic poem by Antimachus.

The arable wealth of Boeotia, a strong contrast with most of Greece, gave it (like Thessaly) a reputation for gluttony, but gluttony that was based on home-grown and not imported produce. The *kollikophage Boiotidion*, 'little bun-eating Boeotian' in Aristophanes' *Acharnians* is a stereotype who eats barley bread, while the bread of Athens was made from imported wheat. The typical meals of fourth century BC Boeotia, as described by the historian Cleitarchus, sound tasty enough but they include dishes of which other Greeks would not have boasted:

> Cleitarchus says that after Alexander had razed their city [of Thebes] their total wealth was computed at under 440 talents; also that they were mean-minded and parsimonious in the mat-

ter of food, cooking for their dinners *thria*, small fry, little gobies, anchovies, sausages, spare ribs and bean soup.

In the fifth century BC, as nearby Athens had grown, the economy of Boeotian cities had become less independent: the *Acharnians* and other sources imply that Boeotia exported to Athens a range of produce the more edible of which were oregano, pennyroyal, ducks, geese, jackdaws, francolins, coots, plovers, grebes, hares and, last but not least, the EELS from Lake Copais. These were certainly the most famous gastronomic product of Boeotia. They were carried in baskets over the short distance that separated the lake from Athens, so that a freshly killed Copaic eel might form the centrepiece at an Athenian dinner.

Among the lesser cities of Boeotia we hear in a food context of Plataea, whose people were to be found at the green cheese market held once a month in Athens (Lysias 23.6); and of Anthedon, a fishing town north of Thebes, with a tree-shaded *agora*, two covered markets and good HAKE or rockling. Was it also a place for good wine? Heracleides Criticus says so, but Aristotle, or at least Plutarch citing Aristotle, denies it (Archestratus *H* 14 Brandt with Olson and Sens *ad l.*; Heracleides Criticus *P* 1.23–4; Plutarch, *Greek Questions* 19 citing Aristotle fragments 596–7 Rose). The small town of ACRAEPHIA is important for its inscription of the second century BC whose purpose is to fix the market price of many kinds of fish.

Aristophanes, *Acharnians* 860–900, *Peace* 1005–14; Antimachus of Colophon 40 Wyss; Plutarch *EC* 995e; Athenaeus *D* 148d quoting Cleitarchus, also 297c–300d quoting Archestratus *H* 8 (see Olson and Sens *ad l.*) and other sources (on Copaic eels), also *D* 417b–418b.

Bonito *see* TUNNY

Botargo *see* GREY MULLET

Boulimos, Greek name for a pathological and insatiable hunger, sometimes affecting individuals, sometimes whole groups. To prevent it the ritual 'driving out of *boulimos*' was performed. The word is the origin of the modern term 'bulimia', but the pathology of this condition is different. Plutarch *QC* 6.1–3, 6.8.

Brain, considered acceptable food among some peoples, tabooed by others. Classical Greeks and Romans in general belonged to the first category. Aristotle, in the course of discussing the anatomy of the brain, speaks as if cooking it were a normal practice; Galen gives detailed information on its dietary qualities.

Thus in several of the recipes for *thria*, stuffed fig leaves (see under FIG), brain is listed as a main ingredient. Yet this point was disputed: Aristophanes of Byzantium argued that it was a misunderstanding based on taking Aristophanes too literally (*Scholia on Aristophanes, Frogs* 134, *Acharnians* 1101; *Suda s.v. thria*). The brain was eaten as part of a traditional delicacy, the split head of a pig or wild boar (see HEAD). It is also explicitly part of the *rodonia lopas* 'rose casserole' with which a fictional cook, in Athenaeus's dialogue set in imperial Rome, impresses his audience. He supplies a recipe.

Others in classical antiquity, however, belonged to the category of those who will not eat brains. PYTHAGORAS was confidently said to have been among them: to him was ascribed the assertion that to eat brains was to eat the heads of one's parents.

Aristotle, *Parts of Animals* 653a22; Plutarch *QC* 8.9; Galen *AF* 6.676–7; Athenaeus *E* 65f–66c, *D* 406a–b; Apicius 2.5.1.

Bread, product of the baking at steady high temperature of cereal flour, especially WHEAT flour. As far as the Old World is concerned bread is an invention of around 6000 BC, as dated by finds of bread ovens in the ancient Near East. Flat breads gradually became a staple of the Old World diet from that time on, a status demonstrated in the Akkadian epic of *Gilgamesh* in which seven loaves at various stages of staleness give evidence that the hero has slept for seven days. In classical Greece and Rome there were other possible STAPLE FOODS but bread was the most appreciated; bread (or, on the march, BISCUIT) was also the standard army food. To the Greeks bread was among the gifts of the cereal goddess Demeter, and to Romans likewise of Ceres. As in the ancient Near East, so in Greek and Roman cultures bread was on certain occasions offered to the gods; examples are supplied by Athenaeus.

Leavened breads are best made from the flour of *Triticum aestivum*, hence called 'bread wheat', a hybrid species that emerged in cultivation early in the first millennium BC. The contrast between leavened and unleavened is significant in the religion of the JEWS. Since bread wheat did not grow well in most of Greece, nor in most of central Italy, classical Athens and Rome (along with other cities that were sufficiently prosperous) came to depend on imported wheat for the leavened bread which became their preferred staple.

Small loaves can be baked in the ashes of a fire. More common in ancient times was the use of a bread crock (Greek *klibanos*, Latin *clibanus*) or an oven (Greek *ipnos*, Latin *furnus*); see COOKING UTENSILS. On farms, and in remote places, when bread was made it was made at home; but, whatever the equipment used, baking requires a hot fire for an extended period, and in crowded cities this was neither practical nor safe for the average small household. Two solutions are possible, and both were certainly used: one is to have communal ovens to which each user brings dough and takes away the finished loaf; the other is for the whole bread-making business to be done commercially and for consumers to buy

their bread. The first solution was used in Roman legionary fortresses (see ARMY FOOD). The second solution had been introduced to Athens by THEARION in the fifth century BC, and the bread on the Athenian market was to be highly praised (Athenaeus D 112a–e); it was no doubt practised in many other ancient cities too. Under the Roman Empire much is known of bread production in a provincial town from the excavation of bakeries at Pompeii. Carbonised loaves of bread have been found there.

The skill of a baker was different from that of a cook. In classical times it was traditionally said that the best bakers came from Lydia and Phoenicia; later, under the Roman Empire, Cappadocia was the favoured source. Pliny describes the ways of making leaven and the adulteration of Roman market bread with bean meal and even with fodder crops. Some types of bread named in ancient sources are set out below; numerous others will be found, especially in lists by Pliny, Pollux and Athenaeus. Aromatics used in baking bread included ajowan, black cumin, poppy seed, linseed and aniseed.

Greek *artos* means 'bread', 'loaf'; *sitos* means 'food', 'staple food', 'cereal food' and in practice often 'bread'. The classical Latin word for bread is *panis*.

Gilgamesh [Standard Babylonian version] tablet 11; Hippocrates *R* 42, *RA* 37, *Ancient Medicine* 14; Archestratus *H* 4–5 Brandt; Pliny *NH* 18.102–8, 18.117, 22.138–9; Pollux *O* 6.72–9; Athenaeus *D* 108f–116a; Aulus Gellius 3.3.14.

Schawe, 'Backen, Bäcker(ei)' in *RA* 1928– ; Buck 1949 pp. 356–63; N. Jasny, 'The daily bread of the ancient Greeks and Romans' in *Osiris* vol. 9 (1950) pp. 227–53; M. Währen, *Brot und Gebäck im Leben und Glauben der alten Ägypter* (Bern, 1963); M. Währen, *Brot und Gebäck im Leben und Glauben des alten Orient* (Bern, 1967); M. Währen, *Brot und Gebäck im alten Griechenland* (Detmold, 1974); Darby and others 1977 pp. 501–28; Joan M. Frayn, 'Home baking in Italy' in *Antiquity* (1978) pp. 28–33; Betty Jo Mayeske, 'Bakers, bakeshops and bread: a social and economic study' in *Pompeii and the Vesuvian Landscape* (Washington: Archaeological

Institute of America, Smithsonian Institution, 1979) pp. 39–58; B.A. Sparkes, 'Not cooking but baking' in *Greece and Rome* vol. 28 (1981) pp. 172–8; Amouretti 1986; E. Battaglia, *Artos. Il lessico della panificazione nei papiri greci* (Milan, 1989) (*Biblioteca di Aevum antiquum*, 2); B.J. Mayeske, 'A Pompeiian bakery on the Via dell'Abbondanza' in *Studia pompeiana et classica in honor of Wilhelmina F. Jashemski* ed. Robert I. Curtis (New Rochelle: Caratzas, 1989) vol. 1 pp. 149–65; Eveline J. van der Steen, 'Fiery furnaces: bread ovens in the ancient Near East' in *Petits Propos culinaires* no. 42 (1992) pp. 45–52; K.D. White, 'Roman bread and cereals' in *Food in Antiquity* ed. John Wilkins and others (Exeter: Exeter University Press, 1995) pp. 38–43; Brewer and others 1995 pp. 29–30; Delwen Samuel, 'Brewing and baking' in *Ancient Egyptian Materials and Technology* ed. P.T. Nicholson and I. Shaw (Cambridge: Cambridge University Press, 2000) pp. 537–76.

- The simplest distinctions, then as now, are between leavened and unleavened and between wholemeal and white. Unleavened bread is *azymos* in Greek, *azymus* in Latin. White bread is *katharos artos* in Greek, *panis mundus* in Latin; wholemeal bread is *ryparos artos* and *autopyros artos* in Greek, *autopyrus* in Latin. The distinction between wholemeal and white is made as far back as the third millennium BC in Mesopotamia; leavened bread was certainly available in Mesopotamia and Egypt by the same period.

Pliny *NH* 22.138; Athenaeus *D* 109b–d quoting Crobylus 2 Kassel, 110c–d quoting Plato Comicus *F* 92 Kassel; *Historia Augusta, Alexander Severus* 37.3, *Aurelian* 9.6; Eustathius, *Commentary on Odyssey* 2.142.

- Breads named for the origin of the flour or meal: *semidalites* from durum wheat, *krithinos artos* and Latin *panis hordeacius* from barley, *khondrites* from emmer meal and *krimmatias* from wheatmeal, *etnitas* and *lekithitas* from legumes (Archestratus *H* 4 Brandt; Athenaeus *D* 109b–c, 111b, also 115d citing Philistion of Locri). An *orindes artos* mentioned by Sophocles was conjectured by Athenaeus to mean either 'rice bread' or 'sawa millet bread': the former conjecture has been widely accepted but both are historically extremely unlikely (Athenaeus *D* 110e citing Sophocles fragment 609 Radt).

- Breads named for the method and equipment used: *artoptikios artos, panis artopticius* (Athenaeus *D* 113a citing Chrysippus of Tyana; Pliny *NH* 18.105); *panis depsticius*, literally 'kneaded bread', which was crock-baked (Cato *DA* 74), see the modern recipe by Leon 1943 pp. 216–17; *artos enkryphias* and *spodites*, baked under ashes (Hippocrates *R* 42, *Epidemics* 7.1.3; Archestratus *H* 4 Brandt; Athenaeus *D* 110b); *klibanites artos*, crock-baked bread (Archestratus *H* 4 Brandt; Athenaeus 109f, 110b–c); *ipnites, panis furnaceus*, oven-baked (Athenaeus *D* 109c; Pliny *NH* 18.105); *obelias artos*, made on a spit, a makeshift idea said to have been invented by the god Dionysus on one of his campaigns (Hippocrates *R* 42; Athenaeus 111b citing Socrates of Cos). Picene bread, a traditional Italian style, was made in an earthenware pot which was then broken to extract the bread (Pliny *NH* 18.106; Martial 13.47): Grant 1999 pp. 140–1 suggests a modern recipe.

Michael Chazen and Mark Lehner, 'An ancient analogy: pot baked bread in ancient Egypt and Mesopotamia' in *Paléorient* vol. 16 no. 2 (1990) pp. 21–35.

- Breads named for their appearance: *boletinos artos*, which rose into a mushroom shape (Athenaeus *D* 113c citing Chrysippus of Tyana), see the modern recipe by Grant 1999 pp. 53–4; *streptikios artos*, made with pepper (Athenaeus *D* 113d citing Chrysippus of Tyana), see the modern recipe by Grant 1999 pp. 54–5; *hapalos artos*, a soft bread said to be typical of Cappadocia (Athenaeus *D* 113b citing Chrysippus of Tyana), see the modern recipe by Grant 1999 pp. 52–3.

- Greek *eskharites* (Aramaic plural *esqarithin*) was a loaf baked over a brazier. Lynceus talks of *diakhristos eskharites*, 'anointed', presumably dipped or covered in a sweet sauce.

Athenaeus *D* 109c–e quoting Lynceus *F* 14; *Mekhilta on Exodus* 16.31 p. 51a (cited by Krauss 1910–12 vol. 1 p. 107 and note 459).

- Greek *kollix* was a spiral-shaped bun of roughly milled barley. A *kollix* was 'slave fodder' according to Hipponax; it was a Boeotian staple according to Aristophanes, a Thessalian delicacy according to Archestratus.

Hipponax 26 West; Aristophanes, *Acharnians* 872; Archestratus *H* 4 Brandt with Olson and Sens *ad l.*; Ephippus 1 Kassel; Galen, *Hippocratic Glossary* 19.113.

- Greek *kyllestis, kyllastis* was Egyptian sourdough emmer bread (the Egyptians used their barley for making beer, Hecataeus observed).

Herodotus 2.77; Athenaeus D 114c–d, also 418e citing Hecataeus.

- Greek *nastos* was a loaf with a filling.

  Aristophanes, *Birds* 567, *Wealth* 1142; F. Sokolowski, *Lois sacrées des cités grecques* (Paris, 1962) no. 52; Athenaeus D 111c.

- Latin *panis militaris* was the Roman 'army bread', made (if the *Historia Augusta* can be trusted) according to two standard recipes, *mundus* 'white' and *castrensis* 'camp style'. Junkelmann (pp. 194–5) reconstructs a recipe based on indications in ancient sources.

  Pliny NH 18.67 [*s.v.l.*]; *Historia Augusta, Aurelian* 9.6.

  Junkelmann 1997.

- Latin *torta* is a round loaf, and perhaps in particular a loaf divided into quarters. In the Vulgate translation of the Old Testament *torta* stands for Greek *artos* 'loaf'. There is no evidence for the usual translation 'twisted loaf'.

  Exodus 29.23; *Numbers* 6.19; *I Samuel* 2.36, 10.3; *Vindolanda Tablets* 2.180.

  W. Meyer-Lübke, *Romanisches etymologisches Wörterbuch* (Heidelberg: Winter, 1930–5) *s.v. torta*.

Bream or porgy, a group of sea fish significant in Mediterranean fisheries. The wealth of ancient nomenclature – only partly listed below – confirms their importance, but the breams, with the exception of the *khrysophrys* or gilthead, were not considered to be of the highest gastronomic quality. Some were good in parts; some were good only at a certain season, like the saupe; some were downright bad.

Thompson 1947 *s.vv.*; Davidson 1981 pp. 74–89.

- Greek *box*, Latin *boca* was the bogue (*Boops Boops*), a small bream feeding on seaweed and offering moderately good food.

  Athenaeus 286e–287b.

- Greek *erythrinos*, Latin *erythinus* was probably the pandora and red bream (*Pagellus Erythrinus* and *P. Bogaraveo*). Eating this fish was a way to settle the stomach, according to Pliny; it was also an aphrodisiac.

Ovid, *Halieutica* 104; Pliny NH 32.101, 32.139; Athenaeus D 300e.

- Greek *hyke* is unidentified, but it was possibly a bream because sources liken it to *erythrinos*. Hycara in Sicily was said to have been so named because these fishes were found spawning there by the first Greek colonists.

  Athenaeus D 327a–c.

  Thompson 1947 p. 272; Andrews 1948.

- Greek *kantharos*, Latin *cantharus* was the griset or black bream (*Spondyliosoma Cantharus*). Ovid found a reason to dislike it, and seems to have modern Provençal gourmets on his side. *La tanudo ni cuecho ni crudo* '[Eat] the black bream neither cooked nor raw' is a local proverb quoted by Alan Davidson. Xenocrates, however, favoured it, as does Davidson himself.

  Acraephia Price List; Ovid, *Halieutica* 103; Xenocrates T 22.

- Greek *khrysophrys* or *khrysopos*, Latin *aurata* or *chrysophrys*, was the gilthead or daurade (*Sparus Aurata*), a pretty fish, spawning near river mouths and said by Archestratus to be at its best at the mouth of the river Selinus near Ephesus. It was called *ioniskos* 'little Ionian' there. It was sometimes dignified with the title *hieros ikhthys* 'holy fish', perhaps because of its good looks, perhaps because it was very good to eat: sweetest and most palatable of all fish, according to Hicesius. Romans liked it enough to keep it in fishponds. To at least one classical Greek author – Archippus – the gilthead was sacred to Aphrodite; to the Christian Jerome it was one of the fish brought ashore by Christ.

  Columella DA 8.16.8; Martial 13.90; Athenaeus D 328a–c quoting Archestratus 12 Brandt (see Olson and Sens *ad l.*), Archippus 18 Kassel and Hicesius; Jerome, *Letters* 72; *Apicius* 4.2.31, 10.2.14–15.

  Higginbotham 1997 p. 48.

- Greek *melanouros*, Latin *oculata* or *melanurus*, was a big-eyed fish, whence no doubt its Latin name. It was the oblade or saddled bream (*Oblada melanura*). It was a 'most deadly' food, according to an opinion cited – to be rejected – in a Hippocratic text. Xenocrates approved it; other sources have little to say of its food qualities, good or bad.

  Hippocrates, *Sacred Disease* 2; *Acraephia*

Price List; Xenocrates *T* 22; Oppian *H* 3.443–81; Athenaeus *D* 313c–e.

- Greek *mormyros*, Latin *mormyr* was the striped bream, known in French as *morme* or *marbré* (*Lithognathus Mormyrus*), a poor fish according to Lynceus, who suggests a pseudo-Hesiodic verse with which to browbeat the fishmonger into reducing its price.

Athenaeus *D* 313e–314a quoting Lynceus *F* 20.

Olson and Sens 2000 p. 201.

- Greek *phagros*, Latin *phager* or *pagrus*, was probably the braize or Couch's sea bream, known in French as *pagre* (*Sparus Pagrus*). The *pagre* was good at Delos and Eretria. There was a NILE FISH of the same name.

Acraephia Price List; Athenaeus *D* 327c–e quoting Archestratus *H* 26 Brandt (see Olson and Sens *ad l.*).

- Greek *salpe*, Latin *salpa* was the fish now known in French as *saupe*, in Spanish as *salema* (*Sarpa Salpa*). If anywhere, they were good at Mitylene and Ibiza. Epicharmus wrote of 'saupes, fat, shit-eating, disgusting, but good to eat in summer'. Archestratus and Diphilus of Siphnos agreed that the best time to eat a saupe was during the grain harvest, and in modern Tunisia, according to Alan Davidson, they say the same.

Pliny *NH* 9.68; Athenaeus *D* 321d–322a quoting Epicharmus 63 Kaibel and Archestratus *H* 28 Brandt, also 356a citing Diphilus of Siphnos.

- Greek *sargos*, Latin *sargus* is now known in French as *sar* or *sargue* (*Diplodus Sargus*). They were best at the beginning of winter, as the vine shed its leaves. There were good *sargues* to be found at Brundisium, according to Ennius.

Ennius *H* 4; Xenocrates *T* 22; *Acraephia Price List* (*kharakias*); Galen *AF* 6.720; Athenaeus *D* 321a–d quoting Archestratus *H* 36 Brandt (see Olson and Sens *ad l.*).

- Greek *sinodon* or *synodous*, Latin *synodon* or *dentex*, was the denté (*Dentex Dentex* and other species), an inshore fish that might be caught by hook and line and was good to eat at the Straits of Messina. It was kept in fishponds in Roman Italy. It could be grilled or baked whole. *Apicius* provides recipes for two suitable sauces, and also for a mixed seafood dish incorporating denté. Greek *synagris* might be this same species or a similar one.

Philoxenus *D* b.14 Page; Columella *DA*

8.16.8; Oppian *H* 1.168–70, 3.610–19; Athenaeus *D* 322b–c quoting Archestratus *H* 17 Brandt; *Apicius* 4.2.31, 10.2.12–13.

- Greek *sparos*, Latin *sparus* or *sparulus*, was the annular bream, known in French as *sparaillon* (*Diplodus annularis*). It is a small and unexciting fish: Martial imagines himself focusing, as client, on a *sparaillon* while his host and patron tucks into a turbot.

Diphilus of Siphnos [Athenaeus *D* 355e]; Martial 3.60; Athenaeus *D* 320c–d.

Brine *see* SALT

Britain (Latin *Britannia*), Roman border province. Literary sources on life in Roman Britain are sparse, but archaeology to some extent fills the gap. It has provided evidence of several kinds. There are finds of plant remains in contexts indicating food use (including rubbish heaps and latrine deposits); there are documents, not only inscriptions on stone and lead but also the letters and memoranda on slips of alder wood found at Vindolanda near the northern frontier of the province. Also relevant, because dated only shortly before the Roman conquest, is the body of 'Lindow Man', drowned in a peat marsh in which his body was preserved. His stomach contents have been analysed. 'Lindow Man's last meal was ... a griddle cake ... baked at *c.*200 deg. C, some of the cake having been exposed to a considerably higher temperature producing charcoal;' the cake was made of hulled barley, spelt, emmer with brome grass and oats (Sales).

It is from archaeobotany (with very little help from Pliny's *Natural History*, and none from other authors) that it is possible to put together a list of plant foods apparently new to Britain in Roman times: for a summary see the tables compiled by Greig. It appears likely that these foods were introduced to Britain by Roman gardeners or army caterers, but that conclusion is necessarily based on negative evidence: archaeobotanists have identified remains of these plants in food contexts from Roman sites but not, so far, from any earlier ones. Pliny adds that cherries were introduced to Britain four years after the invasion by Claudius, in AD 47. Tacitus implies that vines were not yet being grown at the end of the first century; they were apparently introduced later, and the late third-century emperor Probus is said (in the unreliable *Historia Augusta*) to have authorised the making of wine in Britain.

Some of these plants disappeared from Britain after the end of the Empire; others, notably vines, continued to be grown.

Pre-Roman Britain exported grain. Known food exports from Roman Britain are limited to one additional commodity, the OYSTERS from Rutupiae, mentioned by several authors of the late first century AD. Rutupiae, a Roman seaport, is modern Richborough in Kent, not very far from the oyster beds of Winchelsea which are still reputed the best in Britain. Known imports to Roman Britain included wine, olive oil, table olives and dried figs.

Strabo 4.5.2; Pliny *NH* 9.169, 15.102, 32.62; Tacitus, *Agricola* 12; Juvenal 4.140–2; *Historia Augusta, Probus* 18.8; Bede, *Ecclesiastical History* 1.1.

R.G. Collingwood in Frank 1933–40 vol. 3 pp. 1–118; H. Helbaek, 'Early crops in southern England' in *Proceedings of the Prehistoric Society* vol. 18 (1952) pp. 194–233; G.H. Wilcox, 'Exotic plants from Roman water-logged sites in London' in *Journal of Archaeological Science* vol. 4 (1977) pp. 269–82; D. Williams, 'A consideration of the sub-fossil remains of *Vitis vinifera* L. as evidence for viticulture in Roman Britain' in *Britannia* vol. 8 (1977) pp. 327–34; D.P.S. Peacock, 'The Rhine and the problem of Gaulish wine in Roman Britain' in *Roman Shipping and Trade: Britain and the Rhine provinces* ed. J. du Plat Taylor and H. Cleere (London, 1978) (*Council for British Archaeology Research Report* no. 24); G.G. Dannell, 'Eating and drinking in pre-conquest Britain: the evidence of amphora and Samian trading, and the effect of the invasion of Claudius' in *Invasion and Response* ed. B.C. Burnham and H.B. Burnham (Oxford: BAR, 1979) pp. 177–84; B.A. Knights, C.A. Dickson, J.H. Dickson and D.J. Breeze, 'Evidence con-

cerning Roman military diet at Beardsden, Scotland, in the 2nd century AD' in *Journal of Archaeological Science* vol. 10 (1983) pp. 139–52; J.R. Greig, 'Plant foods in the past: a review of evidence from northern Europe' in *Journal of Plant Foods* vol. 5 (1983) pp. 179–214; P. Galliou, 'Days of wine and roses? Early Armorica and the Atlantic wine trade' in *Cross-Channel Trade between Gaul and Britain in the Pre-Roman Iron Age* ed. S. Macready and F. H. Thompson (London, 1984) pp. 24–36; *Lindow Man: the body in the bog* ed. I.M. Stead, J.B. Bourke and D. Brothwell (London, 1986); G. Jones and A. Legge, 'The grape (Vitis vinifera L.) in the Neolithic of Britain' in *Antiquity* vol. 61 (1987) pp. 452–5; K.D. Sales and others in Renfrew 1991 pp. 51–8; C. Dickson, 'The Roman army diet in Britain and Germany' in *Archäobotanik: dissertationes botanicae* vol. 133 (1989) pp. 135–54; T. Unwin, 'Saxon and early Norman viticulture in England' in *Journal of Wine Research* vol. 1 (1990) pp. 61–75; *Britain in the Roman Period: recent trends* ed. R.F.J. Jones (Sheffield, 1991) (includes papers by M. Jones and A.C. King on 'Food production and consumption'); Karen Meadows, 'The appetites of households in early Roman Britain' in *The Archaeology of Household Activities* ed. Penelope M. Allison (London: Routledge, 1999) pp. 101–20; Joan P. Alcock, *Food in Roman Britain* (Brimscombe Port: Tempus, 2001); A.G. Brown and others, 'Roman vineyards in Britain: stratigraphic and palynological data from Wollaston in the Nene valley, England' in *Antiquity* vol. 75 (2001) pp. 745–57; Alison Locker, 'Fish bones and English food history' in *Petits propos culinaires* no. 70 (2002) pp. 38–57. See also references for ARMY FOOD.

Brome grass (*Bromus* sp.), a minor cereal. Brome grass was gathered from the wild in western Europe in prehistoric and probably in Roman times. It was used in southern France by 500 BC. It formed part of Lindow Man's last meal (see BRITAIN).

Buffalo *see* WATER BUFFALO

Bulbs, the usual English translation for Greek *bolboi*, Latin *bulbi* or *bulbi Megarici*, the bulbs of the grape-hyacinth (*Muscari comosum*); they are known in modern Greek as *volví*, in Italian as *lampascioni*. These have been eaten in Greece ever since classical times as an appetiser or relish. They require long baking, traditionally under hot ashes, and generous seasoning, an expenditure of effort possibly redeemed by their lasting fame as APHRODISIACS. Megara was the traditional producer for the Athenian market. Bulbs were no less popular in classical Italy. The 'strengthening foods' prescribed for a case of impotence in Petronius's *Satyricon* are 'bulbs, snails' necks served without sauce, and a little unmixed wine'. Ovid confirms the aphrodisiac reputation of bulbs, as does the uxorious Varro, quoted thus in the recipe book *Apicius*:

> Bulbs. Serve in oil, fish sauce, vinegar, with a little cumin sprinkled over. – Or, mash and boil in water, then fry in oil. Make a sauce thus: thyme, pennyroyal, pepper, oregano, honey, a little vinegar and, if liked, a little fish sauce. Sprinkle pepper over and serve. – Or, boil and squeeze into a pan, adding thyme, oregano, honey, vinegar, concentrated must, *caryota* date, fish sauce and a little oil. Sprinkle pepper over and serve. Varro says: '*What of bulbs?*' '*Boil them in water, I said, if you fancy knocking at Venus's door. Or serve them at dinner, as people do at proper weddings. But you might add pine kernels, or pounded rocket and pepper.*'

Galen suggests a comparable variety of cooking methods. The flavour of bulbs, though somewhat bitter even at the end of the cooking process, was sufficiently attractive that bulbs were often combined with other foods, for example *bolbophake* 'bulb and lentil soup', served, for whatever good reason, at a courtesan's establishment in one Greek anecdote (Lynceus). In this particular combination they were found to confer a general feeling of warmth. *Bolbophake d'hoion ambrosie psykhous kryoentos*, said an ancient proverb recorded by Chrysippus: 'Bulb and lentil soup is like ambrosia when the cold weather bites.'

In addition to the uses of whole bulbs as food and aphrodisiac, the juice of bulbs had medicinal uses, as specified for example in Hippocratic texts.

The Latin word *bulbus* is occasionally used generically, of all edible bulbs, as in two passages of Pliny, *NH* 19.93, 20.102–5. In English the grape-hyacinth (*Muscari comosum*) has also been called 'pursetassels' and 'tassel hyacinth'.

Aristophanes, *Clouds* 187–90, *Assemblywomen* 1091–2; Hippocrates, *Epidemics* 7.101, *Nature of Woman* 93; Plato Comicus *F* 188–9 Kassel; Alexis *F* 167 Kassel with Arnott *ad l.*; Theophrastus *HP* 7.12–13; Lynceus *F* 24 [Athenaeus *D* 584d]; Theocritus 14.17 with Gow *ad l.*; Chrysippus of Soli [Athenaeus *D* 158a]; Cato *DA* 7; Ovid, *Art of Love* 2.421–2; Dioscorides *MM* 2.170; Petronius *S* 130; Columella *DA* 10.105–6; Pliny *NH* 20.105–6; Galen *AF* 6.652–4, *SF* 11.851; Athenaeus *E* 63d–64f quoting Philemon 113 Kassel and Nicander *F* 88 Schneider; *Apicius* 7.12 quoting Varro.

Patience Gray, *Honey from a Weed* (London, 1986) pp. 190, 202; Dalby 1996 p. 83 and note 155.

• Unwary translators sometimes render the Greek and Latin terms with 'onion' (which has very different effects) or 'iris bulb' or even 'tulip bulb' (please don't eat either of these). See also pp. xv–xvi. Ground iris bulb in small quantities was really employed in sexual therapy, to combat premature ejaculation, according to Dioscorides (*E* 2.103).

Bull's blood *see* POISONS

Burbot, freshwater fish of the northern hemisphere. The burbot is said by Pliny to be found in the big Alpine lakes, and to grow there as big as a moray. This is not necessarily exaggeration: specimens of the same species in Alaska have reached sixty pounds weight. The burbot was kept in fishponds, and well repaid the cost of doing so. Its liver was the special delicacy in Roman times (as it has been even recently), and a well-grown burbot claimed a place, as Ausonius says, at the most richly supplied of feasts.

The burbot or eel-pout (*Lota Lota*) is Latin *mustela*.

Columella *DA* 8.17.8; Pliny *NH* 9.63; Ausonius, *Mosella* 101–14.

Bustard, large game bird. The bustard is native to southern Europe and north Africa; many were brought to Alexandria from all around the country.

The bustard (*Otis Tarda*) is Greek *otis*; in Latin its name is *avis tarda* 'the slow bird'.

Xenophon, *Anabasis* 1.5.2–3; Hippocrates, *Sacred Disease* 2; Aelian, *Nature of Animals* 5.24; Pliny *NH* 10.57; Galen *AF* 6.703; Oppian, *Cynegetica* 2.407; Athenaeus *D* 390d (confused); Anthimus *OC* 33.

Butchers *see* MEAT

Butter, a milk product not very familiar in the ancient Mediterranean world. Butter in its typical modern European form would not keep in this climate without refrigeration; unlike cheese, it was therefore not an economical way of using milk.

In translations of ancient Near Eastern texts 'butter' should generally be understood as 'ghee' – butter which has been heated and allowed to solidify, after which it keeps well and can be re-melted for use in cooking. In this form butter was frequently offered to the gods: note for example Gilgamesh's offering to the sun god Shamash (*Gilgamesh* [Standard Babylonian version] tablet 8). When *boutyron* 'butter' is mentioned by Strabo as a commodity of Arabia and Sudan, and is described in the *Periplus* as a typical article of trade in the Indian Ocean, ghee is certainly what these authors mean.

In classical Greece and Rome, both of them enthusiastically cheese-eating cultures, butter was relatively little known in any form, though again sometimes serving as a divine offering, as at the temple of Venus at Eryx. To Greeks its use became a marker of typical northern barbarians: Thracians were called *boutyrophagoi* 'butter-eaters' in a lost play by Anaxandrides. Pliny, however, gives instructions for making butter; and at the

end of the Roman Empire, writing in northern Gaul, Anthimus recommends unsalted butter with honey for patients with consumption.

A perfume (*myron*) was made with butter, according to Dioscorides. Galen had heard that in northern countries, where there is no olive oil, people when washing rub themselves with butter instead of oil.

Dioscorides is right to say that butter can be made from the milk of various animals, but Galen is also right to insist that it is usually a product of cows' milk. The Greek name for it (*boutyron, boutyros*; Latin *butyrum*), means literally 'cow cheese'.

Genesis 18.8; *Deuteronomy* 32.14; Hippocrates, *Affections of Women* 65; Anaxandrides 42 Kassel; Strabo 16.4.24, 17.2.2; Dioscorides *MM* 1.54, 2.72; *Periplus Maris Erythraei* 14; Pliny *NH* 11.239, 28.133–5 (instructions); Plutarch, *Against Colotes* 1109b–c; Galen *AF* 6.683–4, *SF* 12.272; Athenaeus *D* 394f–395a; *Diocletian's Price Edict* 4.50; Anthimus *OC* 77 with Grant *ad l.*

Marten Stol, 'Milk, butter and cheese' in *Bulletin on Sumerian Agriculture* vol. 7 (1993) pp. 99–113.

Byzantium, early Greek colony (from about 660 BC) at the entrance to the Black Sea. Refounded as Constantinople by the Roman emperor Constantine in AD 330, the city would become the capital of the later Roman Empire. Its modern name is Istanbul.

The importance of Byzantium was as a nexus of trade and transport. All Greek traffic to the Black Sea passed this way; all Scythian and Black Sea products that were exported to Greece and beyond came by way of Byzantium. In addition, the fishing business at Byzantium itself produced a copious supply of seafood, both fresh and conserved.

The city's inhabitants were, not unnaturally, seen by critical observers as spending all their time at markets and in taverns. Gastronomes, however, recommended Byzantium for the high quality of several specific foods to be found there, from the small parrot wrasse to the very large swordfish, and for the salted and cured fish which Byzantium exported and which is all that most other Greeks, unless they travelled, would have known at first hand of the city's products. Most unusually among Greek peoples, but in common with other Thracians, the fishermen of Byzantium hunted the dolphin: no author, however, comments on its flavour.

The staple of Byzantian trade was the bonito (see TUNNY). This large and meaty fish has an annual pattern of migration that takes it away from the Black Sea, through the Bosporus and Hellespont, into the Mediterranean, every autumn; it returns in the spring. Strabo describes the migration in some detail, explaining why it benefits Byzantium in particular, and hints broadly at its commercial signifi-cance, from which not only Byzantium but the city's successive overlords, from Macedon to Rome, benefited financially. Three surviving quotations from Archestratus' *Hedypatheia* name Byzantium as source of fine bonito and tunny.

Eastward across the Bosporus lay the smaller city of Calchedon. This was the place to buy a sea squirt (Archestratus *H* 56 Brandt, cf. 13 [*s.v.l.*]).

Archestratus *H* 13, 34, 35, 37, 40 Brandt; Theopompus 115 F 62 Jacoby [Athenaeus *D* 526e]; Oppian *H* 5.519–88, cf. Aristotle *HA* 533b9–14; Athenaeus *D* 116e citing Hicesius.

J. Dumont, 'La pêche du thon à Byzance à l'époque hellénistique' in *Revue des études anciennes* vol. 78/9 (1976/7) pp. 96–119; D. Braund, 'Fish from the Black Sea: classical Byzantium and the Greekness of trade' in *Food in Antiquity* ed. John Wilkins and others (Exeter: Exeter University Press, 1995) pp. 162–70.

C

Cabbage, garden vegetable well known in Greece and Rome. How far back into prehistory its cultivation may go is not known because of the lack of certain archaeobotanical finds, either in Mediterranean lands or in the Near East.

Cabbage was usually prepared by boiling: Theophrastus shows that it was sometimes boiled in *nitron* to improve its flavour and, presumably, colour. It might then be chopped, and fried with olive oil.

Cabbage was popular (or, at least, famous) for its health-giving qualities. These are most fully stated in two sections of Cato's *De Agricultura*, the second of which may be by another hand. A recipe for cabbage as a prophylactic against drunkenness, included there (*DA* 157.7), had an eight-hundred-year vogue: it had been recorded in an earlier version by Mnesitheus of Athens (*c*.400 BC) and would be repeated by Oribasius (*c*.AD 360). Dalby and Grainger 1996 p. 50 and Grant 1999 p. 142 give modern interpretations of this recipe.

The two oldest varieties of cultivated cabbage (*Brassica oleracea*) can already be distinguished in ancient nomenclature. The headed cabbage is Greek *krambe*, Latin *brassica* or *olus*. The open, leafy cabbage or kale is Greek *raphanos*, Latin *caulis*.

Hippocrates *R* 54; Theophrastus *HP* 7.4.4, 7.6.1–2, *CP* 2.5.3; Cato *DA* 157–8; Dioscorides *MM* 2.120–1; Pliny *NH* 19.136–43, 20.78–95; Galen *AF* 6.630–3; Athenaeus *D* 369e–370f; Palladius *OA* 3.24.5–7; Oribasius *CM* 4.4.1 citing Mnesitheus; Anthimus *OC* 50 with Grant *ad l.*

Buck 1949 p. 373; Darby and others 1977 p. 669; Zohary and Hopf 1993 p. 186; E. de Saint-Denis, 'Éloge du chou' in *Latomus* vol. 39 (1980) pp. 838–49.

- Latin *cyma*, Greek *krambosparagon* or *ormenos*, was apparently a young cabbage sprout; the suggestion that it was a Brussels sprout has been scouted. Whatever exactly it was, it was expensive.

Diocletian's Price Edict 6.11.

- Seakale (*Crambe maritima*), Latin *brassica marina*, was counted by Romans as one of the wild varieties of cabbage, of interest both as a wild food and for its medicinal properties.

Pliny *NH* 20.96, cf. Dioscorides *MM* 2.122.

Caecalus of Argos, Greek author of a poem on fish, now lost.

Athenaeus *E* 13b.

Caecuban wine (Latin *Caecubum*; Greek *Kaikoubos*) from a small territory, *ager Caecubus*, at Amyclae, between Terracina and Fundi, in coastal Latium. Varro, around 70 BC, already regarded this district as a place of legendary wealth. To many in the first century BC Caecuban was the best of all wines, smoother than Falernian, fuller than Alban, strong and intoxicating. It was a white wine which turned fire-coloured as it aged. Dioscorides describes it as *glykys* 'sweet'. The vineyard afterwards declined, eventually to be abandoned (according to Pliny) when Nero planned a ship canal across the land. In Martial's time (to rely on the light evidence of a gift poem by him) Caecuban wine was still maturing in cellars at Amyclae. Galen is the last person on record to have tasted Caecuban, nearly a century after it ceased to be made.

Varro, *Menippean Satires* 38 Bücheler; Strabo 5.3.6; Horace, *Odes* 2.14.25–8; Vitruvius 8.3.12; Dioscorides *MM* 5.6.7, 5.6.11; Columella *DA* 3.8.5; Pliny *NH* 14.61, 23.35; Galen *BM* 6.805, 6.809, *On Therapeutic Method* 10.834; Athenaeus *E* 27a; *CIL* 15.4545–8.

Tchernia 1986 esp. p. 342; Dalby 2000a pp. 46, 215.

Caesar, C. Iulius, Roman politician, eventually appointed Dictator for life shortly before his assassination. Caesar offers numerous examples of the successful use of large-scale entertainment in building patronage. It was by no means his only method, but he spent a good deal on it. The first such event recorded by Suetonius is a public banquet given in memory of his daughter: here, as later, he took steps to ensure the maximum of favourable publicity. His choice of wines for such events is recorded by Pliny:

> Did not Caesar, at his triumphal dinner as dictator, provide an amphora of Falernian and a jar of Chian to each party? Again, at his Spanish triumph, Caesar gave Chian and Falernian, but at the feast in his third consulship it was Falernian, Chian, Lesbian, Mamertine – the first time, apparently, that four kinds of wine were served.

Pliny adds that it was precisely Caesar's selection that gave MAMERTINE WINE its high status in Rome. Some of Caesar's less public entertainments are on record, including the dinner he presented to the college of high priests at Rome on the occasion of the appointment of Lentulus's inauguration as Flamen Martialis, around 70 BC. Caesar himself was at that time Flamen Dialis, priest of Jupiter: it is the only such event for which a menu survives.

> As hors-d'oeuvres sea urchins, as many raw oysters as they wanted, palourdes, mussels, thrushes under a thatch of asparagus, a fattened chicken, a patina of oysters and palourdes, black piddocks, white piddocks; then more mussels, clams, sea anemones, beccafici, loin of roe deer and wild boar, fowl fattened on wheatmeal, beccafici, *Murex trunculus* and *Murex brandaris*.
>
> The dinner was udder, the split head of a wild boar, patina of fish, patina of udder, ducks, roast teal, hares, roast fowl, frumenty and Picentine loaves.

Caesar's troops were confident enough of his generosity to them to make jokes, at his triumph, about the dreadful food his stinginess had forced them to live on while they were besieging Pompey. On the real identification of their emergency food at Dyrrachium see ARUM.

Caesar, *Civil War* 3.48 (quoted at ARUM); Pliny *NH* 14.66, 14.97, 19.144; Plutarch, *Life of Caesar* 17.9–10, 39.1–2; Suetonius, *Julius* 26, 38, 43, 48, 53; Macrobius *S* 3.13.10–12 citing Metellus Pius.

Lily Ross Taylor, 'Caesar's colleagues in the pontifical college' in *American Journal of Philology* vol. 63 (1942) p. 385–412; Dalby 2001.

Cakes, like bread, are typically baked from cereal flour: other ingredients are added, before or after baking, to alter the texture and flavour. In classical Greece and Rome bread was the staple constituent of a main meal, while cakes were eaten, alongside wine, dried fruits and nuts, at dessert and at symposia. There were many kinds and many names. The chances of survival mean that we know only a few brief recipes (or rather, lists of ingredients); in numerous cases no details at all are known.

Cakes were often offered to the gods: for examples see below. Their importance in a religious context is signalled by the fact that many different kinds of cakes are mentioned in Greek tragedy. But to what extent were these offertory cakes eaten by the participants? To what extent were they edible at all? How closely did they resemble cakes that were eaten on less religious occasions? In general we have few answers to such questions. It has been suggested that Cato, in his Latin manual *On Farming*, includes a section of cake recipes because they would be needed for religious reasons; it has also been suggested that they would be a profitable cash sideline for a suitably located farm.

In modern cuisines shape and colour are often important to the identification of particular cakes. On the colour and shape of ancient cakes occasional information in the sources is supplemented by equally occasional information from iconography. Greek vase paintings that depict symposia sometimes show cakes on the tables; similarly, images of sacrifice can be found showing cakes on the altar.

The most general terms are Greek *plakous* and *pemma*, Latin *libum*. *Pemma*, if a distinction can be made, was a small cake or sweetmeat in which the cereal element might be absent, supplanted entirely by richer and sweeter ingredients such as nuts and dried fruits.

Philoxenus D e.1–19 Page; Cato DA 75–82; Galen AF 6.491–2; Pollux O 6.72–9; Athenaeus D 108f–116a, 643e–649a.

Orth, 'Kuchen' in RE 1893–1972; Leon 1943; G. Behrens, 'Römische Milchkocher' in *Germania* vol. 30 (1952) pp. 110–11.

- Greek *popanon* is the commonest term for an offertory cake. Alongside four *popana* a fifth cake, the *pemptos bous* 'fifth ox', might be offered. The *pelanos* appears also to have been an offertory cake.

Aristophanes, *Wealth* 676–81; Euripides fragment 912 Nauck; Polybius 6.25.7; *Suda s.v. anastatoi* quoting Euripides fragment

350 Nauck; Eustathius, *Commentary on Iliad* 4.263.

- The usual Roman offertory cake, to judge by the sources, was *libum*. Leon 1943 p. 217, Dalby and Grainger 1996 pp. 92–4 and Junkelmann 1997 p. 196 give interpretations of Cato's recipe for *libum*, but there were also very different recipes; millet was an ingredient in the version mentioned by Ovid, which was offered to Vesta.

Cato DA 75 with Dalby ad l.; Ovid, *Fasti* 3.761, 4.743–4; Athenaeus D 125f.

André 1981 pp. 211–12.

- The Greek *pankarpia* was an offering of 'every kind of fruit' in the form of a cake. The cake involved perhaps took different forms; it is described by Euripides as a *pelanos* (see above), by Theophrastus as a *melitoutta* (see below). Theophrastus was told by the root-cutters that you should bury such a cake, as an offering, after gathering a particular medicinal herb. Presumably you would not afterwards return to eat it.

Sophocles fragment 398 Radt; Euripides fragment 912 Nauck; Theophrastus HP 9.8.7; F. Sokolowski, *Lois sacrées de l'Asie Mineure* (Paris, 1955) no. 52.

- Among Greek sacrificial cakes of special form were the Athenian *amphiphon*, a cheesecake with lighted candles stuck into it, offered to Artemis on the day of the full moon in the month Munychion (Pollux O 6.75; Athenaeus D 645a citing Philochorus; *Suda s.v. anastatoi*; Eustathius, *Commentary on Iliad* 4.263 citing Pausanias); the Delian *basynias*, a honey cake garnished with a dried fig and three walnuts and offered to Iris (Athenaeus D 645b citing Semus; Grant 1999 pp. 152–3); the Athenian *elaphos*, shaped as a deer and offered at the Elaphebolia (Athenaeus D 646e; Grant 1999 p. 61); the *hebdomos bous* 'seventh ox', a crescent-shaped cake offered in sacrifice alongside six *phthoeis* (F. Sokolowski, *Lois sacrées des cités grecques* [Paris, 1962] no. 25; Pollux O 6.76; Eustathius, *Commentary on Iliad* 4.263 citing Pausanias); the Sicilian *myllos*, shaped like female genitals and offered to the goddesses Demeter and Persephone (Athenaeus D 647a with Gulick ad l.). Beside all these there was the *phthois*, a round sacrificial cake apparently also called *selene* 'moon'. It was made with bread-wheat flour, cheese and honey, and was eaten with the entrails of a sacrificial animal (Athenaeus D 489d citing Asclepiades of Myrlea, 647d citing Chrysippus of

Tyana; Eustathius, *Commentary on Odyssey* 2.64). Grant 1999 p. 64 suggests a modern recipe, following Chrysippus; perhaps wisely, he leaves out the entrails. Eustathius also offers a recipe.

Emily Kearns in *Ancient Greek Cult Practice from the Epigraphical Evidence* ed. R. Hägg (Athens, 1994) pp. 64–70.

- Greek *ames* is often translated 'milk cake'; there were also little ones called *ametiskoi*.

Aristophanes, *Wealth* 999; Philo, *On Drunkenness* 217; Athenaeus 644f quoting Menander fragment 425 Körte and Telecleides 1 Kassel.

- Greek *enkhytos*, Latin *encytum* was made by injecting a narrow stream of cheesy batter into hot fat. The analogy between this operation and the sexual act seems to have occurred to Hipponax. One served this pastry with honey or with MULSUM, says Cato. For modern interpretations of the ancient recipes see Leon 1943 p. 219; Grant 1999 p. 150.

Cato *DA* 80 with Dalby *ad l.*; Athenaeus *D* 370a citing Hipponax 104.49 West [*s.v.l.*], also 644c citing Menander fragment 451 Körte, also 647d citing Chrysippus of Tyana.

- Greek *enkris* and Latin *globus* or *globulus* was a doughnut, deep fried in fat or oil and soaked in honey. Leon 1943 pp. 219–21, Dalby and Grainger 1996 pp. 54–5, Junkelmann 1997 p. 198 and Grant 1999 pp. 57–8, 108–9 give interpretations of these hints and recipes.

Stesichorus 179 Davies; Cato *DA* 79 with Dalby *ad l.*; Varro, *On the Latin Language* 5.107; Petronius *S* 1.3; Athenaeus *D* 645e; Hesychius, *Lexicon s.v. enkris*.

- Greek *gastris* was a Cretan speciality made with various nuts, poppy-seeds and sesame seeds. For modern interpretations see Dalby and Grainger 1996 pp. 80–1; Grant 1999 pp. 151–2.

Athenaeus *D* 647f quoting Chrysippus of Tyana.

C. Perry, 'Baklava not proven Greek' in *Petits Propos culinaires* no. 27 (1987) pp. 47–8.

- Latin *laterculi* were poppy-seed cakes, if Plautus is describing them accurately. Grant 1999 pp. 106–7 gives an interpretation of this recipe.

Plautus, *Poenulus* 325–6.

- Greek *melipekton* and *melitoutta* (properly adjectives, 'honey-curdled', 'honey-flavoured') were cakes or sweets of which nothing is known beyond their names.

Herodotus 8.41 (*melitoessa*); Aristophanes, *Clouds* 507, *Lysistrata* 601; Philoxenus *D* e.16 Page (*melipakton*); Philo, *On Drunkenness* 217.

- Greek *oinoutta* 'wine cake' perhaps resembled Latin *mustaceus*, whose special feature was that must, with its natural yeast content, made the cakes rise. Like Cato's *libum* these were baked on bay leaves: the suitable leaves were called *mustaces*. *Mustacei* were a snack and dinner delicacy and are incorporated in a recipe for shoulder of pork in *Apicius* where their function is to soak up some of the sauce. Dalby and Grainger 1996 pp. 109–11, Junkelmann 1997 pp. 195–6 and Grant 1999 pp. 109–11 give interpretations of Cato's recipe.

Aristophanes, *Wealth* 1121 with scholia; Cato *DA* 121; Cicero *Letters to Atticus* 5.20.4; Pliny *NH* 15.127; Statius, *Silvae* 1.6.19; Juvenal 6.202; Athenaeus *D* 647d citing Chrysippus of Tyana; Palladius *OA* 11.21; *Apicius* 7.9.3.

- Greek *plakous* is often translated 'cheesecake'; cheese, honey and flour were the chief ingredients according to a suggestive description by Antiphanes. The *plakous* was good in Athens, because Attic honey was good. No recipe survives in Greek sources. The Latin *placenta* is named after this Greek cake and no doubt had some resemblance to it. Leon 1943 p. 218, Dalby and Grainger 1996 pp. 94–6 and Grant 1999 pp. 104–6 suggest modern recipes based on the very complicated instructions given by Cato.

Archestratus *H* 62 Brandt; Athenaeus 449c quoting Antiphanes; Cato *DA* 76; Lucilius 585 Marx; Martial 5.39.

- Greek *pyramis* and *pyramous* were evidently pyramidal like some of the cakes depicted on Greek vases. The *pyramous*, so Callimachus suggests, was given as a prize for staying awake at all-night festivals. Athenaeus connects the *kharisios* with this idea of a prize (Athenaeus *D* 646b citing Aristophanes fragment 211 Kassel and Eubulus *F* 1 Kassel, also 668c); the *Scholia on Aristophanes* connect the *sesamous* with it. Grant 1999 pp. 42–3 devises a modern recipe for *pyramous*.

Aristophanes, *Acharnians* 1092, *Thesmophoriazusae* 570, *Knights* 277 and scholia; Athenaeus *D* 647c with Gulick *ad l.*, also 668c quoting Callimachus 227 Pfeiffer.

Henderson 1991 p. 160.

- Latin *savillum* was a kind of soufflé. Leon 1943 p. 220 and Grant 1999 pp. 60–1 suggest modern recipes.

  Cato *DA* 84.

- Latin *scriblita* was a big cake, or at least one of the same weight as the *placenta*, if Petronius is to be trusted; and you might pour Spanish honey over it when serving. This ties in with Cato's brief recipe, which specifically excludes honey.

  Cato *DA* 78; Petronius *S* 35, 66; Athenaeus *D* 647d [*s.v.l.*].

- Greek *sesame*, *sesamis* was a mixture of roasted sesame seeds and honey, a sweetmeat served at Athenian weddings. For a modern recipe see Grant 1999 pp. 154–5.

  Stesichorus 179 Davies; Aristophanes, *Peace* 869; Athenaeus *D* 646f.

- Greek *tagenites*, *teganites* or *tagenias* was a 'pancake' (from Greek *tegano* 'frying pan', 'skillet'); perhaps, as implied by Galen's description, it was thicker than most modern pancakes. Dalby and Grainger 1996 p. 38 and Grant 1999 pp. 62–3 suggest recipes. The *staitites* was a pancake with honey, sesame and cheese: Grant 1999 p. 97 suggests a modern version as 'honey and sesame pizza'.

  Galen *AF* 6.490–1 (on which see Grant 1997 p. 117); Athenaeus *D* 110b, 646b, 646e.

  John Wilkins and Shaun Hill, 'Eat up your dormice' in *Ad familiares* no. 3 (Autumn 1992) pp. 8–9.

Calene wine (Latin *Calenum*; Greek *Kalenos*),

from the hills of northwestern Campania on the borders of Latium. Named alongside Falernian and Statan by Strabo, and in the *Epitome of Athenaeus* is said to be easier on the digestion than Falernian.

Horace, *Odes* 1.20, 1.31, 4.12; Strabo 5.4.3; Pliny *NH* 3.60, 14.65; Juvenal 1.69; Athenaeus *E* 27a.

Tchernia 1986 pp. 159–60, 345–7.

Caltrops,

a water plant with a chestnut-like seed. The seed was collected from the wild for food in classical Greece; the Thracians made bread from it, according to Pliny.

Caltrops (*Trapa natans*) are Greek *tribolos*, Latin *tribulus*.

Theophrastus *HP* 4.9.1–3; Pliny *NH* 21.98, 22.27.

Calydon,

coastal city of Aetolia in northwestern Greece. Calydon is not prominent in literature but was a trading centre, being a likely landfall on the sea route from Greece to southern Italy. Bass (locally known as *akarnax*) was good at Calydon. There was a lake or lagoon nearby which was rich in *opson*: in seafood, that is.

Archestratus *H* 45 Brandt with Olson and Sens *ad l.*; Strabo 10.2.3.

Dalby 1995.

Camel,

domesticated animal of the Near East and central Asia. Camel meat was eaten, says Galen, only by people who were 'mentally and physically camel-like'; Aristotle, by contrast, had stated that camel meat and camel milk are exceptionally palatable, and that the milk was drunk mixed with water.

The camel (*Camelus* spp.) is Greek *kamelos*, Latin *camelus*.

Aristotle *HA* 578a10–16; Pliny *NH* 11.236–7, 28.123; Galen *AF* 6.664.

Campania,

region of Roman Italy southeast of Latium. Campania was an early meeting-place of Etruscans, Greeks and Oscan (Italic) peoples, and its early metropolis, Capua, was a centre of trade between these peoples and others – a centre of the spice trade in particular.

Campania was characterised in Roman times as the most fertile region of Italy. Middle Campania produced the best emmer (the traditional cereal of ancient Italy). Inland Campania, from the hillsides bordering on Samnium, produced the best olive oil. Southern Campania, around Abella, was rich in fruit, notably hazelnuts or filberts (*nuces Abellanae*) and apples.

The coastal hills produced the best wine of Italy. The coast itself, with its fisheries and fish farms, produced fine seafood. Coastal Campania became a fashionable resort area where many Romans owned villas and many others spent their leisure time. BAIAE was the most fashionable locality of all, but the ancient Greek foundation of Neapolis (NAPLES) had many attractions. For fine Campanian wines see CALENE WINE; FALERNIAN WINE; GAURAN WINE; NEAPOLITAN WINES; STATAN WINE; SURRENTINE WINE; TRIFOLINE WINE.

Among the most fertile districts of Campania were the slopes of Mount Vesuvius and the plains surrounding the mountain. They were devastated by the eruption of Vesuvius in AD 79, which obliterated POMPEII and many farms in its neighbourhood.

Cato, *On the Agrarian Law* 2.95; Pliny *NH* 3.60–3.

D'Arms 1970; M. Frederiksen, *Campania* (London: British School at Rome, 1984); Dalby 2000a pp. 48–56, 60–3.

Camphor, an aromatic native to Borneo. Camphor is recorded in Mediterranean use as a medicinal spice in the sixth century AD, but has also been identified in an Egyptian tomb of Hellenistic date.

Camphor, the crystallised resin of the tree *Dryobalanops aromatica*, is Greek *kaphoura*.

Aetius, *Medicine* 16.130.

Laufer 1919 pp. 478–9; Miller 1969 pp. 40–2; G.R. Schoff, 'Camphor' in *Journal of the American Oriental Society* vol. 42 (1922) pp. 355–70; R.A. Donkin, *Dragon's Brain Perfume: an historical geography of camphor* (Leiden: Brill, 1999).

Cancamum *see* MYRRH

Cannabis, plant of central Asian origin, cultivated in the classical world and useful for its fibre and for its seeds. Cannabis seed was recognised in ancient times as an antaphrodisiac. For this reason cannabis figured among the *tragemata* chewed after dinner, favoured by those who wished to observe ritual purity by abstaining from sex.

Cannabis or hemp (*Cannabis sativa*) is Greek *kannabis*, Latin *cannabis*.

Herodotus 4.74–5; Ephippus 13 Kassel (quoted at TRAGEMATA); Pliny *NH* 19.173–4, 20.259; Galen *AF* 6.549–50.

Laufer 1919 pp. 289–90; Zohary and Hopf 1993 pp. 126–7; Brian M. du Toit, 'Pot by any other name is still ... a study of the diffusion of cannabis' in *Ethnology* vol. 19 (1996) pp. 127–35.

Cannibalism, the eating of human flesh (Greek *anthropeia krea*). The practice is occasionally recorded in the ancient world in famines, in myths and legends, and among the most distant of BARBARIANS.

As to famines, the eating of corpses is reported on several occasions, the killing of people to eat also more than once. Such incidents sometimes form part of the narratives of siege warfare: for example, Thucydides's narative of the siege of Potidaea, Appian's version of the siege of Athens by Sulla and Caesar's report of his own siege of the Gaulish stronghold Alesia. Sometimes they are features of narratives of lengthy famines, such as the story of the famine in Samaria in *II Kings*.

According to a story told by Clearchus, about the overthrow in 345 BC of Dionysius the Younger, king of Syracuse, his wife and children were killed and shared out as food among the citizens in revenge for his sexual abuse of the children of others. There are episodes involving cannibalism in two Greek romances.

Galen's aside in his survey *On the Properties of Foods* must be counted among urban myths (as they are now called):

> The flesh of pigs and of human beings must be similar, since people have eaten human flesh in place of pork without suspecting either the taste or the smell; the possibility has been discovered, before now, by unscrupulous innkeepers and others.

Juvenal agrees on the similarity of human flesh to pork.

In legendary history, Cambles, a king of Lydia, a man of insatiable hunger, was said (in a story told by Xanthus) to have eaten his wife, committing suicide next day when he woke to find her hand in his mouth. In the narrative of Odysseus in the *Odyssey*, the CYCLOPS, visited by Odysseus and his crew, eats several of them before Odysseus devises an escape from his cave. Cannibalism is described as man's first state, before the invention of cookery, in a comic prehistory in a Greek play of unknown date by Athenion.

Cannibalism recurs in several myths; it brought swift retribution from the gods. Tydeus was caught eating Melanippus' brain; Nyctimus, son of Lycaon, was served as food to Zeus. Tereus was tricked into eating his infant son. Most famously, Tantalus cooked his son Pelops in a stew which he served to the visiting Olympian gods, either because he was short of food or to test the omniscience of his guests. Tantalus was punished with eternal torment.

Cannibalism was theoretically recommended by CYNICS, but they are not accused of practising it. The dietician XENOCRATES, in the late first century AD, reported successful experiments with the use of human blood, brain, liver and muscle meat, and also bone ash, as medicines. Galen summarises these reports with strongly expressed disapproval, adding that the practice was illegal.

Atrahasis tablet 2; Homer, *Odyssey* 9.287–97; *II Kings* 6.28–9; Thucydides 2.70.1; Lycophron, *Alexandra* 479–83, 1066; Athenion 1 Kassel [Athenaeus D 660e]; Caesar, *Gallic War* 7.77; Diodorus Siculus 34/35.2.20; Lollianus, *Phoenicica* [for translation see *Collected Ancient Greek Novels* ed. B.P. Reardon (Berkeley: University of California Press, 1989) p. 811]; Juvenal 14.98; Galen *AF* 6.663, *SF* 12.248; Appian, *Mithridatic War* 38; *Lucius or the Ass* 6; Achilles Tatius, *Leucippe and Cleitophon* 1.15, 3.15, 5.3–5; Athenaeus D 415c citing Xanthus; Porphyry *DA* 2.53–7; Pseudo-Joshua Stylites, *Chronicle* 40, 76–7.

Darby and others 1977 pp. 86–90; John J. Winkler, 'Lollianos and the desperadoes' in *Journal of Hellenic Studies* vol. 100 (1980) pp. 155–81; A. Henrichs, 'Human sacrifice in Greek religion: three case studies' in Jean-Pierre Vernant and others, *Le Sacrifice dans l'antiquité* (Geneva: Fondation Hardt, 1980) (*Entretiens sur l'antiquité classique*, 27) pp. 195–235; S. Wall and others in *Annual of the British School at Athens* vol. 81 (1986) pp. 334–88; Garnsey 1988 pp. 29–30, *al.*; D. Hughes, *Human Sacrifice in Ancient Greece* (London, 1991); S. Brown, *Late Carthaginian Child Sacrifice and Sacrificial Monuments in their Mediterranean Contexts* (Sheffield, 1991).

Capers, spiny Near Eastern plant grown for its buds and small fruits, both of which can be pickled and used as relish. In some cuisines they are also a culinary flavouring incorporated in the course of cooking: this was perhaps rare in Greek and Roman cuisine. The Stoic philosopher Zeno swore by the caper, says the *Suda*, as Socrates swore by the dog.

Capers were collected at Franchthi by 7000 BC. They continued to be gathered from the wild throughout classical times: 'I fell in love with Phryne when she was still gathering capers,' said a character in a comedy by Timocles about a famous Athenian *hetaira*, and whether he means it literally or metaphorically of the lady herself, the status of capers as wild food sold cheaply at street stalls is clear. Indeed, as Aristotle points out, caper bushes grow in rebarbative and apparently inhospitable places, such as among tombstones, and do not respond well to cultivation. Columella gives instructions for planting them, but only in districts where they are not found growing wild.

Capers (*Capparis spinosa*) are Greek *kappari*, Latin *capparis*.

Aristotle, *Problems* 924a1–24; Theophrastus *HP* 6.5.2; Plautus, *Curculio* 90; Dioscorides *MM* 2.173; Columella *DA* 11.3.17, 11.3.54–5, 12.7.1; Pliny *NH* 13.127, 20.165–7; Martial 3.77; Galen *AF* 6.615, *SF* 12.9; Polyaenus 4.3.32; Athenaeus D 567e quoting Timocles; *Apicius* 4.1.1; *Suda s.v. kappari*.

Cappadocia, region of inland Asia Minor. Cappadocia under the early Roman Empire was a source of slaves, and particularly of skilled bakers; it was also a region where the naked variety of barley grew. Better represented in literature than either of these, the Cappadocian type of lettuce was commonly grown in Italy: it was planted in February.

Hippolochus *D* [Athenaeus *D* 129e]; Columella *DA* 10.184, 10.191; Martial 5.78; Galen *AF* 6.520; Athenaeus *D* 112b, cf. Persius 6.77.

Caraway, plant native to central Europe whose seeds are a spice used in flavouring sweet dishes. Unknown in classical Greece, its use spread under the Roman Empire. Because of its name it was supposed to originate from Caria.

Caraway (*Carum Carvi*) is Latin *careum*, Greek *karon*. Some English translators of classical texts wrongly write 'caraway' in place of 'cumin' for Greek *kyminon*.

Pliny *NH* 19.164; Galen *VA* 20, *AF* 6.668; *Apicius* 7.6.10, *al.*

Junkelmann 1997 p. 146.

Cardamom, spice originating in southeastern India. Cardamom consists of aromatic seeds enclosed in a small pod. It was known to a Hippocratic author and to Theophrastus before 300 BC but remained relatively unfamiliar in the classical world. However, it is called for in some medicines. A related species was apparently the source of AMOMUM.

Cardamom (*Elettaria Cardamomum*) is Greek *kardamomon*, Latin *cardamomum*. In spite of a confusion originating with Miller, which has misled some later scholars, Greek *kardamon* means CRESS; it never means cardamom.

Hippocrates, *Affections of Women* 34, *al.*; Theophrastus *HP* 9.7.2–3, *O* 32; Dioscorides *MM* 1.6, *al.*; Pliny *NH* 12.50, *al.*; Plutarch, *On Isis and Osiris* 383e–384b.

Laufer 1919 pp. 481–2; Miller 1969 pp. 71–3.

Cardoon *see* ARTICHOKE

Caria, region of southwestern Asia Minor. Caria was known to Greeks and Romans as a source of dried figs. The Carian city of Caunus was a centre of the trade, which was so firmly associated with this region that in Latin dried figs are called simply *caricae* 'Carians' or *Cauneae*.

The neighbouring island of Rhodes, whether as a second source or an entrepôt, had links with the Carian fig trade. Caria is listed by Archestratus as a place to buy octopus, and the Carian city of Iasus for shrimp. That Iasus took seafood seriously we know also from a story told by Strabo.

Archestratus *H* 25, 53 Brandt; Cicero, *On Divination* 2.84; Strabo 14.2.21; Petronius *S* 44.13; Athenaeus *D* 75e–76a.

Carob, tree fruit native to the Near East. Carob trees spread westwards around the Mediterranean in cultivation in classical times. The fruits (which grow in pods) were occasionally used in classical times as food and in medicines. *Praedulces* 'surpassingly sweet' according to Pliny, they were disliked by Galen for their constipating effect.

The carob (*Ceratonia Siliqua*) is Greek *keratia*. The usual Latin name *siliqua* means literally 'pod'; the bean is occasionally called *faba suriaca* 'Syrian bean' in Latin.

Theophrastus *HP* 4.2.4, cf. 1.11.2; Columella *DA* 5.10.20 (*siliqua Graeca*); Pliny *NH* 13.59, 14.103 (*siliqua Syriaca*), 15.95, 23.151; Galen *AF* 6.615, *SF* 12.23; Palladius *OA* 3.25.27.

Laufer 1919 pp. 414–26; Darby and others 1977 pp. 699–701; Brewer and others 1995 p. 62.

Carp, river fish of the Danube and of other rivers of Europe (see also MOSELLE FISH). The carp could be fattened in pens, and might lose its sexual characteristics, says Aristotle, the resulting flesh being all the fatter and all the better to eat. The carp is in fact artificially spayed by fish-farmers, but Aristotle does not mention the fact.

- Greek *balagros* (variously spelt) is noted by Aristotle as a river fish that may become asexual, like the carp; such specimens are the best for eating. It may be identical with a fish called *barakos* sold at Acraephia, and appears to be a species of carp.

  Aristotle *HA* 538a15, *al.*; *Acraephia Price List*.

  Thompson 1947 pp. 24, 25.

- Greek *kyprinos* is the carp (*Cyprinus Carpio*) as described by Aristotle, presumably from observation in the rivers of northern Greece and the southern Balkans; it is found also in the Danube and neighbouring waters of the Black Sea. Its unusual fleshy palate, sometimes called 'tongue', was observed. The Danube carp was brought as a costly delicacy to the table of Theodoric, Ostrogothic king of Italy.

  Aristotle *HA* 533a29, 538a14, *al.*; Aelian, *Nature of Animals* 14.23, 14.26; Oppian *H* 1.101 with Thompson *ad l.*; Athenaeus *D* 309a–b; Cassiodorus, *Variae* 12.4 (*carpa*).

  Thompson 1947 p. 135.

Carrot, garden plant now grown for its swollen red root. An early form of the carrot apparently began to be cultivated in the last few centuries BC. Its Greek and Latin names are ancestral to modern terms such as English 'carrot'. It is first mentioned in the third century BC by Diphilus of Siphnos. It was diuretic; it was also juicier and more digestible than the parsnip, with which it naturally invited comparison. But it was not red: this feature is thought to have emerged in varieties developed in post-classical times, as a result of hybridisation with a central Asian species in the early Middle Ages. The first European author who mentions red and yellow carrots is the Byzantine dietician Simeon Seth, in the eleventh century.

The carrot (*Daucus Carota*) is Greek *karo*, Latin *carota*.

Dioscorides *MM* 3.57, *E* 2.101; Galen *AF* 6.654, *SF* 11.862; Athenaeus *D* 371d–e citing Diphilus of Siphnos (read *karo*); Simeon Seth p. 35 Langkavel.

Laufer 1919 pp. 451–4; M. Grant on Anthimus *OC* 51 (p. 107); V.H. Heywood, 'Relationships and evolution in the Daucus carota complex' in *Israel Journal of Botany* vol. 32 (1983) pp. 51–65; A.C. Andrews, 'The carrot as a food in the classical period' in *Classical Philology* vol. 44 (1949) pp. 182–96; J.A.C. Greppin, 'Some etymological notes on Greek *staphylinos* carrot' in *Glotta* vol. 64 (1986) p. 248–52.

- Wild carrots (of *Daucus Carota* and several other species) are more in evidence than cultivated carrots in classical sources. They had edible leaves and thin, strong-tasting, white roots which were prescribed for medicinal purposes. Names include Greek *keras*, *staphylinos agrios*, *daukos* and Latin *daucus*, *pastinaca rustica*. One kind of wild carrot, known as *staphylinos agrios* in Greek and *pastinaca erratica* 'wayside parsnip' in Latin, was an aphrodisiac according to Pliny and Dioscorides.

  Dioscorides *MM* 3.52; Pliny *NH* 19.89, also 20.30–2 citing 'Orpheus', also 25.110–12; Galen *SF* 12.129.

Carthage, trading city of north Africa, near modern Tunis. A Phoenician colony, Carthage was itself the mother city of many colonies. The city's trading relations covered much of the western Mediterranean, extending westwards along the Atlantic coasts of Europe and Africa beyond the 'Pillars of Hercules' and eastwards to Phoenicia itself. After its destruction by Rome at the end of the Third Punic War, Carthage was soon refounded as a Roman colony.

The importance of the city in food history derives from the agricultural skills that flourished in Carthaginian north Africa. Owing to skilful irrigation and the development of crop varieties (notably fruit varieties), the region was probably more productive under Carthaginian government than ever before or since. Rome benefited in several ways from its Carthaginian inheritance. Farmers grew African crops and varieties; they learned new methods from the Punic agricultural manual by MAGO, which was translated at the expense of the Roman Senate; and Roman proprietors took over Carthaginian estates in what became the Roman province of Africa.

Archestratus had praised the parrot wrasses of Carthage. For the specialities of the region under Roman rule see AFRICA. Carthaginians are said by Aristotle to have been the developers of the salted TUNNY business at Gades (Cadiz). This trade continued, and its product continued to receive high praise, in Roman times, but is no longer linked with Carthage. They also traded in SILPHIUM from inland Cyrenaica, breaching the attempted monopoly of the Greek city of Cyrene.

Archestratus *H* 13 Brandt; Aristotle, *On Marvellous Things Heard* 844a24–34.

S.F. Bondì, 'L'alimentazione nel mondo feniciopunico' in *L'alimentazione nell'antichità* (Parma, 1985) pp. 167–84; M.L. Uberti, 'Qualche noti sull'alimentazione fenicia e punica: i principali costituenti energetici' in *Rivista storica dell'antichità* vol. 17/18 (1987/8) pp. 189–97; Joseph A. Greene, 'The beginnings of grape cultivation and wine production in Phoenician/Punic north Africa' in *The Origins and Ancient History of Wine* ed. Patrick E. McGovern, Stuart J. Fleming and Solomon H. Katz (London, 1995) pp. 311–22.

Casinum, town of inland southern Latium, a hundred miles from Rome. Casinum was supposed to be the best source of *oleum viride* 'green olive oil', made by pressing less-ripe olives.

Lucilius 961 Marx; Varro quoted by Macrobius *S* 3.16.12.

Dalby 2000a p. 60.

Castagnole, group of sea fish of family *Bramidae*. Few of these are found in the Mediterranean; those that are have many modern names. Classical Greek *korakinos*, literally 'crow-like', might sometimes be identified with *Chromis Chromis*, French *petite castagnole*, or with a larger relative, a fish of the western Mediterranean called Ray's bream, French *brème de mer* or castagnole (*Brama Brama*). *Korakinos* may sometimes also be the name of the MEAGRE. It is also the name of a

DANUBE FISH. For yet another, better species with this Greek name, a freshwater fish that is a close relative of the *petite castagnole*, see NILE FISH.

Archestratus *H* 19 Brandt with Olson and Sens *ad l.*; Aristotle *HA* 570b21–6, *al.*; *Acraephia Price List*; Galen *AF* 6.746; Aelian, *Nature of Animals* 13.17; Athenaeus *D* 308d–309a.

Thompson 1947 pp. 122–3; Davidson 1981 pp. 106–8.

- Latin *chromis*, although based on the Greek name for a meagre species, appears to denote a smaller fish than its Greek equivalent: the 'dirty *chromis*' of Ovid and the nest-building *chromis* of Pliny may be the *petite castagnole*.

  Ovid, *Halieutica* 121; Pliny *NH* 32.153.

- Greek *saperdes* was a kind of salt fish from the Black Sea. Disliked by most of the ancient authors who mention it, it is sometimes said to be made from the *korakinos*.

  Athenaeus *D* 116f–118c quoting Archestratus *H* 38 Brandt (see Olson and Sens AD *l.*), also 308e citing Euthydemus of Athens; cf. Galen *AF* 6.746.

  Thompson 1947 p. 226 (his references to Egypt are mistaken).

Castor oil, product of a plant that was domesticated in prehistoric times either in Ethiopia or in Egypt. The seeds are highly poisonous; the oil, though edible, has an unpleasant flavour. One of the five oils taxed under Ptolemy II (see EGYPT), castor oil was used for lamps but seldom for food. It was a well-known laxative.

The castor oil plant (*Ricinus communis*) is Greek *kiki*, Latin *cici*. The oil is (*elaion*) *kikinon* in Greek, (*oleum*) *cicinum* in Latin.

Herodotus 2.94; Theophrastus *HP* 1.10.1; Diodorus Siculus 1.34.11; Strabo 17.2.5; Dioscorides *MM* 1.32; Pliny *NH* 12.25, 15.25; Galen *ST* 6.220.

Laufer 1919 pp. 403–4; Darby and others 1977 pp. 782–3; Brewer and others 1995 pp. 44–5.

Catacecaumenite wine *see* ASIAN WINES

Cato, M(arcus) Porcius (234–149 BC), Roman politician. Cato is known for his strong traditionalist position: he opposed luxury expenditure and the spread of Greek fashions. His chief importance to this book, however, is as the author of a handbook *De Agri Cultura, On Farming.* Evidently drawing on his own experience of farming near VENAFRUM and at Tusculum, this work provides information of varying detail and completeness on olive farming, the making of olive oil and of wine and the growing of cereals, fruit and other crops. Cato advises on the selection of crops and crop varieties, focusing both on a property near Rome which would sell produce at city markets, and on a slave-run country farm in Campania, where the aim would be to make a profit from oil while maintaining reasonable self-sufficiency in everyday supplies. Information is included on the farmer's religious obligations. There are also about twenty recipes, mainly for various CAKES: whether these are for home use, for sale or for use in religion is not stated and is controversial. Modern interpretations of some of Cato's recipes are given by Leon 1943, Dalby and Grainger 1996, Junkelmann 1997 and Grant 1999.

On Farming is the oldest surviving work of Latin prose. Composed to assist a farm owner and a *vilicus* (slave farm-manager), and showing few literary pretensions, it provides evidence of Latin style and vocabulary at a time when Greek influence was not all-pervasive. The recipes have some interesting points of resemblance with those compiled, perhaps a little later, by CHRYSIPPUS OF TYANA.

K.D. White, 'Roman agricultural writers I' in *Aufstieg und Niedergang der römischen Welt* ed. H. Temporini, part 1 vol. 4 (Berlin: De Gruyter, 1973).

Cato DA: *De Agri Cultura.* Text, translation and commentary: Cato, *On Farming* ed. Andrew Dalby (Totnes: Prospect Books, 1998). Critical text, French translation and commentary: Caton, *De l'agriculture* ed. R. Goujard (1975, *CUF*).

Cat's ear (*Hypochoeris radicata*), meadow plant and potherb, Greek *hypokhoiris* (Theophrastus *HP* 7.7.1).

Caunus *see* CARIA

Celery, garden plant related to parsley, now usually grown for its stem. Ancient varieties of celery were of the strongly aromatic, bitter type now called smallage or leaf celery rather than the more familiar modern kind with juicy, blanched stem. Celery was, however, used as now as an hors d'oeuvre (*Apicius* 4.5.1) and its seed was used as a culinary flavouring. Its use in aromatic wreaths is far more prominent in the texts; a wreath of celery was the victor's prize at the Nemean Games.

Celery was sufficiently interesting to appear in a folk-song ('Where are my roses, where are my violets, where is my pretty celery? Here are your roses, here are your violets, here is your pretty celery!') and sufficiently eye-catching to give its name to several places in the Greek world, from the River Selinous near Miletus to the city of Selinus in eastern Sicily. Its distinctive appearance (the *polygnampton selinon* of Theocritus, 'crinkly celery') apparently gave it the additional meaning of 'women's pubic hair' in comic *double entendre.*

Celery or smallage (*Apium graveolens*) is Greek *selinon*, Latin *apium, apii.*

Homer, *Iliad* 2.776, *Odyssey* 5.72; Anacreon 65 Page; 'Carmina popularia' 6 Page; Herodotus 4.71; Aristophanes, *Wasps* 480 with scholia; Hippocrates *R* 54; Diphilus Comicus 31 Kassel; Theophrastus *HP* 7.4.6, 7.6.3–4; Theocritus 3.23, 7.68; Vergil, *Eclogues* 6.68; Horace, *Odes* 1.36.16, 2.7.24, 4.11.3; Dioscorides *MM* 3.64; Pliny *NH* 19.124, 19.158, 20.112–17; Juvenal 8.226; Pausanias 8.48.2; Galen *AF* 6.637–9, *SF* 12.118; Athenaeus *E* 61c; *Apicius* 3.2.5, 4.2.13, 7.6.14; Anthimus *OC* 55 with Grant *ad l.*

A.C. Andrews, 'Celery and parsley as foods in the Graeco-Roman period' in *Classical Philology* vol. 44 (1949) pp. 91–9; Darby and others 1977 p. 670; Henderson 1991 p. 136.

- Parsley (*Petroselinum sativum*) was regarded as a variant of celery. It is Latin *petroselinum*, Greek *petroselinon* 'rock celery' and *oreioselinon* 'mountain celery'. The two Greek names represent distinct types, and are both loan-translations from a Near Eastern language such as Egyptian; *petroselinon* is sometimes equated with what was afterwards called *Makedonikon*. Parsley served, like celery, as an aromatic. By the time of *Apicius* it had become a much more common culinary ingredient than celery.

Dioscorides *MM* 3.65; Galen *SF* 12.99; Palladius *OA* 12.22.5; *Apicius* 1.27.1, *al.*

Darby and others 1977 pp. 680–1.

Celsus, A(ulus) Cornelius (early first century AD), Latin encyclopaedic author whose surviving work is *De Medicina* 'On Medicine'. It is the oldest Latin compilation on the subject. The dietary properties of foods are dealt with in book 2 chapters 18–33. Celsus clearly translated most of his material from Greek medical writings, many of which are now lost.

His work *Res Rusticae* 'Agriculture' is lost except for a few borrowings by later writers, notably Columella, who cites it thirty-five times. Celsus devoted one book of this work to vines and wine.

Celsus DM: *De Medicina*. Text and translation: Celsus, *DM* ed. W.G. Spencer, 3 vols (1935–8, LCL).

Celts, widespread population of western and central Europe. Celtic languages and people spread by conquest as far west as northwestern Spain, and as far east as Galatia in central Asia Minor, in the few centuries that preceded the Roman conquest of these regions, which took place from the mid second to the late first centuries BC. The Roman conquest of Gaul, the central Celtic territory, was completed by Caesar in the 50s BC.

At the time of the conquest Celtic grain farming was in some ways more advanced than Roman. It was probably the Greeks of Massalia (Marseille) who had introduced olives and vines to Gaul, and the growing of vines had already spread some way north by the Roman conquest, but Roman traders had also been able to make considerable profits by selling Italian wine to wealthy Celts; it was said that an amphora of wine could be exchanged for a slave. On the other hand, Celts had generally not been gardeners or fruit-growers, and after the conquest the Romans introduced many fruit and vegetable species. Hare, and to a lesser extent deer, were hunted, but by late pre-Roman times hunting was not a significant source of food for most people. The Celts of Gaul had kept sheep, cattle, and particularly pigs, and had exported salt pork to Italy.

Celtic dining customs of the late pre-Roman period were described by Poseidonius, on whose writings later authors including Strabo, Diodorus and Athenaeus depend. A similarity to the 'heroic' lifestyle described in the *Iliad* and *Odyssey* was noted, by Diodorus for example: 'They invite strangers to their banquets, and ask them after the meal who they are and what they want.'

Strabo 4.4.3, 4.5.2; Diodorus Siculus 5.28; Athenaeus *D* 150d–154c quoting Phylarchus 81 *F* 2 and 9 Jacoby and Poseidonius *F* 15 and 16 Jacoby.

C. Feuvrier-Prévotat, 'Echanges et sociétés en Gaule indépendante: à propos d'un texte de Poseidonios d'Apamée' in *Ktema* vol. 3 (1978) pp. 243–59; Patrice Méniel, 'Les animaux dans l'alimentation des Gaulois' in *L'Animal dans l'alimentation humaine: les critères de choix: actes du colloque international de Liège 26–29 nov. 1986* ed. Liliane Bodson (Liège, 1988) pp. 115–22; Michael Dietler, 'Driven by drink: the role of drinking in the political economy and the case of early Iron Age France' in *Journal of Anthropological Archaeology* vol. 9 (1990) pp. 352–406; P. Marinval, 'Recent developments in palaeocarpology in western and southern France' in *New Light on Early Farming: recent developments in palaeoethnobotany* ed. Jane M. Renfrew (Edinburgh: Edinburgh University Press, 1991) pp. 247–54; Diarmuid A. Ó Driscoil, 'An experiment in Bronze Age cooking: the Fulacht Fiadh, Castlemary, 1993' in *Petits Propos culinaires* no. 45 (1993) pp. 43–50; P.J. Reynolds, 'The food of the prehistoric Celts' in *Food in Antiquity* ed. John Wilkins and others (Exeter: Exeter University Press,

1995) pp. 303–15; Philippe Marinval, 'Agriculture et structuration du paysage agricole à Marseille grec et dans les sociétés indigènes aux premier et second âges du fer' in *Paysage et alimentation dans le monde grec* ed. Jean-Marc Luce (Toulouse, 2000) pp. 183–94.

Cepola rubescens, a long, ribbon-like fish. Now not much sought after, this was a delicacy to classical Greeks. Athenaeus, native of Egypt, knew it as plentiful near Canopus and near Seleucia in Syria. Epicharmus, writing in Sicily in the fifth century BC, describes it as 'thin but good-tasting, and requiring little fire'. The only surviving recipe by Europe's oldest cookbook author, MITHAECUS, also from Sicily, is an instruction for dealing with this fish. 'Gut, discard the head, rinse, slice; add cheese and oil.'

Cepola rubescens, classical Greek *tainia*, has no English name: it is *cepola* in Italian, *kordella* in modern Greek

Aristotle *HA* 504b34; Oppian *H* 1.100; Athenaeus *D* 325f–326a quoting Epicharmus 56 Kaibel and Mithaecus, also 329f citing Speusippus.

Thompson 1947 p. 258; Davidson 1981 p. 106.

Cereals *see* GRAIN

Ceres, Roman goddess of the sowing and harvesting of grain. She was later identified with the Greek DEMETER. The name is often used poetically to mean 'wheat', 'bread' or 'staple food', as in Terence's *sine Cerere et Libero friget Venus*: 'without Ceres and Liber, Venus will freeze', or rather, 'without food and wine, love will freeze'. At Rome the *Cerialia* were celebrated, with games in the Circus, on 19 April.

Cato *DA* 134; Terence, *Eunuch* 732; Ovid, *Fasti* 1.657–704, 4.389–620; Martial 13.47.

Barbette Stanley Spaeth, *The Roman Goddess Ceres* (Austin: University of Texas Press, 1996).

Chalybonian wine, grown in eastern Syria. Chalybonian wine was the favourite of the kings of Persia, who transplanted Persian varieties of grapes to the Chalybonian district; it was also exported westwards by way of Tyre, according to Ezekiel. It is not heard of later, unless, under another name, it is one of the PHOENICIAN WINES which were in demand in Roman times in Italy, Egypt and India.

Ezekiel 27.18 (*Khelbon*); Strabo 15.3.22 (*Khalymonios*); Athenaeus *E* 28d citing Poseidonius *F* 115 Jacoby (*Khalybonios*).

Dalby 1996 pp. 96–7 and note 12.

Charity (or euergetism) included the provision, by rulers and by wealthy private citizens, of food and drink to poorer fellow-citizens. Sometimes this generosity was extended in the form of public banquets. Sometimes it was slimmed into the distribution of a monetary SPORTULA. The term 'charity' is reserved by many modern authors for benefactions with a Christian motivation; 'euergetism' is then the term used for donations and acts of benefaction in Greek and Roman societies before the establishment of state Christianity.

Such benefactions were a feature of Hellenistic city life, including that of later republican Rome. Under the Roman Empire the emperor himself was a generous donor of food supplies, notably to the populace of Rome itself; wealthy citizens continued the practice of generosity to the inhabitants of provincial cities.

H. Francotte, 'Le pain à bon marché et le pain gratuit dans les cités grecques' in *Mélanges Nicole* (Geneva, 1905) pp. 135–57; A.R. Hands, *Charities and Social Aid in Greece and Rome* (London, 1968); J.-M. Carrié, 'Les distributions alimentaires dans les cités de l'Empire romain tardif' in *Mélanges de l'Ecole Française de Rome. Antiquité* vol. 87 (1975) pp. 995–1101; H. Pavis d'Escurac, *La Préfecture de l'Annone: service administratif impérial d'Auguste à Constantin* (Rome, 1976); P. Veyne, *Le Pain et le cirque: sociologie historique d'un pluralisme politique* (Paris, 1976), abridged translation *Bread and Circuses: historical sociology and political pluralism* (London, 1990); Pauline Schmitt-Pantel, 'Evergétisme et mémoire du mort: à propos des fondations de banquets publics dans les cités grecques' in *La Mort, les morts dans les sociétés anciennes* ed. G. Gnoli and Jean-Pierre Vernant (Cambridge, 1982); P. Gauthier, *Les Cités grecques et leurs bienfaiteurs* (Paris, 1985) (*Bulletin de correspondance hellénique*, supplément 12); S. Mrozek, *Les Distributions d'argent et de nourritures dans les villes italiennes du Haut-Empire romain* (Brussels, 1987); A.J.B. Sirks, *Food for Rome: the legal structure of the transportation and processing of supplies for the imperial distributions in Rome and Constantinople* (Amsterdam, 1991); C. Virlouvet, *Tessera frumentaria: les procédures de la distribution de blé public à Rome à la fin de la République et au début de l'Empire* (Rome, 1995).

- *Alimenta* were regular distributions of money made by local foundations specifically to provide food for children. Such foundations are first recorded, as set up by private individuals, in the Roman Empire of the early first century AD. By the end of the century, benefactors were often the emperors themselves.

Pliny the Younger, *Letters* 7.18.
Peter Garnsey, 'Trajan's *Alimenta*' in *Historia* vol. 17 (1968) pp. 367–81; *OCD* 1996 s.v. *Alimenta*, with references.

Chaste-tree seeds, believed to be antaphrodisiac. They were roasted and chewed at dessert by those who wished to abstain from sexual intercourse for reasons of ritual purity.

The chaste-tree or agnus castus (*Vitex Agnus-castus*) is Greek *agnos* or *lygos*, Latin *vitex*.

Pliny *NH* 24.59–64; Galen *AF* 6.550, *SF* 11.807–10.

Norbert M. Borengässer, 'Agnus Castus: ein Kraut für alle Fälle' in *Chartulae: Festschrift für Wolfgang Speyer* (Münster: Aschendorff, 1998) (*Jahrbuch für Antike und Christentum, Ergänzungsband* 28) pp. 4–13.

Cheese, fine food and an excellent way to store milk, retaining many of its nutritional qualities and improving its digestibility. The milk of several animals might be used, as the following observation by Aristotle shows. The milk of goats and sheep was the best known in classical Greece and Italy.

Goat's milk is mixed with sheep's milk in Sicily, and wherever sheep's milk is abundant ... Mare's milk and milk of the she-ass are mixed in with Phrygian cheese. And there is more cheese in cow's milk than in goat's milk; for graziers tell us that from nine gallons of goat's milk they can get nineteen cheeses at an obol apiece, and from the same amount of cow's milk, thirty.

Cheese-making skills are hinted at in the Cyclops episode of the *Odyssey* but they existed in Greece long before, because finds of what appear to be cheese-strainers at Thessalian sites are to be dated around 3000 BC. Making cheese required the addition of a rennet to the milk to make it curdle. Rennet in general is Greek *tamisos*; the usual kind was *pyetia*, *pytia* 'rennet from animal's stomach'. The best is that of the young deer, says Aristotle, but cow's rennet is also good. Alternatively fig sap, Greek *opos*, could be used to curdle milk. 'The fig sap is first squeezed out into wool. The wool is then washed and rinsed, and the rinsing put into a little milk, and if this be mixed with other milk it curdles it.' The young cheeses were placed in a *talaros* or cheese-basket to let the whey run off; or they might be shaped in a mould, Latin *forma*, *formella*.

Cheese was eaten with honey – one might guess that the most suitable to eat in this way would be a relatively fresh cheese, though any cheese kept in brine, and then washed, is likely to be good with honey. Cheese was eaten at the end of a full meal, with sweet fruits and other desserts. It was also sufficiently nourishing to be eaten with bread as the chief relish of a modest meal, hence its new name *prosphagion* 'relish' in early Byzantine and in modern Greek.

In Rome there was a fashion for fresh-from-the-farm cheese: this is the *neospastos tyros* 'newly curdled cheese', 'cottage cheese' of Pollux's phrase-book (Pollux *KH* 83). A similar product at Athens was *ho khloros tyros* 'the green cheese', the name of a market held monthly and frequented (as producers, one must suppose) by the people of Plataea.

Small shaped cheeses, popular in Europe now, were already popular in ancient times. In Greek we know of the *trophalis*, of which one good and expensive kind came to Athens from Cythnos (Aristophanes, *Wasps* 838 with scholia; Alexis *F* 178 Kassel; Pollux *O* 6.48). Specific or unspecific, we also find Greek *tyriskos*, Latin *caseolus*, meaning literally 'little cheese' (*Copa* 17; Longus, *Daphnis and Chloe* 1.19), the *meta* or pyramid from Sassina in northeastern Italy (Martial 1.43, 3.58), and the square *quadrae* of Tolosa (Toulouse: Martial 12.32).

As in modern Greece, cheese was often kept in brine (and washed before use to reduce its saltiness). Smoked cheeses were also made (smoked in apple wood, according to Columella): good smoked cheese came from the Velabrum district of central Rome. Instructions for the making and storage of cheese are given by Palladius and in the *Geoponica*.

Cheese is *tyros* in Greek, *caseus* in Latin.

Homer, *Odyssey* 9.237–49; Lysias 23.6; Hippocrates *R* 51; Aristotle *HA* 522a22–b12 (above extracts translated by D'A.W. Thompson); Cato *DA* 76; Columella *DA* 7.8, 12.13; Pliny *NH* 11.240–2, 28.131–2; Galen *AF* 6.696–9, *SF* 12.269–72; Athenaeus *D* 658a–d; Palladius *OA* 6.9; Oribasius *CM* 4.3.6; Anthimus *OC* 79–81 with Grant *ad l.*; *Geoponica* 18.19 quoting Berytius.

Kroll, 'Käse' in *RE* 1893–1972; Buck 1949 p. 387; Flower and Rosenbaum 1961 pp. 25–6; Marten Stol, 'Milk, butter and cheese' in *Bulletin on Sumerian Agriculture* vol. 7 (1993) pp. 99–113.

Cherry, tree fruit of which two species are in common use as fruits in Europe. Both are known as 'cherry' in English, but in most other European languages they have separate names.

The sour cherry, source of the finest cultivated varieties (including some that are relatively sweet), reached Greece in early classical times, probably from eastern Anatolia. The name *kerasos*, perhaps borrowed from a Semitic language, was well known to those Greeks of Sinope who named their colony in northeastern Anatolia *Kerasous* 'place of cherries' (modern Giresun). From this point onwards the trees slowly spread westwards in cultivation. Pliny believes that they were first brought to Rome by Lucullus after his campaigns in Anatolia, and adds that in AD 47 the Romans introduced them to Britain. Their spread may have been assisted by the fact that they can be grafted on wild cherries, as Palladius rightly says.

Dietary authors make relatively little mention of cherries. To his royal patron Anthimus recommends cherries that are sweet and well ripened on the tree.

The sour cherry (*Prunus Cerasus*) is *kerasos* in Greek, *cerasus* or *cerasum* in Latin.

Theophrastus *HP* 3.13.1–3; Varro *RR* 1.39.2; Columella *DA* 11.2.96; Persius 6.36; Pliny *NH* 15.102–4, 23.141; Galen *SF* 12.22; Athenaeus *E* 50b–51b; Palladius *OA* 11.12.4–8; Anthimus *OC* 85; *Scholia on Aristophanes, Wealth* 586.

Zohary and Hopf 1993 pp. 171–2.

- The sweet cherry or bird cherry (*Prunus avium*), which grows wild in many parts of Europe, is *cerasus silvestris* in Latin. It is hard to find in classical texts but has been recognised uncertainly in two sources.

  Theophrastus *HP* 3.3.1, 3.6.1 (*lakare*); Palladius *OA* 11.12.4 (*cerasus silvestris*).

Chervil, an aromatic meadow plant which might be picked for wreaths and might also be used as a potherb. Classical authors mention the meadows and the wreaths more often than the stews. Chervil was a tonic and an aphrodisiac especially useful to older men, according to Pliny.

Chervil (*Anthriscus Cerefolium*) is *enthryskon* (variously spelt) in Greek, *enthriscum* in Latin.

Sappho 96 Davies; Pherecrates 14 Kassel; Theophrastus *HP* 7.7.1; Pliny *NH* 21.89, 22.81; Athenaeus *D* 685a–c; Hesychius, *Lexicon s.v. enthryskon*.

- The plant called 'wild chervil' in English (*Scandix Pecten-Veneris*) is *skandix* in Greek, *scandix* in Latin. This also was a potherb: Euripides's mother was supposed to have sold wild chervil on the Athenian market.

Aristophanes, *Acharnians* 478 with scholia, also *Knights* 19, *Frogs* 840 with scholia; Pliny *NH* 21.89, 22.80; Galen *AF* 6.640, 6.794, *SF* 12.124.

Chestnut, tree fruit. The sweet chestnut was one of the group of fruit trees that spread rapidly in western Anatolia and southern Europe after about 1200 BC (see also POLLEN ANALYSIS). In the classical period sweet chestnuts came to Athens (so their Greek names indicate) both from Euboea, where there must have been extensive forests, and from Sardis in Lydia, thus ultimately from inland western Anatolia; Galen adds a third geographical name, from a forest on Mount Ida called Leuce. Pliny names several varieties, adding that the variety grown at Tarentum, one of the best, was 'light and digestible, with a flat shape'.

Chestnuts were among the typical TRAGEMATA at Greek dinners. They could be eaten boiled or roasted, as Anthimus specifies. In parts of the ancient world a kind of bread was made from chestnut flour; in Rome, according to Pliny, this was used as an alternative to bread by women who were fasting. Xenophon, who ate chestnut bread in Armenia, reports that it was 'headachy'.

The sweet chestnut (*Castanea sativa*) is in Greek *diosbalanos*, or (*balanos*) *Euboikos* or *Sardianos* or *Leukenos*; the usual name later is *kastanos* or *kastania*. In Latin it is *castanea*. The multiplicity of Greek names (there are others not listed here) suggests the operation of some kind of taboo.

Hermippus 63 Kassel (*Dios balanos*); Hippocrates *R* 55 and Xenophon, *Anabasis* 5.4.29

(*karya platea* 'flat nuts'); Theophrastus *HP* 1.12.1, 4.5.4, *al.*; Dioscorides *MM* 1.106; Vergil, *Eclogues* 1.81; Ovid, *Art of Love* 2.268 (*nux castanea*); Pliny *NH* 15.92–5; Galen *AF* 6.621, *BM* 6.777, Athenaeus *E* 52a–54d; Gargilius Martialis *DH* 4; Palladius *OA* 12.7.17–22; Oribasius *CM* 4.7 quoting Dieuches; Anthimus *OC* 88.

Zohary and Hopf 1993 pp. 178–9.

Chian wine (Greek *Khios*; Latin *Chium*), from the island of Chios in the eastern Aegean. 'Black wine' (presumably this means red wine) was said in Greek legend to have originated here, its making taught by the founder of Chios, Oenopion, son of Dionysus.

Chian is one of the most enduring names in fine wine, already well known in Athens in the fifth century BC and retaining its reputation at least until the second century AD. The test of the good life, in a legal argument put to the disapproving Areopagus at Athens, was to be a drinker of Chian wine (so says Hegesander). Chian wines was exported in some quantity, and at high prices, to Hellenistic Egypt and to late republican and early imperial Rome. It was easily recognisable in its distinctive jars: *khion* and *hemikhion* are used in Ptolemaic papyri as measurements of volume.

Galen once specifies 'Chian without seawater', as if some Chian did include seawater. Whether or not this signals a decline in quality, Chian is little heard of after Galen's time.

Aristophanes, *Assemblywomen* 1119–39; Theopompus [Athenaeus *E* 26b]; Hegesander [Athenaeus *D* 167e]; Plautus, *Curculio* 78; Dioscorides *MM* 5.6; Pliny *NH* 14.96–7; Galen *DA* 14.162; Athenaeus *E* 28f–33a.

Dalby 2000a p. 136; Dalby 2000c.

- The vineyards of Ariusium at the northwest extremity of the island produced the finest Chian wine, and therefore, according to some estimates, the very best wine in the world (Plutarch couples 'drinking Ariusian' with 'having sex with Lais', the most expensive courtesan ever). According to a source of unknown date used by Athenaeus, there are three styles: one austere, one very sweet, and one midway between the two and known as *autokratos*, self-regulated. The austere is good-flavoured, nourishing, rather diuretic. The very sweet is nourishing, filling, laxative. The *autokratos* is midway between.

Ariusian (Greek *Ariousios*; Latin *Ariusium*) was tawny in colour and aromatic.

Strabo 14.1.35; Pliny *NH* 14.73; Silius Italicus 7.210; Plutarch, *Living Like Epicurus* 1099a; Galen *VA* 94, *ST* 6.334–5, *BM* 6.803, *On Compounding* 12.517, *DA* 14.28; Athenaeus *E* 32f.

- The vineyards of Phanae, a harbour in southeastern Chios, are obliquely ennobled by Vergil in the phrase *rex ipse Phanaeus*, as if they produced the king of wines (either Chian wine itself, or that of a separately named terroir). Vergil is on his own here.

Strabo 14.1.35; Vergil, *Georgics* 2.98 with Servius *ad l.*

Chicken, the domestic or barnyard fowl, native to India; source of meat and of eggs. The earliest sources for the presence of chickens in Europe are Laconian vases dated to the sixth century BC (the chickens identified by some in early Egyptian and Minoan wall paintings are in fact GUINEA FOWL). Greek texts of the fifth century call chickens *alektryones* 'awakeners' (a salient trait) or more fully 'Persian awakeners': the name seems to show that at that date they were more common to the east, in what was then the Persian Empire, than in Greece itself. In the course of the classical period they rapidly supplanted the goose, which had been the farmyard egg-layer of prehistoric Greece but is much less productive. Geese were still kept, but as a luxury rather than an everyday food supply. 'Every woman knows how to keep hens,' writes Palladius. As Aristotle had said of pigs and dogs so Oppian said of the chicken: it lives alongside man, *synestios anthropoisin*.

Chickens were a convenient sacrificial animal, cheaper than any other, hence their popularity on Delos (see also FATTENING) where many people went to sacrifice. There are numerous chicken recipes in *Apicius*. Capons, castrated and fattened, not only on Delos, are often mentioned as providing tasty and juicy meat. Chicken soup (or, rather, old cock soup) is recommended by Galen to re-establish regularity of the bowels without compromising one's diet. The most familiar 'cuts' of today – leg (Latin *femur*, Martial 2.37), wing, breast – are almost absent from ancient sources, but a word for gizzard is already found (Latin *gigeria*, *gizeria*: Lucilius 309 Marx; Petronius *S* 66; *Apicius* 4.5.1), and the TESTICLES are separately treated by dietary authors.

Several varieties of chicken are mentioned in ancient sources (see below and, for further details, Thompson 1936 pp. 39–40). The 'mountain-bred chickens' recommended by Galen as relatively unfattening are evidently not a distinct variety. Varro and Columella name in parallel three kinds of fowl, *gallinae villaticae* or barnyard hens, *gallinae Africanae* or GUINEA FOWL, and *gallinae rusticae* or WOODCOCK.

At a period when nocturnal time-keeping was difficult, cock-crow was a practical, indeed indispensable, marker of approaching dawn; people referred also to 'the second cock-crow' and 'the third cock-crow'. Examples are supplied by Juvenal and in the familiar narrative of Mark's *Gospel*. Chickens were also used in divination. Cock-fighting was a familiar sport.

The domestic fowl (*Gallus gallinaceus*, a phrase borrowed by Linnaeus from Cicero) is Greek *ornis*, literally 'bird'; the cock also *alektor*, *alektryon*, literally 'awakener'; the hen also *alektoris*, the chick *neossos*. In Latin the words are *gallus* cock, *gallina* hen.

Theognis 864; Aeschylus, *Eumenides* 866; Philoxenus *D* b.34 Page; Cicero, *For Murena* 29; Varro *RR* 3.9; Columella *DA* 8.2; Pliny *NH* 10.46–50; Juvenal 9.107; Mark, *Gospel* 14.30–72; Galen *AF* 6.700–2, *VA* 51, 69; Oppian *C* 3.118; Athenaeus *D* 373a–374d; Palladius *OA* 1.27; Anthimus *OC* 23 with Grant *ad l.*

Thompson 1936 pp. 33–44; Buck 1949 pp.

174–7; B. West and Ben-Xiong Zhou, 'Did chickens go north? New evidence for domestication' in *Journal of Archaeological Science* vol. 15 (1988) pp. 515–33; K.C. MacDonald and D.N. Edwards, 'Chickens in Africa: the importance of Qasr Ibrim' in *Antiquity* vol. 67 (1993); Brewer and others 1995 p. 124; Toynbee 1996.

- The Adrian variety of chicken, from the neighbourhood of Adria in Italy, is concisely described by Aristotle. 'The Adrian hens [*Adrianai alektorides*] are small-sized, but they lay every day; they are cross-tempered, and often kill their chickens; they are of all colours.' They were bantams, or some very similar variety, according to Thompson (above), who identifies them with the *pumiles aves* 'small chickens' of Columella.

  Aristotle *HA* 558b16–21; Columella *DA* 8.2.13; Athenaeus *D* 285e citing Chrysippus of Soli; Stephanus, *Geography s.v. Adria*.

- The breed called variously *Medica* or *Melica* appears by its name to recall the eastern origin of the species. These, along with the Rhodian variety, were better at fighting than at breeding and laying.

  Varro *RR* 3.9.6, 3.9.19; Columella *DA* 8.2; Pliny *NH* 10.48; Martial 3.58; Hesychius, *Lexicon s.v. Medikoi orneis*.

  Thompson 1936 p. 203.

- Two further varieties apparently of Greek origin are the Tanagraean (Pausanias describes two Tanagraean breeds) and the Chalcidic.

  Varro *RR* 3.9.6; Columella *DA* 8.2; Pliny *NH* 10.48; Pausanias 9.22.4.

Chickpea, one of the oldest cultivated pulses of the Near East. Chickpeas were grown in Palestine by 8000 BC. They had been gathered from the wild in the Mediterranean region even before cultivation began locally; in southern France, for example, by 7000 BC. Theophrastus says that the chickpea was not grown in India, but this is incorrect: it had reached India by 2000 BC, the date of the oldest archaeobotanical finds of chickpea in the subcontinent.

In the classical world chickpeas were served among TRAGEMATA, variously eaten green, or roasted, or dried and boiled. Chickpea soup (*cicer tepidum*, literally

'hot chickpea') was a common and cheap street food in classical Rome; a helping cost one as, said Martial. Anthimus recommends that chickpeas be boiled till soft and seasoned with oil and salt. Modern recipes for chickpeas based on ancient sources are suggested by Grant (1999 pp. 148–9).

Chickpea or garbanzo bean or Bengal gram (*Cicer arietinum*) is Greek *erebinthos*, Latin *cicer*. It is clear from Aristophanes that the Greek word carried the double meaning 'penis' or 'glans penis'.

Homer, *Iliad* 13.589; Hippocrates *R* 45; Aristophanes, *Peace* 1136, *Assemblywomen* 606; Plato, *Republic* 372c; Archestratus *H* 62 Brandt with Olson and Sens *ad l.*; Theophrastus *HP* 4.4.9, 8.5.1; Dioscorides *MM* 2.104; Pliny *NH* 18.124–5, 22.148–50; Martial 1.103; Galen *AF* 6.532–4, *SF* 11.876; Athenaeus *E* 54e–55b quoting Sappho 143 Lobel, Xenophanes 18 Diehl and Alexis *F* 167 Kassel (see Arnott *ad l.*); Anthimus *OC* 66 with Grant *ad l.*

Darby and others 1977 pp. 685–7; Patience Gray, *Honey from a Weed* (London, 1986) pp. 69–70; Henderson 1991 p. 119; Zohary and Hopf 1993 pp. 101–6.

Chicory *see* ENDIVE

Children, as ancient physicians were aware, were nourished before birth through the umbilical cord, afterwards with the milk supplied by mother or wet-nurse (see BABIES). Weaning, which might come as late as two years old in ancient societies, meant their gradual adaptation to adult foods, or at least to that selection of adult foods believed by adults to be appropriate to them. Ancient physicians and moralists were as bold as modern ones in prescribing regimes for children.

Children were believed to be 'hot' constitutionally and therefore to require 'cold' foods. Rich girls, as they grew into a secluded lifestyle, must be even further 'cooled', not only because they were physically inactive but also to avoid sexual excitement. These supposed requirements would have led to a restricted and almost meatless diet. Some thought that children should drink wine very diluted and not quite cold. Others, including Plato, recommended no wine at all till the age of 18. Clement of Alexandria follows Plato in this: not only is wine conducive to madness, it also inflames sexual feelings and causes precocious sexual maturing.

The extent to which such beliefs were applied in everyday life and their influence on the children of poor people and slaves are largely unknown: evidence of nutritional status from archaeological bone analysis is beginning to provide answers.

Hippocrates *A* 30, 40–2, *RS* 6, *Dentition* 1–17; Plato, *Laws* 666a; Clement of Alexandria, *Paidagogos* book 2; Aulus Gellius 4.19 citing Varro; Oribasius, *Liber Incertus* 18–22 (for summary translation see Garnsey 1999 pp. 101–2).

Emily Vermeule, 'The care and feeding of the child in antiquity' in *The Brearley Bulletin* (Fall 1980) pp. 8–17; R.S.J. Garland, *The Greek Way of Life* (London: Duckworth, 1990); J.N. Bremmer, 'Adolescents, symposion, and pederasty' in *Sympotica: a symposium on the symposion* ed. Oswyn Murray (Oxford: Oxford University Press, 1990) pp. 135–48; A. Booth, 'The age for reclining and its attendant perils' in *Dining in a Classical Context* ed. W.J. Slater (Ann Arbor: University of Michigan Press, 1991) pp. 105–20; Hanne Sigismund Nielsen, 'Roman children at mealtimes' in *Meals in a Social Context: aspects of the communal meal in the Hellenistic and Roman world* ed. Inge Nielsen and Hanne Sigismund Nielsen (Aarhus: Aarhus University Press, 1998) pp. 56–66; Garnsey 1999 pp. 52–61, 100–12, *al.*

Chios, wealthy and mountainous island of the eastern Aegean. Apart from its wine (see CHIAN WINE) Chios has been best known for its MASTIC, which was and is obtainable nowhere else.

The fifth century BC author Ion of Chios, whose varied works survive only in fragments, gives some indication of the style of life and entertainment in his home city: especially evocative is his story of a conversation with the Athenian poet Sophocles.

Ion of Chios 392 F 6 Jacoby [Athenaeus *D* 603e–604d].

Chios: a conference at the Homereion ed. J. Boardman and C.E. Vaphopoulou-Richardson (Oxford: Oxford University Press, 1986).

Chondrilla juncea, a broom-like wild plant used as a potherb. The spelling of its Greek and Latin names is variable.

Theophrastus *HP* 7.7.1 (*andryala?*); Dioscorides *MM* 2.133 (*khondrile*); Pliny *NH* 21.89, 21.105 (*candryala, achendryla*); Galen *BM* 6.794.

Christians, religious group distinguished partly by their food behaviour. Pliny is one of the first external observers to mention early Christian communal meals (see AGAPE). The Christian EUCHARIST took the place of the SACRIFICE practised in other religions of the ancient Mediterranean.

Christians gradually differentiated themselves from Jews in their food rules, but not totally. While Jews refused to eat meat slaughtered by non-Jews partly because it might contain blood, many Christians continued to refuse it (as both Paul and Pliny indicate) because it might have been sacrificed to a pagan god. Christian festivals, too, are not wholly divorced from earlier tradition. With their Easter lamb Christians were continuing to celebrate the Jewish PASSOVER; the festivities at Christmas, with their exchanges of gifts, borrow from the Roman SATURNALIA. Christians soon became distinctive in the extent to which some of their number practised ASCETICISM and FASTING.

Paul, *I Corinthians* 10.25–32; Luke, *Acts* 10.10–15, 11.2–3, 15.29, 27.33–6, *al.*; Pliny the Younger, *Letters* 10.96.

G. Feeley-Harnik, *The Lord's Table: Eucharist and Passover in early Christianity* (Philadelphia: University of Pennsylvania Press, 1981); Robin Lane Fox, *Pagans and Christians* (Harmondsworth: Viking, 1986); Grimm 1996; papers by Geert Hallbäck and L. Michael White in *Meals in a Social Context: aspects of the communal meal in the Hellenistic and Roman world* ed. Inge Nielsen and Hanne Sigismund Nielsen (Aarhus: Aarhus University Press, 1998); Garnsey 1999 pp. 95–9, *al.*; Michael Symons, 'From agape to eucharist: Jesus meals and the early church' in *Food and Foodways* vol. 8 (1999–2000) pp. 33–54.

Chrysippus of Tyana, author of a Greek work on bread and cake-making of which some fragments survive. He wrote notably bad Greek with many Latin loanwords. His recipes have some stylistic features in common with those of CATO: it seems probable that he worked in Italy in the second or first century BC. Surviving recipes from his book have links with Asia Minor (his region of origin), Crete, Syria and Egypt as well as Italy.

Athenaeus *D* 113a, 308f, 647c, 648b.

Bilabel 1921; Dalby 1996 p. 164.

- Whether the same Chrysippus, or another, wrote *Georgika* 'On Farming' and *Peri Lakhanon* 'On Vegetables' is unknown.

  Diogenes Laertius 7.186; Hesychius, *Lexicon s.v. pholia*; *Scholia on Nicander, Theriaca* 845.

Chub, river fish of Europe. The chub resembles the grey mullet and is likened to it from a nutritional point of view by Galen. It is mentioned by Latin authors as a common fish that, like the grey mullet, could easily be kept in fishponds. It was good to eat, but must be eaten within six hours of catching.

The chub (*Leuciscus Cephalus*) is Greek *leukiskos*; in Latin it was known as *squalus* in Italy, as *capito* in Gaul.

Varro *RR* 3.3.9; Pliny *NH* 9.162; Galen *AF* 6.713; Ausonius, *Mosella* 85–7.

Thompson 1947 pp. 37, 150, 251.

Chufa, edible tuber of a marsh plant. Chufa has been eaten in Egypt since the fifth millennium BC. No doubt it is the unnamed sweet root that kept Abba Or from starvation during his years of asceticism in the Theban Desert.

Chufa, also known in English as nut-grass, tigernut and earth almond (*Cyperus esculentus*) is apparently Greek *mnasion* and *malinathalle* [*s.v.l.*], Latin *anthalium*.

Theophrastus *HP* 4.8.6, 4.8.12; Pliny *NH* 21.88, 21.175; *Historia Monachorum in Aegypto* 2.

Miller 1969 pp. 77–9; Darby and others 1977 pp. 649–50; Zohary and Hopf 1993 p. 186.

- The related sedge plant *Cyperus auricomus*, likewise Egyptian, has been identified tentatively with the edible root *sari* described by Theophrastus.

  Theophrastus *HP* 4.8.5; Pliny *NH* 13.128 (*saripha*).

  Darby and others 1977 p. 651.

Cicada, edible insect. The cicada was a better-known food in Greece than in Rome. The grubs or nymphs were nicer to eat than the mature insects, says Aristotle. Boiled cicada was recommended in the treatment of bladder disorders.

The cicada (*Cicada plebeia* and *C. Orni*) is Greek *tettix*, Latin *cicada*.

Aristophanes fragments 53, 581 Kassel; Alexis *F* 167 Kassel with Arnott *ad l.*; Aristotle *HA* 556a14–b20; Dioscorides *MM* 2.51; Pliny *NH* 11.92–5; Athenaeus *D* 133b.

Malcolm Davies and J. Kathirithamby, *Greek Insects* (London: Duckworth, 1986); I.C. Beavis, *Insects and Other Invertebrates in Classical Antiquity* (Exeter: Exeter University Press, 1988).

Cigale, sea creature resembling the lobster but with short claws. Cigales were good at Parium, on the coast of Asia Minor, according to Archestratus, and at their best as food in winter and spring, while carrying eggs, according to Aristotle; the Hippocratic *Regimen* classes them as laxative. In later times, according to Aelian, many considered them sacred and would not eat them.

The cigale or flat lobster (*Scyllarus Arctos* and *Scyllarides Latus*) is classical Greek *arktos*. This name later fell from use, replaced by *tettix*: the creature is named after the cicada in many languages because of the noise it can make with its feet.

Hippocrates *R* 48 (*arkos*); Archestratus *H* 56 Brandt; Aristotle *HA* 549b23; Aelian, *Nature of Animals* 13.26 (*tettix*); Athenaeus *D* 105b citing Speusippus.

Thompson 1947 pp. 17, 259; Davidson 1981 p. 181.

Cilicia, region of coast and mountains in southeastern Asia Minor. Cilicia was the most famous source of SAFFRON in the ancient world: it was grown there in the limestone depression of Corycus, watered by an underground river. Cilicia also provided hyssop to Greek and Roman herbalists, and fruit trees to Roman growers. For the Cilician sweet wine listed by Pliny see ABATE WINE.

Hippocrates, *On Diseases* 3.10, *On the Nature of Woman* 32; Pomponius Mela 1.71–5; Dioscorides *MM* 5.40; Pliny *NH* 14.81, 14.109, 21.31–3; Martial 8.14.

Dalby 2000a pp. 167–8.

Cinnamon and cassia, modern terms referring to two similar aromatics. Both were much prized in the ancient world as incenses, perfumes and medicines.

Their origin was thought by nearly all ancient writers to be in southern Arabia or the neighbouring shore of northeastern Africa. Herodotus gives an exciting, entirely false description of their harvesting; later authors continue to list cinnamon among the legendary aromas of Arabia. In fact cassia came from southeast Asia, and probably was ultimately dispatched from a seaport on the coast of the South China Sea. Cinnamon may also have come from here, or may have originated from Sri Lanka. The southeast Asian supply was probably transshipped in southern India or Sri Lanka; both products were offered to Greek and Roman merchants at the harbours of southern Arabia and Somalia. In classical times they were scarcely used in food, but were valued medicines, also used in sacrifices and at funerals and in perfumed oils.

The English term 'cinnamon' derives from and probably equates with Hebrew *kinnamon*, Greek *kinnamomon*, Latin *cinnamum* or *cinnamomum*. The English word 'cassia' derives from and probably equates with Hebrew *kiddah*, *kesi'ah*, Greek *kitto*, *kasia* and Latin *cassia*: for precise identifications see below.

Sappho 44 Lobel; Ezekiel 27.19; *Proverbs* 7.17; Herodotus *H* 3.107–11; Theophrastus *HP* 9.5.1–3, 9.7.2–3, *O* 30–5, *On Fire* 148; *Song of Songs* 4.14; Strabo 1.4.2, 2.1.13, 2.5.35, 15.1.22 citing Aristobulus, 16.4.14, 16.4.20; Vergil, *Georgics* 2.463–8; Dioscorides *MM* 1.13–14 (*kitto*), 5.121; *Periplus Maris Erythraei* 8–13; Pliny *NH* 12.85–97; Galen *DA* 14.56–73 *passim*.

Laufer 1919 pp. 541–3; Miller 1969 pp. 42–7, 74–7; M.G. Raschke, 'New studies in Roman commerce with the East' in *Aufstieg und Niedergang der römischen Welt* part 2 vol. 9 section 2 (Berlin, 1978) pp. 650–81; Lionel Casson, 'Cinnamon and cassia in the ancient world' in his *Ancient Trade and Society* (Detroit: Wayne State University Press, 1984) pp. 225–46; J.M. Riddle, *Dioscorides on Pharmacy and Medicine* (Austin, 1985) pp. 98–104; Casson 1989 pp. 122–4, 130; Federico De Romanis, *Cassia, cinnamomo, ossidiana. Uomini e merci tra Oceano Indiano e Mediterraneo* (Rome: L'Erma di Bretschneider, 1996); Waruno Mahdi, 'The dispersal of Austronesian boat forms in the Indian Ocean' in *Archaeology and Language* ed. Roger Blench and Matthew Spriggs (London: Routledge, 1997–9) vol. 3 pp. 144–79; Dalby 2000b.

- In modern English, some specialists define cinnamon as the inner bark of *Cinnamomum zeylanicum*, a tree native to Sri Lanka, and cassia as the inner bark of *C. Cassia, C. Loureirii* and other species native to southern China, Indochina and Java (others, however, call all these products cinnamon). The same distinction is possibly valid for the equivalent terms in ancient languages, if one accepts that the cinnamon of Ceylon was exploited in ancient times, but that is uncertain. Casson argues that it was not; Mahdi assumes that it was. Laufer and Raschke (pp. 652–5 and nn. 1058–127) take a third view, arguing that ancient cinnamon and cassia were East African products (as many ancient sources assert) and were thus different from the substances now called cinnamon and cassia. Miller supposes a very long southerly route for Indochinese cinnamon, via Madagascar and East Africa, but on inadequate evidence.

Citron, aromatic fruit originating in eastern Asia. This large, irregular, pithy yellow fruit is now common in Mediterranean countries.

The citron was gradually transplanted westwards in prehistoric times and was known in central Asia by the fourth century BC. It is first described (c.310 BC) by Theophrastus, who regards it as a product of northwestern Iran. From that point it continued to spread westwards. The Jews of Roman Palestine gave the citron a ritual use (claims that it was used in ritual by Jews at earlier periods lack proof). By the fifth century AD the citron was familiar as far west as Spain: the late Roman agricultural author Palladius gives full instructions for growing citron trees from seed and from cuttings.

The zest (rind) of citrons is a widely used flavouring: the inside is of less use. The seeds, says Pliny, when cooked in Parthian dishes for the nobility, served to freshen these nobles' breath. The leaves are used in *Apicius* in an imitation rose wine.

The citron (*Citrus medica*) is Latin *citreum*, *citrium*. Theophrastus calls the fruit 'Persian apple' (but that name was eventually given to the PEACH) and 'Median apple'. The latter term, *melon Medikon*, was standard in Hellenistic Greek. It was eventually replaced by the Latin loanword *kitrion*.

Theophrastus *HP* 4.4.2 (*melon to Medikon e to Persikon*); Nicander *A* 533 (*medon*); Dioscorides *MM* 1.115.5; Pliny *NH* 12.15–16 (*malus Assyria vel Medica*), 13.103 (*citrus*), 23.105 (*citreum*); Plutarch *QC* 8.9; Galen *AF* 6.617, *SF* 12.77; Athenaeus *D* 83a–85c (*kitrion*); Macrobius *S* 3.19.2–5 (confused); Palladius *OA* 4.10.11–18; *Apicius* 1.4.2.

S. Tolkowsky, *Hesperides: a history of the culture and use of citrus fruits* (London, 1938); E. Isaac, 'Influence of religion on the spread of citrus' in *Science* vol. 129 (1959) pp. 179–86; A.C. Andrews, 'Acclimatization of citrus fruits in the Mediterranean region' in *Agricultural History* vol. 35 no. 1 (1961) pp. 35–46; Darby and others 1977 pp. 703–5;

Zohary and Hopf 1993 p. 173; Dalby 1996 pp. 143–4; Junkelmann 1997 p. 143 (*Zitronatzitrone* 'citron').

- Lemons (*C. Limon*) are possibly to be recognised in Roman wall paintings of the early Empire (see Jashemski), and in written sources of the second century AD, which discuss the fact that the *kitrion* was formerly not eaten but now is. This evidence is inconclusive, and some believe that the lemon was first introduced to the Mediterranean under Arab influence.

Plutarch *QC* 8.9; Athenaeus *D* 83a–85c.

Berthold Laufer, 'The lemon in China and elsewhere' in *Journal of the American Oriental Society* vol. 54 (1934) pp. 143–60; H.W. Gladden, 'The lemon in Asia and Europe' in *Journal of the American Oriental Society* vol. 57 (1937) pp. 381–96; Jashemski 197–93 pp. 29, 240.

- Bitter or Seville oranges (*C. Aurantium*) were transplanted westwards during the period of Arab expansion: they appear as *nerantzion* in Byzantine sources. Sweet oranges (*C. sinensis*) are first heard of in Europe at the end of the medieval period.

Citronwood, an aromatic and beautiful wood of north African origin. In Rome of the first century AD a single slice across a citronwood trunk formed the fashionable dinner-table top, to be fitted with ivory legs.

Citronwood or sandarac or pounce (*Callitris quadrivalvis*) is Greek *thya*, Latin *citrus*.

Varro, *Menippean Satires* 182 Bücheler; Petronius *S* 119.27–32; Pliny *NH* 13.91–102; Statius, *Silvae* 4.2.48–9; Martial 10.80, 14.89–91.

Dalby 2000a pp. 108–9.

Claudius, Roman emperor (ruled AD 41–54). Claudius's dining habits figure in Suetonius's biography, notably his immoderate greed and his affection for the city taverns, on which several other emperors attempted to impose tight regulations. His liking for mushrooms provided the opportunity for his poisoning, according to Suetonius and others.

Seneca was a courtier under Claudius, and criticises him and others for the practice of VOMITING to make room for more food. Seneca's satirical squib *Apocolocyntosis* is also severe on the subject of Claudius's gourmandising ways.

Seneca, *Consolation to Helvia* 10.3, *Apocolocyntosis passim*; Suetonius, *Claudius* 8, 32–3, 44, cf. *Nero* 33, *Domitian* 14; Dio Cassius 60.34.2–3.

R. Gordon Wasson, *The Death of Claudius* (Cambridge, Mass.: Harvard University Press, 1972); Dalby 2001.

Clazomenian wine *see* ASIAN WINES

Clibanus *see* COOKING UTENSILS

Clients and patrons *see* COMMENSALITY

Cloves, the spice that defines the 'Spice Islands' of Ternate and Tidore in eastern Indonesia. This was the only locality where cloves grew until modern transplantings. Cloves, the immature, sun-dried bud of a small tree, had reached the Mediterranean world (and also China) by the first century AD. This exotic spice remained a rarity in classical and medieval Europe, used only in costly medicines.

Cloves (*Syzygium aromaticum*) is *gariofilum* in Latin, *karyophyllon* (variously spelt) in Greek.

Pliny *NH* 12.30, 13.18; Cosmas Indicopleustes, *Christian Topography* 11.15; Aetius, *Medicine* 1.131.

Miller 1969 pp. 47–51; Dalby 1996 pp. 138, 183; Dalby 2000b pp. 49–52.

- Nutmeg and mace come from a tree (*Myristica fragrans*) native to the Banda Islands, which are significantly more remote than Ternate and Tidore. Nutmeg has sometimes been conjecturally identified in classical texts but in all probability did not reach the Mediterranean (or indeed China) until around the eighth century AD.

  Miller 1969 pp. 58–60; Dalby 1996 p. 264 note 26; Dalby 2000b pp. 53–5.

Cnidian wine (Greek *Knidios*; Latin *Cnidium*), from Cnidos on the Asia Minor coast, facing Cos. Cnidian was said to be nourishing, but laxative if taken in large quantity. It made good vinegar, too. Pliny lists *protropum Cnidium*, a sweet wine from free-run must, as in the third rank of Transmarine wines.

Strabo 14.1.15; Pliny *NH* 14.75; Athenaeus *E* 32e, 67c; *CIL* 4.5535.

Coan wine (Greek *Koios*; Latin *Coum*), from the island of Cos in the eastern Aegean. Coan was of no note in classical Athens, to judge by its absence from the lists of wines mentioned in Greek comedy.

Its success appears to have come from the addition of seawater to the must at the beginning of fermentation. This was first done, according to Pliny, by a cheating slave who added seawater to make up the amount of must he was expected to produce each day. Such wines already existed (see ANTHOSMIAS). This feature of Coan is confirmed by Dioscorides and Athenaeus. The demand for Coan spread extremely rapidly in the third century BC and after. Already, in the mid second century, Cato in distant Rome is providing a detailed recipe for the imitation of Coan wine. This includes sea water or brine, as available, and directs that the AMPHORAE be left four years in the sun to mature. The result might have resembled the *rancio* wines of modern Languedoc, but with an additional salty tang. In the following centuries the popularity of Coan and its imitations can be traced by the spread of amphorae of Coan type.

Coan is never listed among fine wines, either in Latin or in Greek sources, with one exception. A prescription for wobbly teeth, quoted by Galen from Heracleides of Tarentum, calls for 'the best Coan' as an alternative to Chian wine. Apart from this, Galen, so garrulous on wines of the eastern Aegean in the second century, never mentions Coan wine at all; he regarded the salting of wines as unwholesome. Cos also exported raisins.

Cato *DA* 112; Strabo 14.1.15, 14.2.19; Horace, *Satires* 2.8.9; Dioscorides *MM* 5.6.9; Pliny *NH* 14.78, 15.66; Galen, *On Compounding* 12.867 citing Heracleides of Tarentum; Athenaeus *E* 32e, 33b; *CIL* 4.1320–1, 2565, 5536–41, 9320–1, 10722.

Tchernia 1986 p. 105; Dalby 2000a p. 135.

- Halicarnassian wine (Greek *Halikarnassios*) was produced at the Greek city of Halicarnassus in Caria. Myndian wine (Greek *Myndios*) came from the small town of Myndus to the north-west of Halicarnassus. Cos lies just offshore. Both of these are listed as wines to which seawater was added: both were evidently analogous to, or imitations of Coan wine.

Athenaeus *E* 32e, 33b.

Coconut, fruit of *Cocos nucifera*, a palm tree of southeast Asian origin. The coconut was seen in India by Cosmas. He gives a drawing of the tree and names it *argellia*, for which cf. Sanskrit *nārikela*.

Cosmas Indicopleustes, *Christian Topography* 11.11.

Colchicum or meadow saffron, flowering plant native to the Caucasus. Meadow saffron was the source of the deadly colchicine, sometimes identified as Medea's favourite poison. It can be mistaken for the salutary BULBS of the grape-hyacinth. Meadow saffron (*Colchicum speciosum*) is *ephemeron* and *colchicon* in Latin and Greek.

Nicander *A* 249–78 with scholia; Horace *Epodes* 5.21–4, 17.35, *Odes* 2.13.8–10; Scribonius Largus 193; Dioscorides *MM* 4.83; Pliny *NH* 28.129.

Dalby 2000a pp. 185–6.

Colocynth, wild relative of the watermelon. The colocynth was sufficiently edible to have some food uses in the classical world: it was a very cold food, according to the Hippocratic *Regimen*, and it was one that Elijah's hosts ought not to have made him a soup from, according to *II Kings*. It was perhaps more attractive to prescribers than to eaters: recipes for preparing it are suggested by Galen. Colocynth oil was one of five oils taxed under Ptolemy II (see EGYPT).

The colocynth or bitter apple or bitter cucumber (*Citrullus Colocynthis*) is Greek *kolokynte, kolokynthis, tolype,* Latin *colocynthis*.

Hippocrates *R* 54, *Epidemics* 6.5.15; Theophrastus *HP* 7.2.9, *al.*; *II Kings* 4.39; Dioscorides *MM* 4.167; Pliny *NH* 20.14–17; Galen *AF* 6.561–4, *SF* 12.33–4; Athenaeus *D* 372b–d; Anthimus *OC* 56.

Zohary and Hopf 1993 pp. 181–2.

Columella, L(ucius) Junius Moderatus, Latin writer on agriculture of the mid first century AD. Columella is one of numerous first-century Latin authors who are of Spanish origin. His is in many ways the fullest and most systematic of ancient farming manuals, drawing on his own experience, on that of his uncle (who farmed in Baetica in the late first century BC), and on numerous earlier writers.

On Agriculture is in twelve books. Topics most immediately relevant to the study of particular foodstuffs are these: cereal crops (*DA* 2.6–10); vines, olives and other fruit trees (3.1–5.12); domestic animals (7.2–8.15); fish (8.16–17); wild animals (9.1); beekeeping and honey (9.2–16); garden plants (10 with 11.3); storing and conserving food, with many detailed recipes (12.5–59). All is in clear prose, except that book 10, on gardening, is in verse: it is intended as a tribute and supplement to Vergil's *Georgics*. Columella's separate work *On Trees* (vol. 3 pp. 342–410 of the edition below) appears to be an early version of books 3–5 of *On Agriculture*.

A. Carandini, 'Columella's vineyard and the rationality of the Roman economy' in *Opus* vol. 2 (1983) pp. 177–204.

Columella DA: *De Agricultura*. Critical text and English translation: Lucius Junius Moderatus Columella, *On Agriculture* ed. and tr. Harrison Boyd Ash, E.S. Forster and Edward H. Heffner, 3 vols (1941–55, *LCL*).

Comber, a small and unexciting sea fish related to the larger BASS and GROUPER. It claims no gastronomic praise, but had medicinal uses detailed by Pliny. The comber is correctly listed by Aristotle among hermaphroditic fish.

The comber or sea perch or serran (*Serranus Cabrilla* and *S. Scriba*) is Greek *perke*, *perkis* and *khanna*, Latin *perca* and *channa*. The second of the two species, sometimes called 'lettered perch' in English because of its unusual markings, will be the *perkai aiolai* 'variegated combers' of Epicharmus's verse and the *perke grammopoikilos* of Athenaeus. For a superficially similar and homonymous river fish see PERCH.

Aristotle *HA* 538a20 with Thompson *ad l.*; Diphilus of Siphnos [Athenaeus D 355b]; Pliny *NH* 32.107, 32.116, 32.126, 32.130, 32.145; Athenaeus D 319b–c quoting Epicharmus 47 Kaibel.

Thompson 1947 pp. 195–7, 283–4; Davidson 1981 p. 73.

Comissatio, a Roman drunken revel. Moralists list this alongside gambling, promiscuous women, holidays at Baiae, dinner parties in bad company and other activities on which young men spend their fathers' money. It evidently falls somewhere between the Greek KOMOS and the English pub crawl. Readers familiar with Oxford may wish to accept Murison's description of the *comissatio* as 'similar to Oxford sconcing, with all present competing'.

Cicero, *Against Verres* 2.3.31, *Against Catiline* 2.10, *For Caelius* 35, *For Murena* 13; Varro, *Latin Language* 7.89; Seneca, *On Benefits* 6.32; Martial 12.48; Tacitus, *Histories* 1.30, 2.76; Suetonius, *Caligula* 55, *Vitellius* 13 with Murison *ad l.*, *Titus* 7; Aulus Gellius 1.9.9 (as translation of Greek *komos*).

Katherine M.D. Dunbabin, 'Scenes from the Roman convivium: frigida non derit, non derit calda petenti (Martial xiv.105)' in *In Vino Veritas* ed. Oswyn Murray and Manuela Tecuşan (London: British School at Rome, 1995) pp. 252–65.

Commensality, or, with whom does one eat? In rural life (in classical as in many modern societies) the matter is compli-

cated by HOSPITALITY, whose rule, frequently obeyed, was that an unknown traveller should be offered food at least as good as that enjoyed by the householder. Which meant, in HOMERIC SOCIETY if not in reality, that you might eat with pirates and with resourceless wanderers as often as with gods in disguise.

Hospitality apart, in Greek society a pervasive emphasis on equality is to be noted. In classical Athens, for example, you invited to your dinners or symposia those who would invite you back, or you shared the cost with others on an equal basis (see also SYMBOLA); in classical Sparta all brought contributions that were in theory equal to the *syssition* or mess. Equality and commensality supported one another at regular dinners organised municipally or by political and clan associations. However, at all MEALS and at every symposion (see SYMPOSION (1); SYMPOSION (2)), real or fictional, of which we know anything, unequals were present and the occasion would have been very different without them. The inequality was patent: those present who were below or above the general social and intellectual level (including those who belonged to the wrong sex or had not reached the right age) 'sang for their supper', by being the butt of jokes, the object of sexual attention, the leader in conversation, the waiter, or the provider of entertainment.

It is said that the number of guests at Athenian private parties was sometimes regulated by law (Athenaeus 245a–c). Reality, in Athens and elsewhere, was more anarchic. Plato's *Symposium*, which makes a praiseworthy attempt at a realistic ambience, depicts the gradual arrival of several wholly unexpected guests, some more drunk than others, all of whom the host is prepared to welcome; they double up on the couches. There was a famous occasion on which Philip of Macedon brought more hangers-on than his host expected. Noticing that the food was running out, Philip retrieved the situation by passing the word to his party to 'Save room for cake' (Plutarch *QC* 7.6).

Roman society, so far as we can grasp its nature, fed on inequality and on relations of patronage. In classical Roman dining, to judge by Horace, Petronius and Plutarch, there was a standard placing of diners in the standard three-couch, nine-person *triclinium*, the host usually placed *summus in imo* and the guest of honour beside him *imus in medio*. But rules are for varying, and the fictional hosts Nasidienus (in Horace's *Satire* 2.8) and Trimalchio (in Petronius) both place themselves contrary to this usual rule. The 'place of honour' is *protoklisia* in Greek; Plutarch, from the point of view of a provincial hosting a Roman governor, calls it the 'consular place'. At Roman dinners on this pattern there were a host and a guest of honour, identifiable by their placing; there were also hangers-on of the host and of guests. No source suggests that diners should be equal; in fact all sources suggest the deference paid to the words and wishes of the host, or, if this indeed was the host's wish, the deference paid to a favoured guest. 'To ask and note down what savouries and sweets the prospective guest likes best, what wines and perfumes he prefers, is quite vulgar and *nouveau-riche*,' says one of Plutarch's speakers (*QC* 7.6); evidently some did just this.

In classical Roman dining the number in each circle was usually nine. However, at a large dinner there might be many circles, and there was plenty of opportunity for distinctions among more-favoured and less-favoured guests, as Martial shows:

> When I'm invited to a meal, now that I'm no longer on the payroll, why don't I get the same meal as you? You swallow fat oysters from the Lucrine lake, I suck at a mussel and cut my mouth. You have champignons, I swallow pig-mushrooms. You square up to turbot, I face a gilthead. A fat-arsed

golden turtle-dove fills you up, I'm served a magpie that died in a coop.

Roman entertaining had a technical term for guests brought along by an invited guest: they were *umbrae* 'shadows'. They comforted themselves with the knowledge that Socrates, on the occasion described in Plato's *Symposium*, brought along a shadow.

On commensality between the sexes see WOMEN.

Plato, *Symposium* 212c–e, *al.*; Horace, *Epistles* 1.5.28, *Satires* 2.8; Petronius *S* 31; Martial 3.60; Plutarch *QC* 1.2–3, 4.3, 5.5–6, 7.4, 7.6; Aulus Gellius 2.2, also 13.11 citing Varro, *Menippean Satires* 333 Bücheler.

Patrons and Clients in Mediterranean Societies ed. E. Gellner and J. Waterbury (London, 1977); J.H. D'Arms, 'Control, companionship and clientela: some social functions of the Roman communal meal' in *Classical Views* vol. 28 (1984) pp. 327–48; N.R.E. Fisher, 'Roman associations, dinner parties and clubs' in *Civilization of the Ancient Mediterranean: Greece and Rome* ed. M. Grant and R. Kitzinger (New York: Scribner's, 1988) vol. 2 pp. 1199–225; *Patronage in Ancient Society* ed. A. Wallace-Hadrill (London, 1990); J.H. D'Arms, 'Slaves at Roman convivia' in *Dining in a Classical Context* ed. W.J. Slater (Ann Arbor: University of Michigan Press, 1991) pp. 171–83; *La Sociabilité à table: commensalité et convivialité à travers les ages. Actes du colloque de Rouen, 14–17 novembre 1990* ed. Martin Aurell, Olivier Dumoulin and Françoise Thelamon (Rouen, 1992) (*Publications de l'Université de Rouen*, 178); Oswyn Murray, 'Forms of sociality' in *The Greeks* ed. Jean-Pierre Vernant (Chicago: University of Chicago Press, 1995) pp. 218–53; Davidson 1997 pp. 49–52, *al.*; Garnsey 1999 pp. 128–38 ('You are with whom you eat'); Wilkins 2000 pp. 63–9, *al.*; N.R.E. Fisher, 'Symposiasts, fish-eaters and flatterers: social mobility and moral concerns in Old Comedy' in *The Rivals of Aristophanes: studies in Athenian Old Comedy* ed. David Harvey and John Wilkins (London: Duckworth, 2000) pp. 355–96.

- In classical Greece, in cities such as Athens, private and dining groups and dining clubs could be seen as – and sometimes evidently were – forms of political protest and hotbeds of political instability. Dining was brought under public and municipal control (if that is an acceptable view of the matter) in the dinners of clans and local political units, as well as in official municipal dinners, which typically took place in the *prytaneion* of a Greek city (see under ARCHITECTURE).

Oswyn Murray, 'The affair of the Mysteries: democracy and the drinking group' in *Sympotica: a symposium on the symposion* ed. Oswyn Murray (Oxford: Oxford University Press, 1990) pp. 149–61; James Davidson, 'Fish, sex and revolution at Athens' in *Classical Quarterly* vol. 43 (1993) pp. 53–66; James Davidson, 'Opsophagia: revolutionary eating at Athens' in *Food in Antiquity* ed. John Wilkins and others (Exeter: Exeter University Press, 1995) pp. 204–13; Davidson 1997.

• The following references relate to commensality at public feasts and festivals. See also *Prytaneion* and *Tholos* under ARCHITECTURE

Pauline Schmitt[-Pantel], 'Le festin dans la fête de la cité grecque hellénistique' in *La Fête: pratique et discours* (Paris, 1981) (*Annales littéraires de l'Université de Besançon* vol. 262) pp. 85–100; John Wilkins, 'Public (and private) eating in Greece 450–300 BC' in *Oxford Symposium on Food and Cookery 1991: public eating. Proceedings* (London, 1991 [1992]) pp. 306–10; Pauline Schmitt-Pantel, *La Cité au banquet*. Rome, 1992; Pauline Schmitt-Pantel, 'Public feasts in the Hellenistic Greek city: forms and meanings' in *Conventional Values of the Hellenistic Greeks* ed. Per Bilde, Troels Engberg-Pedersen, Lise Hannestad and Jan Zahle (Aarhus: Aarhus University Press, 1997) pp. 29–47; Wilkins 2000 pp. 52–6.

Comportment, behaviour and etiquette. Not all meals are formal, but all food behaviour accords with customs and rules. In the case of formal Greek and Roman meals and drinking parties the rules appear in sharp focus in ancient sources, and have been very systematically described in modern scholarship. On the subject of food behaviour more widely, taking into account less formal situations, there is much to find out (see also COMISSATIO; CONVIVIUM; KOMOS; MEAL TIMES; MEALS; SYMPOSION (1); SYMPOSION (2)).

In the street, at a shop counter, and when snatching a breakfast, one ate and drank standing. At home, and in a bar or tavern, one often ate and drank sitting,

occasionally reclining. In general one was less likely to recline to eat if one was not a free, leisured adult male. The custom of reclining at formal and leisurely meals and drinking parties goes back to the third millennium BC in Mesopotamia. It had reached Greece by the time of the earliest poetry (Alcman, for example) although in HOMERIC SOCIETY one sat to eat. In Greece of the fifth and fourth centuries the choice between sitting and reclining was charged with implications (see Aristophanes; Xenophon). In Macedonia in the fourth century a young man did not recline until he had killed his first wild boar. Among the Etruscans, as among the Romans later, husbands and wives reclined together, but this was another charged issue: in Rome, as in Greece, the implication of tomb reliefs is that those who were not free adult males sat or stood in attendance and did not recline (see also COMMENSALITY; OPEN-AIR DINING; TRICLINIUM).

One removed footwear and washed the hands before beginning to eat (Athenaeus D 408b–411a). One reclined on the left elbow. One took food with the fingers of the right hand, placing it on one's table or perhaps straight into the mouth. When it came to drinking, the cup, too, was held in the right hand.

Diners were, in the ideal, equal. Food was offered, in dishes or trays, to all; wine was served to all. Equality was varied in Roman practice by the identifying of a place of honour, whose occupant had the best attention of the host and best-chosen portions of each dish. In both Greek and Roman practice, since large dinners were broken up into smaller circles, the circle surrounding the host and the guest of honour got the best of things; sometimes foods and wines served outside this circle were identifiably cheaper or poorer; sometimes the food that was served did not stretch.

When the main course was over the tables were taken away. They ought not to be taken away empty, says Plutarch:

was food being saved for unexpected guests? Compare the proverb (as it probably is) which Varro used as the title of a *Menippean Satire* in which he discussed the number of guests at a dinner, *Nescis quid vesper serus vehat*, 'You don't know what the late evening may bring' (Plutarch *QC* 7.4; Aulus Gellius 13.11 quoting Varro, *Menippean Satires* 333 Bücheler). The lamp must not be put out, Plutarch adds.

Diners entertained themselves – covering their head with their cloak if repeating something indecent (Aulus Gellius 19.9) – with songs (Plutarch *QC* 1.1; Athenaeus *D* 693f–697d), riddles (Antiphanes 180 Kassel; Plutarch *QC* 5.preface; Athenaeus *D* 448b), dancing (Athenaeus *D* 134a–d quoting Alexis *F* 102 Kassel (see Arnott *ad l.*)), the reciting of poetry, some genres of which were intimately linked with drinking parties, and the playing of party games, notably KOTTABOS. Sometimes, at more expensive parties, ENTERTAINMENT was hired; among typical entertainers were musicians and dancers, and (in Greek practice) prostitutes and (in Roman practice) story-tellers.

For more on the specifically Greek ambience of the symposion see SYMPO-SION (1) and SYMPOSION (2). It was sufficiently distinct that CAESAR, when he was on campaign in Gaul, used to hold Greek and Roman dinners simultaneously for visitors and members of his entourage.

Lynceus *F* 9 [Athenaeus *D* 294f]; Petronius *S* 26–78; Clement of Alexandria, *Paidagogos* book 2; Plutarch *QC* 1.1, 2.1, 2.10, 5.6, *al.*; Aulus Gellius 2.2; Athenaeus *D* 227b quoting Anaxandrides, also 418d–422d, *al.*

W. Deonna, 'Vases à surprise et vases à puiser le vin' in *Bulletin de l'Institut Genevois* vol. 38 (1908) pp. 3–29; Carcopino 1940 chapter 9; Waldemar Deonna and Marcel Renard, *Croyances et superstitions de table dans la Rome antique* (Brussels: Latomus, 1961); G. Giangrande, 'Sympotic literature and epigram' in *Entretiens: Fondation Hardt* vol. 14 (1968) pp. 91–174; E.L. Bowie, 'Early Greek elegy, symposium and public festival' in *Journal of Hellenic Studies* vol. 106 (1986) pp. 13–35; J.N. Bremmer, 'Adolescents, symposion, and

pederasty' in *Sympotica: a symposium on the symposion* ed. Oswyn Murray (Oxford: Oxford University Press, 1990) pp. 135–48; Catharine Edwards, *The Politics of Immorality* (Cambridge: Cambridge University Press, 1993); E.L. Bowie, 'Greek table talk before Plato' in *Rhetorica* vol. 11 (1993) pp. 355–71; Wolfgang Rösler, 'Wine and truth in the Greek symposion' in *In Vino Veritas* ed. Oswyn Murray and Manuela Tecuşan (London: British School at Rome, 1995) pp. 106–12; Schäfer 1997.

• Dinners and drinking parties in the ancient Near East (under different names in different languages) had considerable resemblance to the pattern described. A good deal is known of them, both from texts and from iconography (note the series of works by Dentzer). Plenty of work remains to be done on the influence of Near Eastern on Greek, Hellenistic and Roman dining and drinking customs.

M. Lichtenstein, 'The banquet motifs in Keret and in Proverbs 9' in *Journal of the Ancient Near East Society* vol. 1 (1968) pp. 19–31; J.-M. Dentzer, 'Aux origines de l'iconographie du banquet couché' in *Revue archéologique* (1971) pp. 215–58; B. Fehr, *Orientalische und griechische Gelage* (Bonn, 1971); J.C. Greenfield, 'The marzeah as a social institution' in *Acta Antiqua Academiae Scientiarum Hungaricae* vol. 22 (1974) pp. 432–5; J.-M. Dentzer, 'Reliefs au banquet dans la moitié orientale de l'Empire Romain: iconographie hellénistique et traditions locales' in *Revue archéologique* (1978) pp. 63–82; P.R.S. Moorey, 'Metal wine-sets in the ancient Near East' in *Iranica Antiqua* vol. 15 (1980) pp. 181–97; J.-M. Dentzer, *Le Motif du banquet couché dans le Proche-Orient et le monde grec du VIIe au IVe siècle avant J.-C.* (Rome, 1982), review by B. Fehr in *Gnomon* vol. 56 (1984) pp. 335–42; G. Selz, *Die Bankettszene. Die Entwicklung eines überzeitlichen Bildmotivs in Mesopotamien, von der frühdynastischen bis zur Akkad-Zeit* (Wiesbaden, 1983); P. Bordereuil and D. Pardee, 'Le papyrus du marzeah' in *Semitica* vol. 38 (1990) pp. 49–68 and plates VII–X; W. Burkert, 'Oriental symposia: contrasts and parallels' in *Dining in a Classical Context* ed. W.J. Slater (Ann Arbor: University of Michigan Press, 1991) pp. 7–24; *Banquets d'Orient* ed. R. Gyselen (Bures-sur-Yvette: Groupe pour l'Etude de la Civilisation du Moyen-Orient, 1992) (*Res orientales*, 4); Julian Edgeworth Reade, 'The symposion in ancient Mesopotamia: archaeological evidence' in *In Vino Veritas* ed. Oswyn Murray and Manuela Tecuşan (London: British School at Rome, 1995) pp.

35–56; Cristiano Grottanelli, 'Wine and death: East and West' in *In Vino Veritas* ed. Oswyn Murray and Manuela Tecuşan (London: British School at Rome, 1995) pp. 62–89; David Stronach, 'The imagery of the wine bowl: wine in Assyria in the early first millennium B.C.' in *The Origins and Ancient History of Wine* ed. Patrick E. McGovern, Stuart J. Fleming and Solomon H. Katz (London: Gordon and Breach, 1995) pp. 175–95.

Conditum or *piperatum*, spiced wine, made according to varied recipes and allowed to mature before drinking. For this Roman idea an early Greek term was *to artyton*, a loan-translation meaning 'the spiced one'. In later Greek the loan-word *konditon* appears. *Apicius* gives one recipe for *conditum*, in a version called *Conditum paradoxum* or 'surprise spiced wine': what is surprising about it is not clear. This is followed by a *Conditum viatorium*, 'traveller's spiced wine', which takes the form of a concentrate to be added to whatever wine was available to the traveller. The need for such a product is evidence of the important health benefits expected from adding spices and herbs to wine in correct proportions; for the same reason, various recipes for *conditum* are found in Oribasius's *Medical Collections* and in similar Byzantine compilations.

Pliny *NH* 14.108; Pollux *KH* 83; Oribasius *CM* 5.33; *Apicius* 1.1.1–2.

Conger eel, fierce and very large sea fish. Some were a man's load, some were a cartload, and Matron used pardonable exaggeration in saying that a conger 'covered nine dinner tables'. The conger had firm but wholesome flesh. By classical Greek gastronomes it was said to be especially good at Sicyon; it was from here that Poseidon brought congers to the dinners of Olympus. They were also large and good in the Atlantic, around Gades (Cadiz).

Archestratus gives a fine recipe for the head and innards of a conger, flavoured with green herbs and slowly stewed in brine – but no one, I think, has yet made a modern version of it.

The conger eel (*Conger Conger*) is Greek *gongros*, Latin *conger*.

Matron *AD* 36–7; *Acraephia Price List*; Plautus, *Aulularia* 398–9, *Persa* 110–11; Strabo 3.2.7; Athenaeus *D* 288c–294c quoting Philemon 82 Kassel and Archestratus *H* 18–19 Brandt (see Olson and Sens *ad l.*).

Conserving, a matter of life and death when food supplies are limited to those of local origin. How long will individual foods keep? What can be done to prolong their life? Will last year's crop last till next year's is ready? Many familiar flavours of the ancient and modern worlds originate in the necessity to conserve food – not only dried fruit but also wine and vinegar, biscuit, cheese, bacon and other salt meats, salted and smoked fish and fish sauce. Although they had more general senses also, the Greek word *tarikhos* and the Latin *salsamentum* most frequently denoted salt fish: hence the instruction by Diphilus of Siphnos, 'All *tarikhoi* should be washed until the water runs odourless and sweet', treatment not universally appropriate to smoked and dried fish and salt meats.

Several conserving methods, including the making of CHEESE and WINE, can be traced far back in the prehistoric period in the Mediterranean world. Much information about conserved foods is found in occasional asides and brief mentions in classical sources. The following longer surveys need to be signalled: Pliny on conserved and dried fruit; Xenocrates on salt fish; Galen on salt fish. The longest single collection of recipes and instructions is given by Columella; these can be compared with the recipes – most of them of Roman origin – scattered through the Byzantine miscellany called *Geoponica*. Recipes are also found for the last stage in the process, the eventual use of conserved foods. *Apicius* includes several examples. A recipe using *krea tarikhera*, salt meat, is given in the *Heidelberg Papyrus*: there is a modern interpretation by Grant 1999 pp. 124–5. Raw-salted meat and fish, *omotarikhos*, held no fears for Greeks and Romans. For botargo (late Greek *oiotarikha*) see GREY MULLET. See also TUNNY.

Columella *DA* 12.5–59; Pliny *NH* 15.58–67; Xenocrates *T* 133–52; Galen *AF* 6.746–7; Athenaeus *D* 116a–121e (there are many errors of identification in Gulick's translation of this passage) quoting Diphilus of Siphnos; Dioscorides *MM* 2.34, *al.*

M. Besnier, 'Salsamentum' in *DAGR* 1877–1919; M. Dembinska, 'Methods of meat and fish preservation in the light of archaeological and historical sources' in *Food Conservation* ed. A. Riddervold and A. Ropeid (London: Prospect Books, 1988) pp. 13–24; Robert I. Curtis, *Garum and Salsamenta: production and commerce in materia medica* (Leiden: Brill, 1991); Curtis 2001.

Convivium, Roman dinner party. At the typical *convivium* guests were invited and both food and wine were consumed; the occasion thus offers partial parallels to the three Greek terms AGAPE, *deipnon* (see MEAL TIMES) and *symposion* (see SYMPOSION (1) and SYMPOSION (2)). It was an occasion for gastronomic and also social pleasures, which might include seduction and even fighting over potential lovers.

M.D. Gallardo, 'El simposio romano' in *Cuadernos de filología clásica* vol. 7 (1974) pp. 91–143; L. Bek, 'Questiones convivales: the idea of the triclinium and the staging of convivial ceremony from Rome to Byzantium' in *Analecta Romana* vol. 12 (1983) pp. 81–107; Ricotti 1983; J.H. D'Arms, 'Control, companionship and clientela: some social functions of the Roman communal meal' in *Echos du monde classique* = *Classical views* vol. 28 = n.s. vol. 3 (1984) pp. 327–48; Griffin 1985 pp. 83–7; J.H. D'Arms, 'The Roman convivium and the idea of equality' in *Sympotica: a symposium on the symposion* ed. Oswyn Murray (Oxford: Oxford University Press, 1990) pp. 308–20; J.C. Yardley, 'The symposium in Roman elegy' in *Dining in a Classical Context* ed. W.J. Slater (Ann Arbor: University of Michigan Press, 1991) pp. 149–55; Catharine Edwards, *The Politics of Immorality* (Cambridge: Cambridge University Press, 1993); Katherine M.D. Dunbabin, 'Scenes from the Roman convivium: frigida non derit, non derit calda petenti (Martial xiv.105)' in *In Vino Veritas* ed. Oswyn Murray and Manuela Tecuşan (London: British School at Rome, 1995) pp. 252–65; Dalby 2000a pp. 243–58.

Cookery as art and science, an approach to the topic which was taken at least half-seriously in Greece by 400 BC, though a good deal of our evidence for the fact comes from ridiculous speeches by comic cooks. Thus the application to cookery of physical science is demonstrated in a play by Alexis, of philology by Straton, of military science by Dionysius, of climatology by Diphilus, of geometry by Nicomachus, of pharmacology by Hegesippus, of HUMORAL THEORY by Damoxenus. The first six are squibs; the seventh, though laughable in detail, parallels the real application of humoral theory to diet, which was already in evidence in the Hippocratic *Regimen* and has been fated to persist for more than two thousand years. Some may think that the most interesting applications of extraneous science to cookery, in these comedy speeches, are of sciences that were as yet unnamed: 'the psychology of the individual' (catch-phrase of a more recent domestic servant) is shown to guide the selection of menus in Menander and in two plays by Diphilus, while the art of public relations is foreshadowed in a cook's speech in a play by Archedicus.

In these cooks' speeches several extended comparisons are pursued. Cookery is compared with music in plays by Damoxenus and Machon (compare the quotation below), with military science by Poseidippus and others, with poetry by Euphron. In the play by Sosipater, a cook claims to belong to the school of SICON, 'the founder of the art' (see also COOKERY SCHOOLS AND TEACHERS), and explains how astronomy, architecture, physical science and military science were all in turn taught to apprentice cooks in this mythical academy.

The evaluation of cookery as an art is not limited to the comedies. 'Socrates', in Plato's *Gorgias*, mischievously imagines that, just as Gorgias was claiming too much on behalf of current politicians, so he might make inflated claims for exponents of the arts of baking, cookery and wine-dealing (the three examples named are THEARION, MITHAECUS and SARABUS). This is satire; but the art of cookery is placed on a level with that of music without any satirical intent in a passage of the Hippocratic *Regimen*:

> From the same notes come different tunes; from sharp, from flat, all notes but all of different sound; the most different combine best, the least different combine worst: if one composes all on the same note, no pleasure at all! The boldest, the most varied sequences give most pleasure. So cooks make dishes for men from dissimilars and similars; varying the ingredients, using the same with different effect, as food and drink for man. If one makes all alike, there is no pleasure; and if one put all together in the same dish, it would not be right.
>
> The notes of music sound some high, some low. The tongue tastes food as music, distinguishing sweet and sharp, discord and concord, in what it encounters. When the tongue is attuned there is pleasure in the music, when out of tune there is agony.

Moving to Rome in the first century BC and to Horace's satirical secondhand report of a gastronomical lecture: although this is certainly not to be taken as praise of the gastronomic art, it is probably fair to conclude from it that lectures on such a topic really might take place and might attract a leisured audience.

The serious observation that remains when all exaggerations are discounted is that there was recognised to be an art or skill of cookery, in Greek *opsartytike tekhne*, in Latin *scientia popinae* (Seneca, who provides the latter phrase, means to be rude to this 'science of the cookshop'). It was a skill which could be studied in books (see COOKERY BOOKS) but was typi-

cally transferred from expert to apprentice. It was not confined to slaves, but free men who took it too seriously risked ridicule.

Hippocrates *R* 18 and *passim*; Plato, *Gorgias* 518b; Alexis [Athenaeus *D* 383c]; Menander fragment 397 Körte [Athenaeus *D* 132e]; Diphilus Comicus 17 Kassel [Athenaeus *D* 132c], also 42 Kassel [*ib.* 291f]; Damoxenus 2 Kassel [Athenaeus *D* 102a]; Dionysius 3 Kassel [Athenaeus *D* 381d]; Machon *C* 20 [Athenaeus *D* 345f] with Gow (pp. 140–3) *ad l.*; Poseidippus [Athenaeus *D* 377b]; Straton Comicus [Athenaeus *D* 382b]; Sosipater 1 Kassel [Athenaeus *D* 377f]; Euphron 10 Kassel [Athenaeus *E* 7d]; Archedicus 2 Kassel [Athenaeus *D* 292e]; Hegesippus Comicus [Athenaeus *D* 290b]; Nicomachus [Athenaeus *D* 290f]; Seneca, *Consolation to Helvia* 10.8.

Cookery books, a genre some way below literature. As a general rule recipes are copied for practical reasons; there is little incentive for a collection to be preserved as it stands from one copying to the next, and every reason to add new recipes and to omit those that are disliked or have become impractical.

The earliest known recipe collection is on a cuneiform tablet in Akkadian (see works by Bottéro). No connection or line of transmission is visible between this and the first Greek recipe books, all of which are known only from exiguous fragments.

MITHAECUS, a Sicilian of the late fifth century BC, was possibly the first Greek compiler of a cookery book. Athenaeus lists the following additional authors of works entitled *Opsartytika* 'Art of Cookery': GLAUCUS of Locri, DIONYSIUS (two of these), Heracleides of Syracuse (two of these), Agis, EPAENETUS, HEGESIPPUS (of Tarentum), ERASISTRATUS, Euthydemus, Criton, Stephanus, Archytas, Acestius, Acesias, Diocles and Philistion. The list may derive ultimately from the catalogue of the Alexandrian library, compiled in the third century BC; however, Athenaeus has added names to it from his own knowledge. DIOCLES and PHILISTION are probably the dietary authors of those names; EUTHYDEMUS is presumably the author of *On Salt Meats* and *On Vegetables*, quoted several times by Athenaeus. Cooking and baking were different professions, and Athenaeus elsewhere provides a list of writers on the latter subject: Aegimius, Hegesippus (again), Metrobius and Phaestus. That list is explicitly derived from the Alexandrian subject catalogue.

It is evident that in the fourth and third centuries, to which period most or all of these names belong, cookery books quickly multiplied. There are several incidental references to them, as by Plato Comicus, Alexis, Anaxippus and Baton. In third-century Athens one could already boast, with a cook depicted by Sotades, that one's skill came *ouk ex apographes oude di' hypomnematon*, not out of written notes or recipe collections.

In the republican period three recipe collections are known from the Roman world: those of CATO (part of his manual *On Farming*) and the now-fragmentary works of PAXAMUS and CHRYSIPPUS OF TYANA, both of whom wrote in Greek. In the eastern Mediterranean, meanwhile, HARPOCRATION of Mendes and IATROCLES wrote on baking, Heracleides of Syracuse, Epaenetus (both already listed above) and PARMENON of Rhodes on cookery. In Carthage, HAMILCAR and MAGO wrote in Punic on farming and food: fragments of the latter's work survive in Greek and Latin translation.

In the Hellenistic and Roman periods dietary works by physicians (such as XENOCRATES, GALEN, ORIBASIUS and ANTHIMUS) often included cooking instructions, sometimes amounting to recipes, for foods that they were recommending. Farming writers, notably VARRO, COLUMELLA and PALLADIUS, followed the example of Cato and gave instructions for baking and for the conserving of farm produce. These authors name others who had written on food or wine, including AMBIVIUS, MAENAS and MATIUS, and two who certainly wrote specifically on wine, ATTICUS and GRAECINUS. Near the end of the Roman period comes APICIUS (4), the only complete surviving cookery book

from the classical world; it is followed in turn by the *Outline Apicius*, a short independent work, ascribed to VINIDARIUS. No doubt the writing of cookery books continued in Greek also. Nothing is known of them, except for the anonymous fragment on the recto of the HEIDELBERG PAPYRUS, which was written (though perhaps a copy of an earlier text) in the third century AD, and the text on the verso of the same papyrus, which was added at least a century later. In addition, ARTEMIDORUS of Tarsus compiled a dictionary of cookery, while ATHENAEUS, a little after AD 200, wrote the *Deipnosophists*, giving extracts from many of the authors here named.

The recipe tradition of the Roman Empire continued after the Empire had fallen. In western Europe there are medieval Latin cookery compilations, in the Byzantine Empire there are Greek dietary texts often of very practical intent, and in the Near East there are medieval Arabic cookery books.

Plato Comicus *F* 189 Kassel; Alexis *F* 140 Kassel; Anaxippus 1 Kassel; Sotades Comicus 1 Kassel; Baton 4 Kassel; Athenaeus *D* 516c, also 643e quoting Callimachus fragment 435 Pfeiffer.

Bilabel 1921; J. Bottéro, 'The cuisine of ancient Mesopotamia' in *Biblical Archaeologist* vol. 48 (1985) pp. 36–47; Eveline J. van der Steen, 'Zukanda and other delicacies: haute cuisine in the days of Hammurabi' in *Petits Propos culinaires* no. 51 (1995) pp. 40–6; J. Bottéro, 'The oldest recipes of all' in *Food in Antiquity* ed. John Wilkins and others (Exeter: Exeter University Press, 1995) pp. 242–7; Jean Bottéro, *Textes culinaires mesopotamiens* (Indiana: Eisenbrauns, 1995); Dalby 1996 pp. 109–14, 160–7; Maxime Rodinson, A.H. Arberry and Charles Perry, *Medieval Arab Cookery* (Totnes: Prospect Books, 2001) esp. pp. 91–115.

Cookery schools and teachers, a topic on which there is practically no evidence for the Roman period but some for the classical Greek world. All of it is in comedy fragments, and in these it is hard to distinguish real information from parody and fiction (which are certainly present), although most names of cooks seem likely to be real: the details are discussed below.

In tracing the culinary art to distant prehistory, and crediting it with the eradication of cannibalism, the cook depicted by Athenion (in a play of unknown date) goes further than his colleagues. Most of the lineages set out in comedy cover only two or three generations. The following quotation (from a cook's speech in a play by Euphron (fragment 1)) exemplifies the style and atmosphere.

> Though I have had many pupils, Lycus, you, because of your constant good sense and spirit, depart from my house a perfect cook, made so in less than ten months, and much the youngest of them all. Agis of Rhodes was the only one who could bake a fish to perfection; Nereus of Chios could boil a conger to suit the gods; Chariades, who came from Athens, could make an egg mosaic with white sauce; black broth [melas zomos] began to exist with Lamprias first, Aphthonetus cooked sausages, Euthynus lentil-soup, Aristion giltheads for club assemblies. After the famous sophists of old, these men have become our second group of Seven Sages.

There are other names to set beside those given in this quotation. The cook in a play by Sosipater lists 'Boidion, Chariades and myself' as preserving 'the teaching of Sicon ... the founder of the art'; a cook in Anaxippus claims to be a pupil of Sophon of Acarnania, who, with Damoxenus of Rhodes, was a pupil of Labdacus of Sicily. A cook in Euphron (fragment 10) claims to be a pupil of Soterides, royal chef to Nicomedes [I] king of Bithynia. A cook in Baton (quoted at COOKS) talks of the cookery books that he studies all night, in which he finds recipes by Sophon, Semonactides of Chios, Tyndarichus of Sicyon, and Zopyrinus.

Of these, Soterides may be a real person (as is King Nicomedes, after all). Chariades of Athens is probably a real person, since he is mentioned in two different plays for no obvious literary reason; so perhaps Boidion is a real person too, and both of them active when Euphron and Sosipater were writing; but whether Sicon is a real person is not clear (see SICON). So perhaps, along with Chariades, the others mentioned in the above quotation from Euphron are real. Again, Sophon may a real person, for the same reason as Chariades. This would seem to make Damoxenus and Labdacus real too, yet the story told of Damoxenus's death (see the Anaxippus reference below) has the ring of fiction and is accompanied by comic repartee. At any rate, if Sophon is real, then Semonactides, Tyndarichus and Zopyrinus are probably real.

Unfortunately for those who wish to trace culinary history, successful names were transferred and repeated all too easily, especially in the case of slaves and others whose living depended on selling their skills. There may be one or more than one real Sicon, and there are certainly fictional Sicons. Likewise there may be more than one Sophon. In the Roman context there were certainly at least three men named Apicius, all three of them cooks or gourmets.

On the implication of the quotation above that certain dishes were attributed to named cooks, see COOKS.

Euphron 1 Kassel (translation above by C.B. Gulick), also 10 Kassel [Athenaeus E 7d]; Sosipater 1 Kassel [Athenaeus D 377f]; Anaxippus 1 Kassel [Athenaeus D 403e]; Athenion 1 Kassel [Athenaeus D 660e]; Baton 4 Kassel (see quotation at COOKS).

Cooking methods, in classical Greek, may be regarded semantically as elaborations on the two verbs hepso 'cook in liquid, boil, fry' and opto 'cook dry, bake, roast, grill' (see Aristotle and Philemon on these two terms). There were in practice many methods, and there were several more specific technical terms, conceptually subordinate to one of these two. For example, Greek *apanthrakizo, epanthrakizo* means 'grill', a thing you typically did with tender little fish, as nowadays with elvers. Hence, used alone, the verb may mean 'to grill sprats'. The same method was adopted also with cakes (which were thus called *apanthrakis*, like English 'griddle-cake') but not with a whole ox, whatever the housemaid may say in Aristophanes' *Frogs*. Other methods include baking under the ashes of a fire (see e.g. Archestratus); frying in a skillet (*teganon*); grilling on skewers (*obeliskoi*) or on a brazier (*eskhara*). A choice of cooking styles can be found described or listed by Cratinus, Antiphanes and Sotades; cooking lessons and instructions were given on stage in plays by Alexis (see quotation at SCAD) and others.

In Latin the semantics of cooking are different. There is one basic verb *coquo*, covering all methods (but if no other details are given, boiling is implied). More specialised terms include *torreo, asso* 'roast', *frigo* 'fry', *ferveo, bullio* 'boil', *elixo* 'stew'.

Flavourings, such as herbs and spices, were ground in a mortar (*thyeia, mortarium*) to form a sauce: note the phrase *tripsantes katakhysma* 'grinding a sauce' used in Aristophanes's *Birds*. Added ingredients might also be sprinkled over the dish during cooking (Greek *passo* 'sprinkle', *epipasso* 'sprinkle [a powder] over'; Latin *aspergo*). Lists of seasonings are supplied by Antiphanes and Alexis, and from the late Roman period by Vinidarius.

For the utensils mentioned in this entry see COOKING UTENSILS.

Homer, *Iliad* 4.218; Aristophanes, *Frogs* 506, *Birds* 534–5, 1546, *Wasps* 1127; Cratinus 150 Kassel; Hippocrates *R* 56; Plato, *Republic* 405e; Archestratus *H* 5, 35 Brandt; Antiphanes 130, 140, 221 Kassel; Alexis *F* 138 Kassel; Sotades Comicus 1 Kassel; Philemon Junior 1 Kassel; Aristotle, *Meteorologica* 380b13–381b22; Varro, *On the Latin Language* 5.109; Pollux *O* 6.61; Athenaeus *D* 110b quoting Diocles of Carystus, also 170a–c quoting Alexis *F* 132, 179, 193 Kassel with Arnott *ad ll.*, also 329b; *Apicius passim*; Anthimus *OC* preface; Vinidarius *BC*.

Buck 1949 pp. 336–9; Sparkes 1962–5; Rosemary Ellison, 'Methods of food preparation in Mesopotamia (*c*.3000–600 BC)' in *Journal of the Economic and Social History of the Orient* vol. 27 (1984) pp. 89–98; Corbier 1989; F.T. van Straten, *Hiera Kala: images of animal sacrifice in archaic and classical Greece* (Leiden, 1995).

- Anthimus discusses the nutritional consequences of eating rare or lightly cooked meat, describing it as *crudior* 'relatively raw' and *sanguinolentus* 'bloody' (compare modern French *saignant*, similarly used of rare meat). He appears to be discussing a practice more typical of northern Gaul than of his native Constantinople. Much earlier, Archestratus had recommended eating hare that was lightly cooked and still bloody.

Archestratus *H* 57 Brandt; Anthimus *OC* preface.

Cooking utensils, studied through objects found in archaeological contexts and also through objects named and described in classical texts. The classic survey by Sparkes, the study by Annecchino and others, and the recent paper by Allison are the best archaeological approaches. There are several short ancient texts whose purpose is to list cooking utensils, though not for culinary reasons: a list of this kind is offered as a dedication to Hermes by a cook freed from slavery, in an epigram by Ariston; this conceivably 'genuine' dedication was followed by imitations that are of chiefly literary interest, by Leonidas and Philip. More useful, because more detailed and well documented, is the section of Athenaeus's *Deipnosophists* which deals with cooking and DINING AND DRINKING UTENSILS: other sections of the same text are also relevant.

Ariston 1 Gow [*Anthologia Palatina* 6.306]; Leonidas 56 Gow [*Anthologia Palatina* 6.305] with Gow *ad l.*; Philip 16 Gow [*Anthologia Palatina* 6.101]; Athenaeus *D* 169b–f, 459a–504e (with *E* 781c–784d), *al.*

Buck 1949 pp. 340–5; B.A. Sparkes and L. Talcott, *Pots and Pans of Classical Athens* (Princeton, 1958) (*Excavations of the Athenian Agora. Picture Book*, 1); Sparkes 1962–5; M. Annecchino and others, *L'instrumentum domesticum di Ercolano e Pompei nella prima età imperiale* (Rome: L'Erma di Bretschneider, 1977); G. Scheffer, *Cooking and Cooking Stands in Italy 1400–400 B.C.* (Stockholm, 1981) (*Acquarossa*, 2 part 1. Acta Inst. Rom. Regni Sueciae, ser. in-4° vol. 38); D.P.S. Peacock, *Pottery in the Roman World: an ethnoarchaeological approach* (London, 1982); Horst Blanck, 'Utensili della cucina etrusca' in *L'alimentazione nel mondo antico: gli Etruschi* by C. Ampolo and others; ed. C. Cerchiai and others (Rome: Istituto Poligrafico, 1987) pp. 107–17; *The Inscribed Economy: production and distribution in the Roman Empire in the light of instrumentum domesticum* ed. W.V. Harris (Ann Arbor: University of Michigan, 1993) (*Journal of Roman Archaeology. Supplementary Series*, 6); Penelope M. Allison, 'Labels for ladles: interpreting the material culture of Roman households' in *The Archaeology of Household Activities* ed. Penelope M. Allison (London: Routledge, 1999) pp. 57–77.

- Latin *catillus*, a flat dish, gives its name to cooked dishes including the *catillus ornatus* for which Chrysippus of Tyana gives a recipe.

  Cato *DA* 84; Horace, *Satires* 2.4.75; Columella *DA* 12.57; Petronius *S* 50.6, 66.7; Athenaeus *D* 647e quoting Chrysippus of Tyana.

- Greek *eskhara*, a brazier, gives its name to *eskharites*, brazier-baked bread.

  Athenaeus *D* 109c–e.

- Greek *igdis* or *thyeia*, Latin *mortarium*, is a mortar for grinding spices and blending dry ingredients; the pestle is Latin *pistillum* and the appropriate verbs are Greek *tribo*, Latin *tero* 'grind'. Lead vessels were favoured in Roman cuisine for the sweet flavour they gave to a sauce.

  Aristophanes, *Peace* 228–31, *Wealth* 718–20; Plautus, *Aulularia* 95; Columella *DA* 12.55; Pliny *NH* 33.123, 34.168; Pollux *O* 10.103 quoting Solon 39 West.

  Sparkes 1962 pp. 125–7.

- Greek *klibanos*, *kribanos*, Latin *clibanus* is a baking-crock, a portable dome-shaped earthenware oven whose most obvious use was to bake bread. For this purpose the dough was slapped on to its inside surface, the crock was placed on a hearth and the

embers were heaped around it. The cooking method is called *sub testu* 'under a crock' in Latin. The shape of a *klibanos* was so familiar that other objects were named after it, including rock caverns and underground vaults (see Liddell and Scott). The paper by Cubberley, with earlier work referred to there, identifies archaeological finds of broken *klibanoi* and discusses their use: see also *klibanites artos* under BREAD.

Aristophanes, *Acharnians* 1123, *Wasps* 1153; Archestratus *H* 4 Brandt; Paxamus [*Geoponica* 10.54]; Petronius *S* 35.6.

Liddell and Scott 1925–40 *s.v. kribanos*; Barbara Santich, 'Testo, tegamo, tiella, tian: the Mediterranean camp oven' in *Oxford Symposium on Food and Cookery 1988: the cooking pot: proceedings* (London: Prospect Books, 1989) pp. 139–42; A. Cubberley, 'Bread-baking in ancient Italy: clibanus and sub-testu in the Roman world' in *Food in Antiquity* ed. John Wilkins and others (Exeter: Exeter University Press, 1995) pp. 55–68.

- In earlier Greek, *klibanos* was the term for all structures for baking food, small or large. Aeschylus, in what is probably a satyr play featuring Eumaeus, describes its use in baking meat:

  > I shall put this plump sucking-pig in a moist *kribanos*: what better *opson* could a man have? ... the piglet is white, why not? and well-singed. Stew away, and don't be afraid of the fire! ... This piglet I have sacrificed is from the same sow that has been a nuisance to me in the house, galloping about and turning things upside down.
  >
  > (Aeschylus, cf. Aristophanes)

- Archestratus recommends cooking a smallish fish in a *klibanos*; baked tunnies in *kribanoi* were offered by the natives of Gedrosia to the sailors of Alexander's expedition.

  Herodotus 2.92.5; Aeschylus fragment 309 Radt [Athenaeus *D* 375d]; Archestratus *H* 13 Brandt with Olson and Sens *ad l.*; Arrian, *Indica* 28.1.

- Greek *ipnos* and Latin *furnus* is an oven. It was well known in classical Greece that Persian cooks used large ovens for roasting whole animals. The idea is ridiculed by a character in Aristophanes's *Acharnians*; at that time the only food use for such structures in Greece was the large-scale baking of bread. Under Persian influence ovens found their way into Hellenistic Greek culinary practice, and eventually into Roman cuisine.

Aristophanes, *Acharnians* 85–7 (*kribanos*); Hippocrates *R* 42; Archestratus *H* 46 Brandt; Plautus, *Casina* 309–10.

- Greek *obeliskos* or *obelos* was the spit on which food was skewered and held over a fire. The method was most likely to be used for steaks or chunks of meat, such as hare; and for firm-fleshed fish, such as the *aulopias* (see under TUNNY) for which Archestratus recommends it; likewise for some kinds of sausage, such as the *khorde* named by Euphron. It might even be a makeshift way of cooking bread (see *obelias artos* under BREAD). Poseidonius observes that 'the Celts' used to cook their meat this way.

Euripides, *Cyclops* 393; Archestratus *H* 33 Brandt with Olson and Sens *ad l.*, also 57 Brandt; Euphron 1 Kassel [Athenaeus *D* 379d]; Poseidonius *F* 15 [Athenaeus *D* 151e]; Anthimus *OC* 43 (*in brido*) with Grant *ad l.*

F.T. van Straten, *Hiera Kala: images of animal sacrifice in archaic and classical Greece* (Leiden, 1995) plates 123–44.

- Latin *patina* is a flat cooking dish with a raised rim, a typical item in the Roman kitchen. *Apicius* gives numerous recipes for dishes named *patina*: many, but not all, are set (using egg) and therefore have some resemblance to a quiche without the surrounding pastry.

Plautus, *Mostellaria* 2, *Pseudolus* 840; Horace, *Satires* 2.8.43; Apicius 4.20, *al.*

- Greek *pinax* is a platter on which slices of meat might be served (yesterday's meat, in the *Odyssey*).

Homer, *Odyssey* 1.141, 16.49; Athenaeus 228c–e.

- Greek *teganon* or *tagenon* is a frying pan or skillet placed directly over the fire and often used to fry seafood, including small fry or APHYE. The enticing smell of grilled fish suggested to many a comic character the mixed pain and pleasure of eating direct from the sizzling pan. This was shallow-frying, using scarcely any oil: the appropriate verbs are *opto* 'cook dry' or *teganizo* 'pan-fry'.

Aristophanes, *Knights* 929; Eubulus *F* 75 Kassel; Athenaeus *D* 107a–108d quoting Alexis *F* 115 Kassel, also 228d–229b, also

284f–285f citing Archestratus *H* 9 Brandt (see Olson and Sens *ad l.*).

Sparkes 1962 p. 129.

Cooks, exponents of a trade which appears to have come into existence (as far as Greece is concerned) in the late archaic period. In the earliest literature there are no specialised cooks, and the work of food preparation is carried out entirely by non-specialists.

Cookery in classical Athens (and in many other Greek cities of the classical period) had become a freelance trade and probably a remunerative one. In most households a professional cook was not required every day, but only at a dinner party or sacrifice. Cooks (*mageiroi*) were typically free men rather than slaves. Chosen by reputation or recommendation (or by price) they helped select a sacrificial animal, sacrificed it, prepared the meal that followed, and resold the meat and offal that was not consumed. Many comedy fragments give evidence of the tense interaction between cook and household slaves whose result would be a proper and successful sacrifice and meal. It need not be assumed that a sacrifice was always part of the event, but it would nearly always be so if fresh meat was to be served. Without a sacrifice, the specialist's role was limited to food preparation: he became an *opsopoios*, 'relish-maker'. If limited to sacrifice he might be called *artamos* instead of *mageiros* (so Xenophon, *Cyropaedia* 2.2.4 [*s.v.l.*]; Epicrates 6 Kassel; see Berthiaume 1982 p. 10), *artamos* meaning literally 'butcher'.

Cookery was a recognised art or skill, *tekhne* (see COOKERY AS ART AND SCIENCE); cooks were tradesmen or *demiourgoi*. They were members of an established profession with cumulative knowledge, as indicated here by a comedy cook, addressing his female sidekick, in a play by Baton:

Right, Sibyne, we don't sleep at nights
– we don't even lie down – with
lighted lamp, with book in hand we
work out what Sophon has bequeathed
to us, or Simonactides of Chios, or
Tyndaricus of Sicyon, or Zopyrinus.

The stock role of cook in Athenian
Middle and New Comedy (which supplies
this and so much more of the evidence on
which our understanding of the real
profession is based) was said by Aristophanes of Byzantium to have been invented by an actor named Maeson of
Megara. There is a great deal of modern
writing about Greek cooks. The status of
the real profession is discussed by
Berthiaume; the stage role and its implications have been examined most recently in
Wilkins 2000.

Cookery in Rome of the late Republic
and early Empire was a slave profession –
even though Romans from Lucullus to
Vitellius and beyond took close interest in
their food and its preparation. Rome's first
cooks (according to Livy) had come from
Greek Asia Minor, and the date of 189 BC
is given for their arrival (as war booty or
as luxury purchases is not clear) after
Gnaeus Manlius Vulso's campaign in Galatia. Slave cooks had evidently already
been at work in the Greek kingdoms of the
Hellenistic East. Large Roman establishments, from the imperial household down-
wards, needed cooks (Latin *coqui*) every
day. The nature of the cook's trade was
therefore entirely different from that in
classical Greece; a further difference is that
in Rome there was no religious require-
ment that domestic animals killed for food
must be offered to a god. Athenaeus
examines at what seems unnecessary
length the question whether classical
Greek cooks were free men, evidently
because Roman cooks in his time were not.

The implication of the quotation from
Baton above, taken with a fragment from
Euphron (quoted at COOKERY SCHOOLS
AND TEACHERS), is that specific dishes
were known to have been invented or

perfected by named cooks and were attributed to them in cookery books. This is
likely enough (on the specific claim in the
Euphron text concerning black broth see
MELAS ZOMOS). Named and 'authored'
dishes are otherwise attested as follows.
Athenaeus (5d) says that there were cakes
called *philoxeneioi* after one or other of
the gourmets named Philoxenus (see PHI-
LOXENUS (1); PHILOXENUS (2)). It has been
guessed that the barley BISCUIT called
paximadion is named after PAXAMUS. The
cookbook *Apicius* attaches personal
names to several recipes. References to
some are given below; for others see
under APICIUS (2), MATIUS and VITELLIUS.

Herodotus 7.31; Livy 38.27, 39.6; Athenaeus
D 170e–174a, also 658e–662d citing Aristophanes of Byzantium and Baton 4 Kassel, also
E 5d (source attribution lost); *Apicius* 4.2.25,
4.3.2, 5.1.1, 5.4.4, 6.8.11, 6.8.12.

Buck 1949 pp. 364–5; H. Dohm, *Mageiros*
(München, 1964); M. Isenberg, 'The sale of
sacrificial meat' in *Classical Philology* vol. 70
(1975) pp. 271–3; G. Berthiaume, *Les Rôles du
mágeiros: étude sur la boucherie, la cuisine et le
sacrifice dans la Grèce ancienne* (Leiden, 1982);
J.C.B. Lowe, 'Cooks in Plautus' in *Classical
Antiquity* vol. 4 (1985) pp. 72–102; Wilkins
2000.

Copa, anonymous Latin poem, perhaps of
about the time of Augustus. This playful
piece, traditionally attributed to Vergil, is
addressed to the tired traveller and his
donkey and describes the welcome that
awaits them at a country inn somewhere in
Italy. It is an inn that makes its own cheese
and its own wine, serves its own fresh and
conserved fruit, and offers its own entertainment, personified by the *copa Surisca*,
'Syrian bar-girl' of the first line.

P. Cutolo, 'The genre of the *Copa*' in *Papers of
the Leeds International Latin Seminar* vol. 6
(1990) pp. 115–19.

Copa: translation in Dalby 2000a pp. 18–20;
text, Italian translation and commentary:
Copa: l'ostessa. Poema pseudovirgiliano ed.
Alessandro Franzoni (Padua: Programma,
1988).

Copais, Lake, *see* BOEOTIA

Corcyra (Greek *Kerkyra*), large island of northwestern Greece, not so very far from Tarentum, a Corinthian colony in south-eastern Italy. Corcyra was well placed on the usual shipping route from Greece to southern Italy. It was a good place for octopus. It was also famed, at least poetically, for its fruit trees; this because the orchards of Alcinous, so attractively described by Odysseus and located by him on the mythical island of Scherie, were universally believed to be 'really' on Corcyra.

Homer, *Odyssey* 7.112–21; Archestratus *H* 53 Brandt; Ennius *H* 10; Statius, *Silvae* 1.3.81–2.

Dalby 2000a p. 143.

Corcyraean wine (Greek *Kerkyraios*), from the Greek island of Corcyra. In the early fourth century BC the best wine made here was ANTHOSMIAS. Later there was something better: Corcyraean was a particularly pleasant wine when well aged, according to a source used by Athenaeus.

Xenophon, *Hellenica* 6.2.6; Athenaeus *E* 33b.

Coriander or cilantro, aromatic plant of the ancient eastern Mediterranean, now grown on all five continents. Both the leaves and the tiny fruits are used in cooking.

A few coriander seeds were found at Franchthi Cave, in levels dated from about *c.*6500 BC and later, and at an archaeological site of the seventh millennium BC in Israel. Coriander was certainly in use in Egypt, the Near East and Greece in the second millennium BC, and is one of the aromatics listed in Linear B tablets (*ko-ri-ja-do-no*, *ko-ri-a-da-na*). It was known as far east as India by the fourth century, under a name of Aramaic origin (Sanskrit *kustumburu*), suggesting that Persian gardeners were involved in its spread; it was also used in northern Europe in Roman times – the seed has been found at sites in Roman Britain and

Roman Germany – though it does not thrive in northern climates.

Coriander leaf, with its pungent (some say soapy) aroma, was a familiar herb in the Greek and Roman kitchen, listed among potherbs by Diocles and others; ground coriander fruit was equally ubiquitous. Coriander root, nowadays seldom encountered except in Thai cuisine, was used in medicine, and is called for along with the leaves in Anthimus's recipe for lentils.

Coriander (*Coriandrum sativum*) is Greek *koriannon, korion*, Latin *coliandrum, coriandrum*. The leaf and fruit, respectively, are distinguished in Greek as *koriannon khloron* 'green coriander' and *koriannon xeron* 'dry coriander'.

Theophrastus *HP* 7.1–5; Pliny *NH* 20.216–18; Dioscorides *MM* 3.63; Galen *SF* 12.36–40, *DA* 14.139; Athenaeus *D* 170a, also 662e quoting Epaenetus, also *E* 68d quoting Diocles of Carystus; Palladius *OA* 4.9.15; Pseudo-Apuleius, *Herbarius* 103; Anthimus *OC* 67.

Laufer 1919 pp. 297–9; Darby and others 1977 pp. 798–9; Zohary and Hopf 1993 p. 188; Benjamin García-Hernández, 'El nombre del coriandro' in *Actes du colloque international 'Les phytonymes grecs et latins' tenu à Nice les 14–16 mai 1992* (Nice: Université de Nice-Sophia Antipolis [1993?]) pp. 189–206.

Cornel, olive-shaped red tree fruit. Cornels were being collected for human food in northern Greece by the fifth millennium BC as they were in other parts of southern Europe. In classical times they were best known, perhaps, for being fed to pigs (as were acorns too) in the story of Circe in the *Odyssey*. The pigs were Odysseus's crew, temporarily transformed. That humans ate them in other circumstances is known from latrine deposits at Cologne in Roman Germany, though from scarcely any literary sources ('edible', says Galen). They had medicinal uses, and Philagrius gives instructions for making cornel cordial, a medicinal drink.

The cornel or cornelian cherry (*Cornus mas*) is Greek *kranon* or *kraneion* or *pittaxis*, Latin *cornum*; the tree, also called dogwood in English, is *kraneia* in Greek, *cornus* in Latin.

Homer, *Odyssey* 10.242 with scholia; Hippocrates *R* 55; Theophrastus *HP* 3.2.1, 3.12.1–2, *CP* 3.1.4; Dioscorides *MM* 1.119; Galen *AF* 6.619–21, *SF* 12.41; Oribasius *CM* 5.20 quoting Philagrius.

Zohary and Hopf 1993 p. 201.

Corn-flag, meadow plant. Corn-flag has a bulbous root which 'boiled, pounded and mixed with flour, makes bread sweet and wholesome', according to Theophrastus. It was also an aphrodisiac. It is never mentioned as a food in general literature.

Corn-flag (*Gladiolus italicus*) is *phasganon* or *xiphion* in Greek, *gladiolus* in Latin.

Theophrastus *HP* 7.12.3; Dioscorides *E* 2.101; Pliny *NH* 21.107–15 (confused); Pseudo-Apuleius, *Herbarius* 79.

Costus or putchuk, aromatic root native to the mountains of Kashmir. This was one of the chief commodities of trade at successive port cities at the mouth of the Indus. Costus provided 'a burning taste and an exquisite scent' (so Pliny says) but was 'otherwise useless'. As Pliny knew well, costus was popular in Roman festivity. It may be because of its festive associations that costus was counted among aphrodisiacs. It was also much used in compound medicines, and was an ingredient in spiced wines.

Costus (*Saussurea Lappa*), known in the perfume trade as putchuk and in Indian English as kushth, is Greek *kostos*, Latin *costus*.

Theophrastus *HP* 9.7.3, *O* 32; Strabo 16.4.26 (*kostaria*); Dioscorides *MM* 1.16; *Periplus Maris Erythraei* 39; Pliny *NH* 12.41; Galen *SF* 12.40; Oribasius *CM* 5.33.13; Justinian, *Digest* 39.4.16.7; Anthimus *OC* 13 (see quotation at HARE).

John A.C. Greppin, 'Gk. *kóstos*: a fragrant plant and its Eastern origin' in *Journal of Indo-European Studies* vol. 29 (1999) pp. 395–408; Dalby 2000b pp. 85–6, *al.*

- The translation 'costmary' for classical *costus* is erroneous. Costmary (*Tanacetum Bal-*

samita) is a medicinal herb introduced to European gardens from the Near East in medieval times. When added to ale it gave an aroma reminiscent of costus, hence its name, but it does not match the descriptions of costus in any other way.

Cow *see* OX

Cowpea *see* BLACK-EYED PEA

Crab, group of water creatures characterised by their hard, round, flat shells. Several of the larger kinds are very good to eat, but ancient sources do not suggest that they were eaten enthusiastically. The various classical names cannot be confidently attached to individual species; they varied in their reference across the ancient world and through time.

Aristotle *HA* 525b3–11; Dioscorides *MM* 2.10; Galen *AF* 6.735.

Thompson 1947 pp. 105, 193; A.C. Andrews in *Plutarch's Moralia*, vol. 12 ed. and tr. H. Cherniss and W.C. Helmbold (1957, *LCL*) pp. 481–6; Davidson 1981 pp. 182–6.

- The two Greek names that are applied to edible marine species are *karkinos* and *pagouros*; these correspond to Latin *cancer* and *pagurus*. Thompson identifies both with the common crab (*Cancer Pagurus*); in general, however, the sources distinguish them. Andrews (above) suggests *Decapoda brachyura* for *karkinos*, *C. Pagurus* for *pagurus*.
- Greek *potamios karkinos* 'river crab', when used as the name of an edible species, usually refers to *Thelphusa fluviatilis*.

Crane, big migratory bird. Cranes were kept in poultry yards and force-fed, according to early Egyptian iconography; Roman sources, too, tell us that they were sometimes farmed, and Plutarch adds that some farmers sewed up their eyes because they would feed better 'in darkness'.

Cranes were 'very bad food', said Epicharmus; tough and inedible, said Galen, unless hung for several days. For all that, cranes appeared on Roman dinner tables, prized for their appearance and their rarity rather than for purely gastronomic reasons. They should be hung for some days before use, and then sprinkled with salt and flour (like a sacrifice) according to Horace's comic gastronomy. *Apicius* offers several cooking methods applicable to this and other large birds.

The crane (*Grus Grus*) is Greek *geranos*, Latin *grus*.

Epicharmus 87 Kaibel; Plato, *Politicus* 263d–264c; Anaxandrides 42 Kassel; Varro *RR* 3.2.14; Horace, *Epodes* 2.35, *Satires* 2.8.86–7; Vergil, *Georgics* 1.307; Pliny *NH* 10.60; Statius, *Silvae* 4.6.8; Plutarch *EC* 997a; Galen *AF* 6.703; Aulus Gellius 6.16.5; *Apicius* 6.2; Anthimus *OC* 27 with Grant *ad l.*

Thompson 1936 p. 68; J. Witteveen, 'On swans, cranes and herons' in *Petits Propos culinaires* no. 24 pp. 22–31, no. 25 pp. 50–9, no. 26 pp. 65–73 (1986–7); Brewer and others 1995 p. 123; Toynbee 1996.

Crateuas 'the Root-Cutter', herbalist at the court of MITHRIDATES Eupator, king of Pontus, around 100 BC. Crateuas is credited with devising the king's famous prophylactic against poison, the *Mithridateion*. Some fragments from Crateuas's writings are to be found in the works of Dioscorides. Other references show that his work formed a crucial stage in the development of ancient pharmacology.

M. Wellmann, *Krateuas* (Göttingen, 1897) (*Abhandlungen der Göttinger Gelehrter Gesellschaft*); J.E. Raven, *Plants and Plant Lore in Ancient Greece* (Oxford: Leopard's Head Press, 2000).

Crateuas F: fragments. Text: *Pedanii Dioscuridis Anazarbei de materia medica libri quinque* ed. M. Wellmann (Berlin: Weidmann, 1907–14) vol. 3 pp. 144–6.

Crayfish, freshwater creature resembling a large shrimp or prawn. Unfamiliar in Greece, it was known in other parts of the Mediterranean. Some ducks and farmed fish were fortunate enough to be fattened on it, according to Columella; ALLEC was made from it, says Pliny; some kinds were even good enough for people to eat their meat. It might be minced and formed into cakes, as specified by Apicius, or – substituted for the yolk of a hard-boiled egg – it might form a surprise dish

(see SURPRISE DISHES) as described by Juvenal. The red colour attained by crayfish in the course of cooking was noted by poets.

The freshwater crayfish (*Astacus fluviatilis*) is regional Greek *kammoros* (spellings vary widely), Latin *cammarus*. For the larger, marine creature sometimes called crayfish (Greek *karabos*) see under LANGOUSTE.

Epicharmus 47, 60 Kaibel (*komaris, kammoros*); Sophron 26 Kaibel (*kammaros*); Aristotle *HA* 530a28 (*astakos ho mikros*); Varro *RR* 3.11.3 (*cammarus*); Columella *DA* 8.15.6, 8.17.14; Pliny *NH* 31.96 [*s.v.l.*]; Martial 2.43; Juvenal 5.84; Galen *AF* 6.735 (*kammaris*); *Historia Augusta, Heliogabalus* 19.7; *Apicius* 2.1.1, 2.1.3, 9.1.1 (*cammarus, cammaris*); Hesychius, *Lexicon s.v. kammaroi*.

Thompson 1947 p. 100.

• There are several European species. 'A. *Leptodactylus*, a southeast European species, is recognised by O. Keller (*Ant. Tierw.* ii, p. 490) on coins of Astacus in Bithynia, and A. *pallipes* on those of Astacus in Acarnania' (Thompson 1947 p. 18).

Cress, garden plant. Cress is used for its young, hot-tasting leaves, which can be produced at all times of year, and its mustard-like seeds. Cress was well known to classical Greeks, but the best-known fact about it was that it was a typical food of the PERSIANS; the food which young Persians used as 'relish', alongside their bread, unless success in the hunt meant that they had meat instead. Both Dioscorides and Pliny state that the best kind of cress is the Babylonian: though easy to grow elsewhere, the plant had thus continued to be associated with the Middle East through several centuries. Cress, according to Pliny, is antaphrodisiac and 'sharpens the senses', clearing the vision and calming a troubled mind; numerous other medicinal uses are listed.

Cress (*Lepidium sativum*) is Greek *kardamon*, a word borrowed from a Middle Eastern language (cf. Assyrian *kuddimmu*). In Latin it is *nasturcium*, which appears to mean 'nose-twist', from the immediate effect of tasting the leaves – a property also alluded to in Aristophanic comedy. The identification is certain. Some scholars, however, avoid the English word 'cress' and use the invented term 'cardamum': this is unnecessary and unwise owing to the likelihood of confusion with CARDAMOM.

Aristophanes, *Wasps* 455, 1357, *Clouds* 234, *Thesmophoriazusae* 616; Hippocrates *R* 54; Xenophon, *Cyropaedia* 1.2.8–11; Theopompus Comicus 18 Kassel; Strabo 15.3.18; Dioscorides *MM* 2.155, 4.164; Columella *DA* 10.230–2, 11.3.14; Pliny *NH* 19.154–5, 20.127–30; Polyaenus 4.3.32; Palladius *OA* 2.14.5; Pseudo-Apuleius, *Herbarius* 20.

Sancisi-Weerdenburg 1995; M. Stol, 'Cress and its mustard' in *Jaarbericht van het Voorasiatisch-Egyptisch Gesellschaft Ex Oriente Lux* vol. 28 (1983–4 [1985]) pp. 24–32.

- Greek *lepidion* and *gingidion*, Latin *lepidium* are probably names for the related plant dittander (*Lepidium latifolium*). A potherb familiar in Greece and Rome, dittander was dried, then cooked with milk and seasoned with salt.

  Dioscorides *MM* 2.174; Columella *DA* 11.3.16, 11.3.41, 12.8.3; Pliny *NH* 19.166, 20.181.

- A second *gingidion*, also a potherb, has been tentatively identified with *Daucus Gingidium*, a relative of carrot.

  Dioscorides *MM* 2.137, *Euporista* 2.119; Galen *AF* 6.640, 6.794, *SF* 11.856.

Cretan wine (Greek *Kretikos*; Latin *Cretense, Creticum*), from the island of Crete. Sweet Cretan wines were imported to Rome in the first and second centuries AD, as is shown not only by literary sources but also by the remains of numerous amphorae at Pompeii marked *Lyttios*, the name of a Cretan city. The term 'Cretan wine' meant a very sweet wine, a PASSUM or PROTROPOS, as is evident from Dioscorides's and Galen's uses of the word. Galen sometimes specifies *glykys Kretikos*, sweet Cretan, but more often leaves the sweetness unstated. It was a white wine, according to Damocrates. We may suppose it is the wine's type and

sweetness, rather than its geographical origin, that concerns Scribonius Largus when he includes *passum Creticum* in his veterinary prescriptions.

Dioscorides *MM* 5.6.4; Scribonius Largus 63, 65, 74; Pliny *NH* 14.81; Martial 13.106; Galen *DA* 14.130 quoting Damocrates, *On Diagnosis by Pulse* 8.775, *On Compounding* 12.437; Fronto, *Letters* vol. 2 p. 50 Haines; *CIL* 4.5526, 6469–78, *al.*

Dalby 2000a pp. 137–8; Antigone Marangou, 'Le vin de Crète de l'époque classique à l'époque impériale' in *La Production du vin et de l'huile en Méditerranée* ed. M.-C. Amouretti and J.-P. Brun (Athens: Ecole Française d'Athènes, 1993) pp. 177–82.

- Theran wine (Greek *Theraios, Therenos*) was 'made in Crete', according to Pollux: the statement serves as a warning that ancient geographical designations of wine were not always what they seemed. It was very sweet, quite 'thick' and black in colour, according to Galen. He often lists it in prescriptions as an alternative to *protropos* and to SCYBELITE WINE. One or two of Galen's listings suggest, without ever saying clearly, that *Theraios* is 'a Cretan wine'.

  Galen *VA* 99, *ST* 6.337, *BM* 6.800, 6.804, *On Compounding* 13.25, 13.50, 13.85, 13.211; Pollux *O* 6.2.

Crete, largest Greek island (see also MINOANS). Crete was known in Roman times, as it is today, as a source of medicinal herbs. Many kinds were said (by Theophrastus, Dioscorides, Galen and Pliny) to come only from Crete or to be at their best on the island. The full development of this trade has been tentatively dated to the time of Nero, whose physician Andromachus came from Crete. Galen describes it in full vigour (for a summary see Dalby 2000a pp. 152–4).

Crete was known also for its sweet wine (see previous entry), and for its CAKES; one cake recipe, *gastris*, was a Cretan speciality. The city of Cydonia (Khania) in western Crete was famous as the place where quinces came from: in Greek the QUINCE is *Kydonion melon*, literally 'Cydonian apple'. This is no legendary association: quince orchards and nurseries of Roman date have been identified in the fields around Khania.

As at classical Sparta, the male population of some Cretan cities ate communally in 'men's houses'; strangers also ate here. Dining customs are well described by Strabo (probably based on a fourth century BC source, Ephorus) and by Athenaeus (quoting Hellenistic sources).

Hippolochus D; Strabo 10.4.16–20; Galen DA 14.4–79 passim; Athenaeus D 143a–f quoting Dosiadas and Pyrgion.

H. Georgiou, 'Aromatics in antiquity and in Minoan Crete: a review and reassessment' in Kritika khronika vol. 25 (1973) pp. 441–56 and plates 18–19; J.L. Melena, 'La producción de plantas aromáticas en Cnoso' in Estudios clasicos vol. 20 (1976) pp. 177–90; A.-M. Rouanet-Liesenfelt, 'Les plantes médicinales de Crète à l'époque romaine' in Cretan Studies vol. 3 (1992) pp. 173–90; Harriet Blitzer, 'Olive cultivation and oil production in Minoan Crete' in La Production du vin et de l'huile en Méditerranée ed. M.-C. Amouretti and J.-P. Brun (Athens: Ecole Française d'Athènes, 1993) pp. 163–76.

Cucumber see MELON

Culleus, the whole skin of an ox, sealed to form a container for wine. When it was to be distributed by road – more often in Italy than in Greece – wine was perhaps usually packed in this way: earthenware containers (see AMPHORAE) were much heavier and were at continual risk of breakage. The culleus was also a standard measure of liquid volume, containing 20 amphorae, 960 sextarii (pints) or 525 litres. Cato explains a method of filling a wineskin to this standard measure, as a farmer would need to do when selling wine in bulk.

The advantages of an ox-skin as temporary storage device for wine were not only its lightness and resilience but also its ability to collapse as its contents were gradually sold. During the distribution process, the wine that remained was thus not brought into contact with air. The modern bag-in-a-box has the same advantages.

Cato DA 154 with Dalby ad l.

Cumin, spice plant probably native to central Asia. Cumin was familiar in Mesopotamia by the second millennium BC and was introduced at that period, if not before, to Greece (it is listed in Mycenaean tablets as ku-mi-no). It was also well known in classical Rome; Poseidonius reports its use by Celts (for fish cookery, and added to wine) in the second century BC. Cumin is listed by Theophrastus as a potherb but the real reason for growing it is its spicy seed.

Often ground before use, cumin seed gives heat and an unmistakeable flavour in cooking. Classical Greek cuisine was sparing in its use of flavourings, so it is to be noted that Archestratus lists cumin as a required ingredient in two of his verse recipes (for shark and for parrot wrasse). In one case he calls for aukhmeron kyminon 'parched cumin', meaning the ground seed, in the other for hales kyminotriboi or cumin-salt. Cumin was, to judge from the sources, an extremely common flavouring in the Greek, Roman and Near Eastern kitchen, and a cheap one. A skinflint could be called a kyminopristes 'cumin-splitter'; Christ in Matthew chapter 23 follows the same pattern of thought in accusing the Pharisees of being 'tithers of mint, dill and cumin'. Apicius calls for cumin in well over a hundred recipes.

Cumin-salt, a preparation mentioned several times in Greek and Latin, was salt flavoured with cumin, a convenient way of seasoning savoury dishes. This, or perhaps pure ground cumin, was placed before diners in a kyminodokon, a cumin-box, in classical Athens (or at least in Athenian comedy: see Pollux; the word has several variant spellings). In Roman cookery Apicius gives two recipes for a cumin sauce, cuminatum, for oysters and other shellfish; several recipes elsewhere in Apicius, including one for lobster, include the instruction 'serve with cuminatum'.

Cumin was important in medicine. Apart from prescribing its use in foods, physicians recommended the chewing of cumin seeds (as one might chew fennel or anise) to settle the stomach. Owing to its ubiquity and cheapness it is seldom included in compound medicines.

Cumin or cummin (*Cuminum Cyminum*) is Hebrew *kammon*, Greek *kyminon*, Latin *cuminum*.

Aristophanes, *Wasps* 1357; Hippocrates *RA* 23, *Epidemics* 2.6.7, 7.2, *al.*; Archestratus *H* 23 Brandt; Aristotle, *Nicomachean Ethics* 1121b27; Theophrastus *HP* 7.3.2–3, *CP* 2.12.1–2, *Characters* 10.13; Theocritus 10.55; Nicander *T* 601; Poseidonius *F* 15 Jacoby [Athenaeus *D* 152a]; Cato *DA* 121, *al.*; Celsus *DM* 4.24.2, *al.*; Dioscorides *MM* 3.59; Pliny *NH* 19.160–1, 20.159–64; Matthew, *Gospel* 23.23; Galen *SF* 12.52; Pollux *O* 10.93; *Apicius* 1.29, cf. 3.4.6, 9.1.3, *al.*

Laufer 1919 pp. 383–4; Darby and others 1977 pp. 799–800, 807; Zohary and Hopf 1993 p. 189; Dalby 1996 p. 139.

- Latin and Greek *ammi*, *ami* are names for the spice now known in English as ajowan or ajwain (*Trachyspermum Ammi*). It was called by some *kyminon to aithiopikon*, Ethiopian cumin, but that name usually belonged to nigella (see below). The uses of ajowan were medicinal rather than culinary.

  Dioscorides *MM* 3.62; Pliny *NH* 20.163–4; Galen *ST* 6.267, *DA* 14.41 quoting Andromachus.

  Miller 1969 pp. 105–6, 112; Darby and others 1977 pp. 795–6; Yule and Burnell 1903 *s.v.* 'omum water'.

- So-called Ethiopian cumin (Greek *kyminon to aithiopikon*, Latin *cuminum aethiopicum*) is probably nigella (*Nigella sativa*), also called kalonji, black cumin, onion-seed, fennel-flower and several other names. The seeds of 'Ethiopian cumin' were supplied to the Persian King's Table, according to Polyaenus; it is called 'royal cumin', *kyminon to basilikon*, in a Hippocratic text. Pliny knows that nigella was used to flavour bread at Alexandria and was included in Alexandrian sauces. It was not generally wanted in the Greek or Roman kitchen, but was prescribed by physicians, to be taken in wine and to be included in compound medicines. *Apicius* calls for Ethiopian cumin only in recipes for DIGESTIVES, including *oxyporum*.

Hippocrates, *Epidemics* 7.6; Pliny *NH* 20.161; Galen *ST* 6.265, *al.*; Polyaenus 4.3.32; *Apicius* 1.32, 3.18.3.

Zohary and Hopf 1993 p. 189; Dalby 1996 p. 139.

- Greek *melanthion* and Latin *git* are the names of love-in-a-mist (*Nigella damascena*), which is the European relative of nigella and is used as a substitute for it.

  Pliny *NH* 19.167, 20.182–4; Galen *SF* 12.69, *On Substitutes* 19.733.

- Greek *kyminon agrion* 'wild cumin' was, according to Dioscorides, a name given to two plants, both used in medicine but not in food. Probable identifications are *Nigella arvensis* (black bread weed) and *Lagoecia cuminoides*.

  Nicander *T* 710; Dioscorides *MM* 3.60, 3.61.

Cupa, a wooden tank for storing wine. Such tanks could be made from the wood of the 'Scotch pine' (Latin *picea*). Piso bought his wine from the wine-dealer's tank, said Cicero superciliously; just such a tank, fitted with a tap, was found in a wine-shop at Pompeii. The *cupa*, eventually superseding the DOLIUM, was a noticeable feature of Roman civilisation: its name not only survives in the Romance languages (French *cuve*) but was borrowed into German (*Kufe*).

Wooden barrels were used in the northwestern provinces of the Roman Empire for transporting wine, in place of the CULLEUS of Italy and the AMPHORAE of seaborne trade. Such barrels had at first no special name either in Latin or in Greek (cf. Strabo 5.1.8 [*xylinoi pithoi*]; Pliny *NH* 16.50 [*vasa viatoria*]; Herodian 8.4.4). Their use spread southwards to Italy in the first three centuries AD, and the meaning of Latin *cupa* extended to include barrels also.

Varro, *Menippean Satires* 116 Bücheler; Strabo 5.1.12; Cicero, *Against Piso* 67 [*s.v.l.*]; Caesar, *Civil War* 2.11.2; Lucan 4.420; Petronius, *S* 60.3; Pliny *NH* 16.42; *Vindolanda Tablets* 2.80, cf. 2.259, with Bowman *ad ll.*; Palladius *OA* 1.18; Justinian, *Digest* 32.93.4 quoting Scaevola, 33.7.8 citing Sabinus, 33.7.12.1

quoting Ulpian.

Tchernia 1986 pp. 285–94.

Cuttlefish, sea creature resembling squid. Cuttlefish are good to eat, and are often named among seafood delicacies in classical texts. They were especially fine at Abdera and Maronea, on the north coast of the Aegean, according to Archestratus.

Cuttlefish ink, produced as a defence against aggressors as carefully described by Aristotle, can be saved and used as an ingredient of the sauce that is served with cuttlefish. Hipponax (if correctly interpreted by Athenaeus) uses the term *hyposphagma* for the ink (see SAUCE). The ink and the 'bone' were used in medicine.

The cuttlefish (*Sepia officinalis*) is *sepia* in Greek and Latin. This was the general term, covering also the various smaller species.

Aristophanes, *Acharnians* 1041, *Assemblywomen* 126, 554; Aristotle *HA* 524b14–21, 621b28–622a3; Plautus, *Rudens* 659; Columella *DA* 6.17.7; Pliny *NH* 9.84, 32.141; Galen *AF* 6.736; Athenaeus *D* 323c–324c quoting Hipponax 166 West and Archestratus *H* 55 Brandt (see Olson and Sens *ad l.*); *Apicius* 9.4.

Thompson 1947 p. 231; Davidson 1981 pp. 209–10.

- The 'little cuttlefish' (*Sepiola Rondeleti*) is the second most often encountered in the Mediterranean. The diminutive terms, Greek *sepidion*, Latin *sepiola*, apply to this and to smaller specimens generally. Little cuttlefish were fried, and could be part of *hepsetos*, as Dorion says.

  Plautus, *Casina* 2.8.57; Athenaeus *D* 300f citing Dorion.

Cyclops, one of the monsters in the narrative of Odysseus in the *Odyssey*. There was a tribe of Cyclopes ('round-eyes', with a single eye in the centre of their foreheads); the name of the one whom Odysseus encountered was POLYPHEMUS. He is depicted as a lawless cannibal, eating several of Odysseus's crew before the remainder blinded him and made their escape. He is also de-scribed as a shepherd, milking his goats and sheep and making cheese with the milk. In later, literary reworkings by PHILOXENUS and others, Polyphemus has become an Arcadian shepherd: he courts the nymph Galatea with gifts of lambs, cheese, wild fruits and flowers, but is doomed to perpetual failure in courtship owing to his unprepossessing appearance.

Homer, *Odyssey* 9.116–564; Euripides, *Cyclops*; Ovid, *Metamorphoses* 13.738–897.

Cydonia *see* CRETE

Cynics, philosophical school of classical Greece. The founder of the lineage was Diogenes, contemporary of Plato and Alexander. Cynics rejected law and convention. The Cynic lifestyle, permitting its exponents to be as rude, greedy and self-centred as was consistent with the continued receipt of invitations to dinner, eventually attracted many less original thinkers than Diogenes, his best pupil Crates, and Crates's lapsed pupil Zeno of Citium, founder of the Stoic school. A Cynics' dinner in Hellenistic Athens is the theme of a curious memoir by Parmeniscus, quoted by Athenaeus. The Cynics of Roman times are depicted and satirised in the 'Cynulcus' of Athenaeus's long dialogue *Deipnosophists*, and in the *Symposium* of Lucian.

In keeping with his rejection of civilisation Diogenes is said to have tried eating raw meat, but to have found it indigestible (Diogenes Laertius 6.34; Plutarch, *Water or Fire* 956b). One story of his death is that to demonstrate the superfluity of food preparation he had tried to eat raw octopus, with fatal results (Diogenes Laertius 6.76; Lucian, *Philosophers for Sale* 10; Plutarch *EC* 995c–d). Cannibalism was recommended theoretically by Cynics but they are not said to have practised it (Diogenes Laertius 6.73; Dio of Prusa, *Orations* 8.14; Theophilus of Antioch, *To Autolycus* 3.5). Diogenes is also said to have recommended vegetarianism (Strabo 15.1.65).

Parmeniscus [Athenaeus *D* 156d–158a]; Diogenes Laertius 6; Athenaeus *D* 113e–114a,
422c–d.

D. Krueger in *The Cynics* ed. R.B. Branham
and M.-O. Goulet-Caze (Berkeley: University
of California Press, 1996) p. 227 n. 33.

Cyrenaica, rich country in what is now
northeastern Libya. The region was relatively arid, even in ancient times, but the
Greeks from Thera who first colonised it
were led by local guides to a place where
there was 'a hole in the sky', a micro-
climate with abundant rain. The Greek–
Libyan city of Cyrene, founded here in the
late seventh century BC, was rich in cattle
and prospered on its exports of wheat and
SILPHIUM.

Herodotus 4.150–9; Theophrastus *HP* 6.3.1–6;
Strabo 17.3.22.

M. Fulford, 'To east and west: the Mediterranean trade of Cyrenaica and Tripolitania in
antiquity' in *Libyan Studies* vol. 20 (1989) pp.
169–91.

Cythnos, island of the Cyclades. Cythnos
was insignificant except as a source of one
of Athens's favourite cheeses, probably
formed as a 'crottin' and (according to
Aelian) once sold at the high price of 90
drakhmai per talent weight.

Alexis *F* 178 Kassel with Arnott *ad l.*; Aelian,
Nature of Animals 16.32 citing Aeschylides;
Stephanus of Byzantium, *Gazetteer s.v. Kyth-
nos*, cf. Pliny *NH* 13.134.

D

Dacia, powerful kingdom of the first centuries BC and AD, lying north of the lower Danube. The philosophical rule of vegetarianism, a Pythagorean tenet, was apparently taught in Dacia under King Burebistas, contemporary of Julius Caesar; he is also to be noted as an early prohibitionist, ordering the destruction of all vineyards in Dacia. After several inconclusive wars Dacia was eventually conquered by the Roman Empire in AD 101–6 in the campaigns commemorated on Trajan's Column. Documents from the subsequent military occupation give interesting information on army provisioning and the food economy.

Dacia was well known for its medicinal and poisonous drugs, a fact confirmed by the plant names in Dacian which are included in some manuscripts of Dioscorides's *Materia Medica*. Names listed include blite, black hellebore, white bryony, nettle, rosemary, Aaron's rod, wild purslane, blackberry, thyme, elderberry, danewort, dill and mint.

Strabo 7.3.5, 7.3.11; Silius Italicus 1.324–5; *Trajan's Column* casts 325–8.

Dimiter Detschew, *Die thrakischen Sprachreste* (Vienna, 1957), review by L. Zgusta in *Archív orientalní* vol. 26 (1958) pp. 684–5; D. Tudor, 'Importul de vin si untdelemn in Provincia Dacia' in *Apulum* vol. 7 (1968) pp. 391–9; J.G. Nandris, 'Aspects of the Dacian economy and high zone exploitation' in *Dacia* n.s. vol. 25 (1981) pp. 231–54.

Dandelion *see* ENDIVE

Danube fish, a rich fauna, unfortunately listed by no ancient source except the easily misled Aelian. As fish of the Danube Aelian lists *korakinoi* (see CASTAGNOLE for the other species that share this name), *myaloi* (possibly grey mullet), *antakaioi* (sturgeon) and *kyprinoi* (carp), which are black; followed by *khoiroi* (one of the NILE FISH shared this name) and *kossyphoi*, which are white; and then *perkai* (perch) and *xiphiai* (swordfish). Most of these, Aelian adds, can be caught through holes cut in the ice when the Danube freezes over in winter. The carp, under its Latin name *carpa*, is named, much later, by Cassiodorus as a fine fish for a Gothic royal table.

Aelian, *Nature of Animals* 14.23, 14.26; Cassiodorus, *Variae* 12.4.

Darnel, a pernicious weed of wheat crops in Mediterranean lands. Darnel could easily be harvested along with the wheat. It caused headache (as Aristotle and Galen say) if taken in small amounts, and might cause serious illness or death if its seeds were infected by ergot; Paxamus remarked on the danger of blindness. Darnel is coupled with OATS, which in classical agriculture were regarded as an equally pernicious weed, in Vergil's gloomy verse: *Infelix lolium et steriles* *dominantur avenae*, 'Unlucky darnel and barren oats become the masters.'

Darnel (*Lolium temulentum*) is Greek *airai*, Latin *lolium*.

Herodotus 6.100; Aristotle, *On Sleep* 456b30; Plautus, *Miles Gloriosus* 321; Paxamus [*Geoponica* 2.43]; Vergil, *Georgics* 1.154; Ovid, *Fasti* 1.691; Matthew, *Gospel* 13.25 (*zizania*); Galen *AF* 6.551–3; Oribasius *CM* 1.1.10 with Grant *ad l.*

E. Lieber, 'Galen on contaminated cereals as a cause of epidemics' in *Bulletin of the History of Medicine* vol. 44 (1970) pp. 332–45; Garnsey 1999 pp. 38–9 and note 13.

Date, a fruiting palm that grows wild from Mauritania in the west to Baluchistan and Sind in the east. The date palm requires very low rainfall but well-watered soil, conditions obtaining in the Saharan oases, Egypt and Mesopotamia. Under domestication the proportion of female fruit-bearing plants is increased beyond the level at which natural pollination is likely; hand-pollination (Akkadian *rukkubu*) thus becomes necessary.

Dates were being gathered for human use, over much or all of the east–west range of the species, by around 6000 BC. There is evidence of domesticated dates from archaeological sites in the Persian Gulf, Mesopotamia and Palestine beginning around 5000 BC. The tree would grow in Greece, and elsewhere north of its usual range – its silhouette was evidently familiar when the poet of the *Odyssey* compared Nausicaa to a young date palm – but it would not fruit there.

Dates were a popular delicacy in classical Rome – distributed, for example, at Domitian's Saturnalia feast as described by Statius. To judge by the recipes of *Apicius* they were also frequently used as a culinary flavouring. *Nicolaos* and *caryota* are two of the varieties recorded by Aramaic and Roman sources; both were grown in Syria, *caryota* also in Egypt. A third kind recognised in Roman trade was the *Thebaica*, evidently from Thebes in Egypt.

Date syrup was an important sweeten-ing agent, perhaps the cheapest source of dietary sugar, in the ancient Near East; it was also known in the classical Mediterranean. The date palm and its fruit had numerous other uses in its native habitat: 'they say there is a Persian song in which three hundred and sixty uses are enumerated,' according to Strabo.

The date (*Phoenix dactylifera*) is Greek *daktylos, phoinix, phoinikobalanos*, Latin *dactylus*. The tree is *phoinix* in Greek, *palma* in Latin.

Homer, *Odyssey* 6.163; Herodotus 1.193, *al.*; Xenophon, *Anabasis* 2.3.15–16; Theophrastus *HP* 2.6.1–8, *CP* 1.2.3; Varro *RR* 2.1.27; Strabo 16.1.14, 16.2.41, 17.1.15, 17.1.51; Dioscorides *MM* 1.109; Petronius *S* 40; Pliny *NH* 13.26–51, 23.97; Statius, *Silvae* 1.6; Plutarch *QC* 8.4; Galen *VA* 91, *AF* 6.606–8, *BM* 6.777–80, *SF* 12.151; Athenaeus *D* 651b–652b; Palladius *OA* 11.12.1–2; Anthimus *OC* 92.

Laufer 1919 pp. 385–91; B. Landsberger, *The Date Palm and its By-products according to the Cuneiform Sources* (Graz, 1967) (*Archiv für Orientforschung. Beiheft*, 17); D.G. Reder, 'La culture du palmier dattier en Egypte et en Palestine pendant la période gréco-romaine' in *Ellinisticheskii blizhnii vostok, Vizantiya i Iran, istoriya i filologiya* ed. V.V. Struve and others (Moscow, 1967) pp. 52–5; Darby and others 1977 pp. 722–30; M.P. Charles, 'Onions, cucumbers and the date palm' in *Bulletin on Sumerian Agriculture* no. 3 (1987) pp. 1–21; Zohary and Hopf 1993 pp. 157–62; Brewer and others 1995 pp. 47–50; Dalby 2000a p. 169; Mark S. Copley and others, 'Processing palm fruits in the Nile valley: biomolecular evidence from Qasr Ibrim' in *Antiquity* vol. 75 (2001) pp. 538–42.

- Greek *phoinikinos oinos*, Latin *vinum palmeum* is not 'palm wine' made from the sap (as Darby and others say) but date wine made from the semi-dried fruit soaked in water: a recipe is given by Pliny. Date wine is also familiar from Sumerian and Akkadian literature.

  'Love song to a king' [Pritchard 1969 p. 496]; Xenophon, *Anabasis* 2.3.15; Pliny *NH* 14.102.

  Darby and others 1977 pp. 614–5.

- Greek *enkephalos phoinikos*, literally 'brain of the date palm', is palm heart, referred to in old-fashioned English translations as the 'cabbage' of the date palm. Palm heart is an ancient Near Eastern delicacy (Akkadian *ukuru*), and necessarily an expensive one, because taking the growing shoots means killing the tree.

Xenophon, *Anabasis* 2.3.16; Athenaeus *E* 71c–e.

Deer and antelope, wild animals of Europe and the Near East. Venison (Greek *kemadeion*, Latin *damma*) was less common on Greek and Roman tables than on those of the hunters of northern Europe. Several species were known in the Near East, in Egypt and in north Africa.

Athenaeus *D* 397a.

Darby and others 1977 pp. 231–5; Toynbee 1996.

- Greek *elaphos*, Latin *cervus* is the red deer (*Cervus Elaphus*) and the fallow deer (*Dama* spp.). Oppian distinguishes the fallow deer as *eurykeros* 'broadhorn'; Pliny knows the name *platyceros* for it.

  Pliny *NH* 11.123; Oppian, *Cynegetica* 2.176–295.

- Greek *zorkas*, *dorkas* and Latin *dorcas* are names used for the roe deer (*Capreolus Capreolus*) by authors writing of Europe, for the gazelle (*Gazella* spp.) by those writing of Asia. Oppian distinguishes the roe deer, *iorkos* from the gazelle, *dorkos*, clearly employing dialect variants of a single word.

  Herodotus 4.192; Aristotle *HA* 499a9; Oppian, *Cynegetica* 2.296–325; Athenaeus *D* 397a.

- Greek *boubalos*, *boubalis*, Latin *bubalus* is a north African antelope (*Bubalis mauretanica*).

  Herodotus 4.192; Aristotle *HA* 515b34; Strabo 17.3.4; Pliny *NH* 8.38; Dio Cassius 48.23.3; Oppian, *Cynegetica* 2.300–14.

- Greek and Latin *oryx* is the beisa or sable antelope of northeastern Africa and the Near East (*Oryx Leucoryx*).

  Aristotle *HA* 499b20; Callixeinus of Rhodes [Athenaeus *D* 200f]; Pliny *NH* 8.214, *al.*; Oppian, *Cynegetica* 2.445–88.

- Latin *alce*, Greek *alke* is the elk (*Alces Alces*), native to northern Europe, seldom seen in Mediterranean lands. Pausanias describes how it was hunted.

  Pliny *NH* 8.39; Pausanias 5.12.1, 9.21.3.

Delos, island in the middle Aegean sacred to Apollo. In the classical period, since its main *raison d'être* was religious, Delos was a place with an *euopsos agora* 'well-stocked food market' and a good supply of cooks, both being essential in the performance of Greek sacrifices. Delos was also a place where chickens were kept (and castrated to fatten them as capons), presumably because chickens are an economical sacrifice and produce relatively little meat: the continual sacrifice of large animals at Delos would have resulted in an excess of meat and offal which the small local population would have been unable to consume. In Hellenistic times Delos became a centre of the slave trade and home to a large Roman business community. Modern excavations give evidence of the mixture of Greek and Roman lifestyles and even Greek and Roman kitchen utensils.

Archestratus considered Delos a good place for two fish species, the *phagros* (see under BREAM) and the *lebias* (see under HAKE).

Archestratus *H* 26, 27 Brandt with Olson and Sens *ad ll.*; Crito Comicus 3 Kassel; Petronius *S* 22; Athenaeus *D* 172f–173c.

Dalby 2000a pp. 149–50; G. Roux, 'Salles de banquet à Délos' in *Etudes déliennes* (*Bulletin de correspondance hellénique* suppl. 1) (Athens, 1973) pp. 525–54; A. Peignard-Giros, 'Habitudes alimentaires grecques et romaines à Délos à l'époque hellénistique: le témoignage de la céramique' in *Paysage et alimentation dans le monde grec* ed. Jean-Marc Luce (Toulouse, 2000) pp. 209–20.

Delphi, sanctuary of Apollo in central Greece. At Delphi, as at Delos, many cooks were needed to officiate at sacrifices.

Athenaeus *D* 173c–f, also 372a quoting Polemon.

Demeter, the Greek goddess of the grain harvest. Demeter was sister of Zeus and mother of *kore* 'the maiden' whose name when spoken was Persephone. Demeter's famous search for her kidnapped daughter was said to have ended at Eleusis, near Athens, where she was refreshed by a KYKEON flavoured with pennyroyal, and where she rewarded her host's son, Triptolemus, with the honour of bringing the knowledge of cereals to humanity. Throughout ancient times mystery and initiation rites sacred to Demeter, the *Eleusinia*, were celebrated at Eleusis. CERES was Demeter's equivalent in the Roman pantheon.

The Homeric Hymn to Demeter ed. N.J. Richardson (Oxford: Clarendon Press, 1974); Helene P. Foley, *The Homeric Hymn to Demeter: translation, commentary, and interpretive essays* (Princeton: Princeton University Press, 1994); G.J. Baudy, 'Cereal diet and the origins of man: myths of the Eleusinia in the context of ancient Mediterranean harvest festivals' in *Food in Antiquity* ed. John Wilkins and others (Exeter: Exeter University Press, 1995) pp. 177–95.

Diet, a strong interest of ancient physicians. In the prevailing HUMORAL THEORY a healthy constitution was seen as continually threatened by imbalance in bodily humours; diet was the most effective among the means available for retaining and restoring balance. Attention was given to the choice of food, its preparation, its spicing, its quantity, to the number of meals per day and their timing. Other aspects of 'regimen' or daily routine, including sexual behaviour (Hippocrates *R* 68, *RS* 1), were also taken in hand.

Thus the oldest text on the subject, the anonymous *Regimen* traditionally attributed to Hippocrates, gives much space to selection of foods (Hippocrates *R* 40–55) and discusses cooking methods (*R* 56) but also deals with exercise, bathing and other aspects of regimen (*R* 57–66, cf. *RA* 65–8). Since each constitution is different (*R* 32–4), physicians prescribed a different diet for each individual, varying with the current state of health, any symptoms of illness (Hippocrates, *Diseases II* 12–75, *Sacred Disease* 2, *al.*), the usual lifestyle, and external influences including the geographical climate (Hip-

pocrates *R* 37–8, *Airs Waters Places*) and the seasons. Attention was sometimes paid to dreams (*R* 86–93). Changes in the pattern of life, such as a long journey, would require adjustments to the diet (see also TRAVELLERS' FOOD).

This approach to diet is parodied in an Athenian comedy by Damoxenus. In general, however, the humoral effects of foodstuffs surface rather seldom in non-medical discussion. There are numerous relevant remarks by Aristotle and some by Plutarch; there are extended statements on the subject in Athenaeus's *Deipnosophists*, but that food-obsessed text may be considered the exception that proves the rule. The extent to which ordinary individuals asked for dietary advice, or took it when offered, remains uncertain.

An early brief statement of seasonal adjustments to the diet is given in the short text *Regimen in Health* attributed to Hippocrates:

In winter eat very copiously, drink very sparingly; the drink must be wine very little diluted, the cereal must be bread, the relish [meat and fish] cooked dry, and vegetables must be very few at this season: this will keep the body effectively dry and hot. When spring comes the drink can gradually be more plentiful, more watery; the cereal should be softer, also smaller in quantity, reducing the bread and using barley-mash; the relish likewise reduced, and all boiled rather than cooked dry; a few vegetables can be taken in spring. And thus a person will be preparing for summer, and will by then eat all soft cereals, boiled relishes, raw and boiled vegetables, and take drinks that are very watery and very copious; but each change must be small, each addition modest and gradual ... In autumn, cereal to be more copious and drier, and relishes likewise; drinks to be more sparing and less diluted. Thus the winter arrives and a person will be drinking with very little added water and in very sparing quantity, and cereals will be very copious and very dry.

(Hippocrates *RS* 1)

Rules of thumb current in later Roman times for regulating food and drink through the year are given concisely in a 'Letter to King Antigonus' falsely attributed to Diocles of Carystus. This text is much more schematic than those compiled by serious physicians, but it is generally in agreement with them: hence it will be useful to give a summary here. For ninety days from winter solstice, water is in excess; one should take the hottest foods, drink wine undiluted or only slightly diluted with water, and take decoctions of oregano. For forty-six days from the spring equinox, phlegm and sweet ichor of the blood are in excess; one should take the most sharp and sour foods. For forty-five days from the rise of the Pleiades, yellow bile and bitter ichors are in excess; one should take sweet and laxative foods. For ninety-three days from summer solstice, black bile is in excess; one takes cold drinks (meaning water, or wine heavily diluted with water, since wine itself is hot in dietary terms) and aromatic foods. For forty-six days from autumn equinox, phlegm and light fluxes are in excess; one takes the sourest and most sappy of foods. For forty-five days from the setting of the Pleiades, phlegm is in excess; one should take the most astringent foods and drink wines of the nicest possible flavour.

A dietary rule urged by Greek philosophers more strongly than by physicians was that *sitos* or staple food, whether cereals or legumes, should have greater importance than *opson* or relish (see MEALS). This was for reasons less of health than of morality: the craving for strong flavours and the concomitant growth of gastronomy were seen as insidious. It was noticed that a vegetarian diet did no harm; however, physicians did not recommend VEGETARIANISM as a normal practice.

For modern scientific approaches to the ancient diet see NUTRITION.

Hippocrates *R*, *RS*, *RA passim*, *Aphorisms* 1.1–20; Damoxenus 2 Kassel [Athenaeus *D* 102a]; Diocles of Carystus *F* 183 van der Eijk [Paul of Aegina, *Medicine* 1.100]; Aristotle, *Problems* 948b35–949a8, *al.*; Plutarch *QC* 2.2; Galen *AF passim*, *ST passim*; Athenaeus *D passim*.

L. Edelstein, 'Antike Diätetik' in *Die Antike* vol. 7 (1931) pp. 255–70, translation 'The dietetics of antiquity' in L. Edelstein, *Ancient Medicine: selected papers* ed. O. and C.L. Temkin (Baltimore, 1967) pp. 303–16.

Dieuches, physician and dietary author of the early third century BC. Dieuches's work does not survive but is cited six times by Oribasius (one quotation concerns the management of sea-sickness) and was also used by Pliny. The poet of fishing, NUMENIUS, was a pupil of Dieuches.

Athenaeus *E* 5b; Oribasius *CM* 5.33, *al.*

J. Bertier, *Mnésithée et Dieuchès* (Leiden, 1972).

Digestives, medicinal drinks taken after a big meal. Dioscorides names lovage root, caraway seed and aniseed as useful ingredients in mixtures of this type. Cheese was sometimes a solid vehicle for the spicy ingredients; some were mixed with salt, or with honey, or taken in wine. The general Greek term, both for the mixture and for the active ingredients, was *oxyporon*.

Dioscorides *MM* 3.51.3, 3.57.1; Statius, *Silvae* 4.9.36; Archigenes fragment 72 Calabrò.

- Latin *dodra* was a digestive drink with nine ingredients which are listed metrically by Ausonius. There is a modern interpretation of the recipe by Grant 1999 pp. 132–3.

  Ausonius, *Epigrams* 86–88.

- Latin *oxyporum* was a highly-spiced digestive to be taken after a meal, or to help down indigestible foods such as lettuce. Recipes are given by Columella and in *Apicius*. It had no precise Greek name, in Galen's view: he once prescribes 'the black *garos* that is called *oxyporon* in Latin', a good description since GARUM provided the liquid vehicle for this mixture. Pepper, ginger and silphium or asafoetida were among the usual ingredients. Grant 1999 pp. 134–5 offers a modern interpretation of the Columella recipe as a 'tangy salad dressing'.

Columella *DA* 12.59.4–5; Statius, *Silvae* 4.9.36; Galen, *On Compounding* 12.637; *Apicius* 1.32, 3.18.2–3; Aetius, *Medicine* 3.91–2.

- The digestive best known as *to dia kalaminthes*, a digestive incorporating *kalaminthe* (probably catmint) was also called *polyetes Galenou*. It could be mixed with salt and sprinkled on to food, or mixed into honey.

Galen *ST* 6.431; Soranus, *Gynaecology* 3.32; Oribasius, *Select Prescriptions* 45.5; Aetius, *On Medicine* 9.24.

- The digestive *to dia trion pepereon* is also credited to Galen. It included 'the three peppers', black pepper, white pepper and long pepper, as well as ginger and cinnamon, making it extremely expensive. It was mixed into honey or taken with wine.

Galen, *On Compounding* 13.153; Oribasius, *Select Prescriptions* 45.5; Aetius, *On Medicine* 9.24; *Scholia on Plato, Symposium* 185d.

Dill, culinary herb native to the eastern Mediterranean. Texts suggest its use in wreaths and other ritual and sensual contexts more frequently than its incorporation in cooked dishes; the recipes of *Apicius*, however, call for dill about forty times. It is usually the fresh leaf that is meant, though the seed was also used in cooking. Dill seed is found by archaeobotanists in Roman contexts indicating food use; for example, it occurs in latrine deposits at Cologne in Roman GERMANY.

As an element in the diet dill was regarded as diuretic and very 'hot'. Dioscorides gives instructions for the making of dill oil, to be used as an ointment. A riddle: *Apicius* has a recipe for *pullus anethatus*, chicken with dill, and Vinidarius for *mulli anethati*, red mullet with dill, but neither recipe calls for dill or for any obvious substitute.

Dill (*Anethum graveolens*) is Greek *anethon*, Latin *anetum*. Greek *anneson*, *annetos*, evidently a dialect variant of the same word, was the name for ANISE in classical Greek.

Aristophanes, *Clouds* 982 with Dover *ad l.*; Hippocrates *R* 54, *Affections of Women* 66, 185; Alexis *F* 132 Kassel with Arnott *ad l.*; Aristotle, *Problems* 949a2; Theophrastus *HP* 1.11.2, *al.*, *CP* 6.9.3; Theocritus 7.63, 11.119; Dioscorides *MM* 1.51, 3.58; Pliny *NH* 20.196; Matthew, *Gospel* 23.23; Galen *AF* 6.641, *SF* 11.832; Athenaeus *D* 674d–e quoting Sappho 81 Lobel [*s.v.l.*]; *Apicius* 6.8.1, *al.*; Vinidarius *BC* 14.

Zohary and Hopf 1993 p. 189.

Dining and drinking utensils cannot be called 'tableware' since in classical festivity tables were themselves merely utensils like the rest. The useful collective term *instrumentum domesticum* 'household equipment' covers both these and COOKING UTENSILS. See also AMPHORAE; MURRINE VASES; ICONOGRAPHY AS SOURCE.

Vindolanda Tablets 2.194; Pollux *O* 6.95–100; Athenaeus *D* 459a–504e (with *E* 781c–784d); Macrobius *S* 5.21.

W. Deonna, 'Vases à surprise et vases à puiser le vin' in *Bulletin de l'Institut Genevois* vol. 38 (1908) pp. 3–29; G.M.A. Richter, *Shapes and Names of Athenian Vases* (New York, 1935); Buck 1949 pp. 344–51; D.E. Strong, *Greek and Roman Gold and Silver Plate* (London, 1966); T. Cullen, 'Social implications of ceramic style in the Neolithic Peloponnese' in *Ancient Technology and Modern Science* ed. W.D. Kingery (Columbus, Ohio: American Ceramic Society, 1984) pp. 77–100; D.C. Kurtz and J. Boardman, 'Booners' in *Greek Vases in the J. Paul Getty Museum, 3* (*Occasional Papers on Antiquities* no. 2) (Malibu, 1985) pp. 35–70; M. Vickers, 'Artful crafts' in *Journal of Hellenic Studies* vol. 105 (1985) pp. 108–28; H. Hoffmann, 'Rhyta and kantharoi in Greek ritual' in *Greek Vases in the J. Paul Getty Museum, 4* (Malibu, 1989) pp. 131–66; *Looking at Greek Vases* ed. T. Rasmussen and N. Spivey (Cambridge: Cambridge University Press, 1991); Miguel Beltrán Lloris, 'La vajilla relacionada con el vino en Hispania' in *El vino en la antigüedad romana (Jerez, 2–4 de Octubre, 1996)* ed. Sebastián Celestino Pérez (Madrid: Universidad Autonoma de Madrid, 1999) pp. 129–200; Wilkins 2000 pp. 33–6.

- 'Vases' is the traditional term in classical art and archaeology for the subset of utensils that were made to contain or display wine and food. There were many kinds of drinking-cups, and therefore many names. At a *symposion* in Greek style there was one universal feature, the *krater*, Latin *cratera*, in which the communal mixture of wine and water was made. Athenaeus gives a long survey of the names of vases as used in earlier Greek literature. Earthenware is the best-known material now, both because it was commoner and because gold, silver and bronze vessels risked being melted for re-use and have survived more rarely than vases and fragments of earthenware. Glassware, called in Greek *ta hyalina*, in Latin *vitramina* (Pollux *KH* 81) gradually became cheaper and more widespread in the course of the classical period.

• There are again many types of serving dishes and many names: note the general terms, Greek *pinax*, Latin *lanx*. Among smaller vessels there was the *paropsis*, a side-dish for appetisers (Athenaeus *E* 63d–64f, *al.*). There was also Greek *oxybaphon*, Latin *acetabulum*, a small bowl for vinegar or sauce, or for appetisers served in vinegar (Philoxenus *D* b.4 Page; Athenaeus *D* 494b–e quoting Cratinus 199 Kassel).

• In both Greece and Rome tables were small and portable. Each was used by one or two diners and they were washed before use and were replaced or wiped clean between courses. Hence the dessert course was called *deuterai trapezai* in Greek, *secundae mensae* in Latin, 'second tables'. Solid food, if not eaten directly from the serving tray, was placed on one's table, which thus served the function of a modern dinner plate.

Diocles of Carystus, Greek medical and dietary author of the fourth century BC. The major works of Diocles are known only from substantial quotations by Athenaeus, Galen and others. Two short texts, *Regimen for Health* and *Regimen for Travellers* (the latter topic scarcely treated by any other classical writer) survive complete, both of them incorporated in medical miscellanies compiled by Oribasius.

W. Jaeger, *Diokles von Karystos* (Berlin, 1963), 2nd edn.

Diocles F: fragments. Text and translation: *Diocles of Carystus: a collection of the fragments with translation and commentary* vol. 1, ed. Philip J. van der Eijk (Leiden: Brill, 2000).

—— RS: *Regimen for Health* [= F 182 van der Eijk = Oribasius *CM libri incerti* 40]. Text and

translation in van der Eijk (above) pp. 296–311.

—— RV: *Regimen for Travellers* [= F 184 van der Eijk = Oribasius, *To Eustathius* 5.31]. Text and translation in van der Eijk (above) pp. 322–5.

Diocletian's Price Edict, recovered in the form of fragmentary inscriptions from several sites, was an attempt to fix the maximum prices for Roman army supplies that would be paid to dealers in food, wine and other products. The price edict was promulgated by the emperor Diocletian shortly before AD 300, and continuing inflation led to its abandonment within a few years. A large proportion of the text survives in both Greek and Latin.

Apart from the prices themselves, the edict is important as an indication of the organisation of army supply at this period and of which commodities were thought worth controlling. It confirms equivalences between Greek and Latin terms, including *liquamen* = *garos* 'fish sauce', *herbilia* = *lathyros* 'grass pea'. It provides evidence of the borrowing of trade terms and food words from Latin to Greek: examples first found here, well established later, include the Greek words *phaba* 'broad bean', *kondeiton* 'spiced wine', '*conditum*'. This text provides the earliest example of the common Greek phrase *oinos khydeos*, equated with Latin *vinum rusticum* 'vin ordinaire', 'table wine'.

Lactantius, *Deaths of the Persecutors 7.6*.

Simon Corcoran, *The Empire of the Tetrarchs: Imperial pronouncements and government AD 284–324* (Oxford: Clarendon Press, 1996).

Diocletian's Price Edict. Text and German commentary: *Diokletians Preisedikt* ed. S. Lauffer (Berlin: De Gruyter, 1971).

Diogenes *see* CYNICS

Dionysius, author(s) of a Greek work *On Cookery*, perhaps of the fourth or early third century BC, cited twice by Athenaeus.

Athenaeus *D* 326f, 516c.

Dionysus or Bacchus, the Greek god of wine. Son of Zeus and Semele (but born from Zeus's thigh), Dionysus was a traveller, bringing the grape and the knowledge of wine to many peoples. His male followers, the Satyrs, led by Silenus, are often pictured treading the grapes, drinking the wine and participating in the KOMOS or drunken revel. In classical and later Greece women took part, as *mainades*, in wild ceremonies in honour of Dionysus.

Bacchus was the usual name for this god in the Roman pantheon. The worship of Bacchus, as a foreign introduction to Rome associated with drunkenness and immorality, was banned for a while in the second century BC. The traditional Roman wine god had been *Liber Pater*, 'Father Liber': the three names Dionysus, Bacchus, Liber became interchangeable in Latin poetry.

Marcel Detienne, *Dionysos mis à mort* (Paris, 1977), translation *Dionysos Slain* (Baltimore, 1979); François Lissarrague, 'Le banquet' and 'Dionysos' in *Hommes, dieux et héros de la Grèce: catalogue de l'exposition du Musée Départemental des Antiquités, Rouen* (Rouen, 1982) pp. 171–85, 259–77; T.H. Carpenter, *Dionysian Imagery in Archaic Greek Art* (Oxford, 1986); *Dionysos: mito e mistero. Atti del convegno internazionale, Comacchio, 3–5 novembre 1989* ed. F. Berti (Comacchio, 1991).

Dioscorides, in full Pedanius Dioscorides of Anazarba, a Roman army physician in the time of Claudius and Nero. Dioscorides is the author of an extremely full and systematic survey of dietary and medicinal substances. The text is in Greek. It contains much information on the origins and local varieties of foods of all kinds and of medicinal herbs. In many cases the usual method of preparation of foods is briefly stated; sometimes, as in the case of flavoured wines, fuller instructions or recipes are given.

The history of the text is complicated. Numerous manuscripts include additions by later editors, since Dioscorides's work remained standard throughout medieval times. There is an early medieval translation into Latin, and numerous Renaissance translations and commentaries. There are also important illustrated manuscripts, including the famous Codex Anicia Juliana of AD 512.

The glosses that appear in some manuscripts, giving equivalents for the Greek names of certain ingredients in Latin, Etruscan, Egyptian and several other languages of the Empire, will have aided the army pharmacist when dealing with local herbalists. The glosses are said to be later additions to the original text – but they cannot be much later, since Etruscan (for example) soon ceased to be spoken and would have been useless under the later Empire.

Several minor works are attributed to Dioscorides: some are in fact by later authors, but the *Euporista* 'Simple Prescriber' is really his.

Scarborough 1985; J.M. Riddle, *Dioscorides on Pharmacy and Medicine* (Austin, 1985); Max Aufmesser, *Etymologische und wortgeschichtliche Erläuterungen zu De materia medica des Pedanius Dioscorides Anazarbeus* (Hildesheim: Olms-Weidmann, 2000).

Dioscorides E: *Euporista*. Critical text in Wellmann (below) vol. 3 pp. 152–317.

—— **MM**: *Materia Medica*. Critical text: *Pedanii Dioscuridis Anazarbei de materia medica libri quinque* ed. M. Wellmann (Berlin: Weidmann, 1907–14), 3 vols, with excellent indexes: note that the principal index, a topic index in Greek, is vol. 3 pp. 359–93. Early translation: *The Greek Herbal of Dioscorides, Illustrated by a Byzantine A.D. 512, Englished by J. Goodyer A.D. 1655*; ed. R.T. Gunther (Oxford, 1934). Partial translation: John Scarborough and V. Nutton, 'The Preface of Dioscorides' Materia Medica: introduction, translation, commentary' in *Transactions and Studies of the College of Physicians of Philadelphia* n.s. vol. 4 (1982) pp. 187–227.

Diphilus of Siphnos, Greek medical author of around 300 BC. Diphilus was physician to King Lysimachus of Thrace, one of the successors of Alexander. His works are lost except in the form of quotations by later writers, notably

Athenaeus, who gives several long and short extracts from his work *On Foods for the Sick and the Healthy*, evaluating the contribution to the diet made by various breads, cakes, fresh and salt fish, vegetables, pulses and fruits.

Athenaeus *E* 51a.

John Scarborough, 'Diphilus of Siphnos and Hellenistic medical dietetics' in *Journal of the History of Medicine* vol. 25 (1970) pp. 194–201.

Dog, domesticated animal. The dietary qualities of the meat of dogs and puppies are listed alongside those of other animals in Hippocratic texts. Dog was somewhat indigestible, while boiled puppy was considered a suitable invalid food; Galen later adds that the meat of young castrated dogs is best. However, dog is never mentioned as a food in comedy discussions of menus, and very seldom in other relevant ancient sources. References are gathered by Greenewalt in the context of a discussion of puppy sacrifices at Sardis, capital of Lydia, in the sixth century BC. There is clear archaeological evidence for these sacrifices, in which puppies were stewed in a pot, but no written confirmation.

The dog (*Canis familiaris*) is Greek *kyon*, also *skylakion* 'puppy', Latin *canis*.

Hippocrates *R* 46, *Epidemics* 7.62, *Sacred Disease* 2; Galen *AF* 6.664, *VA* 68.

Buck 1949 pp. 178–81; C.H. Greenewalt, *Ritual Dinners in Early Historic Sardis* (Berkeley, 1976); Darby and others 1977 pp. 239–52; Simoons 1994 pp. 200–52; S. Bökönyi in *History of Humanity* ed. S.J. De Laet (Paris, 1994) pp. 389–97; Stanley J. Olsen, 'Dogs' in *CWHF* 2000 vol. 1 pp. 508–17.

Dogfish, group of large sea fish related to the sharks. The dogfish are less dangerous to man and make slightly better eating than their sharp-toothed relatives. Several species are common in the Mediterranean, and they are prominent – perhaps more prominent than modern gourmets would have expected – in Greek gastronomic literature. These fish have a bad smell (as

noted by Mnesitheus) during the short period that they require to mature before cooking, but not afterwards.

The general terms in Greek for the dogfish are *galeos*, *skylion* and *kyon* – the latter means literally 'dog' and may cover the SHARK and SWORDFISH as well.

Archestratus *H* 46 Brandt; Aristotle *HA* 565a13–b17, *al.*; *Acraephia Price List*; Aelian, *Nature of Animals* 1.55; Oppian *H* 1.373–82 with Mair *ad l.*; Athenaeus *D* 294c–295b (confused) citing Aristotle fragment 310 Rose, also 357c citing Mnesitheus.

Thompson 1947 pp. 6, 12, 19, 39–42, 107, 175, 204, 221, 246; Davidson 1981 pp. 26–32.

- Greek *galeos alopekias*, literally 'foxy dogfish', or *alopex*, literally 'fox', or *kyon pion*, literally 'fat dog', and Latin *vulpes marina*, are names for the thresher shark (*Alopias vulpinus*). Perhaps surprisingly this species was said by Diphilus to resemble the terrestrial fox in the flavour of its meat. Archestratus, who in general does not rate the dogfish highly, recommends the thresher shark of Rhodes, and Lynceus is equally enthusiastic.

  Pliny *NH* 9.145; Athenaeus *D* 285e quoting Lynceus *F* 8, also 295a quoting Archestratus *H* 21 Brandt and Lynceus *F* 9, also 356c citing Diphilus of Siphnos.

- Greek *galeos asterias* is the huss (*Scyliorhinus stellaris*), one of the better dogfish from a gastronomic point of view.

  Athenaeus *D* 294c citing Hicesius, also 356c citing Diphilus of Siphnos.

- Greek *rine*, Latin *squatus*, *squatina*, is the monkfish or angel shark (*Squatina Squatina*). The monkfish is strange in shape but was correctly recognised by Aristotle as belonging to the dogfish group. Its skin was sufficiently rough to be used for polishing wood, hence the second meaning of *rine* 'file'. The monkfish was said to be best in the Gulf of Smyrna and around Miletus. As food it is easily digestible and light, according to Diphilus; Mnesitheus had said the same.

  Aristotle fragment 310 Rose; *Acraephia Price List*; Pliny *NH* 9.78, 32.150; Athenaeus *D* 319d–e quoting Archestratus *H* 46 Brandt and Dorion, also 356d citing Diphilus of Siphnos, also 357c citing Mnesitheus.

- Greek *galeos* (*leios*), well described by Aristotle, is the smoothhound (*Mustelus Muste-*

lus and M. Asterias). A cook in a play by Sotades explains how to proceed with this fish: 'A big galeos came next. I've baked the middle pieces; I'm boiling the rest of the stuff, with a mulberry sauce ready.' For a modern version of this recipe see Dalby and Grainger 1996 pp. 62–4.

Aristotle HA 565a13–b17; Sotades Comicus 1 Kassel (see extended translation at FISH).

- Other specific names, not individually noted as food sources in classical texts but no doubt eaten like the rest, are as follows. Greek galeos nebrias is perhaps the rough-hound (Scyliorhinus Canicula). Greek galeos poikilos may be the chien espagnol (Galeus melastomus). Greek (galeos) akanthias is the spur dog (Squalus Acanthias and S. Blainvillei). Greek kentrine, named after its spines, is probably Oxynotus Centrina.

Aristotle HA 565a13–b17 and fragment 310 Rose; Oppian H 1.373–82; Aelian, Nature of Animals 1.55.

Dolium (Greek pithos), a deep earthenware vat, often half-buried to ensure a more even temperature, for the fermenting and maturing of wine. Roman villas in wine-growing country – such as those near Pompeii – were equipped with large numbers of dolia. Dolium is also the name for the specially designed jars in which dormice were fattened.

Dolphin see AVOIDANCE OF FOODS

Dolphin-fish, large deep-sea fish. This is the fish illustrated on the 'fisherman fresco' from the Minoan town of AKROTIRI on Thera; the species was thus familiar to some inhabitants of the Aegean around the sixteenth century BC. Archestratus says that the best dolphin-fish is to be found at Carystus. Its meat was indigestible and not especially nourishing, according to Xenocrates. It was a seasonal fish, says Pliny, seldom caught in winter.

The dolphin-fish (Coryphaena Hippurus) is Greek hippouros, Latin hippurus.

Aristotle HA 543a20–4 with Thompson ad l.; Acraephia Price List; Ovid, Halieutica 95;

Xenocrates T 14; Pliny NH 9.57; Oppian, Halieutica 4.404–36; Athenaeus D 304c–d quoting Archestratus H 50 Brandt.

Thompson 1947 p. 94; Davidson 1981 pp. 106–7; Dalby and Grainger 1996 p. 63.

Domestication, the process of adapting an originally wild species to life under human supervision. Many such species are sources of food or drink. The process may be said to harness the mechanisms of natural selection: the selected mutations will be those which permit survival in a farmed environment and also maximise the product's usefulness to humans.

In general the farmed species used in the classical world had already been domesticated in prehistoric times. Domestication takes a long time, hundreds and perhaps thousands of years. In a sense it continues indefinitely, because breeders and farmers continue to select for yield, nutritional quality, flavour and other variables. The result may be many hundreds of varieties of any one species.

The place where each species was originally domesticated is often uncertain: it may sometimes happen in more than one place, as farmers independently select specimens from the wild and begin to breed them. Botanists have posited the past existence of centres of domestication where many now-domesticated plant species seem to originate. One major centre extended from the southern Caucasus to northern Syria and Iraq; Ethiopia was another. However, not all species fit this Procrustean bed.

Botanists and zoologists investigate the history of domestication using geographical knowledge of wild plants and animals ancestral to, or related to, the domesticated species; they now also use gene studies to trace ancestry and relationships. Archaeobotanists and archaeozoologists investigate the same history using finds of plant and animal remains (usually seeds and bones); these may match later domesticated varieties, or they may show a gradual development from wild to domesticated types.

V. Hehn, *Kulturpflanzen und Haustiere* (Berlin, 1911), expanded 8th edn by O. Schrader and others. Note English translation of 4th edn: *The Wanderings of Plants and Animals from Their First Home* (London, 1885), reprinted as: *Cultivated Plants and Domesticated Animals in Their Migration from Asia to Europe* ed. J.S. Stallybrass and J.P. Mallory (Amsterdam, 1976); N. Vavilov, *The Origin, Variation, Immunity and Breeding of Cultivated Plants* (Waltham, Mass., 1950); W.T. Stearn, 'The origin and later development of cultivated plants' in *Journal of the Royal Horticultural Society* vol. 90 (1965) pp. 279–341; *The Domestication and Exploitation of Plants and Animals* ed. P. Ucko and G.W. Dimbleby (London, 1969); *The Origin and Domestication of Cultivated Plants* ed. C. Barigozzi (Amsterdam, 1986); *Foraging and Farming: the evolution of plant exploitation* ed. D.R. Harris and G.C. Hillman (London, 1989); Zohary and Hopf 1993; H.P. Olmo, 'The origin and domestication of the vinifera grape' in *Origins and Ancient History of Wine* ed. Patrick E. McGovern, Stuart J. Fleming and Solomon H. Katz (London: Gordon and Breach, 1995) pp. 31–43.

Domitian, Roman emperor (ruled AD 81–96). Domitian was personally a sparing eater. His lavish public entertainments made him popular, though not popular enough to escape assassination. His Saturnalia feast in the Colosseum is described fulsomely by Statius; it must have been fun, though sticky. Similar public festivities are described more briefly by Suetonius and Dio Cassius. The latter also narrates at length the 'black dinner' once given by Domitian to selected terrified guests and often evoked in later literature. Almost as frequently mentioned is his sweeping decree that forbade further planting of vines in Italy and ordered the uprooting of those in the provinces, a hasty reaction to an over-productive vintage. This decree, according to Suetonius, was never implemented.

Statius, *Silvae* 1.6; Martial, *Spectacula*; Suetonius, *Domitian* 4, 7, 21; Dio Cassius 67.9.

Phyllis P. Bober, 'The black or Hell banquet' in *Oxford Symposium on Food and Cookery*

1990: feasting and fasting (London: Prospect Books, 1991) pp. 55–7; Brian W. Jones, *The Emperor Domitian* (London: Routledge, 1992); Dalby 2001.

Dorion, Greek author of a work *On Fish*, which would be unknown but for forty-five brief quotations in the *Deipnosophists* of Athenaeus. The work has been dated to the first century BC, although one of the speakers in Athenaeus's dialogue suggests that the only Dorion who had any real connection with the subject was a flute-player and fish-lover of Philip of Macedon's time.

Athenaeus D 337b–338b, cf. 435b.

M. Wellmann, 'Dorion' in *Hermes* vol. 22 (1888) pp. 179–93.

Dormouse, the smallest European mammal that was used as human food in classical times. Greek authors say little of it, but Romans considered it a delicacy. There is an unforgettable description in the *Satyricon* of an elaborate array of appetisers, featuring dormice, served at Trimalchio's fictional feast:

> On the trolley there was a Corinthian bronze donkey with panniers on its back, green olives in one, black in the other. Over the top of the donkey were two trays. Along the edge of them it said 'Property of Trimalchio' and '*x* pounds silver'. These two dishes were joined together by little bridges soldered on, carrying a row of dormice glazed in honey and rolled in poppy seeds.

Avery (below) observes that the poppy seeds in this recipe, being at least symbolically narcotic, are especially suitable to a hibernatory animal.

Varro describes the making of a *glirarium* or dormouse warren. When they were to be fattened for the table, dormice were kept indoors in a specially designed jar (*dolium*), which was filled with their favourite acorns, walnuts and chestnuts, and then closed; they fed continually when left in the dark.

The edible dormouse (*Glis Glis*) is Greek *eleios*, Latin *glis*.

Aristotle *HA* 600b13; Varro *RR* 3.15; Petronius *S* 31; Pliny *NH* 8.223–5; Martial 3.58, 13.59; *Diocletian's Price Edict* 4.38; Ammianus Marcellinus 28.4.13.

William T. Avery, 'More Petroniana' in *Hermes* vol. 107 (1979) pp. 118–21; Toynbee 1996.

Doum palm, a tree of upper Egypt whose large sweet fruits were eaten locally – and offered to the Egyptian gods – but were unknown elsewhere in the ancient world. Its fibres were used in matting, as Strabo says and as archaeologists confirm.

The fruit of the doum palm (*Hyphaene thebaica*) is Greek *kouki*, Latin *cuci*.

Theophrastus *HP* 4.2.7; Strabo 17.2.5 (read *koukina*); Pliny *NH* 13.62.

Darby and others 1977 pp. 730–3; Brewer and others (1995 ?) p. 50.

Dove *see* PIGEON

Drinking parties *see* SYMPOSION (1); MEALS

Drunkenness, intoxication caused by alcohol. The symptoms are, in some societies and in some circumstances, desired, shortly before the after-effects are regretted. Historians, a sober bunch, do not always distinguish as clearly as they might between evidence of habitual drunkenness and evidence of alcoholism (see also ALCOHOLIC DRINKS).

In classical Greece the SYMPOSION (1) was a socially approved ambience for drunkenness. It took place in the late evening, after the main meal of the day. Wine was mixed with water (which moderated its effect) in the communal *krater* or mixing-bowl. Thus the ruling mixture was decided for all and all were expected to drink equally, in spite of the recognition that people differ in their response to alcohol: Aristotle, for example, explores why old men get drunk more easily and

women get drunk more slowly. One could, of course, go home (see quotation); for those who did not, the *symposion* might continue all night or might end in a KOMOS, in which abandoned behaviour associated with drunkenness was *de rigueur*. The progressive effects of wine are summarised by the god Dionysus in a lost play by Eubulus, quoted by Athenaeus:

> I mix just three *krateres* for right-thinking people. One, which they drink first, is for health. The second is for love and pleasure. The third is for sleep, and when they have drunk it those who are called wise go home. The fourth is not mine any more: it is for insult, and the fifth for yelling, and the sixth for the *komos*, and the seventh for black eyes, and the eighth for the guardsman, and the ninth for vomiting, and the tenth for madness ...

Aristotle gives careful and detailed observations of drunkenness and its effects. The *symposion* was not a Greek invention: similar gatherings, equally associated with communal drunkenness, took place in early Egypt, Palestine, Phoenicia and Mesopotamia.

The classical *symposion* was less in evidence in Hellenistic and Roman cultures; these, however, adopted from Macedonians and other northerners the custom of drinking wine stronger, with little admixture of water. Examples of communal drunkenness are less frequent in sources for these later periods, but individual heavy drinkers are common enough. By contrast with classical Greece, excessive drinking now becomes a trait for which individuals (particularly monarchs and rich men, but not only those: see Pliny) are criticised: it becomes an example of EXCESS. From this period, chronic drunkenness is described convincingly enough by Lucretius, Plutarch and Seneca. Plutarch, in particular, observes that regular heavy drinkers appear to be in better control of themselves than those who are just tipsy.

Aristotle, *Problems* 871a1–878a27, 953a32–953b25; Lucretius 3.476–83; Seneca, *Letters* 83.11–26; Pliny *NH* 14.137–49; Plutarch *QC* 1.7, also 3.3 citing Aristotle *S* 108 Rose, also 3.8, also *Precepts on Health* 127f; Athenaeus *E* 36a–38f quoting Eubulus and others.

J.D. Rolleston, 'Alcoholism in classical antiquity' in *British Journal of Inebriety* vol. 24 (1927) pp. 101–20; A. McKinlay, 'Ancient experience with intoxicating drinks: non-Attic Greek states' in *Quarterly Journal of Studies on Alcohol* vol. 10 (1949) pp. 289–315; A. McKinlay, 'Attic temperance' in *Quarterly Journal of Studies on Alcohol* vol. 12 (1951) pp. 61–102; E.M. Jellinek, 'Drinkers and alcoholics in ancient Rome' in *Journal of Studies on Alcohol* vol. 37 (1976) pp. 1718–41; N. el-Guebaly and A. el-Guebaly, 'Alcohol abuse in ancient Egypt: the recorded evidence' in *International Journal of the Addictions* vol. 16 (1981) pp. 1207–21; P. Villard, 'Pathologie et thérapeutique de l'ivresse dans l'antiquité classique' in *Cahiers de nutrition et diététique* vol. 19 (1984) pp. 225–7; J.C. Sournia, 'L'alcoolisme dans la Grèce antique' in *Archéologie et médecine: septièmes rencontres internationales d'archéologie et d'histoire d'Antibes* (Juan-les-Pins, 1987) pp. 523–30; M.B. Lancon, 'Vinolentia: l'ivrognerie en Gaule à la fin de l'antiquité d'après les sources littéraires' in *Archéologie de la vigne et du vin* (Paris, 1990) (*Caesarodunum* no. 24) pp. 155–61; John H. D'Arms, 'Heavy drinking and drunkenness in the Roman world: four questions for historians' in *In Vino Veritas* ed. Oswyn Murray and Manuela Tecuşan (London: British School at Rome, 1995) pp. 304–17; *OCD* 1996 *s.v.* Alcoholism.

Duck, group of aquatic birds. Several species are caught from the wild and are good to eat. The wild mallard was already eaten in Neolithic Greece; in the classical period it was one of the game birds exported from Boeotia to Athens, to judge from a list in Aristophanes's *Acharnians*. Herodotus says that ducks were eaten raw-salted in Egypt, and this is confirmed by Egyptian wall paintings.

Greek sources of the classical and Hellenistic periods say nothing of domesticated ducks. The mallard, a particularly good source of meat, was perhaps first domesticated in Italy in late republican times; Varro and Columella give the apparently Greek name *nessotrophion* to a duck enclosure, but there is no other evidence that the development took place in a Greek-speaking region. Columella supplies plenty of information about the business, observing that full-grown ducks taken from the wild are slow to begin to lay. He remarks on a point already hinted at by Cicero, that duck chicks reared by barnyard hens are the best adapted to captivity.

In late Roman and Byzantine sources duck is listed among the most nourishing of foods.

The mallard (*Anas Platyrhynchos*) is Greek *nessa*, *netta*, Latin *anas*.

Herodotus 2.77; Aristophanes, *Acharnians* 875; Hippocrates *R* 47; Hippolochus *D*; Cicero, *On the Nature of the Gods* 2.124; Varro *RR* 3.5.14, 3.11; Columella *DA* 8.15; Plutarch, *Life of Cato the Elder* 23; Galen, *On Compounding* 13.174; Longus 2.12; Athenaeus *D* 395c–f; Oribasius *CM* 6.38.16; *Apicius* 6.2.1–6; *Geoponica* 14.23 citing Didymus.

Thompson 1936 p. 205; Buck 1949 p. 178; Darby and others 1977 p. 282; Toynbee 1996; Rosemary Luff, 'Ducks' in *CWHF* 2000 vol. 1 pp. 517–24.

- Greek *kerkeris*, Latin *querquedula* is the teal (*Anas Crecca*), classed by Columella among ducks that can be kept in captivity. Greek *boskas*, Latin *boscis* is a similar species, if not the same; the male is brightly coloured, says Athenaeus.

Aristotle *HA* 593b17; *Zenon Papyri* 186.10; Varro *RR* 3.3.3, 3.11.4, *On the Latin Language* 5.79; Columella *DA* 8.15.1; Athenaeus *D* 395d citing Alexander of Myndus; Macrobius *S* 3.13.12 quoting Metellus Pius.

E

Economics, an aspect of the anthropological study of human societies. General theories of economics can be applied in observing any community. However, past societies cannot really be observed (see also ANTHROPOLOGY): problems therefore arise through lack of evidence (and particularly of statistical and financial evidence). These problems have to be alleviated by the use of comparative material from better-known societies and by bold extrapolation from the meagre and partial evidence that does exist.

The best evidence of the economic aims of ancient producing households (those of farmers in particular) comes from a sequence of Latin FARMING manuals: their authors assume that farmers will aim at self-sufficiency, and in addition at producing a marketable surplus in one or more crops. If this impression is true, specialisation in profitable lines, though it existed, was limited by the need to produce also sufficient essential foods for the household. Such households were often far larger than the name implies, since they included the slave labour force which worked the land.

Ancient consuming households, on the impressionistic basis of similar source materials, appear to have aimed to store sufficient essential foods to weather seasonal shortages. Wheat, barley, salt meat, salt fish, olive oil and wine all lend themselves to long-term storage, and the manuals already cited give instructions for CONSERVING many other foods. It is equally true that the inhabitants of large cities such as Rome came to depend on regular distribution of foods organised by their government, and were surely far less provident than large country households and than the notional ideal.

The role of TRADE in the food supply was therefore smaller, proportionally, than it is in typical modern developed societies. The role of money was smaller still, since gifts, exchange and payment in kind were common. Ancient governments involved themselves directly in food distribution in case of famine; some, as said above, made regular distributions. Although the place of money in the food economy was relatively small, the place of taxation was potentially larger, since taxation in kind, in various forms, was common.

R.P. Duncan-Jones, *The Economy of the Roman Empire: quantitative studies* (Cambridge, 1982), 2nd edn; *Trade in the Ancient Economy* ed. Peter Garnsey, K. Hopkins and C.R. Whittaker (London, 1983); A. Carandini, 'Columella's vineyard and the rationality of the Roman economy' in *Opus* vol. 2 (1983) pp. 177–204; P. Veyne, 'Mythe et réalité de l'autarcie à Rome' in *Revue des études anciennes* vol. 81 (1979) pp. 261–80; Garnsey 1999 pp. 22–33.

Eel, European river fish that breeds in the Atlantic. The eel was one of the most sought-after of ancient delicacies. Why it is described as one of the 'most deadly' of foods, in a view cited in the Hippocratic text *Sacred Disease*, is unknown.

Eel was good at Rhegium, says Archestratus, but also – and here other ancient sources agree with him – from Lake Copais in BOEOTIA and from the River Strymon in MACEDONIA: according to Aristotle, the eel-fishing there took place at the rising of the Pleiades, when the water was troubled and muddy. From Copais eels came in large baskets, *spyrides*, to the Athenian market. The question of how there could be eels in the landlocked Lake Copais, since all eels migrate between sea and fresh water, has puzzled modern researchers: Wilkins (with references) explains that eels must have reached Lake Copais, and departed from it to breed, by way of the underground River Cephissus.

Eels were not farmed. The job of *enkhelyotrophoi* 'eel-keepers' in Aristotle's time, as more recently, was to transfer the eels from river or lake to tanks, thus eventually transporting them to market over considerable distances and keeping them healthy meanwhile. They must be sold absolutely fresh if not already cooked or cured. Eel could be fine and nourishing food, Galen advises, but you must find out where it was caught and test it for freshness by look and smell.

Eel could be cooked in beet leaves (see Aristophanes and Athenaeus) or chopped and grilled on a skewer (see Anthimus).

The eel (*Anguilla Anguilla*) is Greek *enkhelys*, Latin *anguilla*.

Aristophanes, *Acharnians* 880–900, *Peace* 1005–14; Hippocrates, *Sacred Disease* 2; Aristotle HA 591b30–592a27; Juvenal 5.103; Pausanias 9.24.2; Galen BM 6.796; Athenaeus D 297c–300d quoting Archestratus H 8 (see Olson and Sens *ad l.*); Anthimus OC 43 with Grant *ad l.*

Thompson 1947 p. 58 (his belief that eels were kept in tanks through the winter is unsupported); Davidson 1981 pp. 50–2; C. Moriarty, *Eels* (New York, 1978); Wilkins 2000 pp. 37–9 and notes 145 and 151.

Egg (Greek *oon*; Latin *ovum*), nourishing food, available in large quantities if barnyard hens are kept (see CHICKEN); the eggs of other birds are somewhat more of a luxury. Hens do not require much space

and it is possible even for some city-dwellers to produce their own eggs. Eggs were also sold: *Diocletian's Price Edict* reckons them at one denarius each, a high price.

Eggs might be eaten very soft-boiled (Greek *oa trometa*, Latin *ova hapala*), removed from their shells and accompanied by *garum* or a pine-kernel sauce: *Apicius* supplies recipes, and Anthimus sensibly emphasises that though the yolk may still be runny it must be properly cooked. Yet Greek *oa ropheta*, Latin *ova sorbilia*, literally 'eggs to be drunk', often prescribed to invalids in the long period between the Hippocratic *Epidemics* and the manual of Anthimus, must be essentially raw eggs made into egg nog or the like. Among other cooking methods we know of Greek *oa ekzesta*, hard-boiled eggs; *oa pnikta*, poached eggs, described by Galen (Grant 1999 p. 100 suggests a modern recipe); and *oa tagenista*, fried eggs. Latin *ova pilleata*, mentioned by Petronius, seems to be a way of presenting soft-boiled eggs, wearing a *pilleus* or cap of liberty.

Eggs are frequently listed among aphrodisiacs (Alexis F 281 Kassel with Austin *ad l.*; Heracleides of Tarentum [Athenaeus E 64a]; Ovid, *Art of Love* 2.423; Alciphron 4.13) and are named by Pliny as an ingredient in an aphrodisiac potion.

Hippocrates R 50, *Epidemics* 7.1.2; Nicomachus Comicus 3 Kassel; Petronius S 65–6; Pliny NH 29.48; Martial 13.40; Galen AF 6.705–9; Athenaeus E 57d–58b; *Diocletian's Price Edict* 6.43; *Apicius* 7.17.1–3 with Flower *ad l.*; Anthimus OC 34–8, 40 with Grant *ad l.*; Alexander of Tralles, *Medicine* 2.7.12; Paul of Aegina, *Medicine* 1.83.

- Latin *spumeum*, Greek *aphraton* was a kind of soufflé, made with chicken or fish or scallops. Anthimus gives instructions, for which Grant (1999 pp. 133–4) offers a modern interpretation.

  Isidore, *Etymologies* 20.2.29; Alexander of Tralles, *On Fevers* 3; Anthimus OC 34.

- Goose and barnyard hen eggs are the most commonly mentioned in ancient sources. There was disagreement among dietary writers as to which species produced the best eggs for human nutrition. Galen says barnyard hen and pheasant, and counts goose and ostrich eggs as the worst. EPAENETUS and Heracleides of Syracuse put peahen eggs at the top of their lists, followed by those of the *khenalopex* (see under GOOSE) and barnyard hen. Anthimus recommends hens', goose and pheasant eggs. Although mallards had been domesticated by the first century BC, duck eggs are not mentioned as food by any ancient source.

Epicharmus 152 Kaibel; Galen *AF* 6.706; Athenaeus *E* 58a citing Epaenetus and Heracleides of Tarentum; Anthimus *OC* 37–8.

Egypt, home of a very ancient civilisation along the lower Nile valley. The food of Pharaonic Egypt (from the later fourth millennium BC to the fourth century BC) is particularly well known, not only from Egyptian texts, but also from the fact that foods were customarily buried with the dead, and foods so buried have sometimes survived in remarkable condition owing to the arid Egyptian climate. For full surveys of Egyptian foods see the works by Darby and others and by Brewer and others. On two especially complete and interesting burial finds see the work by Emery below and the references given at TUTANKHAMUN. The menu of the funeral meal found by Emery at Saqqara in a lady's tomb dated around 3000 BC is: ground barley porridge; a whole cooked quail, the head tucked under the wing; two cooked kidneys; a pigeon stew; a cooked fish with the head removed; ribs of beef; small triangular loaves of emmer bread; small circular cakes; stewed fruit, possibly figs.

Having been an independent kingdom for many centuries, Egypt became part of the Persian Empire under Cambyses. Alexander's conquest of the Persian Empire led to the foundation of ALEXANDRIA and to the establishment of Greek as the ruling language of Egypt. which was ruled by a Greek-speaking dynasty, from Ptolemy I to Cleopatra VII, from 305 to 30 BC. From this period the *Revenue Laws* of Ptolemy II Philadelphus, 259 BC (see Grenfell and Bingen below) list products of sufficient value to be taxed, including five oils (sesame oil, castor oil, safflower oil, colocynth oil and linseed oil). Egypt was thereafter a part of the Roman Empire, with the special status of a personal possession of the emperor, who benefited from the 25 per cent taxation of imports of spices and aromatics from Arabia and India as they passed across Egyptian territory.

The special food habits of Egypt are described at some length by Herodotus, who visited the country in the mid fifth century BC while it was under Persian rule. Many authors observe the importance of fish in the Egyptian diet, and the Egyptian use of BEER alongside wine. The wealth of Ptolemaic Egypt was displayed in lavish ceremonial and luxurious banquets: among the latter Athenaeus describes at length, citing the historian Socrates of Rhodes, the entertainments arranged by Cleopatra for her Roman lover Marcus Antonius. Athenaeus himself, a native of the old Greek trading post of Naucratis, speaks with authority on the foods and dining customs of Egypt around AD 200.

Egypt was remarkable to Greeks and Romans for the food rules and avoidances which were an especially noticeable feature of its everyday life (see also AVOIDANCE OF FOODS). Many Egyptian towns had their own special food taboo, usually connected with a feature of divine worship, often irrelevant elsewhere in Egypt, but sometimes the source of dispute with rival towns. Darby and others (1977 pp. 380–94) deal in particular detail with local rules concerning fish. Several ancient authors describe (with varying and contradictory detail) the special food rules followed by Egyptian priests. They were said to abstain from salt during periods of ritual purity, or to avoid sea salt and to use only rock salt (Plutarch *QC* 5.10, 8.8, *On Isis and Osiris* 352f).

Herodotus already mentions some of the unique animals and plants of Egypt. Many more details of these are given in due course by Diodorus Siculus and Strabo. See also entries for NILE FISH; ARGUN PALM; CASTOR OIL; CHUFA; DOUM PALM; LOTUS (1); LOTUS (2); MOLOKHIA; PAPYRUS; PERSEA; SEBESTEN; SORGHUM; SYCAMORE FIG; TARO.

Herodotus 2.77–8, 2.93; Diodorus Siculus 1.10, 1.34; Strabo 17.1.16–17, 17.2.4; Plutarch, *On Isis and Osiris* 352e–354b; Galen *AF* 6.669; Athenaeus *D* 147e–148c quoting Socrates of Rhodes, also 149d–150d, also 196a–206d, also 549d–550b; Clement of Alexandria, *Protrepticus* 2.39; Heliodorus, *Ethiopian Story* 1.5, 2.22–3, 3.11; Porphyry *DA* 4.6–4.8.

M.A. Ruffer, 'Food in Egypt' in *Mémoires présentés à l'Institut Égyptien* vol. 1 (1919) pp. 1–88; Walter Wreszinski, *Löwenjagd im alten Agypten* (Leipzig, 1932) (*Morgenland*, 23); Allan Chester Johnson in Frank 1933–40 vol. 2; *The Revenue Laws of Ptolemy Philadelphus* edited from a Greek papyrus in the Bodleian Library by B.P. Grenfell; re-edited by J. Bingen (Oxford: Oxford University Press, 1952); Hildegard von Deines and Hermann Grapow, *Wörterbuch der ägyptischen Drogennamen* (Berlin: Akademie-Verlag, 1959) (*Grundriss der Medizin der alten Aegypter*, 6); W.B. Emery, *A Funerary Repast in an Egyptian Tomb of the Archaic Period* (Leiden, 1962); D.J. Crawford, 'The opium poppy: a study in Ptolemaic agriculture' in *Problèmes de la terre en Grèce ancienne* ed. M.I. Finley (The Hague, 1973) pp. 223–51; D.J. Crawford, 'Garlic-growing and agricultural specialization in Graeco-Roman Egypt' in *Chronique d'Égypte*

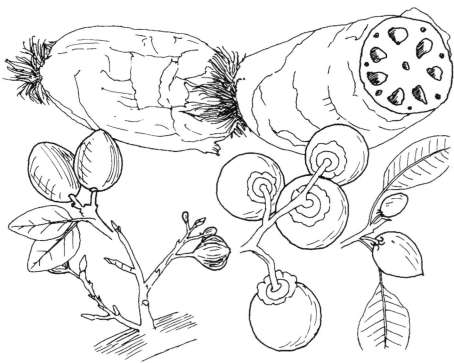

Figure 4 Useful plants of Ancient Egypt. Top: sections of root of the pink lotus or Egyptian bean (*Nelumbo nucifera*), Greek *kyamos ho Aigyptios*, Latin *faba Aegyptia*. Bottom, left to right: Egyptian balsam (*Balanites aegyptiaca*), the source of zachum oil, Greek and Latin *balanites*. Sycamore fig (*Ficus Sycomorus*), Greek *sykomoron*, Latin *sycomorum*. Sebesten or gunda (*Cordia Myxa*), Latin *myxa*. Persea (*Mimusops Schimperi*), Greek and Latin *persea*.

vol. 48 no. 2 (1973) pp. 350–63; *LA* 1975–92; Darby and others 1977; Angela Steimeyer-Schareika, *Das Nilmosaik von Palestrina und eine ptolemäische Expedition nach Athiopien* (Bonn, 1978); D.J. Crawford, 'Food: tradition and change in Hellenistic Egypt' in *World Archaeology* vol. 11 no. 2 (1979) pp. 136–46; N. el-Guebaly and A. el-Guebaly, 'Alcohol abuse in ancient Egypt: the recorded evidence' in *International Journal of the Addictions* vol. 16 (1981) pp. 1207–21; Gérard Charpentier, *Recueil de matériaux épigraphiques relatifs à la botanique de l'Egypte antique* (Paris: Trismégiste, 1982); D. Rathbone, 'Italian wines in Roman Egypt' in *Opus* vol. 2 no. 1 (1983) pp. 81–98; J. Boessneck, *Die Tierwelt des alten Ägypten* (Munich: C.H. Beck, 1988); D.J. Brewer and R.F. Friedman, *Fish and Fishing in Ancient Egypt* (Warminster: Aris, 1989); Lise Manniche, *An Ancient Egyptian Herbal* (London: British Museum Press, 1989); F. Nigel Hepper, *Pharaoh's Flowers* (London, 1990); Dimitri Meeks, 'La production de l'huile et du vin dans l'Egypte pharaonique' in *La Production du vin et de l'huile en Méditerranée* ed. M.-C. Amouretti and J.-P. Brun (Athens: Ecole Française d'Athènes, 1993) pp. 3–38; Dimitri Meeks, 'Migration des plantes, migration des mots dans l'Egypte antique' in *Des hommes et des plantes: plantes méditerranéennes, vocabulaire et usages anciennes* ed. M.-Cl. Amouretti and G. Comet (Aix-en-Provence, 1993) pp. 71–92; D. Thompson, 'Food for Ptolemaic temple workers' in *Food in Antiquity* ed. John Wilkins and others (Exeter: Exeter University Press, 1995) pp. 316–25; Salima Ikram, *Choice Cuts: meat production in ancient Egypt* (Leuven: Peeters, 1995) (*Orientalia Lovaniensia analecta*, 69); Mu-Chou Poo, *Wine and Wine Offering in the Religion of Ancient Egypt* (London: Kegan Paul International, 1995); Brewer and others (1995 ?); T.G.H. James, 'The earliest history of wine and its importance in ancient Egypt' in *The Origins and Ancient History of Wine* ed. Patrick E. McGovern, Stuart J. Fleming and Solomon H. Katz (London: Gordon and Breach, 1995) pp. 197–213; Delwen Samuel, 'Approaches to the archaeology of food' in *Petits propos culinaires* no. 54 (1996) pp. 12–21; *Ancient Egyptian Materials and Technology* ed. P.T. Nicholson and I. Shaw (Cambridge: Cambridge University Press, 2000); E. Panagiotakopulu, 'New records for ancient pests: archaeoentomology in Egypt' in *Journal of Archaeological Science* vol. 28 (2001) pp. 1235–46.

Egyptian bean *see* LOTUS (1)

Egyptian wines, product of a long tradition. Wine was certainly familiar in Egypt from the first dynasty onwards (thus from around 3000 BC). In Pharaonic Egypt, as in classical Greece, wine was the central feature of parties at which music and dancing entertained the participants and from which some had to be helped home. Wine was also important in medicine.

In TUTANKHAMUN's tomb several named and dated wines, laid down in 1327 BC, provide evidence of a tradition of vintages and wine districts, a tradition that had even then been in existence for a thousand years (similar offerings are recorded in honour of King Unas, *c.*2423 BC) and was thus more than two thousand years older than that of Italy.

Wines named in ancient Egyptian texts are listed and studied by Darby and others and by Lesko. The list below is confined to wine districts named in Greek and Latin sources. All, as it happens, are from lower Egypt; Athenaeus, alone among literary authors, mentions the wine of the Thebais in upper Egypt, singling out that of the city of Coptos.

Herodotus 2.60; Strabo 17.1.14; Martial 13.122; Athenaeus E 33d–f.

L.H. Lesko, *King Tut's Wine Cellar* (Berkeley, 1977); Darby and others 1977 pp. 551–618; Jean-Yves Empereur, 'La production viticole dans l'Egypte ptolémaique et romaine' in *La Production du vin et de l'huile en Méditerranée* ed. M.-C. Amouretti and J.-P. Brun (Athens: Ecole Française d'Athènes, 1993) pp. 39–47; Dimitri Meeks, 'La production de l'huile et du vin dans l'Egypte pharaonique' in *La Production du vin et de l'huile en Méditerranée* ed. M.-C. Amouretti and J.-P. Brun (Athens: Ecole Française d'Athènes, 1993) pp. 3–38; Jeremy Black, 'Egypt' in *The Oxford Companion to Wine* ed. Jancis Robinson (Oxford: Oxford University Press, 1994) pp. 355–7; Mu-Chou Poo, *Wine and Wine Offering in the Religion of Ancient Egypt* (London: Kegan Paul International, 1995); T.G.H. James, 'The earliest history of wine and its importance in ancient Egypt' in *The Origins and Ancient History of Wine* ed. Patrick E. McGovern, Stuart J. Fleming and Solomon H. Katz (London: Gordon and Breach, 1995) pp. 197–213; Leonard H. Lesko, 'Egyptian wine production during the New Kingdom' in *The Origins and Ancient*

History of Wine ed. Patrick E. McGovern, Stuart J. Fleming and Solomon H. Katz (London: Gordon and Breach, 1995) pp. 215–30.

- Mareotic wine (Greek *Mareotes, Mareotikos*; Latin *Mareoticum*) came from Mareia in lower Egypt. Strabo says that it was aged; Horace imagines Cleopatra over-indulging in it. Athenaeus describes it as white and lists its dietary qualities. The *mareotica* vine (see GRAPE VARIETIES) may be supposed to have originated here.

  Strabo 17.1.14; Horace, *Odes* 1.37; Athenaeus *E* 33d; *Fayum Papyri* 134.6; *Rylands Papyri* 227.26.

- Saite wine (Greek *Saites, Saeites*; Latin *Saitum*), from the territory of Sais, was one of the seven named wines of the Empire allowed a special high price in *Diocletian's Price Edict*.

  Diocletian's Price Edict 2.5 [*s.v.l.*].

- Sebennytic wine (Latin *Sebennyticum*), from Sebennytus, was made from the three grapes locally counted as most 'noble', *thasia, aethala, peuce*.

  Pliny *NH* 14.74.

- Taeniotic wine (Greek *Tainiotikos*) was lightly yellow, 'oily', aromatic, slightly astringent. The *tainia* or ribbon from which it came is supposed by Darby and others (1977 p. 601) to be the sandy cultivated strip on either side of the black earth of the Nile Delta; it might, however, be the *tainia* described by Strabo, along the Mediterranean coast between Alexandria and Canobus.

  Strabo 17.1.16; Athenaeus *E* 33e.

Einkorn, one of the two most primitive kinds of cultivated wheat. Einkorn grows wild from western Anatolia to southwestern Iran; it was collected for human food in Syria before 12,000 BC, and was cultivated by 8000 BC (early evidence comes from Jericho in Palestine). In the early Neolithic period einkorn spread rapidly eastwards – reaching Baluchistan by 6000 BC – and westwards to Greece and southeastern Europe. Einkorn was not grown in Egypt (where the traditional wheat crop was EMMER) and was unimportant in the western Mediterranean. Although it is named in classical Greek

sources einkorn was rapidly declining in importance by the classical period, supplanted first by emmer, later by durum WHEAT and bread wheat.

Einkorn (*Triticum monococcum*) is Greek *tiphe*. Greek *zeiai* is sometimes used as a general term for the two hulled wheats, einkorn and emmer.

Hippocrates *R* 43; Theophrastus *HP* 8.4.1; Dioscorides *MM* 2.89; Pliny *NH* 18.81, 18.93; Galen *AF* 6.510–23 *passim*; Athenaeus *D* 115f citing Mnesitheus.

B. Gunda, 'Cultural ecology of old cultivated plants in the Carpathian area' in *Ethnologia Europaea* vol. 13 no. 2 (1983) pp. 146–79; Zohary and Hopf 1993 pp. 32–8.

Elagabalus or Heliogabalus, Roman emperor (ruled 218–22), previously a Syrian priest. Elagabalus was noted for his unabashed pursuit of luxury. This included gastronomic extravances which are listed in loving detail (but with uncertain reliability) in his biography in the *Historia Augusta*. A recurrent feature is his experimentation with the colours of foods.

Historia Augusta, Heliogabalus 19–33 *passim*.

E. Alföldi-Rosenbaum, '*Apicius de re coquinaria* and the *Vita Heliogabali*' and 'Notes on some birds and fishes of luxury in the *Historia Augusta*' in *Bonner Historia-Augusta-Colloquium 1970* ed. J. Straub (Bonn, 1972) pp. 5–18.

Elderberry, wild fruit of 'wine-like' but unexciting flavour. Elderberry was gathered from the wild in prehistoric and classical Europe, and was sometimes planted for its fruit, its aromatic flowers and its leaves, which were used in medicine.

Elderberry (*Sambucus nigra*) is Greek *akte*, Latin *sambucum*.

Dioscorides *MM* 4.173; Galen *SF* 11.820.

Zohary and Hopf 1993 pp. 200–1.

- Greek *khamaiakte*, Latin *ebulum* are names for danewort (*Sambucus Ebulus*), a related wild fruit already gathered for food in prehistoric southern Europe.

Dioscorides *MM* 4.173.2; Galen *SF* 11.820; Pseudo-Apuleius, *Herbarius* 92.

Elecampane, a medicinal herb said to have sprung from the tears of Helen. If correctly identified in all the references below (which is uncertain), elecampane root was a medicine for women, particularly a tonic and a means of enhancing beauty and sex-appeal. Bitter in taste, it was eaten in combination with honey, grape syrup, raisins or some other sweet flavour, and was said to have been taken daily as a food supplement, with pepper or thyme, by Augustus's daughter Julia. The leaf is occasionally mentioned as a potherb.

Elecampane (*Inula Helenium*) is Greek *helenion*, Latin *inula*, *inula Campana* or *helenium*.

Hippocrates, *Nature of Woman* 32; Chaeremon 71 F 14 Snell; *Moretum* 72; Dioscorides *MM* 1.28–9; Pliny *NH* 14.108, 15.30, 19.91–2, 20.38, 21.59, 21.159; Palladius *OA* 3.24.13; Pseudo-Apuleius, *Herbarius* 96.

Sarah Currie, 'Poisonous women and unnatural history in Roman culture' in *Parchments of Gender: deciphering the bodies of antiquity* ed. Maria Wyke (Oxford: Clarendon Press, 1998) pp. 147–67; Davidson 1999 p. 272.

Emmer, one of the two early cultivated forms of wheat (see also EINKORN). Emmer is a hulled wheat, requiring to be parched before threshing to release the grain.

Wild emmer is now found in Palestine, Syria and Iraq. Emmer was being cultivated at Jericho by *c*.9000 BC and had spread in cultivation as far east as Baluchistan by 6000 BC: it was a significant crop in the Indus Valley (Harappan) culture before 2000. Looking westwards, emmer was a major crop in the later Neolithic period and the Bronze Age throughout the Mediterranean. For a long time it rivalled barley for the position of the major cereal staple (hence Homer's traditional formula for earth, *zeidoros aroura* 'the emmer-producing field'); it

was more nourishing, but in Mediterranean climates it was a less reliable crop. Just as Greeks sprinkled sacrifices with *alphita* (barley meal) and salt, so Romans offered *mola salsa*, salted emmer groats, to their gods, and the gods (says Pliny) liked it better than all the aromatics offered by the rich. In the classical period durum wheat and bread wheat (see WHEAT) steadily supplanted emmer in popularity; both had the advantage of being naked or free-threshing wheats and bread wheat was particularly attractive because it could be used to make raised bread.

Emmer (*Triticum turgidum* subsp. *dicoccum*) is *olyra* and *zeia* (sometimes *zeia dikokkos*) in Greek, *adoreum*, *semen* and *far* in Latin. These and other words are used in some sources to distinguish among varieties of emmer; the vocabulary of emmer in Sumerian, Akkadian and Egyptian is equally rich. Greek *zeiai*, *zea* often means 'hulled wheat' in general, including both einkorn and emmer. In English translations of classical texts 'spelt' is often written instead of emmer; the obsolete English term 'rice-wheat' may also be encountered. These terms are confusing and best avoided.

Homer, *Iliad* 8.486; Hippocrates *R* 43; Theophrastus *HP* 8.9.2; Strabo 15.1.18; Dioscorides *MM* 2.89; Pliny *NH* 12.83, 18.81–4; Galen *AF* 6.510–23.

B. Gunda, 'Cultural ecology of old cultivated plants in the Carpathian area' in *Ethnologia Europaea* vol. 13 no. 2 (1983) pp. 146–79; Zohary and Hopf 1993 pp. 39–47; Brewer and others 1995 pp. 23–8; T. Braun, 'Barley cakes and emmer bread' in *Food in Antiquity* ed. John Wilkins and others (Exeter: Exeter University Press, 1995) pp. 25–37; M.A. Murray, 'Cereal production and processing' in *Ancient Egyptian Materials and Technology* ed. P.T. Nicholson and I. Shaw (Cambridge: Cambridge University Press, 2000) pp. 505–36; David Downie, *Cooking the Roman Way* (New York: Harper Collins, 2002) p. 10.

- Greek *khidra* is a name for unripe emmer. At this stage the seeds could be rubbed in the hand to extract them from the ear, and then roasted or boiled. *Polphoi* was perhaps (the definitions are inadequate) a thick porridge made from *khidra* and other grains.

Alcman 96 Davies; *Leviticus* 2.14–16; Aristophanes, *Knights* 806 with scholia, *Peace* 595 with scholia; Nicander F 68 [Athenaeus D 126b]; Pollux O 6.61–2; Hesychius, *Lexicon s.v. polphoi*; *Suda s.v. khidra*.

• As the first stage in its use emmer normally had to be pounded in a mortar shaped like a hollow cylinder, with a heavy wooden pestle made from part of a tree trunk. This backbreaking task was given, says Pliny, to convicts as hard labour. The emmer-mortar is in Greek *holmos*, in Latin *fistula farraria*.

Hesiod OD 423 with West *ad l.*; Cato DA 10.3 with Dalby *ad l.*; Pliny NH 18.112.

• Greek *khondros* (this word is occasionally used of barley meal) and *alix*, Latin *alica*, Aramaic *chaliqa*, is emmer meal (which had various uses) and a smooth porridge or pudding made from this, evidently light enough to be served among desserts in classical Greek dinners. In Roman Italy the best kind, made in Campania, was whitened with chalk from *collis Leucogea* between Puteoli and Naples. A recipe for the porridge is given by Pliny. PULS was an earthier or more traditional porridge based on *alica*.

Ephippus 8, 13 Kassel; Chrysippus of Tyana [Athenaeus D 647d]; Dioscorides MM 2.96; Pliny NH 18.112–16, cf. 22.128–9; Galen, *Commentary on Hippocrates RA* 15.455; Athenaeus D 126f–127c; *Diocletian's Price Edict* 1.25.

• Greek *tragos*, *traganos* (modern Greek *trakhanas*), Aramaic *tragos* is the name for a most useful food. Cracked emmer was boiled with milk and dried in the form of lumps. These could be conveniently stored and carried, and, when wanted, boiled again to make a porridge. Pliny describes it as resembling *alica* (see above) but whitened with milk instead of chalk. The *Geoponica* gives a recipe. In the fourth century BC Diocles had described a travellers' drink consisting of *alphita*, barley meal, with water and a moderate amount of salt: he does not call it *tragos*, but this is certainly a predecessor or variant of *tragos*.

Diocles of Carystus RV; Dioscorides MM 2.93; Pliny NH 18.76, 18.116 (*tragum*); Galen AF 6.517, 6.520, BM 6.761; *Geoponica* 3.8.

S. Hill and A. Bryer, 'Byzantine porridge: tracta, trachanas and tarhana' in *Food in Antiquity* ed. John Wilkins and others (Exe-

ter: Exeter University Press, 1995) pp. 44–54; Charles Perry, 'Trakhanas revisited' in *Petits propos culinaires* no. 55 (1997) pp. 34–9 (the link made by Perry between Latin *tracta* [see under PASTRY] and Greek *trakhanas* is controversial).

• Greek *athare* or *athera* is emmer gruel, something to be supped as a soup, rather more liquid than the 'porridge' which sometimes serves as an English equivalent. Dioscorides and Pliny give definitions. Later sources, including Eustathius and the Scholia on Aristophanes, define *athera* as boiled *semidalis* (see WHEAT).

Aristophanes, *Wealth* 676–95 with scholia; Dioscorides MM 2.92; Pliny NH 22.121; Eustathius, *Commentary on Odyssey* vol. 1 p. 403 Stallbaum.

Endive, garden vegetable, comparable to lettuce; but, unlike lettuce, endive is often cooked before serving to reduce its bitterness. Endive (*Cichorium Endivia*) is Greek *seris*, Latin *intibus*.

Theophrastus HP 7.7–10 *passim*; Nicander F 71 Schneider; Dioscorides MM 1.132; Pliny NH 19.129, 20.73–7, 21.88; Galen SF 12.119; Anthimus OC 51 with Grant *ad l.*

Laufer 1919 pp. 400–2; Darby and others 1977 pp. 672–3; Lambraki 1997 pp. 47–8.

• Chicory (*Cichorium Intybus*) is Greek *seris*, *kikhore*, *kikhorion*, Latin *cichorium*. Chicory, regarded as a variety of endive, was used medicinally and as a salad or potherb.

Dioscorides MM 1.132; Thessalus, *Powers of Herbs* 2.1 (translation and comment in John Scarborough, 'The pharmacology of sacred plants, herbs and roots' in *Magika Hiera: ancient Greek magic and religion* [New York: Oxford University Press, 1991] pp. 155–6); Galen BM 6.794, *al.*; Aetius, *Medicine* 9.35.186.

• Classical Greek *pikrides* 'bitters' refers to bitter leaves gathered as salad and potherb, overlapping the wider category of *agria lakhana* 'wild herbs', and the more scientific *kikhoriode* 'chicory-like plants' of Theophrastus. It includes the leaves of wild chicory and related species; also, probably, dandelion (see below), wild LETTUCE, CAT'S EAR and CHONDRILLA JUNCEA. Similar plants are discussed by Pliny under the general heading of *lactuca sponte nascens* 'wild lettuce'. These bitter leaves were prescribed to Jews, to eat with unleavened bread, at

PASSOVER. They made a suitable food for severe ascetics.

Exodus 12.8; Aristotle *HA* 612a30; Theophrastus *HP* 7.7.1–3, 7.11.3–4; Dioscorides *MM* 2.132; Pliny *NH* 20.58–68; Eusebius, *On Easter* [*PG* 24.696]; *History of the Monks in Egypt* 20.17 Festugière; Augustine, *Sermon to Catechumens* 4 fin. (*picridine*).

Lambraki 1997 pp. 37–53.

• Dandelion, a familiar potherb in modern Europe including Italy and Greece, was surely used in classical times but is not clearly distinguishable by name among the bitter leaves. Dandelion (*Taraxacum officinale*) is *pikralis* in later Greek. The author of the sermon *On Unleavened Bread*, the first to use the word, identifies dandelion as the 'bitter leaves' eaten at Passover (see above).

Pseudo-Athanasius, *On Unleavened Bread* [*PG* 26.1328].

Lambraki 1997 pp. 50–3.

Ennius, author of major early Latin poetry and also of an adaptation or imitation of the Greek gastronomic poem by ARCHESTRATUS. The work was entitled *Hedyphagetica* 'Pleasant eating', and it was in even rougher hexameter verse than Archestratus's own. One fragment of eleven lines survives. It mentions local specialities of southern Italy, including Ennius's native Tarentum, and of nearby Corcyra and northwestern Greece.

Ennius H: *Hedyphagetica*. Text, translation and notes: Olson and Sens 2000 pp. 241–5.

Entertainment at ancient dinners, often provided by the diners themselves. Sometimes one of these was present, with or without prior invitation, because he was expected to entertain the rest (see COMPORTMENT; PARASITOS). There were also professional entertainers of various kinds.

In classical Greece these included slave dancers, musicians and acrobats; it was apparently not unusual to hire a prostitute, at whose entrance some diners would keep their heads down and nibble the desserts (so Plutarch suggests, quoting Menander); fellow diners might wonder

whether this was from fear of incurring extra expense, or rather from 'fear of the flute-girl', a phobia observed by an author of the Hippocratic *Epidemics*.

Roman dinners were sufficiently different from those of classical Greece that Julius Caesar, while on campaign in Gaul, regularly hosted twin dinner parties, one Greek and one Roman. Among traditional Roman entertainments may be mentioned the professional story-tellers whom Augustus sometimes employed when he had guests to dinner. Under the Roman Empire dinner entertainment included performances of mimes and classic plays (or perhaps extracts from plays) and the singing of poetry by professionals. Dancing-girls, including those from Gades (Cadiz) and those from Syria, found plenty of customers.

Hippocrates, *Epidemics* 5.81=7.6; Plutarch *QC* book 5 preface, also 7.5 quoting Menander fragment 741 Körte, also 7.7–8; Suetonius, *Augustus* 74; Aulus Gellius 19.9; Athenaeus *D* 607a–f, *al.*

C.G. Starr, 'An evening with the flute-girls' in *Parola del passato* vol. 33 (1978) pp. 401–10;

Figure 5 An acrobat performs a handstand on a revolving wheel spun by an assistant. Possibly a scene from a play, since the acrobat is not nude and the assistant wears 'phlyax' costume. Redrawn from a south Italian vase of the fourth century BC.

D. and M. Gourevitch, 'Phobies' in *L'Evolution psychiatrique* vol. 47 (1982); D. Gilula, 'Menander's comedies best with dessert and wine (Plut. *Mor.* 712E)' in *Athenaeum* vol. 65 (1987) pp. 239–96; E. Pellizer, 'Outlines of a morphology of sympotic entertainment' in *Sympotica: a symposium on the symposion* ed. Oswyn Murray (Oxford: Oxford University Press, 1990) pp. 177–84; C.P. Jones, 'Dinner theater' in *Dining in a Classical Context* ed. W.J. Slater (Ann Arbor: University of Michigan Press, 1991) pp. 185–98; Hartmut Leppin, *Histrionen: Untersuchungen zur sozialen Stellung von Bühnenkünstler im Westen des Römischen Reiches zur Zeit der Republik und des Principats* (Bonn: Habelt, 1992) (*Antiquitas. Reihe I: Abhandlungen zur Alten Geschichte*, 41); Schäfer 1997.

Epaenetus, Greek author of a cookery book. Epaenetus is possibly to be dated to late Hellenistic times. He is cited fourteen times by Athenaeus. Two of these are verbatim quotations of the same passage, a list of fish names; one other is a complete recipe (see quotation at MYMA).

Athenaeus *D* 313b, 328f, 662d; *Scholia on Nicander T* 585.

Bilabel 1921; Dalby 1996 p. 163.

Ephesian wines, those from the vicinity of Ephesus in southern Lydia (the Roman province of Asia). They included some of high quality.

- Mesogite wine (Greek and Latin *Mesogites*), from the slopes of Mount Messogis, east of Ephesus and not far south of the vineyards that produced Tmolite wine (see ASIAN WINES). Mesogite was headachy, according to Pliny. Strabo says that the best Mesogite wine, *Aromeus*, came from the vineyards of the hill village of Aroma, above Nysa.

Strabo 14.1.15, 14.1.47; Dioscorides *MM* 5.6.9; Pliny *NH* 14.75.

- Phygelite wine (Greek *Phygelites*), from seaside vineyards in the neighbourhood of Ephesus, known in the first century AD. It was good for the bowels, said Dioscorides. Strabo thought Ephesian wine good, but Pliny describes it as unwholesome owing to the admixture of seawater and grape syrup.

Strabo 14.1.15; Dioscorides *MM* 5.6.9, 5.6.11; Pliny *NH* 14.75.

- Strabo names two other wines of the neighbourhood. Metropolite wine (Greek *Metropolites*) came from Ephesian Metropolis on the north slope of Mount Gallesion. There was also good wine at Larisa, a village above Tralles.

Strabo 9.5.19, 14.1.15.

- Also in the Roman imperial period, Latoreia, a mountain village near Ephesus, was one of several sources of 'PRAMNIAN WINE'.

Athenaeus *E* 31d.

Ephesus, city of the eastern Aegean. Ephesus was a religious centre and an exporter of wine (see previous entry). It is praised for two kinds of seafood: the *kheme leia*, a species of VENUS CLAM, and the *khrysophrys* or gilthead BREAM.

Archestratus *H* 12, 56 Brandt.

Epicharmus, Sicilian author of Greek comedies of the early fifth century BC. Most of the surviving brief fragments of Epicharmus's works are quoted by Athenaeus because they include names of fish or shellfish.

Comicorum Graecorum fragmenta. Vol. 1 pt 1: Doriensium comoedia, mimi, phlyaces ed. G. Kaibel (Berlin, 1899).

Epicurus, influential Greek philosopher of the third century BC. His prolific writings are largely lost. They included a *Symposium*: the five surviving verbatim fragments of this are to be found in Arrighetti's edition (no. 21), but they are to be supplemented from Plutarch, who summarises (*QC* 3.6) the discussion in this work of the proper time for coitus.

Plutarch *QC* 1.preface, 3.6; Athenaeus *D* 546e–547b.

Epicuro, *Opere* ed. G. Arrighetti (Turin: Einaudi, 1973).

Epimenides, legendary early Greek sage. Epimenides claimed MALLOW and ASPHODEL as his *alimon* and *adipson*, his 'prophylactics against hunger and thirst'.

PYTHAGORAS, following Epimenides's lead, made compound drugs under the names *alimon* and *adipson* whose purpose was to repress the appetites during religious vigils; so at least we are assured by Porphyry, writing in the third century AD, who supplies recipes.

Plato, *Laws* 642d; Aristotle, *Constitution of Athens* 1 with Rhodes *ad l.*; Diogenes Laertius 1.109–15; Scholia on Hesiod *OD* 641 = Plutarch fragment 26 Sandbach, cf. Athenaeus E 58f; Porphyry, *Life of Pythagoras* 29, 34.

M.L. West, *The Orphic Poems* (Oxford: Clarendon Press, 1983) pp. 45–53.

Erasistratus, author of a Greek work on cookery, perhaps of the third century BC. Whether this Erasistratus is the same as the eminent medical writer of the early third century, physician to Seleucus I of Syria, is unknown. Athenaeus quotes from the cookery book a recipe for a sauce: '*Hyposphagma* for roast meat: the blood to be blended with honey, cheese, salt, cumin, silphium – these heated together.'

Athenaeus D 324a, 516c.

Dalby 1996 p. 162.

Eringo, a wild sea-shore plant of which 'the Greeks use both the stem and root as food, served boiled or raw as preferred'. Eringo (*Eryngium maritimum*) is Greek *eryngion*.

Pliny *NH* 22.20, cf. Dioscorides *MM* 3.21.

Etiquette *see* COMPORTMENT

Etruscans, people of Etruria (Tuscany) in central Italy. The Etruscan language has not been shown to be related to any other and is largely undeciphered. Etruscan culture was strongly influenced by that of early Greece, and in turn exerted a powerful influence on Rome.

Etruscan banqueting is depicted in tomb paintings and was described with disapproval by the Greek authors Timaeus and Poseidonius (both quoted by Athenaeus). Social behaviour at meals evidently resembled that of later Rome. Little is known specifically of the food or wine, but modern scholars have made perceptive use of archaeological evidence, notably from cooking and dining utensils.

Athenaeus 153d–154a, 517d–518b.

S. De Marinis, *La tipologia del banchetto nell' arte etrusca arcaica* (Rome, 1961); J.P. Small, 'The banquet frieze from Poggio Civitate (Murlo)' in *Studi etruschi* vol. 39 (1971) pp. 25–61; B. Bouloumié, 'Le vin étrusque' in *Quaderni della Scuola di Specializzazione in Viticoltura e Enologia* vol. 7 (1983) pp. 165–88; M. Gras, *Trafics tyrrhéniens archaïques* (Rome, 1985) (*Bibliothèque des écoles françaises d'Athènes et de Rome*, 258); Oswyn Murray, 'At the Etruscan banquet' in *Times Literary Supplement* (30 August 1985) pp. 948, 960; C. Weber-Lehmann, 'Spätarchaische Gelagebilder in Tarquinia' in *Römische Mitteilungen* vol. 92 (1985) pp. 19–44; *L'alimentazione nel mondo antico: gli Etruschi* [by C. Ampolo and others; ed. C. Cerchiai and others] (Rome: Istituto Poligrafico, 1987); J.P. Small, 'Eat, drink and be merry: some thoughts on Etruscan banquets' in *Murlo and the Etruscans: essays in memory of Kyle Meridith Phillips* ed. R. de Puma and J.P. Small (Wisconsin, 1994) pp. 85–94; A. Rathje, 'Banquet and ideology: some new considerations about banqueting at Poggio Civitate (Murlo)' in *Murlo and the Etruscans: essays in memory of Kyle Meridith Phillips* ed. R. de Puma and J.P. Small (Wisconsin, 1994) pp. 95–9; Flandrin and Montanari 1996.

Euboea, large island off the east coast of Greece. For classical Athens Euboea was a source of fruits and nuts (so-called 'Euboean nuts' were chestnuts). Euboean cities are also noted for seafood: Eretria for the *phagros*, a species of bream, which you bought at the shops along the harbour; Chalcis for the *bouglossos* or sole; Carystus for the big tunny and the little *mainis* or mendole.

Antiphanes 191 Kassel; Archestratus H 26, 32, 34 Brandt; Dio of Prusa, *Orations* 7.65–79; Athenaeus E 54b citing Mnesitheus.

Euboean wine (Greek *Euboikos*), one of the local wines of the classical world that is specifically said to have been resinated:

see also RESINATED WINE.

Plutarch *QC* 5.3; Athenaeus *E* 30f.

Eubulus, Athenian comedy playwright of the mid fourth century BC. His plays survive only in fragments, many of them quoted by Athenaeus for their relevance to food and cooking.

Eubulus F: fragments. Text and commentary: Eubulus, *The Fragments* ed. R.L. Hunter (Cambridge: Cambridge University Press, 1983); text in *PCG: Poetae comici Graeci* ed. R. Kassel and C. Austin (Berlin: De Gruyter, 1983–); English translation in *The Fragments of Attic Comedy* ed. J.M. Edmonds (Leiden, 1957–61). References elsewhere in the present book are to the fragment numbering established by Kassel and Austin, which differs slightly from those of Edmonds and Hunter.

Eucharist or communion, the symbolic Christian meal in which, in sharing bread and wine, participants are said to share also in the body and blood of Christ. The institution derives from the LAST SUPPER, when, according to some manuscripts of Luke's *Gospel*, in the course of distributing bread and wine Jesus instructed his disciples to 'do this in memory of me'.

Luke, *Gospel* 22.17–20; John, *Gospel* 6.48–58.

E. Jastrzebowska, 'Les scènes de banquet dans les peintures et sculptures chrétiennes des IIIe et IVe siècles' in *Recherches augustiniennes* vol. 14 (1979) pp. 3–90; G. Feeley-Harnik, *The Lord's Table: Eucharist and Passover in early Christianity* (Philadelphia: University of Pennsylvania Press, 1981).

Euergetism *see* CHARITY

Euthydemus of Athens, author of Greek works *On Salt Fish* and *On Vegetables* which are several times quoted by Athenaeus. One such quotation (*D* 116a–c) includes thirteen lines of verse on salt fish, lines which Euthydemus attributed, in spite of obvious anachronisms, to Hesiod. Euthydemus is also in Athenaeus's summary list (*D* 516c) of writers *On Cookery*.

He may perhaps have written in the fourth or early third century BC.

Dalby 1996 p. 162 and note 40.

Excess, exemplified in the conspicuous consumption of food and wine, was noticed in both Greek and Roman culture. The god HERACLES was the classical Greek example of shameless greed. Among their human contemporaries, classical Greeks identified ATHLETES as the group most likely to over-eat. The overeating was, specifically, of meat; and the corollary was not that Heracles and the athletes were lazy and obese, but that they were strong and unusually active. In classical Greek sources individual excess in drinking is scarcely mentioned as a problem. At classical symposia the fashion was for all to drink equally; both at symposia and at certain festivals DRUNKENNESS was socially acceptable. Aristotle remarks that excessive drinking impairs sexual function.

In Hellenistic times we hear of competitive drinking, exemplified at the courts of ALEXANDER THE GREAT and MITHRIDATES; we also hear of obesity resulting from habitual excessive eating. Gastronomic extravagance (see LUXURY) is a feature of the wealthy courts of Hellenistic monarchs.

In this respect Rome adopted Hellenistic rather than classical Greek patterns of behaviour – identifying these patterns as Greek and foreign, and setting alongside them a continuing tradition of moralistic disapproval. Though strongly expressed, this tradition was insufficient to discourage excessive eating and drinking by rich Romans of the Empire. Among emperors, Claudius and Vitellius were roundly criticised for over-eating; Vitellius, Elagabalus and others for excessive expenditure on gastronomic luxury. Heavy drinkers are listed by Aelian and Plutarch.

Frugality was recommended by philosophers, both Greek and Roman, and by religious thinkers, notably Clement of Alexandria: see also VEGETARIANISM and ASCETICISM.

Antiphanes 47 Kassel; Eubulus *F* 93 Kassel with Hunter *ad l.*; Aristotle, *Problems* 871a1–878a27; Plutarch *QC* 1.6; Aelian, *Varia Historia* 12.26; Clement of Alexandria, *Paidago-gos* 2; Athenaeus *D* 411a–422d, 427e–437d.

Corbier 1989; Emma Dench, 'Austerity, excess, success and failure in Hellenistic and early Imperial Italy' in *Parchments of Gender: deciphering the bodies of antiquity* ed. Maria Wyke (Oxford: Clarendon Press, 1998) pp. 121–46; Wilkins 2000 pp. 69–86.

F

Falernian wine (Latin *Falernum*; Greek *Phalernos*, *Phalerinos*), the most famous wine of Roman Italy, and according to most judges the second best. Polybius in about 140 BC (cited by Athenaeus) mentions an incomparable wine grown 'at Capua', and this can most plausibly be taken as the earliest contemporary reference to fine wine of the Falernian district. The first sign that the name *Falernum* was in current use as an 'appellation' is the inscription *fal mas*, perhaps *Falernum Massicum*, on an amphora that also bears the consular date 102 BC. According to Cicero, writing in 55 BC, a Falernian wine of the Anician vintage (160 BC) might still be found, but would hardly still be drinkable.

Pliny places Falernian second among Italian wines, after Caecuban and ahead of Alban; some of his contemporaries, including Dioscorides, rank it first. Pliny identifies three wine styles for Falernian, and Galen (writing a century later) describes two of them more fully. The *austerum* was astringent, but not extremely so, as Signine and Marsian wine were. The *dulce* was fairly sweet; both of these were *kirros*, amber in colour, and light enough to be translucent, according to Galen. A *glykazon* wine was made in years when the south wind blew as the vintage was approaching, adds the *Epitome of Athenaeus*; this *glykazon* wine

was 'blacker'. The *tenue* 'thin' style is mentioned only by Pliny.

In general Falernian wine was *ardens* 'burning', *forte* 'strong', *thermos* 'hot', *oinodes* 'winy'. Falernian became darker as it aged, tending in colour towards *fuscum* 'brown' and even *niger* 'black'. It needed at least ten years' ageing and was at its best from fifteen to twenty years old, according to the *Epitome* again.

Falernian was the only wine that would catch fire, said Pliny imaginatively. In Roman literature of the late Republic and early Empire, Falernian is the almost ubiquitous symbol of fine wine and convivial pleasures. Could all the 'Falernian' drunk in Rome in the first and second centuries really be genuine? Galen raises the question and leaves it in the air. Falernian was still sought-after at the end of the third century: it was one of the seven named wines of the Empire allowed a special high price in *Diocletian's Price Edict*.

Pliny distinguishes three named terroirs of Falernian: see below. It has been suggested that Falernian in a wider sense included the neighbouring MASSIC WINE; it might also have englobed Calene (see CALENE WINE) and Statan (see STATAN WINE), since all three names disappear from later sources.

Cicero, *Brutus* 287; Horace, *Odes* 2.11.19, *Satires* 2.4.24; Strabo 5.3.6; Dioscorides *MM* 5.6; Pliny *NH* 14.55, 14.62–3 with André *ad l.*;

Martial 2.40, 8.77, 9.49, *al.*; Galen *BM* 6.801–3, *SF* 11.604, *DA* 14.27–9, *On Therapeutic Method* 10.831–6, *To Glaucon on Therapeutic Method* 11.87, *On Theriac to Piso* 14.267, *On Compounding* 13.404–5; Athenaeus *E* 31d citing Polybius 34.11.1; *CIL* 4.2553, 15.4553–4; *Diocletian's Price Edict* 2.7.

Griffin 1985 p. 67; Tchernia 1986 esp. pp. 60–6, 342–3; Dalby 2000a pp. 48–50; P. Arthur, 'Territories, wine and wealth: Suessa Aurunca, Sinuessa, Minturnae and the Ager Falernus' in *Roman Landscapes: archaeological survey in the Mediterranean region* ed. G. Barker and J. Lloyd (London, 1991) pp. 153–9.

- *Caucinum* (Greek *Kaukinos*) was grown on the high slopes.

  Pliny *NH* 14.63; Athenaeus *E* 27b.

- *Faustianum* (Greek *Phaustianos*) came from the lower slopes. It was the best for some medicinal purposes, said Galen: if unable to get it you should use one of the similar sweet yellow wines such as the ASIAN WINES *Therinos* and *Karyinos*.

  Pliny *NH* 14.62–3; Galen *ST* 6.338, *BM* 6.801, *On Therapeutic Method* 10.832, *DA* 14.20; Fronto, *Letters* vol. 2 p. 6 Haines.

- *Falernum* in its narrowest sense was the wine of the lowlands.

Famine and food shortage, ever-present threats in the ancient Mediterranean. In spite of the productivity of the region, occasional climatic variation may lead to the failure of a harvest or to unexpected mortality among farm animals. The absence of a surplus elsewhere, the slowness of communication, and various difficulties in the long-distance transport of food are factors that may in such circumstances contribute to a catastrophic food shortage.

War (and large-scale population movements from any other cause) may also cause shortages and famines. The precipitating factor may be that a population is trapped by siege, or that a large army or a group of refugees makes impossible demands on local food supplies, or that army service has deprived farms of their labour force at a crucial time, or that crops and farm animals have been destroyed or confiscated.

In most ancient societies the first result of catastrophic food shortage will be a sudden rise in price. This will mean that the poor are unable to buy their usual foods; the rich have more options. In such circumstances ancient governments often intervened, with greater or less success, to control supplies and prices. The gift of essential foods by one state to another ('food aid') is by no means a modern innovation: in Hellenistic times many Greek cities recorded their gratitude to monarchs of the larger eastern Mediterranean kingdoms for relieving their citizens from sudden food shortage by sending urgently needed supplies of wheat.

Some famines, but surely not all, are recorded in historical sources: see works by Garnsey for citations and analysis.

Philo of Byzantium, *Poliorcetica* 88.25–89.46 Thévenot.

Garnsey 1988; Peter Garnsey and Ian Morris, 'Risk and the polis: the evolution of institutionalised responses to food supply problems in the ancient Greek state' in *Bad Year Economics: cultural responses to risk and uncertainty* (Cambridge, 1989) pp. 98–105; C. Virlouvet, *Famines et émeutes à Rome des origines de la République à la mort de Néron* (Rome, 1985); *Hunger in History: food shortage, poverty and deprivation*, ed. L.F. Newman (Oxford, 1990); T.W. Gallant, *Risk and Survival in Ancient Greece: reconstructing the rural domestic economy* (Oxford: Polity Press, 1991), review by Emily Vermeule in *Classical Journal* vol. 89 (1993) pp. 215–17; Garnsey 1999.

- Famine foods are those used only or principally when there is a disastrous shortage of normal food. Garnsey suggests a scale of famine foods 'in descending order of desirability'. He cites a schematic list from the *Talmud* of the foods supposed to have been used, year by year, during the seven-year famine in Samaria which is described in *II Kings*. Garnsey's list, which will be found useful in evaluating anecdotes and narratives of famine, is as follows. First, 'livestock not in ordinary circumstances destined for slaughter'. Second, 'inferior cereals': for Greece, these included various semi-wild and cultivated LEGUMES such as black-eyed pea, grass pea, lupin and vetch; all four were counted as human food, but any who relied on them as staples risked serious illness, as a Hippocratic text reminds us (see also GRASS

PEA). Third, 'regular animal food': for Italy, this would include vetch (compare above); for most of Greece, acorns. Fourth, 'last resort natural products or non-foods' such as roots, twigs, leaves, bark and leather; Galen describes the use during famines in his native Asia Minor of 'twigs and shoots of trees and bushes, bulbs and roots of plants that produce bad humours; they dish up the so-called wild vegetables ... and cook and eat green grass.' Fifth, human flesh (see CANNIBALISM).

Alexis *F* 167 Kassel with Arnott *ad l.*; *II Kings* 6.24–8.3; Hippocrates, *Epidemics* 2.4.3=6.4.11; Galen *BM* 6.750, cf. *AF* 6.622; *Babylonian Talmud* Taanit 5a.

Garnsey 1988 pp. 28–9, *al.*; Garnsey 1999 pp. 34–41, *al.*

Farming, the principal source of food and drink in sedentary societies. The early development of farming parallels that of DOMESTICATION. In the Mediterranean region by classical times domestication had made available a range of GRAIN crops, LEGUMES, VEGETABLES and FRUIT. For the major domesticated animals used for food see PORK; SHEEP; GOAT; OX (but the ox was principally a working animal). Several BIRDS were also domesticated. By Roman times further animals and birds were being kept in a semi-wild state in *leporaria* and *vivaria* (see, for example, Varro *RR* 3.3; Aulus Gellius 2.20) or were being regularly trapped from the wild and reared or fattened for the table: see also FATTENING.

The evidence suggests that most farming in classical Greece was on a relatively small scale, a matter either of subsistence farming or of the use of a few labourers (normally slaves). There were farming manuals, but none survives. From Rome, however, there is a sequence of surviving farming manuals, all of which provide interesting information on food production and preparation: see CATO; VARRO; COLUMELLA; PALLADIUS; GARGILIUS MARTIALIS. It is clear from these authors and from contemporary sources of other kinds that in Roman Italy, alongside small subsistence farms, there was an increasing

number of extensive estates which were worked by large teams of slaves. Roman landowners also gathered properties in the provinces. Thus the typical pictures from literature (which can bear only an oblique relationship to the real typical situation) are of a Greek citizen who lived in town but had some land, worked by his family with the help of a slave or two, contrasted with a Roman landowner who owned several large farms, run by tenant farmers and by slave managers (*vilici*). This typical Roman, when entertaining, boasted of the freshness of the produce that was served at dinner, specially brought from his own estates. See also GARDENING.

A. Aymard, 'Les capitalistes romains et la viticulture italienne' in *Annales: économies, sociétés, civilisations* (1947) pp. 257–365, reprinted in *Etudes d'histoire ancienne* (Paris, 1968) pp. 585–660; Buck 1949 pp. 135–81, 486–533; A. Salonen, *Agricultura Mesopotamica nach sumerisch-akkadischen Quellen* (Helsinki, 1968) (*Annales Academiae Scientiarum Fennicae = Suomalaisen Tiedeakatemian Toimituksia B* vol. 149); *The Domestication and Exploitation of Plants and Animals* ed. P. Ucko and G.W. Dimbleby (London, 1969); C. Clark and M. Haswell, *The Economics of Subsistence Agriculture* (London, 1970), 4th edn; White 1970; K.D. White, *A Bibliography of Roman Agriculture* (Woking, 1970); J. Pecirka, 'Homestead farms in classical and Hellenistic Hellas' in *Problèmes de la terre en Grèce ancienne* ed. M.I. Finley (The Hague, 1973) pp. 113–47; C. Vatin, 'Jardins et vergers grecs' in *Mélanges helléniques offerts à Georges Daux* (Paris, 1974) pp. 345–57; A.B. Cooper, 'The family farm in Greece' in *Classical Journal* vol. 75 (1977/8) pp. 162–75; Joan M. Frayn, *Subsistence Farming in Roman Italy* (London: Centaur Press, 1979); P. Veyne, 'Mythe et réalité de l'autarcie à Rome' in *Revue des études anciennes* vol. 81 (1979) pp. 261–80; D.J. Thompson, 'Agriculture' in *The Cambridge Ancient History* vol. 7 part 1, (Cambridge, 1984), 2nd edn; S.J. Hodkinson, 'Animal husbandry in the Greek polis' in *Papers of the Ancient History (Greece and Rome) Section of the 9th International Economic History Congress* (Bern, 1986); K. Greene, *The Archaeology of the Roman Economy* (London: Batsford, 1986); K.W. Russell, *After Eden: the behavioral ecology of early food production in the Near East and North Africa* (Oxford: BAR, 1988) (*BAR International Series* vol. 391); S. Isager and J.E. Skydsgaard, *Ancient Greek Agriculture: an introduction* (London: Routledge, 1992); S. Bergqvist, 'Considerations on yields, the distribution of crops and the size of estates. Three Roman agricultural units' in *Classica et medievalia* vol. 43 (1993) pp. 111–39; Brewer and others 1995; *OCD* 1996 *s.vv.* Agriculture, Greek, Agriculture, Roman; H. Kroll, 'Agriculture and arboriculture in mainland Greece of the first millennium B.C.' in *Paysage et alimentation dans le monde grec* ed. Jean-Marc Luce (Toulouse, 2000) pp. 61–8.

Fasting, abstinence from all solid food. The emperor Vespasian was no doubt not the only Roman who fasted for one day each month for (presumably) health reasons. Ritual fasting was practised occasionally by Greeks (the word is *apastia*) and by Jews, for reasons of mourning and atonement. Athenian women celebrating the annual *Thesmophoria* in honour of Demeter fasted on the third day of this festival; Romans observed an annual *ieiunium Cereris* 'fast for Ceres' or 'fast from cereal food' (Grimm 1996 p. 40 for both examples). Jews fasted regularly on the Day of Atonement each year, and in case of drought observed three days of fasting in expiation of presumed sins. Mondays and Thursdays were regarded as suitable days for frugality or fasting. Jews were regarded by Greek and Latin authors, perhaps with some exaggeration, as habitual fasters. By contrast with Jews, Christians regarded Wednesdays and Fridays as suitable days for fasting or for abstinence from certain foods, though at first this was a matter of individual piety, not of general rule. Among some Christians in late antiquity and after, fasting eventually became far more than an occasional act of repentance; it became a way of life.

Fasting was sometimes undertaken in the hope of prophetic visions; examples in a Judaeo-Christian context are found in the biblical romance of *Daniel* and in the apocalyptic *Fourth Book of Ezra*.

Plutarch discusses why it is that those who fast find that the practice arouses thirst more urgently than hunger.

Numbers 29.7–11; Aristophanes, *Clouds* 621; *Daniel* 10.2–4; *Fourth Book of Ezra* 5.20, 6.35, *al.* [for translation see *The Old Testament Pseudepigrapha* ed. J.H. Charlesworth (London, 1983–5) vol. 1 pp. 516–59]; Philo, *On the Special Laws* 1.186; Suetonius, *Vespasian* 20; Luke, *Gospel* 18.12; *Didache* 8.1; Plutarch *QC* 6.1; Tertullian *On Fasting*; Clement of Alexandria, *Stromateis* 7.11; *Mishnah*, tractates *Yoma* and *Taanith*; Theodoret, *History of the Monks* 1.7.

Rudolph Arbesmann, 'Fasting and prophecy in Pagan and Christian antiquity' in *Traditio* vol. 7 (1949–51) pp. 1–71; R.M. Bell, *Holy Anorexia* (Chicago, 1985); Daniel L. Smith-Christopher, 'Hebrew satyagraha: the politics of biblical fasting in the post-exilic period (sixth to second century B.C.E.), in *Food and Foodways* vol. 5 (1991–4) pp. 269–92; Veronika E. Grimm, 'Fasting women in Judaism and Christianity in late antiquity' in *Food in Antiquity* ed. John Wilkins and others (Exeter: Exeter University Press, 1995) pp. 225–40; Grimm 1996.

Fat *see* MEAT

Fat hen *see* ORACH

Fattening, farming practices aimed at producing bigger animals, with better-tasting or more tender meat, than would be the case without intervention. Details vary depending on the species; they may include castration, the use of special foods, confinement and force-feeding. Fattening was a familiar business in Mediterranean farming of the first millennium BC.

Fattening of calves is mentioned in Hebrew and Greek sources from around 600 BC. 'Fatted ox, I think, is good to eat at midnight and midday,' wrote the Greek poet Ananius, meaning that it was always good. 'Fatted calves' are a rude simile for the mercenary soldiers of Egypt, about the same date, in the biblical book of Jeremiah; fattened veal is distinguished from grazing veal in a later biblical text, the romantic history of Solomon which forms the first part of *I Kings*. Later still a 'fatted calf' is a feature of a well-known parable in the Gospels. The growth and fattening of calves, pigs and chickens was promoted by castration or spaying, as is clear from Greek sources. The Greek verb *piainomai*, 'fatten', applies to these cases.

The Greek verb *siteuomai*, 'feed', applies to geese and to smaller birds. With these (and in Roman times also with the DORMOUSE and the SNAIL) fattening was carried out largely by intensive feeding, and eventually forced feeding, with selected foods. Again, both Greek and Hebrew sources of the mid first millennium BC show that some of these practices were in use. In the *Odyssey* Penelope, with the suitors on her mind, dreams of twenty geese fattening in her farmyard; fattened birds are probably also mentioned in *I Kings*, though some details in this text are uncertain. Greek *siteutos*, Latin *altilis* are the usual terms for a fattened bird.

Late Greek and late Latin terms for 'liver', *sykoton*, *ficatum*, have the literal meaning 'stuffed with figs', because, as Pliny, Galen and Pollux explain, pigs were fed with dried figs to produce large and fine-flavoured liver. Pliny attributes the invention of the method to APICIUS (2). Fattened goose liver (see under GOOSE) is possibly first mentioned by Eubulus in the fourth century BC, but that is uncertain; it is certainly familiar to Horace.

Homer, *Odyssey* 19.536; Ananius 5 West; Jeremiah 46.21; *I Kings* 4.23; Archestratus *D* 58 Brandt; Aristotle *HA* 595a15–595b22, 632a21–6; Cato *DA* 89–90; Horace, *Epistles* 1.7.35, *Satires* 2.8.88; Luke, *Gospel* 15.23; Fronto, *Letters* vol. 2 p. 6 Haines; Galen *AF* 6.679, 6.704, *BM* 6.771, *Commentary on Hippocrates RA* 15.657; Aulus Gellius 15.8.2; Pollux *O* 6.49, *KH* 83; Polyaenus 4.3.32; Athenaeus *D* 384a–c quoting Archestratus *H* 58 Brandt and Eubulus *F* 99 Kassel, also 656e–657c.

Fennel, culinary and medicinal herb. Fennel is probably native to the Near East. The earliest certain sign of it in human use is the term *ma-ra-tu-wo* found in

Linear B tablets and confidently identified with classical Greek *marathon*.

Both leaves and seeds of fennel give a characteristic flavour. Fennel was a favourite ingedient (as it still is) in preparing table olives, and it was also used in cooked dishes. The roots were useful in medicine.

Fennel (*Foeniculum vulgare*) is Greek *marathon*, Latin *feniculum*. Florence fennel or finocchio, the variety with swollen edible bulb, was unknown in ancient times.

Epicharmus 159 Kaibel; Hermippus 75 Kassel; Theophrastus *HP* 6.1.4; Cato *DA* 117; Columella *DA* 12.7.1, 12.9.1, *al.*; Pliny *NH* 20.254–61; Galen *AF* 6.641, *SF* 12.67; Pseudo-Apuleius, *Herbarius* 125; *Apicius* 1.35.1, *al.*

Darby and others 1977 p. 801; Dalby 1996 pp. 50, 83.

- The seeds and preserved stems of giant fennel (*Ferula communis*: Latin *ferula*) were eaten in Italy, says Pliny.

  Pliny *NH* 19.175, 20.260–1.

Fenugreek, fodder plant, legume and aromatic herb. Domesticated by the fourth millennium in the Near East and Egypt, fenugreek became familiar to Greeks and Romans only in Hellenistic times. It was more important as animal fodder than as human food, but some ate the seeds – boiled and flavoured with fish sauce, as Galen and *Apicius* agree. Fenugreek also served as the basis of a perfume, *telinon*, *telinum*.

Fenugreek (*Trigonella Foenum-graecum*) is Greek *telis, tele, boukeras, aigokeras*, Latin *silicia, fenum Graecum*.

Theophrastus *HP* 8.8.5, *CP* 5.15.5, 6.4.10; Pliny *NH* 13.13, 24.184–8; Galen *AF* 6.524, 6.537, *SF* 12.141, *On Compounding* 12.448, 12.622; *Apicius* 5.7.

Laufer 1919 pp. 446–7; Darby and others 1977 pp. 801–2; Zohary and Hopf 1993 pp. 116–17; K.T. Achaya, *Indian Food: a historical companion* (Delhi: Oxford University Press, 1994) pp. 214–15; Dalby 1996 p. 146.

Fig, tree fruit native to the Near East. Figs were being collected by humans from the wild by about 8000 BC across a swathe of territory from southern France to Iran. At some later date selection and planting of the female trees must have begun. By classical times – and much earlier in Mesopotamia – there was a range of varieties available and the fig had become one of the standard constituents of the human diet, an especially convenient one because figs dry well and the dried fruit is a rich source of dietary sugar. Both fresh and dried figs were rightly regarded as effective laxatives.

Fertilisation of the ancient varieties of cultivated figs (as of the Smyrna group of modern varieties) required the presence nearby of male wild fig trees. The process of fertilisation is accurately described by Herodotus, and in the following outline by Aristotle:

> The fruit of the wild fig contains the fig-wasp. This creature is a grub at first; but in due time the husk peels off and the fig-wasp leaves the husk behind it and flies away, and enters into the fruit of the domesticated fig tree through its orifice, and causes the fruit not to drop off. With a view to this phenomenon, country folk are in the habit of tying wild figs on to fig trees, and of planting wild fig trees near domesticated ones.

Because of this last practice wild figs are found almost everywhere that cultivated figs are grown, and the original range of the species is now hard to trace. Figs may, depending on the variety and the climate, appear two or three times a year, but not all will ripen. The main crop is borne in early autumn. The fig tree provided two seasonal landmarks to farmers, the date when the trees come into leaf and the date when the first fig ripens (Latin *prima ficus*). Apart from the fruit, the tree is useful for its bitter, milky sap,

which may be used as a rennet in cheese-making.

Wild fig trees and their fruit occur in Greek myth. In one story the seers Mopsus and Calchas competed to answer how many figs there were on a certain tree at Colophon: Mopsus had the answer right.

In linguistic double entendre Greek *sykon* 'fig' often stands for the vagina. As a bad joke, *iskhas* 'dried fig' is given the double meaning 'anus' in Greek literature; a further bad joke made *Iskhas* the name of a courtesan (Philip 75 Gow [*Anthologia Planudea* 240]; Menander, *Kolax* fragment 4 Sandbach [Athenaeus D 587d]).

Figs are such an important fruit in the eastern Mediterranean that languages of the region have special vocabularies for fig cultivation and for distinguishing the fruit by colour, quality and place of origin. Among terms often encountered in Greek are *syke*, cultivated fig tree, *erineon*, wild fig, *olonthos*, male fig in which fig wasps breed, and *erineos*, wild fig tree. The fig wasp is *psen* is Greek.

The following varieties of figs are relatively prominent in classical texts. Greek *lakonika* were grown around Athens and were among the most profitable of varieties in classical Greece. Greek *khelidonia*, Latin *chelidonia*, are among the most frequently named: this variety flourished in fourth-century BC Athens as in first-century AD Rome. Latin *africa, africana*, Greek *aphrikana*, was a variety grown near Rome, presumably originating in north Africa. Latin *chalcidica*, Greek *khalkidika*, were likewise grown near Rome and perhaps came originally from Chalcis in Euboea. Latin *pompeiana* were named after a certain Pompeius who introduced them; this was an early variety and, no doubt for that reason, the best for sun-drying.

The fig (*Ficus carica*) is Greek *sykon*, Latin *ficus*.

Hesiod *OD* 679–82; Herodotus 1.193; Hippocrates *R* 55, *Epidemics* 6.7.9; Alexis *F* 167 Kassel with Arnott *ad l.*; Aristotle *HA* 557b25–31 (extract above translated by D'A.W.

Thompson) with Thompson *ad l.*; Theophrastus *HP* 2.8.1–4, 4.14.2–12, *al.*; Machon *C* 18.427 [Athenaeus *D* 582f] with Gow *ad l.*; Lycophron, *Alexandra* 426–30, 979–81; Dioscorides *MM* 5.32; Columella *DA* 11.2.56; Pliny *NH* 15.68–83, 23.117–30; Athenaeus *D* 74c–80e; Macrobius *S* 3.20.1–5; Palladius *OA* 4.10.23–36; Anthimus *OC* 87, 93.

Laufer 1919 pp. 410–14; Erich Ebeling, 'Feige(nbaum)' in *RA* 1928– ; I.J. Condit, *The Fig* (Waltham, Mass., 1947); Buck 1949 pp. 377–8; V. Reichmann, 'Feige' in *RAC* 1950– ; V. Buchheit, 'Feigensymbolik im antiken Epigramm' in *Rheinisches Museum* vol. 103 (1960) pp. 200–29; A. Goor, 'The history of the fig in the Holy Land from ancient times to the present day' in *Economic Botany* vol. 19 (1965); G. Scarpat, 'Il fico e le sue foglie nella tradizione classica e cristiana' in *Studi linguistici in onore di V. Pisani* (Brescia, 1969) pp. 873–90; Darby and others 1977 pp. 708–11; Henderson 1991 p. 134; Zohary and Hopf 1993 pp. 150–6; Brewer and others (1995 ?) pp. 51–2; Grant 1999 pp. 92–5.

- Greek *iskhas*, Latin *carica, caunea* is a dried fig. Much more concentrated in flavour than fresh figs, these were available to add sweetness to the diet throughout the year. They were eaten among TRAGEMATA or desserts. Columella gives careful instructions for sundrying and storage: they were typically trodden into cakes (he observes that one should first wash one's feet) with the addition of fennel and other aromatics. In Greek there is a separate term, *palathai*, for caked dried figs.

  Columella *DA* 12.15.1–5; Athenaeus *D* 74c–80e, 652b–653b.

- *Thria* are fig leaves. They had several culinary uses in the ancient world; they were, for example, used for wrapping bonito (see TUNNY) in Archestratus's excellent recipe for that fish. They also gave their name to a series of recipes for stuffed fig leaves. The development of this idea is traced in the article by Dalby (below); Grant interprets some of the recipes for the modern kitchen, substituting vine leaves for fig leaves in accordance with a statement by Hesychius.

  Aristophanes, *Frogs* 134, *Acharnians* 1101, *Knights* 954 with scholia on all three; Pollux *O* 6.57; Athenaeus 148e citing Cleitarchus; Hesychius, *Lexicon s.v. thria*; *Suda s.v. thria*.

  Andrew Dalby, 'On thria' in *Petits propos culinaires* no. 31 (1989) pp. 56–7; Grant 1999.

Fig-pecker *see* BECCAFICO

Fish, a major source of food to Mediterranean peoples. The oldest evidence of the use of fish in human food is the find of tunny bones at Franchthi Cave, in a layer dated to the seventh millennium BC. By classical times (and no doubt long before) many species of fish were being regularly caught and eaten.

Fish is prominent in Greek literature (in the lost play *The Fishes* by Archippus, a contemporary of Aristophanes, the chorus impersonated fishes). Fish is also well represented in writings by medical dieticians, including EUTHYDEMUS and XENOCRATES who devoted whole works to the subject.

However, the proportion of fish in the Greek diet and its availability to poorer people are controversial. Gallant has argued that fish was in short supply and expensive, while James Davidson and others have explored the political meanings of the quest for fine fish which seems so ubiquitous in the fragments of Athenian comedy. Dried fish and salt fish (see under CONSERVING) and fish sauce (see GARUM) are forms in which fish might form part of the diet of those who could not afford good fresh fish, or did not live close enough to the sea to be able to get it, as many Romans of the Empire did not. But even in these forms fish was not necessarily cheap: Grant has argued that while the Roman rich used fish sauce, the poor were limited to salt (Grant 1999 pp. 19, 28).

Extensive materials for the discussion of fish cookery are provided in the section of Athenaeus's *Deipnosophists* devoted to this subject. Athenaeus supplies numerous extracts from Athenian comedy as well as copious selections from Archestratus and other poets. If a general trend of argument can be extracted from these fragments, it is that fish must be carefully selected at market and keenly bargained for, and that each species will have its own best recipes (some liked the addition of grated cheese and olive oil in almost every case; others, including Archestratus, disapproved). The quotation that follows is from a cook's speech in a lost play by Sotades: it exemplifies the range of possible methods.

> Shrimps I took first: I cooked them all in a frying pan. A big smoothhound came next: I've baked the middle pieces, I'm boiling the rest of the stuff, with a mulberry sauce ready. I fetch two very large head steaks of bluefish: into a casserole with that, with a few herbs, cumin, salt, water and a drop of olive oil. Now then, I bought a very fine sea bass: it's to be cooked in stock with oil and herbs when I have taken off the steaks that are going to be grilled on spits. I bought fine red mullets and wrasses: I put them straight on the grill, adding oregano to an oily sauce. Beside these I bought cuttlefish and squid: a boiled stuffed squid is nice, and so are the tentacles of a cuttlefish, simply roasted. I have made a side salad of all sorts of greens to go with these. Then there was some *hepsetos* [see below], for which I made a well-shaken oily dressing. Then I bought a very sturdy conger, and drowned it in a stock with strong herb flavours. Some gobies and some little rock-fish, naturally: I chopped their heads off, dredged them in a bit of flour, and sent them off to follow the shrimps. Then a lonely bonito, a very fine beast, which I dipped in oil, wrapped in fig-leaves, sprinkled with oregano, and hid like a firebrand under heaped ashes. Beside this I got some little Phalerum anchovies: a cup of water over these is plenty; chopping up lots of herbs finely I tip them on with a good jug of oil. What else? Nothing at all. That's the art, and you don't learn it from books and notes.

Very small fish could be fried up together in the *tagenon* or skillet. Alexis and Plautus provide lists. In such dishes many species could be used, and the particular species available hardly mattered: hence the Greek terms *hepsetos* 'fish for frying, fish for the skillet' (the word is used in the above extract) and *epanthrakides* or *anthrakides* or *apopyrides*, 'fish to be grilled' (Aristophanes, *Acharnians* 670, *Wasps* 1127; Teles p. 41 Hense). For the small fish that typically went into such dishes see APHYE. As a further exception, rules stated more than once by the gastronomic poet Archestratus apply cheese and oil as flavourings to any 'coarse fish' (Mithaecus quoted by Athenaeus D 325f; Archestratus H 36, 46 Brandt, *al.*). In the case of larger fish, gastronomic interest often focuses on the head, *kephale*, the belly cut, *hypogastrion*, the tail cut, *ouraion*, or steaks or slices, *temakhos*.

Separate entries will be found for ANGLER-FISH; BARBIER; BASS; BREAM; BLUEFISH; CASTAGNOLE; COMBER; CONGER EEL; DOGFISH; DOLPHIN-FISH; EEL; FLATFISH; FLYING FISH; GREY MULLET; GURNARD; HAKE; LAMPREY; MEAGRE; MORAY EEL; PICAREL; RAY; RED MULLET; SHARK; SKATE; TRIGGER-FISH; and WRASSE. Among freshwater fish entries will be found for bleak (see under MOSELLE FISH); BURBOT; CARP; CHUB; GRAYLING; gudgeon (see under GOBY); PERCH; PIKE; SHAD; SHEATFISH; DANUBE FISH; and NILE FISH. Sea creatures that were not eaten (see AVOIDANCE OF FOODS) include the dolphin and pilot-fish, both (especially the latter) thus sometimes called 'holy fish' – but this name could also be given to the *anthias*, gilthead (see BREAM) and sturgeon.

Some fish named in Greek and Latin sources (especially Greek) are now hard to identify. For the *anthias* see BARBIER. For the *elops* see STURGEON. For the *glaukos* and *glaukiskos* see BLUEFISH. For *hepatos*, *lebias*, *onos* and other terms said to be synonymous with these see HAKE. For *korakinos* see CASTAGNOLE and NILE FISH. For *kapriskos* and *hys* see TRIGGER-FISH.

Hippocrates *R* 48; Alexis *F* 115 Kassel [Athenaeus *D* 107b] with Arnott *ad l.*; Plautus, *Casina* 490–503; Xenocrates *T*; Plutarch *EC* 995c; Athenaeus *D* 224b–361e quoting Sotades Comicus 1 Kassel, Philemon 82 Kassel.

F. Dölger, *Ikhthys: das Fisch-Symbol in frühchristlicher Zeit* (Munich, 1922–43); L. Lacroix, *La Faune marine dans la décoration des plats à poissons: étude sur la céramique grecque d'Italie méridionale* (Verviers, 1937), review in *Journal of Hellenic Studies* vol. 57 (1937) pp. 268–9; G. Bini, *Atlante dei pesci delle coste italiane*, 8 vols (Rome, 1960–70); *Catalogue of Names of Fish, Molluscs and Crustaceans of Commercial Importance in the Mediterranean* ed. G. Bini (Food and Agriculture Organization, Milan, 1965); T.W. Gallant, *A Fisherman's Tale: an analysis of the potential productivity of fishing in the ancient world* (Gent, 1985) (his list of fish should be checked against other sources); I. McPhee and A.D. Trendall, *Greek Red-figured Fish-plates* (Basel, 1987) (*Antike Kunst. Beiheft*, 14); J. Delorme and Ch. Roux, *Guide illustré de la faune aquatique dans l'art grec* (Juan-les-Pins, 1987); I. McPhee and A.D. Trendall, 'Addenda to *Greek Red-figured Fish-plates*' in *Antike Kunst* vol. 33 (1990) pp. 31–51; J. Davidson, 'Fish, sex and revolution at Athens' in *Classical Quarterly* vol. 43 (1993) pp. 53–66; N. Purcell, 'Eating fish: the paradoxes of seafood' in *Food in Antiquity* ed. John Wilkins and others (Exeter: Exeter University Press, 1995) pp. 132–49; D.J. Brewer and R.F. Friedman, *Fish and Fishing in Ancient Egypt* (Warminster: Aris, 1989); B.A. Sparkes, 'A pretty kettle of fish' in *Food in Antiquity* ed. John Wilkins and others (Exeter: Exeter University Press, 1995) pp. 150–61.

- The ancient three-way scientific classification of fish, as adopted by Aristotle and others, relates to their habitat: Greek and Latin *pelagia*, 'deep sea fish'; Greek *aigialode*, Latin *litoralia*, 'inshore fish'; Greek *petraia*, Latin *saxatilia*, 'rock fish'. To those who spoke familiarly of marine gastronomy, such as physicians and the characters in comic plays, *petraia* and more specifically *petraia ikhthydia* 'little rockfish' was a category to be despised. These *petraia*, taking the term most specifically, seem always to include the wrasse group, often also the goby group.

Archestratus *H* 45 Brandt with Olson and Sens *ad l.*; Aristotle *HA* 488b6–8; Plautus, *Rudens* 299; Columella *DA* 8.16.6–10; Athenaeus *D* 355a–357f citing Diphilus of Siphnos.

- Fishing was apparently conducted as a

small-scale business throughout classical times. The principal exception was the trapping of migratory and seasonal shoals, notably of TUNNY and bonito, which required a numerous labour force. Along the coasts of Greece – and of most other Mediterranean regions – many smaller cities and villages will have depended on fishing for a large share of their economic activity. In many of these the fishermen themselves, or their households, probably traded directly with consumers; in large cities, however, fishmongers were different from fishermen, and the two groups were sometimes in dispute. Influential Greek and Roman thinkers regarded hunting as a noble pastime, fishing as despicable: 'it is more noble to buy fish than to catch them', so Plutarch expresses it.

Plato, *Laws* 823d–e; Plutarch, *Intelligence of Animals* 965e–966b; Heliodorus, *Ethiopian Story* 5.18–20.

J. Engemann, 'Fisch, Fischer, Fischfang' in *RAC* 1950– ; D. Sperber, 'Some observations of fish and fisheries in Roman Palestine' in *Zeitschrift der Deutschen Morgenländischen Gesellschaft* vol. 118 (1968) pp. 265–9; A. Salonen, *Die Fischerei im alten Mesopotamien* (Helsinki, 1970) (*Annales Academiae Scientiarum Fennicae = Suomalaisen Tiedeakatemian toimituksia B*, 166); A. Guest-Papamanoli, 'Pêche et pêcheurs minoens: proposition pour une recherche' in *Minoan Society: proceedings of the Cambridge colloquium 1981* ed. O. Krzyszkowska and L. Nixon (Bristol: Bristol Classical Press, 1983) pp. 101–10; T.W. Gallant, *A Fisherman's Tale: an analysis of the potential productivity of fishing in the ancient world* (Gent, 1985); D.J. Brewer and R.F. Friedman, *Fish and Fishing in Ancient Egypt* (Warminster: Aris, 1989).

- Fish farming was developed in Italy in the late republican period. It took two forms (both of which are still practised). One involved the dividing off of stretches of sea, alongside jetties or the open shore, with fences or nets. Within these divisions certain fish and shellfish could be kept, fed, encouraged to breed, and 'harvested'. Other species, including some that were too powerful to be restrained by such fences, could be kept and (in some cases) bred in fishponds, an idea developed by Romans including Vedius Pollio (who was said to have fed recalcitrant slaves to his moray eels), Sergius ORATA (his cognomen may mean 'gilthead bream'), Licinius Murena (whose cognomen might be interpreted as 'moray eel') and

LUCULLUS. Details of both methods, including lists of suitable seafood species, are given by Varro and Columella; Pliny supplies historical details. Higginbotham (pp. 69–226) provides a gazetteer of fishponds in Roman Italy.

Varro *RR* 3.3, 3.17 with Flach *ad l.*; Columella *DA* 8.16–17; Pliny *NH* 9.167–72; Macrobius *S* 3.15–16.

D'Arms 1970 pp. 41–2 and *passim*; J. Kolendo, 'Parcs à huîtres et viviers sur un flacon en verre du Musée National de Varsovie' in *Travaux du Centre d'Archéologie Méditerranéenne de l'Académie Polonaise des Sciences* vol. 17 (Warsaw, 1976) pp. 143–58; L. Giacopini, B.B. Marchesini and L. Rustico, *L'itticoltura nell'antichità* (Rome, 1994); Higginbotham 1997 (his identifications of fish species should be checked against other sources).

Flamingo, large marsh bird. The flamingo was occasionally eaten by Romans (not, apparently, by earlier Greeks) and *Apicius* suggests a recipe. The special delicacy – and it was truly conspicuous consumption to kill the bird for this – was its tongue, included in a famous dish prepared for the Roman emperor Vitellius. Pliny attributes the vogue for flamingoes' tongues to APICIUS (2).

The flamingo (*Phoenicopterus antiquorum*) is Greek *phoinikopteros*, Latin *phoenicopterus*.

Seneca, *Letters* 110.12; Pliny *NH* 10.133; Martial 3.58, 13.71; Juvenal 11.139; Suetonius, *Vitellius* 13; *Apicius* 6.6.1.

Toynbee 1996.

Flatfish, sea fish belonging to the order *Pleuronectiformes*. They are dealt with here as a group because of the uncertainties in matching ancient names to species. The principal zoological difference is between the dextral species (such as the sole and flounder) and the sinistral species (most of the others). The flatfish as a whole are called *plateis* by Xenocrates, *plani* by Pliny. Pliny uses Latin *rhombus* as a name for the whole sinistral group: in his usage *passer* and *solea* exemplify the dextral group.

Xenocrates *T* 2; Pliny *NH* 9.72.

Davidson 1979 pp. 143–59; Davidson 1981 pp. 154–64.

- Greek *bouglossos*, *bouglottos*, literally 'ox tongue', is the sole (*Solea vulgaris*) and no

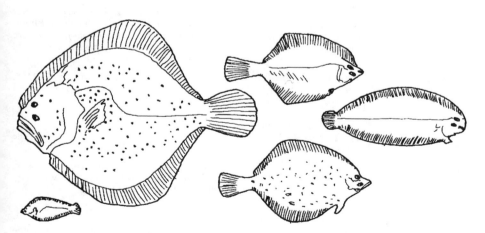

Figure 6 Flatfish. Top left: turbot (*Psetta maxima*), Greek *rombos*, Latin *rhombus*. Bottom left: fausse limande (*Citharus* sp.), Greek *psetta*. Top right: flounder (*Platichthys Flesus*), Greek *kitharos*, Latin *passer*. Bottom right: plaice (*Pleuronectes Platessa*), late Latin *platessa*. Far right: sole (*Solea vulgaris*), Greek *bouglossos*, Latin *solea*.

doubt also the various smaller species related to it. From its shape the sole is named 'tongue' in many modern languages. It was good in summer at Chalcis in Euboea, said Archestratus.

Epicharmus 65 Kaibel; *Acraephia Price List* (*bogglot.*); Xenocrates *T* 2, 24; Galen *AF* 6.724; Athenaeus *D* 288a–b quoting Archestratus *H* 32 Brandt, also 356b quoting Diphilus of Siphnos.

Thompson 1947 p. 33.

- Greek *kitharos* appears to be a flatfish species. An identification with the flounder, *Platichthys Flesus*, might be suggested. Ancient sources often liken the *kitharos* to flatfish such as *rombos*; it was the worst of them, says Pliny, and Galen agrees that the flesh of the *kitharos* is less tender than that of the *rombos*. Archestratus agrees too, since he suggests stewing a large, white specimen, grilling a smaller one with cheese and olive oil. The identification of *kitharos* with the guitar fish, *Rhinobatus Rhinobatus* (certainly *rinobatos* in Greek: see RAY) was proposed doubtfully by Thompson, and accepted by me in *Siren Feasts*, but seems to be ruled out because both names occur in the *Acraephia Price List*.

Aristotle *HA* 508b16–17; *Acraephia Price List*; Xenocrates *T* 30; Pliny *NH* 32.146; Galen *AF* 6.720 quoting Phylotimus, 6.724; Athenaeus 305f–306b quoting Archestratus *H* 31 Brandt.

Thompson 1947 p. 114, cf. p. 222.

- Latin *passer* is the same colour as the *solea*, according to Ovid, and lies on the same side, according to Pliny. It is therefore certainly the flounder (*Platichthys Flesus*).

Horace, *Satires* 2.8.29; Ovid, *Halieutica* 125; Columella *DA* 8.16.7; Pliny *NH* 9.72.

Thompson 1947 p. 295.

- *Platessa*, in the Latin of Gaul, is the plaice (*Pleuronectes Platessa*). This is a North Atlantic fish, unknown in the Mediterranean, and is mentioned only in late texts.

Ausonius, *Letters* 4.60 (*platessa*); Anthimus *OC* 42 (*platensis*) with Grant *ad l.*

- Greek *psetta*, *psessa* is probably a name for sinistral flatfish smaller than the brill and turbot. The word is often translated 'plaice', but this is inaccurate. For linguistic reasons Thompson's identification with the flounder is improbable. Modern Greek and Turkish *pisi* has a range of meanings similar to that proposed here for ancient *psetta*. The term

would include flatfish belonging to the genera *Citharus, Lepidorhombus, Arnoglossus* and *Bothus*; the English names 'megrim' and 'scaldfish' apply to some, but several Mediterranean species have no English names. The best *psettai* were found off Eleusis in Attica, it was agreed by numerous authors; they could be fried in a skillet.

Alexis *F* 115 Kassel; Matron *AD* 27; Xenocrates *T* 2, 24; Galen *AF* 6.724; Athenaeus *D* 329e–330b quoting Archestratus *H* 32 Brandt and Lynceus *F* 8, also 356b quoting Diphilus of Siphnos.

Thompson 1947 p. 294.

- Latin *rhombus* serves as the equivalent of the two Greek terms *rombos* and *psetta*. It was, however, the turbot (*Psetta maxima*) that they had in mind when Ovid and Pliny both express admiration at the size and quality of the *rhombi* on the Adriatic coast. Juvenal's fourth satire begins to tell the grandiose story of a *rhombus* from this sea, brought ashore at Ancona and destined by its proud captor to be presented to the emperor Domitian. The eventual theme of the story turns out to be the council meeting called by Domitian to help him decide how to cook the monster.

Horace, *Satires* 2.8.30; Ovid, *Halieutica* 125; Columella *DA* 8.16.7; Pliny *NH* 9.169; Juvenal 4.37–136; Athenaeus *D* 330b.

Higginbotham 1997 pp. 50–1.

- Greek *rombos* denotes the largest and finest sinistral flatfish, brill (*Scophthalmus Rhombus*) and turbot (*Psetta maxima*). They were good food, but much too big for frying, said Galen; they had to be baked.

Xenocrates *T* 2, 30; Galen *AF* 6.724–5; Athenaeus *D* 356b quoting Diphilus of Siphnos.

Thompson 1947 p. 223.

- Latin *solea*, literally 'sandal', is the sole (*Solea vulgaris* and other species).

Plautus, *Casina* 495; Ovid, *Halieutica* 124; Columella *DA* 8.16.7; Pliny *NH* 9.52; Anthimus *OC* 42.

Flavour, a sensation evoked with a range of technical terms in Greek and Latin (see also WINE TASTING). It should be remembered that in ancient medicine flavour indicated the presence of particular humours, and as such determined the dietary effect of foods. Depending on constitution, state of health and the seasons, certain humours, and thus certain flavours, were to be emphasised or avoided (for a summary of these rules see DIET). Because of this unquestioned link with humoral theory, ancient flavour terms have different reference from those in modern European languages, and any English equivalents are far from precise.

The commonest specific flavour terms in Greek are *drimys* 'sour'; *pikros* 'bitter'; *oxys* 'sharp'; *liparos* 'oily'; *opodes* 'sappy'; *styphizon* 'astringent'; *hedys* 'pleasant'; *glykys* 'sweet'. More general than these are the two matched pairs, *thermos* 'hot' and its opposite, *psykhros* 'cold'; *xeros* 'dry' and its opposite, *hygros* 'wet'. Still more general is the matched pair *eukhylos* and *kakokhylos* 'producing good humours', 'producing bad humours'.

Flavourings important in classical cuisine include various spices, HERBS and SWEETENERS, but also two more general flavour enhancers, SALT and GARUM. The latter, to judge by its southeast Asian analogues, was not only very salty but was also a plentiful natural source of umami: it was added both to savoury and to some sweet dishes.

Aristotle, *On the Senses* 440b26–442b26; Plutarch, *Animals are Rational* 990a–c.

P. Rozin, 'The use of characteristic flavorings in human culinary practice' in *Flavor* ed. C.M. Apt (Boulder, 1978) pp. 101–27; John Wilkins and S. Hill, 'The flavours of ancient Greece' in *Spicing up the Palate: proceedings of the Oxford Symposium on Food and Cookery 1992* (Totnes: Prospect Books, 1993) pp. 275–9; J. Alcock, 'Flavourings in Roman culinary taste with some reference to the province of Britain' in *Spicing up the Palate: proceedings of the Oxford Symposium on Food and Cookery 1992* (Totnes: Prospect Books, 1993) pp. 11–22.

Flying fish, the usual name for two different Mediterranean fish species. Both regularly emerge from the sea; the true flying fish can achieve a flight of as much as 100 metres. The two species had different names, both in Greek and Latin, but were nonetheless sometimes confused.

Thompson 1947 pp. 90, 285; Davidson 1981 p. 58.

- Greek *hirax*, *hierax* and Latin *milvus* are names for the flying gurnard (*Dactylopterus volitans*). Both names mean literally 'hawk'. The flesh of this fish was coarser than that of gurnards in general, but otherwise had similar dietary qualities, says Diphilus.

  Horace, *Epistles* 1.16.51; Athenaeus *D* 329a quoting Epaenetus, also 356a quoting Diphilus of Siphnos.

- Greek *khelidon* and Latin *hirundo* are names for the true flying fish (*Exocoetus volitans*). Both names mean 'swallow'. As food this species produced bad humours and had a bad smell; however, it made a good table display, says Xenocrates.

  Aristotle *HA* 535b28; Xenocrates *T* 21; Athenaeus *D* 324f quoting Speusippus, also 329a quoting Epaenetus.

Food poisoning, sickness caused by microbial contamination of foods and drinks. The problem is scarcely recognised by ancient observers, who were unaware of microbes.

A search among cases reported by physicians, and in other relevant sources, will show that food poisoning was in fact widespread. Anthimus gives a brief description of what would now be called salmonella poisoning and rightly recommends thorough cooking as a way of preventing it. WATER was often boiled before drinking, and before mixing with wine: this will have been an effective means of averting sickness caused by drinking contaminated water.

Anthimus *OC* preface.

E. Lieber, 'Galen on contaminated cereals as a cause of epidemics' in *Bulletin of the History of Medicine* vol. 44 (1970) pp. 332–45.

Forbidden foods *see* AVOIDANCE OF FOODS

Force-feeding *see* FATTENING

Foreigners *see* ACCULTURATION; BARBARIANS

Formian wine (Latin *Formianum*; Greek *Phormianos*), from vineyards on the coast of Latium. Formiae was a pleasant holiday resort where you could fish in the fish farms just offshore. Its wine, neighbour to the famous Caecuban (to the northwest) and the equally famous Massic (to the southeast) was not as good as either of these; it matured quickly and was more 'oily' even than Regian.

Horace, *Odes* 1.20.11, 3.16.34; Martial 10.30; Athenaeus E 26e.

Fox, wild animal. The taste of fox was not unknown to hunters of classical times, who used this animal as food particularly in autumn when the foxes had fattened on grapes. The meat is discussed briefly by the dietary writers.

The fox (*Vulpes Vulpes*) is Greek *alopex*, Latin *vulpes*.

Ananius 5 West; Hippocrates R 46; Theocritus 1.48–9; Galen AF 6.665, VA 68.

Franchthi, cave in southern Argolis, of great archaeological importance since it was inhabited (with interruptions) over a very long period, from c.23,000 to 3000 BC. Plant, mammal and seafood finds contribute to knowledge of foods in late Palaeolithic, Mesolithic and Neolithic southern Greece. Neolithic crops were introduced here c.6000 BC. At that date some wild foods used earlier (including local wild forms of the newly introduced crops, such as lentil and barley) ceased to be gathered.

Judith C. Shackleton, *Marine Molluscan Remains from Franchthi Cave* (Bloomington: Indiana University Press, 1988) (*Excavations at Franchthi Cave, Greece*, 4); Julie Hansen, *The Palaeoethnobotany of Franchthi Cave* (Bloomington: Indiana University Press, 1991) (*Excavations at Franchthi Cave, Greece*, 7); S. Payne, 'Faunal change at Franchthi from 20,000 B.C. to 3,000 B.C.' in *Archaeozoological Studies* ed. A.T. Clason (New York: Academic Press, 1975) pp. 120–31; J.M. Hansen and Jane M. Renfrew, 'Palaeolithic-Neolithic seed re-

mains at Franchthi Cave, Greece' in *Nature* vol. 271 (1978) pp. 349–52; T.W. Jacobsen, 'Franchthi Cave and the beginning of settled village life in Greece' in *Hesperia* vol. 50 (1981) pp. 303–19; Tj. H. van Andel and C.N. Runnels, *Beyond the Acropolis: a rural Greek past* (Stanford: Stanford University Press, 1987); Tj. H. van Andel and S.B. Sutton, *Landscape and People of the Franchthi Region* (Bloomington: Indiana University Press, 1987); J.M. Hansen, 'Franchthi Cave and the beginning of agriculture in Greece and the Aegean' in *Préhistoire de l'agriculture* ed. P.C. Anderson-Gerfaud (Paris, 1992) pp. 231–47.

Francolin, marsh bird, a delicacy in ancient as in modern cuisine. Francolins were brought from Boeotia to market at Athens, according to a list in Aristophanes's *Acharnians*, and were also to be found at Marathon, but were rather typical of the eastern Aegean. This is shown both by their first mention in a fragment of Hipponax (who wrote in an Ionic and Lydian milieu) and their Latin epithet, the *Ionicae attagenae* of Martial. The francolin, originally native to western Asia, had probably spread westwards with human encouragement. Nowadays it is no longer found in Greece or Italy, though it was observed in Samos as late as the eighteenth century and in Sicily in the nineteenth.

The francolin (*Francolinus Francolinus*) is Greek *attagas* and Greek and Latin *attagen*.

Aristophanes, *Acharnians* 875, *Birds* 247, 761; Horace, *Epodes* 2.54; Pliny NH 8.228, 10.133; Martial 2.37, 13.61; Athenaeus D 387f–388b quoting Hipponax 26a West; *Suda s.v. attagas*.

Thompson 1936 pp. 60–1; Toynbee 1996; Dalby 1996 pp. 64–5.

Frankincense, the pre-eminent incense of the ancient world. An aromatic resin from southern Arabia, Socotra and Somalia. It was not used in food but its heady aroma was much in evidence at banquets and sacrifices, both in the ancient Near East and in the classical world.

Frankincense (*Boswellia sacra* and

related species) is Greek *libanotos*, Latin *thus*.

Herodotus 3.107; Theophrastus *HP* 9.4, O 12, 21; *Periplus Maris Erythraei* 27–32 with Casson *ad l.*; Pliny *NH* 12.51–65.

G.W. van Beek, 'Frankincense and myrrh in ancient South Arabia' in *Journal of the American Oriental Society* vol. 78 (1958) pp. 141–52; G.W. van Beek, 'Frankincense and myrrh' in *Biblical Archaeologist* vol. 23 (1960) pp. 69–95; F. Nigel Hepper, 'Arabian and African frankincense trees' in *Journal of Egyptian Archaeology* vol. 55 (1969) pp. 66–72; N. Groom, *Frankincense and Myrrh* (London, 1981).

Fruit, already a major source of food before the beginning of agriculture, retained and perhaps increased its importance as fruit-growing techniques were gradually developed in later Neolithic times. Many fruits are useful both fresh and dried; among Mediterranean fruits the grape is notable for a third pattern of use (equally important nutritionally) as the source of wine.

In the Near East and Mediterranean it is logical to distinguish two groups of fruit trees as regards their potential for domestication. The first group includes plants that are propagated by cuttings and suckers, notably the olive, vine, fig, date, pomegranate and sycamore fig. The second group includes plants that are propagated by seed, including almonds, walnuts, apples, pears, plums and cherries.

With the last four in this list, an important second step was taken with the development of cultivated varieties that can only be propagated by grafting – a technique first recorded around 300 BC and invented at some earlier date now unknown. Grafting is described by Theophrastus, and afterwards in more detail by Cato and other Latin agricultural writers.

Throughout the prehistoric and ancient periods the range of fruits available in the Mediterranean region increased with the transplanting of species domesticated elsewhere. Examples of introductions in clas-

sical times include pistachio, peach, citron and apricot.

Theophrastus *HP* 2.5.3, *CP* 1.6, 5.5; Cato *DA* 40–2; Fronto, *Letters* vol. 1 p. 140 Haines.

Buck 1949 pp. 374–81; D. Zohary and P. Spiegel-Roy, 'Beginnings of fruit-growing in the Old World' in *Science* vol. 187 (1975) pp. 319–27; Zohary and Hopf 1993 pp. 134–83.

Fundan wine (Latin *Fundanum*; Greek *Phoundanos*) from the neighbourhood of Fundi (and close to the vineyard where CAECUBAN WINE was produced) on the coast of Latium. The vines here were trained on trees. Fundan in the first century was strong, full, affecting head and stomach – and so it was not often served at symposia, according to the *Epitome of Athenaeus*. By Pliny's time its reputation was not so high. Martial writes a gift-poem for wine that claims to be Fundan of the Opimian vintage, 220 years old.

Strabo 5.3.6; Pliny *NH* 14.65; Martial 13.113; Aretaeus p. 128 Hude; *CIL* 15.4566–9.

Funeral feast, a usage observed in several societies in the ancient Mediterranean and Near Eastern world. We know of funeral feasts either because evidence of the foods consumed still survives entombed, or because texts refer to them. Depictions of feasts in tomb paintings or on reliefs may represent a funeral feast, or a feast that the deceased had enjoyed while alive, or one to be enjoyed in the afterlife.

Perideipnon is the classical Greek term for a funeral feast. In classical Greek practice this special meal, at which one may suppose the qualities of the deceased were commemorated, gave its name to a literary form of which (according to Diogenes Laertius) at least two examples were recorded, by SPEUSIPPUS and by Timon of Phlius.

Diogenes Laertius 9.109–15.

H. Helbaek, 'Vegetables in the funeral meals of pre-urban Rome' in *Early Rome* vol. 2 (Lund, 1956); W.B. Emery, *A Funerary Repast in an Egyptian Tomb of the Archaic Period* (Leiden, 1962); P.A. Février, 'A propos du repas

Figure 7 Small fruits of the Mediterranean. Upper row, left to right: sloe (*Prunus spinosa*), bullace and damson (*Prunus domestica* subspecies): for Greek and Latin names see PLUM. Medlar (*Mespilus germanica*), Greek *mespilon*, Latin *mespilum*. Myrtle (*Myrtus communis*), Greek *myrton*, Latin *myrtum*. Far right: Christ's thorn (*Paliurus Spina-Christi*), Greek *paliouros*, *lotos*, Latin *paliurus*. Lower row, left to right: wild sour cherry (*Prunus Cerasus*), wild sweet cherry (*Prunus avium*), Morello cherry (variety of sour cherry), Greek *kerasos*, Latin *cerasus* and *cerasus silvestris*. European strawberry (*Fragaria vesca*),Latin *fragum*. Arbutus or tree strawberry, Greek *mimaikylon*, Latin *arbutus*, *unedo*.

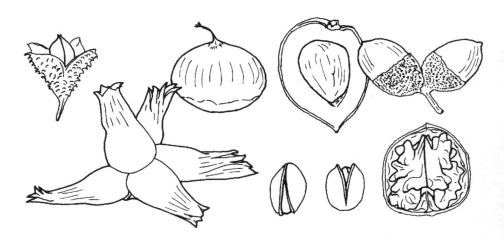

Figure 8 Nuts of the classical Mediterranean. Upper row, left to right: beech mast (*Fagus sylvatica*), fruit of Greek *oxye*, Latin *fagus*. Chestnut (*Castanea sativa*), Greek *diosbalanos*, *balanos Euboikos*, *kastanos*, Latin *castanea*. Almond (*Prunus dulcis*), Greek *amygdalon*, *karyon Thasion*, Latin *amygdalum*. Acorn (*Quercus* spp.), Greek *balanos*, Latin *glans*. Lower row, left to right: hazelnut (*Corylus avellana*), Greek *karyon Pontikon*, *leptokaryon*, Latin *nux avellana*. Pistachio (*Pistacia vera*), Greek *pistakion*, Latin *pistacia*. Walnut (*Juglans regia*), Greek *karyon*, *karyon basilikon*, Latin *iuglans*, *nux*.

funéraire. Culte et sociabilité' in *Cahiers archéologiques* vol. 26 (1977) pp. 29–45; N.H. Ramage, 'A Lydian funerary banquet' in *Anatolian Studies* vol. 29 (1979) pp. 91–5; R. Hägg, 'Funerary meals in the geometric necropolis at Asine?' in *The Greek Renaissance of the Eighth Century B.C.: tradition and innovation. Proceedings of the Second International Symposium at the Swedish Institute in Athens, 1–5 June, 1981* ed. R. Hägg (Stockholm, 1983), pp. 189–94; C. Compostella, 'Banchetti pubblici e banchetti privati nell'iconografia funeraria romana del I secolo d.C.' in *Mélanges de l'Ecole Française de Rome: antiquité* vol. 104 (1992) pp. 659–89; Hugh Lindsay, 'Eating with the dead; the Roman funerary banquet' in *Meals in a Social Context: aspects of the communal meal in the Hellenistic and Roman world* ed. I. Nielsen and H.S. Nielsen (Aarhus: Aarhus University Press, 1998), pp. 67–80.

Furniture required in classical Greek dining of the typical kind included a high couch, *kline*, and a small low table, *tripous* or *trapeza*. They are depicted on innumerable vases of the sixth, fifth and fourth centuries BC; most scenes allot one couch and one table to each guest, though it is clear from others, and from literary texts, that two or even three diners might crowd on to a couch. In later Greek practice, as in classical Rome, one reclined on a low dais or on built-in larger couches (see ARCHITECTURE); the number of tables (Latin *mensa*) was also probably reduced.

Athenaeus *E* 47e–49d.

E.M. Smith, 'Some Roman dinner tables' in *Classical Journal* vol. 50 (1955) pp. 255–60; G.M.A. Richter, *The Furniture of the Greeks, Etruscans and Romans* (London, 1966); J. Boardman, 'Symposion furniture' in *Sympotica: a symposium on the symposion* ed. Oswyn Murray (Oxford: Oxford University Press, 1990) pp. 122–31.

G

Galanga *see* GINGER

Galbanum *see* ASAFOETIDA

Galen (born 129, died after 210). Galen was important in his lifetime, as physician to the emperor Commodus, and even more important later as author of a range of medical textbooks which remained classics until early modern times.

An informal, indeed garrulous, writer, Galen is significant in studies of food history both for works focusing directly on the subject and for asides on food and wine elsewhere in his writings. In *On the Properties of Foods* he provides the classic statement of the flavour and dietary properties of most of the foods that were used in classical cultures. His insatiable curiosity and his interest in what would now be called medical demography led him to include information on foods eaten by the poor as well as the rich. *On the Properties of Simples* (not yet available in English) performs the same task for spices, medicinal plants and other substances used as drugs.

Galen is cited elsewhere in this book by volume and page number of Kühn's edition. This standard reference system will be found in the margins of the later editions (but not the English translations) listed separately below.

Galeni opera omnia ed. and Latin tr. C.G.

Kühn (Leipzig, 1821–33); John Scarborough, 'The Galenic question' in *Sudhoffs Archiv* vol. 65 (1981) pp. 1–31; *Galen: Problems and Prospects. A collection of papers submitted at the 1979 Cambridge conference* ed. V. Nutton (London, 1981); Richard J. Durling, *A Dictionary of Medical Terms in Galen* (Leiden: Brill, 1993); V. Nutton, 'Galen and the traveller's fare' in *Food in Antiquity* ed. John Wilkins and others (Exeter: Exeter University Press, 1995) pp. 359–70; *Galen on Pharmacology: philosophy, history and medicine. Proceedings of the Vth International Galen Colloquium, Lille, 16–18 March 1995* ed. Armelle Debru (Leiden: Brill, 1997); John Wilkins, 'Eating à l'ancienne: the lesson of Galen' in *Petits propos culinaires* no. 68 (2001) pp. 18–28.

Galen AF: *De alimentorum facultatibus* 'On the properties of foods'. Translation in *Galen on Food and Diet* tr. Mark Grant (London: Routledge, 2000) pp. 68–190; note that there is additional relevant commentary in Grant 1997. Critical text: *Galeni de sanitate tuenda, de alimentorum facultatibus, de bonis malisque sucis, de victu attenuante, de ptisana* ed. K. Koch, G. Helmreich and others (Leipzig: Teubner, 1923).

—— BM: *De rebus boni malique suci* 'On substances containing good and bad humours'. Text and Latin translation: Kühn (above) vol. 6 pp. 749–815.

—— DA: *De antidotis* 'On antidotes'. Text and Latin translation: Kühn vol. 14 pp. 1–209.

—— DP: *De ptisane* 'On barley gruel'. Translation in *Galen on Food and Diet* tr. Mark Grant (London: Routledge, 2000) pp. 62–7. Text and Latin translation: Kühn vol. 14 pp. 1–209.

—— SF: *De simplicium medicamentorum temperamentis ac facultatibus* 'On the properties of simples'. Text and Latin translation: Kühn vol. 11 p. 379 to vol. 12 p. 377.

——*ST: De sanitate tuenda* 'On retaining health'. Text and Latin translation: Kühn vol. 6 pp. 1–452.

——*VA: De victu attenuante* 'On the thinning diet'. Translation in Galen, *Selected Works* tr. P.N. Singer (Oxford: Oxford University Press, 1997) pp. 305–24. Text, Italian translation and commentary: Galeno, *La dieta dimagrante* ed. Nino Marinone (Turin: Paravia, 1973). Critical text: Koch and others (above) pp. 433–51.

Game *see* HUNTING

Gardening, in the usual ancient and modern classifications, is separate from farming. Ancient gardens produced vegetables and roots for household consumption, as well as culinary and medicinal herbs. Fruit-growing was sometimes regarded as a subdivision of gardening rather than farming. Monthly instructions for the gardener are included in Palladius's farming manual.

Columella *DA* 10, 11.3; Pliny *NH* 19.49–63; Palladius *OA passim*.

Jashemski 1979–93; *Ancient Roman Villa Gardens* ed. E.B. MacDougall (Washington: Dumbarton Oaks, 1987) (*Dumbarton Oaks Colloquia on the History of Landscape Architecture*, 10); M.A. Tomei, 'Nota sui giardini antichi del Palatino' in *Mélanges de l'Ecole Française de Rome: antiquité* vol. 104 (1992) pp. 917–51; *Garden History: garden plants, species, forms and varieties from Pompei to 1800: symposium, Ravello, June 1991* ed. Dagfinn Moe, James H. Dickson and Per Magnus Jorgensen (Rixensart: PACT Belgium, 1994).

Gargilius Martialis, Q(uintus), Latin technical author of the third century AD. His works are known only in fragmentary form. They are relatively difficult of access and have not been translated into English. The incomplete text *On Gardens* is occasionally cited in this book: he also wrote *Medicines from Vegetables and Fruits, The Care of Oxen* and *Martial's Vegetables*. He used and cited Mago, Diophanes of Nicaea, Celsus, Columella and 'Aristotle *On Farming*'.

Gargilius Martialis DH: *De hortis* 'On Gardens'. Text and Italian translation: *Q. Gargilii*

Martialis De hortis ed. Innocenzo Mazzini (Bologna: Patròn, 1978).

Garlic, important culinary and medicinal plant of the Old World. Garlic was grown by the third millennium BC in Egypt and Mesopotamia. It has an important place in the MESOPOTAMIAN RECIPE COLLECTIONS. Garlic was familiar in Greece and Rome throughout classical times.

Garlic grows well in southern Europe, so long as it is kept well drained. When harvested in early summer it can be hung up in the smoke and kept till next year (see Palladius for instructions). It came from MEGARA to market at Athens in the fifth century BC and after.

The good things about garlic are that it is a health-giving food and adds relish to the flavour of cooked dishes. The bad thing about garlic is that it gives a strong odour to the breath (and not only the breath) of those who eat it copiously. It was good for those on a journey, says Anthimus; it was not so good for those who had to live crowded together. Its unwanted effects explain why garlic incurs some obloquy in Greek comedy and some disapproval in Roman literature, from Horace among others. These effects also explain why it occurs very little in the recipes of *Apicius*, and why it is often forbidden in the rules followed by ascetics and monks.

Garlic (*Allium sativum*) is Greek *skorodon*, Latin *allium*. In Greek the head is *kephale*, the clove *aglis* or *skelis*.

Aristophanes,. *Acharnians* 520–2, *Wealth* 718; Hippocrates *R* 54; Theophrastus *HP* 7.4.11; Callimachus 495 Pfeiffer; Cato *DA* 48, 70 with Dalby *ad l.*; Horace, *Epodes* 3.1–3; Columella *DA* 11.3.19–23; Pliny *NH* 19.111–16, 20.50–7; Palladius *OA* 12.6; Anthimus *OC* 61 with Grant *ad l.*

D.J. Crawford, 'Garlic-growing and agricultural specialization in Graeco-Roman Egypt' in *Chronique d'Égypte* vol. 48 no. 2 (1973) pp. 350–63; Darby and others 1977 pp. 656–60; H. Waetzoldt, 'Knoblauch und Zwiebeln nach den Texten des 3. Jt.' in *Bulletin on Sumerian Agriculture* no. 3 (1987) pp. 23–56; M. Stol, 'Garlic, onion, leek' in *Bulletin on Sumerian*

Agriculture no. 3 (1987) pp. 57–92; Gowers 1993 pp. 280–310; Zohary and Hopf 1993 pp. 183–5; Simoons 1998 pp. 136–57.

Garum (Greek *garos*; Latin *garum, liquamen*; Aramaic *tser*), a fermented fish sauce familiar in the Mediterranean world from the fifth century BC to the end of antiquity. *Garum* is frequently mentioned in ancient literature. This evidence is amply supported by finds of amphorae that once contained the product and by excavations of salteries, from Portugal and Spain to the Crimea, where it was manufactured.

Textual evidence ranges from fragments of satyr plays by Aeschylus and Sophocles (evoking the odour of 'stinking *garos*') to full-scale recipes supplied in the Byzantine *Geoponica*: these recipes are unattributed but probably, like most of the rest of the collection, derive from sources of the Roman imperial period. Various fish and parts of fish (innards of mackerel and tunny were the preferred ingredients) were mixed with plentiful salt and allowed to stand in the sun for about two months, after which a liquid (whence the alternate Latin name *liquamen*) was allowed to flow off. This salty, fishy liquid was *garum*; the solid residue was ALLEC. Both products had a strong smell, which no authors praise.

The best *garum* was the same colour as amber Falernian wine. A good name in ancient fish sauce was *garum sociorum* 'partners' *garum*', mentioned several times in literature and also evoked in amphora inscriptions. This was the *garum* in which the gourmet APICIUS (2) prescribed that red mullet should be drowned (Pliny *NH* 9.66, cf. Manilius, *Astronomica* 4.681; Ausonius, *Epistles* 21).

Curiously, very little information is forthcoming about how *garum* was used, until, towards the end of the classical period, the recipes of *Apicius* give an unambiguous answer. It was a culinary ingredient, called for in almost every dish, including many sweets. It is possible that *garum* was also used as a table condiment, but the evidence for this is weak.

This product was clearly quite different from anything now made in Europe, and few modern scholars grasped its nature until, in 1952, Grimal and Monod showed its close resemblance to the fish sauce of modern Vietnam and southeast Asia. This is the product of fermenting fish with salt for several weeks in the sun. It is a free-flowing liquid, the best quality being sherry-coloured while cheaper varieties are dark brown or black. It has a strong smell and is much more often used as a culinary ingredient than as a table sauce. Southeast Asian fish sauce is very salty and is the usual way to add salt in cooking; it is also a plentiful natural source of umami or monosodium glutamate. One notes that scarcely any recipes in *Apicius* call for salt, and that *garum* is added to many sweet dishes as well as to practically all the savoury ones: in Roman cuisine, as in southeast Asian, we may conclude, *garum* was the usual culinary flavour enhancer.

Don't try the recipes for fermented *garum*: the result may contain carcinogens.

Strabo 3.4.6; Pliny *NH* 31.93–7; Galen *SF* 12.377; Pollux *O* 6.65; Athenaeus *E* 67b–c quoting Aeschylus fragment 211 Radt; Anthimus *OC* 9 with Grant *ad l.*; *Geoponica* 20.46 (for translation see Flower and Rosenbaum 1961 pp. 22–3).

P. Grimal and T. Monod, 'Sur la véritable nature du garum' in *Revue des études anciennes* vol. 54 (1952) pp. 27–38; M. Ponsich and M. Tarradell, *Garum et industries antiques de salaison dans la Méditerranée Occidentale* (Paris, 1965); R. Etienne, 'A propos du garum sociorum' in *Latomus* vol. 29 (1970) pp. 297–313; I.M. Mackie, R. Hardy and G. Hobbs, *Fermented Fish Products* (Rome: Food and Agriculture Organization, 1971); D.P.S. Peacock, 'Amphorae and the Baetican fish industry' in *Antiquaries' Journal* vol. 54 (1974) pp. 232–43; D.J. Georgacas, *Ichthyological Terms for the Sturgeon* (Athens, 1978) pp. 192–6; J.C. Edmondson, *Two Industries in Roman Lusitania: mining and garum production* (Oxford: BAR, 1987) (*BAR International Series*, 362), review by K. Greene in *Classical Review* vol.

42 (1992) pp. 407–9; Robert I. Curtis, *Garum and Salsamenta: production and commerce in materia medica* (Leiden: Brill, 1991); Grant 1999 pp. 19, 28.

- *Liquamen ex piris* was an alternative to *garum*, made from pears instead of fish, and is specifically recommended to vegetarians by Palladius. For a modern interpretation of the recipe see Grant 1999 pp. 30–1.

  Palladius *OA* 3.25.12.

- Latin *muria*, *salimoria*, Greek *halmyris*, Aramaic *muriyes* was a product with a family resemblance to *garum*. It was both salty and fishy, but was perhaps not fermented, and was at any rate sufficiently respectable in odour to be used as a table sauce. At Antipolis (Antibes), according to Martial, *muria* was made from tunnies, and it was good. At Barcino (Barcelona) they made a *muria* which Paulinus sent as a present to Ausonius; the latter complained that there was no classical Latin word for it but put it on his table anyway.

  Vindolanda Tablets 1.4=2.190; Martial 13.103; Galen *SF* 12.377; Ausonius, *Epistles* 21; Anthimus *OC* 29, 43 with Grant *ad l.*

- Greek *halme*, Aramaic *chalmi* is a more general term than the last; it is sometimes the salty liquor in which fish is stewed, sometimes a salty table dip (e.g. for tuna steak), sometimes a sauce or dressing for fish or for salad vegetables.

  Archestratus *H* 18, 37 Brandt; Antiphanes 221 Kassel; Axionicus 4 Kassel; Athenaeus *D* 329b with an inaccurate quotation of Aristophanes, *Wasps* 1127; Hesychius, *Lexicon s.v. halme*; Theodoret, *History of the Monks* 2.4.

- *Garum* was the chief ingredient in some standard mxtures used in cookery and medicine. *Hydrogaron* is fish sauce diluted with water, sometimes with herbs added. *Oxygaron* is fish sauce mixed with vinegar.

  Arrian, *Epictetus* 2.20.30; Galen *AF* 6.534; Athenaeus *E* 67e, *D* 366c.

Gastronomy means taking food seriously – its sources, its preparation, and principally its sensory qualities (aroma, flavour, texture) when eaten. There will be no gastronomy if no one has the resources to make food choices. There is gastronomy when there is enthusiasm for finding, making and savouring food, and

when relevant information and skills are shared and transmitted.

The resources have existed in all societies in which some people have wealth and leisure: for more than five thousand years in the Near East, for at least four thousand years in Greece, for at least three thousand years in Italy. The oldest pieces of evidence of the actual existence of gastronomy are these. First, the MESO-POTAMIAN RECIPE COLLECTIONS. Second, collections of varied foods and, especially, varied wines in Egyptian burials, from as early as 3000 BC and most notably in the tomb of TUTANKHAMUN. Third, the beginning of literary writing about foods and wines and the choices among them: there is little sign of this in ancient Near Eastern literature, but there are hints of it in the very oldest Greek literary texts, from HESIOD (about 700 BC) onwards. Fourth, by about the same date, in Greece, the identification and valuing of LOCAL SPECIALITIES.

By the fourth century, again in Greece, a varied and copious gastronomic tradition existed. There were professional COOKS; there was copious public talk about food (for example, in Athenian comedy) to which many were prepared to listen; there was writing about dinners (see PHILOXENUS (1)) and about cuisine (see ARCHESTRATUS). Greeks of this period traced some of their gastronomic traditions to LYDIA and SICILY. At the same period there are signs of a developed gastronomic tradition among the PERSIANS, though we have less information about this.

Gastronomy in the HELLENISTIC KINGDOMS continued earlier Greek and Persian traditions. In this context Rome takes its place as the last and greatest Hellenistic state. The beginnings of Roman gastronomy, including cooks, recipe collections (see CATO; CHRYSIPPUS OF TYANA; PAXAMUS), food writing (see ENNIUS) and wine appreciation, all except the last showing strong signs of Greek influence, were dated by Romans themselves to the second century BC. Conspicuous gastronomy at Rome peaked, according to Tacitus (*Annals* 3.55), in the last century BC and the first century AD. But gastronomy did not wither under the later Roman Empire; in the fourth century the recipe collection *Apicius* (see APICIUS (4)) demonstrates the range of ingredients that were sought and the subtlety of flavouring that was expected.

E.S. Ramage, *Urbanitas: ancient sophistication and refinement* (Norman: University of Oklahoma Press, 1973) (*University of Cincinnati Classical Studies*, 3); J.-F. Revel, *Un Festin en paroles: histoire littéraire de la sensibilité gastronomique de l'antiquité à nos jours* (Paris: Pauvert, 1979); J. Goody, *Cooking, Cuisine and Class* (Cambridge: Cambridge University Press, 1982), review by Jean-Louis Flandrin in *Annales* (1987) no. 2 pp. 645–52, reviews in *Food and Foodways* vol. 3 (1988–9) pp. 177–221; Griffin 1985 pp. 82–3; Gowers 1993; Dalby 1996 esp. pp. 93–112, 152–67; Dalby 2000 esp. pp. 25–30, 243–57; Wilkins 2000 esp. pp. 257–311.

Gaul, region of the Roman Empire roughly equating with modern France. On food and wine in pre-Roman Gaul see CELTS. The Celtic inhabitants of Gaul had been farmers but not gardeners: many food vegetables and cultivated fruits were introduced to Gaul in Roman times, and by the early medieval period France was a place for fine fruit varieties. Vines had been introduced to southeastern Gaul long before Roman times (see NARBONENSIAN WINES), but it was probably after the Roman conquest (in the 50s BC) that vines were first planted in central and northern Gaul. By late antiquity there were good wines in several regions, including the neighbourhood of Bordeaux and the Moselle valley.

Among food specialities of Roman Gaul Ausonius lists oysters from the Atlantic coast – the territories of the Santones, Pictoni and Meduli (modern Médoc) and the region of Aremorica (Brittany) – and from Narbo and Massilia on the Mediterranean shores. It is known from archaeological finds that GARUM and salt fish were manufactured along both these coasts. Ausonius also gives a poetic catalogue of the fish of the River Moselle. Martial names a square cheese, *quadra*, from Tolosa (Toulouse).

Martial 12.32; Ausonius, *Epistles* 9, *Mosella*.

A. Grenier in Frank 1933–40 vol. 3 pp. 379–644 [article in French]; R. Sanquer and P. [Galliou], 'Garum, sel et salaisons en Armorique gallo-romaine' in *Gallia* vol. 70 (1972) pp. 199–223; Jean-Pierre Brun, 'L'oléiculture et la viticulture antiques en Gaule d'après les vestiges d'installations' in *La Production du vin et de l'huile en Méditerranée* ed. M.-C. Amouretti and J.-P. Brun (Athens: Ecole Française d'Athènes, 1993) pp. 307–41; Dalby 2000a pp. 88–99.

Gauran wine (Latin *Gauranum* Greek *Gauranos, Gaurianos*), a wine from the volcanic hills near Puteoli in Campania. The local *calventina* grape variety was one of those grown here.

Gauran was a fine wine, contending with Massic (in the classification given by Pliny) for fourth place among Italian wines. It was produced in small quantities and was therefore expensive. It was more 'oily' than Praenestine and Tiburtine, according to Athenaeus's source; 'watery' and light enough to be drunk young, according to Galen.

Pliny *NH* 3.60, 14.38, 14.64; Statius, *Silvae* 3.5.99; Juvenal 9.57; Marcus Aurelius, *Letters* [Fronto vol. 1 p. 177 Haines]; Galen *ST* 6.335, *BM* 6.806, *DA* 14.16, *On Therapeutic Method* 10.833; Athenaeus *E* 26f; Symmachus, *Letters* 1.8; *CIL* 4.5511.

Tchernia 1986 pp. 202–3.

Gazelle *see* DEER

Geoponica, an extensive manual of farming in Greek, compiled (like several other encyclopaedic works) under the Byzantine emperor Constantine Porphyrogennetus in the tenth century AD, based on earlier materials in Greek and Latin. Most chapters are ascribed to authors of the Roman imperial period or before; some are unattributed. The works of many of the authors thus excerpted are otherwise lost. PAXAMUS, who wrote on cookery, is among them. No modern English translation of the *Geoponica* is available.

W. Gemoll, *Untersuchungen über die Quellen, der Verfasser und die Abfassungszeit der Geoponica* (Berlin, 1883); E. Fehrle, *Richtlinien zur Textgestaltung der griechischen Geoponica* (Heidelberg, 1920); John A.C. Greppin, 'The Armenian and the Greek Geoponica' in *Byzantion* vol. 57 (1987) pp. 46–55.

Geoponica. Critical text: *Geoponica sive Cassiani Bassi scholastici de re rustica eclogae* ed. H. Beckh (1895, reprinted 1994, *BT*).

Germany, a region which in spite of efforts at conquest remained independent of the Roman Empire. The Roman historian Tacitus, in a monograph written in his youth, provides information, somewhat romanticised, on the lifestyle of Germany, emphasising the differences between German and Roman diet. Further information comes from Pliny, who had served on the German frontier: he tells us that the Germans grew oats and lived on *puls* 'porridge' made from oats. Both these sources relate to the first century AD. The extent of eventual Roman influence on Germany can be judged by archaeological finds of trade goods and by Latin loanwords in German, which include many cultivated fruits and vegetables (*Bohne* 'bean', *Pflaume* 'plum', *Fenchel* 'fennel') and other foods (*Käse* 'cheese', *Wein* 'wine').

Although ethnically indistinguishable from GAUL, the two Roman provinces along the Rhine, bordering on Germany, were officially called *Germania*. Several legions were stationed along the border. Much archaeological work has been done on the legionary headquarters and border forts; food information includes latrine deposits (see the table given by Knörzer, p. 44).

Mela, *Geography* 3.3.28; Pliny *NH* 18.149–50; Tacitus, *Germania* 23, *al.*

K.-H. Knörzer in *New Light on Early Farming: recent developments in palaeoethnobotany* ed. Jane Renfrew (Edinburgh: Edinburgh University Press, 1991) pp. 31–50; Junkelmann 1997;

J.R. Greig, 'Plant foods in the past: a review of evidence from northern Europe' in *Journal of Plant Foods* vol. 5 (1983) pp. 179–214; C. Dickson, 'The Roman army diet in Britain and Germany' in *Archäobotanik: dissertationes botanicae* vol. 133 (1989) pp. 135–54.

Gilthead *see* BREAM

Ginger, culinary and medicinal spice. Ginger probably originated in southern China but is easily transplanted in warm climates. By Roman times, assuming classical authors are correctly informed, it was grown in Sri Lanka and in Trogodytica (modern Eritrea). Its Greek and Latin names are loans from an Indic language (cf. Pali *singivera*).

Dioscorides gives a good description of ginger and adds that producers in Trogodytica were already pickling ginger and exporting it in that form, in jars, to Italy: it was good to eat, pickle and all. Its medicinal effect, Dioscorides adds, is 'warming, digestive, gently laxative, appetising: it helps in cases of cataract and is an ingredient in poison antidotes.' It was frequently an ingredient in DIGESTIVES.

Ginger (*Zingiber officinale*) is Greek *zingiberi*, Latin *zingiber*.

Dioscorides *MM* 2.160; Pliny *NH* 12.28; Galen *SF* 11.880; Apicius 1.32, *al.*

Laufer 1919 pp. 545, 583; Miller 1969 pp. 53–7, 107–8; Dalby 2000a p. 181; Dalby 2000b pp. 21–6.

- Galanga (*Alpinia Galanga*) is the spicy root of a plant resembling ginger, native to southeast Asia. The root was used in medicine and cuisine in late antique and medieval Europe; it is first prescribed in the early sixth century by Aetius. It is *galanga* in late Greek and Latin.

  Aetius, *Medicine* 1.131, 11.13.116.

  Laufer 1919 pp. 545–6; Miller 1969 pp. 51–3.

- Zedoary is the root of *Curcuma Zedoaria*, grown in India. As with galanga, the first record of zedoary in the Mediterranean region comes in a prescription by Aetius for a kidney complaint. It is Greek *zador*.

  Aetius, *Medicine* 11.13.116.

Glaucus of Locri, author of a Greek work on cookery. Glaucus is probably to be dated to the fourth century BC. Athenaeus quotes from him one brief recipe, for a sauce to serve with meat: 'But *hyposphagma*: fried blood and silphium and grape syrup (or honey) and vinegar and milk and cheese and chopped aromatic herbs.' Athenaeus also attributes to Glaucus the view, stated in verse, that cookery was a profession for free men.

Athenaeus D 324a, 516c, 661e.

Bilabel 1921; Dalby 1996 pp. 110–11.

Gluttony *see* EXCESS

Glykismos, an aperitif, a sweet wine or spiced wine offered at municipal entertainments in Hellenistic Greek cities.

Pauline Schmitt-Pantel, 'Rite cultuel et rituel social: à propos des manières de boire le vin dans les cités grecques' in *In Vino Veritas* ed. Oswyn Murray and Manuela Tecuşan (London: British School at Rome, 1995) pp. 93–105.

Goat, domesticated animal important for its milk and its meat. The goat was domesticated in the Near East at the beginning of the Neolithic period. Goats were being kept in Greece and the southern Balkans by 6000 BC. Their milk was used for CHEESE by 3000 BC, because objects that appear to be cheese-strainers have been found at Thessalian sites of about that date. Goat's milk cheese was surely the commonest kind in classical Greece, and common enough in Roman Italy also.

Those with the leisure to choose find that goat meat is better at certain times of year, having a rank taste and smell at other times. It was considered highly nourishing by the dietary writers. A story was told of a Theban athlete who ate little else and was the star performer of his time, though his rivals mocked him for the smell of his sweat.

By classical times suckling kids were regarded as a delicacy – an expensive one,

since goats are not especially prolific and the animal provides much more meat when it is closer to its adult size. Philoxenus mentions an *eriphos galaktotrophos*, a milk-fed kid, among the centrepieces of a banquet.

The domesticated goat (*Capra Hircus*) has several names in Greek and Latin. In Greek the female is *aix*, the kid *eriphos*; the meat is *aigeion*. In Latin the female is *capra*, the kid *haedus*.

Homer, *Odyssey* 17.213–14; Hesiod *OD* 591; Hippocrates *RA* 49; Philoxenus D b.29 Page; Machon C 18.462 [Athenaeus D 583d]; Cleitomachus of Carthage [Athenaeus D 402c]; Athenaeus D 402c–d.

W. Richter, 'Ziege' in *RE* 1893–1972; Bökönyi 1974; Darby and others 1977 pp. 222–7; Toynbee 1996; Dalby 1996 p. 43, *al.*

- The wild goat of Europe (subsp. *Ibex*, also known as ibex and chamois) is often distinguished as *aigagros* in Greek. Wild goats were hunted in Greece and southern Europe in prehistoric times, and they continued to be hunted in the classical period.

  Hesiod, *Shield of Heracles* 407; Oppian, *Cynegetica* 2.326–76.

Goby, small sea fish, plentiful, sometimes nice and fat, but not delicate in flavour, and thus a fish eaten by the poor and underprivileged. They were sometimes counted among *petraioi*, 'rock-fish', like the WRASSE. Galen goes into some detail on their dietary quality.

The goby (*Gobius niger* and several other species) is Greek *kobios*, Latin *gobius, gobio*.

Machon C 5.31–45 with Gow *ad l.*; Martial 13.88; Juvenal 11.37; Galen *AF* 6.718–20; Athenaeus D 309b–e, also 300f citing Dorion, also 355b citing Diphilus of Siphnos.

Thompson 1947 p. 137; Davidson 1981 p. 135.

- The same Greek and Latin words sometimes designate a river fish, which the goby is not. In these cases a gudgeon (*Gobio Gobio*) is probably intended.

  Athenaeus D 309e citing Dorion; Ausonius, *Mosella* 130–4.

Golden Age, a myth, or series of myths, developing through ancient literature. The earliest recorded version is Hesiod's myth of the five successive races, the golden race, the silver, the bronze, the heroes, and the iron race. The earth bore its fruits for the golden people without the need for labour.

This five-member sequence does not recur in later narratives, but the Golden Age persists. The basic theme, used in varied ways by authors pursuing different purposes, is accompanied by varied images of the foods that offered themselves, unsown and unharvested, to the fortunate people of that age: sometimes fine foods, sometimes nearer to famine foods (such as acorns), sometimes almostmagical foods such as MANNA, nearly always vegetarian foods. Animal foods came into use following the offering by Prometheus of the first SACRIFICE.

Hesiod *OD* 106–26 with West *ad l.*; Vergil, *Georgics* 1.118–59; Ovid, *Fasti* 4.395–402, *Metamorphoses* 1.89–112; Plutarch *EC* 993c–994b; Athenaeus *D* 267e–270a.

Bodo Gatz, *Weltalter, goldene Zeit und sinnverwandte Vorstellungen* (Hildesheim: Olms, 1967) (*Spudasmata*, 16); Jean-Paul Brisson, *Rome et l'âge d'or: de Catulle à Ovide, vie et mort d'un mythe* (Paris: Editions La Découverte, 1992).

Golden thistle, a root vegetable familiar in parts of southern Europe, little known elsewhere. As a typically rustic food this was served by Icarius and Erigone to their anonymous visitor Bacchus in a lost poem by Eratosthenes (see HOSPITALITY).

Golden thistle (*Scolymus hispanicus*), also known as Spanish salsify and Spanish oyster plant, is Greek *skolymos*, Latin *scolymus*.

Hesiod *OD* 582; Theophrastus *HP* 6.4.3–7; Pliny *NH* 22.86–7 citing Eratosthenes 34 Powell; Galen *SF* 12.125; Athenaeus *D* 371c quoting Numenius.

- Salsify (*Tragopogon porrifolius*) is Greek *tragopogon*.

Theophrastus *HP* 7.10.1; Dioscorides *MM* 2.143; Pliny *NH* 21.89, 27.142.

Gold-of-pleasure or false flax (*Camelina sativa*), a plant native to southeastern Europe whose seeds provide edible oil. Seeds are found at late prehistoric and classical sites in Europe, but the plant has not been identified in classical texts.

Zohary and Hopf 1993 pp. 131–2; Junkelmann 1997 p. 147 (*Leindotter*).

Goose, group of large birds domesticated in prehistoric times in the Near East and southern Europe. The goose was a domesticated animal by the time of the earliest Greek literature.

The goose was surely the commonest farmyard bird in early Greece until the spread of the chicken, from India and Iran, around 600 BC. The relative ubiquity of chickens, from that date onwards, explains why geese are less frequently mentioned in Greek and Latin literature. They continued to be kept, however, both for their meat and for their eggs, which are good food, though not so plentiful as hens' eggs. FATTENING of geese is mentioned in the *Odyssey*; for the later practice of force-feeding to produce foie gras see below.

The greylag goose (*Anser Anser*), the species domesticated in Europe, is Greek *khen*, Latin *anser*. The white-fronted goose (*Anser albifrons*) was equally familiar in early Egypt; this species, in fact, is thought to have been domesticated there in Pharaonic times.

Homer, *Odyssey* 19.536; Herodotus 2.72; Aristophanes, *Acharnians* 878; Ovid, *Fasti* 1.453; Pliny *NH* 10.52–6; Galen *AF* 6.703; Athenaeus *D* 384a–c quoting Archestratus *H* 58 Brandt; Palladius *OA* 1.30; *Apicius* 6.5.5, 6.7; Anthimus *OC* 22 with Grant *ad l.*

Thompson 1936 p. 325; Buck 1949 p. 177; Darby and others 1977 pp. 283–6; Brewer and others (1995 ?) pp. 121–3; Toynbee 1996; Kevin C. MacDonald and Roger Blench, 'Geese' in *CWHF* 2000 vol. 1 pp. 529–31.

- Greek *khenalopex*, in texts referring to

Greece, is possibly the ruddy shelduck (*Tadorna ferruginea*). When writing of Egypt, Greek authors probably intend by *khenalopex* the Nile goose (*Alopochen aegyptiacus*), a familiar wild bird.

Herodotus 2.72; Aristophanes, *Birds* 1295 with Sommerstein *ad l.*; Aristotle *HA* 559b29; Herondas 4.31; *Zenon Papyri* 562.17; Pliny *NH* 10.56; Aelian, *Nature of Animals* 5.30; Athenaeus *E* 58b citing Epaenetus and Heracleides of Syracuse.

- The liver of force-fed geese, known as foie gras, is nowadays an expensive delicacy. The first reference to this gourmet product may possibly be in a fragment by Eubulus, writing in the mid fourth century BC: the point is discussed by 'Plutarch' in Athenaeus's dialogue. However, goose livers are good to eat whether or not the goose is specially fattened, so a reference to goose liver does not prove that foie gras is intended. Pliny is certain that the idea of foie gras was Roman, and names two possible inventors in the first century BC, one of whom is Metellus Scipio, governor of Syria in 49–48. Foie gras is certainly mentioned by Horace and Martial. The Greek phrase *trypheron sykoton*, literally equivalent to *foie gras*, occurs first in the late second century AD in a text by Pollux.

Athenaeus *D* 384a–c quoting Eubulus *F* 99 Kassel; Horace, *Satires* 2.8.88; Ovid, *Fasti* 1.453; Pliny *NH* 10.52; Persius 6.71; Juvenal 5.114; Martial 13.58; Galen *AF* 6.704; Pollux *KH* 83.

Silvano Servienti, *La Grande Histoire du foie gras* (Paris: Flammarion, 1993).

Goosefoot *see* ORACH

Gourd, large fruit whose flesh may be cooked and eaten as a vegetable. It dried well, making a basis for a good cheap winter vegetable soup for slaves (Nicander gives instructions).

The gourd or bottle gourd (*Lagenaria siceraria*) is Greek *sikya*, Latin *cucurbita*. Translation of these words as pumpkin, squash or marrow and identification with *Cucurbita maxima* and *C. Pepo* are erroneous: these are South American plants, introduced to Europe in modern times.

Theophrastus *HP* 7.2.9, 7.3.5; Nicander *F* 72 Schneider [Athenaeus *D* 372e–f]; Pliny *NH*

19.69–74; Athenaeus *E* 58f–59f; Palladius *OA* 4.9.16; Anthimus *OC* 56.

J. Organ, *Gourds* (London, 1963); M. Stol, 'The cucurbitaceae in the cuneiform texts' in *Bulletin on Sumerian Agriculture* no. 3 (1987) pp. 57–92; Waruno Mahdi, 'Linguistic data on transmission of Southeast Asian cultigens to India and Sri Lanka' in *Archaeology and Language* ed. Roger Blench and Matthew Spriggs (London: Routledge, 1997–9) vol. 2 pp. 390–415.

Graecinus, Julius (executed AD 39 or 40), author of a Latin work on vines and wine. Graecinus was the father of Julius Agricola, Roman governor of Britain under Domitian. He farmed at Forum Julii, modern Fréjus. His work survives only in borrowings by later authors, notably Columella, who cites him eleven times, and Pliny.

Seneca, *De Beneficiis* 2.21.5; Tacitus, *Agricola* 4 with Ogilvie and Richmond *ad l.*

Grain or cereal, the principal and preferred staple food of the classical world. It is suggested by Foxhall and Forbes (below) that grain made up 70 to 75 per cent of total food intake. LEGUMES, neither principal nor preferred, were a secondary staple and a lifeline for many poorer people.

During the classical period the availability of bread WHEAT was gradually increasing. The other major cereal crops were BARLEY and EMMER, both of which were used for porridges and cakes more than for bread. Relatively minor cereal crops were MILLET (two species) and EINKORN. On the edges of the classical world, SPELT, RYE, SORGHUM and OATS were to be found.

Cereals were spoiled and contaminated by weeds (notably DARNEL and oats), by crop diseases (to avert this the Romans observed the festival *Robigalia* on 25 April) and by the attack of insect pests on stored grain (see under ARCHAEOZOOLOGY).

As staple foods, necessary for survival, cereals attracted the attention of ancient governments as most other foods did not. They attempted to facilitate their import, to locate supplies when usual sources proved inadequate, to regulate the price and prevent profiteering, and thus to ensure that an adequate ration was available to citizens, either at a standard price or free of charge. *Annona* was the Latin name for Rome's grain supply and for a citizen's grain ration; it was also the name for the imperial administrative office dealing with grain and other food supplies.

N. Jasny, 'Competition among grains in classical antiquity' in *American Historical Review* vol. 47 (1941–2) pp. 747–64; N. Jasny, 'Wheat prices and milling costs in classical Rome' in *Wheat Studies* vol. 20 no. 4 (1944); Buck 1949 pp. 506–18; Lionel Casson, 'The grain trade of the Hellenistic world' in *Transactions of the American Philological Association* vol. 85 (1954) pp. 168–87; E. Lieber, 'Galen on contaminated cereals as a cause of epidemics' in *Bulletin of the History of Medicine* vol. 44 (1970) pp. 332–45; E. Tengström, *Bread for the People: studies of the corn-supply of Rome during the late Empire* (Stockholm, 1974); R.P. Duncan-Jones, 'The price of wheat in Roman Egypt under the Principate' in *Chiron* vol. 6 (1976) pp. 241–62; G. Rickman, *The Corn Supply of Ancient Rome* (Oxford: Clarendon Press, 1980); L. Foxhall and H.A. Forbes, '*Sitometreia*: the role of grain as a staple food in classical antiquity' in *Chiron* vol. 12 (1982) pp. 41–90; Peter Garnsey, 'Grain for Rome' in *Trade in the Ancient Economy* ed. Peter Garnsey, K. Hopkins and C.R. Whittaker (London, 1983); A.J.B. Sirks, *Food for Rome: the legal structure of the transportation and processing of supplies for the imperial distributions in Rome and Constantinople* (Amsterdam, 1991); Garnsey 1999 pp. 12–21.

Grape, fruit of the grape vine, useful as a fresh fruit, a dried fruit (raisin) and as the source of MUST and WINE. In all these roles, but especially the last, the grape was a major component of the diet of the ancient Mediterranean.

The grape vine is native to southern Europe and the Near and Middle East (wild grapes have disappeared from much of this region only in very recent times). The vine is thought to have been brought into cultivation in the Caucasus region (in or near modern Georgia) about 4000 BC, though wine from wild grapes was already being made by that time. Cultivated varieties spread to northern Mesopotamia, Syria, Palestine, Egypt and north Africa; also eastwards to Iran, Bactria and Sogdiana and (about 120 BC) onwards to China; also westwards through Anatolia and on to Greece and the Balkans, Italy and the western Mediterranean. It was under the Roman Empire that the vine was introduced to the Moselle and Rhine valleys and to southern Britain. It is likely (see GRAPE VARIETIES) that as knowledge of vine cultivation spread to new areas local wild grapes were taken into cultivation and crossed with already cultivated varieties.

The vine is a very long-lived plant if properly cared for. By classical times vine cultivation had reached a high level of skill: details are given in Latin agricultural writers. Something of Greek and Carthaginian knowledge of the subject survives in these and in the Byzantine agricultural compendium GEOPONICA.

The grape vine (*Vitis vinifera*) is *ampelos* in Greek, *vitis* in Latin.

Hippocrates *R* 55; Theophrastus *HP* 4.13.5–6, al.; Cato *DA passim*; Columella *DA* 5.1–5; Dioscorides *MM* 5.1–6; Pliny *NH* 14.8–150, 23.10–16; Galen *AF* 6.576–80; Athenaeus *D* 653e–654c; Palladius *OA passim*.

Laufer 1919 pp. 220–45; Buck 1949 pp. 378–9, 533–4; Darby and others 1977 pp. 711–16; Zohary and Hopf 1993 pp. 143–50; Jane Renfrew, 'Palaeoethnobotany and the origins of wine' in *The Oxford Companion to Wine* ed. Jancis Robinson (Oxford: Oxford University Press, 1994) pp. 702–4; Brewer and others (1995 ?) pp. 54–60; H.P. Olmo, 'The origin and domestication of the vinifera grape' in *The Origins and Ancient History of Wine* ed. Patrick E. McGovern, Stuart J. Fleming and Solomon H. Katz (London: Gordon and Breach, 1995) pp. 31–43; H. Kroll, 'Vor- und frühgeschichtliche Weinreben: wild oder angebaut? Eine abschließende Bemerkung' in *Trierer Zeitschrift* vol. 62 (1999); M.A. Murray, N. Boulton and C. Heron, 'Viticulture and wine production' in *Ancient Egyptian Materials and Technology* ed. P.T. Nicholson and I. Shaw (Cambridge: Cambridge University Press, 2000) pp. 577–608.

- Raisins (dried grapes) are Greek *astaphis*, *staphis*, Latin *uva passa*. The Greek term *botrys ex heliou* 'sun-dried grapes' is also found, prescribed as an invalid food in the Hippocratic text *Epidemics*. Palladius gives a detailed method for preparing *uva passa Graeca*, Greek raisins.

Herodotus 2.40; Hermippus 63 Kassel; Hippocrates, *Epidemics* 7.80; Palladius *OA* 11.22.

- Smoked raisins were a Roman favourite. These strongly flavoured dried grapes came from the Alban and Raetic vineyards (the latter being the ones that Augustus liked); also from north Africa, and these were the ones preferred by Tiberius.

Horace, *Satires* 2.4.72; Pliny *NH* 14.16.

- Wild grapes had their uses, particularly in medicine. For *oenanthe*, a wild grape conserve, a recipe is given by Palladius (*OA* 7.11).

Grape varieties were numerous in ancient times: perhaps there were already thousands of them, as there are today. Pliny cites Democritus as believing that the grape varieties of Greece could be counted; other people, Pliny adds, regarded them as uncountable and infinite. There is some evidence that, as has happened again in more recent times, the great range of varieties resulted partly from crossing with local races of the wild grape as vine cultivation spread across the ancient world. Varieties were developed and selected for suitability to particular climates and soils; for heavy cropping; for the suitability of their grapes for marketing fresh and for drying as raisins; and for the flavour and other qualities of the wine that could be made from them, either alone or blended.

The rapidity of development in this technical field is indicated by Pliny's information (which could be paralleled in modern wine-growing countries) as to the number of varieties which are clearly named after specific places, but are not grown in those places, having, one must usually presume, been completely replaced there by others that were found to do better. A second, direct indication of the rapid spread of varieties is the following, also from Pliny:

Within the last seven years there was discovered at Alba Helvia [Viviers] in Provence a vine whose blossoms are normally shed within a single day, rendering it very secure against bad weather. They call it *carbonica*, and the whole province now grows it.

The names given in classical sources can represent only a small proportion of the varieties that existed – the ones that spread beyond their place of origin and became known as sources of fine wine or table grapes. Names and spellings varied, as they do nowadays. Some varieties significant over a wide area and mentioned in literature are listed below.

Columella *DA* 3.2, *al.*; Pliny *NH* 14.36–47, *al.*; Macrobius *S* 3.20.7.

Jacques André, 'Contribution au vocabulaire de la viticulture: les noms des cépages' in *Revue des études latines* vol. 30 (1952) pp. 126–56; Tchernia 1986, especially pp. 184–8, 350–7.

- *Albuelis*, a variety of secondary quality for wine, was, according to Celsus, better on hill than plain, better on tree than trellis, better at top of tree than on lower branches. Hence plant it with *visulla*, said Pliny, which did best on the lower branches.

Columella *DA* 3.2.24 citing Celsus; Pliny *NH* 14.31.

- *Alexandrina*, with especially small and sweet grapes, perhaps identical with the variety briefly described by Theophrastus as growing on Mount Ida, is often identified with the modern currant grape, *Vitis vinifera* var. *corinthiaca*.

Theophrastus *HP* 3.17.6; Pliny *NH* 14.43.

- *Allobrox* was a group of varieties named for a region of Gaul, in the hills around Vienne southeast of Lyon, where it had been developed (see also NARBONENSIAN WINES). It included the three varieties *taburnum*, *sotanum* and *helvicum*. Their black grapes produced in the first century AD fine wine with a natural pitchy flavour. They gave a poorer quality when transplanted elsewhere, but they stood up well to a cold climate.

Columella *DA* 3.2.16; Pliny *NH* 14.18, 14.26; Plutarch *QC* 5.3.

- Greek *amethystos* 'unintoxicated', equated by Columella with Latin *inerticula nigra*.

The variety was supposed to make 'strong but non-intoxicating' wine.

Columella *DA* 3.2.24; Pliny *NH* 14.31.

- *Aminnia*, Greek *aminaia*, *aminnaia*, a recognised group of grape varieties typical of parts of Sicily and Italy, later transplanted successfully to Bithynia, producing fine wine. The yield was low; the wine aged well. In Columella's time growers were uprooting *aminnia* in favour of high-yielding varieties. The group included *aminnia minuscula* (or *germana minor*), *aminnia maior* (or *germana maior*, or *scantiana*), *gemina minor* (or *gemella*), *gemina maior*, *singularis*, *lanata*, *aminnia nigra* (or *syriaca*). *Aminnia maior* could be conserved as table grapes. Both the fruit and the resulting wine are described by Galen as 'austere' in flavour. For the varietal wine based on the *aminnia* grape see AMINNIAN WINE.

  Cato *DA* 6–7 with Dalby *ad l.*; Archigenes 21 Brescia; Dioscorides *MM* 5.19; Columella *DA* 3.2.7–13, 3.9.1–9; Pliny *NH* 14.21–2, 14.41, 14.47; Galen *ST* 6.335, *DA* 14.16, *al.*; *Geoponica* 4.1.3 and 5.17 both quoting Florentinus.

- *Apiana* was a pair of varieties, one early, one late. They produced fine, sweet, heady wine which became drier with age. They suited a cooler climate and did well in Etruria. Cato has a variety name *apicia*, perhaps identical, good for conserving as well as for wine. Columella gives a special recipe for PASSUM, raisin wine, made from *apiana* grapes.

  Cato *DA* 6–7; Columella *DA* 3.2.17–18, 12.39.3; Pliny *NH* 14.24, 14.81.

- *Arcelaca* gave the highest yield of any known variety. Pliny and others thought it was the same as Vergil's *argitis*, but Columella denies this.

  Columella *DA* 3.2.27; Pliny *NH* 14.35 [*s.v.l.*].

- *Argitis*, a variety of the second quality, very robust and productive in less fertile ground.

  Vergil, *Georgics* 2.99–100; Columella *DA* 3.2.21.

- *Balisca* or *basilica*, grown around Dyrrachium (in modern Albania), is said to be the same as the *coccolobis* grown in Spain. It had a high yield.

  Columella *DA* 3.2.19–20; Pliny *NH* 14.30–1.

- *Biturica* or *biturigiaca* was more robust and

higher in yield than any of the fine wine varieties, and came nearest to them in quality. It was presumably developed in the territory of the Bituriges Vivisci in Gaul, the region of modern Bordeaux.

Columella *DA* 3.2.28; Pliny *NH* 14.27.

- *Duracina* was a group of varieties or category of fruit especially suitable for marketing as table grapes. The name implies firmness of flesh and resilience of skin, and thus suitability for transport to market.

  Cato *DA* 7.2 with Dalby *ad l.*; Columella *DA* 3.2.1; Pliny *NH* 14.42; Suetonius, *Augustus* 76 (quoted at AUGUSTUS).

- *Eugenea* had been transplanted from Tauromenium in Sicily to the Alban district near Rome. The name is supposed to be identical with that of *ugni blanc*, grown now in southern France and Bulgaria. ALBAN WINE exemplified the best that *eugenia* could do.

  Cato *DA* 6; Varro *RR* 1.25; Columella *DA* 3.2.16; Pliny *NH* 14.25.

- *Graecula*, grown in Italy, is treated by Pliny as a variety originating in Chios or Thasos. It produced fine wine but was so low in yield that it was only worth growing on very fertile soil. By Columella *graecula* is treated as a group of varieties, 'Greeklings'. The group includes *mareotica*, *thasia*, *psithia* (see separate paragraphs for these three) and *sophortia*.

  Columella *DA* 3.2.24; Pliny *NH* 14.25.

- *Hedanos*, a grape variety in Nicander's verse, a formulaic adjective elsewhere.

  Nicander *A* 162, 181, cf. Hesychius, *Lexicon s.v. edane*, Homer, *Iliad* 14.172, Aeschylus, *Agamemnon* 1407.

- *Helvenaca* was a group of varieties, high-yielding but of poor quality, native to Gaul. It included the varieties *marcus*, *longa* (or *cana*) and *minor*. The latter alone, in some districts, might give wine that was good enough to last out the year. Pliny has a more nuanced estimate of *helvenaca*, appealing to the authority of Graecinus, who farmed in Gaul. The variety needed to be severely pruned in the way that was already typical of Gaul; failure to do this had led to the lack of success of *helvenaca* in Italy.

  Columella *DA* 3.2.25, 5.5.16; Pliny *NH* 14.32–3 citing Graecinus.

- *Helvola* or *varia* or *variana* was variable in colour. The darker grapes gave the largest quantity of must; the lighter made the best-flavoured wine. They did well when trained on trees. Cato names *helvola minuscula*.

Cato *DA* 6; Columella *DA* 3.2.23; Pliny *NH* 14.29.

- *Kapneos* (variously spelt) was a variety that bore sometimes black, sometimes white grapes; in fact neither, says Theophrastus, but a 'smoky' colour between the two. It was one of the varieties grown at Thurii, according to Pliny.

Aristotle, *Generation of Animals* 770b17–24; Theophrastus *HP* 2.3.2, *CP* 5.3.1–2; Pliny *NH* 14.39 (*capnios*); *Scholia on Aristophanes, Wasps* 151.

- *Lagea*, named by Vergil. Pliny describes it as a foreign variety not grown in Italy.

Vergil, *Georgics* 2.91, cf. Pliny *NH* 14.40.

- *Mainomene*, a prolific variety: for the choice of name compare the modern *folle blanche*.

Aristotle, *On Marvellous Things Heard* 846a38; Theophrastus *CP* 1.18.4.

- *Mareotica*, one of the varieties grouped by Columella as *graecula* (see above). Columella implies that it was grown in Italy; Pliny says flatly that it was not. Its origin appears to be Egypt (see under EGYPTIAN WINES).

Vergil, *Georgics* 2.91, cf. Pliny *NH* 14.40; Columella *DA* 3.2.24.

- *Murgentina* originated in Sicily; was grown in small quantity around Vesuvius and was also typical of Clusium (Chiusi): it flourished only on rich soil. An alternative name was *pompeiana*.

Cato *DA* 6; Varro *RR* 1.25; Columella *DA* 3.2.27; Pliny *NH* 14.35, 14.38.

- *Nomentana* was a group of grape varieties, said in Italy in the first century AD to produce fine wine comparable with *aminnia*, and including the varieties *nomentana minor* (or *rubellana*) and *nomentana scissa*. It was presumably named after Nomentum near ROME. Columella equates *faecenia* with *nomentana*, but Pliny distinguishes them.

Columella *DA* 3.2.14–15; Pliny *NH* 14.23, 14.27.

- *Praecia* or *pretia* included a larger and a smaller variety. Of secondary quality as wine grapes but of high yield, these were good for conserving.

Columella *DA* 3.2.23; Pliny *NH* 14.29.

- *Psithia*, a group of varieties well known in classical and Hellenistic times, suitable (when unripe) for making verjuice, but, more important, yielding grapes that when semi-dried made fine PASSUM or raisin wine. *Psithia* was counted among the Greek varieties (*graeculae*) grown in Italy, but it was unproductive when grown there. The scholia on Nicander identify *psithia* with PRAMNIAN WINE; Dioscorides links these names without explicitly identifying them.

Nicander *A* 181 with scholia; Vergil, *Georgics* 2.93, 4.269; Dioscorides *MM* 5.5, 5.6; Columella *DA* 3.2.24 (*pithia*); Pliny *NH* 12.130 (*psitia*); Statius, *Silvae* 4.9.38; Athenaeus *E* 28f.

Lambert-Gócs 1990; Dalby 2000a p. 137.

- *Raetica* was presumably the native variety used in RAETIAN WINE. It also produced the conserved table grapes that Augustus liked. A quite different and much poorer variety, grown in the Alpes Maritimae, shared the same name. Pliny classed *raetica* high, Columella low.

Columella *DA* 3.2.27; Pliny *NH* 14.16, 14.26, 14.41.

- *Spionia* was particular to the neighbourhood of Ravenna, where it liked the fogs and autumn rains. It was also planted elsewhere for its high yield.

Columella *DA* 3.2.27 [*s.v.l.*]; Pliny *NH* 14.34; cf. Strabo 5.1.7.

- *Thasia*, one of the varieties grouped by Columella as *graecula* (see above). Columella implies that it was grown in Italy; Pliny says flatly that it was not. Its origin appears to be Thasos in the north Aegean.

Vergil, *Georgics* 2.91, cf. Pliny *NH* 14.40; Columella *DA* 3.2.24.

- *Venucula, vennuncula* (and other names) did well in southern Campania between Surrentum and Vesuvius. At Tarracina in Latium they called it *numisiana*. It also provided table grapes.

Horace, *Satires* 2.4.71; Pliny *NH* 14.34.

- *Visulla* was a pair of varieties, *minor* and *maior*, much grown in the Sabine country (see SABINE WINE).

Columella *DA* 3.2.21–2; Pliny *NH* 14.28, 14.31.

Grass pea, legume once commonly used as human food in Europe, now seldom seen. Lathyrism, a dangerous disease, can result from over-use of grass peas in the diet.

The grass pea was domesticated either in the Near East or in southern Europe. *Lathyrus Cicera* may have been the wild ancestor, but this is uncertain. The domesticated species spread westwards along the northern shores of the Mediterranean, reaching southern France by the early first millennium BC. In classical Greece the grass pea was food for the poor, perhaps most commonly made into a thick soup, resembling lentil soup. Galen observed that poor people used grass pea in this way in his native Asia Minor.

The grass pea or chickling vetch (*Lathyrus sativus*) is Greek *lathyros*, Latin *ervilia*.

Hippocrates *R* 45, *Epidemics* 2.4.3=6.4.11; Alexis *F* 167 Kassel with Arnott *ad l.*; Theophrastus *HP* 8.3.1–2; Pliny *NH* 18.98; Galen *AF* 6.540–6 *passim*.

F. Kupicha, 'The infrageneric structure of *Lathyrus*' in *Royal Botanic Garden Edinburgh: notes* vol. 41 (1983) pp. 209–44; Zohary and Hopf 1993 pp. 114–16; Garnsey 1999 p. 38.

- The seeds of *Lathyrus Aphaca*, *L. Cicera*, *L. hirsutus*, *L. grandiflorus*, *L. Ochrus* and other related species, known as vetchling and birds' pease in English, were being collected from the wild as food, in southern France and Sicily, by 7000 BC; similar finds are reported from Franchthi Cave from levels dated to 10,000 BC. The various wild species of *Lathyrus* and *Vicia* (see VETCH) are very difficult to identify in Greek and Latin texts. Greek terms include *aphake* and *okhros*, the latter common in the sources and probably a cultivated species; Latin terms include *aphaca*, *cicera* and *cicercula*.

  Alexis *F* 167 Kassel with Arnott *ad l.* (*okhros*); Theophrastus *HP* 8.3.1–2 (*okhros*); Pliny *NH* 18.124 (*cicercula*), 27.38 (*aphaca*); Palladius *OA* 2.5 (*cicercula*), 4.6 (*cicera*).

- Theophrastus mentions *arakhidna* and another unnamed species, both related to the grass pea, as useful for their edible tubers. These are presumably *Lathyrus tuberosus* and *L. amphicarpus*.

Theophrastus *HP* 1.1.7, 1.6.12; Pliny *NH* 21.89 (*arachidna*).

Grayling, river fish of northern Europe. This is the 'light *umbra*, deceiving the eye with its rapid swimming' described by Ausonius in the River Moselle. Aelian and Ambrose know of it in the Ticino of northern Italy.

The grayling (*Thymallus Thymallus*) is *thymallus* in the Latin of Italy, *umbra* in the Latin of Gaul.

Aelian, *Nature of Animals* 14.22; Ambrose, *Hexaemeron* 5.2; Ausonius, *Mosella* 90.

Greece. For food behaviour and food specialities of Greek regions and cities see AMBRACIA; ARCADIA; ATHENS; BOEOTIA; BYZANTIUM; CALYDON; DELPHI; HELLESPONT; MACEDONIA; MEGARA; SICYON; SPARTA; THESSALY. On the Greek islands see CHIOS; CORCYRA; CRETE; CYTHNOS; DELOS; EUBOEA; LESBOS; RHODES; SAMOS; THASOS. On prehistoric Greece see also FRANCHTHI (a site in the Peloponnese); KASTANAS (in southern Thrace); MINOANS; MYCENAEANS. On Greek wines see CHIAN WINE; COAN WINE; CORCYRAEAN WINE; CRETAN WINE; EUBOEAN WINE; LESBIAN WINE; LEUCADIAN WINE; MENDAEAN WINE; PEPARETHAN WINE; RHODIAN WINE; THASIAN WINE; see also BIBLINE WINE and PRAMNIAN WINE.

J.A.O. Larsen in Frank 1933–40 vol. 4 pp. 259–498; K.F. Vickery, *Food in Early Greece* (Urbana, 1936); G.E.M. Jones, 'Interpretation of archaeological plant remains: ethnographic models from Greece' in *Plants and Ancient Man* ed. W. van Zeist and W.C. Casparie (Rotterdam, 1984) pp. 43–61; J.M. Hansen, 'Palaeoethnobotany in Greece: past, present and future' in *Contributions to Aegean Archaeology. Studies in honor of W.A. McDonald* ed. N.C. Wilkie and W.D.E. Coulson (Minneapolis, 1985) pp. 171–82; S. Payne, 'Zooarchaeology in Greece: a reader's guide' in *Contributions to Aegean Archaeology. Studies in honor of W.A. McDonald* ed. N.C. Wilkie and W.D.E. Coulson (Minneapolis, 1985) pp. 211–44; Dalby 1996; Flandrin and Montanari 1996; Martine Leguilloux, 'L'alimentation carnée au 1er millénaire avant J.-C. en Grèce continentale et dans les Cyclades: premiers résultats archéozoologiques' in *Paysage et alimentation dans le monde grec* ed. Jean-Marc Luce (Toulouse, 2000) pp. 69–95; Catherine Perlès, *The Early Neolithic in Greece: the first farming communities in Europe* (Cambridge: Cambridge University Press, 2001).

Grey mullet, important group of sea and river fish. Newly caught grey mullet provided much-appreciated and fairly expensive food along Mediterranean coastlines. The marine grey mullet was the best, says Xenocrates; however, the grey mullet of the Nile was extensively salted (see below) and was familiar well beyond the borders of Egypt.

The grey mullet was to be bought at Aegina, Abdera and Sinope, according to Archestratus; it was at its best in autumn, as Dorion, Lynceus and Xenocrates agree. Aristotle describes how grey mullet were caught off the coast of Phoenicia, the males taken when they cluster around a previously trapped female. The proper way to cook this prized fish is specified grandiosely in a play by Antiphanes (216):

> The mullet which has fasted for a whole day and night, nicely sealed, sprinkled with salt, turned out flat, well browned, as one reaching the end of his race, is now sizzling and shrieking, while a boy stands by to sprinkle him with vinegar, and the crushed stalk of silphium from Libya is at hand to aid with its divine rays.

The reference to 'fasting' in this quotation takes up one of the alternative names of the grey mullet in Greek, *nestis*, literally 'faster'; Athenaeus gives numerous examples of literary play based on this name, which his speakers explain from the fact that the grey mullet has a vegetarian diet and will not take a live bait.

Greek *kestreus* is the commonest term for the grey mullet species. When used generally it covers the whole group; some authors, however, use *leukos* and *leukiskos* as general terms for the group. There were numerous names for grey mullet in Greek; only those used in a food context are listed below. For other terms see especially Athenaeus. The general Latin term, more commonly used than any of the Greek ones, is *mugil*.

Archestratus *H* 43 Brandt; Hippocrates, *Sacred Disease* 2; Antiphanes 216, 221 Kassel; Aristotle *HA* 541a19–22, 591a17–592b4; *Acraephia Price List*; Xenocrates *T* 5, 28, 30; Athenaeus *D* 118b–c citing Dorion, also 306d–308d, also 313f quoting Lynceus *F* 20.

Thompson 1947 *s.vv.*; Darby and others 1977 pp. 372–9; Davidson 1981 pp. 140–4; Higginbotham 1997 pp. 46–7.

- Greek *kephalos*, literally 'head', is very commonly encountered in texts as the name of a grey mullet species; it is the same as *khelon*, says Aristotle; the best of all grey mullets in terms of food quality, says Hicesius; at its peak at Miletus where the Gaeson joins the sea, says Archestratus, and at its best more generally – as Galen explains – in bays that are fed by great rivers. The *kephalos* is probably to be identified with *Mugil Cephalus*. The evidently equivalent Latin term *capito* occurs in classical texts only once in this sense, but is supported by reflexes in Romance languages.

  Archestratus *H* 45 Brandt; Cato *DA* 158 (*capito*); Galen *AF* 6.708–13; Athenaeus *D* 306d–308d citing Hicesius.

- When used as a specific name Greek *kestreus* applies probably to *Liza Ramada*.

  Athenaeus *D* 118c, 306d–308d citing Hicesius.

- The *kestreus* of the Nile (*Liza Ramada* and other species) was the commonest food fish of the great river, and frequently illustrated in reliefs and paintings from the Pharaonic period. This is apparently the *leukos*, the sacred 'fish that they call white' mentioned in a fragment of a lost poem by Theocritus on an Egyptian theme. The grey mullet of the Nile was conserved and, evidently, widely marketed in that form. For the Roman period details are provided by Xenocrates. The salt mullets called *Mendesioi*, evidently named after the city where they were prepared, are mentioned by Sopater of Paphos, about 300 BC, and also in the dialogue of Athenaeus's *Deipnosophists*, as if still familiar about AD 200. *Apicius* provides two recipes for sauce for salt mullet, *ius in mugile salso*.

Strabo 17.2.4–5; Xenocrates *T* 149 (see translation at NILE FISH); Athenaeus *D* 118f–119a quoting Sopater 12 Kaibel, also 284a quoting Theocritus fragment 3 Gow; *Apicius* 9.10.6–7.

Darby and others 1977 pp. 372–8.

- Reliefs from Pharaonic Egypt clearly show the salting of mullet roe, now called in Arabic *butarikh*, and in English botargo. Both words derive from Greek *ootarikhos* 'salt fish egg'. The Greek word is recorded from classical times only in the form of a paraphrase by Diphilus of Siphnos, a third-century BC author, who says that *ta ton tarikhon oa* 'the eggs of salt fish' are hard to digest and hard to excrete. It may be guessed that the sauce *ius in mullo taricho*, for which *Apicius* provides a recipe, is for mullet roe or botargo.

Athenaeus *D* 121c citing Diphilus of Siphnos (on this text see also Georgacas pp. 167–87); *Apicius* 9.10.9; Simeon Seth, *On the Properties of Foods* p. 125 Langkavel.

John P. Hughes and R. Gordon Wasson, 'The etymology of botargo' in *American Journal of Philology* vol. 68 (1947) pp. 414–8; D.J. Georgacas, *Ichthyological Terms for the Sturgeon and Etymology of the International Terms Botargo, Caviar and Congeners* (Athens, 1978).

- Greek *khelon*, *khellon* (sometimes identified with *bakkhos*) was the smallest grey mullet according to Diphilus. It might be identified with *Liza saliens*.

Athenaeus *D* 306e–f citing Hicesius, also 356b citing Diphilus of Siphnos.

- Greek *myllos* was a fish of the Danube and the Black Sea, where it was salted. The word is thought to denote one of the grey mullet species.

Aelian, *Nature of Animals* 14.23 (*myalos*); Galen *AF* 6.729, 6.746–7; Athenaeus *D* 118c–d.

- Greek *myxinos* was one of the smaller grey mullets, possibly *Liza aurata*.

Aristotle *HA* 543b14 (*myxon*); Athenaeus *D* 306e–f citing Hicesius, also 356b citing Diphilus of Siphnos.

- According to Epicharmus and Polemon the grey mullet was called *plotis*, 'floater'. Other sources apply this name to the MORAY EEL as found in the sea off Rhegium in southern Italy.

Athenaeus *D* 307b quoting Epicharmus 44 Kaibel and Polemon.

- For the freshwater chub, which resembles the grey mullet and is likened to it by ancient authors, see CHUB.

Groundsel (*Senecio vulgaris*), a potherb used in Greece and Italy. Pliny cites it from Callimachus, possibly from the episode in which Hecale offered HOSPITALITY to Theseus. It is Greek *erigeron*, Latin *senecio*.

Pliny *NH* 25.167 citing Callimachus fragment 585 Pfeiffer.

Grouper, big sea fish related to BASS. The grouper was in demand at Athens, according to Aristophanes, and good at Rhodes according to Lynceus.

The grouper or mérou (called a sea-perch by Thompson, an old-fashioned English usage) is *Epinephelus Guaza*. The Greek name is *orphos*, whence Latin *orphus*. These names may also belong to the rarer *Epinephelus aeneus* and to the similar wreckfish, stone bass or cernier, *Polyprion americanus*.

Aristophanes, *Wasps* 493; Athenaeus *D* 315a–c, also 285e quoting Lynceus *F* 8.

Thompson 1947 pp. 187–8; Davidson 1981 pp. 67–71.

Grouse, large game bird of Europe and the Near East. The sand-grouse or ryper (*Bonasa Bonasia* and other species) is Greek and Latin *tetrax*, Latin also *tetraon*.

Aristophanes, *Birds* 884; Pliny *NH* 10.56; Athenaeus *D* 398b–399a.

Thompson 1936 p. 282; Toynbee 1996.

Gudgeon see GOBY

Guinea fowl, farmyard bird domesticated in prehistoric Africa south of the Sahara. The guinea fowl (unlike the CHICKEN) was familiar in Pharaonic (and later) Egypt. However, the gradual spread westwards in the mid first millennium BC of the chicken, a more amenable and productive species, ensured that the guinea fowl would be a curiosity, rather than a farmyard staple, in classical Greece and Rome. They were 'the latest exotic bird to reach our dinner tables', according to Varro; they were a suitable sacrifice, for poorer worshippers who could not afford a large animal, at the biennial festival for the Egyptian goddess Isis at Tithorea in Phocis, central Greece. Instructions for rearing them are given by Columella, who clearly distinguishes between the two major varieties (one of which had in fact originated in northeastern Africa, the other in west Africa).

The guinea fowl (*Numida Meleagris*) is Greek and Latin *meleagris*, Latin also (*gallina*) *Numidica, Africana*.

Scylax 112; Varro *RR* 3.9.18; Horace, *Epodes* 2.53; Strabo 16.4.5; Columella *DA* 8.2.2; Petronius *S* 93 (*Afrae volucres*); Pliny *NH* 10.74, 10.132; Statius, *Silvae* 2.4.28; Suetonius, *Caligula* 22; Martial 3.58, 13.45, 13.73; Pausanias 10.32.16; Athenaeus *D* 655a–e, also 201b quoting Callixeinus of Rhodes; *Apicius* 6.8.4 (*pullus Numidicus*).

R.A. Donkin, *Meleagrides: an historical and ethnogeographical study of the guinea fowl* (London: Ethnographica, 1991).

Gunda *see* SEBESTEN

Gurnard and piper, small sea fish, not without their attractions to the gastronome. 'Shining gurnards,' says a character in a lost play by Epicharmus: 'we split them, grilled them, seasoned them, and took bites.' Dorion, not disputing the method, provides a fuller recipe: 'They should be split along the spine, grilled, and seasoned with fresh herbs, cheese, silphium, salt and olive oil. Then they should be turned, more oil added, salt sprinkled on; and finally taken off the fire and soused in vinegar.'

The gurnards and pipers, belonging to the genera *Trigla, Trigloporus* and *Chelidonichthys*, are *kokkyx* in Greek and *rubellio* in Latin. For the flying gurnard see under FLYING FISH.

Hippocrates *R* 48, *Internal Medicine* 21; Acraephia Price List (*kokkoux*); Pliny *NH* 32.138 (*rubellio*); Galen *AF* 6.727; Athenaeus *D* 309e–f quoting Epicharmus 164 Kaibel and Dorion, also 324f quoting Speusippus; *Apicius* 10.1.15 (*rubellio*).

H

Hadrian wine (Greek *Adriakos, Adrianos;* Latin *Hadrianum*) from the neighbourhood of Adria in Picenum on the Adriatic coast of central Italy – and not, in spite of Pliny's careless assertion, from Adria in Venetia at the head of the Adriatic gulf. The wine is frequently named in papyri from Egypt, to which it began to be exported as early as the fourth century BC. It is perhaps the Picene wine (Latin *Picenum,* Greek *Pikenos*), one of the seven named and high-priced wines of the Empire, in *Diocletian's Price Edict.*

Antiphilus 22 Gow [*Anthologia Graeca* 6.257] with Gow *ad l.;* Philip 42 Gow [*Anthologia Graeca* 9. 232]; Dioscorides *MM* 5.6.7; Pliny *NH* 14.67; Galen *ST* 6.275, 6.334–5, *On Therapeutic Method* 10.485, 10.833, *To Glaucon on Therapeutic Method* 11.87; Athenaeus *E* 33a; *Diocletian's Price Edict* 2.1.

Tchernia 1986 pp. 55, 167–8, 260, 348–9; D. Rathbone, 'Italian wines in Roman Egypt' in *Opus* vol. 2 no. 1 (1983) pp. 81–98.

- The *Praetutianum* vineyards, in the neighbourhood of Adria and Truentum, were (as shown by Tchernia) either adjacent to, or incorporated in, the *Hadrianum* wine region. Praetutian was ideal for making MULSUM, according to Pliny.

 Dioscorides *MM* 5.6.7–8, 5.6.11; Pliny *NH* 3.110–12, 14.67, 14.75 [*s.v.l.*]; Silius Italicus 15.568.

 Tchernia 1986 pp. 131, 348–9.

- *Palmense* wine, named alongside Praetutian, apparently came from neighbouring vineyards.

Pliny *NH* 14.67.

Hake, rockling and whiting, group of sea fish. In dietary texts these species are placed midway between tough and tender. They are often mentioned, but are not so often said to be good to eat.

There were many names for them, and the names are variously defined; to many who dealt with them, the distinctions of species were not worth noticing. The fishes concerned include the rockling (*Gaidropsarus tricirratus* and other species), the forkbeard (*Phycis blennioides*), the blue whiting (*Micromesistius Poutassou*), the ling (*Molva macrophthalma*), the Mediterranean hake (*G. mediterraneus*) and the common hake (*Merluccius Merluccius*). The hake grows larger than any of the others, at up to a metre in length.

Acraephia Price List (*gelabrias*); Xenocrates *T* 2 (*oniskos, bakkhos*); Pliny *NH* 9.61 (*asellus, collyrus, bacchus*), 32.146; Galen *AF* 6.720–4; Athenaeus *D* 118b–d citing Dorion, also 315e–316a quoting Archestratus *H* 14 Brandt (see Olson and Sens *ad l.*) and Dorion.

Thompson 1947 *s.vv.;* Andrews 1949; Davidson 1979 pp. 51–70; Davidson 1981 pp. 59–64.

- The most general terms are Greek *onos, oniskos,* Latin *asellus.* Minor terms, now difficult to distinguish, are Greek *bakkhos, gale, delkanos, gados, hepatos, lebias, mazeas, maxeinos* and *kallarias* (also spelt *galleria* and *khellares*). Dorion (see reference above) identifies the *onos* with the *gados,* distinguishing it from the *galleria*. He gives *bakkhos* and *oniskos* as alternative names for the latter. Archestratus identifies the *onos* and *kallarias*. Greek *hepatos* and *lebias* are synonyms, Archestratus seems to say; *hepatos* and *mazeas*, according to Xenocrates; *hepatos* and *gale*, according to Aelian; *lebias* and *delkanos* according to Dorion. Later authors, from Galen onwards, identify *onos* and *oniskos*, and the Latin *asellus* clearly equates to both. The English translation 'cod' is sometimes used for some or all of these names; this is inaccurate, since cod are not found in the Mediterranean.

- Latin *asellus*, literally 'little donkey', is a name for the common hake, the Mediterranean hake and the forkbeard: the name corresponds to Greek *oniskos* and *onos*. The only recipe in *Apicius* uses the minced flesh of *asellus* as an ingredient in a 'milk patina', a distant ancestor of blancmange.

  Ovid, *Halieutica* 133; *Apicius* 4.2.13.

- Greek *hepatos* was good at Delos and Tenos in the central Aegean; it was palatable and moderately nourishing; but what was it? It was like *phagros* and *erythrinos*, according to Speusippus, and these are breams; it was a 'rock fish' like a wrasse, according to Diocles of Carystus; it was like the *gale* (see below) but with a shorter beard, according to Aelian. Andrews (above) suggests an identification with the ling.

  Xenocrates *T* 27; Galen *AF* 6.720; Aelian, *Nature of Animals* 15.11; Athenaeus *D* 108a, also 301c quoting Archestratus *H* 27 Brandt and Diocles of Carystus, also 327c citing Speusippus, also 329d citing Mnesimachus.

- Greek *oniskos*, literally 'little donkey', is probably the common hake. As a food it was nourishing and productive of good humours, but its quality depended on what it had been feeding on.

  Xenocrates *T* 2, 36; Galen *AF* 6.721–4, *al.*; Athenaeus *D* 315e–316a.

- Greek *onos*, literally 'donkey', when used specifically, is the Mediterranean hake, a soft-fleshed fish, according to Phylotimus; sometimes also the forkbeard.

  Galen *AF* 6.720–1 citing Phylotimus; Athenaeus *D* 315e–316a quoting Epicharmus 67 Kaibel.

- Latin *mustela* (*marina*) and Greek *gale* are names for the rockling and forkbeard. Its liver was prescribed medicinally in cases of epilepsy. For the freshwater *mustela* see BURBOT.

Ennius *H* 1; Pliny *NH* 32.112; Aelian, *Nature of Animals* 15.11.

Hamilcar, Punic author on food or wine, mentioned by Columella but otherwise unknown.

Columella *DA* 12.4.2.

Hare, an important animal in Greek food writing since this was the largest game animal likely to be encountered near Athens. Most of Xenophon's brief manual of hunting is in fact about hunting the hare. Hare was therefore a prestigious food, a typical lover's gift (as seen in vase paintings of the sixth and fifth centuries BC), a fine presentation for a dinner or an intimate supper. A recipe is given by Archestratus (his only surviving instruction for a meat dish):

> There are many ways, many rules for the preparation of hare. This is the best, that you should bring the roast meat in and serve to everyone while they are drinking, hot, simply sprinkled with salt, taking it from the spit while still a little rare. Do not worry if you see the ichor seeping from the meat, but eat greedily. To me the other recipes are altogether out of place, gluey sauces, too much cheese, too much oil over, as if one were cooking a weasel.

In Roman Italy the position of hare was different. Larger game, in the form of wild BOAR, was available close to Rome. Hares were farmed, giving their name in fact to the *leporaria* – enclosures in which not only hares but other 'wild' animals might be kept. Both these reasons help to explain why hare was a less prestigious food in Rome than in earlier Greece. It was, however, recommended by dieticians, as by Anthimus here:

> Hares, if they are quite young, can be taken with a sweet sauce including

pepper, a little cloves and ginger, seasoned with putchuk and spikenard or tejpat leaf. Hare is an excellent food, good in cases of dysentery, and its bile can be taken, mixed with pepper, for earache.

Modern interpretations of these recipes are given by Dalby and Grainger 1996 pp. 75–6 and Grant 1999 pp. 123–4. In ancient iconography hares are often depicted feeding on grapes, their favourite delicacy.

Hare (*Lepus capensis*) is Greek *lagos* (also *dasypous* 'swift-foot' and *ptox* 'cowerer'), Latin *lepus*.

Eupolis 174 Kassel; Aristophanes, *Acharnians* 1112 with scholia; Xenophon, *On Hunting* 2–8; Varro *RR* 2.preface.5, 3.3, 3.12 with Flach *ad l.*; Oppian, *Cynegetica* 3.504–25; Athenaeus D 399d–401b quoting Archestratus H 57 Brandt (see Olson and Sens *ad l.*), also 656c–e; Anthimus *OC* 13 with Grant *ad l.*

Liliane Bodson, 'Données antiques de zoogéographie. L'expansion des léporidés dans la Méditerranée classique' in *Les Naturalistes belges* vol. 59 (1978) pp. 66–81; D.W. Rathbone, 'Breeding hares for medicinal uses' in *Zeitschrift für Papyrologie und Epigraphik* vol. 47 (1982) pp. 281–4; B. Laurioux, 'Le lièvre lubrique et la bête sanglante: réflexions sur quelques interdits alimentaires du haut Moyen Age' in *L'Animal dans l'alimentation humaine: actes du colloque international de Liège, 1986* ed. Liliane Bodson (Liège, 1988) pp. 127–32; Gamkrelidze and Ivanov 1995 pp. 440–1; Toynbee 1996.

- In Greek cuisine the offal and blood of hare were prepared separately in the traditional dish *mimarkys*, briefly described by Pollux.

  Aristophanes, *Acharnians* 1112 with scholia; Pollux O 6.57; Hesychius, *Lexicon s.v. mimarkys* citing Pherecrates 255 Kassel.

Harpocration of Mendes, Egyptian author of a Greek work *On Cakes*, possibly to be dated to late Hellenistic times. It is cited once by Athenaeus.

Athenaeus D 648b–c.

Bilabel 1921; Dalby 1996 p. 164.

Hartwort (*Tordylium* spp.), genus of wild plants, used in Greece in drugs and medicinal wines and also as potherbs and culinary herbs. *Tordylium Apulum*, small hartwort, is said to be still used for food in Greece. According to Aristotle, a deer will find and eat hartwort immediately after giving birth to young.

Ancient Greek names are *seseli* (Hippocrates *RA* 23, *Epidemics* 7.101; Alexis F 132 Kassel [*s.v.l.*]: see the judicious Arnott *ad l.*; Aristotle *HA* 611a18; Theophrastus *HP* 9.15.5; Dioscorides *MM* 3.53), *tordilon* (Nicander *T* 841; Dioscorides *MM* 3.54; Pliny *NH* 24.177), *kaukalis* (Theophrastus *HP* 7.7.1–2; Dioscorides *MM* 2.139); Latin also *sili* (Pliny *NH* 20.36–7, 22.83).

S. Facciola, *Cornucopia: a source book of edible plants* (Vista: Kampong Publications, 1990) p. 19; Dalby 1996 p. 236 n. 176, p. 250 n. 13.

Hazelnut and filbert. Trees of these species spread gradually from northeastern Turkey after the last ice age and were widespread across Europe by the later Mesolithic period. In classical times, as now, they were much grown in Mediterranean lands but the big plantations remained in the region of Pontus (northern Turkey) from which supplies of hazelnuts came to Greece. To Romans hazelnuts were typical of, or at least named after, Praeneste near Rome and Abella in Campania. Like other dried fruits and nuts, their usual use in classical dining was to munch after a meal, alongside wine. Hazelnut oil, known in medieval Iran, is not recorded in ancient use.

The hazelnut (*Corylus avellana* and related species) is Greek *karyon Herakleotikon*, *karyon Pontikon*, *leptokaryon* and other names, Latin (*nux*) *avellana*, *nux Praenestina*.

Hippocrates R 55 (*karya strongyla* 'round nuts'); Theophrastus *HP* 3.6.5; Cato *DA* 8, 133 (*nux Abellana, nux Praenestina*); Dioscorides *MM* 1.125; Pliny *NH* 15.88–9, 23.150; Galen *AF* 6.609, *SF* 12.15; Athenaeus E 52a–54d; Macrobius S 3.18.5–7; Palladius *OA* 3.25.31; Anthimus *OC* 89.

Zohary and Hopf 1993 pp. 179–80.

Head, a source of nourishing and tasty meats and of varied textures. Note Herodotus's assertion – which may have been partly intended to shock his Greek audience – that after sacrifice in Egypt an animal's head would be cut off, cursed, and if there was a market at hand with Greek traders, sold to them; if there was not, it would be thrown in the river.

Greek *hemikraira*, Latin *sinciput*, was a traditional delicacy, the split head of a pig, of which a character in a fragmentary comedy by Crobylus claims, 'By Zeus, I didn't leave a single bit.' The split head of a wild boar was also of high repute.

Herodotus 2.39.4; Crobylus 6 Kassel; Pliny *NH* 8.209; Persius 6.70; Macrobius *S* 3.13.12 quoting Metellus Pius.

Heart, one of the 'vital organs' grouped as SPLANKHNA in Greek terminology. In classical sacrifice heart was roasted, tasted by the participants and shared with the god. It was a special item, not a forbidden food. From the dietary point of view, Galen observes, it is nourishing food if well cooked. The philosopher PYTHAGORAS, however, forbade the eating of animal hearts.

Diogenes Laertius 8.19; Galen *AF* 6.680, *BM* 6.771.

Hecale *see* HOSPITALITY

Hecate, Greek underworld goddess. Offerings to Hecate were made at crossroads, and when left behind by the celebrants were eaten by beggars or by sacrilegious revellers like the club of *Triballoi* at Athens. Hence the *mainis*, a cheap fish, was 'food for Hecate' in a Greek comedy by Antiphanes, food that you would not mind leaving as a wayside sacrifice, knowing that it would be filched from the altar.

Semonides 7.56 West; Demosthenes, *Against Conon* 39, cf. Eubulus *F* 75 Kassel (see Hunter *ad l.*).

D.R. West, *Some Cults of Greek Goddesses and Female Daemons of Oriental Origin* (Kevelaer: Butzon & Bercker, 1995) (*Alter Orient und Altes Testament*, 233).

Hegesippus of Tarentum, author of Greek works on cookery and on cake-making, perhaps of the fourth century BC. Athenaeus cites Hegesippus for a list of the ingredients of KANDAULOS: 'fried meat and grated bread and Phrygian cheese and dill and rich broth'.

Athenaeus *D* 516c–d, also 643e citing Callimachus fragment 435 Pfeiffer.

Bilabel 1921; Dalby 1996 p. 111.

Heidelberg Papyrus, a fragment containing recipe collections in Greek on both sides of the papyrus sheet. The text on the recto is part of a collection of recipes made or copied in the third century AD. Recipes include fish soup, ham, liver and *laganophake* (see PASTA). The text on the verso was added at least a century later and is perhaps part of an informal collection of recipes or notes gathered by the then owner of the papyrus. Interpretations of several recipes are given by Grant 1999 pp. 124–7, 131, 137. These are the first extensive English versions from the Heidelberg Papyrus.

Heidelberg Papyrus: text, German translation and commentary: F. Bilabel, *Opsartytiká und Verwandtes* (Heidelberg, 1920) (*Sitzungsberichte der Heidelberger Akademie der Wissenschaften, Stiftung Heinrich Lanz. Philosophisch-historische Klasse* 1919 no. 23; *Mitteilungen aus der Heidelberger Papyrussammlung* no. 1).

Hellebore, medicinal plant, a dangerous purge well known to ancient physicians. Its powerful reputation is demonstrated by the fact that Cato gives a recipe for a purging wine made from vines around whose roots hellebore had been buried.

True hellebore (*Helleborus cyclophyllus* and *Helleborus niger*) is to be distinguished from white hellebore or false hellebore (*Veratrum album*). Hellebore is Greek *helleboros*, Latin *veratrum*.

Hippocrates *R* 35, *RA* 23, *Aphorisms* 4.13–16, *al.*; Theophrastus *HP* 9.10.1–4, 9.17.1–3; Cato *DA* 115; Dioscorides *MM* 4.148, 4.162; Pliny *NH* 25.47–64; Aulus Gellius 17.15.

- Greek *to pharmakon*, 'the medicine', when the term is used in a specific sense, is hellebore, the purge par excellence, taken as a drastic cure for the madness caused by drinking.

  Hippocrates, *Epidemics* 5.2 with Smith *ad l.*

Hellenistic kingdoms, those established in succession to the empire of ALEXANDER THE GREAT, and, more generally, the monarchies of the Greek world in the last three centuries BC. Like Alexander himself, his Hellenistic successors appear to have taken an interest in the transplanting of plant species and varieties, particularly in spreading food plants that were familiar in the Greek diet to regions to which Greek culture was newly spreading, notably MESOPOTAMIA and EGYPT. Hellenistic foods and food customs were in practice a conflation of those of classical Greece with those of the earlier cultures of the Near East.

Hellenistic courts were noted for the LUXURY of their lifestyle, and particularly of their dinners and symposia, which resembled those of earlier Greece but were far more lavish and costly. There are some lively descriptions in Athenaeus's *Deipnosophists*.

Several dietary authors were physicians to early Hellenistic kings: ERASISTRATUS (if correctly identified) to Seleucus I of Syria, APOLLODORUS (if correctly identified) to an early Ptolemy of Egypt, DIPHILUS OF SIPHNOS to Lysimachus of Thrace. One would almost like to believe that the 'Letter of DIOCLES of Carystus to King Antigonus' is genuine, and so to add Diocles to the list – but it is certainly a forgery. Aśoka, king of northern India in the third century BC, prided himself on encouraging his fellow monarchs in the west to transplant medicinal plants: the only evidence that his interest was shared is provided by the unusual hobby of

ATTALUS Philometor, who grew POISONS in his palace garden. However, both Seleucids and Ptolemies presided over important experiments and successes in the naturalisation of Greek food plant species and varieties in the Near East.

Aśoka, *Rock Edict* 2 [for translation see N.A. Nikam and Richard McKeon, *The Edicts of Aśoka* (Chicago: University of Chicago Press, 1959)]; Strabo 15.3.11; Athenaeus *D* 193c–196a, 210c–211e, 438c–440b, 540a–c, 549d–550c.

D.J. Crawford, 'Food: tradition and change in Hellenistic Egypt' in *World Archaeology* vol. 11 no. 2 (1979) pp. 136–46; D.J. Thompson, 'Agriculture' in *The Cambridge Ancient History* vol. 7 part 1 (Cambridge, 1984), 2nd edn; Oswyn Murray, 'Hellenistic royal symposia' in *Aspects of Hellenistic Kingship* ed. Per Bilde, Troels Engberg-Pedersen, Lise Hannestad and Jan Zahle (Aarhus: Aarhus University Press, 1996) pp. 15–27; Daniel Ogden, *Polygamy, Prostitutes and Death: the Hellenistic dynasties* (London: Duckworth, 1999); Andrew Dalby, 'To feed a king: tyrants, kings and the search for quality in food and agriculture' in *Paysage et alimentation dans le monde grec* ed. Jean-Marc Luce (Toulouse, 2000) pp. 133–44.

Hellespont, the strait linking the Propontis (Sea of Marmara) with the northern Aegean. The Hellespont was rich in seafood, whence the epic formula *Hellesponton ep' ikhthyoenta* 'to the fishy Hellespont' used in the *Iliad* – though, as Plato observed, the Greeks besieging Troy are never described as eating any of this seafood. Bonito (see TUNNY) was naturally to be found there in large quantity, since the biennial migration of this species took it from the Black Sea to the Aegean. Oysters were also plentiful, and there was excellent lobster.

Homer, *Iliad* 9.360; Hipponax 26 West; Plato, *Republic* 404c; Archestratus *H* 24, 35, 56 Brandt; Aristotle *HA* 549b15–17; Ennius *H*; Catullus fragment 1; Vergil, *Georgics* 1.207.

Dalby 2000a pp. 158–9.

Heracleides (1) 'Criticus' or 'Creticus', obscure author of a brisk topography of Greece in the third century BC, surviving in fragments, that sometimes refer to food and wine. The text has also been called 'Pseudo-Dicaearchus'.

W.H. Duke in *Essays and Studies Presented to William Ridgeway* (Cambridge, 1913) pp. 228–48.

Heracleides P: *Periegesis.* Text and German translation: F. Pfister, *Die Reisebilder des Herakleides* (Vienna, 1951) (*Sitzungsberichte der Österreichische Akademie der Wissenschaften, philosophisch-historische Klasse,* 227 part 2). Text and Latin translation: in *Fragmenta historicorum Graecorum* ed. C. Müllerus (Paris: Didot, 1841–83) vol. 2 pp. 254–64.

Heracleides (2) of Syracuse, Greek cookery author. 'Heracleides of Syracuse *On Cookery*' is cited five times by Athenaeus, on subjects ranging from the JOHN DORY to the dietary qualities of eggs.

Athenaeus *D* 105c, 114a, 328d, 661e, *E* 58b.

Bilabel 1921; Dalby 1996 p. 161.

- In his list of cookbook writers Athenaeus says that two authors, both called Heracleides of Syracuse, had written on the subject. There is one citation of 'Heracleides of Syracuse *On Regulations*', and this may perhaps be the second author: it concerns the cakes called *mylloi,* shaped like women's sexual parts, which were made in Syracuse for the festival *Thesmophoria.*

  Athenaeus *D* 647a with Gulick *ad l.,* cf. 516c.

Heracleides (3) of Tarentum, Greek medical author of the first century BC. Among other works Heracleides wrote a *Symposium* which is several times cited by Athenaeus. To judge by these citations it consisted of discussions of food and diet.

Athenaeus *D* 79e, *E* 53c, *al.*

Heracles, Greek god (Greek *Herakles,* Latin *Hercules*), a latecomer to Mount Olympus. In Athenian Old and Middle Comedy (fifth and fourth centuries BC) Heracles is frequently depicted as an unashamed glutton, greedy for beef. Heracles has a quite different renown as the hero who brought the first olive tree from the land of the Hyperboreans, beyond the north wind, to the sanctuary of Olympia. Roman olive traders therefore honoured *Hercules Olivarius* 'the olive-farmer'.

Pindar, *Olympians* 3.11–15; Athenaeus *D* 411a–412b, cf. 512e.

D. Noël, 'Du vin pour Héraklès' in *Image et céramique grecque: colloque Rouen 25–26 novembre 1982* ed. François Lissarrague and F. Thelamon (Rouen, 1983) pp. 141–50.

Herbalists. The traditional experts in Greece were *rizotomoi* 'root-cutters', who gathered and sold herbs traditionally known to have medicinal uses. Many of their observations and beliefs are recorded by THEOPHRASTUS, NICANDER and DIOSCORIDES. Sophocles's lost play *Rizotomoi* centred on Medea and her expertise in drugs. The first century BC pharmacologist CRATEUAS was himself honoured with the nickname *rizotomos.*

Similar skills were to be observed among other peoples. The people of DACIA were renowned for their knowledge of medicinal plants. Young PERSIANS of the empire were taught the skills of 'root-cutting', according to Strabo. The Indian emperor Aśoka, in the third century BC, encouraged the planting of medicinal herbs not only in his own country but among the Hellenistic kingdoms of south-western Asia.

Following the *Odyssey* story, Circe is credited with professional herbalist skills by Ovid and others. She was believed to have lived somewhere near Circeii in coastal Latium. Medicinal plants really were gathered in the hills around Circeii; however, the finest medicinal plants of the Roman Empire were agreed to come from CRETE, where the imperial pharmacy obtained its supplies.

Homer, *Odyssey* 10.230–40; Strabo, *Geography* 15.3.18; Aśoka, *Rock Edict* 2 [for translation see N.A. Nikam and Richard McKeon, *The Edicts of Aśoka* (Chicago: University of Chicago Press, 1959)]; Ovid, *Metamorphoses* 14.264–7; Macrobius *S* 5.19.9–10 quoting Sophocles.

A. Delatte, *Herbarius. Recherches sur le cérémonial usité chez les anciens pour la cueillette des simples et des plantes magiques* (Brussels,

1961), 3rd edn; John Scarborough, 'Theophrastus on herbals and herbal remedies' in *Journal of the History of Biology* vol. 11 (1978) pp. 353–85; Jerry Stannard, 'Medicinal plants and folk remedies in Pliny, *Historia Naturalis*' in *History and Philosophy of the Life Sciences* vol. 4 (1982) pp. 3–23; Scarborough 1985; John Scarborough, 'The pharmacology of sacred plants, herbs and roots' in *Magika Hiera: ancient Greek magic and religion* (New York: Oxford University Press, 1991).

Herbs, aromatic plants used in cuisine important both in Greek and Roman cookery; there were significant differences between the two.

In classical Greece few exotic spices were yet available, and fewer still were used in everyday food; therefore fresh and dried native herbs (and seeds) were almost the only aromatics that were used. Important culinary herbs included CORIANDER, OREGANO, THYME and PENNYROYAL. The Greek terms *khloe* and *hedysmata khlora* 'green herbs' refer to a chopped or pounded mixture of fresh herbs used as a culinary flavouring. Greek *phyllas* is the name of a dish of bitter herbs, perhaps a salad, served, according to sources cited by Athenaeus, at the end of the main course of a meal.

In Roman cookery of the Empire many spices were available, from all over the known world, but, although less expensive and less prestigious, fresh garden herbs continued to be used liberally. Important herbs in Roman cuisine included coriander and oregano again, LOVAGE, RUE, PARSLEY, CELERY seed and MINT. The recipes in *Apicius* call for one or more fresh herbs in nearly every dish.

Archestratus *H* 18, 49 and cf. 23 Brandt; Antiphanes 140 Kassel; Alexis *F* 84 Kassel; Pollux *O* 6.71; Athenaeus *D* 133f quoting Diphilus Comicus, also 140e quoting Callias, also 403b; *Apicius passim.*

Guido Majno, *The Healing Hand: man and wound in the ancient world* (Cambridge, Mass.: Harvard University Press, 1975); Jerry Stannard, 'Medicinal plants and folk remedies in Pliny, Historia Naturalis' in *History and Philosophy of the Life Sciences* vol. 4 (1982) pp. 3–23; John Scarborough, 'The pharmacol-ogy of sacred plants, herbs and roots' in *Magika Hiera: ancient Greek magic and religion* (New York: Oxford University Press, 1991) pp. 138–74; Hellmut Baumann, *The Greek Plant World in Myth, Art and Literature*, translated and augmented by William T. Stearn and Eldwyth Ruth Stearn (London: Herbert Press, 1993); J.E. Raven, *Plants and Plant Lore in Ancient Greece* (Oxford: Leopard's Head Press, 2000).

Herculaneum *see* POMPEII

Hermits *see* ASCETICISM

Hesiod, author of two Greek hexameter poems of about 700 BC. The *Theogony* tells of the origin and genealogy of the gods; the *Works and Days* is a collection of farming wisdom, much of it evidently proverbial. The latter poem is the oldest literary text focusing on food and food sources.

T.P. Howe, 'Linear B and Hesiod's breadwinners' in *Transactions of the American Philological Association* vol. 89 (1958) pp. 44–65; J.C.B. Petropoulos, *Heat and Lust: Hesiod's midsummer festival scene revisited* (Lanham, Md: Rowman and Littlefield, 1994).

Hesiod OD: *Works and Days*. Translation: *Hesiod's Works and Days: a translation and commentary for the social sciences* tr. David W. Tandy and Walter C. Neale (Berkeley, London: University of California Press, 1996). Critical text and commentary: Hesiod, *Works and Days* ed. M.L. West (Oxford: Clarendon Press, 1978).

Hestiatorion *see* ARCHITECTURE

Hetairai, in classical Athens and other Greek cities, women who kept company with men: the term means literally 'companions'. Unlike the wives and daughters of citizens, who lived in seclusion, *hetairai* attended dinner parties and *symposia*: indeed, they sometimes hosted them, though it was the men who paid. The term is used in several overlapping senses; it is sometimes extended to include prostitutes (*pornai*) and entertainers such as flute-girls, the implication being that women of all three groups mixed publicly with men and were regarded as sexually available.

Diphilus Comicus 42 Kassel [Athenaeus *D* 292d]; Athenaeus *D* 572d–599b with quotations from Machon, Lynceus, Hermesianax and others.

I. Peschel, *Die Hetäre bei Symposion und Komos in der attisch-rotfigurigen Vasenmalerei des 6.–4. Jahrh. v. Chr.* (Frankfurt, 1987); Davidson 1997; Leslie Kurke, *Coins, Bodies, Games and Gold: the politics of meaning in archaic Greece* (Princeton: Princeton University Press, 1999) pp. 175–219.

Hippocrates, legendary (but real) Greek physician who practised and taught at Cos in the late fifth century BC. In spite of the wealth of Greek literature from this period, there is no contemporary evidence at all concerning Hippocrates. Many surviving medical texts of various kinds are attributed to him, but these texts are best treated as anonymous; they were clearly written at different periods and from very different scientific standpoints.

The books *On Regimen* and *On Regimen in Acute Diseases* belong to this collection. They are both relatively early texts, from about 400 BC or slightly before, and provide useful evidence of foods and nutritional beliefs then current. To later medical authors, including GALEN, they were classics.

Oeuvres complètes d'Hippocrate ed. and French tr. E. Littré (Paris, 1839–61); *Hippocrates* ed. and tr. W.H.S. Jones and others (1923– , *LCL*); I.M. Lonie, 'The Hippocratic treatise *Perì diaítes oxéon*' in *Sudhoffs Archiv* vol. 49 (1965) pp. 50–79; J.-H. Kühn, U. Fleischer and others, *Index Hippocraticus* (Göttingen, 1986–9); E.M. Craik, 'Hippocratic diaita' in *Food in Antiquity* ed. John Wilkins and others (Exeter: Exeter University Press, 1995) pp. 343–50; H. King, 'Food and blood in Hippocratic gynaecology' in *Food in Antiquity* ed. John Wilkins and others (Exeter: Exeter University Press, 1995) pp. 351–8.

Hippocrates R: *On Regimen*. Text and translation in Jones and others vol. 4 pp. 224–447. Critical text and French translation: *Hippocrate: Du régime* ed. R. Joly (Berlin: Akademie-Verlag, 1984) (*Corpus medicorum Graecorum*, 1.2.4).

—— **RA**: *On Regimen in Acute Diseases*. Text and translation in Jones and others vol. 2 pp. 62–125. Critical text and French translation:

Hippocrate, tome VI, 2e partie: Du régime des maladies aiguës, Appendice, De l'aliment, De l'usage des liquides ed. R. Joly (1972, *CUF*).

—— **RS**: *Regimen in Health*. Text and translation in Jones and others vol. 4 pp. 44–59.

Hippodamantian wine (Greek *Hippodamanteios*; Latin *Hippodamantium*), from the neighbourhood of Cyzicus in northwestern Asia Minor. Galen prescribes it when aged.

Pliny *NH* 14.75; Galen, *On Therapeutic Method* 10.836; Hesychius, *Lexicon s.v. Hippodamanteios*.

Hippolochus, Greek author of about 300 BC. Hippolochus was a correspondent of Lynceus and addressed to him a letter narrating the wedding feast of Caranus – presumably a relative of the Caranus who was a companion of Alexander the Great. The letter is summarised, with a long verbatim extract, by Athenaeus in the *Deipnosophists*. It is the fullest surviving description of a Macedonian banquet; it provides evidence of the mingling of native customs with Greek and Persian fashions.

Athenaeus *D* 128a–130e.

Hippolochus D: *Dinner*. Translation and commentary: Andrew Dalby, 'The wedding feast of Caranus the Macedonian by Hippolochus' in *Petits propos culinaires* no. 29 (1988) pp. 37–45, reprinted in *The wilder shores of gastronomy* ed. A. Davidson and H. Saberi (Berkeley: Ten Speed Press, 2002) pp. 288–97. Text and translation in Gulick's edition of Athenaeus vol. 2 pp. 90–101.

Hittites, rulers of an empire in northern Anatolia in the second millennium BC. Hittite cuneiform texts have been deciphered; they show that the language belonged to a now-extinct subgroup, Anatolian, of the Indo-European language family. Literature and culture were influenced by Mesopotamia. The names of many foods have been identified in Hittite: see Hoffner for discussion and references.

H.A. Hoffner, *Alimenta Hethaeorum* (New Haven, 1974); H. Klengel, 'The economy of the Hittite household (É)' in *Oikumene* vol. 5 (1986) pp. 23–31; Ronald L. Gorny, 'Viticulture and ancient Anatolia' in *The Origins and Ancient History of Wine* ed. Patrick E. McGovern, Stuart J. Fleming and Solomon H. Katz (London: Gordon and Breach, 1995) pp. 133–74.

Homeric society, the way of life depicted with great clarity and consistency in the *Iliad* and *Odyssey*. It has been an article of faith with many readers of the poems, from the fifth century BC to the present day, that a real society is being described, though answers to the question when and where this society existed have varied (the German series *Archaeologia Homerica* is the fullest systematic exploration of the similarities between this poetic world and the finds made by archaeologists). Real or not, Homeric society influenced the behaviour and thinking of later Greeks. Its rules of hospitality are set out in two formulaic scenes that recur several times in the *Odyssey*, the communal meal (which always consists of meat, bread and wine) and the feeding of a newly arrived guest. Sacrifices are also fully described.

Homer, *Odyssey* 1.109–60, 3.1–66, *al.*; Athenaeus E 8e–19a, 24b–25f, 177a–182b, 186d–193c.

G. Bruns, *Küchenwesen und Mahlzeiten* (Göttingen, 1970) (*Archaeologia Homerica* vol. 2 chapter Q); H.-G. Buchholz and others, *Jagd und Fischfang* (Göttingen, 1973) (*Archaeologia Homerica* vol. 2 chapter J); G. Nagy, 'Six studies of sacral vocabulary relating to the fireplace' in *Harvard Studies in Classical Philology* vol. 78 (1974) pp. 71–106, revised text in G. Nagy, *Greek Mythology and Poetics* (Ithaca: Cornell University Press, 1990) pp. 143–80; J.L. Perpillou, 'Vinealia 1. Vignes mycéniennes, homériques, historiques: permanence de formules?' in *Revue de philologie* 3rd ser. vol. 55 (1981) pp. 41–55; E. Minchin, 'Food fiction and food fact in Homer's Iliad' in *Petits Propos culinaires* no. 25 (1987) pp. 42–9; S. Reece, *The Stranger's Welcome: oral theory and the aesthetics of the Homeric hospitality scene* (Ann Arbor: University of Michigan Press, 1993); Hans van Wees, 'Princes at dinner: social event and social structure in Homer' in *Homeric Questions* ed. Jan Paul Crielaard (Amsterdam: Gieben, 1995) pp. 147–82; James Davidson, 'On the fish missing from Homer' in *Food in European*

Literature ed. John Wilkins (Exeter: Intellect, 1996) pp. 57–64; Garnsey 1999 pp. 72–7.

Honey, product of the honey-bee (*Apis mellifera*). Since cane SUGAR was as yet little known and very costly in the Mediterranean world, honey was the best available sweetener and the most concentrated source of dietary sugar throughout prehistoric and classical times. As such it was used in cuisine, it was mixed with wine and other fluids to make sweet drinks (see below) and in these and other forms it was very commonly used in medicine.

Honey was still gathered from the wild in classical Greece and Rome, as it had evidently been for many millennia. We can learn this, if little else, from the sad and silly story told by Conon and Antiphilus of the honey-collector who used to let himself down a cliff face by a rope: the rope became smeared with honey, his dog chewed it through and the honey-collector fell to his death. Bee-keeping, however, had already begun in Egypt in the third millennium BC and was familiar in Minoan Greece – an ancient beehive was found in the excavation of AKROTIRI. Information on classical bee-keeping comes not only from archaeology but also from detailed instructions given by Varro and Columella in prose and by Vergil in verse.

Honey often had a smoky taste, for the simple reason that smoke was used to drive the bees away while it was taken from the hive. It was well known that honey varied in flavour and aroma depending on which flowers had been available to the bees. The best honey was agreed to be that of Mount HYMETTUS in Attica, which had the special taste of thyme. Certain honeys, deriving from poisonous plants, were poisonous themselves: this was a problem, according to Roman sources, with the honey of Corsica and Sardinia.

In the ancient Near East honey was frequently offered to the gods: note for example Gilgamesh's offering to the sun god Shamash. Honey was included in the sacrifices of MITHRIDATES of Pontus. *Melisponda*, offerings of honey, were also made in Greece, for example to the Eumenides as described by Plutarch.

Honey is Greek *meli*, Latin *mel*. These terms were also sometimes used for MANNA.

Gilgamesh [Standard Babylonian version] tablet 8; Hippocrates *RA* 53–7, *Epidemics* 7.8; Aristotle *HA* 553a17–554b21, 623b5–627b22; Conon, *Narratives* 35; Antiphilus 18 Gow [*Anthologia Palatina* 7.622] with Gow *ad l.*; Varro *RR* 3.16 with Flach *ad l.*; Vergil, *Georgics* book 4; Dioscorides *MM* 2.101–3; Columella *DA* 9.2–16; Pliny *NH* 21.70–85, 22.107–15; Plutarch *QC* 4.6; Appian, *Mithridatic War* 66; Athenaeus *E* 46e–47a; Palladius *OA* 1.37–8, *al.*

M. Schuster, 'Mel' in *RE* 1893–1972; Buck 1949 p. 383–4; G. Kuény, 'Scènes apicoles dans l'ancienne Egypte' in *Journal of Near Eastern Studies* vol. 9 (1950) pp. 84–93; A.J. Graham, 'Beehives from ancient Greece' in *Bee World* vol. 56 (1975) pp. 64–75; J.E. Jones, 'Hives and honey of Hymettus' in *Archaeology* vol. 29 no. 2 (1976) pp. 80–91; F. Ruttner, 'Minoische und altgriechische Imkertechnik auf Kreta' in *Bienenmuseum und Geschichte der Bienenzucht* (Bucharest: Apimondia, 1979) pp. 209–29; C. Zymbragoudakis, 'The bee and beekeeping in Crete' in *Apiacta* vol. 14 no. 3 (1979) pp. 134–8; Eva Crane, *The Archaeology of Beekeeping* (London: Duckworth, 1983); H. Chouliara-Raïos, *L'Abeille et le miel en Egypte d'après les papyrus grecs* (Yoannina, 1989) (*Epistimoniki epetiris filosofikis skholis Dhodhoni*, 30); Claire Balandier, 'Production et usages de miel dans l'antiquité gréco-romaine' in *Des hommes et des plantes: plantes méditerranéennes, vocabulaire et usages anciennes* ed. M.-Cl. Amouretti and G. Comet (Aix-en-Provence, 1993) pp. 93–125; Brewer and others (1995 ?) pp. 125–9; *OCD* 1996 *s.vv.* Beekeeping, Honey; Eva Crane, *The World History of Beekeeping and Honey Hunting* (London: Duckworth, 1999).

- Honey was mixed with water (or sometimes with milk) at various strengths to make a medicinal drink known in Greek as *hydromeli*, *melikreton* or *eukratomeli*. Recipes are given by Dioscorides and others.

  Hippocrates *RA* 53–7; Dioscorides *MM* 5.9; Pliny *NH* 14.113; Palladius *OA* 8.7; *Geoponica* 8.28.

- Greek *oxymeli* is honey mixed with vinegar. This medicinal drink is mentioned no fewer than 221 times in the works of Galen. Recipes are given by Dioscorides and others.

  Hippocrates *RA* 58–61; Dioscorides *MM* 5.14; Pliny *NH* 14.114, 23.60; Galen *ST* 6.271, *Commentary on Hippocrates RA* 15.676–7.

- Other compounds incorporating honey include *melitites*, which is honey mixed with must and a little salt (Pliny *NH* 14.85). The most important of such mixtures, both health-giving and pleasurable, were MULSUM and CONDITUM.

Horehound, wild plant whose leaves and seeds were used in a medicinal wine effective against coughs and colds. An amphora at the Roman fort at Carpow, Scotland, had contained horehound wine.

Horehound (*Marrubium vulgare*) is Greek *prasion*, Latin *marrubium*.

Dioscorides *MM* 3.105; Columella *DA* 12.32; Pliny *NH* 20.241–4; *Journal of Roman Studies* vol. 53 (1963) pp. 160–7, no. 51; Pseudo-Apuleius, *Herbarius* 45.

Mrs M. Grieve, *A Modern Herbal* ed. H. Leyel (London, 1931) pp. 415–6; Lindsay Allason-Jones, 'Health care in the Roman North' in *Britannia* vol. 30 (1999) pp. 133–46, esp p. 140.

Horse, domesticated animal. Horse meat was seldom eaten by Greeks and Romans, except in emergencies and catastrophic food shortages, although the Hippocratic *Regimen* lists the dietary qualities of horse along with other meats. Horse MILK was rumoured to be a favourite beverage of the horse-riding barbarians of the steppes north of the Black Sea; the Geloni and Concani, more barbaric in this than their neighbours, drank their horses' blood.

The horse (*Equus Caballus*) is Greek *hippos*, Latin *equus*.

Hippocrates *R* 46; Strabo 15.2.10; Horace, *Odes* 3.4.34; Vergil, *Georgics* 3.461–3; Tacitus, *Annals* 2.24, *Histories* 4.60.

Buck 1949 pp. 167–71; S. Bökönyi, 'Horses and sheep in East Europe in the copper and bronze ages' in *Proto-Indo-European: the archaeology of a linguistic problem. Studies in honor of Marija Gimbutas* ed. S.N. Skomal and E.C. Polomé (Washington: Institute for the Study of Man, 1987) pp. 136–44; Simoons 1994 pp. 168–93; Toynbee 1996.

Hospitality was enjoined on Greeks and Romans by divine precept. The routine of welcoming, feeding and questioning a guest, as observed in HOMERIC SOCIETY, is further exemplified in several retellings of myth.

Many stories make it clear that poverty did not absolve a householder from the obligation, which was to provide guests with the best food available even if the host had to go without. Stories exemplifying this include Eumaeus's welcome for the disguised Odysseus (Homer, *Odyssey* 14; Aeschylus fragment 309 Snell); Hecale's for Theseus (Callimachus, *Hecale*); Molorchus's for Heracles (Callimachus, *Aetia* 54–59 Pfeiffer); Icarius and Erigone's for Bacchus (Eratosthenes, *Erigone* 22–36 Powell; Nonnus, *Dionysiaca* book); Falernus's for Bacchus (Silius Italicus 7.166–211); Baucis and Philemon's for Jupiter and Mercury (Ovid, *Metamorphoses* 8.626–91); Hyrieus's for Jupiter and Mercury (Ovid, *Fasti* 5.493–522); Brongus's for Bacchus (Nonnus, *Dionysiaca* 17.37–86). Poets found opportunities in these tales to catalogue rustic foods that seldom appeared in literature, such as samphire and sow-thistle with which Hecale regaled Theseus and the salsify offered to Bacchus by Erigone.

A Roman custom was the *cena adventicia*, a dinner given in honour of the arrival of a friend (Suetonius, *Vitellius* 13.2; Plutarch *QC* 8.7; cf. Petronius, *Satyricon* 90.5; Martial 12.preface).

In Greece there were few inns (the relevant terms are *katagogion* and *pandokeion*). Those that existed were, like the caravanserais of the Near East, not convivial, and travellers did in fact very generally rely on the hospitality of householders. Italy and the western Mediterranean in general were better supplied with inns; travellers still often preferred to stay and eat with friends, or friends of friends, or in houses belonging to friends, as Horace makes clear (Horace, *Satires* 1.5). See also under TRAVELLERS' FOOD.

D. Gorce, *Les Voyages, l'hospitalité et le port des lettres dans le monde chrétien des IVe–Ve siècles* (Paris, 1925); P. Gauthier, 'Notes sur l'étranger et l'hospitalité en Grèce et à Rome' in *Ancient Society* vol. 4 (1973) pp. 1–21; C. Grottanelli, 'Notes on Mediterranean hospitality' in *Dialoghi di archeologia* vols 9/10 (1976/ 7) pp. 186–94; R.E.F. Smith and D. Christian, *Bread and Salt* (Cambridge, 1984); Callimachus, *Hecale* ed. A.S. Hollis (Oxford: Clarendon Press, 1990) pp. 341–54; S. Reece, *The Stranger's Welcome: oral theory and the aesthetics of the Homeric hospitality scene* (Ann Arbor: University of Michigan Press, 1993); R. Seaford, *Reciprocity and Ritual: Homer and tragedy in the developing city-state* (Oxford: Clarendon Press, 1994).

Hound's tongue (*Cynoglossum officinale*), edible wild plant, occasionally listed as a potherb. Its nutlet had medicinal uses. Hound's tongue is Greek *kynoglosson* and *leimonion*.

Nicander *F* 71 Schneider; Pliny *NH* 25.81; Galen *SF* 12.57, *On Compounding* 13.241; Hesychius, *Lexicon s.v. kynoglosson*; Aetius, *Medicine* 1.246.

Humoral theory, the generally accepted approach among ancient physicians and medical authors to DIET, human metabolism and the pathology of disease. The theory can be seen at an early stage in Hippocratic writings; see especially *Nature of Man*, and, on the origin of different human 'constitutions', *Regimen*.

As humoral theory developed, dieticians found themselves generally, though not always, in agreement on the humoral effects of individual foodstuffs: for full details and much discussion see several works by GALEN including *On the Properties of Foods* and *On the Thinning Diet* (both now available in translation). Controversy over such evaluations did occur: note for example Plutarch's discussion of whether wine is hot or cold.

With the translation of Hippocratic and Galenic texts into Arabic in the early medieval period, humoral theory, complete with the detailed evaluations of each food ingredient, was adopted into Islamic medicine. From this source it was transmitted to late medieval Europe, where it continued to hold the field until early modern times. It still influences everyday dietary practice in Muslim countries.

Hippocrates *R* 32–4, *Humours passim, Nature of Man* esp. 4–5; Plutarch *QC* 3.5; Galen *AF passim, SF passim, BM passim, ST passim, VA passim, Commentary on Hippocrates RA passim*.

Hunting, source of meat for the ancient diet: meat that was high in status but very small in quantity in proportion to the total food intake. On hunting and gathering as a means of subsistence, see also WILD FOODS.

In the classical world you hunted if you had leisure and energy. Hunters were often boys or young men (this is as true of ancient Persia and Macedonia as it is of classical Greece); when older they continued to hunt only if they had nothing else to do, as might apply to gods, kings and nobles rather than to those who had to make a living. Having hunted, you ate the catch or presented it as a love gift, as young men can be seen to do in Athenian vase paintings.

The Persians, in succession to earlier empires, had hunting parks, admired by Xenophon. The Greek word for these is *paradeisos*, a Persian loanword; the same word is used in the Septuagint translation of the Old Testament for the Garden of Eden.

Greeks hunted hares: in most of Greece not much larger game was to be found, except the occasional wild boar. Macedonians hunted bears and lions. Persians hunted antelopes, gazelles and tigers. Romans hunted wild boars in central Italy. The Roman Empire included many wilder regions (notably north Africa) in which varied hunting was to be had, and the results sometimes reached Rome, live or freshly killed. Sallust told in his *Histories* of the Roman dinner at which Metellus Pius served 'several previously unknown species of birds and animals from Mauritania'.

Genesis 2.8; Xenophon, *Anabasis* 1.5.2–4, *al.*, *On Hunting*; Columella *DA* 9.1; Dio of Prusa, *Orations* 7.67–79; Macrobius *S* 3.13.9 quoting Sallust.

J.K. Anderson, *Hunting in the Ancient World* (Berkeley, 1985); F. Ghedini, 'Caccia e banchetto: un rapporto difficile' in *Rivista di archeologia* vol. 16 (1992) pp. 72–88 with 15 plates; Toynbee 1996; Alain Schnapp, *Le Chasseur et la cité: chasse et érotique dans la Grèce ancienne* (Paris, 1997).

Hymettus, mountain of Attica close to Athens. The famous honey of Mount Hymettus, redolent of the thyme of the mountain slopes, lent its sweetness to Attic cakes. Under the Roman Empire Hymettus honey was a commonplace of the gastronomy of Rome itself, being one of the two classic ingredients in MULSUM.

Archestratus *H* 62 Brandt with Olson and Sens *ad l.*; Horace, *Odes* 2.6.13; Strabo 9.1.23; Pausanias 1.32.1.

Dalby 2000a pp. 141–2.

Hyssop, strong-smelling herb native to northern Anatolia and central and southeastern Europe. Hyssop was used medicinally in classical Greece and in the Roman Mediterranean. The Hippocratic text *On Diseases* is the first to specify Cilician hyssop – Cilicia being a known source of aromatics under the Persian Empire and of fruits later. Dioscorides and Pliny describe a medicinal wine *hyssopites*, made by adding Cilician hyssop to must or wine.

Hyssop was seldom employed in cuisine, but Archestratus recommends it chopped, with vinegar, as a dip for the fish *hys*, perhaps TRIGGER-FISH, caught at Aenus in Thrace or in the Pontus. These are places where hyssop was native.

Hyssop (*Hyssopus officinalis*) is Greek *hyssopos*, Latin *hyssopus*. The identification is controversial. Olson and Sens 2000 p. 102, following some earlier scholars, identify *hyssopos* with oregano, but they are on shaky ground; well-informed classical sources distinguish hyssop and oregano. See Andrews for details.

Hippocrates *R* 54, *On Diseases* 3.10, *On the Nature of Woman* 32; Archestratus *H* 22 Brandt; Nicander *A* 603, *T* 872; Dioscorides *MM* 3.25, 5.40; Scribonius Largus 121; Pliny *NH* 14.109; Galen *SF* 12.149.

A.C. Andrews, 'Hyssop in the classical era' in *Classical Philology* vol. 56 (1961) pp. 230–48.

- Greek *hyssopos*, Latin *hyssopus* and English *hyssop*, in translations from the Old Testament, represent Hebrew *'ezob*. The plant referred to here, one little known in the classical world but familiar in Egypt and Palestine, is Syrian marjoram or za'tar (*Origanum Maru*). Za'tar was also the only luxury of a group of Jewish ascetics in northern Egypt in the first century AD; they used it to flavour the salt that was their *opson* or relish.

Exodus 12.22; *Leviticus* 14.4, 14.52; *Psalms* 51.7; Philo, *On the Contemplative Life* 37, 73, 81; Paul, *Epistle to the Hebrews* 9.19.

I

Iatrocles, Greek author of a work *On Bread-Making* and (possibly the same work under another name) *On Cakes*. He perhaps wrote in Hellenistic times.

Dalby 1996 p. 160 with notes 29–31.

Ibex *see* GOAT

Iconography as source. The concept includes imagery both painted and sculpted, and covers illustrations on utensils (especially Greek vase painting), domestic wall paintings and mosaics, funerary paintings and reliefs, public and religious statuary and reliefs. The paper by Meirano deals with a category sometimes overlooked: clay models (in this case, of fruits) as divine offerings. Iconography is useful in its depiction of (or commentary on) everyday life and also in its representation or idealisation of foods and food sources.

Jashemski 1979–93; *La Cité des images: religion et société en Grèce antique* ed. Claude Bérard, Jean-Pierre Vernant and others (Lausanne: Fernand Nathan, 1984), translation: *A City of Images: iconography and society in ancient Greece* (Princeton: Princeton University Press, 1989); R. Hurschmann, *Symposienszenen auf unteritalienischen Vasen* (Würzburg, 1985); François Lissarrague, *Un Flot d'images: une esthétique du banquet grec* (Paris: Biro, 1987), translation: *The Aesthetics of the Greek Banquet: images of wine and ritual* (Princeton: Princeton University Press, 1990); François Lissarrague, 'Around the krater: an aspect of banquet imagery' in *Sympotica: a symposium on the symposion* ed. Oswyn Murray (Oxford:

Oxford University Press, 1990) pp. 196–209; *Looking at Greek Vases* ed. T. Rasmussen and N. Spivey (Cambridge: Cambridge University Press, 1991); Toynbee 1996; Valeria Meirano, 'Mets et végétaux en Grande Grèce: nouvelles données de la coroplathie' in *Paysage et alimentation dans le monde grec* ed. Jean-Marc Luce (Toulouse, 2000) pp. 167–80.

India, source of one food spice important in the classical Mediterranean, PEPPER, and of several other aromatics used in festivity and medicine, CARDAMOM, AMOMUM (probably Nepaul cardamom), COSTUS (putchuk) and SPIKENARD. SUGAR, regarded in classical Europe as a medicinal substance rather than a food spice, was imported from India.

The staple diet of much of southern India was well known to be RICE; it was known also that India grew two species of MILLET. Typical Indian meals were described briefly by Megasthenes around 300 BC, and classical authors were impressed by India's fertility and productivity in food, adequate to the huge population of the country.

Several food animals and plants were transplanted from India westwards either before or during the classical period. They include the CHICKEN and PEAFOWL, also SESAME, JUJUBE and probably the SEBESTEN and pink lotus (see LOTUS (1)). For Indian foods occasionally encountered by classical observers see BANANA; JACKFRUIT; MANGO; URD.

Small quantities of Greek and Italian wine were exported to Barygaza and Muziris on the west coast of India.

Theophrastus *HP* 4.4.10; Diodorus Siculus 2.36; Strabo 15.1.20; Philo, *On Drunkenness* fragment 5; *Periplus Maris Erythraei* 49, 56; Athenaeus *D* 153d citing Megasthenes.

Om Prakash, *Food and Drinks in Ancient India* (Delhi, 1961); E. Warmington, *The Commerce between the Roman Empire and India* (Cambridge: Cambridge University Press, 1974), 2nd edn; Vimala Begley and Richard Daniel de Puma, *Rome and India: the ancient sea trade* (Madison: University of Wisconsin Press, 1991); M.D. Kajale, 'Current status of Indian palaeoethnobotany' in *New Light on Early Farming: recent developments in palaeoethnobotany* ed. Jane M. Renfrew (Edinburgh: Edinburgh University Press, 1991) pp. 155–89; K.T. Achaya, *Indian Food: a historical companion* (Delhi: Oxford University Press, 1994) (unreliable in its use of non-Indian sources); Dalby 2000a pp. 191–7.

Inns *see* HOSPITALITY; TRAVELLERS' FOOD; TAVERNS

Instrumentum domesticum *see* COOKING UTENSILS; DINING AND DRINKING UTENSILS

Invitation to dinner, a literary form frequently employed, and as frequently subverted, in Rome in the first centuries BC and AD. The oldest surviving example is in Greek; it is by the lively philosopher–poet Philodemus, inviting his patron Piso to a simple dinner in memory of Epicurus. It is followed, probably within a few years, by Catullus's invitation to 'Fabullus', who is required to bring the food, the wine, the salt, the girl and the laughter. Horace's invitations are addressed to his patron Maecenas, to Torquatus and to Vergil. Horace can promise food and wine – but Torquatus is enjoined to bring a better wine if he has it, while Vergil must pay his admission fee with a pot of nard unguent.

Martial and Juvenal boast, with studied carelessness, of the farm-fresh food that they will fashionably fetch from non-existent estates. Pliny, finally, turns the genre upside down with a non-invitation; he upbraids 'Septicius Clarus' for failing to attend, and tells him what he missed.

If the real can be distinguished from the ironic, the invitations can be made to tell us a good deal of Roman dining at this period.

Philodemus 23 Gow [*Anthologia Palatina* 11.44] with Gow *ad l.*; Catullus 13; Horace, *Epistles* 1.5, *Odes* 3.29, 4.12; Martial 5.78, 10.48, 11.52; Juvenal 11; Pliny the Younger, *Letters* 1.15.

Gowers 1993; Dalby 2000a pp. 243–56.

Italy. For regions of Italy with their own gastronomic character see APULIA; CAMPANIA; ETRUSCANS; LATIUM; MESSANA; ROME; SICILY; SYBARIS; TARENTUM; VENAFRUM.

For the wines of Italy see ANCONITAN WINE; BABBIAN WINE; HADRIAN WINE; MAMERTINE WINE; MARSIAN WINE; PUCINE WINE; RAETIAN WINE; RAVENNA WINE; ROMAN WINES; SABINE WINE; SPOLETINE WINE; TARENTINE WINE; THURINE WINE; TUSCAN WINE; and the additional cross-references at CAMPANIA and LATIUM.

Frank 1933–40 vols 1 and 5, esp. vol. 5 pp. 138–68; White 1970; Joan M. Frayn, *Subsistence Farming in Roman Italy* (London: Centaur Press, 1979); J.J. Rossiter, 'Wine and oil processing on Roman farms in Italy' in *Phoenix* vol. 35 (1981) pp. 345–61; M. Tagliente, 'Elementi del banchetto in un centro arcaico della Basilicata (Chiaromonte)' in *Mélanges de l'École Française de Rome. Antiquité* vol. 97 no. 1 (1985) pp. 159–91; Joan M. Frayn, *Markets and Fairs in Roman Italy* (Oxford: Clarendon Press, 1993); Mario Lombardo, 'Food and frontier in the Greek colonies of south Italy' in *Food in Antiquity* ed. John Wilkins and others (Exeter: Exeter University Press, 1995) pp. 256–72; Dalby 2000a pp. 21–81.

J

Jackfruit (*Artocarpus heterophyllus*), very large fruit native to southern Asia. Jackfruit was apparently observed in the course of Alexander's expedition, as a result of which Theophrastus is able to give a brief description.

Theophrastus *HP* 4.4.5.

Jews followed a set of precise dietary rules which – uniquely in the context of the ancient Mediterranean – were laid down in writing as a religious imperative. The general rules appear in the books of *Leviticus* and *Deuteronomy*, which probably took their final form in the sixth and fifth centuries BC.

The most obvious prohibition is that of pork, a rule also observed by the Egyptians and some other Near Eastern peoples. Numerous other specific foods were prohibited. The prohibition of BLOOD was, by late Hellenistic times, observed by many Jews. This was why Daniel and his comrades in captivity, in the biblical romance of *Daniel*, refused meat; this was why Jewish priests, while imprisoned in Rome in the first century AD, lived on figs and nuts only, according to Josephus.

Other Jewish religious rules had effects on food behaviour. On the Sabbath, as a day of rest, food could not be prepared (but it could be eaten: classical authors who say otherwise are in error). The annual festival of PASSOVER included a feast with specified constituents. For Jewish fasts, not undertaken as frequently in reality as classical obervers believed, see FASTING.

Leviticus 3.1–17, 11.1–47; *Deuteronomy* 14.3–29; *Daniel* 1.8–18; Strabo 16.2.37; Josephus, *Autobiography* 13–14; Plutarch *QC* 4.5–6; Porphyry *DA* 2.26.

S. Stein, 'The dietary laws in Rabbinic and Patristic literature' in *Studia Patristica: papers presented to the 2nd International Conference on Patristic Studies, Oxford, 1955*, ed. K. Aland and F.L. Cross, vol. 2 (Oxford, 1957); J. Soler, 'Sémiotique de la nourriture dans la Bible' in *Annales: économies, sociétés, civilisations* vol. 28 (1973) pp. 943–55, English translation as 'The semiotics of food in the Bible' in *Food and Drink in History* ed. R. Forster and O. Ranum (Baltimore, 1979) pp. 126–38; J. Soler, 'Les raisons de la Bible: règles alimentaires hébraiques' in *Histoire de l'alimentation* ed. Jean-Louis Flandrin and Massimo Montanari (Paris, 1996) pp. 73–84; Grimm 1996 pp. 14–33, 106; papers by David Noy, Per Bilde and L. Michael White in *Meals in a Social Context: aspects of the communal meal in the Hellenistic and Roman world* ed. Inge Nielsen and Hanne Sigismund Nielsen (Aarhus: Aarhus University Press, 1998); Garnsey 1999 pp. 91–5.

John Dory, sea fish of distinctive physiognomy – ugly would be another way to put it – and with fine-tasting flesh. The John Dory was common around Cyzicus in the Propontis in ancient times and was also one of the many delicacies of Gades (modern Cadiz) in southwestern Spain. It was sometimes salted.

The John Dory (*Zeus Faber*) is Greek *khalkeus*, Latin *faber, zeus*.

Ovid, *Halieutica* 110; Columella *DA* 8.16.9; Pliny *NH* 9.68; Athenaeus *D* 328d citing Euthydemus and Heracleides.

Thompson 1947 pp. 73–4, 281–2; Davidson 1981 pp. 65–6.

Jujube, tree fruit resembling a small date. The jujube grows wild in eastern Iran and central Asia; it was being gathered for human food in Baluchistan by 6000 BC. It is as an Indian fruit that it is very briefly described by Theophrastus. In Hellenistic times the tree spread westwards in cultivation; by the first century BC it was grown in the Near East and north Africa, and it was from Africa that it was introduced to Italy by Sextus Papinius in Augustus's last years.

The jujube (*Zizyphus Jujuba*) is Latin *ziziphum*, Greek *zizyphon* (the word may sometimes refer to local wild species, for which see LOTUS (2)). For the fruit named *tuber*, sometimes identified as a variety of jujube but more probably an azarole, see under MEDLAR.

Theophrastus *HP* 4.4.5 (unnamed); Columella *DA* 9.4.3; Pliny *NH* 15.47; *Diocletian's Price Edict* 6.56; Palladius *OA* 5.4.1–3.

Juniper, group of aromatic evergreen trees and shrubs (genus *Juniperus*). The general names for the group are Greek *kedros*, Latin *cedrus*.

Juniper berries, particularly those of *Juniperus communis*, when dried resemble peppercorns and are used like pepper as a spice. They have some similar medicinal properties. According to the recipe given by Plutarch, 'two kinds of juniper berry' were used in the Egyptian purge KYPHI. In Greek the tree is *arkeuthos*, the berry *arkeuthis* and *kedrion*; in Latin the tree is *iunipirus*, the berry often simply *baca* 'berry'.

Cedar sap, particularly that of *Juniperus excelsa* (Greek *kedrelate*), was a preservative, used in embalming in Egypt; it was used also as a contraceptive, applied to the male member before coitus.

Theophrastus *HP* 3.12.3; Dioscorides *MM* 1.75–7; Pliny *NH* 24.17–20, 24.54–5; Plutarch, *On Isis and Osiris* 383e–384b; Sidonius, *Letters* 8.11.3 line 46.

- Savin (*Juniperus sabina*), an aromatic shrub, is *brathy* in Greek, *herba Sabina* in Latin. It was used medicinally.

  Cato *DA* 70; Pliny *NH* 24.102; Pseudo-Apuleius, *Herbarius* 86.

K

Kandaulos, one of the contributions of LYDIA to Greek cuisine. This luxury dish came in three forms, according to Athenaeus. One of them was sweet, and is described by one source as a kind of *plakous* 'cake'. A second was apparently savoury, consisting of meat and meat broth with breadcrumbs; Athenaeus quotes a brief recipe for this (see quotation at HEGESIPPUS). What these two kinds of *kandaulos* had in common with one another or with the third kind is none too clear. The term *kandaulos* appears to be related to Lydian words recorded by Hipponax and Herodotus.

Herodotus 1.7; Pollux O 6.69; Athenaeus D 516d–517a quoting Alexis F 178 Kassel (see Arnott *ad l.*) and Hegesippus of Tarentum; Hesychius, *Lexicon s.v. kandylos*; *Scholia on Aristophanes, Peace* 123; Photius, *Lexicon s.v. kandytos*; Tzetzes, *Commentary on Chiliades* 6.477 quoting Hipponax 3a West.

Dalby 1996 p. 111 and note 59; Wilkins 2000 pp. 284–9, *al.*

Kapnias, a cooked wine style, literally 'smoky'. *Kapnias* is the name used in classical Greek sources. According to Athenaeus, the best wine of this type later came from Beneventum in Italy. Martial expresses repeated disgust at the smoked wine of Massilia.

Pherecrates 137 Kassel; Anaxandrides 42 Kassel; Martial 3.82, 10.36, 13.123, 14.118; Athenaeus E 31e.

Karyke *see* SAUCE

Kastanas, village in southern Thrace not far from the Aegean coast, inhabited in the second and early first millennia BC and an important source of archaeobotanical information. Field crops and fruits identified at Kastanas are likely to have been familiar in early classical Greece.

H. Kroll, *Kastanas: Ausgräbungen in einem Siedlungshügel der Bronze- und Eisenzeit Makedoniens 1975–1979. Die Pflanzenfunde* (Berlin, 1983); H. Kroll, 'Bronze Age and Iron Age agriculture in Kastanas' in *Proceedings of the Sixth Symposium of the International Work Group for Palaeoethnobotany, 1983: plants and ancient man* ed. W. van Zeist and W.A. Casparie (Rotterdam, 1984) pp. 243–6.

Kid *see* GOAT

Kidney *see* MEAT

Kitchen, a room for cooking, seldom to be found in Greek houses before the fourth century BC. In the earlier period, Greek cooking equipment (see COOKING UTENSILS) – even the *klibanos* which played the role of an oven – tended to be mobile and was set up where wanted, indoors or outdoors. In Hellenistic and Roman houses kitchens are more commonly found.

J. Liversidge, 'Roman kitchens and cooking utensils' in Flower and Rosenbaum 1961 pp. 29–36; Sparkes 1962–5; M. Annecchino and others, *L'instrumentum domesticum di Ercolano e Pompei nella prima età imperiale* (Rome: L'Erma di Bretschneider, 1977).

Klibanos *see* COOKING UTENSILS

Komos, in classical Greek society, a drunken revel. The nearest Roman parallel to the classical Greek *komos* is Latin COMISSATIO. The *komos* is known from two aspects.

Literary sources describe it as the culmination of a *symposion* (see SYMPOSION (1)) (but not of every *symposion*); the participants progressed through the streets, musically and noisily, serenading acquaintances and lovers, misbehaving in a predictable fashion. Alcibiades, when he interrupts the *Symposium* narrated by Plato, is engaged in a *komos*, accompanied by friends and a flute-girl, draped in ribbons; his fate is (though already very drunk, so he says) to be invited to participate in the *symposion* of Agathon, whom he had come to serenade.

Vase paintings (most of them one to two hundred years older than this literary scene) depict the *komos* as involving promiscuous sexual acts. The participants are sometimes drunken humans but very often they are SATYRS.

Aristophanes, *Wasps* 1292–449; Plato, *Symposium* 212c–213b, 223b.

C. Bron, 'Le lieu du comos' in *Third Symposium on Ancient Greek and Related Pottery, Copenhagen, 1987* ed. J. Christiansen and T. Melander (Copenhagen, 1988) pp. 71–9; François Lissarrague, 'The sexual life of satyrs' in *Before Sexuality: the construction of erotic experience in the ancient Greek world* ed. D.M. Halperin and others (Princeton: Princeton University Press, 1990); A. Seeberg, 'From padded dancers to comedy' in *Stage Directions: essays in ancient drama in honour of E.W. Handley* ed. A. Griffiths (London, 1995) pp. 1–12; Tyler Jo Smith, 'Dances, drinks and dedications: the archaic komos in Laconia' in *Sparta in Laconia: the archaeology of a city and its countryside* ed. W.G. Cavanagh and S.E.C. Walker (London, 1998) pp. 75–81; Tyler Jo Smith, 'Dancing spaces and dining places: archaic komasts at the symposion' in *Periplous: papers on classical art and archaeology pre-*

sented to Sir J. Boardman* ed. G.R. Tsetskhladze, A.J.N.W. Prag and A.M. Snodgrass (London: Thames and Hudson, 2000) pp. 309–19.

Kottabos, favourite party game of classical Greece. The game consisted of tossing an almost-empty wine cup with the finger in such a way as to project the last drops of wine at a target. The target, generally of earthenware, was either floating in a bowl of water or balanced on a stand; the object was to sink the target or to make it fall. Typical prizes (*kottabeia*) were TRAGEMATA (such as nuts and raisins) or kisses. In later times, when the game had fallen out of fashion, *kottabeia* were 'prizes' for any society game; as a joky metaphor the verb *kottabizein* came to mean not 'play *kottabos*' but 'vomit'.

Many vase paintings show the game in progress or depict men or women in the act of tossing a wine cup. Quotations supplied by Athenaeus give additional details. 'In the old days' the target was a slave, some said.

Pollux *O* 6.109–11; Athenaeus *D* 665d–668f quoting Critias 2 West and other sources.

Schneider, 'Kottabos' in *RE* 1893–1972; H.W. Hayley, 'The *kóttabos kataktós* in the light of recent investigations' in *Harvard Studies in Classical Philology* vol. 5 (1894) pp. 73–82; M. Vickers in *American Journal of Archaeology* vol. 78 (1974) p. 158; Schäfer 1997.

Krater *see* DINING AND DRINKING UTENSILS; WINE-MIXING

Kronia, a summer festival celebrating the god Kronos. According to Accius, 'Most of the Greeks, Athens especially, perform rites which they call Cronia: when they celebrate this day they feast joyfully in country and in city alike, and attend upon their slaves' – a custom which may be compared with the Roman SATURNALIA.

Machon *C* 17.335 [Athenaeus *D* 581a] with Gow *ad l.*; Accius, *Annales* 3 Dangel.

Hesiod, *Theogony* ed. M.L. West (Oxford, 1966) p. 205.

Figure 9 The game of *kottabos*. The target is a model of a bird, balanced above a basin of water, on which, to make all clear, the word *kotabos* is written. Redrawn from an Athenian *kylix* by Apollodorus, about 490 BC.

Figure 10 Two women playing *kottabos*. One says, 'This [throw] is for you, Euthymides!' Redrawn from an Athenian *hydria* by Phintias, about 520 BC, at Munich.

Kykeon, a 'potion', a magical and medicinal drink based on pearl barley with water, wine or milk, and with added foods or drugs whose effects were either salutary or dangerous. PENNYROYAL, an important gynaecological herb, was often an ingredient. Hanson observes that texts in the Hippocratic corpus prescribe *kykeon* frequently, but *kykeon* with pennyroyal only for women patients. It seems clear also that *kykeon* with pennyroyal was the ritual drink of the Eleusinian rites of Demeter.

The verb from which the word *kykeon* derives is *kykao* 'mix': the same verb is used of one who churns milk. The resulting mixture is characterised by Homer as *sitos* 'cereal food'. At a much later period the lexicographer Hesychius equates *ptisane* 'barley gruel' with *kykeon*; Galen, however, had specifically distinguished these two terms, on the grounds that *kykeon* might incorporate flavourings such as cumin.

Modern recipes for *kykeon* are suggested by Dalby and Grainger 1996 p. 40 and by Grant 1999 p. 81.

Homer, *Iliad* 11.623–41, *Odyssey* 10.233–8, 10.316–18; *Homeric Hymn to Demeter* 209 with Richardson *ad l.*; Hippocrates *R* 41; Theophrastus, *Characters* 4.1; Plutarch *QC* 7.1; Galen *AF* 6.503; Polyaenus 4.3.32; Hesychius, *Lexicon s.vv. kykeon, ptisane*.

W.H. Roscher, 'Der Kykeon des Hipponax' in *Jahrbücher für klassische Philologie* vol. 34 (1888) pp. 522–4; A. Delatte, *Le Cycéon, breuvage rituel des mystères d'Eleusis* (Paris, 1955); P. Mingazzini, 'Su un particolare della cucina omerica' in *Rendiconti delle sedute dell'Accademia Nazionale dei Lincei*, Classe di scienze morali, storiche e filologiche vol. 31 (1976) pp. 3–7; Helene P. Foley, *The Homeric Hymn to Demeter* (Princeton: Princeton University Press, 1994) pp. 46–8, 68–70; Ann Ellis Hanson, 'Talking recipes in the gynaecological texts of the Hippocratic corpus' in *Parchments of Gender: deciphering the bodies of antiquity* ed. Maria Wyke (Oxford: Clarendon Press, 1998) pp. 71–94.

Kyphi, Egyptian aromatic compound, used medicinally as a purge. There were usually said to be sixteen ingredients; the mixture might be taken in wine. Egyptian and Greek sources provide several different recipes.

Dioscorides *MM* 1.25; Plutarch, *On Isis and Osiris* 383e–384b; Galen *DA* 14.117 quoting Damocrates.

V. Loret, 'Le kyphi, parfum sacré des anciens Egyptiens' in *Journal Asiatique* 8th series vol. 10 (1887) pp. 76–132.

L

Lablab bean, legume domesticated in the Middle East. Cultivation of the lablab bean had spread eastwards as far as the Indus valley before 2000 BC. It was in due course familiar in classical Greece. An *etnos* or bean soup was made with these beans, but it receives no commendations from the dietary writers such as Galen and Oribasius. The lablab bean, under its various names, is still a significant crop in India and the Levant.

The lablab bean or bonavist bean or hyacinth bean (*Dolichos Lablab*) is Greek *dolikhos* (and later *lobos*). Dioscorides names the seeds *lobia*, the plant *smilax kepaia* 'garden bindweed', and gives a full description.

Hippocrates *R* 45; Cato *DA* 70 (*fabuli albi*); Dioscorides *MM* 2.146; Pliny *NH* 16.244 (*dolichos*); Galen *VA* 53; Oribasius *CM* 4.8.7–18.

Lamb *see* SHEEP

Lamprey, primitive bloodsucking 'fish' (actually member of a distinct order of vertebrates). The lampreys of southern Gaul are unmistakably mentioned by Pliny in the course of his discussion of the *muraena*, moray eel; the lamprey had previously been noticed by Dorion under the name of the 'river moray'. Lampreys are possibly also mentioned by Galen, categorised by him as a 'dogfish' much liked by Romans and unknown in Greek waters. Anthimus is the first author to use a form of the name under which lampreys are now known in western Europe.

The lamprey's scientific name is *Petromyzon marinus*. The term 'lamprey' is often used in translations of classical texts to render Greek *myraina* and Latin *muraena*, but in fact these words nearly always refer to the MORAY EEL.

Pliny *NH* 9.73, 9.76 (*muraena*); Galen *AF* 6.727 (*galaxias*); Athenaeus *D* 312d citing Dorion (*myraina he potamia*); Anthimus *OC* 47 with Grant *ad l.* (*nauprida* or *lamprida*); *Corpus glossariorum Latinorum* 3.570.36 (*lampetra*).

Thompson 1947 pp. 162–5; Andrews 1949 p. 10 (on *galaxias*); Davidson 1979 pp. 176–7; Davidson 1981 pp. 24–5.

Langouste and langoustine, lobster-like sea creatures. Beloved of ancient gourmets, the langouste was an expensive luxury and deserved elaborate cooking, as seen in the six recipes offered in *Apicius*. It is indigestible, according to Galen; its broth or cooking liquor was, however, recommended to invalids. Langoustes were found in rough and rocky places, said Aristotle, such as at Sigeum (near Troy) and off Mount Athos. The langoustine has 'long hands and small feet', says Epicharmus: Archestratus would say the same of the LOBSTER.

The spiny lobster, rock lobster, crawfish or langouste (*Palinurus Elephas*) and the langoustine, scampo, crayfish or Dublin Bay prawn (*Nephrops norvegicus*) are Greek *karabos* and Latin *locusta*. The langouste is occasionally called *astakos*, lobster, in Greek; for the langoustine Greeks also used the diminutive forms *karabis* and *karabion*.

Karabos 'langouste' was the nickname of the Greek orator Callimedon 'owing to his love for this food' (Athenaeus *D* 339e–340e, *al.*).

Hippocrates *R* 48; Aristotle *HA* 525a30–527a34, 549a14–549b29, 590b13–21; Pliny *NH* 9.95–7, 11.152, 37.89; Aelian *Nature of Animals* 1.32, *al.*; Suetonius, *Tiberius* 60; Galen *AF* 6.735; Oppian *H* 1.259–79, 2.389–418; Athenaeus *D* 104c–106e quoting Alexis *F* 57 Kassel (see Arnott *ad l.*) and Epicharmus 57 Kaibel; *Apicius* 2.1.1, 9.1.1–6; Vinidarius *BC* 17.

Thompson 1947 p. 102; Davidson 1981 pp. 177–80.

Last Supper, the last meal shared between Jesus and his disciples. The occasion was a PASSOVER meal; a lamb was cooked and eaten, but the narratives of the event emphasise the sharing of bread and wine, prefiguring the Christian EUCHARIST.

Mark, *Gospel* 14.12–25; Matthew, *Gospel* 26.17–29; Luke, *Gospel* 22.7–38; John, *Gospel* 13.1–30.

Latium, region of Italy extending southeastwards from Rome. For gastronomic specialities of Latium see CASINUM; ROME; VENAFRUM. For the wines of Latium see ALBAN WINE; CAECUBAN WINE; FORMIAN WINE; FUNDAN WINE; MASSIC WINE; ROMAN WINES; SETINE WINE; SIGNINE WINE; TIBURTINE WINE.

Lead, malleable metal. In Roman times lead was customarily used to line the channels of aqueducts, and thus added its sweetish flavour to city water supplies. Lead vessels were recommended by some, for the flavour they contributed, when boiling down MUST to make grape syrup (*defrutum*), an ingredient widely used in cooking and in flavoured wines; others,

however, were aware that lead might be poisonous.

Vitruvius 8.6.10; Pliny *NH* 14.136, 32.68, *al.*

Leek, the typical garden vegetable in the early eastern Mediterranean. The Greek term for garden plot or bed, *prasia*, means literally 'leek-bed'. Similarly the ancient Egyptian term for leek also means 'vegetables' in general. Leeks are planted in summer and harvested in mid to late winter, an unusual timetable which helps to explain the apparently vapid proverb recorded by Cato, 'If you plant leeks every year, you will have leeks to pull every year.' Leeks also gave their name in Greek and Latin to the colour *prasinos*, *prasinus* 'green', which for many centuries was the livery of one of the two teams of charioteers at the Roman Circus.

Leeks were an important vegetable and aromatic in both Greek and Roman cuisine, called for over sixty times in the recipes of *Apicius*. They spread northwards in cultivation in Roman times. Leek seeds are found in excavations of sites from Roman Gaul, Britain and Germany, and in all three regions the leek, once introduced, continued to be grown in later times.

They were also valued as a medicinal plant; in particular they were supposed to add brilliance to the voice, which is why the emperor Nero ate cutting leeks, *porra sectiva* – and nothing else – on certain prescribed days each month.

The leek (*Allium Porrum*) is Greek *prason*, Latin *porrum*. Two cultivated varieties were recognised, the cutting leek (Greek *karton*, Latin *porrum sectivum*) and the 'headed leek' (Greek *kephaloton*, Latin *porrum capitatum*). The latter, rightly said by Athenaeus to be 'more juicy', corresponds to the modern Middle Eastern varieties, which have a distinct bulb: some botanists treat them as a separate species, *A. Kurrat*.

Homer, *Odyssey* 7.127; Hippocrates *R* 54; Cato *DA* 47; *Moretum* 73; Pliny *NH* 19.108–10,

20.44–9; Galen *AF* 6.658; Athenaeus *D* 371e–372b quoting Diphilus of Siphnos (*karton* is to be translated 'cutting leek', not 'carrot'); Palladius *OA* 3.24.11–12; *Apicius* 2.3.1, *al.*

Darby and others 1977 pp. 673–5; M. Stol, 'Garlic, onion, leek' in *Bulletin on Sumerian Agriculture* no. 3 (1987) pp. 57–92; Zohary and Hopf 1993 p. 183; Davidson 2000 p. 447.

- Greek *ampeloprason* is the wild leek (*Allium Ampeloprasum*).

  Dioscorides *MM* 2.150; Athenaeus *D* 371f.

- Cultivated varieties of this wild leek species are now called Levant garlic. Classical sources also describe this as a kind of garlic: in Greek it is *skorodon to Kyprion*, Cypriot garlic, and in Latin *ulpicum*. It was well known as a country food in the classical world. It foamed when beaten with oil and vinegar.

  Columella *DA* 11.3.21; Galen *AF* 6.632.

Legumes, the generally less-favoured staple food of the classical Mediterranean (for the more-favoured see GRAIN). Although Greeks and Romans sometimes talk of the *etnos* (Greek: bean soup) or *cicer tepidum* (Latin: hot chickpea soup) that kept them going, they seldom praise it.

The legumes of the ancient world were BEAN (fava bean), BLACK-EYED PEA, CHICKPEA, FENUGREEK, GRASS PEA, LABLAB BEAN, LENTIL, LUPIN, PEA, VETCH; see also URD.

Galen *AF* 6.524–47; Athenaeus *D* 406b–408b.

G. Ladizinsky, 'Origin and domestication of the Southwest Asian grain legumes' in *Foraging and Farming: the evolution of plant exploitation* ed. D.R. Harris and G.C. Hillman (London, 1989) pp. 374–89; K.B. Flint-Hamilton, 'Legumes in ancient Greece and Rome: food, medicine, or poison?' in *Hesperia* vol. 68 (1999) pp. 371–85.

Lentil, one of the major legumes of the ancient Near East. Lentils were being gathered from the wild in Syria by 12,000 BC, at Franchthi Cave in southern Greece before 10,000 BC and in southern France by 7000 BC. Lentils were being cultivated in Greece before 6000 BC. These small, brightly coloured seeds are easily stored and were to be one of the three dietary staples of classical Greece (with wheat and barley), in the familiar form of lentil soup, *phake*.

Greek *phake*, like the comparable Roman staple PULS, was prepared in many ways. In its most basic form the lentils were simply boiled until they formed a smooth soup, which could be flavoured, so Anthimus suggests, with vinegar and sumach (Grant 1999 pp. 138–9 suggests a modern interpretation of Anthimus's instructions). To add expensive aromatics would be inappropriate – 'the myrrh on the lentil soup', *toupi tei phakei myron*, proverbial overkill – but sumach was available from the earliest classical times and was not expensive. There were other combinations, however. One was *bolbophake*, bulb and lentil soup (see BULBS); another was *phakoptisane*, lentil and barley soup, for which Galen gives a recipe (followed by Oribasius, and in due course by Grant 1999 p. 69). One more alternative, *laganophake*, incorporating a kind of PASTA, is described in the *Heidelberg Papyrus*. Again, Grant (1999 p. 137) suggests a modern interpretation. Lentils, though familiar in classical Rome, are less prominent in Roman than in Greek sources.

Lentil (*Lens culinaris*) is Greek *phakos*, Latin *lens*, *lenticula*.

Solon 38 West; Hippocrates *R* 45; Theophrastus *HP* 8.5.1–3; Dioscorides *MM* 2.107; Pliny *NH* 18.123, 22.142–5; Galen *AF* 6.527–8; Athenaeus *D* 156c–160c quoting Chrysippus of Soli [Athenaeus *D* 158a]; Palladius *OA* 3.4; *Apicius* 5.2; Oribasius *CM* 4.1.22–3; Anthimus *OC* 67 with Grant *ad l.*

Darby and others 1977 pp. 687–9; Zohary and Hopf 1993 pp. 88–94; Brewer and others (1995 ?) pp. 70–1; Wilkins 2000 pp. 13–16.

Leopard, wild animal of Africa and Asia. Its flavour was not unknown to classical hunters.

The leopard (*Panthera Pardus*) is Greek *pardalis* and *panther*, Latin *pardus* and *panthera*.

Galen *AF* 6.665.

Lesbian wine (Greek *Lesbios*; Latin *Lesbium*), from the big island of Lesbos in the northeastern Aegean. Lesbian wines are scarcely heard of in Greek literature of the fifth century BC but are warmly spoken of in the fourth. Can it be true, as implied by Eubulus, that this was because of a tax break for Lesbian wine at Athens? In any case, Lesbian wine achieves fulsome praise from Archestratus, who rates it above Thasian and Phoenician, without even a mention (in surviving fragments) of Chian, the other first-class wine of Greece at this period.

Until the Roman period we have no information on different styles of Lesbian wine, or on the terroirs of the Lesbian region. Galen talks of the 'very aromatic Lesbian' of which there is a little from Mitylene, more and better from Methymna and Eresus. Pliny thinks that Lesbian wine 'tastes of the sea by its own nature', but Galen carefully insists that the Lesbian to which seawater is added must be avoided in favour of the pure sort, which they call *aparakhytos*. Lesbian wine was tawny in colour, according to Galen, 'hot' and light in dietary terms.

Archestratus *H* 56 Brandt; Hippolochus *D*; Callimachus [*Anthologia Palatina* 13.9]; Dioscorides *MM* 5.6; Pliny *NH* 14.73–4; Galen *ST* 6.334–5, *BM* 6.803, *SF* 11.604, *On Therapeutic Method* 10.832–5, *On Compounding* 13.405; Athenaeus *E* 28e–29d quoting Eubulus 136 Kassel and Archestratus *H* 59–60 Brandt.

Dalby 2000c.

- Eresus, birthplace of Theophrastus, at the western extremity of the island, was the best of the terroirs of Lesbos according to Galen.

  Galen *DA* 14.28, *On Therapeutic Method* 10.832, *On Compounding* 13.405, 13.659.

- Methymna on the north coast (modern Molyvos) was second best. Horace's ridiculous gastronome, Nasidienus, claims to get his vinegar from Methymna.

  Horace, *Satires* 2.8.52; Silius Italicus 7.210; Galen *DA* 14.29, *On Therapeutic Method* 10.832, *On Compounding* 13.405, 13.659.

- Mitylene, administrative capital of the island, was third best for quality of wine.

  Galen *DA* 14.29, *On Therapeutic Method* 10.832, *On Compounding* 13.405.

- There was a Lesbian PROTROPOS, known in Mitylene as *prodromos* 'forerunner', a sweet wine made from free-run must.

  Vitruvius 8.3.12; Athenaeus *E* 30b, 46e.

Lesbos, large island in the northeast Aegean. In the ancient world Lesbos was famed not only for its wine (see LESBIAN WINE) but for the barley of Eresus: 'if the gods eat *alphita*, this is where Hermes goes shopping for it,' Archestratus assures his readers. Methymna and Mitylene, in the eastern half of the island, fished for the SCALLOP that was found in the straits between Lesbos and the Anatolian coast. It was conserved in brine for export.

Archestratus *H* 4 Brandt with Olson and Sens *ad l.*; Philyllius 12 Kassel with Kassel *ad l.*; Aristotle *HA* 603a21–3; Xenocrates *T* 56–71.

Lettuce, salad vegetable. Lettuce was familiar in Egypt as early as the third millennium BC. In Greece and Rome lettuce was familiar throughout the classical period, but no evidence of its prehistoric use has been found. Lettuce was eaten among the hors d'oeuvres: it was said to 'float' in the stomach and thus to be indigestible if eaten towards the end of the meal. Anthimus, wisely, advises that it be eaten when freshly gathered.

Lettuce was apparently regarded in Egypt as an aphrodisiac. It is easier to explain the fact that in Greek and Roman medicine lettuce was said to cause 'bodily weakness' (thus in the Hippocratic text *Regimen*), or, more bluntly, to be an antaphrodisiac:

> Don't serve me *thridakinai* at table, woman, or you will have yourself to blame. In a lettuce bed, they say, once upon a time the dead Adonis was laid to rest by Aphrodite. So it is food for corpses.

The milky sap of lettuce has a real sedative effect, though it is weaker in modern cultivated varieties than in the wild species. Lettuce was sometimes eaten with rocket, which was regarded as aphrodisiac; the two salad vegetables thus counterbalanced one another, as Pliny explains. Plutarch discussed why it is that women do not eat the heart of lettuce, but the discussion does not survive.

Lettuce (*Lactuca sativa*) is Greek *thridax*, Latin *lactuca*. Greek *thridakine*, when intended specifically, is a name for the wild species of southern Europe sometimes called prickly lettuce (*L. serriola*).

Hippocrates *R 54*; Theophrastus *HP* 7.4.5, 7.6.2; Horace, *Satires* 2.8.8; *Moretum* 74; Pliny *NH* 19.125–8, 19.155, 20.64–8; Plutarch *QC* 4.10; Athenaeus *E* 68f–70a; Palladius *OA* 2.14.1–4; Anthimus *OC 51* with Grant *ad l.*

Laufer 1919 pp. 400–2; Darby and others 1977 pp. 675–80; Zohary and Hopf 1993 p. 186; Brewer and others (1995 ?) pp. 74–5.

Leucadian wine (Greek *Leukadios*; Latin *Leucadium*) from the Greek island of Leucas. Leucadian wine is heard of from the fourth to the second century BC.

Eubulus 129 Kassel; Plautus, *Poenulus* 699; Pliny *NH* 14.76 citing Apollodorus; Athenaeus *E* 33b (source attribution lost).

Libation, a form of sacrifice (Greek *sponde*, Latin *libamen*). To associate a god with a solemn human act, unmixed wine was poured into a cup, was tasted by participants and was spilled on to an altar or on to the ground. A libation was made towards the end of a Greek dinner, at the beginning of the drinking or *symposion*.

Libations are very frequently depicted on Greek vase paintings and reliefs in memory of the dead. This is not because libations were made at funerals: it is because they were made at parting. The icon thus represents a farewell. Greek *spondai* means also 'truce, treaty' because a libation was poured to solemnise an agreement.

Herodotus 1.132, 2.39; Aristophanes, *Peace* 1059–110; Menander, *Dyscoluss* 621–4, *Kolax* fragment 1 Sandbach; Athenaeus 692f–693f.

Liddell and Scott 1925–40 *s.v. sponde* and related words; P. Veyne, 'Divinités à la patère' in *Metis* vol. 5 (1990) pp. 17–30; François Lissarrague, 'Un rituel du vin: la libation' in *In Vino Veritas* ed. Oswyn Murray and Manuela Tecuşan (London: British School at Rome, 1995) pp. 126–44; Mu-Chou Poo, *Wine and Wine Offering in the Religion of Ancient Egypt* (London: Kegan Paul International, 1995).

Limpet, group of univalve shellfish, proverbial for clinging tightly to the rocks. Limpets are edible but their flesh is tough, and gets tougher as they grow.

The limpet (*Patella caerulea* and other species) is Greek *lepas*.

Aristophanes, *Wasps* 105, *Wealth* 1096; Aristotle *HA* 530a17; Xenocrates *T* 88; Galen *BM* 6.769; Athenaeus *D* 85f–87e *passim*.

Linseed or flax, an important oil and fibre plant first domesticated in the Near East. Flax was being cultivated in Syria by 10,000 BC and gradually spread westwards in prehistoric times. Cultivation had reached the western Mediterranean by the last few centuries BC.

Linseed oil was probably the usual food oil of the ancient Near East, but it is inconvenient as a food oil because it rapidly goes rancid. It was therefore superseded in food use by SESAME oil in Mesopotamia when sesame became available there, perhaps around 1000 BC, and by OLIVE OIL to the north and west, wherever it was found that the olive would grow. By classical times linseed oil was little used in food, though it was still important enough economically to be one of five oils taxed under Ptolemy II (see EGYPT). It was used in a rustic food of northern Italy, according to Pliny.

The seeds, like those of sesame, are aromatic when roasted. Alcman, the poet of early Sparta, hints that they might be sprinkled on bread before baking.

Linseed or flax (*Linum usitatissimum*) is Greek *linon*, Latin *linum*, apparently one of the few plant names inherited by both languages from proto-Indo-European.

Pliny *NH* 19.16, 20.249–51; Athenaeus *D* 110f quoting Alcman 19 Davies; Palladius *OA* 11.2.

Laufer 1919 pp. 288–96; H. Helbaek, 'Notes on the evolution and history of Linum' in *Kuml. Ärbog for Jysk Arkaeologisk Selskab* (1959) pp. 103–29; J.N. Postgate, 'The oil plant in Assyria' in *Bulletin on Sumerian Agriculture* vol. 2 (1985) pp. 145–52; Zohary and Hopf 1993 pp. 119–26.

Lipara, one of the Aeolian islands north of Sicily. Lipara was good for lobster, the fine fish called *aulopias* (see TUNNY) and sprats.

Archestratus *H* 24 and cf. 33 Brandt; Diodorus Siculus 5.10.3; Aelian, *Nature of Animals* 13.17; Pollux *O* 6.63; Athenaeus *E* 4d.

Liquorice, aromatic root native to southern Russia and central Asia. Liquorice was familiar in the classical Mediterranean and had medicinal uses. In particular, sweet *protropos* wine, whether Scybelite or Theran, formed the basis of a medicinal wine in which liquorice was an ingredient, according to Galen. It was also an ingredient in a compound which was used for doctoring young wine to give it age: Damegeron supplies a recipe. By late Roman times liquorice was grown plentifully in northern Anatolia.

Liquorice (*Glycyrrhiza glabra*) is Greek *glykyrriza*, Latin *glycyrrhiza*.

Theophrastus *HP* 9.13.2 (*Skythike riza, glykeia riza*); Dioscorides *MM* 3.5 (gives Latin as *dulciradix*); Pliny *NH* 22.24–6; Soranus, *Gynaecia* 2.54; Galen, *On Compounding* 13.85; Oribasius *CM* 11.g.8; *Geoponica* 7.24.4 quoting Damegeron.

Literature as source

- This is a selection of papers dealing with food and dining as they arise in specific genres of ancient literature.

Griffin 1985 pp. 65–87; N.A. Hudson, 'Food in Roman satire' in *Satire and Society in Ancient Rome* ed. S.H. Braund (Exeter: Exeter University Press, 1989) pp. 69–87; Gowers 1993; Norman Kiell, *Food and Drink in Literature: a*

selectively annotated bibliography (Lanham: Scarecrow Press, 1995); D. Gilula, 'Comic food and food for comedy' in *Food in Antiquity* ed. John Wilkins and others (Exeter: Exeter University Press, 1995) pp. 386–99; E.L. Bowie, 'Wine in Old Comedy' in *In Vino Veritas* ed. Oswyn Murray and Manuela Tecuşan (London: British School at Rome, 1995) pp. 113–25; John Wilkins, 'Eating in Greek comedy' in *Food in European Literature* ed. John Wilkins (Exeter: Intellect, 1996) pp. 46–56; John Wilkins, 'Edible choruses' in *The Rivals of Aristophanes: studies in Athenian Old Comedy* ed. David Harvey and John Wilkins (London: Duckworth, 2000) pp. 341–54; Wilkins 2000; Kirk Freudenberg, *Satires of Rome: threatening poses from Lucilius to Juvenal* (Cambridge: Cambridge University Press, 2001).

- This is a selection of papers concerned with food and dining as they arise in the work of single classical authors. There is a separate entry for ARISTOPHANES.

Alcman: M. Pizzocaro, 'Alcmane e la gastronomia poetica' in *Aion* vol. 12 (1990) pp. 285–308; Andrew Dalby, 'The vineyards of Laconia' in *Classica* (São Paulo) vol. 11/12 (1998–9) pp. 281–8. **Horace:** C.J. Classen, 'Horace: a cook?' in *Classical Quarterly* vol. 28 (1978) pp. 333–48; R. Mayer, 'Horace on good manners' in *Proceedings of the Cambridge Philological Society* no. 211 (1985) pp. 33–46; Oswyn Murray, 'Symposium and genre in the poetry of Horace' in *Journal of Roman Studies* vol. 75 (1985) pp. 39–50; Deena Berg, 'The mystery gourmet of Horace's *Satires* 2' in *Classical Journal* vol. 91 (1996) pp. 141–51. **Juvenal:** R. Cuccioli, 'The banquet in Juvenal *Satire* 5' in *Papers of the Leeds International Latin Seminar* vol. 6 (1990) pp. 139–43. **Lucilius:** L.R. Shero, 'Lucilius's *Cena rustica*' in *American Journal of Philology* vol. 50 (1929) pp. 64–70. **Menander:** D. Gilula, 'Menander's comedies best with dessert and wine (Plut. *Mor.* 712E)' in *Athenaeum* vol. 65 (1987) pp. 239–96. **Pindar:** B. van Groningen, *Pindare au banquet* (Leiden, 1960); review by Emily Vermeule in *Classical Philology* vol. 57 (1962) pp. 184–7. **Plautus:** J.C.B. Lowe, 'Cooks in Plautus' in *Classical Antiquity* vol. 4 (1985) pp. 72–102; S.A. Frangoulidis, 'Food and poetics in Plautus, *Captivi*' in *L'Antiquité classique* vol. 65 (1996) pp. 225–30; C. Connors, 'Scents and sensibility in Plautus' *Casina*' in *Classical Quarterly* vol. 47 (1997) pp. 305–9. **Solon:** Maria Noussia, 'Solon's symposium (frs. 32–4 and 36 Gentili-Prati² = 38–40 and 41 West²)' in *Classical Quarterly* vol. 51 (2001) pp. 353–9. **Vergil:** Jasper Griffin, 'Regalis inter mensas laticemque Lyaeum: wine in Virgil and others' in *In Vino Veritas* ed. Oswyn Murray and

Manuela Tecuşan (London: British School at Rome, 1995) pp. 283–96. **Xenophanes:** C.M. Bowra, 'Xenophanes on songs at feasts' in his *Problems in Greek Poetry* (Oxford, 1953) pp. 1–14; J. Defradas, 'Le banquet de Xénophane' in *Revue des études grecques* vol. 75 (1962) pp. 344–65; M. Marcovich, 'Xenophanes on drinking-parties and Olympic games' in *Illinois Classical Studies* vol. 3 (1978) pp. 1–26.

Liver, one of the 'vital organs' grouped as SPLANKHNA in Greek terminology. The liver of all animals has thick humours and is heavy on the digestion, according to Galen; he lists it first among vital organs and gives it more space, suggesting it was in practice more significant in the diet than was heart.

For foie gras see GOOSE. For a similar feeding method for pigs, used to produce succulent liver, see FATTENING. Anthimus gives a recipe for pig's liver: see the modern version by Grant 1999 pp. 127–8.

Liver is Greek *hepar*, Latin *iecur*.

Galen *AF* 6.679–80; Pollux *O* 6.49; Athenaeus *D* 106f–107f; Anthimus *OC* 21.

- Greek *khoria* is a dish difficult to define, possibly liver or other offal cooked in the caul, possibly cooked with milk and honey.

  Athenaeus *D* 106e–107a, 646e; *Scholia on Theocritus* 9.19; cf. *Apicius* 7.10.1.

Lobster, well-armed sea creature. Its most noticeable external traits were its 'long hands and small feet' (Archestratus), its 'bent fingers' (Epicharmus) and its dark colour (Pliny). It is very good, albeit somewhat complicated, to eat; simpler for the eventual diner if the cook minces the meat and forms it into cakes, as described in *Apicius*. Archestratus says that the lobster was at its best at the volcanic island of Lipara, north of Sicily; lobsters were plentiful in the Hellespont. and (as noted by Aristotle) at Thasos.

The lobster (*Homarus Gammarus*) is Greek *astakos* (occasionally *leon*), Latin *astacus* and *elephantus*; the latter name is seldom attested in classical texts but was certainly in use, since it survives in modern Italian dialects.

Aristotle *HA* 525b33–526b18, 549a14–549b29; Matron *AD* 66–8; Machon *C* 5.29 [Athenaeus *D* 244b]; Pliny *NH* 9.10, 32.148 (*elephantus*), 9.97, 32.149 (*leon*); Aelian, *Nature of Animals* 8.23 (*astakos*), 14.9 (*leon*); Galen *AF* 6.735; Oppian *H* 1.259–79; Athenaeus *D* 104f–106e quoting Archestratus *H* 24 Brandt and Epicharmus 30 Kaibel; *Apicius* 2.1.1.

Thompson 1947 pp. 18, 150; Davidson 1981 pp. 177–8.

Local specialities in food and wine scarcely come to notice in ancient Near Eastern or Egyptian cultures. For whatever reason, the recognition of local specialities and local food excellence appears to be an ancient Greek innovation, balanced by the equally novel idea that food preferences, also, vary from place to place (Athenaeus 131f–132f).

Several lists of local fine produce are quoted by Athenaeus from texts of the sixth to fourth centuries BC: see also POLYCRATES. The classic statement on the subject was the gastronomic poem of ARCHESTRATUS, which survives in fragments. Written *c.*350 BC, this drew on local traditions that were older – but of unknown age – most of which are otherwise unrecorded. A summary list of the best-known specialities is given by Pollux in the late second century AD on the basis of earlier texts:

> You must know that the ancients approved moray eel from the Straits and from Tartessus, tunny from Tyre, *kestreus* grey mullet from Sciathos, kid from Melos, shellfish from Cape Pelorus (which is how the shellfish now called *pelorides* got their name), beet from Ascra, sprats from Lipara, turnips from Mantinea, scallops from Methymna, dogfish from Rhodes, flatfish from Eleusis, *aphyai* from Phalerum, red mullet from Aexone, Copaic eels from Boeotia, 'floaters' [moray eels] from Sicily, Thasian brine,

Thasian radishes, Cythnian and Sicilian cheese, and salt of Tragasae: Tragasae is a marsh near Troy.

The idea was possibly first transmitted to Rome in Ennius's translation from Archestratus in the early second century BC. It was taken up by Varro, more than a century later, in a verse satire 'On foods' which no doubt owed something to Ennius's example and certainly draws on earlier Greek material. Neither Ennius's nor Varro's poem survives, but Aulus Gellius gives a summary from Varro:

M. Varro, in the satire which he entitled *Peri Edesmaton*, in verses written with great charm and cleverness, treats of exquisite elegance in banquets and viands. He has set forth and described in iambic trimeters the greater number of things of that kind which such gluttons seek out on land and sea.

As for the verses themselves, he who has leisure may find and read them in the book which I have mentioned. So far as my memory goes, these are the varieties and names of the foods surpassing all others, which a bottomless gullet has hunted out and which Varro has assailed in his satire, with the places where they are found: a peacock from Samos, a francolin from Phrygia, Melic cranes, a kid from Ambracia, a bonito from Chalcedon, a moray eel from Tartessus, young [wild] asses from Pessinus, oysters from Tarentum, a scallop [from Mitylene?], an *elops* from Rhodes, parrot wrasses from Cilicia, walnuts from Thasos, dates from Egypt, an acorn from Spain.

Varro is also quoted on the same subject by Macrobius. This time the extract is from Varro's prose work *Human Antiquities*: 'As regards food, Campanian farms produce the best wheat, Falernian wine, Casinan olive oil, Tusculan figs, and the Tiber the best fish.'

Regulations on the naming and quality of local produce, a concept ancestral to the appellation regulations of modern Europe, are as yet very rarely found: see THASIAN WINE for one example.

Aulus Gellius 6.16.1–5 citing Varro, *Menippean Satires* 403 Bücheler; Pollux O 6.63; Athenaeus E 26c–33c; Macrobius S 3.16.12 quoting Varro.

Dalby 1996 pp. 97–106, 124–9; Dalby 2000a pp. 21–208; Dalby 2000c.

Locust, edible insect. Classical sources that hint at the eating of locusts by human beings are not, in general, positive and unambiguous. That locusts could be eaten by ascetics, and by others when necessary, is shown by the Gospel references to John the Baptist's food while in the desert; indeed, four species of locusts (see the *Leviticus* reference for a list) were specifically permitted as a food for Jews. One of the barbarian tribes of northeastern Africa listed by Diodorus Siculus and Strabo is called by them *Akridophagoi* 'locust-eaters'.

The locust (*Schistocerca gregaria*) is Greek *akris*, Latin *locusta*.

Leviticus 11.22; Aristophanes, *Acharnians* 1116–17; Diodorus Siculus 3.29.1; Strabo 16.4.12; Dioscorides MM 2.52; Mark, *Gospel* 1.6; Matthew, *Gospel* 3.4; Galen, *Commentary on Hippocrates' Aphorisms* 17b.484; Athenaeus E 63c quoting Epicharmus.

Lotus (1). Group of edible water plants typical of Egypt. They are frequently described by classical authors, and almost as frequently confused with one another and with the TARO, simply because the plants and their uses, though easily distinguished, were all quite unfamiliar in Greece and Italy. The Greek and Latin words listed below are used consistently with these senses by well-informed authors but are often misunderstood and misapplied by others.

The pink lotus or Egyptian bean (*Nelumbo nucifera*) is native to India. When Alexander saw it growing in the River

Acesines, a tributary of the Indus (having, presumably, previously seen it in Egypt), he believed he must have found the headwaters of the Nile. The pink lotus is believed to have been introduced to Egypt in the mid first millennium BC: at any rate it does not appear in earlier Egyptian wall paintings. It has a large fruit which is honeycombed and contains edible nuts. Its use is first described by Herodotus, who describes it as a rose-like lily. Later authors observe that the root, too, is honeycombed and is edible. The fruit is called *kiborion* in Greek, *ciborium* in Latin; the nut is *kyamos ho Aigyptios* or 'Egyptian bean' in Greek, and similarly *faba Aegyptia* in Latin.

Herodotus 2.92; Theophrastus *HP* 4.8.7–11; Diodorus Siculus 1.10.1, 1.34.6–7; Strabo 15.1.25, 17.1.15, 17.2.4; Dioscorides *MM* 2.106; Pliny *NH* 18.121–2, 22.56; Athenaeus *D* 677d, also *E* 72a–73c quoting Nicander *F* 81–2 Schneider (in Nicander fragment 82 read *kyamous*).

Darby and others 1977 pp. 619–41; Hepper 1990 p. 11; Davidson 2000 pp. 460–1.

- The white lotus (*Nymphaea Lotus*) has a fruit or seed-head which can be dried, ground into meal and baked as 'bread'. Its root is edible once the dark skin is removed; it can be eaten raw, but is better boiled or roasted. This plant is *ssn* in Egyptian and *shoshan* in Hebrew. This and the blue lotus are both called *lotos* in Greek, *lotus* in Latin (Herodotus says that the name *lotos* is Egyptian, but this is not true). The edible root is *korsion* in Greek, *corsium* in Latin.

  Herodotus 2.92 with How and Wells *ad l.*; Theophrastus *HP* 4.10.1–7; Diodorus Siculus 1.10.1; Strabo 17.2.4; Dioscorides *MM* 4.113; Pliny *NH* 13.110.

- The blue lotus (*Nymphaea caerulea*), *srpt* in Egyptian and *sirpad* in Hebrew, is used as food only during famines. People are often seen smelling the flowers in Egyptian wall paintings: some say the aroma is a sexual stimulant.

  Diodorus Siculus 1.10.1; Athenaeus *D* 677d (*lotinos*).

  Hepper 1990 p. 16.

Lotus (2). Group of small tree fruits

related to the JUJUBE. Of these the best-known, the Christ's thorn, is now cultivated in Egypt, and its fruit and timber have been used there since pre-dynastic times. The fruits are among those found in Tutankhamen's tomb.

The Christ's thorn (*Paliurus Spina-Christi*) is *paliouros* or *lotos* in Greek, *paliurus* in Latin.

The related Jew's thorn (*Zizyphus Lotus*) is native to north Africa. This is imagined to be the fruit of the lotus-eaters, *Lotophagoi*, of the *Odyssey*; it is *lotos* in Greek, *lotus* in Latin. The white lotus (see LOTUS (1)) and the Jew's thorn, both called *lotos* by Herodotus, have nothing at all in common except that they are foods unfamiliar to Greeks and eaten in north Africa, where the lotus-eaters of the *Odyssey* were supposed to live.

The hackberry (*Celtis australis*) and barberry (*Berberis vulgaris*) were known as edible wild fruits of southern Europe. They share the names *lotos* in Greek, *lotus* in Latin; one or both may also be called *appendix* in Latin.

Homer, *Odyssey* 9.82–96; Herodotus 2.96, 4.177; Theophrastus *HP* 3.18.3, 4.3.1–4, 5.8.1; Strabo 16.4.17; Pliny *NH* 13.104–6, 13.111, 14.101, 24.114–15; Galen *AF* 6.621 (*zizyphon*); Athenaeus *D* 649e–650b; Aetius, *Medicine* 11.13.115.

Darby and others 1977 pp. 641–3, 702; Zohary and Hopf 1993 pp. 198–9; Brewer and others (1995 ?) pp. 62–3.

Lovage, bitter culinary herb. Lovage was said by Dioscorides to grow wild in its native Liguria. The statement that it originates there, rather than in the Near East, has been doubted, but it is a fact that lovage was unknown to Greeks before the Roman imperial period, which suggests that Dioscorides may be right. 'The local people use it instead of pepper, as an ingredient in sauces,' he adds. Its popularity evidently spread rapidly. It was of very common use in the later Roman kitchen if *Apicius* is to be believed; it added a bitterness (resembling that of parsley) to almost every savoury dish – and cured wind, according to Galen.

Lovage (*Levisticum officinale*) is Greek *ligystikon, libystikon*, Latin *liguisticum*.

Dioscorides *MM* 3.51; Pliny *NH* 19.165, 20.187; Galen *VA* 20, *ST* 6.267, *AF* 6.668, *SF* 12.62; *Apicius passim*; Alexander of Tralles, *Eight Books of Medicine* 8.2.

A.C. Andrews, 'Alimentary use of lovage in the classical period' in *Isis* vol. 33 (1941–2) pp. 514–18.

Lucanica *see* SAUSAGE

Lucian, Greek essayist and satirist (born *c*.AD 120, died after 180). One of his works is *The Symposium, or the Lapiths*, a fictional narrative of a dinner party that ended in fighting. Many of Lucian's other works are relevant to dining and related pleasures. They are complicated to use as sources for social history because Lucian often sets his scenes in the classical past and always employs to the full his excellent knowledge of earlier Greek literature and history.

Lucian ed. and tr. A.M. Harmon, K. Kilburn and M.D. Macleod, 8 vols (1913–67, *LCL*); H.-G. Nesselrath, *Lukians Parasitendialog: Untersuchungen und Kommentar* (Berlin, 1985).

Lucullus, L(ucius) Licinius (117–56 BC), Roman general. Lucullus shares the distinction with the Greek philosopher Epicurus of having given his name to a style of pleasure: a Lucullan feast is lavish, costly and anything but vulgar. Lucullus, having waged a long war successfully, though not conclusively, against MITHRIDATES of Pontus, was peremptorily recalled to Rome. He retired gracefully to his houses, his dining-rooms and his cultural pursuits. His house at Rome is said by Plutarch to have resembled a *prytaneion* for cultured Greek visitors. The fishponds at his villa at Naples, which were fed with seawater obtained by tunnelling through a mountain, were famous; his aviaries were the only out-of-season source for thrushes. His death was widely mourned.

Varro *RR* 3.17.9; Pliny *NH* 9.170; Plutarch, *Life of Lucullus* 39–42, *Life of Marius* 34.2.

D'Arms 1970 pp. 184–6, *al.*

Lupin, a legume and garden plant. The seed is bitter (hence *tristis lupinus* 'sad lupin' in Vergil's verse); indeed, it is poisonous when raw, but can be eaten after boiling. Lupin was one of the STAPLE FOODS of the poor in Greece and the Graeco-Roman East; also a favourite with CYNICS for its association with poverty and, yes, its tendency to cause flatulence (see Krueger). It was 'shared by humans and hoofed quadrupeds', says Pliny, meaning that it was also used, as it still is, for animal fodder. In fixing a rule for the handling of lupins, Jewish law varies between defining them as 'food for the poor' and 'food for goats'.

Lupin (*Lupinus albus*) is Greek *thermos* (cf. Akkadian *tarmuš*, Aramaic *tormos*, Coptic *tharmos*), Latin *lupinus*.

Hippocrates *R* 45; Alexis *F* 167, 268 Kassel with Arnott *ad ll.*; Theophrastus *HP* 8.7.3, 8.11.8; Vergil, *Georgics* 1.75; Dioscorides *MM* 2.109; Columella *DA* 2.10–15 *passim*; Pliny *NH* 18.133–6, 22.154–7; Athenaeus *E* 55c–f; *Mishnah* Shabbath 18.1.

Darby and others 1977 pp. 689–90; W. Hondelmann, 'The lupin: ancient and modern crop plant' in *Theoretical and Applied Genetics* vol. 68 (1984) pp. 1–9; Zohary and Hopf 1993 p. 117; D. Krueger in *The Cynics* ed. R.B. Branham and M.-O. Goulet-Cazé (Berkeley: University of California Press, 1996) p. 227 n. 33.

Luxury means spending more than one needs to, and, in the view of those who concern themselves with the matter, more than one ought to, on comforts and pleasures. Luxury is not an issue in every culture, but it has been an issue in Graeco-Roman and Christian society.

Since eating and drinking are (to most people) pleasures, luxury may take the form of lavish spending on eating and drinking, and that is the form of luxury relevant to this book. Consider the possibilities. You can eat more than you need to stay alive and healthy (see EXCESS). You can drink more wine than is consistent with sobriety (see DRUNKEN-NESS). You can choose foods and drinks for their flavour, their appearance, their rarity, their cost or their reputation, rather than because they are handy and nourishing (see GASTRONOMY). You can also make choices of dining companions and of ambience that others consider luxurious.

Classical Athenians commonly considered that luxury (Greek *tryphe*) lay to the east: the Greeks of Ionia, the Lydians who lived just beyond Ionia, and the Persians who conquered the Lydians, were shown in literature to have become soft through luxury. Gluttony lay to the north: the Greeks of Boeotia and Thessaly and the Macedonians and Thracians beyond them ate too much meat and drank unmixed wine, and it made them dull and stupid. There was yet more luxury to the west: the prosperous Greeks of southern Italy (notably SYBARIS) and those of SICILY spent too much time on food and sex. These places were also credited as the sources of classical Greek gourmandise: bakers and fancy dishes from Lydia, cooks and gastronomic poetry from Sicily. Athenians worried additionally about the luxury of their fellow-citizens, focusing on excessive enthusiasm for tasty *opson* as opposed to solid *sitos* (see MEALS), and focusing most particularly on expensive fish. Davidson (below) explores the issue.

At the courts of the HELLENISTIC KINGDOMS large, lavish and costly banquets followed the patterns already established in Persia and the Greek cities. Rome's conquests in the East, particularly in ANATOLIA in the second century BC, brought both the wealth and the skills that enabled Rome in turn to enjoy luxury (Latin *luxuria*) on a Hellenistic scale. At Rome, in particular, the custom of generous entertaining had a political dimension in that it defined and reinforced the relations of patron and client on which Roman political life largely depended

until the entrenchment of the monarchy in the later first century AD. Emperors were not the only luxurious diners, but they were the latest and best. Caligula, VITELLIUS and Elagabalus were famed for their use of ridiculously costly ingredients, comparable with the *allec* recipe invented by APICIUS (2) made exclusively from red mullet livers; hence the vogue for flamingoes' tongues and nightingales' tongues.

Condemnation of the practices of luxury was voiced, at least from the fourth century BC onwards, by philosophers. Others favoured them. The ambivalence is natural: many philosophers, from Plato and ARISTIPPUS to Seneca, were attached to courts and partook of such pleasures themselves. Among the various schools of philosophy CYNICS such as Diogenes, and Stoics such as Seneca himself, were the fiercest despisers of luxury; early Christian thinkers fall into the same category, and it was among Christians, not long after the end of the period dealt with in this book, that luxury was defined as a mortal sin.

The attitude of classical literary authors, like that of philosophers, shows no unanimity (though Wilkins, below, attempts to define a shared view of Athenian comedy authors and audiences). Some enjoyed luxurious banquets and *symposia*; some did not, or were not invited; some criticised luxury and conspicuous consumption. Both philosophers and literary authors were clearly reflecting popular views and also helping to shape them. Sumptuary laws, restricting certain forms of expenditure, existed in many ancient jurisdictions and were sometimes effective. In fourth-century Athens, for example, the number of guests at a private party is said to have been restricted to thirty.

Plato, *Letter 7* 326b, *Republic* 404d; Livy 39.6; Seneca, *On the Happy Life* 11; Pliny *NH* 9.63, 9.66; Juvenal 14.1–14, *al.*; Suetonius, *Caligula* 22, *Galba* 12, *Vitellius* 13; Aulus Gellius 2.24; Athenaeus *D* 510b–554f; Macrobius *S* 3.17; *Historia Augusta, Heliogabalus* 19–33 *passim*.

Jasper Griffin, 'Augustan poetry and the life of luxury' in *Journal of Roman Studies* vol. 66 (1976) pp. 87–105, reprinted in Jasper Griffin, *Latin Poets and Roman Life* (London, 1985) pp. 1–31; Emma Dench, 'Austerity, excess, success and failure in Hellenistic and early Imperial Italy' in *Parchments of Gender: deciphering the bodies of antiquity* ed. Maria Wyke (Oxford: Clarendon Press, 1998) pp. 121–46; Davidson 1997 pp. 3–69; Wilkins 2000 pp. 257–311, *al.*

Lycia, region in southwestern Anatolia, tributary kingdom of the Persian Empire, gradually Hellenised. Banquet scenes on Lycian reliefs show the interplay of Persian and Greek influences.

Susanne Ebbinghaus, 'A banquet at Xanthos: seven rhyta on the northern cella frieze of the Nereid monument' in *Periplous: papers on classical art and archaeology presented to Sir John Boardman* ed. G.R. Tsetskhladze and others (London: Thames and Hudson, 2000).

Lydia, kingdom of western Anatolia in early classical times. To Greeks of the seventh and sixth centuries BC Lydia was a wealthy neighbour and the inventor or immediate source of some of the usages of luxury, including the dish called KANDAU-LOS.

Lydia, then ruled by King Croesus, was conquered by the Persians under Cyrus in 546 BC but remained of gastronomic interest. Some of the best bakers came from Lydia, according to Archestratus in the fourth century.

The region eventually became the heartland of the Hellenistic Greek kingdom of Pergamum, which was incorporated into the Roman Empire as the province of Asia, proverbial for the wealth that it supplied to the Roman treasury and to unscrupulous administrators. Under Rome this was an area of fine

wines: see ASIAN WINES, EPHESIAN WINES. The slopes of Mount Tmolus, south of Sardis, were clothed in vines and were also a source of saffron, like the better-known Corycus in Cilicia.

Herodotus 1.6–94; Archestratus *H* 5 Brandt; Vergil, *Georgics* 1.56; Columella *RR* 3.8.4; Athenaeus *D* 515d–517a.

C.H. Greenewalt, *Ritual Dinners in Early Historic Sardis* (Berkeley, 1976); N.H. Ramage, 'A Lydian funerary banquet' in *Anatolian Studies* vol. 29 (1979) pp. 91–5; D. Harvey, 'Lydian specialities, Croesus' golden baking-woman, and dogs' dinners' in *Food in Antiquity* ed. John Wilkins and others (Exeter: Exeter University Press, 1995) pp. 273–85; Dalby 1996 pp. 106–7; Stavros A. Paspalas, 'A Persianizing cup from Lydia' in *Oxford Journal of Archaeology* vol. 19 (2000) pp. 135–74.

Lynceus of Samos, Greek gastronomic author (*c.*300 BC), pupil of Theophrastus and brother of the historian Duris. Lynceus wrote a comedy, *Centaur*, whose opening scene (which alone survives) discussed local food preferences. He also wrote *Anecdotes*, *Memoirs of Menander* and some literary *Letters*. His letter to Diagoras included an extended comparison of Rhodian with Athenian culinary delicacies. His letter *Shopping for Food* (*F* 20 [Athenaeus *D* 313f]) quotes phrases playfully from Archestratus and Hesiod. He and his works would be practically unknown but for numerous quotations by Athenaeus.

Athenaeus *D* 128a–b, *al.*

Lynceus F: fragments. Text: Andrew Dalby, 'Lynceus and the anecdotists' in *Athenaeus and his World* ed. David Braund and John Wilkins (Exeter: University of Exeter Press, 2000) pp. 372–94. Translation in Gulick's edition of *Athenaeus.*

M

Macedonia, kingdom located immediately north of classical Greece (its traditional territory lies largely within modern Greece). Macedonia was under strong Greek cultural influence from the fifth century BC onwards. Its political ascendancy under Philip II, his son ALEXANDER THE GREAT and Alexander's successors reversed the direction of influence and spread a mixed Greek–Macedonian culture through the HELLENISTIC KINGDOMS.

Classical Greek narratives of meals in Macedonia, by Herodotus and Demosthenes, emphasise their barbarism. An extended narrative of a wedding feast around 300 BC, by HIPPOLOCHUS, focuses on elements that would have been out of place in contemporary Greece. Traditionally Macedonia differed from Greece in its use of wine, which was taken stronger and was consumed in a competitive spirit.

Macedonian gastronomy is never praised in classical sources; Macedonia had its local specialities nonetheless. The eels of the River Strymon, dividing Macedonia from Thrace, were salted for export (Aristotle *HA* 592a7–9; Athenaeus *D* 297c–300d quoting Archestratus *H* 8 [see Olson and Sens *ad l.*] and Antiphanes 104 Kassel). Shrimp was plentiful along the Gulf coast (Archestratus *H* 25 Brandt). The *khromis* or ombrine was to be enjoyed at Pella (Archestratus *H* 30 Brandt); the *kyon karkharias*, a kind of shark, at Torone (Archestratus *H* 23 Brandt).

Herodotus 5.18–5.20; Demosthenes, *On the Embassy* 196–8, cf. Aeschines, *On the Embassy* 154–8; Hippolochus *D*; Persaeus of Citium [Athenaeus *D* 607a–e]; Athenaeus *D* 155a–d, 434a–435d.

E.N. Borza, 'The natural resources of early Macedonia' in *Philip II, Alexander the Great and the Macedonian Heritage* ed. W.L. Adams and E.N. Borza (Lanham, Maryland, 1982) pp. 1–20; *Macedonia and Greece in Late Classical and Early Hellenistic Times* ed. B. Barr-Sharrar and E.N. Borza (Washington, 1982); Dalby 1996 pp. 152–60; Andrew Dalby, 'Alexander's culinary legacy' in *Cooks and Other People: proceedings of the Oxford Symposium on Food and Cookery 1995* ed. Harlan Walker (Totnes: Prospect Books, 1996) pp. 81–93.

- Lake Bolbe, in southeastern Macedonia, was noted for its fish. Bass was good there. It also produced, once a year in spring, large numbers of a certain freshwater fish which were taken in the little river that flowed northwards from Olynthus into Lake Bolbe. They were salted for local consumption, and the fish or the annual catch was known as *apopyris*. The fish of Bolbe are celebrated on the coins of Apollonia, which lay on its southern shore (Archestratus *H* 45 Brandt with Olson and Sens *ad l.*; Athenaeus *D* 334e–f citing Hegesander 40 Müller). Finally, Archestratus recommends shopping for the *glaukos* (see BLUEFISH) at Olynthus (Archestratus *H* 20 Brandt; Dalby 1995 p. 404; Olson and Sens 2000 p. xxii).

Macellum *see* MARKETS

Machon, poet working in Alexandria in the early third century BC. He wrote plays in imitation of Athenian comedy, but his major work, surviving in long fragments quoted by Athenaeus, was a book of humorous verse anecdotes of convivial life in Athens around 300 BC. In common with similar prose works by LYNCEUS and others, it will have served as a handbook for jokers (Gow p. 24).

Dioscorides 24 Gow [*Anthologia Palatina* 7.708]; Athenaeus *D* 241f, 664a.

Machon C: *Khreiai*. Text and commentary: Machon, *The Fragments* ed. A.S.F. Gow (Cambridge: Cambridge University Press, 1965). Translation in Gulick's edition of *Athenaeus*.

Mackerel, oily and nutritious sea fish. Mackerel are good for conserving (salted or smoked) as well as for eating fresh; among other species of which this is true, they fall between the pilchard and the tunny in size. They are also good ingredients for fermented fish sauces such as the ancient GARUM, and were used for this purpose in Roman times, especially at the big salteries along the Spanish Mediterranean coast. At an earlier period Greeks found that the best mackerel came from Parium (it was *kolias* according to Euthydemus, *skombros* according to Xenocrates).

Epicharmus 62 Kaibel; Xenocrates *T* 20, 143; Columella *DA* 8.17.12; Pliny *NH* 31.94; Martial 13.102; Oppian *H* 3.576–95; Athenaeus *D* 116a–121a (there are several errors of identification in Gulick's translation of this passage) quoting Euthydemus of Athens.

- Greek *kolias* and Latin *lacertus, lacerta* are names of the chub mackerel or 'Spanish mackerel' (*Scomber japonicus*). In a dinner invitation Martial promises chub mackerel dressed with rue and topped with slices of egg; another epigram suggests that chub mackerel was among the *mezedes* or *tapas* (to use modern Mediterranean terminology) available at the bars at Roman baths. Chub mackerel was fished – by holidaymakers, as well as commercially – along the coast of Latium south of Rome.

Cicero, *Letters to Atticus* 2.6.1; Xenocrates *T* 20; Martial 10.48, 12.19; Juvenal 14.131; Athenaeus *D* 116a–121a.

- Greek *skombros* and Latin *scomber* are names of the common or Atlantic mackerel (*Scomber Scombrus*). Its dietary qualities are dealt with by Xenocrates alongside those of tunny. Conserved mackerel was palatable but difficult to break down, and provoked thirst.

Hermippus 63 Kassel; Archestratus *H* 38 Brandt; Aristotle *HA* 597a22, 599a2, *al.*; Catullus 95.8, cf. Martial 4.86; Oppian *H* 3.576–95; Athenaeus *D* 321a.

- Salted mackerel (no doubt also bonito and tunny) from the salteries at Malaga and neighbouring places in southeastern Spain was known in general as *Saxitanon* or *Exitanon*. Some of the salt fish and garum factories on this coast have been excavated.

Strabo 3.4.2; Martial 7.78; Pliny *NH* 9.49, 32.146; Galen *AF* 6.728; Athenaeus *D* 121a citing Diphilus of Siphnos.

- References to *lacertae cum muria sua*, 'chub mackerel in their liquor', are to a different method of conserving.

Ulpian [Justinian, *Digest* 33.9].

Macrobius, Latin scholarly author of the fifth century AD. Macrobius's chief work is the *Saturnalia*, an extended literary symposium with some resemblance to the *Deipnosophists* of ATHENAEUS. Participants quote extensively from earlier Latin literature, much of it otherwise lost. Macrobius was learned in Roman law, religion and history, and these preoccupations form the main subjects of his work. Food and entertainment are among other topics discussed at length.

Macrobius S: *Saturnalia*. Translation: Macrobius, *The Saturnalia* tr. Percival Vaughan Davies (New York: Columbia University Press, 1969); critical text: *Ambrosii Theodosii Macrobii Saturnalia* ed. J. Willis (1970, *BT*).

Maenas Licinius, Latin author on food or wine, mentioned by Columella but otherwise unknown.

Columella *DA* 12.4.2.

Mageiroi *see* COOKS

Mago, Carthaginian author of an extensive manual of farming in Punic, based partly on earlier Greek texts. After the Roman conquest of Carthage in 146 BC Mago's work was translated into Greek (by Cassius Dionysius) and Latin (by Decimus Silanus), the latter at the expense of the Roman Senate. The Greek version was later abridged by Diophanes of Nicaea. These works served as sources for Columella (by whom Mago is cited eighteen times), for Pliny and for other Latin authors, and in due course for the Byzantine *Geoponica*. In this way some Carthaginian recipes for conserves and other farm-produced foods, including an early recipe for PASSUM, reached the Roman mainstream.

Varro *RR* 1.1.10; Columella *DA* 1.1.10, 12.4.2, 12.39.1; Pliny *NH* 1.18, 18.22.

J.P. Mahaffy, 'The work of Mago on agriculture' in *Hermathena* vol. 7 pp. 29–35; V. Lundström, 'Magostudien' in *Eranos* vol. 2 pp. 60–7.

Malabathron, popular aromatic in the Roman Empire, used both in cosmetics and in food. The leaves, native to Sichuan (southwestern China), were dried locally and gathered into bundles by size, as described in detail in the *Periplus*. Exported from a port at the Ganges mouth, they reached Rome by way of Egypt, where much of the supply was processed for perfumed oil.

Greek *malabathron*, *phyllon*, Latin *folium*, *folium indicum*, *malobathrum*, are usually identified as tejpat, the leaf of *Cinnamomum Tamala*. The ancient name is borrowed from Sanskrit *tamālapattra* 'dark leaf', used occasionally as a designation of this product. Laufer argues that malabathron was modern patchouli, *Pogostemon Cablin*, and other identifications have been tried.

Horace, *Odes* 2.7.8; Ovid, *Tristia* 3.3.69; Celsus, *DM* 5.23.3b; Dioscorides *MM* 1.12; *Periplus Maris Erythraei* 56, 65, cf. Pliny *NH* 12.44; Pliny *NH* 12.129, 23.93; Martial 11.18, 14.146; Ptolemy, *Geography* 7.2.16, *Apicius*

1.29.1, 1.30.2, 9.1.3, 9.7.

Yule and Burnell 1903 pp. 543–4, 912; Berthold Laufer, 'Malabathron' in *Journal Asiatique*, 11th series vol. 12 (1918) pp. 5–49; Casson 1989 pp. 241–2; Dalby 2000a pp. 198–9.

Mallard *see* DUCK

Mallow, a common wild plant of Europe. Mallow was a potherb in Greece and Rome, more useful as such to the poor than to the rich, and particularly useful because it alleviated hunger. An aside by Lucian suggests that it was used, like lettuce nowadays, as a garnish on trays of food at banquets. It also had medicinal uses.

Mallow (*Malva sylvestris*) is Greek *malakhe*, *molokhe*, Latin *malva*.

Hesiod *OD* 41 with West *ad l.*; Aristophanes, *Wealth* 544; Theophrastus *HP* 7.7.2; Horace, *Epodes* 2.58, *Odes* 1.31.16 with Nisbet *ad l.*; *Moretum* 72; Pliny *NH* 20.222–8; Lucian, *On Salaried Posts in Great Houses* 26; Athenaeus E 58d–f; Porphyry, *Life of Pythagoras* 34; Palladius *OA* 11.11.3; Anthimus *OC* 50 with Grant *ad l.*

• Marshmallow (*Althaea officinalis*), Greek *althaia*, Latin *hibiscus*, a plant resembling mallow, was used to treat wounds, and was an ingredient in a medicinal wine taken for coughs.

Theophrastus *HP* 9.18.1; Pliny *NH* 20.29, 20.229–30.

Malnutrition *see* NUTRITION

Mamertine wine (Greek *Mamertinos*; Latin *Mamertinum*), from the territory of Messana in Sicily. Mamertine was an 'Italiote' wine: though not from mainland Italy it was treated as if Italian by Roman drinkers, served with the main course and in larger quantities than *transmarina* or overseas wines. It was one of those chosen by Caesar to serve at his public banquets. In this particular context it held fourth place among wines, after Caecuban, Falernian and Alban, according to Pliny. It was pleasant in taste, easy drinking, forceful.

Vitruvius 8.3.12; Dioscorides *MM* 5.6.7, 5.6.11; Pliny *NH* 14.66, 14.97; Martial 13.117; Athenaeus *E* 27c (read *Italiotes* with Desrousseaux).

- After Martial, Mamertine wine is no longer heard of. The name is possibly supplanted by the *Sikelikos aminaios*, Sicilian wine from the *aminnia* grape variety, recommended by Galen.

  Galen, *On Therapeutic Method* 10.834, *On Compounding* 13.659.

Mango, fruit of *Mangifera indica*. It appears on the classical scene only once: Alexander's soldiers ate mangoes, in India in 326 BC, and got stomach-ache.

Theophrastus *HP* 4.4.5.

Manna, a group of substances, white or clear in colour, sweet in taste, sometimes collected for food or for medicinal uses. Manna is the exudate from leaves of various plant species or the excretion of insects that feed on them. The Greek word *manna* can be traced to Egyptian and Hebrew: the word was in current use in all three languages, presumably to denote local forms of manna. In Greek, from Herodotus onwards, the terms *meli* 'honey' and *aeromeli* 'air honey' are also used. In Latin, local mannas are known as *mel* 'honey' – or *mel ex aere* 'honey from the air', or the *roscida mella* 'dewy honey' of Vergil – though later, in biblical contexts, the word *manna* also occurs.

The manna collected by the Israelites in Sinai during their exodus from Egypt may be identifiable with that of a TAMARISK (see Donkin p. 70). Herodotus mentions a local manufacture in eastern Lydia of so-called 'honey' made from *myrike* 'tamarisk manna' mixed with wheat flour. A well-known manna of Roman Italy was that of the holm-oak, listed by Ovid as one of the foods of the Golden Age. Onesicritus reported a manna from a fig-like tree called *occhi* used in Gedrosia by troops on Alexander's expedition; this has

been identified tentatively with a species of sainfoin, *Alhagi Maurorum*.

Hippocratic texts prescribe *manna* in gynaecological practice and *to mannodes* 'the manna-like substance' to soothe the mouth; it is not known whether the manna used by physicians in this tradition came from a consistent source, and if so which.

Exodus 16.15; Herodotus 7.31; Hippocrates, *Epidemics* 7.2, 7.47; Josephus, *Jewish Antiquities* 3.1.6; Vergil, *Eclogues* 4.30; *Aetna* 14; Ovid, *Metamorphoses* 1.111; Pliny *NH* 12.34 citing Onesicritus; Galen, *On Therapeutic Method* 10.329, *al.*; Athenaeus *D* 500d.

R.A. Donkin, *Manna: an historical geography* (The Hague: Junk, 1980) (*Biogeographica*, 17).

- Confusion may occur with a low grade of frankincense known as *manna* (*libanou*) in Greek, *manna* (*turis*) in Latin (Pliny *NH* 12.62; Galen, *On Substitutes* 19.734).
- The manna ash, *Fraxinus Ornus*, has been the main source of manna in southern Europe (notably Sicily) in recent times.

Marjoram, an aromatic plant not popular in ancient food but commonly used in perfumes. Marjoram (*Origanum Majorana*) is Greek *amarakon*, *sampsoukhon*, Latin *sampsuchus*. In older translations, written when Mediterranean herbs were unfamiliar to English-speaking classicists, 'marjoram' often stands for the related OREGANO.

Theophrastus *HP* 9.7.3; Dioscorides *MM* 3.39; Pliny *NH* 13.14, 21.163–4; Athenaeus *D* 681b quoting Diocles of Carystus, also 689e quoting Antiphanes 105 Kassel.

A.C. Andrews, 'Marjoram as a spice in the classical era' in *Classical Philology* vol. 56 (1961) pp. 73–82.

Markets, temporary locations for selling food and other goods. Three kinds of markets occur in many parts of the world: daily markets, usually in larger towns and cities; occasional markets held as part of large fairs and festivals; and periodic markets, repeated in each location every five to fifteen days on a regular timetable.

There is evidence for all three kinds in the classical world.

The *agora* of a Greek city and the *forum* of a Roman town were places for buying, selling and other forms of social interaction. There is considerable evidence for food sales in the market at ATHENS. Republican ROME had a *Forum Boarium*, *Forum Holitorium* and a *Macellum* (see below) at which fresh meat was sold. Rome, and perhaps other cities, had a *Forum Cuppedinis* (variously spelt) whose stallholders, *cuppedinarii*, sold cooked meats, sauces and savoury foods (Terence, *Eunuch* 256 with Donatus *ad l.*; Apuleius, *Metamorphoses* 1.24–2.2).

Parts of Italy, from at latest the second century BC, had nine-day market cycles, recorded in inscriptions and occasionally mentioned in literature (see Frayn with references). Elsewhere in the Mediterranean region, under the Roman Empire, similar systems existed but on cycles that varied from region to region. Some information is available for north Africa, for Syria and for Anatolia (see Shaw and de Ligt with references). Classical Greece, like modern Greece, had few periodic markets; this may be attributed to the fact that so much travel in Greece is seaborne and weather-dependent. Instead, in Greece, impromptu markets are set up when a ship arrives or when the fishing boats come in. A bell was rung to announce a market (Strabo 14.2.21; Plutarch *QC* 4.4).

Jean Andreau, 'Pompéi: enchères, foires et marchés' in *Bulletin de la Société Nationale des Antiquaires de France* vol. 9 (1976) pp. 104–26; P.V. Stanley, 'Agoranomoi and metronomoi' in *Ancient World* vol. 2 (1979) pp. 13–19; B.D. Shaw, 'Rural markets in North Africa and the political economy of the Roman Empire' in *Antiquités africaines* vol. 17 (1981) pp. 37–83; J. Nollé, *Nundinas instituere et habere: epigraphische Zeugnisse zur Einrichtung und Gestaltung von ländlichen Märkten in Afrika und in der Provinz Asia* (Hildesheim, 1982); Joan M. Frayn, *Markets and Fairs in Roman Italy* (Oxford: Clarendon Press, 1993), reviews in *Journal of Roman Studies* (1994) pp. 235–7; L. de Ligt, *Fairs and Markets in the Roman Empire: economic and social aspects of periodic trade in a pre-industrial society* (Amsterdam: Gieben, 1993).

- Latin *macellum*, Greek *makellon*, was a covered market typical of Hellenistic and Roman cities. *Macella* were centres of butchery and the trade in fresh meat.

C. de Ruyt, *Macellum* (Louvain, 1983); Joan M. Frayn, 'The Roman meat trade' in *Food in Antiquity* ed. John Wilkins and others (Exeter: Exeter University Press, 1995) pp. 107–14.

Marrow, meaty substance inside marrowbones. The softness of bone-marrow made of it a rich food for lucky children, as is said by Andromache in the Homeric *Iliad*. It was eaten by others too; it contributed to the food value of soups; it was often prescribed by physicians.

'White marrow' is sometimes a poetic euphemism for spilt brains, as observed by Athenaeus. It also served as a simile for foods rendered soft and succulent by nature or the cook's art, such as the oysters described by Matron (but this is a Homeric pun, *ostrea myeloenta* 'marrowy oysters' replacing the *ostea myeloenta* 'marrowy bones' crunched by the Cyclops in the *Odyssey*). In the minds of the more decadent poets, marrow made a good comparison for the softness of the buttocks.

Homer, *Iliad* 22.501, *Odyssey* 9.293; Aeschylus, *Agamemnon* 76 with Fraenkel *ad l.*; Alexis F 191 Kassel with Arnott *ad l.*; Matron AD 16; Nicander T 101, A 59; Catullus 25; Dioscorides 10 Gow [*Anthologia Palatina* 12.37]; *Priapeia* 64; Galen AF 6.677–8, SF 12.331–3; Athenaeus E 66a–c.

Marsian wine (Latin *Marsicum, Marsum*; Greek *Marsikos, Marsos*) grown by the Paeligni and Marsi, north of Rome. In the first century this was said to be an 'austere' wine, but easy on the stomach. Martial's view, around AD 100, is unenthusiastic: 'Don't drink it: give it to your freedman to drink.' Its reputation improved in the second century, with a change of fashion among drinkers or a change of style among winemakers: Philumenus recommended the austere Marsian as astringent, while Galen favoured a sweet Marsian.

Scribonius Largus 57; Pliny *NH* 17.171; Martial 1.26, 13.121, 14.116; Marcus Aurelius, *Letters* [Fronto vol. 1 p. 177 Haines, *s.v.l.*]; Philumenus, *Latin Fragments* 114; Galen *ST* 6.337, *SF* 11.441, *DA* 14.15, *On Therapeutic Method* 10.831–2, *On Compounding* 13.659; Athenaeus *E* 27f.

Massic wine (Latin *Massicum*) from the slopes of Mons Massicus at the southern extremity of Latium in central Italy. Sinuessa was a centre of trade in Massic wine. This was one of the best names in wine for roughly a century, from perhaps 30 BC to AD 70. Massic was counted by Columella, in the mid first century AD, as one of the four supreme wines. What became of it afterwards? It may be that the name of Falernian, a name which sold more wine, was stretched northwards from the adjacent vineyards on the northern edge of Campania and that Massic ceased to be considered a separate appellation. In some later sources the two seem synonymous (Columella omits Falernian from his list of four). At any rate, after about AD 100 Massic is not mentioned at all. It was apparently forgotten by the date of Servius's commentary on Vergil.

Vergil, *Georgics* 2.143 with Servius *ad l.*; Horace, *Satires* 2.4.51, *Odes* 1.1.19, 2.7.21, 3.21.5; Columella *DA* 3.8.5; Pliny *NH* 3.60, 14.62–4 with André *ad l.*; Silius Italicus 7.207; Statius, *Silvae* 4.3.64; Martial 13.111, *al.*; Florus 1.115; *CIL* 15.1554.

Tchernia 1986 esp. pp. 283, 342.

Massilia (Greek *Massalia*), modern Marseille. As a Greek colony founded around 600 BC, Marseille was for many centuries a centre of Greek culture in the western Mediterranean. It was from here that the cultivated vine gradually spread into southern Gaul, and eventually further north; olive-growing, too, is said by Justin to have been introduced to Gaul by the Greeks. Excavations at the Massilian colony of Olbia, near modern Hyères, and elsewhere in the region, have provided important information on acculturation. For Massilian wine see NARBONENSIAN WINES.

Justin, *Epitome of Trogus* 43.4.

M. Bats, *Vaisselle et alimentation à Olbia de Provence, v. 350 – v. 50 a.C.: modèles culturels et catégories céramiques* (Paris, 1988); M. Gras, 'De la céramique à la cuisine: le mangeur d'Olbia' in *Revue des études anciennes* vol. 91 (1989) pp. 65–71; Philippe Marinval, 'Agriculture et structuration du paysage agricole à Marseille grec et dans les sociétés indigènes aux premier et second âges du fer' in *Paysage et alimentation dans le monde grec* ed. Jean-Marc Luce (Toulouse, 2000) pp. 183–94.

Mastic, resin of a local variety of the lentisk tree (see also TEREBINTH) which grows only in the southwestern part of the Greek island of Chios. The principal and most obvious use of mastic was to clean the teeth and freshen the breath, a habit more practised by women than men, according to some ancient stereotypes. Mastic was thus an eastern Mediterranean equivalent of pine resin and of chicle (the latter now used as the basis of commercial chewing gum).

There is a likeness between one who chews mastic and one who gnashes or grinds the teeth in anger, a likeness observed in the Lucianic sketch *Ocypus*. It is the familiarity of mastic, and of this image, at the very beginning of the historical period, that leads to the metaphorical use of the verb *mastikhoo* 'chew mastic', 'gnash the teeth' of a fierce wild boar in the *Shield of Heracles* attributed to Hesiod.

Mastic was important medicinally: the word occurs over ninety times in Galen's works (and even more frequently in later medical authors), generally as an ingredient in compound medicines, used either solid or in the form of mastic oil. Dioscorides provides instructions for making the oil. The real effectiveness of mastic in treating diseases of the gums and mucosa is now being rediscovered.

The white mastic of Chios, Pliny says,

fetched 10 denarii to the pound. Galen, like Pliny, sometimes specifies Chian mastic: there were no other sources of the genuine product, but there were substitutes. The poorer 'black mastic' mentioned by Pliny, selling at a fifth of the price, is probably terebinth resin, as is the 'Egyptian mastic' of Galen.

The mastic tree (*Pistacia Lentiscus* var. *Chia*) is *skhinos* in Greek, the fruit *skhinis*, the resin *mastikhe*. In Latin the tree is *lentiscus*, the resin *mastiche*.

Hesiod, *Shield of Heracles* 389; Aristophanes, *Wealth* 720 with scholia; Theophrastus *HP* 9.4.7; Dioscorides *MM* 1.42, 1.70; Pliny *NH* 12.72, 24.43; Lucian, *The Ignorant Book-Buyer* 23, *Ocypus* 122; Galen *SF* 12.68–9, *DA* 14.52 quoting Andromachus, *al.*; Clement of Alexandria, *Educator* 3.15.1, 3.71.1; Gregory of Nyssa, *On Beneficence* 9.101.

F.N. Howes, 'Age old resins of the Mediterranean regions and their uses' in *Economic Botany* vol. 4 (1950) pp. 307–16; K. Browicz, '*Pistacia Lentiscus* L. var *Chia* (Desf. ex Poiret) DC. on Chios island' in *Plant Systematics and Evolution* vol. 155 (1987) pp. 189–95; Andrew Dalby, 'Mastic for beginners' in *Petits Propos culinaires* no. 65 (2000) pp. 38–45.

- The gummy exudation of the pine-thistle (*khamaileon leukos* or *ixia* in Greek: *Atractylis gummifera*) was used by women 'in place of mastic'. The leaves of this plant are listed among potherbs by Galen.

  Theophrastus *HP* 6.4.9, 9.1.2; Dioscorides *MM* 3.8; Pliny *NH* 22.45; Galen *AF* 6.623.

Matius, C. (Gaius), Latin author of three books on food, *Cocus* 'The Cook', *Cetarius* 'The Fisherman', *Salgamarius* 'The Pickler'. They included, says Columella, instructions for city dinners and fancy parties. These instructions may have been simply recipes; the titles are reminiscent of those of the individual books of Apicius.

The author's connection with C. Matius who was a friend of Caesar and Cicero, and with a namesake who was a contemporary of Augustus, is uncertain; some suppose him to be identical with the second of these. The *matiana* variety of APPLES may have been named after one of these people.

Columella *DA* 12.4.2, 12.46.1.

Matron of Pitane, Greek author of around 300 BC. Matron wrote a comic description of a lavish dinner at Athens (since real names are used, it may be that a real occasion is being evoked) in the form of a parody of Homeric epic. The poem is quoted in fairly complete form by Athenaeus (*D* 134d–137c).

E. Degani, 'Problems in Greek gastronomic poetry: on Matro's *Attikon Deipnon*' in *Food in Antiquity* ed. John Wilkins and others (Exeter: Exeter University Press, 1995) pp. 413–28.

Matron AD: *Attic Dinner*. Text, translation and commentary: S. Douglas Olson, Alexander Sens, *Matro of Pitane and the Tradition of Epic Parody in the Fourth Century BCE* (Atlanta: Scholars Press, 1999).

Mattye (Latin *mattea*: both words variously spelt), a dish or dishes served for dessert at ancient dinners. According to Gow, Greek *mattye* 'would appear to denote a course, rather than a dish of more or less standard ingredients, and … served much as a savoury serves in modern dinners'; the Latin word appears to have similar connotations. However, one recipe for *mattye* is available, quoted by Athenaeus from Artemidorus of Tarsus. A link is visible in comic word-play between the *mattye* and fellatio: the nature of the link eludes me.

Aristophanes, *Clouds* 451 [*s.v.l.*]; Petronius *S* 65; Martial 10.59, 13.92; Athenaeus *D* 141d, also 662e–664f quoting Machon *C* 19.463 (see Gow *ad l.*), Alexis *F* 208 (see Arnott *ad l.*) and Artemidorus; Ammianus Marcellinus 15.5.4; Arnobius, *Against the Gentiles* 7.25.

Henderson 1991 p. 167 note 75; Dalby 1996 pp. 156–7 with notes 13–16; Wilkins 2000 pp. 287–8.

Mead, a wine made by fermenting diluted honey. The English word is now used commercially for grape wines flavoured with honey.

Mead was not widely known in the ancient Mediterranean world, since must was available there in much larger quantity than honey and is a better raw material for wine. However, Aristotle reports that mead was made by the Taulantii of Illyria. He describes the process in detail and adds, convincingly, that the result tasted like old wine. Pliny says that mead was also made in Phrygia.

Aristotle, *On Marvellous Things Heard* 832a5; Pliny *NH* 14.113 (*hydromeli*); Anthimus *OC* 15 (*medus*).

Buck 1949 p. 389; J.H. Dickson, 'Bronze Age mead' in *Antiquity* vol. 205 (1978) pp. 108–13.

Meagre, fish of the family *Sciaenidae*, related to the squeteague and drumfish of North America. Two noticeable features of fish of this family is that they have large otoliths (traditionally used medicinally) and that they communicate under water by grunting.

Mediterranean fish of this group include the meagre, French *maigre* (*Argyrosomus regius*), the corb, French *corvine* (*Sciaena Umbra*) and two other species without common English names, known in French as *ombrine* (*Umbrina cirrosa* and *U. canariensis*).

Thompson 1947 pp. 241, 291; Davidson 1981 pp. 97–9.

- The Greek name *khromis*, *khremes* (literally 'neigher') belongs usually to the ombrine. This fish was good in spring and early summer. It was worth buying at Pella in Macedonia and at Ambracia. The term becomes uncommon in post-classical Greek.

  Aristotle *HA* 535b16–17, *al.*; Aelian, *Nature of Animals* 9.7 (*khromis*), 15.11; Oppian *H* 1.112 with Mair *ad l.*; Athenaeus *D* 282b quoting Epicharmus 58 Kaibel and Ananius 5 West, also 328a quoting Archestratus *H* 30 Brandt.

- Greek *korakinos* (see CASTAGNOLE) is occasionally used as the name of a large sea fish. This is probably the maigre, a fish that is rare in Greek waters but common towards Egypt.

  Aristotle *HA* 543a31, 599b3.

- Greek *skiaina* is perhaps the name of the corb. Various similar terms, which may or may not all have the same meaning, are

found in Greek texts, beginning with the 'fat *skiathides*' of Epicharmus. Xenocrates describes the *skiaina* as having flesh between coarse and tender, not excessively nourishing but generally good for the digestion.

Aristotle *HA* 601b30 (*skiaina*); Xenocrates *T* 3, 38 (*skias*, *skiadeus*); Pliny *NH* 32.151 (*sciaena*, *sciadeus*); Galen *AF* 6.720 quoting Phylotimus (*skinis*), also 6.724 (*skiaina*); Aelian, *Nature of Animals* 9.7; Oppian *H* 4.616–34; Athenaeus *D* 322f quoting Epicharmus *F* 44 Kaibel (*skiathis*) and Numenius (*skiadeus*).

- The Latin name *umbra* belongs to all these fish (the Greek names also occur in Latin as loanwords). Columella distinguishes two species, one regarded by him as native Italian and the other as typically Punic. The former probably represents the corb, the latter the maigre, a fish of the southern Mediterranean. For the freshwater fish also known as *umbra* in Latin see GRAYLING.

  Ennius *H* 7 (*umbra marina*); Ovid, *Halieutica* 111–12; Columella *DA* 8.16.8.

Meal times. In classical Greece there were some who took one meal a day, some two, according to the Hippocratic text *Regimen in Acute Diseases*. The one meal was *deipnon*, taken in the evening, and sometimes extended into or followed by a symposion (see SYMPOSION (1)). When there were two, the other was *ariston*, customarily translated 'breakfast' but usually taken, like a modern lunch, about noon. This meal was perhaps more often taken in summer than in winter: it is a noon picnic that Hesiod recommends for hot June days, while the dietician Diocles of Carystus sensibly advises those making a long journey in summer – the assumption is that they are walking – to pause for lunch and to take a siesta before continuing (Diocles of Carystus *RV*).

The principal meal for Romans of the Empire was *cena*, taken in the evening: it had slipped later in the day, as a Greek fashion, having once been an early afternoon meal which would be followed by a *vesperna* or supper. Romans ate more, and certainly they ate more frequently, than Greeks. The Roman *ientaculum* or breakfast was bread, or maybe bread and cheese; the *prandium* or lunch was bread, cold meat, salad, fruit, accompanied by wine; but (for some) these were still the kind of meals for which one did not need a table and after which one did not need to wash one's hands.

These are not the only terms found in classical texts. Greek *akratisma* was a nip of wine and a bite of food, taken early (Aristotle *HA* 564a20; Athenaeus *E* 11d). Latin *merenda* was an afternoon snack or (so to speak) tea; the term *merenda* is still used in Portuguese. The emperor Marcus Aurelius provides a menu (Marcus Aurelius, *Letters* [Fronto vol. 1 p. 182 Haines]).

Hesiod *OD* 585–96; Hippocrates *RA* 28–33; Martial 8.67, 13.31; Pliny the Younger, *Letters* 3.5.10; Suetonius, *Nero* 27; Plutarch *QC* 8.6.

Carcopino 1940 chapter 9; Buck 1949 pp. 352–6.

Meals. The typical full ancient Greek meal consisted of a cereal staple (Greek *sitos*), plus relish (Greek *opson*), plus wine (Greek *oinos*). The typical full Roman meal had a similar makeup, though the words have a different range of meaning: Romans ate cereal (Latin *panis*, bread, or *puls*, porridge) plus vegetables and meats (there is no commonly used collective Latin term) plus wine (Latin *vinum*). In everyday meals, in both cultures, a bean or legume soup could take the place of the bread or the relish or both.

But there might be more, and there are certainly more possible subdivisions. The full list begins with a *propoma*, a drink before dinner (Plutarch *QC* 8.9; Athenaeus *E* 58b–66f). This might be followed by *paropsides*, appetisers. The *bolbos* (see BULBS) exemplified the apparently typical bitter flavour of ancient *paropsides*, a flavour rejected by the Heracles of Eubulus as sacrilegious and by Aristophanes's speaker more picturesquely as *katapygo-syne* 'buggery'. In later Greek *paropsis* meant a small serving-dish (see DINING AND DRINKING UTENSILS) rather than its

contents. The word *paropsis* also served as a sexual metaphor – a favourite, apparently, of the dramatist Plato – hinting sometimes at foreplay, sometimes (like British English 'a bit on the side') at extramarital activities (Archedicus 2 Kassel; Alexis *F* 89 Kassel with Arnott *ad l.*; Philoxenus *D* b.4 Page; Pollux *O* 6.69 quoting Aristophanes fragment 128 Kassel, also 10.88; Athenaeus *E* 63d–64f quoting Archestratus *H* 6 Brandt and Eubulus *F* 6 Kassel, also *D* 367b–368e quoting Plato Comicus *F* 32, 43 and 190 Kassel). One Latin equivalent for *paropsis* – but a relatively rare word – is *mantusa* 'amuse-gueule', said to be Etruscan in origin. 'The amuse-gueule [*mantusa*] defeats the main dish [*obsonia*],' said the satirist Lucilius. But the best equivalent is Latin *gustus* (or occasionally *gustatio*), literally a 'taster', and the commonness of this term shows that this preliminary course of hors d'oeuvres was a more standard feature of Roman than of Greek dining.

The main course of a full and formal meal was more disparate than in northern European cuisines, rather resembling the succession of dishes that are served in Middle Eastern, Indian or Chinese entertaining. Substance was provided by (in Greek terms) *sitos*, the cereal staple, whether bread-like (Greek *artos*, Latin *panis*), polenta-like (Greek *maza*, Latin *polenta*) or soup-like (Latin *puls*: there are many other terms). In the view of Greek philosophers, from Socrates onwards, people ought to concentrate on this *sitos*. If one devoted too much attention, if one reserved too much of one's capacity, to its accompaniment *opson*, one merited the name *opsophagos*, which meant 'relish-eater' but implied 'gourmand, glutton' (see EXCESS). *Opson* is usually and conveniently translated 'relish' (Plutarch *QC* 4.4, *EC* 995c, *Animals are Rational* 991c–d; Athenaeus *D* 153d–e; Moeris *s.v. opson*); it included whatever one ate to help the bread (etc.) on its way, from a simple splash of olive oil to the costliest fish and the choicest morsels of meat. Although Greek *opson* can perfectly well denote the vegetables that accompany bread in a vegetarian diet (cf. *Epidemics* 7.115) the word often implies 'fish': the diminutive, Greek *opsarion* (Athenaeus D 385b–386c), and modern *psari*, simply mean 'fish'. Except when translating from Greek, Romans do not make a comparable distinction between worthy cereal and luxurious relish.

Discussing the new fashion for the *propoma*, Plutarch observes that the ancients did not drink anything, even water, before the TRAGEMATA (Plutarch *QC* 8.9). The main courses having been eaten and the tables cleared away, with the second tables (Greek *deuterai trapezai*, Latin *secundae mensae*: Athenaeus D 639a–658e) came wine and desserts. For these the literal Greek rendering is *epidorpismata* or *epiphoremata*; more often encountered is the term *tragemata* which means, specifically, chewy things such as dried fruits and nuts. Also served at this stage were CAKES and sweets. The nearest equivalent for Greek *tragemata* and *pemmata* is Latin *bellaria*, desserts. In both Greek and Latin usage there was the option of a savoury dessert, sometimes called MATTYE in Greek, *mattea* in Latin.

Aristophanes, *Acharnians* 1088–94; Machon C 16.266–70 [Athenaeus D 579e] with Gow *ad l.*; Poseidippus 124 Austin [*Anthologia Palatina* 5.183]; Asclepiades 25 Gow [*Anthologia Palatina* 5.181]; Petronius S 26–78; Aulus Gellius 13.11.6–7 citing Varro, *Menippean Satires* 333 Bücheler; Macrobius S 3.18–21.

Meat, a food which was less commonly eaten by classical Greeks and Romans than by most of their modern students. Its desirability and perceived importance were all the greater; hence the startling frequency with which fresh meat is eaten in the imaginary HOMERIC SOCIETY.

In the real world, those Greeks and Romans whose diet is known to us ate meat sparingly. It is thought that in Greece domestic animals (usually pig [see PORK], SHEEP, GOAT, CHICKEN, GOOSE) were routinely sacrificed to a god when slaughtered for food. However, thanks to a thriving trade in SAUSAGES, fat and offal (see below) and an established system of salting, an animal (especially a pig) stretched a long way. It is therefore misleading to suggest that Greeks only ate meat immediately after a SACRIFICE. In Rome there was no unbreakable link between slaughter and sacrifice (Varro *RR* 2.5.11) and fresh meat was perhaps more prominent in the average weekly diet. Both Greeks and Romans will have eaten beef (see OX) very seldom. In both cultures large game (BOAR, HARE and others) will have contributed insignificantly to most people's diet; smaller birds were probably easier to get. These categories of meat were available without religious formality.

Greek terms for 'butcher' (*boutypos*, *artamos*, *mageiros*) all have religious overtones. *Mageiros* became the usual term, and included the sense of 'cook', since the tasks involved extended from supplying and sacrificing the chosen animal, through preparing it for the sacrificial feast, to abstracting and re-selling the offal. The name of a Roman butcher, *macellarius*, came from the covered markets, MACELLA, where meat was typically sold.

See also: RAW MEAT; VEGETARIANISM.

Berthiaume 1972; Liliane Bodson, 'Redécouvrir les animaux antiques' in *Antiquité classique* vol. 48 (1979) pp. 146–53; P. Halstead, 'Man and other animals in later Greek prehistory' in *Annual of the British School at Athens* vol. 82 (1987) pp. 71–83; *L'Animal dans l'alimentation humaine: les critères de choix: actes du colloque international de Liège 26–29 nov. 1986* ed. Liliane Bodson (Liège, 1988) (*Anthropozoologica*, numéro spécial, 2); Corbier 1989; Joan M. Frayn, 'The Roman meat trade' in *Food in Antiquity* ed. John Wilkins and others (Exeter: Exeter University Press, 1995) pp. 107–14; Paul Stokes, 'Debris from Roman butchery: a new interpretation' in *Petits Propos culinaires* no. 52 (1995) pp. 38–47, with note in no. 54 (1996) p. 67; Martine Leguilloux, 'L'alimentation carnée au 1er millénaire avant J.-C. en Grèce continentale et dans les Cyclades: premiers résultats archéozoologiques' in *Paysage et alimentation dans le monde grec* ed. Jean-Marc Luce (Toulouse, 2000) pp. 69–95; S.H. Lonsdale, 'Attitudes towards animals in ancient Greece' in *Greece and Rome* vol. 26 (1979) pp. 146–59.

- The (relatively small) portion of meat that was burned in honour of the god was wrapped in fat. Animal fat was sometimes used for other non-food purposes but, as in the modern Mediterranean, had few dietary uses (Galen *AF* 6.678–9). For the 'vital organs', which in Greece had special religious significance, see SPLANKHNA. For these and other offal see BRAIN; HEAD; HEART; LIVER; MARROW; TESTICLES; TONGUE; TRIPE; UDDER; WOMB. Kidneys appear to have been seldom eaten (Galen *AF* 6.675, 6.680; see also EGYPT). Some of these kinds of offal, alongside salt pork, formed the stock of the boiled meat shops, *hephthopolia*, of Alexandria (Athenaeus *D* 94c–101e).

Medlar, tree fruit domesticated in the Near East or southern Europe. The medlar is a small apple-like fruit which must either be rotted or cooked before eating. It is clearly described in ancient sources and its seeds have been found in contexts indicating cultivation and food use (e.g. in latrine deposits at Cologne in Roman GERMANY).

The medlar (*Mespilus germanica*) is Greek *mespilon* and *epimelis*, Latin *mespilum*. The medlar and the *Crataegus* species seem to be treated as a single group in the classical languages. The fruit called *ypomelis* by Palladius (*OA* 13.4) cannot be identified but may be a member of this group.

Hippocrates *R* 55; Theophrastus *HP* 3.12.5, 3.15.6; Dioscorides *MM* 1.118; Pliny *NH* 15.47, 15.84, 16.75, 23.141, 24.108; Dio of Prusa, *Orations* 7.75; Galen *AF* 6.606, *SF* 12.71; Palladius *OA* 4.10.19–22.

J.R. Baird and J.W. Thieret, 'The medlar (Mespilus germanica, Rosaceae) from antiquity to obscurity' in *Economic Botany* vol. 43 (1989) pp. 328–72; Zohary and Hopf 1993 pp. 197–8.

- The small-fruited, thorny species known as hawthorn and Oriental thorn in English (*Crataegus Heldreichii*, *C. pubescens*, *C. monogyna*, *C. oxyacantha*) are common in Mediterranean lands. Greek *anthedon*, *akanthion* and Latin *anthedon*, *anthedon Gallicus* and *spina alba* are names for these trees and their fruit. The *spina alba* or hawthorn was celebrated in legend as providing torches for the mass wedding of the founders of Rome with the Sabine women.

- The azarole (*Crataegus laciniata*, *C. Aronia*, *C. Azarolus*), now known in several varieties both white- and red-fruited, may sometimes be intended by Greek *mespilon* and may possibly be the tree-fruit called *tuber*, *tubur* in Latin: of this, too, red and white kinds were known. It was introduced to Italy from Syria by Sextus Papinius in Augustus's time. It did well if grafted on quince stock.

Columella *DA* 11.2.96; Pliny *NH* 15.47; Palladius *OA* 10.14.

Megara, Greek city sometimes dominated economically by Athens. Megara was a source of garlic, salt, cucumber, hares, sucking-pigs and BULBS (most of this information comes from Aristophanes's *Acharnians*: its reliability must be evaluated delicately). The fishermen of Megara offered the excellent fish called *glaukos* in Greek, possibly BLUEFISH.

Aristophanes, *Acharnians* 520–3, 760–4; Archestratus *H* 20 Brandt; Antiphanes 191 Kassel; Callimachus 495 Pfeiffer; Nicander *F* 88 Schneider; Cato *DA* 7.

Melas zomos or 'black broth', a hearty food typical of ancient Sparta and possibly liked by some in Athens too. Geoffrey Arnott characterises it as 'a thick, meatless soup that owed its colour presumably to ingredients such as the black variety of chick-pea or Bengal gram. Gypsies still served this dish at fairs in northern England up to the 1940s.' This sounds convincing; but what variety of chickpea or other pulse, available in classical Greece, would have given it a black colour (compare Plutarch *QS* 2.1)?

Pherecrates 113, 137 Kassel; Alexis *F* 145 Kassel with Arnott *ad l.*; Nicostratus 16 Kassel; Euphron 1 Kassel; Matron *AD* 94; Plutarch, *Lycurgus* 12.6.

Melon, large thick-skinned fruit. The melon is usually thought to have originated in west Africa. Its cultivation had reached the Mediterranean by around 1000 BC; melon seeds from that period are found at Kastanas, in southern Thrace, and afterwards at other sites. This was not yet, however, the sweet, round melon familiar today. It was an older variety, the cucumber-shaped chate melon, still well known in the eastern Mediterranean. It was good food – the Israelites during their exodus are said to have longed for the melons of Egypt.

Melons, watermelons and eventually cucumbers, all of them creeping plants, were grown by gardeners in a bed set aside for the purpose, known as *sikyela-ton*. Cultivation of the melon – for which Palladius gives instructions – ceased in the Roman West after the fall of the Roman Empire, as indicated by Anthimus (it was later reintroduced under Arab influence).

The typical shape of the chate melon led to the use of *sikyos* as a metaphor for 'penis'; for a clever example see the poem by Strato.

The chate melon (*Cucumis Melo* var. *Chate*) and the cucumber (see below) are Greek *sikyos*, Latin *cucumis*. Many references to 'cucumber' in English translations of ancient texts should be understood as 'chate melon'.

Numbers 11.5; Hippocrates *R* 55 (*sikyos omos* 'unripe melon'), *Epidemics* 5.71; Theophrastus *HP* 7.4.6; Strato [*Anthologia Palatina* 12.197]; *Moretum* 76; Pliny *NH* 19.64–8, 20.6–12; Plutarch *QC* 8.9; Athenaeus *E* 73d–74b; Palladius *OA* 4.9.6–9; *Apicius* 3.7; Anthimus *OC* 57.

A.C. Andrews, 'Melons and watermelons in the classical period' in *Osiris* vol. 12 (1956) pp. 368–75; Darby and others 1977 pp. 693–5, 717–18; R. Norrman and J. Haarberg, *Nature and Language: a semiotic study of cucurbits in literature* (London, 1980); M.P. Charles, 'Onions, cucumbers and the date palm' in *Bulletin on Sumerian Agriculture* no. 3 (1987) pp. 1–21; M. Stol, 'The cucurbitaceae in the cuneiform texts' in *Bulletin on Sumerian Agriculture* no. 3 (1987) pp. 57–92; Zohary and Hopf 1993 pp. 182–3; Brewer and others 1995 p. 65; David Maynard and Donald N. Maynard, 'Cucumbers, melons and watermelons' in *CWHF* 2000 vol. 1 pp. 298–313.

- The sweet melon, distinguished by shape as well as flavour, is Greek (*sikyos*) *pepon*, Latin *pepo*: this occasionally appears as 'ripe cucumber' in English translations of classical sources. It is first mentioned in Greek – as a constituent of a bad diet – in a Hippocratic text; however, 'sweet' or 'ripe' melons are already known from Akkadian texts in the second milennium BC. Some people, said Plutarch, were unable to get the taste for it.

  Hippocrates, *Epidemics* 5.71; Pliny *NH* 19.65, 20.11–12; Plutarch *QC* 8.9; Athenaeus *E* 68c–f.

- Another variety of melon, now known as snake-cucumber, with a snake-like shape and a taste of cucumber, was well known by Hellenistic and Roman times. The snake-cucumber or snake melon (*C. Melo flexuosus* group) is Greek *drakontias*, Latin *anguinus*.

  Pliny *NH* 20.9–10; Athenaeus *D* 74b citing Euthydemus.

- At some time probably in the archaic or early classical period the cucumber (*Cucumis sativus*) reached Mediterranean lands; the species is native to Himalayan India. The difficulty is to say when it arrived. There is no archaeological evidence, since cucumber seeds, soft and usually eaten with the surrounding fruit, have not been found by archaeobotanists. There is also no literary evidence: the cucumber was regarded at first as a variety of chate melon, which it resembles in size and shape. In Greek lands the term *angourion* eventually came to be used for 'cucumber' as distinct from *sikyos* 'chate melon'. In the West Latin *cucumis* eventually came to mean 'cucumber' alone.

- The root and fruit of squirting cucumber (*Ecballium Elaterium*), Greek *elaterion* or *sikyos ho agrios*, Latin *elaterium*, regarded as a 'wild melon', were used medicinally as a purge.

  Hippocrates, *Epidemics* 5.7 with Jouanna *ad l.*; Theophrastus *HP* 9.4.1–2, 9.9.2; Dioscorides *MM* 4.150; Pliny *NH* 19.74, 20.3–6; Pseudo-Apuleius, *Herbarius* 114.

Men *see* WOMEN

Mendaean wine (Greek *Mendaios*), from Mende in Chalcidice. Mendaean was a favourite wine in Athens in the fourth century and in Macedonia in the third. It was fresh and white, but needed to age a little (hence the covert comparison with an adolescent boy in a play by Cratinus).

Demosthenes, *Against Lacritus* 10; Hippolochus *D*; Athenaeus *E* 29d–f quoting Hermippus 77 Kassel and Cratinus 195 Kassel.

Dalby 2000c.

Mercury (*Mercurialis* spp.), genus of plants with ancient medicinal uses. Annual mercury (*Mercurialis annua*), Greek *linozostis*, was a purge (Hippocrates, *Epidemics* 7.5, *al.*; Dioscorides *MM* 4.189). The male and female forms of dog's mercury (*M. perennis*), Greek *arrenogonon, thelygonon*, were eaten before coitus to ensure, respectively, male or female offspring (Theophrastus *HP* 9.18.5–6).

Mesopotamia, region 'between the rivers' (the Tigris and Euphrates) corresponding roughly with modern Iraq. The oldest literate civilisation in Mesopotamia is that of the Sumerian cities, which flourished in southern Iraq in the third millennium BC. Akkadian is the language of the two best-known of subsequent civilisations in Mesopotamia, those of the Assyrians and Babylonians; for the surviving recipes in Akkadian see MESOPOTAMIAN RECIPE COLLECTIONS.

Mesopotamian food is known from archaeology and written records on cuneiform tablets, including bilingual Sumerian–Akkadian word lists. These sources indicate the importance of barley bread, of which many kinds are named, and barley and wheat cakes, and grain and legume soups; of onions, leeks and garlic; of vegetables including chate melon, and of fruits including apple, fig and grape; of honey and cheese; of several culinary herbs; and of butter and vegetable oil. Sumerians drank beer often, wine seldom if at all; wine was better known in northern Mesopotamia and in later times. Animal foods included pork, mutton, beef, fowl including ducks and pigeons, and many kinds of fish. Meats were salted; fruits were conserved in honey;

various foods, including apples, were dried. A kind of fermented sauce is identified in Akkadian texts.

Mesopotamia became a part of the Persian Empire and, after the Macedonian conquest by Alexander the Great, fell to the Hellenistic kingdom of the Seleucids. In Seleucid times experiments were made with transplanting Mediterranean crops to Mesopotamia: the 'Macedonians' were the first to succeed with vines in southern Mesopotamia, Strabo tells us. As the Seleucid dominion shrank to Syria, Mesopotamia in the first century BC became the heartland of the empire of the PARTHIANS.

Herodotus 1.192–3, 1.200–2; Strabo 15.3.11.

J. Bottéro, 'Getränke' ['Les boissons': the article is in French] in *RA* (1928–) vol. 3 pp. 302–6; K.V. Flannery, 'The ecology of early food production in Mesopotamia' in *Science* vol. 147 (1965) pp. 1247–56; A. Salonen, *Die Fischerei im alten Mesopotamien* (Helsinki, 1970) (*Annales Academiae Scientiarum Fennicae B*, 166); H. Limet, 'L'étranger dans la société sumérienne' in *Gesellschaftsklassen im alten Zweistromland und in den angrenzenden Gebieten: Rencontre Assyriologique Internationale XVIII* ed. D.O. Edzard (Munich, 1972) pp. 123–38; J. Kinnier-Wilson, *The Nimrud Wine Lists: a study of men and administration at the Assyrian capital in the eighth century B.C.* (London: British School of Archaeology in Iraq, 1972); A. Salonen, *Vögel und Vogelfang im alten Mesopotamien* (Helsinki, 1973) (*Annales Academiae Scientiarum Fennicae B*, 180); I.M. Diakonoff, 'Earliest Semites in Asia: agriculture and animal husbandry according to linguistic data (VIIIth–IVth millennia BC)' in *Altorientalische Forschungen* vol. 8 (1981) pp. 23–74; Rosemary Ellison, 'Methods of food preparation in Mesopotamia (*c.*3000–600 BC)' in *Journal of the Economic and Social History of the Orient* vol. 27 (1984) pp. 89–98; J. Bottéro, 'The cuisine of ancient Mesopotamia' in *Biblical Archaeologist* vol. 48 (1985) pp. 36–47; G.C. Hillman, 'Traditional husbandry and processing of archaic cereals in recent times: the operations, products and equipment which might feature in Sumerian texts' in *Bulletin on Sumerian Agriculture* vol. 1 (1984) pp. 114–52, vol. 2 (1985) pp. 1–2; H. Limet, 'The cuisine of ancient Sumer' in *Biblical Archaeologist* vol. 50 (1987) pp. 132–47; J.N. Postgate, 'Some vegetables in the Assyrian sources' and 'Notes on fruit in the cuneiform sources' in *Bulletin on Sumerian Agriculture* no. 3 (1987); J. de Moor,

'Eating out in the ancient Near East' in *Oxford Symposium on Food and Cookery 1991: public eating. Proceedings* (London, 1991) pp. 213–21; V. Blažek and C. Boisson, 'The diffusion of agricultural terms from Mesopotamia' in *Archív orientalní* vol. 60 (1992) pp. 16–37; Eveline J. van der Steen, 'Zukanda and other delicacies: haute cuisine in the days of Hammurabi' in *Petits Propos culinaires* no. 51 (1995) pp. 40–6; J. Bottéro, 'The oldest recipes of all' in *Food in Antiquity* ed. John Wilkins and others (Exeter: Exeter University Press, 1995) pp. 242–7; Jean Bottéro, *Textes culinaires mesopotamiens* (Indiana: Eisenbrauns, 1995); Marvin A. Powell, 'Wine and the vine in ancient Mesopotamia: the cuneiform evidence' in *The Origins and Ancient History of Wine* ed. Patrick E. McGovern and others (London: Gordon and Breach, 1995) pp. 97–122; Richard L. Zettler and Naomi F. Miller, 'Searching for wine in the archaeological record of ancient Mesopotamia of the third and second millennia B.C.' in *The Origins and Ancient History of Wine* ed. Patrick E. McGovern and others (London: Gordon and Breach, 1995) pp. 123–31; David Stronach, 'The imagery of the wine bowl: wine in Assyria in the early first millennium B.C.' in *The Origins and Ancient History of Wine* ed. Patrick E. McGovern and others (London: Gordon and Breach, 1995) pp. 175–95; Suzanne Amigues, 'Végétation et cultures du Proche-Orient dans l'Anabase' in *Pallas* no. 43 (1995) pp. 61–78; Flandrin and Montanari 1996.

Mesopotamian recipe collections, three cuneiform tablets at Yale University (*YOS* XI.25–7) containing recipes in Akkadian. Probably originating from southern Mesopotamia in the seventeenth century BC, these are the oldest known food recipes anywhere in the world. As such they are landmarks of early GASTRONOMY and provide crucial information on Mesopotamian cuisine.

J. Bottéro, 'The oldest recipes of all' in *Food in Antiquity* ed. John Wilkins and others (Exeter: Exeter University Press, 1995) pp. 242–7; J. Bottéro, *Textes culinaires mesopotamiens* (Indiana: Eisenbrauns, 1995).

Messana (older Greek *Zankle*) and Rhegium, cities that faced one another across the straits that divided Italy from Sicily. These cities, lying astride an important route from Greece and south Italy to the Greek cities of Sicily, were much frequented by travellers. They were a source of fine seafood, including eel, moray eel, swordfish and palourdes. For the last-named see under VENUS CLAM: they were believed to get their name from Cape Pelorus, the long sandy peninsula north of Messana, noted equally for its fishing and its hunting.

Archestratus *H* 8, 16, 17, 40, 56 Brandt; Solinus 5.3.

Dalby 1995.

Methodius, Greek Christian author of the early fourth century AD. Methodius, a literary disciple of Plato, wrote philosophical dialogues including a *Symposium*, which survives.

Miletus, coastal city of western Anatolia. Miletus was said to be a good place for sea bass, from around the mouth of the River Gaison. Some sharks and rays were also good here. The nearby harbour of Teichiussa was a place to buy red mullet.

Archestratus *H* 41–2, 45–6 Brandt with Olson and Sens *ad ll.*

Milk had an unusual status as a food item in the classical world, because milk, as such, will not keep (without the use of refrigeration or other modern techniques). So the drinking of fresh milk was a luxury shared by farmers and nomadic shepherds with those in cities and royal courts who were rich enough to pay for express delivery. The Persian King's Dinner demanded large supplies (100 Attic *khous*) of fresh milk of the day, *gala authemerinon*. Much later, there were apparently hawkers of *lac venale* through the streets of classical Rome.

Aristotle observes that sheep, goats and cows all produce more milk than is needed for their own offspring. These were the sources of most of the milk that Greeks and Romans used; mare's milk and ass's milk were also sometimes used. The milk of any of these five animals might be used as an ingredient in KYKEON. Aristotle also refers to the drinking of camel's milk.

Much of the milk that domestic animals produced was turned into cheese, a far more stable substance and an excellent food. Both milk and cheese were typical foods of shepherds – thus of the Cyclops Polyphemus, according to Odysseus in the *Odyssey*, and of Ganymede before his translation to Olympus, according to Zeus in one of Lucian's humorous dialogues. Cheese is not the only potential milk product. For curds and yoghourt see below; see separate entries for BUTTER and CHEESE.

For milk, especially human milk, as baby food see BABIES. Milk was prescribed in various diseases: in Hippocratic texts there are mentions of *to oneion* 'ass's milk' and *boeion gala* 'cow's milk' in dysentery, also of *oros aigeios* 'goat's whey' and *gala aigeion* 'goat's milk'. The existence of lactose intolerance was observed; hence Anthimus prescribes not goat's milk but bread soaked in boiling goat's milk.

Milk is *gala* in Greek, *lac* in Latin.

Homer, *Iliad* 13.5–6, *Odyssey* 9.244–7; Hippocrates *RA* 33, 40, *R* 41, *Aphorisms* 5.64, *Epidemics* 7.3–4, 7.115; Aristotle *HA* 521b21–523a12, 578a10–16; Varro *RR* 2.11.1; Pliny *NH* 11.236–8, 28.123–30; Lucian, *Dialogues of the Gods* 4.3; Polyaenus 4.3.32; Anthimus *OC* 75–8 with Grant *ad l.*

G. Herzog-Hauser, 'Milch' in *RE* 1893–1972; K. Wyhs, *Die Milch im Kultus der Griechen und Römer* (Giessen, 1914); Buck 1949 pp. 385–8; R.G. Ussher, 'A comment on unmixed milk' in *Hermathena* vol. 89 (1957) pp. 59–64; K. Deichgräber, 'Zur Milchtherapie der Hippokratiker (Epid. VII)' in *Medizin-Geschichte in unserer Zeit: Festgabe E. Heischkel-Artelt und W. Artelt* ed. H.H. Eulner (Stuttgart: Enke, 1971) pp. 36–53; F. Graf, 'Milch, Honig und Wein' in *Perennitas: studi in memoria di A. Brelich* (Rome, 1980) pp. 209–21; Marten Stol, 'Milk, butter and cheese' in *Bulletin on Sumerian Agriculture* vol. 7 (1993) pp. 99–113.

- Greek *oxygala* was yoghourt, or something closely approaching it. *Oxygala* was easier to digest than fresh milk, said Anthimus: when eaten it should be mixed with honey or with oil. Full instructions are given by Columella. A cheese, *oxygalaktinon*, was made from *oxygala*. Plutarch and Polyaenus both indicate that *oxygala* (sweetened, according to Polyaenus) was a food of the ancient Persians.

  Strabo 7.4.6; Columella *DA* 12.8; Plutarch, *Life of Artoxerxes* 3.2; Galen *AF* 6.689, 6.697; Polyaenus 4.3.32; Oribasius *CM* 1.13.4 with Grant *ad l.*; Hesychius, *Lexicon* s.v. *hippake* citing Theopompus 115 F 45 Jacoby; Anthimus *OC* 78.

- Latin *melca* 'curds' appears to be the equivalent of earlier Greek *gala sympakton*. Anthimus was to equate *melca* with Greek *oxygala*, but perhaps inaccurately, since *melke* had meanwhile been borrowed into Greek with this meaning. For a modern version of Paxamus's recipe see Grant 1999 p. 80. Greek *hypotyrides* is another term belonging to the same semantic region. Grant 1999 pp. 79–80 gives a modern version of Chrysippus' recipe for *hypotyrides* as 'curds with honey'.

  Philoxenus b.36 Page; Athenaeus *D* 647f citing Chrysippus of Tyana; Anthimus *OC* 78; *Geoponica* 18.21 citing Paxamus.

Milk-vetch or tragacanth (*Astragalus* spp.), a spiny plant whose leaves are listed among potherbs by Galen. It is *tragakantha* in Greek.

Theophrastus *HP* 9.1.3, 9.15.8; Pliny *NH* 13.115; Galen *AF* 6.636.

Millet, a general English name for cereals not belonging to the genera of wheat, barley, rye and oats. None of the millets were favourite crops in the classical Mediterranean; the best known in Greece and Rome was broomcorn millet. This had been domesticated, probably in the region of the Caucasus, before 5000 BC. It spread both westwards to central Europe (it was being cultivated in eastern France before 4000 BC) and eastwards to China. It was known in Greece and Italy by late prehistoric times. It must have been a convenient crop in certain special circumstances, since it will ripen in Mediterranean lands even if planted as late as the second half of June. Millet was made into a kind of porridge; Grant 1999 pp.

40–1 develops a recipe from hints by Anthimus.

Broomcorn millet (*Panicum miliaceum*) is Greek *kenkhros*, Latin *milium*.

Hesiod, *Shield of Heracles* 398; Herodotus 1.193, 4.17; Xenophon, *Anabasis* 1.2.22, 2.4.13; Hippocrates *R* 45; Theophrastus *HP* 8.7.3; Dioscorides *MM* 2.97–8; Columella *DA* 2.9.17–19; Seneca, *Letters* 86.16; Pliny *NH* 18.99–102, 22.130; Oribasius *CM* 4.7.15 quoting Dieuches; Anthimus *OC* 71.

M.S. Spurr, 'The cultivation of millet in Roman Italy' in *Papers of the British School at Rome* vol. 51 (1983) pp. 1–15; Zohary and Hopf 1993 pp. 78–83; *Millet = Hirse = Millet: actes du congrès d'Aizenay, 18–19 août 1990* ed. E. Hörandner (1995) (*Grazer Beiträge sur europäischen Ethnologie*, 4); J.M.J. de Wet, 'Millets' in *CWHF* 2000 vol. 1 pp. 112–21.

- Greek *elymos*, *meline*, Latin *panicum* is foxtail millet or Italian millet (*Setaria italica*). In English translations 'panic' often stands for foxtail millet. This species was domesticated in northern China, as early as 6500 BC, and reached southern Europe in late prehistoric times. Herodotus assumes that it will be known to his audience. Foxtail millet was also in due course known to Roman authors and is said by Pliny to have been cultivated in Roman Gaul; this statement is not yet supported by archaeological finds.

  Herodotus 3.117; Pliny *NH* 18.52–4, 18.101, 22.131; Oribasius *CM* 1.15 with Grant *ad l.*

- Sawa (*Echinochloa colona*), a millet now cultivated in India, was probably gathered from the wild in early Egypt as it still is in time of famine. Seeds have been identified in mummy intestines from Naga ed-Dar. This species is possibly mentioned, unnamed, by Theophrastus, as having a seed no larger than sesame but good to eat.

  Theophrastus *HP* 4.8.14 (cf. Athenaeus *D* 110e).

  D.M. Dixon, 'A note on cereals in ancient Egypt' in *The Domestication and Exploitation of Plants and Animals* ed. P.J. Ucko and G.W. Dimbleby (London, 1969) pp. 131–42.

- Ragi or finger millet (*Eleusine coracana*) and bajra or bulrush millet (*Pennisetum glaucum*) are the two major cultivated millets of India. They are occasionally mentioned in classical sources, one simply as *kenkhros* 'millet', the other as *bosmoron* or *bosporos*.

Diodorus Siculus 2.36 (*bosporos*); Strabo 15.1.13, 15.1.18 (*bosmoron*).

Minoans, bearers of a culture which was indigenous to CRETE and influenced much of Greece in the mid second millennium BC. The non-Greek languages of prehistoric Crete, represented in Linear A and other scripts, have not been deciphered. Minoan uses of foods, wine and aromatics are studied by interpreting Linear A tablets and Minoan paintings and through archaeological finds. At a slightly later period records at the palace of Knossos were kept in Greek in Linear B script, which can be read (see MYCENAEANS).

H. Georgiou, 'Aromatics in antiquity and in Minoan Crete: a review and reassessment' in *Kritika khronika* vol. 25 (1973) pp. 441–56 and plates 18–19; J.L. Melena, 'La producción de plantas aromáticas en Cnoso' in *Estudios clasicos* vol. 20 (1976) pp. 177–90; A. Guest-Papamanoli, 'Pêche et pêcheurs minoens: proposition pour une recherche' in *Minoan Society: proceedings of the Cambridge colloquium 1981* ed. O. Krzyszkowska and L. Nixon (Bristol: Bristol Classical Press, 1983) pp. 101–10; N. Marinatos, *Minoan Sacrificial Ritual: cult practice and symbolism* (Stockholm, 1986) (*Skrifter utgivna av Svenska institutet i Athen, 8°* vol. 9); Ruth Palmer, 'Wine and viticulture in the Linear A and B texts of the Bronze Age Aegean' in *The Origins and Ancient History of Wine* ed. Patrick E. McGovern, Stuart J. Fleming and Solomon H. Katz (London: Gordon and Breach, 1995) pp. 269–85; James C. Wright, 'Empty cups and empty jugs: the social role of wine in Minoan and Mycenaean societies' in *The Origins and Ancient History of Wine* ed. Patrick E. McGovern, Stuart J. Fleming and Solomon H. Katz (London: Gordon and Breach, 1995) pp. 287–309; Yannis Hamilakis, 'Wine, oil and the dialectics of power in Bronze Age Crete: a review of the evidence' in *Oxford Journal of Archaeology* vol. 15 (1996) pp. 1–32; Yannis Hamilakis, 'Food technologies, technologies of the body: the social context of wine and oil production and consumption in Bronze Age Crete' in *World Archaeology* vol. 31 (1999) pp. 38–54.

Mint, aromatic plant of Europe and elsewhere. Mint was well known in classical Greece and in Roman Italy, where, according to Pliny, it was a scent familiar at country feasts. In Greece, however, mint is seldom mentioned in the context of food and dining. At least two reasons can be suggested. One is that it was considered antaphrodisiac: 'if eaten often it melts the seed and makes it runny, preventing erections and weakening the body,' according to the Hippocratic *Regimen*. Minthe was said to have been a nymph who became Pluto's lover; in revenge Persephone turned her into a plant – and one with undesirable side-effects when eaten. A second reason is that mint had an unfortunate name: *minthe* in Greek meant mint, but *minthos* meant shit; this was avoided by giving it a second and euphemistic name, *hedyosmon* 'nice smell'.

Spearmint, horsemint and field mint (*Mentha spicata*, *M. longifolia* and *M. arvensis*) are Greek *minthe* and *hedyosmon*, Latin *menta*. Water mint (*M. aquatica*) is Greek *sisymbrion*, Latin *sisymbrium*. This word served in double entendre for 'women's pubic hair'. Other names such as Greek *kalaminthe* and Latin *mentastrum* and *nepeta* belonged to related herbs but are not easy to identify precisely; they were in any case seldom used in food.

Aristophanes, *Birds* 160; Hippocrates *R* 54; Theophrastus *HP* 2.4.1; Nicander *T* 60 with scholia; Strabo 8.3.14; Dioscorides *MM* 3.34–5; Pliny *NH* 19.159–60, 20.144–51, 20.158, 20.247–8; Matthew, *Gospel* 23.23; Galen *SF* 11.882–3; Pseudo-Apuleius, *Herbarius* 91.

A.C. Andrews, 'The mints of the Greeks and Romans and their condimentary use' in *Osiris* vol. 13 (1958) pp. 127–56.

Mithaecus, cook and cookbook author of the late fifth century BC. Mithaecus was a Sicilian who brought good cooking to Sparta, where it was not welcomed (this according to a late source, Maximus of Tyre), and to Athens, where it was. He earned a backhanded compliment from 'Socrates' in Plato's *Gorgias*, and lasting, albeit limited, fame. His book, the first known cookbook in Greek, was written in the Doric dialect. It is lost except for

two citations and one short verbatim quotation by Athenaeus: the latter is a recipe for the fish CEPOLA RUBESCENS (see quotation there).

Plato, *Gorgias* 518c; Maximus of Tyre, *Dissertations* 17; Athenaeus *D* 282a, also 325f quoting Mithaecus, also 516c.

Bilabel 1921; Dalby 1996 pp. 109–10; Shaun Hill and John Wilkins, 'Mithaikos and other Greek cooks' in *Cooks and Other People: proceedings of the Oxford Symposium on Food and Cookery 1995* ed. Harlan Walker (Totnes: Prospect Books, 1996) pp. 144–8.

Mithridates Eupator (*c.*132–66 BC), king of Pontus. Mithridates was famous not only for his poison antidote, the *Mithridateion* (see below), but also for the eating and drinking competitions staged at his court. The king himself won the prizes in both competitions: some said it was because of his capacity for heavy drinking that he gained the nickname Dionysus. A sacrificial feast conducted by Mithridates is described briefly by Appian. He or his courtiers drank from aromatic MURRINE VASES, carved from Parthian fluorspar; such things were unknown at Rome until displayed in the booty from Mithridates's defeat.

Plutarch *QC* 1.6; Appian, *Mithridatic War* 66.

- The *Mithridateion* was a prophylactic against poisons formulated by CRATEUAS. Mithridates's antidote served him well – until his final defeat by the Romans, when he decided to commit suicide by taking poison and the poison would not work. The oldest surviving recipe is given by Celsus, a century after Mithridates's time. Clearly, however, there was no authoritative record. Galen reproduces three conflicting recipes from different authorities. Pliny knew another, with fifty-four ingredients, but does not quote it.

Celsus, *DM* 5.23.3; Pliny *NH* 29.24; Galen *DA* 14.115 quoting Damocrates, also 14.154 citing Andromachus, also 14.164 citing Xenocrates.

Mnesitheus of Athens, physician of the early fourth century BC. His best-known work was *On Foods*, now lost but cited eighteen times by Athenaeus, twenty-eight times by Galen, and occasionally by others.

Pausanias 1.37.4.

J. Bertier, *Mnésithée et Dieuchès* (Leiden, 1972).

Molokhia, a fibre plant – the source of jute – whose leaves are traditionally used as food in the eastern Mediterranean, especially in Egypt. It is listed among potherbs by Theophrastus; Pliny names it as a plant eaten at Alexandria. It was proverbial for its bitterness: *korkoros en lakhanoisi,* 'molokhia among potherbs', not unlike 'a rose among thorns'.

Molokhia or melokhia or Jew's mallow (*Corchorus olitorius*) is Greek *korkoros.*

Aristophanes, *Wasps* 239 with scholia; Theophrastus *HP* 7.7.2 (*korkhoros*); Nicander *T* 626; Pliny *NH* 21.183 (*corchorum*).

Darby and others 1977 pp. 670–2.

Moly, the name among gods of the plant which was Odysseus's prophylactic against the drugs of Circe. It was identified with garlic by some later Greeks. The summer snowflake, *Leucojum aestivum,* a plant of Arcadia, was identified with the Homeric *moly* and credited with magical properties.

Homer, *Odyssey* 10.304–6; Theophrastus *HP* 9.15.7.

Jerry Stannard, 'The herb called moly' in *Osiris* vol. 14 (1962) 254–307; John Scarborough, 'The pharmacology of sacred plants, herbs and roots' in *Magika Hiera: ancient Greek magic and religion* (New York: Oxford University Press, 1991) pp. 139, 141 and notes 24, 51; Suzanne Amigues, 'Des plantes nommées moly' in *JS* (1995) pp. 3–29.

Moray eel, one of the larger Mediterranean fish. 'They have a dangerous bite and are both cunning and greedy,' according to Alan Davidson, but ancient gastronomes thought them well worth the trouble of someone else's catching; as nourishing as eels, said Hicesius; easiest to pick at when cold, according to a speaker in Plautus's *Persa.* They were good in the Atlantic, around Gades (Ca-

diz). Another good place to catch them was off Rhegium at the southern extremity of Italy, where they grew to great size, basked on the sea surface and were called *plotai* in Greek, *flutae* in Latin.

Roman lovers of luxury foods kept moray eels in fishponds – but separately from other fish, which they were fierce enough to kill. Vedius Pollio was said to punish slaves by feeding them to his morays; this may be an abridgment of the truth, but need not be a falsification, since the bite of a moray will often fester and can therefore kill. The emperor Augustus, present on the occasion of one such execution, intervened to reprieve the victim. Crassus wept as bitterly for a pet moray as Domitian wept for his three wives, in a story told by Plutarch.

The usual Greek name for the moray eel (*Muraena Helena*) was *smyraina* or *myraina.* The word was also used (like English 'shark') as a term of abuse. The corresponding Latin word is *muraena*; this was also the surname, not as uncomplimentary as it might seem, of a family in the Roman *gens Licinia.*

Aristophanes, *Frogs* 474–5; Archestratus *H* 16 Brandt with Olson and Sens *ad l.*; Matron *AD* 73; Nicander *T* 823–5; Plautus, *Aulularia* 398–9, *Persa* 110–11; Strabo 3.2.7; Columella *DA* 8.17.2; Seneca, *On Clemency* 1.18; Pliny *NH* 9.73–7, 9.170; Juvenal 5.99–102; Plutarch, *Intelligence of Animals* 976a; Oppian *H* 1.141–2; Athenaeus *D* 312b–e citing Hicesius; Macrobius *S* 3.15.1–10.

Thompson 1947 pp. 162–5 (he believes that the *muraena* kept in fishponds was a LAMPREY); Davidson 1981 p. 54; Higginbotham 1997 pp. 43–6 (his identification of *muraena* with EEL is certainly mistaken).

Moretum, name of a short hexameter poem, traditionally attributed to Vergil. It is not by him but is probably of about the same date, the late first century BC. It describes a day in the life of a peasant farmer, with a special focus on the *moretum,* a mixture of cheese with olive oil, herbs and garlic (especially garlic) that is to be his lunch.

Another *Moretum*, also in hexameters, was written by the obscure poet Sueius in the mid first century BC. The only surviving fragment is quoted by Macrobius (*S* 3.18.12).

Moretum. Text, translation and commentary: *Moretum: the ploughman's lunch, a poem ascribed to Virgil* ed. E.J. Kenney (Bristol: Bristol Classical Press, 1986).

- *Moretum* was a nourishing, pungent and vegetarian food to eat with bread. The recipe incorporated in the poem *Moretum* has been interpreted by Dalby and Grainger 1996 pp. 85–8, Junkelmann 1997 pp. 109–11 and Grant 1999 pp. 72–3. Four further recipes are given by Columella, though he does not use the term *moretum*.

Ovid, *Fasti* 4.367; Columella *DA* 12.59.1–4.

M. Visser, 'Moretum: ancient Roman pesto' in *Spicing Up the Palate: proceedings of the Oxford Symposium on Food and Cookery 1992* (Totnes: Prospect Books, 1993) pp. 263–74.

Moselle fish, a rich fauna from a big river of northern Gaul, a tributary of the Rhine. The fish of the Moselle are warmly evoked in the hexameter poem *Mosella* by Ausonius, written around AD 400. See BURBOT; CHUB; GOBY; GRAYLING; LAMPREY; PERCH; PIKE; SALMON; SHAD; SHEATFISH; TROUT (two species). The following are not mentioned by any classical author other than Ausonius: they can be identified because the names he uses, evidently current in the spoken Latin of Gaul, have survived in French or another of the Romance languages.

- Latin *alburnus* is the bleak, French *ablette* (*Alburnus Alburnus*). The bleak is a small fish easily caught by children, a fact noted by Ausonius and by more recent authors.

Ausonius, *Mosella* 126.

Thompson 1947 p. 10.

- Latin *barbus* is the barbel (*Barbus Barbus*), a carp-like fish of western European rivers. It is best when old and well-grown, says Ausonius, and better in the Moselle than the Sarre.

Ausonius, *Mosella* 91–6, 134.

Thompson 1947 p. 25.

- Latin *redo* may possibly be the roach (*Leuciscus rutilus*). Thompson suggests instead the burbot, which others prefer to identify with Ausonius's *mustela*.

Ausonius, *Mosella* 89.

Thompson 1947 p. 220.

- Latin *tinca* is the tench (*Tinca Tinca*), 'solace of the common people' according to Ausonius.

Ausonius, *Mosella* 125.

Thompson 1947 p. 262.

Mulberry, tree fruit. The dark-fruited species, more familiar in Europe, was perhaps domesticated in southeastern Europe or Anatolia. It can be eaten fresh or conserved; as Galen observes, it cannot be dried.

The mulberry (*Morus nigra*) is Greek *moron* and *sykaminos*, Latin *morum* (*domesticum*). The superficially similar BLACKBERRY was not always distinguished by name.

Hippocrates *R* 55; Theophrastus *HP* 1.10.10, *CP* 6.6.4; Diodorus Siculus 1.34.8; Dioscorides *MM* 1.126; Pliny *NH* 15.97, 23.135–40; Galen *AF* 6.584, *BM* 6.785; Athenaeus *E* 51b–52a; Palladius *OA* 3.25.28–30; Anthimus *OC* 86 with Grant *ad l.*

Mullet *see* GREY MULLET; RED MULLET

Mulsum, wine sweetened with honey (and sometimes spiced). *Mulsum* was a typical aperitif, served by Romans before or alongside the first course of an evening meal, and freshly mixed for the occasion. The best *mulsum*, it was commonly said, was made with Falernian wine and Hymettan honey – in other words, the finest and most expensive wine available and the finest and most expensive honey – but others less vocal may have taken the same view as Flower and Rosenbaum (below). *Mulsum* was good for you: Romilius Pollio claimed (to the emperor Augustus) to have reached the age of 100 by regular application of *mulsum* on the inside and oil on the outside. 'When drunk cold it relaxes the bowels,' Pliny specifies; 'hot, most people find that it settles them.'

Mulsum is less common in later texts, perhaps because it was driven from fashion by the ready-made product CONDITUM. Columella had already given a recipe for a ready-prepared *mulsum* made from must and honey and aged in smoke.

The equivalent Greek term is *oinomeli*. This also occurs in Latin: a recipe for *ynomelli* is supplied by Palladius.

Poseidonius *F* 1 Jacoby [Athenaeus *D* 153c]; Columella *DA* 12.41; Pliny *NH* 22.113–14; Palladius *OA* 11.17.

Flower and Rosenbaum 1961 pp. 25–6 ('one can use very cheap wine, which in its pure form would hardly be drinkable'); S.D. Goitein, *A Mediterranean Society* (Berkeley, 1967–88) vol. 3 pp. 260–1.

Muria *see* GARUM

Murrine vases (Latin *murrina*), a luxury for which Romans were prepared to pay a great deal. They were carved from fluorspar, a fissile crystalline substance which – to prevent breakage during manufacture – had to be gradually impregnated with resin as it was carved. Thus they gave a slight, attractive aroma to wine. Various resins might be chosen; if myrrh was often used (and Romans liked wine aromatised with myrrh) this would explain the Latin name. Murrine vases were a product of Parthia, where fluorspar is found. They first reached Rome in the booty of MITHRIDATES's defeat in 63 BC.

Pliny *NH* 33.5, 36.198, 37.20–2; Martial 10.80, 11.70 with Kay *ad l.*, 14.113 with Leary *ad l.*

Mushrooms, plant-like organisms of which many species are good to eat. The first evidence that mushrooms were used as human food in prehistoric Europe is the recent find of a bowl of field mushrooms in a Bronze Age house near NOLA in Italy.

Mushrooms were gathered from the wild. Classical Greek authors tend to treat them as famine food, on a level with acorns. By Romans, however, they were so highly regarded that the Stoic writer Seneca gave up mushrooms (*boleti*) as unnecessary luxuries – an approach to the vegetarianism and asceticism that he toyed with. Recipes are suggested by Diphilus of Siphnos, in the third century BC, and in *Apicius* in the fourth century AD. For modern interpretations see Grant 1999 pp. 146–7 and Dalby and Grainger 1996 p. 113.

The danger of poisoning was also recognised (see Athenaeus). Antidotes for mushroom poisoning are mentioned in the Hippocratic text *Epidemics VII* and other sources; eat pears afterwards, Pliny advises. It was a commonplace that a *boletus*, a mushroom, comprised the last, poisonous or poisoned, meal of the emperor Claudius (Pliny *NH* 22.92; Martial 1.20; Juvenal 5.147; Suetonius, *Claudius* 44.2, *Nero* 33.1).

The general terms for mushroom are Latin *boletus*, Greek *mykes*. The word *boletus* gives its name to a mushroom-shaped cooking pot, Latin *boletar*.

Hippocrates, *Epidemics* 7.102; Theophrastus *HP* 1.1.11; Scribonius Largus 198; Seneca, *Letters* 95.25, 108.15; Pliny *NH* 22.92–9; Martial 13.48; Juvenal 14.8; Pliny the Younger, *Letters* 1.7.6; Galen *AF* 6.655–6; Athenaeus *D* 372e quoting Nicander *F* 72 Schneider, also *E* 60b–61f citing Diphilus of Siphnos and others; *Apicius* 7.13.

W. Houghton, 'Notices of fungi in Greek and Latin authors' in *Annals and Magazine of Natural History* ser. 5 vol. 5 (1885) pp. 22–49; G. Maggiulli, *Nomenclatura Micologica Latina* (Genoa: Istituto di Filologia Classica e Medievale, 1977); M.D. Grmek, 'Intoxication par les champignons dans l'antiquité grecque et latine' in *Littérature, médecine, société* vol. 4 (Nantes, 1982) pp. 17–52.

• On the identification of classical names with scientific species see Houghton and Maggiulli (above). Names used for edible mushrooms are Greek *amanites* (Galen *AF* 6.656; Athenaeus *E* 61a quoting Nicander *F* 78 Schneider); Latin *boletus* in a narrow sense (Pliny *NH* 16.31; *Apicius* 7.13.4–6); Greek *bolites* (Galen *AF* 6.655–6); Latin *farneus* (*Apicius* 7.13.1–3); Greek *mykes Italikos* (Plutarch, *Precepts on Health* 124f); Greek *mykes prininos* (Athenaeus *E* 60d quoting Antiphanes); Greek *pezix* (Theophrastus *HP* 1.6.5, cf. Athenaeus *E* 61e–f; Pliny *NH* 19.38); Latin *suillus* (Pliny *NH* 16.31, 22.96–8; Martial 3.60); Latin *mussirio* (Anthimus *OC* 38), the last being ancestral to English *mushroom*. The *suillus*, a new taste in Pliny's time, grew under the oak *Quercus Robur*; it could be dried. The *mykes prininos* grew under the kermes-oak *Q. coccifera*.

W. Meyer-Lübke, *Romanisches etymologisches Wörterbuch* (Heidelberg: Winter, 1930–5) *s.vv.* boletus, farneus, mussiro, suillus.

• Petronius, in a mood of fantasy, talks of the sending of 'mushroom seed' from India for planting in Italy. In reality, cultivation of mushrooms is a modern development.

Petronius *S* 38.4.

Mussel, group of bivalve shellfish. Mussels are easily cooked, without removing from the shells, and just as easily eaten, though Martial notes the risk of a cut lip from a broken shell.

They produced better humours than venus-shells and were regarded as laxative (or worse) and diuretic. Not only in Cato's practical manual, but also in Horace's satirical gastronomy, mussels and other cheap shellfish are recommended as a cure for constipation. Drinking the cooking liquor, according to Pliny, promotes growth.

Mussels were good at Aenus, according to Archestratus, followed in this by Ennius. Both Diphilus, the dietician, and Hicesius, the culinary author, prefer the mussels of Ephesus to all others. The shells (*myakes* in Greek) had medicinal uses. Diphilus adds that they are best in spring; Aristotle concurs, because that is when they bear their 'so-called eggs'. It is likely, as observed by Thompson, that Mitylene, chief city of the Greek island of Lesbos, is named for the abundance of mussels in the neighbouring straits and bays.

The mussel (*Mytilus galloprovincialis* and other species) is Greek *mys*, Latin *mitulus*. Greek *mys* also means 'mouse'; therefore *mys thalattios*, literally 'sea mouse', is occasionally used in texts to distinguish the shellfish from its terrestrial homonym.

Hippocrates *R* 48; Aristotle *HA* 528a15–29; Ennius *H* 2 (*mus*); Plautus, *Rudens* 298; Horace, *Satires* 2.4.28; Dioscorides *MM* 2.5; Xenocrates *T* 90–1; Pliny *NH* 32.95–8, 32.111; Martial 3.60; Athenaeus *D* 85d–92e *passim* quoting Archestratus *H* 56 Brandt, Diphilus of Siphnos and Hicesius; *Apicius* 9.9.

Thompson 1947 p. 166; Andrews 1948; Davidson 1981 p. 198.

• Greek *myiskos* is the name of the smaller and more definitely bearded species *Modiolus barbatus*. They are sweet, productive of good humours and nourishing, according to Diphilus.

Athenaeus *D* 90d quoting Diphilus of Siphnos; Xenocrates *T* 92–3; Pliny *NH* 32.98 (*myisca*).

Must, fresh grape juice. Must is a product which in normal conditions begins to ferment into wine almost as soon as it flows from the press, and therefore is soon somewhat alcoholic – whence the rude remark made about the apostles, 'They are full of *gleukos*!' meaning that they had been at the new wine.

Grape juice or must is *gleukos, ho glykys, to glyky* in Greek, *mustum* in Latin.

Aristophanes, *Wasps* 878; Dioscorides *MM* 5.6; Pliny *NH* 14.80, 23.29–30; Luke, *Acts of the Apostles* 2.13; Martial 3.60; Galen *AF* 6.575; *Diocletian's Price Edict* 2.15–16.

• Grape syrup, i.e. boiled-down must (Greek *hepsema*, Latin *defrutum*), a more stable product than fresh must, was of great importance. In cooking it added both sweetness and flavour (*Apicius passim*). It was – and occasionally still is – an ingredient in the making of flavoured wines and cooked wines, such as the typical *vinum Graecum* 'Greek wine' of the Roman and later West (Cato *DA* 23, 105). Careful instructions for *defrutum* are given by Pliny (*NH* 18.318; cf. Palladius *OA* 11.18). *Caroenum* was grape juice boiled down to two-thirds of its volume.

- If further boiled to one third of its volume, grape syrup was known as *sapa* in Latin; for a recipe see Pliny *NH* 23.62. Greek *siraion* was a similar product (Galen, *On Compounding* 13.612, cf. *AF* 6.667), and there was also a cooked must product with medical uses, known as *adynamos oinos* 'impotent wine' (Dioscorides *MM* 5.6).

- Greek *omphakion* and Latin *omphacium* are names for verjuice, the juice of unripe grapes (of the *psithia* and *aminnaia* varieties, according to Dioscorides). This was used medicinally and as a culinary ingredient. The same Greek and Latin term is used for the oil of unripe olives.

  Dioscorides *MM* 5.5; Pliny *NH* 12.131, 23.7; Galen, *On Compounding* 12.902; Anthimus *OC* 94.

- Greek *oinanthe* is the name of an oil or extract made from the wild vine and used in perfumes and medicinally.

Pliny *NH* 12.132, 23.8–9, 23.19–20.

Mustard, the hottest of northern spices. Mustard was in use in northern Greece before 2000 BC and was thoroughly familiar in classical Greece and Rome. In ancient sources it is generally listed as a herb, not a spice: this reflects its local origin and cheapness – the same could be said of coriander – rather than its actual uses, for it was and is generally the seed of mustard that is of most interest to humans. These seeds can be used directly in flavouring cooked dishes, but in Europe, certainly since Roman times, their usual fate is to form the main ingredient of a sauce with an unmistakable yellow colour, a biting taste and a tendency to make the nose smart. The earliest recipes for mustard sauce are given by Columella and Palladius; Columella already describes it as 'brightly coloured'. You ate it with ham, with other meats and with certain fish including swordfish.

The word 'mustard' and its equivalents in many other languages refer to at least three plant species (*Brassica nigra*, black mustard; *Sinapis alba*, white mustard; *Brassica juncea*, brown mustard), of which the first two were certainly known

in the classical Mediterranean. The Greek term is *napy*, the Latin *sinapi*.

Hippocrates *R* 54; Theophrastus *HP* 7.3.2; Columella *DA* 12.57; Pliny *NH* 19.170–1, 20.236–40; Macrobius *S* 6.5.5 quoting Ennius; Palladius *OA* 8.9, 11.11.2.

Darby and others 1977 pp. 803–4; Zohary and Hopf 1993 p. 132.

- The Greek name *anarrinon* may refer to the related vegetable now called mustard greens (*Sinapis arvensis*).

  Aristotle, *Problems* 925a30; Athenaeus 369b citing Speusippus.

Mutton *see* SHEEP

Mycenaeans, bearers of the culture represented by the palaces of Mycenae and Pylos (in mainland Greece) and Knossos (in Crete) in the later first millennium BC. Aspects of the culture are recorded in Linear B tablets, written in an early form of Greek, which were used for accounting in these palaces. Mycenaean uses of foods, perfumes and wines have been studied by way of the tablets and also through archaeological investigations of these and other contemporary sites.

The traditional view is that the adventures narrated in the *Iliad* and *Odyssey*, in so far as they took place at all, are to be dated to the Mycenaean period. Mycenae itself was a significant place in those stories: in archaeological reality it was significant at this period and not at any later date. However, HOMERIC SOCIETY as described in the two epics has little resemblance to the way of life and the social structure represented by the Mycenaean palaces.

A.J.B. Wace, 'Mycenae 1939–1952: the house of the oil merchant' in *Annual of the British School at Athens* vol. 48 (1953) pp. 9–15; E.D. Foster, 'An administrative department at Pylos dealing with perfumery and offerings' in *Minos* vol. 16 (1975) pp. 19–51; G. Säflund, 'Sacrificial banquets in the Palace of Nestor' in *Opuscula Atheniensia* vol. 13 (1980) pp. 237–46; J.L. Perpillou, 'Vinealia 1. Vignes mycéniennes, homériques, historiques: permanence de formules?' in *Revue de philologie* 3rd ser.

vol. 55 (1981) pp. 41–55; J.L. Melena, 'Olive oil and other sorts of oil in the Mycenaean tablets' in *Minos* vol. 18 (1983) pp. 82–123; C.W. Shelmerdine, *The Perfume Industry of Mycenaean Pylos* (Göteborg, 1985); P. Halstead, 'The Mycenaean palatial economy: making the most of the gaps in the evidence' in *Proceedings of the Cambridge Philological Society* vol. 38 (1992) pp. 57–86; Ruth Palmer, 'Wine and viticulture in the Linear A and B texts of the Bronze Age Aegean' in *The Origins and Ancient History of Wine* ed. Patrick E. McGovern, Stuart J. Fleming and Solomon H. Katz (London: Gordon and Breach, 1995) pp. 269–85; James C. Wright, 'Empty cups and empty jugs: the social role of wine in Minoan and Mycenaean societies' in *The Origins and Ancient History of Wine* ed. Patrick E. McGovern, Stuart J. Fleming and Solomon H. Katz (London: Gordon and Breach, 1995) pp. 287–309; Yannis Hamilakis, 'Wine, oil and the dialectics of power in Bronze Age Crete: a review of the evidence' in *Oxford Journal of Archaeology* vol. 15 (1996) pp. 1–32; Yannis Hamilakis, 'Food technologies, technologies of the body: the social context of wine and oil production and consumption in Bronze Age Crete' in *World Archaeology* vol. 31 (1999) pp. 38–54.

Myma, a meat dish that incorporated the blood of the animal. Athenaeus quotes a recipe from EPAENETUS:

A *myma* of any sacrificial animal, or chicken, is to be made by chopping the lean meat finely, mincing liver and offal with blood, and flavouring with vinegar, melted cheese, silphium, cumin, thyme leaf, thyme seed, Roman hyssop, coriander leaf, coriander seed, Welsh onion, peeled fried onion (or poppy seed), raisins (or honey) and the seeds of a sour pomegranate. You may also use it as a relish.

Grant 1999 pp. 128–9 gives a modern interpretation of Epaenetus's recipe.

Athenaeus *D* 662d citing Epaenetus and Artemidorus.

Myrrh, aromatic resin with many uses in ancient religion and medicine. Myrrh was an aroma familiar at feasts, including weddings. Theophrastus and several later authors note its use as an ingredient in spiced wine. It has a 'slightly bitter' taste, according to Pliny, but was added to wine not for the sake of the taste but for its heady aroma with its festive and erotic associations. Myrrh comes from southern Arabia and the nearby Somali coast (and nowhere else: it has never been naturalised elsewhere). It had been familiar to Egyptians and Assyrians in the second millennium BC; in classical times it reached Mediterranean lands by way of the Red Sea trade.

Myrrh, the resin of *Commiphora Myrrha*, is *smyrna* in Greek, *murra* or *myrra* in Latin (compare Akkadian *murru*). The alternative Greek term *stakte* corresponds to Hebrew *nātāf* and properly denotes a high-quality myrrh, 'droplet' or 'tear', containing no impurities.

Sappho 44 Lobel; *Exodus* 30.34; *Psalms* 45.8; *Proverbs* 7.17–18; Herodotus *H* 2.73; Theophrastus *HP* 9.4.1–10, *al.*, *O* 21, 32, 34; Horace, *Odes* 3.14.21–4; Dioscorides *MM* 1.64; Pliny *NH* 12.66–71; John, *Gospel* 19.39; Plutarch, *On Isis and Osiris* 383c; Galen *SF* 12.127; *Geoponica* 8.22 citing Didymus.

Laufer 1919 pp. 460–2; Miller 1969 pp. 104–5, 108; N. Groom, *Frankincense and Myrrh* (London, 1981); Casson 1989 pp. 118–20; Dalby 2000b pp. 113–22.

- The resin called *bdolah* in Hebrew, *bdella* or *bdellion* in Greek, *bdellium* in Latin, resembled myrrh. Bdellium was one of the products of the Garden of Eden according to *Genesis*; in *Numbers* the appearance of MANNA is likened to it. The Septuagint translators of the Bible did not understand the Hebrew term. Bdellium, now usually called gum guggul, is in fact a product of the tree *Commiphora Mukul*, which is native to Baluchistan and Sind; however, in Greek scientific sources before the first century AD, this product is not separately named but is identified with myrrh. Bdellium was exported in the first and second centuries from the Indo-Scythian port Barbarice at the mouth of the Indus, hence Galen's term *bdellion skythikon* 'Scythian bdellium'.

Genesis 2.12; *Numbers* 11.7; Theophrastus *HP* 4.4.13; Strabo 15.2.3; Dioscorides *MM* 1.67; *Periplus Maris Erythraei* 39, *al.*; Pliny *NH* 12.35–6; Galen *SF* 11.849, *To Glaucon* on *Therapeutic Method* 11.106; Oribasius *CM* 14.38.8.

Laufer 1919 pp. 464–7; Miller 1969 pp. 69–71; Yule and Burnell 1903 pp. 76, 386.

- Greek *kankamon*, Latin *cancamum* was another resin resembling myrrh. *Cancamum* was exported in classical times by Arab traders at Malao (probably modern Berbera, Somalia). It is the resin now called bisabol, African bdellium and sometimes opopanax; it comes from the trees *Commiphora erythraea* and *C. Kataf*. An alternative identification with turmeric (Sanskrit *kunkuma*) goes against the evidence.

Dioscorides *MM* 1.24; *Periplus Maris Erythraei* 8 with Casson *ad l.*; Pliny *NH* 12.98.

Myrtle, a decorative and aromatic plant which also bears edible berries. Native to southern Europe and the Near East, myrtle was a garden shrub in the classical world. Theophrastus, who seldom mentions central Italy at all, observes how prolifically myrtle grew in Latium.

Myrtle was more important to Greeks and Romans symbolically than as a fruit. It was sacred to Aphrodite and Venus – and 'myrtle berry' alluded in comic double entendre to the clitoris. However, there is a better reason why myrtle berries were chewed by the protagonists of Menander's play *Synaristosai* 'Women lunching together': according to Pliny (*NH* 23.159), they keep the breath fresh.

The aromatic leaves were worn as a wreath at dinners and symposia. A myrtle branch called *aisakos*, Plutarch assures us, was passed from one participant to another at symposia and the eventual recipient was supposed to sing or play the lyre. Myrtle berries were chewed fresh, but were perhaps most often used dried, as a condiment, a European predecessor of and occasional substitute for pepper. As such myrtle berries gave a name to the dish *myrtatum*, and in classical Roman

cuisine were still regarded as necessary to the sauce served with wild boar. Myrtle oil was used as an aromatic and myrtle wine was used medicinally: recipes for both are given by Palladius.

The myrtle shrub (*Myrtus communis*) is Greek *myrrine*, Latin *myrtus*. The berry is Greek *myrton*, Latin *myrtum*.

Aristophanes, *Birds* 160, 1100, *Lysistrata* 632, 1004, *Knights* 964 with scholia; Plato Comicus F 188 Kassel with Kassel *ad l.*; Plato, *Republic* 372c; Theophrastus *HP* 1.12.1, 5.8.3, *Characters* 11.4; Dioscorides *MM* 1.112, 5.28; Pliny *NH* 12.3, 15.118–26, 23.159–66; Plutarch *QC* 1.1, cf. Hesychius *s.v. aisakos*; Palladius *OA* 2.17–18, 3.27, 3.31; *Suda s.v. myrton*.

Henderson 1991 pp. 134–5.

- The bilberry (*Vaccinium Myrtillus*), a low-growing plant which has a superficially similar fruit, was regarded as a kind of wild myrtle. Pliny describes it under the name *chamaemyrsine*, but this name was also sometimes used for butcher's broom (*Ruscus aculeatus*).

Pliny *NH* 15.27.

Mysian wine (Greek *Mysios*), from Hellespontine Mysia, a wine that is likened by Galen to Surrentine.

Galen *ST* 6.334–5, *On Therapeutic Method* 10.833, *On Compounding* 13.660 (read *Mysios*).

Myttotos, a garlic sauce familiar in archaic and classical Greek cuisine. *Myttotos* was to be eaten with tunny, according to Ananius. In a passage in Aristophanes's *Peace* that is laden with unreliable meanings, a *myttotos* recipe is sketched incorporating leeks, garlic, cheese and honey, standing respectively for Prasiae (a play on words: *prason* 'leek'), Megara, Sicily and Attica.

Hipponax 26 West; Ananius 5 West; Aristophanes, *Peace* 227–58; Galen, *Hippocratic Glosses* 19.124.

N

Names and identifications. Work on the identification of plant and animal sources of foods mentioned in Greek and Roman texts uses the following forms of evidence, which are not in order of importance: (1) the descriptions in the texts; (2) the history of Greek and Latin words, their origin if traceable, and their linguistic descendants if any; (3) the present flora and fauna of Greece, Italy and their neighbours; (4) modern knowledge and use of plants and animals (ethnobotany and ethnozoology) in the region; (5) the recorded history of plant and animal discovery, use and transplanting; (6) AR-CHAEOBOTANY and ARCHAEOZOOLOGY. Problems are caused by inadequate information, by difficulties and confusions over identification in all these forms of evidence, and by conflicts among them.

In each culture, and therefore in each language and dialect, names and classifications correspond to local observations and needs; 'species' and groups named in, say, Latin will therefore not equate precisely with those named in English, and will not correspond consistently with any particular level in scientific taxonomy. In addition, words are used with different meanings from place to place and from time to time, and each particular author may have a preferred usage. Finally, not everything said in the texts is the result of first-hand observation; even the most careful of authors may be wrong or confused on occasion.

Those unfamiliar with scientific nomenclature need to be aware that the fact that a generic or specific name in scientific Latin coincides with a classical Latin or Greek name is no positive evidence for an identification: the scientific names, as such, have been freshly devised by Linnaeus and later taxonomists, and historical continuity has not been their chief criterion. However, Linnaeus, when choosing to re-use a Latin or Greek name, did so on the basis of enviable familiarity with classical sources and often in the light of continuous use of the name through medieval Latin and down to his own time: that is why so many of the binomials chosen by Linnaeus himself (see the index of scientific names) do in fact correspond with classical names for the same species.

Thompson 1936; L. Lacroix, 'Noms de poissons et noms d'oiseaux en grec ancien' in *Antiquité classique* vol. 6 (1937) pp. 265–302; Thompson 1947; R.C. Thompson, *Dictionary of Assyrian Botany* (London, 1949); Jacques André, *Lexique des termes de botanique en latin* (Paris, 1956); Jacques André, *Notes de lexicographie botanique grecque* (Paris, 1958); H.A. Hoffner, *Alimenta Hethaeorum* (New Haven, 1974); *Actes du colloque international 'Les phytonymes grecs et latins' tenu à Nice les 14–16 mai 1992* (Nice: Université de Nice-Sophia Antipolis [1993?]); *Des hommes et des plantes: plantes méditerranéennes, vocabulaire et usages anciennes* ed. M.-C. Amouretti and

G. Comet (Aix-en-Provence, 1993); Iohannes Stirling, *Lexicon nominum herbarum, arborum fruticumque linguae Latinae ex fontibus Latinitatis ante saeculum XVII scriptis* (Budapest: Encyclopaedia, 1995–); Françoise Gaide, 'Les noms latins des plantes médicinales comme vestiges d'une tradition orale' in *Les Structures de l'oralité en latin: colloque du Centre Alfred Ernout, juin 1994* ed. Jacqueline Dangel and Claude Moussy (Paris, 1996) pp. 99–108; José Fortes Fortes, 'Anatolische und griechische Pflanzennamen: Methodologie ihrer etymologischen Erforschung' in *Faventia* vol. 21 (1999) pp. 15–28; J.E. Raven and others, *Plants and Plant Lore in Ancient Greece* (Oxford: Leopard's Head Press, 2000).

Naples (Greek and Latin *Neapolis*), Greek colony on the coast of Campania. A centre of the Greek way of life, Naples was also renowned for its wine (see NEAPOLITAN WINES; GAURAN WINE) and for its seafood, not all of which came from the sea: there were many fishponds in the neighbourhood, including those created by LUCULLUS. For a while, in the later first century AD, the beautiful and costly *scarus* or parrot wrasse (see under WRASSE) abounded. There were good chestnuts, too.

Strabo 5.4.7; Pliny *NH* 15.94; Martial 5.78.

D'Arms 1970 *passim*; Dalby 2000a pp. 54–5.

Narbonensian wines, from modern Provence and Languedoc, the Roman *Provincia* (known more explicitly as *Gallia Narbonensis*). The cultivated grape vine was introduced to the region, in all probability, by Phoenicians or by the Greeks of MASSILIA. By Roman imperial times the high quality of some of the wines of Narbonensis, and the low quality of others, was already noted.

A. Aymard, 'L'interdiction de plantations de vignes en Gaule transalpine sous la République romaine' in *Mélanges Faucher* (Toulouse, 1948) pp. 27–47, reprinted in *Etudes d'histoire ancienne* (Paris, 1968) pp. 409–17; A. Tchernia, 'Italian wine in Gaul at the end of the Republic' in *Trade in the Ancient Economy* ed. Peter Garnsey, K. Hopkins and C.R. Whittaker (London, 1983) pp. 87–104; Jean-Pierre Brun, 'L'oléiculture et la viticulture antiques en Gaule d'après les vestiges d'installations' in *La Pro-*

duction du vin et de l'huile en Méditerranée ed. M.-C. Amouretti and J.-P. Brun (Athens: Ecole Française d'Athènes, 1993) pp. 307–41.

- 'A different kind of raisin wine, known locally as *dulce*' was produced among the Vocontii. The name (*vinum*) *dulce* is the direct ancestor of French *vin doux*. The district now produces Clairette de Die, not a *vin doux* but a sweet sparkling wine.

Pliny *NH* 14.83–4.

- A wine with a natural flavour of pitch, produced around Vienna (modern Vienne, south of Lyon), was sold locally at a higher price than wines of more usual flavour. This wine was supposed to be colder (in terms of humoral theory) than any other. For the *allobrox* group of grape varieties originating here see under GRAPE VARIETIES.

Pliny *NH* 14.18, 14.26, 14.57; Martial 7.88, 13.107; Plutarch *QC* 5.3.

- Massilian wine (Greek *Massalietes, Massaliotes*) is said in the *Epitome of Athenaeus*, in a list originating in the first century AD, to be a fine wine, produced in small quantities, thick and fleshy. Pliny knows of this type, describing it as sappy and fat. He adds that there is another type, and that might be the one listed by Galen among wines that are light, white and with little astringency.

Pliny *NH* 14.68; Galen, *To Glaucon on Therapeutic Method* 11.87; Athenaeus E 27c.

- The wine of Baeterrae, modern Béziers, is said by Pliny to have a high reputation locally. Other wines of Narbonensis, excluding those named above, come in for Pliny's disapproval. They are smoked and (he wishes he did not have to say this) flavoured with aromatics such as aloes. These are no doubt the 'musts cooked in Massilian smoke' of which Martial, also, strongly disapproved.

Pliny *NH* 14.68; Martial 3.82, 10.36, 13.123, 14.118.

Dalby 2000a pp. 95–6.

Nard, or in full spikenard, aromatic root originating in the Himalayas – 'Himalaya, producer of many perfumes, rich with hundreds of magical drugs' (*Milindapañha* 4.8.16) – and reaching the Mediterranean by way of the Indian Ocean trade. Spikenard was much prized in the ancient West; so much so that Seleucus, presumably Seleucus I of Syria in the early third century BC, was said to have tried without success to transplant it to Arabia. It was a perfume, costly enough to be presented in a glass bottle; it was frequently used in compound medicines, and occasionally in cuisine. It is called for twice in the recipes of *Apicius*.

Spikenard (*Nardostachys Jatamansi*) is Greek *nardon* or *nardostakhys*, Latin *nardus*.

Theophrastus *HP* 9.7.2–4; Antiphilus 1 Gow [*Anthologia Palatina* 6.250]; Dioscorides *MM* 1.7–12; Pliny *NH* 12.42–6, 16.135, 21.135–6; Arrian, *Anabasis* 6.22.5; Galen *ST* 6.339, *SF* 12.15, *On Compounding* 12.606, cf. *DA* 14.71.

Laufer 1919 pp. 455–6; W.H. Schoff, 'Nard' in *Journal of the American Oriental Society* vol. 43 (1923) pp. 216–28; Miller 1969 pp. 88–92; Egon Brucker, 'Ai. *nálada* = *Nardostachys jatamansi*: ein Beitrag zur indischen Pflanzenkunde' in *Asiatische Studien* vol. 19 (1975) pp. 131–6.

- The Latin name *nardum rusticum* 'country nard' was occasionally given to the medicinal plant *Asarum europaeum*, hazelwort, according to Pliny. Known in Greek as *asaron*, this was the source of the classical Greek perfume *bakkaris* (on which see Athenaeus) and was later used in medicinal drinks, for which Oribasius supplies a recipe.

Pliny *NH* 12.47, 21.30; Athenaeus *D* 690a–c quoting Hipponax 104.21–2 West; Oribasius *CM* 5.33.8; Hesychius, *Lexicon s.v. bakkaris*.

Neapolitan wines, from the neighbourhood of Naples in Campania. In the late second century Galen sometimes specifies a Neapolitan wine made with an *aminnia* grape (*Neapolites ho Aminaios*). This designation had possibly supplanted those listed below.

Galen *ST* 6.335, *BM* 6.806, *DA* 14.16, *On Therapeutic Method* 10.833.

- Trebellic wine (Latin *Trebellicum*, Greek *Trebillikos*) came from a district 'at the fourth milestone' from Naples. This wine was briefly esteemed in the mid first century AD.

Pliny *NH* 14.69; Athenaeus *E* 27c.

- Vesuvine wine (Latin *Vesuvinum*) came from the slopes of Vesuvius in the first century. Here the commonly grown grape variety was *gemina minor* of the *aminnia* group. It liked a western breeze in summer; it gave a wine that was harsher than some, but kept well. The *murgentina* or *pompeiana* grape was also grown. Both had been transplanted from Sicily. The vineyards were destroyed in the volcanic eruption of AD 79.

Columella *DA* 3.2.10; Martial 4.44.

- Pompeian wine (Latin *Pompeianum*) would improve for up to ten years in amphora, said Pliny, but was betrayed as unwholesome by the fact that it caused headache.

Pliny *NH* 14.70.

Nectar *see* AMBROSIA AND NECTAR

Nero, Roman emperor (ruled AD 54–68). Nero's lavish public banquets, in common with some of his less amiable pastimes, were famous long after his death. The splendid dining rooms in his grandiose *Domus Aurea* or 'Golden House' were destroyed soon after his death, as was the rest of the palace, parts of which are now being excavated. His contribution to gastronomy was equivocal. He is said to have put an end to the production of CAECUBAN WINE, the vineyard having been abandoned because his planned ship canal from Puteoli to Rome would have passed through it. On the credit side, he devised a system of boiling water and then chilling it in snow, a relatively safe way of adding ice-cold water (*decocta*) to wine for summer drinking (see under WATER).

Pliny *NH* 14.61, 19.38, 31.40; Suetonius, *Nero* 26–7, 31, 48; Dio Cassius 62.15.1–6.

D. Hemsoll, 'Reconstructing the octagonal dining room of Nero's Golden House' in *Architectural History* vol. 32 (1989) pp. 1–17; J. Goddard, 'The tyrant at table' in *Reflections of Nero: culture, history and representation* ed. Jas Elsner and Jamie Masters (London, 1994) pp. 67–82.

Nettle, a stinging plant all too familiar in Mediterranean lands, but also an important potherb and medicinal plant. Nettle was not a gourmet item but was a regular part of the ancient diet. Young nettle tops were gathered in late winter and early spring 'before the swallow comes' or 'when the sun is in Aries'. Boiling removes the sting.

Nettle (*Urtica dioica* and other species) is Greek *knide, akalephe*, Latin *urtica*.

Aristophanes, *Knights* 422 with scholia; Hippocrates *R* 54; Theophrastus *HP* 7.7.2; Dioscorides *MM* 4.93; Pliny *NH* 22.31–8; Persius 6.70; Galen *AF* 6.639; *Apicius* 3.17.

Mrs M. Grieve, *A Modern Herbal* ed. H. Leyel (London, 1931) *s.v.* 'Nettles'; Lambraki 1997 pp. 145–53.

Nicander of Colophon, Greek poet, apparently of the mid second century BC. His two surviving poems are catalogues of antidotes to poisons and venoms; they give a good deal of information on edible plants and other foods. Several fragments of a lost poem on farming, *Georgica*, including recipes, are quoted by Athenaeus. Another of Nicander's works was dedicated to ATTALUS Philometor. However, there are doubts whether all the poems ascribed to Nicander are by the same person, and there are also contradictions in the sources concerning his date.

John Scarborough, 'Nicander's toxicology, part 1: snakes' in *Pharmacy in History* vol. 19 (1977) pp. 3–23; John Scarborough, 'Nicander's toxicology, II: spiders, scorpions, insects and myriapods' in *Pharmacy in History* vol. 21 (1979) pp. 3–34, 73–92; Scarborough 1985.

Nicander A: *Alexipharmaca*. Critical text, translation and commentary: *Nicander* ed. A.S.F. Gow and A.F. Scholfield (Cambridge: Cambridge University Press, 1953).

—— T: *Theriaca*. Critical text, translation and commentary as above.

—— F: fragments. Critical text: Otto Schneider, *Nicandrea* (Leipzig: Teubner, 1856). Text, translation and commentary on selected fragments in Gow and Scholfield (above).

Nigella *see* CUMIN

Nightshade, a climbing plant grown in gardens as a potherb. The Greek name was also applied to some poisonous plants of the same botanical family: see Theophrastus and Dioscorides. Pliny is aware of the possibilities for confusion between the garden plant and its dangerous relatives and for this reason discourages its use.

Nightshade (garden nightshade, black nightshade: *Solanum nigrum*) is Greek *strykhnos*, Latin *solanum*.

Hippocrates *R* 54; Theophrastus *HP* 7.7.2, 7.15.4, 9.11.5–6; Dioscorides *MM* 4.72; Pliny *NH* 21.177–82, 27.132.

Lambraki 1997 pp. 65–9; Davidson 1999 p. 533.

Nile fish, a highly important nutritional source in ancient Egypt. Many species were regarded as sacred at one or other of the towns of Egypt (examples below: see also Plutarch), but this did not prevent their being eaten elsewhere. Information on the use of fish in Pharaonic Egypt comes from finds of mummified and dried fish and fish bones, also from the many reliefs and paintings on which fish are carefully and accurately depicted, and finally from Egyptian texts, notably medical prescriptions.

The fish of the Nile were largely of different species from those familiar elsewhere in the Mediterranean basin, and were (as observed by Diodorus) far more plentiful and varied than those of any other river known to Greeks and Romans. Herodotus, in the fifth century, had already remarked on the income derived by the Egyptian kingdom from taxing the fisheries. Some fish were trapped and caught in backwaters as the annual Nile flood receded; traps, nets, fishing lines and harpoons were also familiar. Lake Moeris, connected with the Nile by a canal, had twenty-two species of fish and a busy salting industry.

Greeks who came to Egypt, before and particularly after the conquest by Alexander, needed to become familiar with Nile fish species that were used for food; they were well prepared for the enquiry, since they themselves came from a culture in which fish (albeit sea fish) were highly valued. The Greek names that they applied to the Nile species are sometimes loanwords from Egyptian, sometimes existing Greek words to which new meanings were applied.

Some fish were eaten fresh – reliefs show them being roasted on a spit. Probably the great majority were salted or sun-dried, and some of these were familiar beyond Egypt, as shown by Lucian and (if read literally) Martial. The dietary writer Xenocrates gives a survey of Nile fish that were salted:

> The river and lagoon fish of the Nile include the big *simos* and *phagros*, which are so extremely oily that they are boiled and eaten with mustard: if too many are eaten, they are not digested. Moving to less extreme items, the *kestreus* [grey mullet] is preserved in several ways: those cut down the spine are called *Mendesioi*, the whole ones are *halykatoi*. The potted ones are *boreis*; sometimes these are skinned, cut into pieces and eaten raw. The ones called *akropastoi*, salt-sprinkled, are good; they are eaten baked, and so are the *halykatoi* and the *Mendesioi*. As to the *korakinos*, when these are preserved they are called *hemineroi*. They, too, are baked, and are like a seasonal fruit – they are not always available, but only towards winter. Finally the preserved fish that are least oily. They are eaten raw, and are nothing very special, but each has its own particular flavour when eaten with bitter vegetables, and they had better be named for completeness' sake. They are called *korakidion, boridion, kolidion, typhlenidion, abramidion*; they are all hard to digest, difficult to break down, and laxative.

Athenaeus, native of the old harbour town of Naucratis, often mentions Nile fish in the *Deipnosophists* and at one point provides a general survey:

> The *latos* of the Nile grows to a weight of over two hundred pounds. It is very white and sweet, whichever cooking method is used, and much resembles the *glanis* of the Danube. The Nile produces many other species of fish, all good to eat, notably the *korakinoi*, of which there are several kinds. It also produces the *maiotes* ... Other Nile fish – if I can still recall them after many years' absence – are these: *narke*, the sweetest of all; *khoiros*; *simos*; *phagros*; *oxyrynkhos*; *allabes*; *silouros*; *synodontis*; *eleotris*; *enkhelys*; *thrissa*; *abramis*; *typhlen*; *lepidotos*; *physa*; *kestreus* [grey mullet]. There are several others as well.

A third list, not quoted here, is given by Strabo in the course of a discussion of animals and plants found only in Egypt.

From these lists, the important fish named *kestreus* is the GREY MULLET, probably the favourite salt fish of Egypt in ancient as in modern times. *Enkhelys* is the EEL; *thrissa* the SHAD. The remaining Nile fish known from these and other classical texts are listed separately below, omitting those that are named in only one source and are unidentified.

Herodotus 2.92, 2.149; Heliodorus, *Ethiopian Story* 1.5; Diodorus Siculus 1.36, 1.43, 1.52; Strabo 17.2.4; Lucian, *The Ship* 15; Xenocrates T 148–52; Athenaeus D 311f–312b, *al.*

Thompson 1947 *passim*; Darby and others 1977 pp. 336–404, with many illustrations; J. Dumont, 'La Pêche dans le Fayoum hellénistique' in *Chronique d'Égypte* vol. 52 no. 103 (1977) pp. 125–42; D.J. Brewer and R.F. Friedman, *Fish and Fishing in Ancient Egypt* (Warminster: Aris, 1989).

• Greek *abramis* and *abramidion* are identified with *Tilapia nilotica* by Thompson. This is problematic because Xenocrates and Athenaeus, who should know, distinguish these names from *korakinos*, which is more confidently identified with *T. nilotica* (see below). Oppian describes *abramis* as a migratory fish which moves in shoals; this does not suit *T. nilotica*.

Xenocrates *T* 152; Oppian *H* 1.244; Athenaeus *D* 312b.

- Greek *allabes*, Egyptian *lbs*, Coptic *labes* and *leifi*, is a relative of the carp, *Labeo niloticus*.

  Strabo 17.2.4; Pliny *NH* 5.51; Athenaeus *D* 312b.

- Greek *khoiros*, literally 'piglet', may be the schall, *Synodontis Schall*, which – like the *khoiros* as described by Aristotle – makes a distinctive noise with its fins.

  Strabo 17.2.4–5; Athenaeus *D* 312b, also 331d citing Aristotle fragment 272 Rose.

  Andrews 1948.

- Greek *korakinos* or *peltes*, Latin *coracinus*, is the bolti, *Tilapia nilotica*, 'the best of all Nile fishes' according to Thompson and frequently illustrated on tomb reliefs and paintings. Athenaeus recalled nice fat *korakinoi* at Alexandria. The salted form of this fish, *hemineros*, is so named by Xenocrates, by Athenaeus and apparently by Diphilus. It was eaten baked or boiled, and Diphilus approved the latter method. It (and its smell) reached as far as Rome, suggesting to Martial the name 'Coracinus' for a subject whose foul breath gave rise to the imputation that he practised cunnilingus. Greek *korakinos* is also the name of a Mediterranean fish (see CASTAGNOLE).

  Martial 4.43, 13.85; Xenocrates *T* 151–2; Athenaeus *D* 118f, also 121b citing Diphilus of Siphnos, also 308d–309a, also 311f, also 356a citing Diphilus of Siphnos.

- Greek *latos* is the Nile perch, *Lates niloticus*, likewise very good to eat. Many specimens of the Nile perch were mummified at the town whose Greek name is Latopolis, where this fish was sacred. Greek *latos* is also the name of an unidentified fish described as 'wonderful food' at the Straits of Messina.

  Strabo 17.2.4; Athenaeus *D* 311e–312b.

- Greek *lepidotos* and Egyptian *bwt* are probably *Barbus Bynni*; for other possible identifications see Thompson. This was a sacred fish at Egyptian Thebes, where many mummified specimens have been found.

  Strabo 17.2.4; Plutarch, *On Isis and Osiris* 358b; Athenaeus *D* 309b, 312b.

- Greek *maiotes* is unidentified, both as a fish of the Nile and as one found in the Sea of Azov. The Egyptian species gave warning of the Nile's annual flood, according to Aelian. It was sacred at Elephantine.

Aelian, *Nature of Animals* 10.19; Athenaeus *D* 312a; Clement of Alexandria, *Protrepticus* 2.39.5.

- Greek *narke* is the electric catfish, *Malapterurus electricus*. Its Greek name is borrowed from that of the Mediterranean electric ray (see RAY), because both species defend themselves with an electric shock. Athenaeus considered this the best to eat of all Nile fish.

  Athenaeus *D* 312b.

- Greek *notidanos* and *epinotideus* may possibly be *Synodontis Batensoda*.

  Athenaeus *D* 294d citing Epaenetus.

- Greek *oxyrynkhos*, so named from its sharp, downturned snout, is *Mormyrus Caschive* and related species. It was sacred to Set and was especially honoured at the Egyptian town named (in Greek) after this fish, Oxyrhynchus. The place is now known for the vast hoard of fragmentary Greek papyri found there. Greek *oxyrynkhos* is also the name of a STURGEON.

  Strabo 17.2.4; Plutarch, *On Isis and Osiris* 358b, 380b; Aelian, *Nature of Animals* 10.46; Athenaeus *D* 312b; Clement of Alexandria, *Protrepticus* 2.39.5.

- Greek *phagros* or *phagrorios*: this species gave warning of the Nile's annual flood, according to Aelian. It was sacred at Syene. It may possibly be the raschal, *Hydrocyon Forskalii*. *Kapriskos* is an alternative name. Greek *phagros* is also the name of a sea fish, a species of BREAM; the river kind was not such good eating, according to Diphilus.

  Strabo 17.2.4, cf. 17.1.26; Pliny *NH* 32.113; Xenocrates *T* 148; Plutarch, *On Isis and Osiris* 358b; Aelian, *Nature of Animals* 10.19; Athenaeus *D* 312b, also 355f citing Diphilus of Siphnos; Clement of Alexandria, *Protrepticus* 2.39.5.

  Andrews 1948.

- Greek *physa* may be the globefish, *Tetraodon Fahaka*.

  Strabo 17.2.4; Aelian, *Nature of Animals* 12.13; Athenaeus *D* 312b.

- Greek *silouros*, Latin *silurus*, when it is the name of a Nile fish, may be a small, not very good, but commonly eaten catfish such as *Clarias anguillaris*: this is frequently illustrated in reliefs and paintings. For other identifications see Thompson. Greek *silouros* is also the name of the SHEATFISH.

Strabo 17.2.4; Juvenal 4.32; Athenaeus *D* 230e quoting Sopater 15 Kaibel.

- Greek *simos, simarion* is unidentified; so is Greek *typhlen, typhlenidion, typhlinos.*

Xenocrates *T* 148, 152; Athenaeus *D* 312b; *Oxyrhynchus Papyri* 1857.1.

- Greek *synodontis* may be the shilbe, *Schilbe Mystus.*

Athenaeus *D* 312b.

Nitron, soda, an *artyma* or condiment, used in ancient Greek cookery – as by our own grandmothers – to 'improve' boiled cabbage; and also in the tenderising of meat.

Theophrastus *CP* 2.5.3, cf. Antiphanes 140 Kassel; Plutarch *QC* 6.10.

Nola, Roman and modern Italian town in Campania. In this neighbourhood an eruption of Mount Vesuvius caused extensive destruction around 1500 BC. Farms and small houses are being excavated: they provide detailed evidence of foods and domesticated animals. In one house shoulders of pork and mutton were still hanging from a beam.

Claude Albore Livadie, 'Une Pompéi de l'âge du bronze' in *Archeologia* no. 387 (March 2002) pp. 14–19.

Numenius of Heracleia, Greek poet of the third century BC, a pupil of the physician Dieuches. Numenius's poem on fishing does not survive, but many short extracts from it are quoted by Athenaeus.

Athenaeus *E* 5b, 13b; *Suda s.v. Timakhidas.*

Numenius H: *Halieuticon.* Text in *Supplementum Hellenisticum* ed. H. Lloyd-Jones and P. Parsons (Berlin: De Gruyter, 1983). Translation in Gulick's edition of *Athenaeus.*

Nutrition, the scientific study of food and diet. The typical ancient diet consisted of cereals or legumes, plus wine, plus olive oil, plus vegetables and fruits, plus, when available and in small quantities, fish and meat; this same statement appears in different words under MEALS. But for

whom was it typical? We know enough of ancient thinking on DIET to know that the diet of men and women, babies, children and adults, young and old, will have varied significantly, but we do not know how closely practice matched theory. We know enough of ancient society to know that the diet of rich and poor, country-dwellers and city-dwellers, householders and dependants (a category including the great majority of slaves) will have varied widely, but we do not know enough of the nutritional consequences.

Malnutrition existed: its presence is clear from a few ancient literary sources and is now abundantly confirmed by analyses of bones and teeth from ancient burials. Garnsey (below) gives an outline of current knowledge on the presence of specific nutritional diseases, focusing on rickets, bladder stone, and eye diseases associated with vitamin A deficiency: again, these are described in ancient sources, if one knows how to recognise them, and are confirmed by archaeobiology. Darby and others explore evidence for nutritional diseases in Egypt.

A.S. Barclay and F.R. Earle, 'Chemical analyses of seeds, 3. Oil and protein content of 1253 species' in *Economic Botany* vol. 28 (1974) pp. 178–236; K.D. White, 'Food requirements and food supplies in classical times in relation to the diet of the various classes' in *Progress in Food and Nutritional Science* vol. 2 (1976) pp. 143–91; N.S. Scrimshaw and V.R. Young, 'The requirements of human nutrition' in *Scientific American* vol. 235 no. 3 (1976) pp. 55–70; Darby and others 1977 pp. 60–83; E.S. Wing and E.B. Brown, *Paleonutrition: method and theory in prehistoric foodways* (New York, 1979); L. Milano, 'Alimentazione e regime alimentari nella Siria preclassica' in *Dialoghi di archeologia* n.s. no. 3 (1981) pp. 85–120; L. Gallo, *Alimentazione e demografia della Grecia antica* (Salerno, 1984); S.C. Bisel and J.L. Angel, 'Health and nutrition in Mycenaean Greece: a study in human skeletal remains' in *Contributions to Aegean Archaeology: studies in honor of William A. McDonald* ed. N.C. Wilkie and W.D.E. Coulson (Minneapolis, 1985); D.V. Sippel, 'Dietary deficiency among the lower class of late Republican and early Imperial Rome' in *Ancient World* vol. 16 (1987) pp. 47–54; S. Bisel, 'Nutrition in first-century Herculaneum' in *Anthropologie* vol. 26 (1988) pp. 61–6; A. Ferro-Luzzi and S. Sette, 'The Mediterranean diet: an attempt to define its present and past composition' in *European Journal of Clinical Nutrition* vol. 43 suppl. 2 (1989) pp. 13–29; S.C. Bisel, *The Secrets of Vesuvius* (Sevenoaks, 1990); R. Sallares, *The Ecology of the Ancient Greek World* (London, 1991), review by Frank Frost in *Ancient History Bulletin* vol. 6 (1992) pp. 187–95; Francesco De Martino, 'Sull' alimentazione degli schiavi' in *Parola del passato* vol. 48 (1993) pp. 401–27; Garnsey 1999 esp. pp. 12–21, 43–61, with quotations and references.

O

Oats, a cereal known but not liked by classical Greeks and Romans. Wild oats had been gathered at Franchthi Cave as early as 11,000 BC, and also elsewhere in Mediterranean lands in prehistoric times, and continued to be used in classical times by those who had no choice. Oats was, however, regarded rather as a weed or degenerative disease of wheat and barley than as a potential crop in its own right. Pliny adds that the Germans grow oats and that a *puls* 'porridge' made from oats is their staple diet (this Latin term is roughly equivalent to the *alphita bromou* 'oatmeal' of Dieuches).

Oats (*Avena sativa*) is Greek *bromos*, *bormos*, Latin *avena*.

Hippocrates *R* 43; Pliny *NH* 18.149–50; Oribasius *CM* 1.14 with Grant *ad l.*, also 4.6.4 quoting Dieuches.

Buck 1949 pp. 517–8; Zohary and Hopf 1993 pp. 73–8; David M. Peterson and J. Paul Murphy, 'Oat' in *CWHF* 2000 vol. 1 pp. 121–32.

Octopus, group of marine cephalopods. Well known to Mediterranean peoples since prehistoric times, the octopus served as human food throughout the classical period. Its flesh must be beaten, against a stone or pillar, to tenderise it before cooking: 'the octopus must be beaten with twice seven blows', said the Greek proverb. A comedy fragment by Ephippus or Eubulus speaks of the custom 'to swing and beat many an octopus tentacle', synonymous in effect with cooking and eating many an octopus.

This was one of the foods that had an enduring aphrodisiac reputation. Athenaeus cites Diphilus of Siphnos on the subject, and in the following quotation cites the comic playwright Alexis:

> Octopus increases sexual vigour, but it is tough and indigestible. The larger species provides better nourishment. When boiled slowly, it settles the stomach and moistens the bowel. Alexis makes clear in *Pamphila* the usefulness of octopus, in these words: 'To a man in love, Cteson, what could be more useful than what I have brought with me? Whelks, scallops, bulbs, a big octopus, and hearty fish.'

The major edible species are enumerated below. Certain others, listed by Aristotle, are bad-smelling and inedible.

Hippocrates *R* 48; Plato Comicus *F* 189 Kassel; Ephippus 3 Kassel = Eubulus *F* 148 Kassel (see quotation at AMPHIDROMIA); Aristotle *HA* 525a13–19, 622a3–34; Pliny *NH* 9.83–93, 32.121; Galen *AF* 6.736; Athenaeus *D* 316a–318f quoting Archestratus *H* 53 Brandt (see Olson and Sens *ad l.*), also 356e quoting Alexis *F* 175 Kassel; *Apicius* 9.5; *Suda s.v. polypous*.

Thompson 1947 pp. 61, 204; Davidson 1981 pp. 213–15.

- The general terms, Greek *poulypous* or *polyps*, Latin *polypus*, apply to the two long-tentacled species, the larger *Octopus vulgaris* and the smaller *O. macropus*.

- Greek *eledone* is the curled octopus, particularly the edible species *Eledone cirrosa*.

Odysseus, hero of the *Odyssey*. Odysseus has his importance in the context of food history. His sack of Ismarus in southern Thrace and acquisition there of strong old wine from the priest Maron led to an allusion by Archilochus to 'Ismaric wine' and to the lasting reputation of nearby Maronea as a place for strong wine; Mucianus, in the first century AD, was persuaded that eight volumes of water must be added to each volume of Maronean wine. Odysseus's encounter with the CYCLOPS Polyphemus, later imagined as inhabiting Sicily, gave rise to later tales of Polyphemus as rustic shepherd and may have helped the classical reputation of Sicilian cheese. Odysseus's travels were evoked in Athenian satyr plays and mythological comedies, with food and cookery often prominent.

Homer, *Odyssey passim*; Archilochus 2 West; Aeschylus fragment 309 Radt (see quotation at *klibanos* under COOKING UTENSILS); Cratinus Junior 1 Kassel (see quotation at SICILY); Pliny *NH* 14.53–4 citing Mucianus ter consul.

Ofellae, Roman dish consisting of bite-sized meat pieces marinaded and cooked in a sauce. It was typical of tavern food. 'Who can live without *offulae*?' asked the emperor Claudius rhetorically in a Senate discussion of the regulation of cookshops. The Latin name is variously *ofellae*, *offulae*, *offlae* or *offae*. There was no better Greek name for this Roman favourite than, as Pollux suggests, *to diazomon* 'the stew'. Six recipes for *ofellae* are provided in *Apicius*.

Petronius *S* 56.8, 58.2; Suetonius, *Claudius* 40; Pollux *KH* 83; *Apicius* 7.4.1–6.

- The Latin word *offa* means literally 'food formed into a lump or ball' and is often used in its literal sense. Thus Psyche is advised to take along a couple of *offae* or *offulae* of

polenta to distract the ravening Cerberus when she visits the underworld.

Apuleius, *Metamorphoses* 6.18–19.

Offal *see* MEAT

Olive, tree fruit native to the eastern Mediterranean. The olive was probably domesticated in or near Syria in the fourth millennium BC (its wild ancestor is identified as *Olea chrysophylla*). It was in fairly intensive cultivation in Palestine and Syria in the third millennium BC. The olive was relatively unfamiliar in the ancient Near East; in most parts of the region it did not grow naturally and the commonly used vegetable oils came from other sources (see LINSEED; SESAME).

In Crete olive cultivation certainly dates to around 2000 BC at the latest. From Crete it spread slowly northwards to mainland Greece; how soon olives there began to be pressed for their oil, and how soon the oil became a staple product, is uncertain and controversial. At any rate, by the mid first millennium BC, under Greek and Phoenician influence, olive cultivation was extremely important in Greece, was familiar in large areas of Italy, and had extended to all the Mediterranean shores. There was a very distinct boundary (there still is) running west to east across southern Europe and Anatolia, north of which the olive will not fruit and is therefore seldom grown. It is a sign of the economic significance of the olive in classical times that this boundary is often mentioned in classical texts, even by authors not usually concerned with biogeography. The importance of the olive in Greece is further signalled by mythology in the story of the first olive tree, planted by ATHENA on the acropolis at Athens; there was an alternative origin myth, however, and Roman olive traders regarded *Hercules Olivarius* 'the olive-farmer' (see HERACLES) as their patron.

Olive trees are deep-rooted and slow to mature: it was an act of reckless war, in some eyes even an act of sacrilege, to destroy an enemy's olive plantations. If spared by war and climate these trees are very long-lived. Olive-growing regions, such as Greece and Italy, can show gnarled trees that are many hundreds of years old and are still fruiting reliably.

The fruit contains a glucoside which makes it very bitter, even when ripe. This bitter principle (or most of it) has to be removed as part of the process of curing olives for eating; however, it separates naturally when the fruit is pressed for OLIVE OIL, its principal product. Instructions for conserving are given by Columella and Palladius: some ancient types of conserved olives are listed below.

Many varieties of olive had been developed by classical times: Cato, Columella and Pliny give information on the subject. They varied both as regards the climate and terrain to which they were adapted, and as to whether they were better for pressing for oil, or for curing. The olive is unusual among cultivated fruits in that no variety has ever been developed that can be eaten raw. It is unique in the contribution that it makes to the human diet in the Mediterranean region, both as cured fruit and as oil.

The olive (*Olea europaea*) is Greek *elaia, elaa*, Latin *oliva*.

Herodotus 8.55; Theophrastus *HP* 1.14.2, 7.2.8–9, *al.*; Cato *DA* 6–7, 45, 64–8, *al.*; Columella *DA* 5.8–9, 12.49–51; Pliny *NH* 12.3, 15.1–34, 23.69–73; Athenaeus *E* 56a–d quoting Aristophanes fragment 408 Kassel; Macrobius *S* 3.20.6; Festus *s.v. orchitis*; Palladius *OA* 12.22; *Suda s.v. gergerimon*.

Buck 1949 p. 380–1; G. Vallet, 'L'introduction de l'olivier en Italie centrale d'après les données de la céramique' in *Hommages à Albert Grenier* vol. 3 (Brussels, 1962) (*Latomus*, 58) pp. 1554–63; J. Boardman, 'The olive in the Mediterranean: its culture and use' in *The Early History of Agriculture* ed. J. Hutchinson and others (London, 1976) (*Philosophical Transactions of the Royal Society of London*,

B 275) pp. 187–96; Darby and others 1977 pp. 718–21; C.N. Runnels and J. Hansen, 'The olive in the prehistoric Aegean: the evidence for domestication in the early Bronze Age' in *Oxford Journal of Archaeology* vol. 5 (1987) pp. 299–308; Zohary and Hopf 1993 pp. 137–43; *World Olive Encyclopaedia* (Madrid: International Olive Oil Council, 1996).

- *Thlastai* were olives crushed and cured in salt, like the Latin *olivae novae fractae* and the modern French *olives cassées*. The process is suited to young olives before they turn colour: Pollux and the *Geoponica* give details. The result of this kind of processing is a good rustic olive, but one that would not last long or travel far before the advent of refrigeration.

  Aristophanes fragment 408 Kassel; Poliochus 2 Kassel; Pollux O 6.45; *Apicius* 6.5.7; *Geoponica* 9.32.

- Among riper but still green olives are *halmades*, to which almost-virgin girls are compared in a fragment by Aristophanes. Fennel might be added to these as a flavouring. Also commonly mentioned are *kolymbades*. Both types were conserved in brine.

  Moeris, Phrynichus and Zonaras *s.v. halmades*, cf. Callimachus, *Hecale* 36 Hollis; Athenaeus *E* 56a–d, also *D* 133a quoting Aristophanes fragment 148 Kassel; Paul of Aegina, *Medicine* 1.81.3.

- Greek *drypepeis*, Latin *druppae*, are black, tree-ripened, wrinkled olives, associated with a simple traditional diet. You might compare *mazai* 'barley-cakes', or indeed old whores, with olives of this kind. Greek *gergerimoi* are another type of black olive.

  Aristophanes, *Lysistrata* 564 with scholia; Archestratus *H* 7 Brandt with Olson and Sens *ad l.*; Pliny *NH* 15.6; Galen *AF* 6.609; Marcus Aurelius, *Meditations* 3.2.2; Athenaeus *E* 56a–e quoting Eupolis 338 Kassel and Telecleides 40 Kassel, also *D* 133a quoting Aristophanes fragment 148 Kassel; Paul of Aegina, *Medicine* 1.81.3.

- Greek *pityrin* is a name for the cheapest olives, says Athenaeus. Latin *epityrum*, evidently the same word in origin, is an olive relish, for which a recipe is given by Cato. See the modern interpretations by Dalby and Grainger 1996 p. 31, Junkelmann 1997 p. 201 and Grant 1999 p. 75.

  Cato *DA* 119; Athenaeus *E* 56c.

Olive oil, the main product of the OLIVE and an extremely important food product of the ancient Mediterranean. Olive oil production involves three processes. The skin of the fruit must first be broken and the flesh crushed, preferably without breaking the stone. The pulp must then be pressed to release the oil. The oil must finally be separated from the watery *amurca* (see below). Oil can be extracted without the use of presses, but mechanisation must have been important in the development of olive oil production. A beam press was in use in Ugarit (Syria) around 1500 BC. Crushing mills and oil presses were widespread throughout the Mediterranean in Hellenistic and Roman times.

Once produced, olive oil must be stored in the dark; contact with air must be restricted. Ancient AMPHORAE were ideal for this purpose, so long as, once they were opened, the oil was used within a limited time. Olive oil, like wine, shows extreme variation in flavour and quality depending on fruit variety, growing conditions, harvesting and production methods, and storage. These variables can make all the difference between a luxury product with an established reputation for which gastronomes will pay very high prices, and a product that is almost unusable and almost unsaleable. Hence ancient authors such as Cato and Columella give close attention to QUALITY CONTROL.

Although olive oil is never a cheap product it is used generously in modern Mediterranean cuisines, as it clearly was in ancient cookery also. It served several food purposes. It was a medium for marinading meat and fish before cooking. It was a cooking medium. It was used as a dressing both for cooked food when served, and for fresh green vegetables; for this purpose it was sometimes used alone, sometimes mixed with vinegar and aromatic herbs. Finally it was used in conserving. Olive oil is one of the best cooking oils, since, apart from its unusual health benefits, it retains a good flavour and its boiling point is high. In ancient times it had no competition from cheaper vegetable oils, while in ancient Mediterranean cuisine animal fat was not used as a cooking medium.

On the edges of the classical world olive oil was less well known. Pharaonic Egypt imported olive oil from Palestine and Crete. By the twelfth century BC olives were growing in Egypt, and Theophrastus confirms that at the time of Alexander's conquest in the fourth century olives were grown for oil in the Thebaid, but this had been small-volume luxury production. In Mesopotamia before Hellenistic times olive oil was a rarity, sesame oil being used for most of the above purposes. In northern and central Europe before the Roman expansion, Poseidonius noted that the Celts found the taste of olive oil unpleasant 'because they are unused to it'. However, wherever the Roman army went, olive oil was needed, and its manufacture and use spread widely under the Roman Empire. There was heavy production in Roman north Africa and Spain. The finest oil, Romans said, came from central Italy: from Venafrum, where Cato had farmed, according to Varro; from the Sabine country, so Galen often asserts. When mature, he tells us, Sabine oil has no astringency and is the best he knows.

As the principal vegetable oil of the ancient Mediterranean, olive oil had many non-food uses. It was a fuel, especially for lamps. It was a soap or cosmetic, used for rubbing on the body (the practice is discussed by Diocles); it was used for oiling clothes (Hippocrates *RS* 3; Machon *C* 18.416 [Athenaeus *D* 582e] with Gow *ad l.*). Perfumed oils, used for burning and as unguents, were made with the addition of various spices and aromatics: some instructions are given by Columella. Both pure oil and perfumed oil were used in religious and social rituals.

Olive oil is Greek *elaion*, Latin *oleum*.

Diocles of Carystus F 185 van der Eijk [Galen SF 11.471–4]; Cato DA 18–22, 64–8, 144–6; Poseidonius F 15 Jacoby [Athenaeus D 152c]; Dioscorides MM 1.30; Columella DA 12.52–4; Pliny NH 15.1–24; Athenaeus E 66f–67b; Galen ST 6.196, 6.220, 6.287–8, AF 6.684, SF 12.513, *On Therapeutic Method* 10.400; Galen ST 6.196; Palladius OA 12.17–21.

Laufer 1919 pp. 415–19; A.G. Drachmann, *Ancient Oil-mills and Presses* (Copenhagen: Levin & Munksgaard, 1932) (Det Kgl. Danske Videnskabernes Selskab, *Archaeologisk-kunsthistoriske Meddelelser* vol. 1 part 1); E.L. Bennett, *The Olive Oil Tablets of Pylos* (Salamanca, 1958) (*Minos* vol. 2 suppl.); A. Wittenburg, 'Zur Qualität des Olivenöls in der Antike' in *Zeitschrift für Papyrologie und Epigraphik* vol. 38 (1980) pp. 185–9; J.J. Rossiter, 'Wine and oil processing on Roman farms in Italy' in *Phoenix* vol. 35 (1981) pp. 345–61; J.L. Melena, 'Olive oil and other sorts of oil in the Mycenaean tablets' in *Minos* vol. 18 (1983) pp. 82–123; M. Ponsich, *Aceite de oliva y salazones de pescado: factores geo-economicos de Bética y Tingitania* (Madrid: Universidad Complutense, 1988), review by K. Greene in *Classical Review* vol. 42 (1992) pp. 407–9; D.J. Mattingly, 'Oil for export? A comparison of Libyan, Spanish and Tunisian olive oil production in the Roman Empire' in *Journal of Roman Archaeology* vol. 1 (1988) pp. 33–56; D.J. Mattingly, 'The olive boom: oil surpluses, wealth and power in Roman Tripolitania' in *Libyan Studies* vol. 19 (1988) pp. 21–41; David J. Mattingly, 'First fruit? The olive in the Roman world' in *Human Landscapes in Classical Antiquity* ed. Graham Shipley and John Salmon (London: Routledge, 1996) pp. 213–53; S. Hadjisavvas, *Olive Oil Processing in Cyprus* (Nicosia: Aström, 1992); *La Production du vin et de l'huile en Méditerranée* ed. M.-C. Amouretti and J.-P. Brun (Athens: Ecole Française d'Athènes, 1993); *World Olive Encyclopaedia* (Madrid: International Olive Oil Council, 1996); *Olive Oil in Antiquity: Israel and neighbouring countries from the Neolithic to the early Arab period. Proceedings of the conference held in Haifa, Israel, 1995* ed. David Eitam and Michael Heltzer (Padova: Sargon, 1996) (*History of the Ancient Near East: Studies*, 7); Yannis Hamilakis, 'Wine, oil and the dialectics of power in Bronze Age Crete: a review of the evidence' in *Oxford Journal of Archaeology* vol. 15 (1996) pp. 1–32; Yannis Hamilakis, 'Food technologies, technologies of the body: the social context of wine and oil production and consumption in Bronze Age Crete' in *World Archaeology* vol. 31 (1999) pp. 38–54.

• *Oleum viride*, green olive oil, was made in Roman Italy from under-ripe olives. Instructions are given by Palladius for making it in October. The best was reputed to come from CASINUM in southeastern Latium. This was a good gastronomic choice for use as a dressing.

Cato DA 65; Suetonius, *Julius* 53; Palladius OA 11.10.

• The oil of unripe olives (Greek *omphakion*, Latin *omphacium*) was used as a vehicle for perfumes. The same Greek and Latin term is used for verjuice (see MUST). The oil of the wild olive, thin and bitter, was used in medicines.

Pliny NH 12.130, 13.12, 15.24, *al.*

• Greek *amorge*, Latin *amurca* is the bitter, watery liquid that separates from olive oil in the pressing. It is inedible but had many uses in traditional agriculture.

Cato DA 66 with Dalby *ad l.*, 91–103; Dioscorides MM 1.102.

Cynthia W. Shelmerdine, 'Shining and fragrant cloth in Homeric epic' in *The Ages of Homer: a tribute to Emily Townsend Vermeule* ed. Jane B. Carter and Sarah P. Morris (Austin: University of Texas Press, 1995) pp. 99–107, esp. p. 105 n. 10.

Onion, aromatic bulb native to the Near East. The onion had been domesticated in the Near East by the mid third millennium BC, and was one of the more important elements in the Greek and Roman food repertoire, frequently called for in recipes. The *cepe maestum* 'tearful onion' of Ennius's verse is easily recognisable.

Onions keep well if stored with adequate circulation of air. They were already in the fifth century BC being kept and sold in net bags, as Aristophanes happens to tell us. They could also be pickled: Columella gives a recipe.

The onion (*Allium Cepa*) is Greek *kromyon*, Latin *cepa*. Several varieties are mentioned in ancient sources, but they are not easy to identify with modern kinds. The shallot (*A. Cepa aggregatum* group) divides and is harvested in groups: it, or something like it, was Greek *kromyon to skhiston* and Latin *schista*. Greek *askalonion*, Latin *ascalonia* is the name of an unidentified variety linked with Ascalon in Palestine, a country 'fertile in onions' according to Strabo. Greek *gethyon, geteion*, Latin *pallacana, getium*, was a kind of onion which had no 'head', only a 'neck', and it was raised from seed, according to Theophrastus: if not the so-called Welsh onion (*A. fistulosum*) it was something like it. Neither of these Latin terms is used by Palladius, who instead has *cepulla*: this is the direct ancestor of French *ciboule* 'Welsh onion'.

For the Marsian variety of onion Columella gives the alternative local name *unio*, literally 'pearl'. This variety, or at least its name, must afterwards have become familiar in Gaul, since it is the origin of French *oignon* (modern English *onion*) and of parallel Provençal and Anglo-Saxon words.

Hippocrates *R* 54; Aristophanes, *Acharnians* 550; Theophrastus *HP* 7.2.3, 7.4.7–10; Strabo 16.2.29; Columella *DA* 12.10.1; Pliny *NH* 19.101–7, 20.39–43; Macrobius *S* 6.5.5 quoting Ennius; Anthimus *OC* 62–3.

W. Meyer-Lübke, *Romanisches etymologisches Wörterbuch* (Heidelberg: Winter, 1930–5) *s.vv. cepa, cepulla, unio*; Darby and others 1977 pp. 660–3; M.P. Charles, 'Onions, cucumbers and the date palm' in *Bulletin on Sumerian Agriculture* no. 3 (1987) pp. 1–21; H. Waetzoldt, 'Knoblauch und Zwiebeln nach den Texten des 3. Jt.' in *Bulletin on Sumerian Agriculture* no. 3 (1987) pp. 23–56; M. Stol, 'Garlic, onion, leek' in *Bulletin on Sumerian Agriculture* no. 3 (1987) pp. 57–92; Zohary and Hopf 1993 p. 185; Simoons 1998 pp. 136–57.

Open-air dining, the normal practice in the warmer months in Mediterranean lands. Open-air meals and symposia are common in the sources, both literary and iconographical. They are less common in the modern stereotypes of classical food because these are largely created by Germans, Britons and northern French, who like to dine under a solid roof.

Greeks dined in circles or semicircles – large parties formed more than one semicircle. Romans of the late Republic and early Empire built permanent three-sided arrangements of couches in their gardens (both house gardens and the gardens of inns), thus replicating the favoured pattern for Roman indoor dining. Eventually Romans, too, adopted the simpler pattern of reclining in a semicircle. If trees or caves did not provide shade, awnings (Greek *skene*, Latin *velum*) became almost indispensable; they are often depicted in Roman paintings and mosaics.

The diners lay sometimes on the ground, sometimes on a raised dais (Greek and Latin *stibas*). The semicircle of diners was often called *sigma* from the shape of the Greek letter C (its modern shape Σ spoils the analogy). ASPHODEL and fleabane (Greek *konyza*, Latin *conyza*: *Inula* spp.) were good to lie on at open-air feasts, since they repelled venomous creatures.

Plato, *Republic* 372b; Menander, *Dyscolus passim*; Theocritus 7.67–8; Nicander *T* 57–79; Dioscorides *MM* 3.121; Athenaeus *D* 138f–139f, *al.*

P. Soprano, 'I triclini all'aperto di Pompei' in *Pompeiana* (Naples, 1950) pp. 288–310; J. Engemann, 'Der Ehrenplatz beim antiken Sigmamahl' in *Jenseitsvorstellungen in Antike und Christentum: Gedenkschrift für Alfred Stuiber* (Münster: Aschendorff, 1982); (*Jahrbuch für Antike und Christentum. Ergänzungsband*, 9) pp. 248–50; E.S.P. Ricotti, 'The importance of water in Roman garden triclinia' in *Ancient Roman Villa Gardens* ed. E.B. MacDougall (Washington, DC, 1987) (*Dumbarton Oaks Colloquia on the History of Landscape Architecture*, 10) pp. 137–84; E.S.P. Ricotti, 'Le tende conviviali e la tenda di Tolomeo Filadelfo' in *Studia pompeiana et classica in honor of Wilhelmina F. Jashemski* ed. Robert I. Curtis (New Rochelle: Caratzas, 1989) vol. 2 pp. 199–239; L. Richardson, 'Water triclinia and biclinia in Pompeii' in *Studia pompeiana et classica in honor of Wilhelmina F. Jashemski* ed. Robert I. Curtis (New Rochelle: Caratzas, 1989) vol. 1 pp. 305–15; Katherine M.D. Dunbabin, 'Triclinium and stibadium' in

Figure 11 An open-air symposium. Redrawn from a *kylix* of about 520 BC in the Ashmolean Museum.

Figure 12 A trick cup. The *kylix* whose interior painting is redrawn in Figure 11 is a trick cup. Its base is modelled like male genitalia with the penis pierced so that wine runs through. Such a cup is shown in use in a vignette redrawn from a *kylix* of about 510 BC in the Metropolitan Museum of Art, New York.

Dining in a Classical Context ed. W.J. Slater (Ann Arbor: University of Michigan Press, 1991) pp. 121–48; Katherine M.D. Dunbabin, 'Scenes from the Roman convivium: frigida non derit, non derit calda petenti (Martial xiv.105)' in *In Vino Veritas* ed. Oswyn Murray and Manuela Tecuşan (London: British School at Rome, 1995) pp. 252–65.

Opimian vintage *see* WINE STORAGE AND AGEING

Oppian, Greek poet of the late second century AD, native of Cilicia. His poem *On Fishing* is dedicated to 'Antoninus', the emperor Marcus Aurelius, and was apparently completed between 176 and 180. It was known to ATHENAEUS. A second poem, *On Hunting*, was written after 212 and is dedicated to 'Antoninus, son of Domna by Severus', i.e. the emperor Caracalla. It is ascribed in the manuscripts to the same Oppian but is in fact by an imitator.

Oppian C: *Cynegetica* 'On Hunting'. Text, translation and commentary: *Oppian, Colluthus, Tryphiodorus* ed. A.W. Mair (1928, LCL).

—— **H:** *Halieutica* 'On Fishing'. Text, translation and commentary: as above.

Opson *see* MEALS

Orach (*Atriplex hortensis*), a potherb of Near Eastern origin, can be prepared and eaten as spinach is. It was familiar, though not relished, in the classical Mediterranean. It is Greek *adraphaxis* (variously spelt), Latin *atriplex*.

Hippocrates *R* 54; Theophrastus *HP* 7.1–5 *passim*; Dioscorides *MM* 2.119; Pliny *NH* 20.219–22; Galen *AF* 6.633; Anthimus *OC* 59 with Grant *ad l.*

A.C. Andrews, 'Orach as the spinach of the classical period' in *Isis* vol. 39 (1948) pp. 169–79.

• Greek *halimon* is sea orach (*Atriplex Halimus*). This was also used as a potherb and was believed to have useful medicinal qualities (Pliny *NH* 22.73–5).

• Greek *adraphaxis agrios* and Latin *atriplex silvestre* are possibly the names of fat hen (*Chenopodium album*), a species of goosefoot whose leaves are used similarly as a potherb. Fat hen grows wild in most parts of Europe. It was gathered from the wild by Neolithic and later prehistoric populations in Greece and the Balkans, and also further west: it was used in western France, for example, by 3000 BC. Fat hen has continued to be an important food source, especially for poorer country people, throughout historic times.

Hippocrates, *Affections of Women* 14, 172; Pliny *NH* 19.117, 20.219–21.

Orata, Sergius, Roman hedonist of the first century BC. Orata is credited with beginning the farming of oysters, and also with establishing the gastronomic preeminence at Rome of the oysters of the Lucrine lake near BAIAE. He is, additionally, held responsible for the beginning of the fashion for hot baths. Whether his cognomen came from the gilthead bream (*aurata*), or from his wearing of two gold rings, was disputed.

Cicero, *De Finibus* 2.70, *Hortensius* 68; Varro *RR* 3.3.10; Pliny *NH* 9.168–9; Festus *s.v. Orata.*

A. Tchernia, 'Le cercle de L. Licinius Crassus et la naissance de la hiérarchie des vins à Rome' in *Comptes-rendus de l'Académie des Inscriptions et Belles-Lettres* (1997) pp. 1247–59.

Oregano, Mediterranean herb typical of classical Greek and Roman cuisine. Oregano was often used as a flavouring for fish, as recommended, for example, by Archestratus. Oregano and other herbs of the same genus had also numerous uses in medicine, though they were said to be bad for the eyes and for the teeth.

Oregano (*Origanum vulgare*: called 'marjoram' in some English translations of classical texts) is Greek *origanon*, Latin *origanum*.

Hippocrates *R* 54, *Epidemics* 5.54=7.76d; Archestratus *H* 35 Brandt, *al.*; Aristotle, *Problems* 925a27–927a2; Theophrastus *HP* 6.2.3;

Nicander *T* 626–8; Dioscorides *MM* 2.27–9; Pliny *NH* 20.169–70, 20.175–80; Pseudo-Apuleius, *Herbarius* 123.

A.C. Andrews, 'Marjoram as a spice in the classical era' in *Classical Philology* vol. 56 (1961) pp. 73–82.

- Other species of this important genus might substitute for oregano in cooking. They are separately named and described in medical texts (references above). *Origanum heracleoticum* is Greek *konile*, *origanos Herakleotike*, Latin *cunila bubula*, *heraclium*. *O. microphyllum* is Greek *origanos he leuke*, Latin *cunila gallinacea*. *O. Onites* is Greek and Latin *onitis*. For za'tar (*O. Maru*) see under HYSSOP.

Oribasius of Pergamum (or Sardis), *c*.325 to *c*.400. Oribasius was physician to the emperor Julian II (ruled 355–63) and compiler of a big and useful medical manual made up almost entirely of extracts from earlier medical writings. Among his sources, Galen's works largely survive, but most of the others do not. Books 1 to 5 of the *Medical Collections* are directly relevant to food and dietetics.

Eunapius, *Lives of the Sophists* 498–9; *Suda* s.v. *Oreibasios*; *Anthologia Planudea* 16.274.

B. Baldwin, 'The career of Oribasius' in *Acta Classica* vol. 18 (1975) pp. 85–97; Mark Grant, 'Oribasius and medical dietetics or the three Ps' in *Food in Antiquity* ed. John Wilkins and others (Exeter: Exeter University Press, 1995) pp. 371–9.

Oribasius CM: *Medical Collections*. Partial translation and commentary: Mark Grant, *Dieting for an Emperor: a translation of books 1 and 4 of Oribasius' Medical Compilations with an introduction and commentary* (Leiden: Brill, 1997). Critical text: *Oribasii collectionum medicarum reliquiae* ed. I. Raeder (Leipzig: Teubner, 1928–33).

Ormer, univalve shellfish looking unexpectedly like an ear – whence its name in many languages. Ormers were plentiful around the Pharos island off Alexandria. They are nourishing but none too palatable, according to Hicesius. They were served fried: that is the only way to make them good to eat, says Xenocrates.

The ormer or sea-ear (*Haliotis tuberculata*) is Greek *otion* and *otarion*.

Aristotle *HA* 529b15 (*thalattion ous*); Xenocrates *T* 130–2; Athenaeus 87f–88a citing Hicesius.

Thompson 1947 p. 296; Davidson 1981 p. 189.

Ostrich, large flightless bird of north Africa and the Near East. According to ancient sources, ostriches were eaten by Africans, Persians and the Roman emperor Elagabalus; the late third-century usurper Firmus is said to have eaten an ostrich a day. Few classical Greeks or Italians imitated these examples. Its meat was tough, said Galen, but the wings were not so bad. Ostrich eggs, like those of geese, were not as good nutritionally as hens' eggs.

The ostrich (*Struthio Camelus*) is Greek *strouthos ho megas*, *strouthokamelos*, Latin *struthio*.

Herodotus 4.175, 4.192 (*strouthos katagaios*); Xenophon, *Anabasis* 1.5.2; Galen *AF* 6.703, 6.706; Aelian, *Nature of Animals* 14.13 (*strouthos khersaios*); Athenaeus *D* 145e quoting Heracleides of Cumae; *Historia Augusta, Heliogabalus* 22, 28, 30, *Firmus* 4; Apicius 6.1.

Toynbee 1996.

Oven *see* COOKING UTENSILS

Over-eating *see* EXCESS

Ox, farm animal domesticated in the Near East or north Africa before 7000 BC. In the societies of the ancient Near East and the classical Mediterranean oxen were first working animals, second producers of MILK, and only in third place likely to be killed for their beef. They were, however, the largest and most prestigious of sacrificial animals. The sacrificial ceremony is described more than once in the Homeric epics, and is often alluded to in later literature both Greek and Latin. The *Bouphonia*, for example, was a ceremony at Athens at which an ox was killed (Aristophanes, *Clouds* 985; Pausanias 1.28.11). Multiple sacrifices of oxen sometimes took place at municipal festivals. In the period preceding the introduction of coinage, both in Greece and Italy, there is evidence for the use of cattle as a standard of value.

On select occasions beef was certainly tasted and relished by Greeks and Romans. Calves were castrated because this made them fatten more rapidly; there are many allusions in Hebrew, Greek and Latin texts to fatted calves and fatted veal (see FATTENING).

But Greeks in particular ate beef rarely, and classical Athenians were ready to criticise others – from the mythological hero Heracles to contemporaries such as their neighbours of BOEOTIA and the Thracians of the north Aegean coast – for eating too much of it. According to the stereotype, ATHLETES were prescribed a diet rich in beef. In consequence, Greeks characterised all these people as physically strong but mentally dull. The assumption among Roman writers on farming, too, is that cattle will be kept as working animals rather than for milk or meat.

Humped cattle are said by Aristotle to be found in Syria; this is now a typical Indian variety. On varieties and breeds generally see the short survey by Columella (*DA* 6.1.1–2).

The domestic ox (*Bos Taurus*) is Greek *bous*, an inherited Indo-European word. Latin *bos* has the same ultimate origin, but (like several other important agricultural words in Latin) shows the signs of borrowing from a neighbouring Italic dialect. For the meat, Greek has the term *boeion* beef; Latin has *bubula* beef, *vitulina* veal.

Homer, *Odyssey* 3.1–66, 3.404–63; Aristophanes, *Peace* 1280; Aristotle *HA* 595b5–22, 606a15; Cato *DA* 4, 6; Columella *DA* 6.1–26;

Oppian, *Cynegetica* 2.43–158; Palladius *OA* 4.11–12.

Buck 1949 pp. 143–55, 365–6; Bökönyi 1974; Darby and others 1977 pp. 85–169; Brewer and others 1995 pp. 77–90; Gamkrelidze and Ivanov 1995 pp. 439–40; Toynbee 1996; Dalby 1996 pp. 59–60, *al.*

- The wild ox or aurochs of central Europe is Latin *urus*, a Celtic loanword. The Gauls used aurochs horns, trimmed with silver, as drinking vessels, says Caesar. By Romans the aurochs was not always clearly distinguished from the BISON and the WATER BUFFALO.

Caesar, *Gallic War* 6.28; Martial, *Spectacles* 22 (*bubalus*), cf. Pliny *NH* 8.38.

Oxygala *see* MILK

Oxyporum *see* DIGESTIVES

Oyster, bivalve shellfish which has been an article of food on Mediterranean coasts since prehistoric times. Heaps of oyster-shells were found by Heinrich Schliemann in his excavations at Mycenae. The classical Hellespont was rich in oysters, the city of Abydos in particular, according to Archestratus. Latin poets agree, adding Cyzicus and Calchedon (opposite Byzantium) to Abydos. In Roman times an oyster geography becomes established. They were good, says Xenocrates, at the mouth of the Nile; at Ephesus near the mouth of the Cayster; at Brindisium, Tarraco, Narbo, in the Lucrine lake, at Leucas, at Actium and in the Syrtes gulfs. At almost the same date Pliny gives another list, crediting it to Mucianus, a Roman consular who wrote enthusiastically of his Eastern posting:

> The oysters of Cyzicus are bigger than the Lucrine, sweeter than the British, smoother than the Medulan, sharper than the Ephesian, fuller than those of Luca, drier than the Coryphantene, more tender than the Histrian, whiter than the Circeian.

Pliny, incidentally, attributes the fame of Lucrine oysters to Sergius ORATA. Three hundred years later Ausonius, in a verse survey, claims knowledge of several of these kinds, and adds to them others; mainly from Gaul. The coast near Narbo was still producing; oysters came from Massilia and from the beds on the Atlantic coast which, nowadays, produce the oysters of Marennes. His favourite, however, came from closest at hand: they were the Medulan, from the peninsula now known as Médoc, close to his home town of Burdigala (Bordeaux), and they had graced imperial tables.

The oysters of Britain, which must have been very new to Rome in Mucianus's time, came from the Kent coast, as they do now; they were associated with the Roman harbour of Rutupiae. Those of the Lucrine lake were farmed, or at least encouraged, and supplied the demand for fine seafood at the Roman holiday resort of Baiae. Pliny notes that the best were found to be Brundisian oysters transported across the Apennines (at what must have been a high cost) and fattened in the Lucrine lake.

Oysters were a rich man's dish – Lucrine oysters were a patron's dish, in Martial's satirical epigram – and wealth was demonstrated by the consumption of large numbers of them (fortunately they slip down easily): a hundred, says Juvenal. Seneca gave up oysters (and mushrooms) as unnecessary luxuries – as symbol of the vegetarianism and asceticism he toyed with.

Oysters are hard to open but easy to eat, Epicharmus rightly says. They have the softest flesh of any shellfish, according to Galen, but some, including the unsmiling Seneca, declared them indigestible. The oyster is the only common shellfish that is customarily opened by the eater and eaten raw. So it was in the ancient world, but this was advisable only if the oysters were good and fresh – otherwise they were no better than poison, says Anthimus. Galen agrees that oysters were sometimes eaten raw, sometimes fried in a skillet. The 'Baian casserole' of *Apicius*, in which 'minced oysters' mingled with mussels and sea urchins, was indeed a rich man's dish.

The fact that British oysters were available in Rome shows that they were preserved – presumably in brine, in barrels or earthenware jars – for dispatch on the long journey from the Channel coast. That fresh British oysters were available at Rome is impossible; though one famous cook, APICIUS (3), found a way of packing fresh oysters to send over a shorter distance, from the Syrian coast to the emperor Trajan's camp, while he was on campaign in Mesopotamia *c.*AD 115, according to the *Epitome* of Athenaeus. The cookbook APICIUS (4) gives instructions for 'making oysters last' in this way by washing them and the container in vinegar.

The oyster (*Ostrea* spp. especially *Ostrea edulis*) is Greek *ostreion, ostreon*, Latin *ostrea*.

Alexis 115 Kassel; Lucilius 440 Marx; Catullus fragment 1; Horace, *Satires* 2.4.33; Vergil, *Georgics* 1.207; Xenocrates *T* 95–6; Lucan 9.959; Seneca, *Letters* 78.23, 95.26, 108.15; Pliny *NH* 9.168–9, also 32.59–65 quoting Mucianus ter consul; Martial 3.60, 10.37; *Priapeia* 75; Juvenal 4.140–2, 8.85; Galen *AF* 6.734; Athenaeus *D* 85d–92e *passim* quoting Archestratus *H* 56 Brandt and Epicharmus 42 Kaibel, also *E* 7d; *Apicius* 1.12, 9.7, 9.11; Ausonius, *Epistles* 9; Anthimus *OC* 49 with Grant *ad l.*

R.T. Gunther, 'The oyster culture of the ancient Romans' in *Journal of the Marine Biological Association* vol. 4 (1897) pp. 360–5; Thompson 1947 p. 190; A.C. Andrews, 'Oysters as a food in Greece and Rome' in *Classical Journal* vol. 43 (1948) pp. 299–303; P.J. Parsons, 'The oyster' in *Zeitschrift für Papyrologie und Epigraphik* vol. 24 (1977) pp. 1–12; Davidson 1981 p. 197 ('lavish your money on these delectable creatures'); R.A. Donkin, *Beyond Price: pearls and pearl-fishing: origins to the age of discoveries* (Philadelphia:

American Philosophical Society, 1998) (*Memoirs of the American Philosophical Society*, 224).

- Greek *spondylos* is the name of a shellfish now called *gaidaropous* in Greek and occasionally 'ass's hoof' in English (*Spondylus Gaedaropus*). It is not closely related to the oyster but is often compared with it; its shell is equally rough and hard to open. Its meat is plentiful but much tougher than that of an oyster, and it needs cooking.

Pliny *NH* 32.154; Galen *AF* 6.734; Macrobius *S* 3.13.12 quoting Metellus Pius; *Diocletian's Price Edict* 5.10.

P

Palaeoethnobotany *see* ARCHAEOBOTANY

Palestine *see* SYRIA

Palladius, Rutilius Taurus Aemilianus, Latin author of the fifth century AD. Palladius's principal work was *Agricultural Work*, which depends on early farming authors such as Columella but also on his own experience. Book 1 is introductory; books 2 to 13 deal with the farmer's work month by month. Palladius also wrote on veterinary medicine and on grafting.

Palladius OA: *Opus Agriculturae*. Critical text: Palladii Rutilii Tauri Aemiliani *Opus Agriculturae, De Veterinaria Medicina, De Insitione* ed. R.H. Rodgers (1975, BT).

Palm heart *see* DATE

Palynology *see* POLLEN ANALYSIS

Pancrates of Arcadia, Greek author of a poem on fish of which three brief fragments are quoted by Athenaeus.

Athenaeus D 283a, 283c, 305c, 321f, E 13b.

Panspermia, traditional gruel consisting as its name suggests of 'all kinds of seeds', or at least of several. Panspermia was made on the day of *khytroi* 'pots' during the Anthesteria festival at Athens; indeed, it was made in the pots. It was said to commemorate those who survived the flood, and in modern scholarship has been seen as a reminiscence of pre-Neolithic food gathering.

Scholia on Aristophanes, Acharnians 1076 and *Frogs* 218, citing Theopompus 115 F 347 Jacoby.

W. Burkert, *Homo Necans: the anthropology of ancient Greek sacrificial ritual and myth* (Berkeley: University of California Press, 1983) pp. 238–9.

Papyrus, Egyptian marsh plant. Papyrus was principally used as writing material in ancient times. In addition, however, the lower stem could be chewed raw and could be eaten after boiling or roasting.

Papyrus (*Cyperus Papyrus*) is Greek *byblos, papyros*, Latin *papyrus*.

Herodotus 2.92; Theophrastus *HP* 4.8.2–5; Diodorus 1.80.5; Strabo 17.1.15; Pliny *NH* 13.68–79.

N. Lewis, *L'Industrie de papyrus dans l'antiquité gréco-romaine* (Paris, 1934); Darby and others 1977 pp. 644–9.

Parasitos, one who in some sense 'dined alongside'. *Parasitoi*, in early Athens and elsewhere, were religious celebrants whose duty was to share a ritual meal with a god or gods. The playwright ALEXIS applied the term, as a nickname, to a comedy character – after whom he named his play *Parasitos* – whose distinguishing feature was that he habitually dined at other people's expense. This was opprobrious behaviour in early Greece, where the prevailing ethos was of equal exchange of hospitality (see SYMBOLA), and where those who were unable to conform to the ethos were indeed designated by nicknames.

As a result of this choice of name by Alexis, the noun *parasitos* became accepted as the ordinary term for someone who behaved in that way, whether as a stock character in comedy or in real life. The development of the character in earlier and later Greek comedy can be traced through the quotations of Athenaeus. The earliest occurrence in drama of a parasite-like figure is in a fragment of the early fifth-century Sicilian playwright Epicharmus; the *kolakes* 'flatterers' of the rich and powerful, satirised in early Athenian comedy such as the play *Flatterers* by Eupolis, contributed in turn to the stereotype. In due course, stylised 'parasites' appear as a feature of the Roman comedy of Plautus and Terence.

Homer, *Odyssey* 18.6–7; Alexis *F* 183 Kassel [Athenaeus *D* 421d]; Athenaeus *D* 234d–245b quoting Epicharmus 34–5 Kaibel and Eupolis 172 Kassel.

J.O. Lofberg, 'The sycophant-parasite' in *Classical Philology* vol. 15 (1920) pp. 61–72; W.G. Arnott, 'Alexis and the parasite's name' in *Greek, Roman and Byzantine Studies* vol. 9 (1968) pp. 161–8; W.G. Arnott, 'Phormio parasitus' in *Greece and Rome* vol. 17 (1970) pp. 32–57; A.S. Gratwick, 'Sundials, parasites and girls from Boeotia' in *Classical Quarterly* n.s. vol. 29 (1979) pp. 308–23; G. Guastella, *La contaminazione e il parassito: due studi su teatro e cultura romana* (Pisa: Giardini, 1988); papers by Oddone Longo and Gianni Guastella in *Homo edens: regime, rite e pratiche dell' alimentazione nella civiltà del Mediterraneo* ed. Oddone Longo and P. Scarpi (Milan: Diapress, 1989); B. Fehr, 'Entertainers at the symposion: the akletoi in the archaic period' in *Sympotica: a symposium on the symposion* ed. Oswyn Murray (Oxford: Oxford University Press, 1990) pp. 185–95; Louise Bruit Zaidman, 'Ritual eating in ancient Greece: parasites and paredroi' in *Food in Antiquity* ed. John Wilkins and others (Exeter: Exeter University Press, 1995) pp. 196–203; Arnott 1996 pp. 336–43, 542–7; Wilkins 2000 pp. 71–87.

Parmenon of Rhodes, author of *Lessons in Cookery*, a work probably of the Hellenistic period, quoted once by Athenaeus on a point of vocabulary.

Athenaeus *D* 308f.

Bilabel 1921; Dalby 1996 p. 164.

Parsley *see* CELERY

Parsnip, root vegetable. Parsnip, domesticated in central or southern Europe, was the best and most health-giving of the roots in classical Greek gardens, since the carrot was at first a small and unprepossessing object. It was less grown in Rome, however, and by the date of *Apicius* (whatever date that may be) the roles had been exchanged: recipes call for carrot, while parsnip is treated as a substitute. Probably introduced to Britain during the Roman period, the parsnip is nowadays little grown in southern Europe (one French reference book describes it as a 'forgotten vegetable') but retains all its popularity in Britain.

The parsnip (*Pastinaca sativa*) is Greek *staphylinos* (sometimes qualified *kepaios* or *hemeros* 'cultivated'), Latin *pastinaca*. Greek *staphylinos* includes carrot and various similar wild species (see CARROT).

Dioscorides *MM* 3.52; Celsus, *DM* 2.26.2; Columella *DA* 11.3.35; Pliny *NH* 19.62, 19.88–9; Galen *AF* 6.654, *SF* 12.129; Athenaeus *D* 371b–e; *Apicius* 3.21; Anthimus *OC* 53 with Grant *ad l.*

A.C. Andrews, 'The carrot as a food in the classical period' in *Classical Philology* vol. 44 (1949) pp. 182–96; A.C. Andrews, 'The parsnip as food in the classical era' in *Classical Philology* vol. 53 (1958) pp. 131–52; J.A.C. Greppin, 'Some etymological notes on Greek *staphylinos* carrot' in *Glotta* vol. 64 (1986) p. 248–52.

- The spring shoots of wild parsnip were gathered as food (not a food but an amuse-gueule, says Pliny). Leaves and roots were used in medicine. Wild parsnip is Latin *pastinaca pratensis, pastinaca silvatica*.

Columella *DA* 12.7.1; Pliny *NH* 21.86; Pseudo-Apuleius, *Herbarius* 81.

Parthians, an Iranian-speaking people from central Asia who, from the mid third century BC to the early third century AD, ruled an extensive territory in the Middle East. The Parthian kingdom was thus the contemporary of later Seleucid Syria (indeed most of its territory had previously been subject to the Seleucids) and was in due course the eastern neighbour of the Roman Empire.

Parthian culture, influenced by that of the earlier Persian Empire and that of the Greeks after Alexander, demanded liberal use of aromatics in religion and festivity. Parthia controlled the westward trade in certain aromatics, including AMOMUM, bdellium (see MYRRH), ASAFOETIDA and its relatives galbanum and sagapenum.

According to Pliny, citron pips were included in Parthian dishes for the nobility, serving to freshen the breath. The leaves of a tree called *bratus* were sprinkled into drinks. 'Parthian chicken' is the name of a dish for which *Apicius* provides a recipe: appropriately it is heavily flavoured with asafoetida.

Pliny *NH* 12.16, 12.78 citing the emperor Claudius, 12.80; *Apicius* 6.8.2.

Dalby 2000a pp. 186–91.

Partridge, a game bird which, in Greece in the orator Hypereides's time, was being regularly farmed in enclosures called *perdikotropheia*. It was not native to Italy or the western Mediterranean, but became familiar there during the Roman imperial period. Its eggs were recognised as good food for invalids.

The rock partridge (*Alectoris graeca* and *A. rufa*, not the same species as the partridge of northern Europe) is Greek and Latin *perdix*.

Jeremiah 17.11; Aristotle *HA* 613b5–614a31; Strabo 14.2.5; Dioscorides *MM* 2.96; Martial 3.58, 13.65, 13.76; Pollux *O* 10.159 citing Hypereides fragment 45 Jensen; Athenaeus *D* 388e–390d; *Apicius* 6.3; Anthimus *OC* 28 with Grant *ad l.*

W. Meyer-Lübke, *Romanisches etymologisches Wörterbuch* (Heidelberg: Winter, 1930–5) *s.v.*

perdix; Thompson 1936 pp. 234–8; Toynbee 1996.

Passover, Jewish annual festival. Passover commemorates events that preceded the exodus from Egypt. The tradition is to slaughter and roast a lamb on the day preceding Passover, then, after Passover has begun at sunset, to eat a meal of lamb and unleavened bread with bitter herbs (see under ENDIVE). The LAST SUPPER shared by Jesus and his disciples was a Passover feast. Christians adopted the Jewish custom of an annual feast on the same evening, which in their terms was the evening of the Thursday preceding Good Friday. The feast, and the lamb which forms its centrepiece, are Hebrew *pešach*, Greek *paskha*, Latin *pascha*.

Exodus 12.1–30; Mark, *Gospel* 14.1–21; Matthew, *Gospel* 26.1–25; Luke, *Gospel* 22.1–16; John, *Gospel* 13.1–30; Paul, *I Corinthians* 5.7.

G. Feeley-Harnik, *The Lord's Table: Eucharist and Passover in early Christianity* (Philadelphia, 1981).

Passum, raisin wine, made from semi-dried grapes. The resulting must is so sweet that not all the sugar will ferment out. Instructions are given by Columella, Pliny and Palladius. The *passum* of the Roman Empire came from Greece (the best, according to Pliny), Cilicia and Africa. How old the practice was in these three regions is not known. One of Columella's recipes is attributed by him to Mago: this makes it far earlier than any other Roman evidence for *passum* and implies that the idea came to Rome from Carthage.

Vergil, *Georgics* 2.93, 4.269; Columella *DA* 12.39.1–4; Pliny *NH* 14.81–2 (read *Graeco*, not *Cretico*); Martial 13.106; Palladius *OA* 11.19.

N.K. Rauh, E.L. Will, 'My blood of the Covenant' in *Odyssey* (Sept./Oct. 2002) pp. 47–51, 62.

- Latin *psythium*, evidently named after the variety *psithia* (see GRAPE VARIETIES), is described by Pliny as a special type of *passum* or raisin wine. This and the next had a distinctive flavour which was not that of wine. Latin *melampsythium*, Greek *melampsithios* was a variant of *psythium*, 'black' in colour, 'thick' and nourishing, according to Dioscorides.

Dioscorides *MM* 5.6; Pliny *NH* 14.80.

Lambert-Gócs 1990; Dalby 2000a pp. 137–8.

Pasta, pressed shaped cakes of flour (especially durum wheat flour) and water. Certain forms of pasta existed in classical antiquity: under what names? The three listed below are relevant. A general Greek term for pasta, though rarely used, is *ryemata*.

Galen *AF* 6.687.

P. Mingazzini, 'Gli antichi Romani conoscevano i maccheroni?' in *Archeologia classica* vol. 6 (1954) pp. 292–4; Charles Perry, 'The oldest Mediterranean noodle: a cautionary tale' in *Petits Propos culinaires* no. 9 (1981) pp. 42–5, with note by Bignia Kuoni in no. 23 (1986) pp. 62–3; Davidson 1999 *s.v.* 'Pasta'; Silvano Serventi, Françoise Sabban, *Les pâtes* (Arles: Actes Sud, 2001).

- Greek *itria*, Aramaic *itriya* was, by later classical times, a pasta-like product made from wheat flour, cooked by boiling, and generally forming part of a sweet dish. It was one of the ingredients of *libum* (see CAKES) as briefly described by Athenaeus (*D* 125f). It was shaped: note the word *plasmata* 'shapes' used by Hesychius in describing it. One of its shapes may already (as believed by Krauss) have been that of vermicelli. This was certainly the meaning of medieval Arabic *itriyah*: see also Perry (above).

  Athenaeus *D* 646d citing Anacreon and Sophocles; Oribasius *CM* 1.9.2, 4.7.33 with Grant *ad l.*; Hesychius, *Lexicon s.v. itria*.

  Krauss 1910–12 vol. 1 p. 107.

- Greek *laganon*, Latin *laganum* was, by later classical times, a flat pasta-like product; in earlier contexts the word is likened to unleavened bread or to pancake. This is the 'pasta', if indeed it was already that, which Horace ate with his leeks and chickpeas. *Laganon* might be eaten with oil; it might be fried (see the interpretation as 'fried pasta' in the recipe suggested by Grant 1999 p. 65) or cooked in chicken broth. *Artolaganon*, presumably a variant, incorporated a little

wine, pepper and milk (Pliny *NH* 18.105; Athenaeus *D* 113d citing Chrysippus of Tyana). The word survives in modern Italian dialects.

Leviticus 2.4, 7.12 [Septuagint and Vulgate versions]; Horace, *Satires* 1.6.115 with Porphyrio *ad l.*; Josephus, *Jewish Antiquities* 7.86; Galen *AF* 6.492, *BM* 6.768; Athenaeus *D* 110a, also 647e–648a quoting Chrysippus of Tyana, also 656f quoting Matron; Oribasius *CM* 1.9.2 with Grant *ad l.*; Apicius 4.2.14–15; Hesychius, *Lexicon s.v. laganon*; Aetius, *Medicine* 7.33.

- Greek *makaria* was a dish made of soup and barley meal, and not pasta, in classical times. Its name is, however, the origin of Italian *maccherone*.

  Hesychius, *Lexicon s.v. makaria*.

Pastry, mixture of flour, fat and water, made into a dough and cooked. Pastry was probably known in Roman times but is not prominent in the sources.

- Latin *crustulum* is a name for a pastry (or the like) that was to be eaten as a cake; but maybe also pastry as a wrapping, as when it formed part of the complex dish TETRAFARMACUM.

  Horace, *Satires* 1.1.25, 2.4.47; Seneca, *Letters* 99.27; Juvenal 9.5; *Historia Augusta*, *Aelius Verus* 5.

- Latin *tracta*, Aramaic *truqta* (variously spelt) appears to be a kind of pastry. It is hard to be sure, because its making is never described fully and it is always wanted as a constituent of a complex dish. Cato uses it in sheets, Apicius in balls; but the two sources are several centuries apart and the meaning of the word may well have changed in the interim. Greek *kapyria* is said by Athenaeus to be the Greek equivalent of *tracta*.

  Cato *DA* 76; Chrysippus of Tyana [Athenaeus *D* 113d]; Pliny *NH* 18.106; Apicius 2.1.5, 4.3.1–7, 5.1.3, 6.8.13, 7.11.5, 8.7.5.

  Krauss 1910–12 vol. 1 p. 106 and note 446; J. Solomon, 'Tracta: a versatile Roman pastry' in *Hermes* vol. 106 (1978) pp. 539–56; Charles Perry, 'What was tracta?' in *Petits Propos culinaires* no. 12 (1982) pp. 37–9, with note in no. 14; Charles Perry, 'Trakhanas revisited' in *Petits Propos culinaires* no. 55 (1997) pp. 34–9 (the link made by Perry between Latin *tracta* and Greek *trakhanas* [see under EMMER] is controversial); Davidson 1999 *s.v.* 'Pastry'.

Patina *see* COOKING UTENSILS

Patronage *see* COMMENSALITY

Paxamus, Hellenistic Greek author of wide interests. He was read in Rome; perhaps he wrote in Rome, reworking Greek technical texts for a new audience. He wrote *On Cookery* and *On Farming* among several other works. Paxamus is cited once by Athenaeus, in the frame narrative of the *Deipnosophists*, for his use of the Latin word *isicia* 'meatballs'. Paxamus is guessed, but without support from ancient texts, to have been the inventor of the barley BISCUIT called *paxamas* or *paximadion*. He is frequently quoted in the Byzantine farming compilation *Geoponica*.

Varro *RR* 1.1.13; Columella *DA* 1.1.13, 12.4.2; Pliny *NH* 18.22; Athenaeus *D* 376d; *Suda s.v. Paxamos*; *Geoponica* 12.17, *al.*

Dalby 1996 pp. 164–5.

Pea, legume domesticated in the prehistoric Near East. Peas were being grown in Palestine by 8000 BC and their cultivation had spread westwards as far as western France before 4000 BC. They were known in Egypt by the early second millennium BC, if not before, and were fully familiar in classical Greece and Rome. They were most commonly dried, in which condition they keep for a long time, and then boiled before eating; boiling might often continue till a smooth soup had been produced.

The pea (*Pisum sativum*) is Greek *pisos*, Latin *pisum*.

Hippocrates *R* 45; Pliny *NH* 18.123; Oribasius *CM* 4.8.7–18.

Buck 1949 pp. 371–2; Darby and others 1977 pp. 690–2; Zohary and Hopf 1993 pp. 94–101; Brewer and others 1995 pp. 71–2.

- In Greek, pea soup could be called *pisinon etnos*; another name was *konkhos*. The Latin equivalent was *conchis* and later *conchicla*. It was typically cooked with a lot of cumin, according to Scribonius Largus, and served with oil, according to Martial. *Apicius* provides several recipes, including one

for *pullus conchiclatus*, chicken with peas. There is no evidence for the usual translation of *conchis* as 'beans cooked with the pods'.

Aristophanes, *Knights* 1171; Scribonius Largus 233; Martial 7.78, 13.7; Juvenal 3.293, 14.131; Marcus Aurelius, *Letters* [Fronto vol. 1 p. 182 Haines]; Athenaeus *D* 159f–160b quoting Timon; *Apicius* 5.4 with Flower and Rosenbaum *ad l.*; Oribasius *CM* 4.8.14.

Peach, tree fruit native to central Asia or China. Peaches are first named in Greek by Theophrastus, according to Athenaeus, but the mention is not in Theophrastus's surviving *History of Plants*. Under the descriptive name 'Persian apple' they certainly became familiar to Greeks at the beginning of the third century BC, probably as a result of Alexander's Persian expedition. Pliny discusses their introduction to Italy, still recent in the mid first century AD, and there is a Pompeiian still-life painting including a half-eaten peach. The variety name *duracinum* 'clingstone', first mentioned by Pliny, is the origin of the later Greek name for this fruit (modern Greek *rodakino*).

The peach (*Persica vulgaris*) is Greek *melon Persikon* and later *dorakinon*, Latin *malum Persicum*.

Pliny *NH* 15.39–45, 23.132; Athenaeus *D* 82e–83a citing Theophrastus (Gulick's translation and note are erroneous) and Diphilus of Siphnos; Galen *BM* 6.785; Gargilius Martialis *DH* 2; Palladius *OA* 12.7.1–8; *Apicius* 1.26 (*duracina persica*); Anthimus *OC* 85 (*persica duracina*).

Laufer 1919 pp. 378, 539–41; Buck 1949 p. 377; Darby and others 1977 pp. 733–5; Zohary and Hopf 1993 p. 172; Dalby 1996 pp. 144–5, 181.

Peafowl, showy bird, domesticated in India and perhaps first introduced to Mediterranean countries at the time of the Persian Empire. At the date of Aristophanes's *Birds* there were peacocks in Athens, exhibited as a rarity; they were also kept, like many other exotic animals and plants, at the sanctuary of Hera on Samos. Eventually they became common at Rome too, and it was apparently not in Greece but in Rome, home of conspicuous consumption, that a European peacock was first eaten (at the table of the orator Quintus Hortensius in the first century BC). Since (as Aristotle had remarked) peafowl are not prolific, they and their eggs would remain a costly delicacy. Peahen eggs were recommended as better than any others, from the dietary point of view, by the Hellenistic authors EPAENE-TUS and Heracleides of Syracuse.

The peafowl (*Pavo cristatus*) is Greek *tahos*, Latin *pavo*.

Aristophanes, *Birds* 102; Cicero, *Letters to Friends* 9.18, 9.20; Varro *RR* 3.3–3.9; Horace, *Satires* 1.2.116, 2.2.23; Petronius *S* 55 quoting Publilius Syrus; Columella *DA* 8.11; Pliny *NH* 10.161–2; Martial 13.70; Suetonius, *Vitellius* 13; Athenaeus *D* 397a–398b quoting Aristotle fragment 351 Rose, also 654d–655b quoting Antiphanes 203 Kassel, also *E* 58a citing Epaenetus and Heracleides of Syracuse; *Diocletian's Price Edict* 4.39–40; Palladius *OA* 1.28; *Apicius* 2.2.6; Anthimus *OC* 24 with Grant *ad l.*

Thompson 1936 p. 277; Joop Witteveen, 'Peacocks in history' in *Petits Propos culinaires* no. 32 (1989) pp. 23–34; Joop Witteveen, 'Preparation of the peacock for the table' in *Petits Propos culinaires* no. 36 (1990) pp. 10–20; Toynbee 1996; Dalby 1996 pp. 146–7 and note 49.

Pear, tree fruit presumably domesticated in the southern Caucasus and northeastern Anatolia. This is the native habitat of the two wild species of which the cultivated pear is a cross. Its westward spread was speeded by grafting on several species native to the Near East and southern Europe, including the Greek species *Pyrus spinosa*.

In classical Greece the cultivated pear was recognised to be a relative of the native wild pear but not a direct offshoot. It is among the typical orchard fruits listed in Odysseus's description of the gardens of Alcinous in the *Odyssey*. From a clever object-lesson taught to a courtesan in a play by Alexis we know that pears were served as a dessert or at symposia in classical Athens:

> 'Did you ever see pears served in water to men while they were drinking?'
> 'Lots. Lots of times. Obviously.'
> 'Doesn't each of the men always look for the ripest of the floating pears for himself and pick that?'
> 'Of course they do.'

From Roman sources we know other ways in which pears were used. They could be cooked with wine and water to make a kind of *pulmentarium*, as Pliny describes it. They were conserved in grape syrup, and also dried, for use over the winter – an important point because pears are at their peak of ripeness only for a short time (which made them a good example for the courtesan's best friend to use) and must be conserved in some way if they are not to be wasted. By late Roman times perry (an alcoholic drink analogous to cider), pear vinegar and pear *liquamen* were all being manufactured, as shown by Palladius; pear *liquamen* served as a vegetarian alternative to GARUM. See Grant 1999 pp. 30, 113, 155 for modern interpretations of recipes for pear conserves.

Numerous varieties were developed, especially in the Roman period. Among the most frequently named are the *crustuminum*, recorded in Aramaic and Roman sources and apparently linked with the town of Crustumeria near Rome; the *mnaia* recorded by Galen, which could be sliced into rings and dried for use in winter and spring; and the *volaema*, supposed to be large enough to fill the hand, one of those good for conserving in grape syrup according to Cato.

The cultivated pear (*Pyrus communis*) is Greek *apios* and *onkhne* (Theophrastus distinguishes the two terms) and Latin *pirus*.

Homer, *Odyssey* 7.115–20; Aristophanes, *Assemblywomen* 355; Hippocrates *R* 55; Alexis *F* 34, 167 Kassel with Arnott *ad l.*; Menander, *Dyscolus* 99 with Handley *ad l.*; Theophrastus *HP* 1.14.4, 2.5.6, 3.11.5; Theocritus 7.120

with Gow *ad l.*; Cato *DA* 7.4; Celsus, *DM* 2.24.2; Dioscorides *MM* 1.116, 5.24; Pliny *NH* 14.103, 15.53–8, 23.115–16; Galen *AF* 6.599–605 *passim*, *SF* 11.834; Athenaeus *D* 650b–e quoting Alexis *F* 34 Kassel; Macrobius *S* 3.19.6; Palladius *OA* 3.25.1–13; Anthimus *OC* 84.

Buck 1949 p. 376; Darby and others 1977 pp. 735–6; Zohary and Hopf 1993 pp. 167–9.

• The wild pears of Greece (*Pyrus spinosa*) were being collected at Franchthi Cave by 9000 BC. Wild pear is Greek *akhras* and *akherdos* (Galen distinguishes the two terms). The spiny tree was used for a defensive hedge (as shown by the *Odyssey*); the small and astringent fruit continued to be gathered from the wild in classical times. An Attic deme, *Akherdous*, was evidently named for its wealth of wild pear trees.

Homer, *Odyssey* 14.10; Aristotle, *On Marvellous Things Heard* 845a15; Theocritus 24.90; Strabo 15.3.18; Galen *AF* 6.619, 6.621.

Pellitory, a potherb. The fresh leaves are listed by Galen among foods that thin the humours. The root was used medicinally. 'Pellitory of Spain', to give it its full name (*Anacyclus Pyrethrum*), is Greek *pyrethron*.

Nicander *T* 938; Galen *VA* 7, *AF* 6.622–3, *SF* 12.110; Aetius, *Medicine* 12.35.

Pennyroyal, a small-leaf species of mint. Pennyroyal is far more important in the Greek and Roman context than mint: it was considered an important medicinal plant. Pennyroyal was a heating food, and in particular it was a women's drug used in childbirth and as abortifacient (indeed, it will have been very effective as such). Its medicinal effects were often achieved in combination with wine or vinegar, as Pliny says, and especially in KYKEON and POSCA, in both of which pennyroyal was frequently an ingredient.

In comic double entendre pennyroyal suggested women's pubic hair.

Pennyroyal (*Mentha Pulegium*) is Greek *glekhon, blekhon* and other forms, Latin *pulegium*.

Homeric Hymn to Demeter 209; Aristophanes,

Acharnians 874, *Lysistrata* 89, *Peace* 712; Hippocrates *R* 54, *Nature of Woman* 32; Dioscorides *MM* 3.31; Pliny *NH* 20.152–7; Galen *SF* 11.857.

E. Kislinger, 'Phoûska und glékhon' in *Jahrbuch der österreichischen Byzantinistik* vol. 34 (1984) pp. 49–53; John Scarborough, 'Contraception in antiquity: the case of pennyroyal' in *Wisconsin Academy Review* (1989) pp. 19–25; John Scarborough, 'The pharmacology of sacred plants, herbs and roots' in *Magika Hiera: ancient Greek magic and religion* (New York: Oxford University Press, 1991) pp. 144–5; Henderson 1991 p. 135.

Peparethan wine (Greek *Peparethios*; Latin *Peparethium*), from the island of Peparethos. Named without enthusiasm in classical sources, Peparethan had its moment of fame in the recommendations of APOLLODORUS to King Ptolemy, in the early third century BC. It was said to require at least six years to mature.

Hermippus 77 Kassel; Aristophanes fragment 334 Kassel; Pliny *NH* 14.76 citing Apollodorus.

P. Bruneau, 'Peparethia' in *Bulletin de correspondance hellénique* vol. 111 (1987) pp. 471–93; Dalby 2000c.

Pepper, fruit of a climbing plant of southern Asia. Two species were known as imports in the classical Mediterranean, long pepper (*Piper longum*) and black pepper (*P. nigrum*).

Pepper became known in classical Greece around 400 BC; it is first mentioned by the comic playwrights Antiphanes, Eubulus and Alexis and in a Hippocratic text. Diphilus of Siphnos, recommending pepper with scallops in the early third century BC, provides the oldest positive evidence of the use of pepper as a condiment. It is generally supposed that until understanding of the monsoons allowed direct sailings from southern India to the Red Sea, shortly before 100 BC, the only pepper available in Mediterranean lands will have been long pepper, which grows in northeastern India. Its name in Prakrit is *pipali*, evidently the source of the classical names

(Greek *peperi*, Latin *piper*). Black pepper was *marica* in Prakrit and Sanskrit, but whenever it first came to Greek and Roman notice the same Greek and Latin names were applied to it: it was evidently regarded as a variety of the same spice.

Long pepper (Greek *peperi to makron*, Latin *piper longum*) is the hotter of the two: Galen compares its heat with that of ginger. It fetched twice the price of black pepper in Roman times. It was separately prescribed by ancient and medieval physicians; food recipes, on the other hand, very seldom specify whether long pepper or black pepper is to be taken. Long pepper practically ceased to be used in Europe at the end of the medieval period and is now very little known outside southern Asia. White pepper, regarded by Pliny and some other authors as a third species, is in fact a ripened form of black pepper.

Pepper was the quintessential spice of the Indian Ocean trade in Roman times. It was for pepper, more than any other single product, that Roman gold and silver coins were exported to India; pepper, when it reached Rome, was stockpiled as another kind of currency in the treasury and in the *horrea piperatoria* 'pepper warehouses' built by Domitian. But it was for use as well as for storing. For those who could afford this costly exotic, pepper is called for no fewer than 452 times in the recipes of *Apicius*.

Hippocrates, *Epidemics* 5.67=7.64; Alexis F 132 Kassel [*s.v.l.*]; Aristotle, *Problems* 1.43; Theophrastus *HP* 9.20.1–2, *On Fire* 166; Horace, *Epistles* 2.1.270; Dioscorides *MM* 2.159; *Periplus Maris Erythraei* 49; Pliny *NH* 12.26–9; Plutarch, *Life of Sulla* 13; Galen *ST* 6.268, *SF* 11.881, *DA* 14.55; Athenaeus *E* 66c–f quoting Antiphanes 274 Kassel, also 90f quoting Diphilus of Siphnos, also 381b; *Apicius passim*.

A. Steier, 'Pfeffer' in *RE* 1893–1972; Laufer 1919 pp. 374–5; Buck 1949 p. 382; Miller 1969 pp. 80–3; M.G. Raschke, 'New studies in Roman commerce with the East' in *Aufstieg und Niedergang der römischen Welt* part 2 vol. 9 section 2 (Berlin, 1978) pp. 650–81 and footnotes pp. 904–1055; P. and M. Hyman,

'Long pepper: a short history' in *Petits Propos culinaires* no. 6 (1980) pp. 50–2, with notes in nos 7, 8 and 12; K.T. Achaya, *Indian Food: a historical companion* (Delhi: Oxford University Press, 1994) pp. 50–2, 192, 214; Dalby 1996 pp. 137, 250; Dalby 2000b pp. 43, 89–94.

- Chilli peppers, red peppers, hot peppers (*Capsicum* spp.) are a New World genus, unknown in the ancient Mediterranean.

Perch, a river fish known to Romans from its presence in the Moselle and Rhine. Ausonius addresses the perch as 'better than any river fish, equal even to the red mullet'.

The perch (*Perca fluviatilis*) is Greek *perke*, Latin *perca*. For the unrelated but superficially similar sea fish, homonymous in Latin and Greek and often called 'perch' by English translators, see COMBER.

Xenocrates *T* 9; Ausonius, *Mosella* 115–17; Anthimus *OC* 39.

Periplus Maris Erythraei, sailing guide to the Red Sea and Indian Ocean, written in Greek by an anonymous merchant between AD 40 and 70 (for the date, which has been disputed, see Casson pp. 6–7). The *Periplus* is a very businesslike survey of trading conditions with detailed information on imports and exports of aromatics – and other exotic products – along the sea routes from Egypt to Arabia, east Africa and the west coast of India.

Periplus Maris Erythraei. Text, translation and commentary: *The Periplus of the Erythraean Sea* tr. Lionel Casson (Princeton: Princeton University Press, 1989).

Persea, tree fruit formerly grown in Egypt, apparently introduced there from Ethiopia, where it is native. Finds in tombs date knowledge of the persea in Egypt to the beginning of the third millennium BC. 'The yellow fruits are about the size of a pigeon's egg and contain two shiny hard seeds', according to Hepper, one of the few modern authors who mentions them at all.

The persea (*Mimusops Schimperi*) is

Greek and Latin *persea*, also Greek *persion*, *persaia*.

'Some say it grows, but is inedible, in Persia,' says Dioscorides in an attempt to explain its name. The story grew, in the hands of Pliny and medieval authors, to the point at which the persea (or occasionally the peach) was said to be a deadly poison in Persia. At least two other explanations of the name were given: that it was introduced from Ethiopia to Egypt by the Persians; and that it was introduced by the Greek mythological hero Perseus.

Hippocrates, *Affections of Women* 90; Theophrastus *HP* 4.2.5; Diodorus Siculus 1.34.7; Strabo 17.2.2; Dioscorides *MM* 1.129; Pliny *NH* 13.60–1, 15.45; Plutarch, *On Isis and Osiris* 378c; Helliodorus, *Ethiopian Story* 8.14.

[A.] Steier, 'Persea' in *RE* 1893–1972; Darby and others 1977 pp. 736–40; Hepper 1990 p. 15; Brewer and others 1995 pp. 63–4.

Persians, people of southern Iran who, in the mid sixth century BC, rapidly gained a vast empire in the Near and Middle East. The Persian Empire lasted from the reign of its founder Cyrus until its conquest by ALEXANDER THE GREAT in the late fourth century. For most of this period it extended from the Aegean coast to the lower Indus valley and from Bactria to Egypt.

In the fifth and fourth centuries many Greeks regarded the Persian Empire as the principal threat to their own freedom. For all that, Greeks were interested by many features of Persian culture. Herodotus's *Histories* are evidence of this interest; so is Xenophon's novelistic *Cyropaedia*, the 'Education of Cyrus'.

The traditional foods for Persian youngsters, unless they improved their rations by successful hunting, were CRESS and TEREBINTH fruits, according to Greek reports. (It is conceivable that by 'terebinth fruits' pistachio nuts are meant: at the relevant period pistachio nuts were unknown in Greece and had no Greek name, and terebinth fruits would be the

nearest approximation.) Strabo adds acorns and wild pears to the list.

Greek sources give interesting details of the supplies regularly required for the Persian King's Dinner. It called for large quantities of domesticated animals and of other farm produce – because it fed not only the king but his courtiers, their families and dependents. The quantity of fattened animals and birds of various species, and the variety of edible oils, are especially interesting. Daily consumption at the King's Dinner is listed, from earlier documents, by Polyaenus and is discussed by Athenaeus. A third indication of the fascination of this topic is the listing of daily supplies for King Solomon's court in the romantic history of Solomon which forms part of *I Kings*: the list is clearly inspired by the Persian King's Dinner. The sauce called *abyrtake* (see under SAUCE), prepared for the King's Dinner, was also known in Greece by the early fourth century, a possible sign of direct Persian influence on Greek cuisine. Note Lewis's important paper on the King's Dinner.

Another commonplace of Persian dining (from the Greek point of view) is the 'prize for a new pleasure', such as a new recipe, that was popularly said to have been offered by the Persian king. The earliest version of the tale is reported from Aristoxenus of Tarentum, possibly built on a report by Xenophon. Plutarch attributes the prize idea to the Assyrians.

Persian sources give a significantly different perspective. Notable here is the information on workmen's supplies during the building of the imperial capital, Persepolis (see Hallock and Lewis). Persian monarchs and governors developed gardens and parks and are known to have transplanted species or varieties across the empire. It is likely that coriander and saffron reached India during this period as a result of their activities.

Herodotus 1.131–40; *I Kings* 4.20–5; Xenophon, *Agesilaus* 9.3, *Cyropaedia* 1.2.8–11, *al.*; Strabo 15.3.18; Plutarch *QC* 1.4 with Clement *ad l.*, also 7.4; Polyaenus 4.3.32; Athenaeus *D*

143f–146d, 513e–515d, also 545d citing Aristoxenus of Tarentum.

Laufer 1919; J.-M. Dentzer, 'L'iconographie iranienne du souverain couché' in *Annales archéologiques arabes syriennes* vol. 21 (1971) pp. 39–50; R.T. Hallock, 'The evidence of the Persepolis tablets' in *The Cambridge History of Iran. Vol. 2* ed. I. Gershevitch (Cambridge: Cambridge University Press, 1985); D.M. Lewis, 'The King's dinner (Polyaenus IV 3.32)' in *Achaemenid History II: the Greek sources* ed. Heleen Sancisi-Weerdenburg and A. Kuhrt (Leiden, 1987) pp. 79–87; Heleen Sancisi-Weerdenburg, 'Gifts in the Persian Empire' in *Le Tribut dans l'Empire Perse* ed. P. Briant and C. Herrenschmidt (Louvain, 1989) pp. 129–46; Pierre Briant, 'Table du roi, tribut et redistribution chez les Achemenides' in *Le Tribut dans l'Empire Perse: actes de la table ronde de Paris, 12–13 Décembre 1986* ed. Pierre Briant and Clarisse Herrenschmidt (Paris, 1989) pp. 35–44; Pierre Briant, 'L'eau du Grand Roi' in *Drinking in Ancient Societies: history and culture of drinks in the Ancient Near East. Papers of a Symposium held in Rome, May 17–19, 1990* ed. Lucio Milano (Padova: Sargon, 1994) pp. 45–65; Jeremy Black, 'Persia: ancient Persia' in *The Oxford Companion to Wine* ed. Jancis Robinson (Oxford: Oxford University Press, 1994) pp. 714–5; Sancisi-Weerdenburg 1995; Pierre Briant, *Histoire de l'Empire Perse: de Cyrus à Alexandre* (Paris: Fayard, 1996); M. Brosius, *Women in Ancient Persia, 559–331 BC* (Oxford: Clarendon Press, 1996) pp. 94–7; Andrew Dalby, 'To feed a king: tyrants, kings and the search for quality in food and agriculture' in *Paysage et alimentation dans le monde grec* ed. Jean-Marc Luce (Toulouse, 2000) pp. 133–44.

Petronius Arbiter, author of a Latin picaresque novel, the *Satyricon*. Parts of books 14 to 16 survive of an original of considerable, but unknown, length. There is much information on food and related matters throughout, but the longest scene and the most important in food history is the 'Dinner of Trimalchio' or *Cena Trimalchionis* (*S* 26–78). A rich, boastful former slave is the host: his slaves, his guests, their conversation and behaviour, and what they eat and drink, are seen through the cynical eyes of the narrator, Encolpius. The menu is showy rather than elegant, and includes dormice rolled in honey and poppy seeds, a dish that has,

ever afterwards, seemed typical of Roman cuisine. The author is generally believed to be the Gaius Petronius who was the emperor Nero's courtier and 'Arbiter of Elegance'. His fame and suicide, in AD 66, are described by Tacitus.

Pliny *NH* 37.20–2; Tacitus, *Annals* 16.17–20.

G. Schmeling, 'Trimalchio's menu and wine list' in *Classical Philology* vol. 55 (1970) pp. 248–51; Edward Courtney, *A Companion to Petronius* (Oxford: Oxford University Press, 2001).

Petronius S: *Satyricon*. Numerous English translations. Critical text and French translation: Pétrone, *Le Satiricon* ed. Alfred Ernout (1923, *CUF*).

Pheasant, game bird of Europe and the Near East. The pheasant was known in classical Greece to be plentiful at the mouth of the River Phasis in Colchis (modern Georgia); it is indeed native to the Caucasus and central Asia. Its spread, with human encouragement, to Greece and other parts of Europe was already under way in the classical period. Palladius gives careful instructions for keeping and breeding. The eggs are recommended by Anthimus.

The pheasant (*Phasianus colchicus*) is Greek *phasianos*, Latin *fasianus*.

Aristophanes, *Clouds* 109 with scholia; Hippocrates *R* 47; Athenaeus *D* 386e–387f, 654b–d; Palladius *OA* 1.29; Anthimus *OC* 22, 38 with Grant *ad l.*

Toynbee 1996 pp. 254–5; Davidson 2000 p. 599.

Philistion of Locri, Greek medical and dietary author, apparently of the fourth century BC. He is cited by Athenaeus, Galen and others; biographical information is scanty.

Die Fragmente der sikelischen Ärzte Akron, Philistion und des Diokles von Karystos ed. M. Wellmann (Berlin, 1901).

Philoxenus (1) of Cythera (*c.*435–380 BC), Greek poet linked with the court of Dionysius of Sicily, at Syracuse. His principal work, very little of which survives, was in the dithyrambic genre.

According to Athenaeus, Philoxenus of Cythera was the author of a florid poem entitled *Dinner*, which was certainly written by someone called Philoxenus shortly before 391 BC. The *Dinner* appears to survive almost complete in several scattered quotations by Athenaeus. Like the fragmentary dithyrambs, the *Dinner* is stuffed with elaborate descriptions and newly invented compound words. It narrates a lavish entertainment in some Greek city – which could be Syracuse, but need not be – focusing unashamedly on the quantity and variety of food that was served.

Philoxenus's poem *Cyclops* or *Galatea* concerned the mythical love of the Cyclops POLYPHEMUS for the nymph Galatea, a tale appropriate to Sicily. This poem is said by Athenaeus and Aelian to have been inspired by a love affair of Philoxenus himself with the royal concubine Galatea. As punishment for this, the poet had been condemned to the Syracusan quarries (but he was always being sent there).

Machon C 9–10 [Athenaeus D 341a–d]; Aelian, *Varia Historia* 12.44; Athenaeus E 6d–7a.

Wilkins 2000 pp. 342–54, *al.*

Philoxenus D: *Deipnon.* Text in *Poetae melici Graeci* ed. D.L. Page (Oxford: Clarendon Press, 1962) pp. 433–41. Translation in Wilkins 2000 pp. 304–6. Commentary: Andrew Dalby, 'The Banquet of Philoxenus' in *Petits Propos culinaires* no. 26 (1987) pp. 28–36.

—— F: fragments. Text in Page (above) pp. 423–32. Text: *Dithyrambographi Graeci* ed. D.F. Sutton (Hildesheim: Weidmann, 1989) pp. 68–77. Translation: *Lyra Graeca* ed. J.M. Edmonds (1922–7, *LCL*) vol. 3 pp. 363–99.

Philoxenus (2) of Leucas, son of Eryxis, legendary Greek gourmand of the fifth or fourth century BC. Stories about him are told by Athenaeus and others. There was, however, confusion among the gluttonous Philoxeni, and some stories of this kind unexpectedly feature Philoxenus of Cythera instead. A kind of cake, *plakountes*

Philoxeneioi, is said to have been named after Philoxenus of Leucas.

The *Dinner* poem discussed at PHILOXENUS (1) was ascribed to Philoxenus of Leucas by Theodor Bergk in the nineteenth century, and many modern editors (including D.L. Page) have followed him, mainly owing to doubt whether its subject and style were suitable to Philoxenus of Cythera. There is little evidence to fortify this doubt, however, and there is no evidence that Philoxenus of Leucas was an author.

Athenaeus E 4b–6d; *Suda s.v. Timakhidas.*

Phoenicia, group of coastal cities at the eastern end of the Mediterranean. Their importance was as emporia at which goods (including foods, wine and aromatics) were transshipped *en route* from east to west and from west to east. The description by the Jewish prophet Ezekiel of the transit trade of Tyre in the sixth century BC is well known.

The Phoenician cities were at their most prosperous from the mid second millennium BC, when Minoan and Mycenaean Greece were beginning to demand supplies from the east, while the already-existing coastal trade with Egypt continued. During the next thousand years Phoenician vessels conducted regular trade from end to end of the Mediterranean. Cyprus was settled partly by Phoenicians, partly by Greeks; Carthage in north Africa (near modern Tunis) was the best known of all the numerous Phoenician colonies and trading posts. The cities were autonomous under the Persian Empire, but ALEXANDER THE GREAT and his successors reduced this autonomy, while Antioch, Gaza and Alexandria took over much of the formerly Phoenician transit trade.

To classical Greeks Phoenicia was a source of wine (see PHOENICIAN WINE), of the wheat called *semidalis* (see WHEAT), of DATES; also of SUMACH, storax, BALSAM and other aromatics. According to Archestratus around 350 BC the best bakers came from Phoenicia. In the Roman period the Phoenician cities were less important, having by now lost their long-distance trade to Antioch and Alexandria; however, Tyre and Sidon were the centres of the purple-dyeing industry.

The luxurious banqueting of 'Straton', king of the Phoenician city of Sidon in the fourth century BC, is described by Theopompus.

Ezekiel 27.17–33; Archestratus *H 5* Brandt; Theopompus 115 F 114 [Athenaeus *D* 531a–d].

M.E. Aubet, *The Phoenicians and the West* (Cambridge, 1993).

Phoenician wine (Greek *Phoinikios*), already familiar in the second millennium BC, was exported to Egypt in the fifth century BC and in Roman times. The best-known appellation then was Laodicean wine (see below); three other cities, Berytus, Tripolis and Tyre, are named as producers by Pliny, and Berytus also exported raisins. Tyrian wine occurs also in the *Ethiopian Story* of Heliodorus. See also CHALYBONIAN WINE.

Sinuhe 82–4 [Pritchard 1969 p. 19]; Herodotus 3.6; Ephippus 8, 24 Kassel [*s.v.l.*]; Heliodorus, *Ethiopian Story* 5.27.9; Pliny *NH* 14.74, 15.66.

Michael Heltzer, 'Olive oil and wine production in Phoenicia and in the Mediterranean trade' in *La Production du vin et de l'huile en Méditerranée* ed. M.-C. Amouretti and J.-P. Brun (Athens: Ecole Française d'Athènes, 1993) pp. 49–54; Albert Leonard, ' "Canaanite jars" and the late Bronze Age Aegeo-Levantine wine trade' in *The Origins and Ancient History of Wine* ed. Patrick E. McGovern, Stuart J. Fleming and Solomon H. Katz (London: Gordon and Breach, 1995) pp. 233–54; Dalby 1996 pp. 96–7.

• Byblos was a major independent city under the Persian Empire. Its wine was liked – though not as much as Lesbian – by Archestratus around 350 BC.

Archestratus *H 59* Brandt [*s.v.l.*].

• The wine of Laodiceia (Greek *Laodikenos*), modern Latakia, was well known in the first centuries BC and AD. The mountain slopes behind the city were covered with vines. Much of the wine of Laodiceia was sold to

Alexandria, according to Strabo; the *Periplus* tells us that some was exported from there to Ethiopia and western India.

Strabo 16.2.9; *Periplus Maris Erythraei* 6 with Casson *ad l.*, 49; *Greek Ostraca in the Bodleian Library* vol. 1 P241, P289, P290.

Phylotimus or Philotimus, Greek medical author of the third century BC. Phylotimus was a pupil of Praxagoras of Cos. He wrote on diet, including a work *On Cookery* (*Opsartytikon*) which is quoted several times by Athenaeus.

F. Steckerl, *The Fragments of Praxagoras of Cos and his School* (Leiden, 1958) pp. 108–23.

Physalis (winter cherry or Chinese lantern: *Physalis Alkekengi*), wild fruit of southeastern Europe and Anatolia, possibly mentioned by Galen under the name *alikakabos*. The same name was used for other, less edible plants.

Dioscorides *MM* 4.71–4; Galen *AF* 6.621.

Picarel and mendole, common and cheap small fish of the Mediterranean. Classical authors, with near unanimity, despise them: the clear conclusion is that they were food for the poor, spurned by any who aspired to wealth or taste.

Thompson 1947 pp. 153–5, 247–8; Davidson 1981 pp. 90–1.

• Latin *gerres*, *gerricula* are general names for both species. The proverbial phrase *addere garo gerrem*, to put a *gerres* into the fish sauce, only produces its expected meaning (to put something bad into what was otherwise good) if it is understood that garum was good and expensive and that the *gerres* was cheap and bad.

Martial 3.77, 12.32.

• Greek *maine*, Latin *maena*, is the specific name for the mendole (*Spicara Maena*). In Rome the mendole provided a kind of *ius* or *muria* (see GARUM), certainly not fine fish sauce but popular among ordinary people, according to Pliny. The *maena* resembled the *smaris* (see below) and the *box* (see BREAM) and was cheap and bad. It was 'food for HECATE' in a Greek comedy by Antiphanes, food that you would leave as a wayside sacrifice to be taken by poor passers-by.

Aristotle *HA* 569b27, 607b9–26; Machon C 5.35–6 (*mainis*); Cato *DA* 23.1 (*mena*); Lucilius 1077 Marx; Ovid, *Halieutica* 120 (*mena*); Persius 3.76; Pliny *NH* 31.83; Martial 11.31, 12.32; Oppian *H* 1.108 (*mainis*); Marcus Aurelius, *Letters* [Fronto vol. 1 p. 182 Haines]; Athenaeus *D* 313a–c quoting Speusippus and Antiphanes.

- Greek and Latin *smaris* is the picarel (*Spicara Smaris*). It was called *kynos eunai*, 'dogs' beds', according to the cookery author Epaenetus; no one knows why.

Aristotle *HA* 607b15–26; Ovid, *Halieutica* 120; Pliny *NH* 32.129 (*zmaris*); Athenaeus *D* 313a–c quoting Epicharmus 29 Kaibel, Speusippus and Epaenetus.

Piddock, a 'boring mollusc' (Thompson). He means that it bores into undersea rock clefts. The animal that protrudes seawards from the long, oval bivalve shell has the look of an acorn, and is good eating. Two species of piddock were on the menu when CAESAR gave a dinner for the college of priests at Rome around 70 BC; they were probably farmed, as described by Columella. According to Diphilus, the Egyptian piddocks were best: 'sweet, tender, palatable, nourishing, juicy, diuretic, laxative; others are rather salty.'

The piddock (*Pholas Dactylus* and *P. crispata*) is Greek *balanos* (literally 'acorn') and *pholas*, Latin *balanus*.

Aristotle *HA* 547b23, *al.*; Theophrastus *HP* 4.6.9 (*drys pontia*); Plautus, *Rudens* 297; Columella *DA* 8.16.7; Athenaeus 85c–91a quoting Diphilus of Siphnos; Macrobius *S* 3.13.10.

Thompson 1947 p. 24.

- Greek *daktylos*, Latin *dactylus*, literally 'date', are names for a similar species, the date-shell (*Lithophaga Lithophaga*). This boring mollusc is edible, but not good enough for high priests. It is luminescent, and remains so even as you eat it, says Pliny.

Pliny *NH* 9.101, 9.184, cf. 32.151.

- Thompson 1947 p. 51.

Pig *see* PORK

Pigeon, group of wild birds of the Near East. Pigeons were probably first domesticated in Pharaonic Egypt, and were at least occasionally used in sacrifice and in food from the second dynasty onwards. The fully domesticated birds were kept in pens. Pigeons could be force-fed to produce a fatter and better-tasting bird. The method is described by Cato, writing in Italy in the mid second century BC, but Cato assumes that the young bird will be taken from the wild, perhaps implying that domesticated pigeons had not then been introduced to Italy.

In late Hellenistic times, not only in Egypt but also in Italy, dovecotes were introduced where flocks of semi-wild pigeons could be kept. Dovecotes are still a feature of the Egyptian rural landscape. In the classical languages these towers are known as *perister(e)on, peristerotrophion* and (in later Latin) *columbarium*. A distinction is made by agricultural writers between the fully domesticated pigeons called *katoikidioi* in Greek and those that live in the dovecote and come and go, *boskades, nomades*. The same distinction is drawn by dietary authors. A prolific breeder and a source of fine food, the pigeon is characterised by Varro as a highly profitable investment.

A general term for pigeon, sometimes covering both wild and domesticated kinds, is Greek *peleia*. The domesticated pigeon is *peristera* in Greek, *columba* in Latin.

Herodotus 1.138; Hippocrates *R* 47; Aristotle *HA* 544a29–544b11, 612b31–613b5; Varro *RR* 3.7; Vitruvius 10.4.2; Columella *DA* 8.8; Pliny *NH* 10.79; Galen *ST* 6.435; Athenaeus *D* 393f–395c, 654a–b; Palladius *OA* 1.24; *Apicius* 6.4; Anthimus *OC* 29 with Grant *ad l.*

Thompson 1936 *s.vv.*; Y. Tepper, 'The rise and fall of dove-raising' in *Adam va-adamah be-Erets-Yi'sra'el ha-kedumah = Man and Land in Eretz-Israel in Antiquity* ed. Aharon Oppenheimer, Aryeh Kasher and Uriel Rappaport (Jerusalem: Yad Yitshak Ben-Tsevi, 1986) pp. 170–96; Brewer and others 1995 p. 123; Arnott 1996 pp. 618–9; Toynbee 1996; Richard F. Johnston, 'Pigeons' in *CWHF* 2000 vol. 1 pp. 561–5.

- Greek *oinas* is the wild rock-dove (*Columba Livia*), the wild form of the domestic pigeon.

  Aristotle *HA* 593a16–19; Aelian, *Nature of Animals* 4.58; Pollux *O* 6.22; Athenaeus *D* 394e.

- Greek *phassa*, Latin *palumbus* is the ring dove or woodpigeon (*Columba Palumbus*).

  Aristophanes, *Acharnians* 1104; Aristotle *HA* 613a20; Theocritus 5.96 with Gow *ad l.*; Columella *DA* 8.9; Pliny *NH* 16.93; Martial 13.67.

- Greek *trygon*, Latin *turtur* is the turtle dove (*Streptopelia Turtur*); in Roman times these were taken from the wild and reared in captivity for the table.

  Hippocrates *R* 47; Columella *DA* 8.9; Palladius *OA* 1.25; Anthimus *OC* 25 with Grant *ad l.*

Pike, river fish of northern Europe. The pike was little known in classical Greece or Italy and is mentioned only by authors writing of northern Gaul. Scarcely fit for the table, it sizzled malodorously in smoky cookshops, according to Ausonius; Anthimus, by contrast, recommended an omelette incorporating minced pike as fit for a king.

The pike (*Esox Lucius*) is Latin *lucius*. For its marine relative (sometimes called 'pike' in English translations) see BARRACUDA.

Ausonius, *Mosella* 120–4; Anthimus *OC* 40 with Grant *ad l.*

Pilot-fish *see* AVOIDANCE OF FOODS

Pine trees, a major feature of the Mediterranean landscape but not a major food source. However, the stone pine (*Pinus pinea*) is the principal source of pine nuts, good to eat and nourishing, though time-consuming to collect. Pine nuts were used in both Greek and Roman cuisine. The tree is *peuke he konophoros* in Greek, *pinus* in Latin; the kernel or nut is *strobilos* in Greek, *nux pinea* in Latin.

Theophrastus *HP* 3.9.1–4; Pliny *NH* 15.35–6, 16.38–41, 23.142–3, 24.28–41; Athenaeus *E* 57b–d; Palladius *OA* 12.7.9–12.

Darby and others 1977 pp. 753–4; Dalby 1996 p. 81.

- The Aleppo pine (*P. halepensis*) and the Scotch pine (*P. sylvestris*) were the principal sources of pine resin, the additive required for RESINATED WINE. These species were called *pitys* in Greek, *picea* in Latin.

  Theophrastus *HP* 9.2.1–2; Pliny *NH* 16.57–8.

- The Scotch pine was used more than other species in the manufacture of pitch. This substance was employed to seal *dolia* in which wine would ferment; it was also used to seal wine-barrels, and these might be made from the wood of the same tree. Powdered pitch was sometimes added to wine for its flavour; in this case, as Palladius observes, it must be checked for good flavour before use.

  Strabo 5.1.12; Pliny *NH* 16.42, 16.52–4; Palladius *OA* 10.11.

Pinna, large bivalve shellfish. The pinna was more valued in ancient times for its wool, which was woven into a costly golden fabric resembling silk, than for its flesh. It was, however, sometimes eaten; Diphilus considers it nourishing, slow to digest, and diuretic. According to Xenocrates the smaller ones were better; they were most tender if previously marinated in wine and vinegar; and they were cooked in 'sweet oil', honey and wine. Artemidorus advises that a dream about the *pine* and its accompanying crab (*pinophylax karkinos* or *pinnoteres*) is a good omen for marriage because of their 'goodwill and fellowship'.

The pinna or fan-mussel (*Pinna nobilis* and other species) is Greek *pine* or *pinne*, Latin *pinna*.

Nicander *A* 394; Xenocrates *T* 98–104; Athenaeus 91e quoting Diphilus of Siphnos; Artemidorus, *Interpretation of Dreams* 2.14.

Thompson 1947 p. 200; Davidson 1981 p. 199; Felicitas Maeder, 'Muschelseide: gesponnenes Gold' in *Mare* no. 13 (1999) pp. 22–6.

Piraeus *see* ATHENS

Pistachio, fruit (nut) of a tree native to central Asia. The pistachio was domesticated in Afghanistan, where archaeobotanical finds demonstrate its use in human food from the third millennium BC. For so-called 'pistachio' in archaeological reports from prehistoric Europe and the Near East, see TEREBINTH.

The earliest description of the pistachio is given by Theophrastus: it is one among the food plants that became known to Greeks in the course of Alexander's expedition, and was mentioned briefly by Aristobulus. Theophrastus had no name for it; Nicander, a century later, recalls Theophrastus's description and is the first to give the fruit a name. Good to eat and very nourishing, it spread rapidly to Mediterranean lands in Hellenistic times, grafted on terebinth rootstocks: this practice, first described by Damegeron and Palladius, is still standard.

Paxamus is the first surviving author who gives instructions for growing the pistachio, but he does not mention grafting. It seems possible that the pistachio was first introduced to Italy in republican times and was known at that time in Latin as *mollusca*; if this identification is correct, the trees did not eventually become established. The successful transplanting of pistachios from Syria to Italy in the mid first century AD by the future emperor Vitellius is recorded by Pliny.

The pistachio (*Pistacia vera*) is Greek *bistakion, pistakion, psittakion*, Latin *pistacia*.

Theophrastus *HP* 4.4.7; Nicander *T* 891; Dioscorides *MM* 1.124; Pliny *NH* 13.51, 15.90–1; Arrian, *Anabasis* 3.28 citing Aristobulus, cf. Strabo 15.2.10; Galen *AF* 6.612, *SF* 12.102; Athenaeus *D* 649c–e citing Poseidonius *F* 3 Jacoby; Macrobius *S* 3.18.9–12 (*mollusca*); Palladius *OA* 11.12.3; Anthimus *OC* 91; *Geoponica* 10.12 citing Damegeron and Paxamus.

Laufer 1919 pp. 246–53; M. Zohary, 'A monographical study of the genus *Pistacia*' in *Palestine Journal of Botany. Jericho series* vol. 5 (1952) pp. 187–228; Zohary and Hopf 1993 p. 180; Dalby 1996 p. 146.

Plato (1). Greek philosopher (*c.*428–349 BC). Plato's *Symposium* is a narrative of a drinking party at the house of the playwright Agathon, held to celebrate his prize at the *Lenaia*, one of the annual dramatic festivals at Athens, in 416. The purpose of the sketch is to exemplify Socrates's participation in philosophical discussions at symposia, to give an interpretation of his relationship with Alcibiades, and to report (or reinvent) a discussion on this particular occasion concerning the nature of love. Incidentally the *Symposium* gives a fine impression of the mechanics of a *symposion*, including the less cerebral side of it (see also XENOPHON).

Elsewhere Plato expresses disapproval of the banquets and luxury foods of Sicily. A speaker probably representing his views is critical of the drunkenness that was typical of Athenian symposia by contrast with the sobriety of Sparta. In the *Republic* Plato attributes to Socrates the recommendation of a largely vegetarian diet in a utopian republic.

Plato, *Symposium passim, Letters* 7.326b, *Republic* 372b–c, *Laws* 636e–637c.

P. Boyancé, 'Platon et le vin' in *Bulletin de l'Association Guillaume Budé. Lettres d'humanité* (1951) pp. 3–19; Livio Rossetti, 'Il momento conviviale dell'eteria socratica e il suo significato pedagogico' in *Ancient Society* vol. 7 (1976) pp. 29–77; Manuela Tecuşan, 'Logos sympotikos: patterns of the irrational in philosophical drinking: Plato outside the *Symposium*' in *Sympotica: a symposium on the symposion* ed. Oswyn Murray (Oxford: Oxford University Press, 1990) pp. 238–60; Roland Brunet, 'Vin et philosophie: le Banquet de Platon; esquisse d'une sympotique platonicienne' in G. Garrier and others, *Le Vin des historiens* (Suze-la-Rousse: Université du Vin, 1990) pp. 21–48; Luciana Romeri, 'Food and forgetfulness at Socratic symposia' in *Food and the Memory: papers of the Oxford Symposium on Food and Cookery 2000* ed. Harlan Walker (Totnes: Prospect Books, 2001) pp. 199–204.

Plato (2) 'Comicus', Athenian comedy playwright (active *c.*425–385 BC). None of his plays survives complete, but Plato is frequently quoted by Athenaeus for evidence of dining and drinking customs, and is often cited in this book.

In his play *Phaon*, produced 391 BC, a character decides to 'sit down and read a new book on cookery by Philoxenus' and proceeds to quote this book on stage (Plato Comicus F 189 Kassel). The quotation is a set of comic hexameter lines, not unlike the (slightly later) work of ARCHESTRATUS in style, overtly discussing gastronomy but continually harping on the subject of APHRODISIACS. The lines must really be by Plato himself, but in modern times they have occasionally been attributed to PHILOXENUS (2) of Leucas on the basis of a statement by the epitomator of Athenaeus (Athenaeus E 5b). These parodic lines serve as evidence that the *Dinner*, by PHILOXENUS (1) of Cythera, was then recently written, though they bear no resemblance to it. They are discussed by Rosen and by Wilkins, both of whom provide translations, and by Olson and Sens.

Ralph M. Rosen, 'Plato Comicus and the evolution of Greek comedy' in *Beyond Aristophanes: transition and diversity in Greek comedy* ed. Gregory W. Dobrov (Atlanta: Scholars Press, 1995) pp. 119–37; Wilkins 2000 pp. 342–50, *al.*; Olson and Sens 2000 pp. xl–xliii.

Plato F: fragments. Critical text in *PCG: Poetae comici Graeci* ed. R. Kassel and C. Austin (Berlin: De Gruyter, 1983–); English translation in *The Fragments of Attic Comedy* ed. J.M. Edmonds (Leiden, 1957–61). References elsewhere in the present book are to the fragment numbering established by Kassel and Austin, differing slightly from that of Edmonds.

Pliny 'the Elder' (Gaius Plinius Secundus), Roman encyclopaedic author (AD 23–79). Pliny the Elder is conventionally so called to distinguish him from his nephew and namesake, author of a collection of letters.

Pliny was a tireless reader and notetaker, as his nephew makes clear. His only surviving work, the *Natural History* (in 37 books), gives evidence of his wide interests. It is a remarkable achievement in recording and classifying the knowl-

edge of the natural world available in the first century AD. On the subject of food the most useful divisions are books 8–11 (animals) and books 12–19 (plants): Pliny gives special attention throughout to their uses to humanity, including food uses. Book 14 deals with the vine and with wine; book 16 is devoted largely to the olive, and book 17 to fruit trees. The next major division, books 20–32, is also noteworthy: it deals with substances useful in medicine and the diet, including important foods such as honey, fruits (again), milk, cheese and butter. Pliny is particularly informative on the spice trade, its practices, its prices and its deceits.

Very large numbers of 'authors consulted' are listed in the preliminary bibliographical section of the *Natural History*. Individual sources are rarely credited in the course of the work; many statements are thus difficult to evaluate. Where it is possible to check Pliny's use of his sources, as with his numerous unacknowledged quotations from THEOPHRASTUS, it becomes clear that he often quotes almost verbatim but also fairly frequently misreads his source and sometimes slants his report to suit his current line of argument.

Pliny the Younger, *Letters* 3.5, 6.16.

Jerry Stannard, 'Medicinal plants and folk remedies in Pliny, Historia Naturalis' in *History and Philosophy of the Life Sciences* vol. 4 (1982) pp. 3–23; John Scarborough, 'Pharmacy in Pliny's *Natural History*' in *Science in the Early Roman Empire* ed. R. French and F. Greenaway (Beckenham, 1986); Jacqueline Vons, 'Il est des parfums sauvages comme l'odeur du désert: étude du vocabulaire des parfums chez Pline l'Ancien' in *Latomus* vol. 58 (1999) pp. 820–38.

Pliny NH: *Natural History*. Text and translation: Pliny, *Natural History* ed. H. Rackham and others 10 vols (1938–63, *LCL*). Note the revised edn of vol. 7, 1980.

Plum, tree fruit of which various species grow wild from western Europe across the temperate zone to China. The cultivated plum of Europe (*Prunus domestica* subsp. *domestica*) descends ultimately from a wild species of southeastern Europe and southwestern Asia; it is not known where domestication took place, but, as with several other fruits, it could have been in Anatolia in the late prehistoric period.

A divergent subspecies, the bullace (*P. domestica* subsp. *insititia*) gave rise to the modern group of cultivated varieties known as damsons. These, nowadays favoured in northern Europe, may be descendants of the type known in Roman times as *damascenum* 'Damascus plum', which at that time was typical of Syria. The name is undoubtedly the same, but the historical link between *damascenum* and damson is tenuous.

The usual wild plum of central and southern Europe is the sloe (*P. spinosa*). Sour though it is, this was being gathered as human food in southern Europe by 7000 BC, and remained familiar in classical times as a food gathered from the wild.

Greeks had many names for plums, uncertainly identified: *kokkymelon* perhaps 'domestic plum', *proumnon* 'bullace', *damaskenon* 'damson', *brabylon* 'sloe'. They were beginning to develop larger, sweeter varieties: we can contrast the wreath of plums mentioned by Hipponax (not sloes, which would be a thorny wreath, but not large plums either) with the engaging simile offered by Alexis two centuries later: 'Did you ever see a cooked calf's stomach, or a boiled stuffed spleen, or a basket of ripe plums? That's what his face looks like!' (he was evidently apoplectic, and the sense demands large, purple plums). Romans, by Pliny's time at any rate, had got a good deal further with plum cultivation: they used the general term *prunum*. They distinguished *damascenum* as one among several varieties (whence *ameixa* 'plum' in Portuguese) and *cereola* as another (whence *ciruela* 'plum' in Spanish).

Hipponax 60 West; Alexis *F* 275 Kassel; Theocritus 7.146; Pliny *NH* 15.41–4, 23.132–3; Galen *AF* 6.619–22; Athenaeus *E* 49d–50b;

Palladius *OA* 12.7.13–16; Anthimus *OC* 85.

T. Weber, 'Damaskena' in *Zeitschrift der deutschen Palästina-Vereins* vol. 105 (1989) pp. 151–65; J. Diethart and E. Kislinger, 'Aprikosen und Pflaumen' in *Jahrbuch der österreichischer Byzantinistik* vol. 42 (1992) pp. 75–8; Zohary and Hopf 1993 pp. 169–71; Davidson 1999 p. 614.

Plutarch of Chaeronea, Greek biographer and essayist (*c.*AD 45–120). Three of Plutarch's writings, listed below, have settings or subjects directly related to food and dining. Of these three, *Symposium Questions* is the most important. It is a long and lively work claiming to report discussions which took place at dinners and symposia attended by Plutarch, members of his family, and his friends. The topics are varied, but many of the discussions focus on food, wine, dining and entertainment. The *Dinner of the Seven Sages* is historical fiction. *On Eating Meat* is an unfinished (or, at any rate, incomplete) text arguing the moral case for vegetarianism. Some scholars doubt that the two latter writings are really by Plutarch.

Many of his other works are occasionally relevant to the subjects of food and dining; for example, banquets and drinking parties figure extensively in several of his biographies.

G. Paul, 'Symposia and deipna in Plutarch's Lives and in other historical writings' in *Dining in a Classical Context* ed. W.J. Slater (Ann Arbor: University of Michigan Press, 1991) pp. 157–69; Judith Mossman, 'Plutarch's Dinner of the Seven Wise Men and its place in symposion literature' in *Plutarch and his Intellectual World* ed. J. Mossman (London: Duckworth, 1997) pp. 119–40.

Plutarch CS: *Dinner of the Seven Sages*. Text and translation in *Plutarch's Moralia*; vol. 2 ed. and tr. F.C. Babbitt (1928, *LCL*). Text, Italian translation and commentary: Plutarco, *Il convito dei sette sapienti* ed. Ferdinando Lo Cascio (Napoli: D'Auria, 1997).

—— **EC**: *On Eating Meat*. Text and translation in *Plutarch's Moralia*; vol. 12 ed. and tr. H. Cherniss and W.C. Helmbold (1957, *LCL*).

—— **QC**: *Symposium Questions*. Text, translation and commentary: *Plutarch's Moralia*; vol. 8 ed. and tr. P.A. Clement and H.B. Hoffleit; vol. 9 ed. and tr. E.L. Minar, F.H. Sandbach and W.C. Helmbold (1969, 1961, *LCL*). Critical text and French translation: Plutarque, *Oeuvres morales. Tome 9: Propos de table* parts 1–2 ed. and tr. F. Fuhrmann (1972–8, *CUF*). Partial commentary: S.-T. Teodorsson, *A Commentary on Plutarch's Table Talks* (Gothenburg: Acta Universitatis Gothoburgensis, 1989).

Poisons, reportedly combined with foods on several famous occasions to effect assassination. The last king of Pergamum, ATTALUS Philometor, was said to have grown poisonous plants and to have used them. The Roman emperors AUGUSTUS and (more unanimously) CLAUDIUS are said to have been poisoned. See also COLCHICUM.

John Scarborough, 'Nicander's toxicology, part 1: snakes' in *Pharmacy in History* vol. 19 (1977) pp. 3–23; John Scarborough, 'Nicander's toxicology, II: spiders, scorpions, insects and myriapods' in *Pharmacy in History* vol. 21 (1979) pp. 3–34, 73–92; Sarah Currie, 'Poisonous women and unnatural history in Roman culture' in *Parchments of Gender: deciphering the bodies of antiquity* ed. Maria Wyke (Oxford: Clarendon Press, 1998) pp. 147–67.

- Bull's blood was widely regarded as a poison. Themistocles killed himself, it was said, by drinking it. Several antidotes were prescribed.

  Aristophanes, *Knights* 83 with scholia; Nicander *A* 312–34 with Gow *ad l.*; Scribonius Largus 196.

  Kenneth F. Kitchell and Lin Allison Parker, 'Death by bull's blood: a natural explanation' in *Alpha to Omega: studies in honor of George John Szemler on his sixty-fifth birthday* ed. William J. Cherf (Chicago: Ares, 1993) pp. 123–41.

Polenta *see* BARLEY

Pollen analysis or palynology, the use of pollen conserved in datable deposits to study historical flora. Some pollens are likely to be preserved in such samples, some are not. Some terrains provide suitable samples, some do not. Although the information available is for these reasons imperfect, it may still be crucial in pinpointing the period at which food plants were introduced to a particular region. One example is the rapid spread of several fruit tree species to western Anatolia, Greece and the Balkans at a date close to 1200 BC in the 'Beyşehir Occupation Phase'.

S. Bottema, 'Palynological investigations in Greece with special reference to pollen as an indicator of human activity' in *Paleohistoria* vol. 24 (1982 [1985]) pp. 257–89; Petra Dark, 'Pollen evidence for the environment of Roman Britain' in *Britannia* vol. 30 (1999) pp. 247–72; S. Bottema, 'The Holocene history of walnut, sweet chestnut, manna-ash and plane tree in the Eastern Mediterranean' in *Paysage et alimentation dans le monde grec* ed. Jean-Marc Luce (Toulouse, 2000) pp. 35–59.

Pollux or Polydeuces, Julius, Greek educator and linguist (late second century AD). Pollux taught Greek to the future emperor Commodus. His *Onomasticon*, a thesaurus of classical Greek terminology, is dedicated to his pupil. Also attributed to Pollux is a series of dialogues in Greek and Latin serving as a textbook for students of Greek. Neither of these works has been translated into English.

Pollux KH: *Kathemerine Homilia* 'Daily conversation in Greek and Latin'. Text: Julius Pollux, *Hermeneumata kai Kathemerine homilia* ed. A. Boucherie (Paris: Imprimerie Nationale, 1872) (*Notices des manuscrits de la Bibliothèque Nationale*, 23 part 2).

—— **O**: *Onomasticon*. Critical text: *Pollucis Onomasticon* ed. E. Bethe (Leipzig: Teubner, 1900–37).

Polycrates, king of the Greek island of SAMOS (538–522 BC). Polycrates is said to have gathered on Samos, 'for luxury's sake', the finest breeds of animals and the finest varieties of crops, including goats of Scyros (likewise said by Pindar to be the best for milk) and pigs from SICILY. This is the earliest record of the recognition of LOCAL SPECIALITIES.

Athenaeus *D* 540a–541a, cf. Pindar fragment 95 Bowra [Athenaeus *E* 28a].

Andrew Dalby, 'To feed a king: tyrants, kings

and the search for quality in food and agriculture' in *Paysage et alimentation dans le monde grec* ed. Jean-Marc Luce (Toulouse, 2000) pp. 133–44.

Polyphemus, the memorable CYCLOPS, blinded by Odysseus in the story told in the *Odyssey*. In this narrative Polyphemus is a man-eater and also a nomadic shepherd skilled in making cheese from the milk of his sheep and goats.

The adventure was localised in SICILY by almost all later readers, and it is a fact that Sicily produced fine cheese from mixed goat's and sheep's milk. Many later poets revisited the Cyclops theme, sharpening the image of Polyphemus as a shepherd, cheese-maker and gatherer of wild herbs and fruits. He was also likened, in the mythological comedy of Cratinus, to a Sicilian cook.

Homer, *Odyssey* 9.218–23; Philoxenus *F* 7 Page; Aristophanes, *Wealth* 290–301 with scholia; Cratinus Junior 1 Kassel; Theocritus 11 with scholia and Gow *ad l.*; Ovid, *Metamorphoses* 13.810–30.

Pomegranate, segmented fruit whose juice can be drunk and whose juice and seeds had many medicinal uses in the classical world. The pomegranate, native to Iran, was familiar in Egypt by the mid second millennium BC: its unmistakeable shape appears frequently on wall paintings from then onwards. By the beginning of the archaic period it was well known in Greece. It is one of the fruit trees that characterises the orchards of Alcinous in the *Odyssey*. By then the pomegranate was evidently spreading further west: it is represented by archaeobotanical finds in southern France in the last few centuries BC. If the Latin name of the fruit, *malum punicum* 'Phoenician apple', can be relied on as evidence, cultivation might have been introduced to Italy (indeed, possibly to Greece and to Gaul also) by the Phoenicians and Carthaginians.

Early medical authors distinguished three kinds of pomegranate by their juice, respectively sweet, winy and acid; they prescribed the juice and also other preparations.

Pomegranates were perhaps more significant mythologically than in the diet. They were offered to the Phoenician goddess Astarte, and to several Greek goddesses. Persephone, while in the underworld, is said to have sucked one pomegranate seed, and thus to have condemned herself to remain there for a third of every year.

The pomegranate (*Punica Granatum*) is Greek *roa*, *side*, Latin *malum Punicum*, *malum granatum*.

Homer, *Odyssey* 7.115; *Homeric Hymn to Demeter* 370–413; Hippocrates *R* 55, *Epidemics* 7.67, 7.80, 7.101; Theophrastus *HP* 4.3.3; Pliny *NH* 13.112–13, 23.106–14; Plutarch *QC* 5.8 quoting Empedocles 80 Diels; Pausanias 7.17.11; Apollodorus 1.5.3; Athenaeus *D* 650e–651b, cf. 82a–b; Palladius *OA* 4.10.1–10.

Laufer 1919 p. 276–87; J. Engemann, 'Granatapfel' in *RAC* 1950– ; Darby and others 1977 pp. 740–4; Zohary and Hopf 1993 p. 162; Brewer and others 1995 p. 64; Simoons 1998 pp. 279–84.

Pompeii, coastal city of Roman Campania. Although a settlement of some size, Pompeii was of only local importance and is infrequently mentioned in classical texts; its moment of fame came with the eruption of Mount Vesuvius in AD 79 by which the city was destroyed.

Since its rediscovery in the late eighteenth century, and especially with wider archaeological perspectives in the twentieth century, Pompeii has been of crucial importance for the information it can provide on daily life under the Roman Empire. Information comes from finds of market gardens, installations for food preparation (including bread ovens), places where food and wine were sold; finds of fossilised foods, including grains, dried fruits, and breads; finds of labelled amphorae, some of which retain the stains and even the smells of their original contents; wall paintings including kitchen still lifes and garden paintings; inscriptions, official and unofficial, including advertisements for inns.

The neighbouring settlements of Herculaneum and Oplontis were also destroyed, as was much of the agricultural region surrounding Pompeii. Here farms have been found equipped with wine and olive presses and with *dolia* for maturing large quantities of wine. The volcanic slopes of Vesuvius and the alluvial soils below had been clothed in vines, notably the *aminnia gemina minor* variety. Many vineyards of the *Vesuvinum* and *Pompeianum* appellations (see NEAPOLITAN WINES) were destroyed or abandoned in the eruption. Villas around Vesuvius were equipped with presses. The relationship between Pompeii and its hinterland is a fruitful topic for study.

Pliny the Younger, *Letters* 6.16; Martial 4.44.

Emilio Magaldi, 'Il commercio ambulante a Pompei' in *Atti dell' Accademia Pontaniana* vol. 60 (1930) pp. 61–88; P. Soprano, 'I triclini all'aperto di Pompei' in *Pompeiana* (Naples, 1950) pp. 288–310; J. Packer, 'Inns at Pompeii' in *Cronache pompeiane* vol. 4 (1978) pp. 12–24; Betty Jo Mayeske, 'Bakers, bakeshops and bread: a social and economic study' in *Pompeii and the Vesuvian Landscape* (Washington: Archaeological Institute of America, Smithsonian Institution, 1979) pp. 39–58; W.F. Jashemski, *The Gardens of Pompeii, Herculaneum and the Villas Destroyed by Vesuvius* (New Rochelle, 1979–93); Robert I. Curtis, 'The garum shop of Pompeii (I.12.8)' in *Cronache pompeiane* vol. 5 (1979 [1982]) pp. 5–23; V. Gassner, *Die Kaufläden in Pompeii* (Vienna, 1986); Tchernia 1986 pp. 176–7; E.S.P. Ricotti, 'The importance of water in Roman garden triclinia' in *Ancient Roman Villa Gardens* ed. E.B. MacDougall (Washington, DC, 1987) (*Dumbarton Oaks Colloquia on the History of Landscape Architecture*, 10) pp. 137–84; S. Bisel, 'Nutrition in first century Herculaneum' in *Anthropologie* vol. 26 (1988) pp. 61–6; B.J. Mayeske, 'A Pompeiian bakery on the Via dell'Abbondanza' vol. 1 pp. 149–65; F.G. Meyer, 'Food plants identified from carbonized remains at Pompeii and other Vesuvian sites' in *Studia pompeiana et classica in honor of Wilhelmina F. Jashemski* ed. Robert I. Curtis (New Rochelle: Caratzas, 1989) vol. 1 pp. 183–229; see also M. Ricciardi and G.G. Aprile in *Studia pompeiana et classica in honor of Wilhelmina F. Jashemski* ed. Robert I. Curtis (New Ro-

chelle: Caratzas, 1989) pp. 317–30; D.P.S. Peacock, 'The mills of Pompeii' in *Antiquity* vol. 63 (1989) pp. 205–14; S.C. Bisel, *The Secrets of Vesuvius* (Sevenoaks, 1990); *Garden History: garden plants, species, forms and varieties from Pompei to 1800: symposium, Ravello, June 1991* ed. Dagfinn Moe, James H. Dickson and Per Magnus Jorgensen (Rixensart: PACT Belgium, 1994); Michael Fulford and Andrew Wallace-Hadrill, 'Unpeeling Pompeii' in *Antiquity* vol. 72 (1998) pp. 128–45.

Pontus or *Pontus Euxinus* (Greek *Pontos* or *Pontos Euxeinos*), the Black Sea. In classical times the Black Sea was surrounded by Greek-established harbour cities and was an important source of seafood, notably the bonito (see TUNNY) that was fished along the southern shore and the fish sauce (see GARUM) that was made at several places on the northern shore. Sinope was also a good place for the *kestreus*, grey mullet. Fish that was salted or dried for trade was necessarily exported to Greece and beyond by way of BYZANTIUM, which commanded seaborne access to the Black Sea. Some of the wheat grown on the wide steppes of what is now Ukraine was exported, by way of the Greek colonies and the Pontic seaways, to classical Athens.

The Hellenistic kingdom on the southern shore, in northeastern Anatolia, was also called Pontus; its most famous and its last ruler was MITHRIDATES. The mountains of Pontus were rich in fruits, notably the HAZELNUT, which was usually called *karyon Pontikon* 'Pontic nut' in Greek.

Archestratus *H* 44 Olson; Athenaeus *D* 118b–c citing Dorion.

Poor and rich people were distinguished by their diet and their nutritional status in Greece and Rome, as they are in modern societies. The definition of 'poor' is complicated by the existence of slavery.

Nutritional differences are not easy to characterise in detail because literary sources emerge from the richer end of society; when they describe the life of the poor – for whatever motive – they may fail to do so accurately. Archaeological information, which in general derives from both poor and rich lifestyles, may redress the balance.

The diet of those unable to choose and get the foods they wanted consisted, in general, of less-nourishing staple foods (barley and dried pulses rather than wheat) and of less varied relishes (WILD FOODS, fruits and greens, replacing meat and fish). Wine and olive oil were not equally available to all. Citizens and their families – of many cities including Athens and Rome – might benefit from charities and from municipal distributions of bread, sacrificial meat and other foods: non-citizens, particularly slaves, had no such opportunities.

V. Neri, 'L'alimentazione povera nell'Italia romana' in *L'alimentazione nell'antichità* (Parma, 1985); N.A. Hudson, 'Food in Roman satire' in *Satire and Society in Ancient Rome* ed. S.H. Braund (Exeter: Exeter University Press, 1989) pp. 69–87; Dalby 1996 pp. 24–9; Garnsey 1999 pp. 113–27.

Poppy, group of wild flowers widely distributed across Eurasia. In the classical Mediterranean the poppy was most important as a medicinal plant, the source of opium. This was harvested by slitting the ripe seed-head in late spring. Owing to the risk of fatal overdose some physicians urged that opium should be avoided in medicine. However, in practice the compound medicine made with opium, *to dia kodyon* in Greek, *diacodion* in Latin, was commonly used: it was by far the best available analgesic. The opium poppy is native to southwestern Europe from the west coast of Italy to Spain and Morocco. It was brought into cultivation in prehistoric Europe and spread rapidly eastwards.

Oil can be extracted from the seeds of the opium poppy, and the seeds themselves have food uses (the oil and the seeds are not narcotic). Both Greek and Latin sources agree that poppy seeds were sprinkled on bread before baking; white

of egg was used to bind the seeds to the crust.

The opium poppy (*Papaver somniferum*) is Greek *mekon he leuke*, Latin *papaver candidum*. The corn poppy (*P. Rhoeas*) is Greek *mekon he melaina*, Latin *papaver nigrum*; this is the species that was cultivated for its oil, which had medicinal uses. The leaves of a wild poppy of Italy and Greece, *P. hybridum*, were used as a salad vegetable or potherb, variously compared to chicory and to rocket. This species was Greek *mekon he roias*, Latin *papaver erraticum*.

Homer, *Iliad* 8.306–7; Hippocrates *R* 45; Theophrastus *HP* 1.12.2, 9.12.4; Plautus, *Poenulus* 326; Cato *DA* 79, 84; Pliny 19.167–9, 20.198–209; Oribasius *CM* 5.18 citing Galen and Philagrius; Pseudo-Apuleius, *Herbarius* 53.

Yule and Burnell 1903 pp. 640–2; A.C. Andrews, 'The opium poppy as food and spice in the classical period' in *Agricultural History* vol. 26 (1952) pp. 152–5; P.G. Kritikos and S.P. Papadaki, 'The history of the poppy and of opium and their expansion in antiquity in the eastern Mediterranean area' in *Bulletin on Narcotics* vol. 19 (1967) no. 3 pp. 17–38 and no. 4 pp. 5–10; D.J. Crawford, 'The opium poppy: a study in Ptolemaic agriculture' in *Problèmes de la terre en Grèce ancienne* ed. M.I. Finley (The Hague, 1973) pp. 223–51; Guido Majno, *The Healing Hand: man and wound in the ancient world* (Cambridge, Mass.: Harvard University Press, 1975) pp. 108–11; M.D. Merlin, *On the Trail of the Ancient Opium Poppy* (Rutherford, 1984); Zohary and Hopf 1993 pp. 128–31; Martin Booth, *Opium: a history* (New York: Simon and Schuster, 1996).

Porgy *see* BREAM

Pork, meat of the pig, domestic relative of the wild BOAR. Pigs had been domesticated by around 7000 BC, at which date they were being kept and bred both in Mesopotamia and in southeastern Europe. It is uncertain whether domestication took place in the two regions independently.

In classical times pigs were probably the commonest source of meat in most people's diet. They are the most specialised of the major domestic animals of

Europe: they produce no wool, and humans do not drink their milk. 'What the pig does produce,' to quote Frost, 'is more pigs': as many as twelve per farrow, and healthy sows may farrow twice a year. Moreover, a young well-grown porker gives far more edible meat than comparable young of the other domesticated species. By classical times (and probably long before) people had worked out various methods of conserving nearly all of this meat, so that the slaughter of an animal would provide a steady food supply over a long period – and, particularly important, so that animals slaughtered at the end of autumn, as fodder becomes scarcer, will provide food through the winter.

Pigs will eat almost anything, from acorns to pork. Their meat is of varied taste, texture and quality. If not thoroughly cooked, pork can indeed be 'disturbing to the digestion' (as in a view cited in the Hippocratic text *Sacred Disease*). It can also be a luxury food. In Greece and Rome there was a market for sucking-pig (see also SUCKLING ANIMALS) and for fatted pig, which Aristotle knew of as a product of Thracian fatteners. Pigs were fed with dried figs because this produced fine-flavoured liver (see FATTENING).

The economic importance of pork comes partly from the fact that not only the muscle meat but practically every other bit of the animal can be used as human food. The stomach and intestines were used not only in their own right but also as SAUSAGE casings. For pork offal see also HEAD; HEART; LIVER; TRIPE; UDDER; WOMB; and under MEAT.

The pig (*Sus Scrofa*) is Greek *hys*, Latin *sus*. The successive stages of the animal's growth are represented by the Greek terms *khoiros* and *delphax* (with diminutive *delphakion*); both terms have the second meaning 'cunt', an ambiguity which is the source of extended word play in Aristophanes's *Acharnians*. Latin *porcus* (with diminutive *porcellus*) had the same

double meaning, as Varro makes clear (*RR* 2.4.10).

Aristophanes, *Acharnians* 729–817, cf. *Thesmophoriazusae* 237, *Lysistrata* 1061; Hippocrates, *Sacred Disease* 2; Philoxenus D b.27 Page; Aristotle *HA* 595a15–595b4; Varro *RR* 2.4; Pliny *NH* 8.209; Galen *AF* 6.679, 6.704, *BM* 6.771; Athenaeus *D* 374d–376b, 655f–656b; Palladius *OA* 3.26; Anthimus *OC* 9–10, 21 with Grant *ad ll.*

Buck 1949 pp. 160–4; Darby and others 1977 pp. 171–209; S. Bökönyi in *History of Humanity* ed. S.J. De Laet (Paris, 1994) pp. 391–3; Brewer and others 1995 pp. 93–7; Bernard Sergent, 'Le porc indo-européen d'ouest en est' in *Mythologies du porc* ed. Philippe Walter (Grenoble: Millon, 1999) pp. 9–39; Frank Frost, 'Sausage and meat preservation in antiquity' in *Greek, Roman and Byzantine Studies* vol. 40 (1999) pp. 241–52.

- Greek *perikomma, perikommation*, Latin *callum* is skin or crackling. Greek *akrokolia*, Latin *ungella* is trotter.

Eubulus *F* 14 Kassel; *Vindolanda Tablets* 2.233; Galen *AF* 6.669–72; *Apicius* 7.1.5.

- Greek *kolen*, Latin and later Greek *perna* is ham, meaning a leg of pork, salted or destined for salting. The best hams were from Gaul, says Athenaeus, but there were also good ones in Asia and Lycia; Strabo knew of fine hams in northern Spain. Instructions on salting pork are given by Cato and Columella. Greek *halipasta* means salt meats or salt pork in general; Latin *abdomen* is belly of pork.

Cato *DA* 162; Strabo 3.4.11; Columella *DA* 12.55; *Vindolanda Tablets* 2.182; Pollux *O* 6.52; Athenaeus *D* 657e–658a; *Apicius* 7.4.2.

- Greek *lardion*, Latin *laridum, lardum* is bacon: in other words, sliced ham (or any other cut of salt pork), re-fried, or added to other foods when cooking for the sake of the flavour. Already known in Roman cuisine, bacon was to become a favourite Frankish delicacy.

Vindolanda Tablets 2.182; Anthimus *OC* 14 with Grant *ad l.*, 20; Nicetas Choniates, *Chronicle* p. 594 van Dieten.

Porphyry (*Porphyrios*), Greek Neoplatonist philosopher (AD 234–*c*.303). A prolific author, Porphyry wrote one work of particular relevance to food, an exposition of vegetarianism.

Porphyry DA: *On Abstinence from Animal Foods*. Text, French translation and commentary: Porphyre, *De l'abstinence* ed. Jean Bouffartigue, Michel Patillon and A.P. Segonds (1977–95, *CUF*).

Posca, a drink based on vinegar heavily diluted with water (Greek *oxykraton*) and infused with herbs. Such mixtures were used medicinally in earlier Greece, sometimes taken as a drink, sometimes applied externally, but they had no general name. As an everyday drink used in the army and by the urban poor, *posca* was a Roman development, and a convenient one economically since faulty storage of wine tends to result in vinegar. The elder Cato liked *posca*, according to Plutarch; other commanders drank it ostentatiously to show solidarity with their troops (*Historia Augusta*). Like it or not, the lower ranks of the Roman army were drinking *posca* and wine on alternate days (*Codex*, a decree of AD 360). *Posca* continued to be an everyday drink in the Byzantine period, both in the army and in the city; the loanword *phouska* is recorded in Greek from the sixth century onwards.

The initial unfamiliarity of *posca* in the Greek-speaking East explains why *oxos* 'vinegar' is the Greek term used for this beverage by Plutarch and in the narratives of the Crucifixion: at that date there was no more precise Greek equivalent. This word *oxos* is rendered literally *acetum* in the Vulgate Latin translation of the Bible and 'vinegar' or its equivalent in many modern versions. *Acetum* is also the term used in the *Codex*.

Plautus, *Truculentus* 609; Mark, *Gospel* 15.36; Plutarch, *Cato the Elder* 1.10; Suetonius, *Vitellius* 12.1; *Historia Augusta, Hadrian* 10.2, *Avidius Cassius* 5.3, *Pescennius* 10.3; Vegetius 3.3; Justinian, *Codex* 12.37.1; Aetius, *Medicine* 3.81–2; Anthimus *OC* 58.

E. Kislinger, 'Phoûska und glékhon' in *Jahrbuch der österreichischen Byzantinistik* vol. 34 (1984) pp. 49–53; Tchernia 1986 pp. 11–19; M.-C. Amouretti, 'Vin, vinaigre, piquette dans l'antiquité' in G. Garrier and others, *Le Vin des historiens* (Suze-la-Rousse: Université du Vin, 1990) pp. 75–87.

Poseidonius (1) of Apameia, Greek Stoic philosopher and traveller of the first century BC. The writings of Poseidonius do not survive, but his important ethnographic observations on the peoples of the western Mediterranean are quoted at some length by Athenaeus.

Poseidonius F: fragments. Text, translation and commentary: L. Edelstein and I.G. Kidd, *Posidonius* (Cambridge: Cambridge University Press, 1972–99). References elsewhere in the present book are to the fragment numbering established by F. Jacoby, to which Edelstein and Kidd provide a concordance.

Poseidonius (2) of Corinth, Greek author of a poem on fish, now lost.

Athenaeus E 13b.

Praetutian wine *see* HADRIAN WINE

Pramnian wine (Greek *pramn(e)ios oinos*), a formulaic phrase used in the *Iliad* and *Odyssey*. The adjective has no obvious meaning in its epic contexts. The phrase was taken up by later poets and antiquarians, who attributed several contradictory senses to it. The most likely, perhaps, is that *pramnios* was an obsolete term for a 'black and austere' wine: so says Galen's *Hippocratic Glossary*. Other conjectures are listed by Athenaeus. It is an austere or dry wine that is called for in the Hippocratic text *Affections of Women*, which is the only source of pre-Roman date in which the word *pramnios* must have had some specific meaning.

Homer, *Iliad* 11.639, *Odyssey* 10.235; Aristophanes, *Knights* 107, fragment 334 Kassel; Hippocrates, *Affections of Women* 90, *al.*; Nicander A 163 with Gow *ad l.*; Pliny *NH* 14.54; Galen, *Hippocratic Glossary s.v. pramnios*; Athenaeus E 30b–e, 31d.

E. Meyer, '*Pramnios, Pramnos, Pramneios oinos*' in *Paulys Real-Enzyklopädie der classischen Altertumswissenschaft: Supplement* (Stuttgart, 1903–) vol. 14; A.J. Papalas, 'Pramnian wine and the wine of Icaria' in *Platon* vol. 34/5 (1982/3) pp. 49–54.

- In Hellenistic and Roman times several vineyards around the Aegean produced a sweet raisin wine or cooked wine that they called 'Pramnian'. Pliny had heard of one grown near Smyrna (see ASIAN WINES); there was another near Ephesus (see EPHESIAN WINES).

Nicander A 162–3; Dioscorides MM 5.6; Pliny NH 14.54; Athenaeus E 31d.

Prawn see SHRIMP

Prometheus, Greek mythological character. Prometheus stole fire from the gods; he recompensed them by offering the first sacrifice; but the share that he reserved for the gods was the animal's bones, wrapped in its fat, and accompanied by the smoke which rose to heaven.

Jean-Pierre Vernant, 'Sacrifice et alimentation humaine à propos du Prométhée d'Hésiode' in *Annali della Scuola Normale di Pisa* vol. 7 (1977) pp. 905–40, available in English as 'The myth of Prometheus in Hesiod' in *Myth, Religion and Society* ed. R.L. Gordon (Cambridge, 1981) pp. 57–79 and in *The Cuisine of Sacrifice among the Greeks* ed. Marcel Detienne and Jean-Pierre Vernant, tr. Paula Wissing (Chicago: Chicago University Press, 1989).

Protropos (Latin *protropum*), wine made from free-run must: this very sweet juice flows in small quantities from the grapes before they are trodden or pressed. Wine of this type (Pliny gives detailed instructions) was produced in several favoured districts around the Aegean. Such wine is known in modern French as 'vin de paille'.

Dioscorides MM 5.6; Pliny NH 14.85.

Prytaneion see ARCHITECTURE

Psithia see GRAPE VARIETIES

Ptisane see BARLEY

Pucine wine (Latin *Pucinum*) from a promontory subject to sea breezes between Aquileia and Tergeste at the head of the Adriatic. Livia, wife of the emperor Augustus, attributed her long healthy life

to drinking this little-known wine regularly.

Pliny NH 3.127, 14.60, 17.31.

Tchernia 1986 p. 192; Roberto Matijasic, 'Oil and wine production in Istria and Dalmatia in classical antiquity and early Middle Age' in *La Production du vin et de l'huile en Méditerranée* ed. M.-C. Amouretti and J.-P. Brun (Athens: Ecole Française d'Athènes, 1993) pp. 247–62.

Puls, a thick porridge made from emmer, a traditional Roman food more basic than bread. The making of *puls* began with hulled emmer or *alica* (see under EMMER). It was completed in many ways; it might incorporate meat (as in recipes in *Apicius*) or cheese. Junkelmann 1997 p. 194 and Grant 1999 p. 39 give recipes for a cheesy version, *puls Punica*, based on Cato and Pliny. Something different again is *puls fabacia*, a heavy mixture incorporating broad beans which was offered along with bacon – ancient and stodgy Roman fare – to the goddess Carna every year on the Calends of June.

Cato DA 85; Ovid, *Fasti* 6.169–72; Pliny NH 18.72, 18.117–18; Macrobius S 1.12.33; *Apicius* 5.1.

Purple-shell, group of univalve shellfish. The purple-shells are edible (and they thicken a soup, Hicesius observes) but their chief use in ancient times – eventually the subject of a Roman imperial monopoly – was in the production of purple dye, an industry which was lost with the fall of Constantinople in 1453. Thompson lists the places where this production was carried on in ancient times. The dye was used in colouring turnips for the table, according to Pliny.

The purple-shell is *porphyra* in Greek. The species were separately named in Latin: *bucinum* is probably *Stramonita Haemastoma*; *murex* is *Murex Trunculus*, the purple-shell used for dyeing at Tyre and Sidon; *purpura* is usually applied to *Murex Brandaris*, the species used for dyeing in Laconia and at Tarentum.

Aristotle HA 546b18–547b11 with Thompson

ad l.; Strabo 5.2.8; Dioscorides *MM* 2.4, 2.7; Xenocrates *T* 78–82; Pliny *NH* 9.129, 18.128; Martial 13.87; Athenaeus *D* 87e quoting Hicesius.

Thompson 1947 pp. 209–18; Davidson 1981 pp. 192–3; *La Porpora: realtà e immaginario di un colore simbolico. Atti del convegno di studio, Venezia, ottobre 1996* ed. Oddone Longo (Venice: Istituto Veneto di Scienze, Lettere ed Arti, 1998).

Purslane, distinctive fleshy-leaved plant, a familiar weed and also a familiar potherb in southern Europe. 'Watery purslane', as Columella calls it when he is in poetic mood, was conserved for winter use by packing it in salt. Galen, not in the least poetically, agrees with Columella: purslane is, in the dietary sense, watery and cold.

Purslane (*Portulaca oleracea*) is Greek *andrakhne*, Latin *portulaca*.

Hippocrates *R* 54; Dioscorides *MM* 2.124, 4.168; Columella *DA* 10.376, 12.13; Pliny *NH* 20.210–15, 25.162, 27.119; Galen *AF* 6.634; Pseudo-Apuleius, *Herbarius* 104.

Lambraki 1997 pp. 70–5.

- Greek *peplis, peplon*, a medicinal plant identified with *Euphorbia Peplis* and *E. Paralias*, sea spurge, has a superficial resemblance to purslane and was sometimes known as *andrakhne agria* or 'wild purslane'; in Latin it was *portulaca minor* or *lactia*. Its medicinal properties were different from those of true purslane but it too could be pickled for winter use. A second *andrakhne agria*, a plant of rocky places, is stonecrop, *Sedum* spp.: this was *illecebrum* in Latin.

Putchuk *see* COSTUS

Pyanepsia or *Pyanopsia*, a festival to Apollo, and a ritual bean soup prepared at this festival, which was held at Athens on the seventh day of the month Pyanepsion. Plutarch gives an Athenian explanation for the practice, which was, however, wider than Athens alone, since the month name Pyanepsion (sometimes *Kyanepsion*) was used in other cities too. An apparently related phrase, *pyanion polton* 'bean

porridge', is quoted by Athenaeus from Alcman.

Plutarch, *Life of Theseus* 22; Athenaeus *D* 408a, also 648b quoting Alcman 96 Davies.

Pythagoras, Greek philosopher of the sixth century BC. Pythagoras wrote nothing: his views were stated in *akousmata*, oral teachings, and in the form of *symbola*, symbolic pronouncements whose inner logic, if any, is now lost or uncertain. Practically every detail of Pythagoras's beliefs was and is controversial.

Many of the *symbola* concern food behaviour, or seem to do so. The most famous of these, often discussed in ancient and modern times, is 'Withhold your hands from beans!' A prohibition of red mullet is asserted by Aelian.

Pythagoras was often said to have enjoined vegetarianism. A good Pythagorean reason for vegetarianism – relating to the transmigration of souls – is mocked by Archestratus à propos of the eating of shark; it also comes in for criticism from Athenian comic poets, including Alexis and Aristophon. A particular avoidance of fish is often said to be a Pythagorean rule; it is discussed by Plutarch. Aristotle, however, is quoted as asserting that 'the Pythagoreans abstained from the womb, the heart, the sea anemone and a few other things, but used all other animal food'. The regimen followed by the community of Pythagoras's disciples is described most fully by Porphyry. Pythagoras, following EPIMENIDES's example, made compound drugs under the names *alimon* and *adipson* whose purpose was to repress the appetite during religious vigils; so we are assured by Porphyry, writing in the third century AD, who supplies recipes. Pythagoras or his followers also had their own names for certain medicinal herbs, according to Dioscorides and the *Herbarius* of Pseudo-Apuleius. Mallow, for example, they called *anathema*. Their communal dining prefigured the Christian AGAPE, according to Clement of Alexandria.

The rules laid down by Pythagoras are listed and discussed (repetitively) by Diogenes Laertius. Independent views of some of them, and the reasons for them, are given in interesting discussions by Plutarch and Aulus Gellius. Even close to his own time the strange pronouncements of Pythagoras and the strict regulations by which his followers lived were the subject of satire (or amused and uncomprehending observation) as from Alexis in *The Pythagoréenne*: 'The feast shall be dried figs, pressed olives and cheese: these are proper offerings, so the Pythagoreans believe;' and from Antiphanes in *The Bag*: 'Well, being a Pythagorean he eats nothing that has a soul: he takes a sunburnt helping of barley mash, an obol's worth at most, and sucks at that.'

Archestratus *H* 23 Brandt with Olson and Sens *ad l.*; Alexis *F* 201–3, 222–3 Kassel with Arnott *ad ll.*; Aristophon 9–12 Kassel; Dioscorides *MM* 2.118, *al.*; Diogenes Laertius 8.12–38 passim; Plutarch *QC* 8.7–8; Aulus Gellius 4.11; Clement of Alexandria, *Stromateis* 1.15; Athenaeus *D* 161a quoting Antiphanes, also 308c–d, 418e–419a; Porphyry, *Life of Pythagoras* 7, 34, 43–5; Pseudo-Apuleius, *Herbarius* 49, *al.*

A. Delatte, 'Faba Pythagorae cognata' in *Serta Leodiensia* (Liège, 1930) pp. 33–57; T.H.D. Arie, 'Pythagoras and beans' in *Oxford Medical School Gazette* vol. 2 (1959) pp. 75–81; Marcel Detienne, 'La cuisine de Pythagore' in *Archives de sociologie des religions* vol. 15 no. 29 (1970) pp. 141–62, revised translation in Marcel Detienne, *The Gardens of Adonis: spices in Greek mythology* (Hassocks: Harvester Press, 1977); W. Burkert, *Lore and Science in Early Pythagoreanism* (Cambridge, Mass., 1972); Simoons 1998 pp. 192–266; Garnsey 1999 pp. 86–90.

Q

Quail, a migratory bird of Mediterranean lands. It is clear from an aside by Eupolis that in Greece by the late fifth century BC quails were trapped in the wild and kept through the summer. They were at their best for eating in autumn. Aristotle explains that bird-catchers found these plump little birds easiest to catch in windy weather. Varro, writing in Italy three centuries later, describes in detail how the young birds were fattened for the table.

Controlling their feeding had the advantage of ensuring that they did not eat poisonous foods, such as hellebore. This was the accepted explanation in ancient times for occasional incidents of fatal poisoning from eating quail. Such poisonings still occur, for uncertain reasons.

Conveniently carried under the arm, quails were evidently a familiar sight in classical cities. In several source texts they play the role of a lover's gift.

The quail (*Coturnix Coturnix*) is Greek *ortyx*, Latin *coturnix*. The *ortygometra* 'mother of quail', supposed to lead their migrations, is the corncrake. The quail enclosure was called *ortygotrophion*, and the quail-farmer in Greek *ortygotrophos*.

Epicharmus 45 Kaibel; Aristophanes, *Birds* 707, 1298, *Peace* 789; Plato, *Lysis* 211e, *Euthydemus* 290d, *Hippias Major* 295d; Aristotle *HA* 597b5–21, 613b6–614a31; Plautus, *Captivi* 1003; Varro *RR* 3.5.2; Pliny *NH* 10.65–69; Dio of Prusa 70.3; Plutarch, *Life of Alcibiades* 10; Galen, *On Theriac to Piso* 14.227; Athenaeus *D* 392a–393c quoting Eu-

polis 226 Kassel; Oribasius *CM* 1.3.4 with Grant *ad l.*

Thompson 1936 p. 215; D.C. Lewis, E.S. Metallinos-Katsaras and L.E. Grivetti, 'Coturnism: human poisoning by European migratory quail' in *Journal of Cultural Geography* vol. 7 (1987) pp. 51–65; Toynbee 1996; Dalby 1996 p. 63 (I was wrong to suppose that quails were fully domesticated).

- Quails were eaten as early as *c.*3000 BC in EGYPT, at which date a quail formed part of a funerary meal found at Saqqara. Herodotus lists quails among the birds whose flesh was eaten raw-salted in Egypt. *Khennion* is the term used in the later Greek of Egypt for the quails of Egypt.

Herodotus 2.77; *Papiri greci e latini* vol. 4 no. 428, vol. 7 no. 862; *Greek Papyri in the British Museum* vol. 2 no. 239; Diodorus Siculus 1.60.10; Athenaeus *D* 393c.

Darby and others 1977 pp. 309–14; Brewer and others 1995 pp. 124–5.

Quality control, an issue that presents itself at several stages of food production. Quality is affected, for better or worse, in breeding or selection, rearing or growing, slaughtering or trapping or harvesting, storage, transport, marketing, preparation and cooking. The issue is scarcely ever discussed in these terms in ancient sources; though it is noted that high production at the expense of quality (e.g. of wine or olive oil) may damage a producer's reputation and is therefore best avoided. Ancient authors have, however, plenty to say of selection for quality by the final purchaser: see further GASTRONOMY.

G. Nebbia, 'Aspetti storici del problema del controllo della qualità delle merci nel mondo antico e nel medioevo' in *Quaderni di merceologia* vol. 1 (1962) pp. 327–80; A. Wittenburg, 'Zur Qualität des Olivenöls in der Antike' in *Zeitschrift für Papyrologie und Epigraphik* vol. 38 (1980) pp. 185–9.

Quince (*Cydonia vulgaris*), orchard fruit typical of southern Europe. Quinces are not always distinguished from apples in classical Greek texts: both equally could be called *melon*. The two fruits look superficially similar, but while apples are shiny, quinces are downy. They suggested both to Aristophanes and to Aristaenetus a comparison with young women's breasts. While many varieties of apples can be eaten fresh, quinces always need to be boiled or baked, as Anthimus rightly says.

The earliest history of the quince is unknown: prehistoric archaeologists have found no signs of it. Apparently not mentioned in the Homeric epics (where apples are conventionally 'shiny-fruited') quinces can be distinguished in archaic Greek lyric poetry and in later written sources, both Greek and Latin, of all kinds. Their characteristic slightly irregular bulges are often to be identified in classical sculpture.

In ancient times two varieties of quince were always recognised – though perhaps not always the same two. The larger, sweeter and less astringent kind were called *strouthion* by the Greeks in Asia, according to Galen. This name had been familiar in earlier Greek (and in Latin as *struthium*). The other variety had been distinguished from it as *kydonion* (*melon*) in Greece, *cydonium* or *cotoneum* in Latin. However, Galen is one of the latest sources to refer to the *strouthion* at all. Either the variety he knew as *strouthion*, or more likely a newer and even sweeter one, was by his time already known as

melimelon 'honey-apple', Latin *melimelum*. This latter variety became sufficiently popular to transmit its variety name to the whole species in modern Spanish (*marmelo*). The other name, Latin *cotoneum*, survives in French (*coing*).

Quinces could be boiled with wine and water to make a kind of *pulmentarium* (Pliny *NH* 15.58). There are many recipes and instructions for conserving them so as to retain their food value through the winter, whether whole or cooked down. They combined particularly well with honey. Recipes can be found for *kydonion syn meliti* 'quince in honey' and *kydonion en staiti* 'quince in fat' (Oribasius *CM* 4.2.20 quoting Rufus of Ephesus): see Grant 1999 pp. 111–12 for modern interpretations of these. A more homogenised product, a distant ancestor of modern quince marmalade or quince cheese, was *kydonomeli* or *melomeli*, mentioned by Columella (*DA* 12.47): a recipe for this is supplied by Dioscorides (*MM* 5.21 = Oribasius *CM* 5.25.16). A fermented drink, essentially a fruit wine, was made from this and was known in Greek as *hydromelon* (Dioscorides *MM* 5.22; Galen *BM* 6.744). There is also a recipe for steeping quinces in grape wine to make what was known in Greek as *kydonites oinos* or *melites oinos* 'quince wine, apple wine' (Dioscorides *MM* 5.20). Finally there is a recipe for a kind of quince jam, known as *cydonites*, a preserve with the consistency of honey (Palladius *OA* 11.20); and one for a quince syrup or cordial, *to apo ton kydonion melon* (Oribasius *CM* 5.20 quoting Philagrius). All these conserves had medicinal uses, and it is generally in medical sources that the recipes are found.

Aristophanes, *Acharnians* 1199, *Clouds* 978; Hippocrates *R* 55; Theophrastus *HP* 2.2.5; Antiphilus 2 Gow [*Anthologia Palatina* 6.252]; Dioscorides *MM* 1.115; Pliny *NH* 15.37–8, 23.100–4; Galen *ST* 6.450; Athenaeus *D* 80e–82e quoting Stesichorus 187 Davies and Ibycus 286 Davies; Gargilius Martialis *DH* 1; Palladius *OA* 3.25.20–6; Aristaenetus 1.1, 1.3; Anthimus *OC* 83 with Grant *ad l.*

J. Trumpf, 'Kydonische Äpfel' in *Hermes* vol. 88 (1960) pp. 14–22; A.R. Littlewood, 'The symbolism of the apple in Greek and Roman literature' in *Harvard Studies in Classical Phi-lology* vol. 72 (1967) pp. 147–81; Zohary and Hopf 1993 pp. 172–3; S. Döpp, 'Malum Cydonium: Quitte oder Apfel?' in *Hermes* vol. 123 (1995) pp. 341–5.

R

Rabbit, wild mammal unfamiliar in early Greece. In the earliest sources rabbits appear as Spanish fauna (they are no doubt the 'hares' which Roman soldiers in Spain were compelled to eat, according to Appian), but they were evidently spreading rapidly eastwards with occasional human encouragement. Polybius is the earliest author to mention them; Poseidonius observed large numbers of them on an island near Naples. Varro explains how to keep them for food.

The rabbit (*Oryctolagus Cuniculus*) is Latin *cuniculus*.

Catullus 25.1, 37.18; Varro *RR* 3.12.6–7; Pliny *NH* 8.217; Martial 13.60; Appian, *Spanish War* 227; Athenaeus *D* 400f–401a quoting Polybius 12.3.10 and Poseidonius *F* 61 Jacoby; *Apicius* 2.2.6.

Liliane Bodson, 'Données antiques de zoogéographie. L'expansion des léporidés dans la Méditerranée classique' in *Les Naturalistes belges* vol. 59 (1978) pp. 66–81; Toynbee 1996.

Radish, vegetable whose root and leaves can be eaten. The roots are to be left to ripen for five days after pulling, says Anthimus carefully.

There were several kinds in classical Greece. Those named after Boeotia, Corinth and Cleonae were noted, according to Athenaeus and Pliny. Radishes were sweet in Egypt and radish-seed oil was made there, says Pliny.

The radish (*Raphanus sativus*) is Greek *raphanis*, Latin *raphanus*. In the Roman imperial period two groups of varieties can be distinguished: the old, familiar, black, woody kinds already known to the Greeks, and a new kind with smaller red roots and a finer flavour, similar to those favoured in northern Europe now. These red varieties are known as *radix* in Latin. The two kinds still have different names in languages of southern Europe (e.g. French *raifort, radis*).

Hippocrates *R* 54; Diphilus Comicus 87 Kassel; Theophrastus *HP* 7.2.5–6, 7.4.1–3; Varro, *On the Latin Language* 5.103; Horace, *Satires* 2.8.8–9; *Moretum* 75; Dioscorides *MM* 2.112; Pliny *NH* 15.30, 19.75–87, 20.22–8, 20.96; Galen *AF* 6.656–7; Athenaeus *E* 56d–57b; Anthimus *OC* 60 with Grant *ad l.*

Darby and others 1977 pp. 663–4; Zohary and Hopf 1993 p. 132.

- Horseradish (*Armoracia rusticana*), native to eastern and central Europe, was apparently known to classical Romans but little used; it is probably Latin *armoracia*.

  Columella *DA* 6.17.8, 12.9.3; Pliny *NH* 19.82, 20.22.

- The related white charlock or hoary mustard (*Raphanus Raphanistrum*) is a wild potherb used in Mediterranean lands. The Greek names for white charlock are *lapsane* and *raphanos he agria*. In Latin it is *lapsana*. It was familiar enough to Caesar's troops that they called their emergency food at Dyrrachium *lapsana*, though it was really ARUM.

Varro *RR* 3.16.25; Dioscorides *MM* 2.116; Columella *DA* 9.4.5; Pliny *NH* 19.144; Galen, *On Distinguishing Fevers* 7.285; Palladius, *Lausiac History* 32.11.

A.C. Andrews, 'Alimentary use of hoary mustard in the classical period' in *Isis* vol. 34 (1942) pp. 161–2.

Raetian wine (Latin *Raeticum*), from the hills near Verona, some distance south of the Roman province of Raetia. Augustus liked it and Strabo confirms its reputation at that period; Vergil is studiously non-committal. Wine of this region matured in wooden vats treated with local pitch, resulting in a flavour which will have surprised most ancient drinkers. Later a fine wine *Acinaticum* came from the same district; Valpolicella originates here today.

Vergil, *Georgics* 2.95–6 with Servius *ad l.*; Strabo 4.6.8, 5.1.12; Celsus 4.12.8; Pliny *NH* 14.67; Martial 10.93, 14.100; Suetonius, *Augustus* 77; Cassiodorus, *Variae* 12.4.

Dalby 2000a p. 90.

Raisin *see* GRAPE

Rascasse or scorpionfish (the large red *Scorpaena Scrofa* and the small brown *S. Porcus*), fish protected by poisonous spines around the head. Smaller specimens were preferred by Archestratus, who adds that they were worth buying at Thasos. Nowadays they are prized for their contribution to the flavour of a bouillabaisse.

The rascasse is Greek *skorpios* and *skorpaina*, Latin *(piscis) scorpio*. The names 'sculpin' and 'bullhead' are sometimes used in English translations but they really belong to fish of a different zoological family.

Acraephia Price List; Ovid, *Halieutica* 116; Petronius *S* 35.4; Pliny *NH* 32.93; Oppian *H* 2.457–61; Athenaeus *D* 320d–321a quoting Archestratus *H* 29 Brandt; *Apicius* 10.2.16; Vinidarius *BC* 7.

Thompson 1947 pp. 245–6; Davidson 1981 pp. 145–7.

Ravenna wine was respectable according to Pliny, worse than water according to Martial. The *spionia* grape variety was typical of the district, suiting its damp climate.

Strabo 5.1.7; Columella *DA* 3.13.8; Pliny *NH* 14.34; Martial 3.56, 3.57.

Tchernia 1986 pp. 223–4.

Raw meat is in general something that other people eat. Germans ate it according to Mela; wild people in inland Aetolia ate it according to Thucydides. It is also a food used in dire emergencies; for example, Alexander's soldiers, having no food and no firewood on their journey towards Bactria, were reduced to eating raw horse-meat.

Closer to civilisation the Cynic philosopher Diogenes tried eating raw meat, in keeping with his rejection of social convention, but found it indigestible (see CYNICS).

For the choice between rare and well-cooked meat, discussed by Archestratus and Anthimus, see under COOKING METHODS.

Thucydides 3.94.5; Strabo 15.2.10; Mela, *Geography* 3.3.28.

J. Schmidt, 'Omophagia' in *RE* 1893–1972; Corbier 1989.

- Raw-salted and raw-dried meat and fish, *omotarikhos*, were relatively unfamiliar to Greeks and Romans. Herodotus observes that the Egyptians ate raw-salted duck. Ammianus Marcellinus describes the raw-salting of meat as practised by the Huns.

  Herodotus 2.77; Ammianus Marcellinus 31.2.3.

Ray, group of stinging fish whose flesh was regarded as good food in ancient times though it is less prized now. They had soft flesh, says Galen. For the innocuous fishes also known as ray in English see SKATE.

Davidson 1981 p. 33.

- The electric ray (*Torpedo marmorata* and other species) is Greek *narke*, Latin *torpedo*. It is soft-fleshed and sweet, according to Galen, but this (says Diphilus) applies only to the flesh near the head; the rest is indigestible. This fish Archestratus would like to see stewed in olive oil and wine with fragrant fresh herbs and a little grating of cheese. Other sources describe it baked, or stuffed and roasted whole. It is the electric ray to which Meno somewhat irreverently compares Socrates in Plato's *Meno*:

> Not only in outward appearance but in other respects as well you are exactly like the flat electric ray that one meets in the sea. Whenever anyone comes into contact with it, it numbs him, and that is what you seem to be doing to me now.

Philoxenus *D* b.11 Page; Plato Comicus *F* 164 Kassel; Plato, *Meno* 80a; Antiphanes 130 Kassel; Alexis 115 Kassel; Aristotle *HA* 620b19–29; Oppian *H* 2.56–85; Galen *AF* 6.737; Athenaeus *D* 314a–e quoting Archestratus *H* 48 Brandt (see Olson and Sens *ad l.*), also 356c–d quoting Diphilus of Siphnos; *Apicius* 9.2.

Thompson 1947 p. 169.

- The stingray (*Dasyatis* spp.) is Greek *trygon*, Latin *pastinaca*. It was said to be with a stingray's spine, given him by Circe, that Telegonus unintentionally killed his father Odysseus.

Epicharmus 66 Kaibel; Aristotle *HA* 620b19–29; Nicander, *Theriaca* 835–6; Pliny *NH* 9.155; Oppian *H* 2.470–505 with Mair *ad l.*, cf. Eustathius, *Commentary on Homer's Odyssey* 1.404; Galen *AF* 6.737.

Thompson 1947 p. 270.

Ray's bream *see* CASTAGNOLE

Razor-shell, group of bivalve shellfish. Razor-shells live buried in the sand on the sea shore, and are quite distinctive in appearance, as indicated in dialogue in a lost mime by Sophron:

> 'Whatever are these, dear, these long shells?'
>
> 'Oh, those are the razor-shells, a little shell sweet of flesh, a joy to widow-women.'

The joke is that the creature which owns the shell has a distinctly phallic shape – and indecently protrudes in the course of cooking. Whether for this reason or another, razor-shells were considered useful in treating gynaecological illnesses. They thicken a soup, observes Hicesius.

The razor-shell (*Ensis Ensis* and other species) is *solen* in Greek and Latin.

Aristotle *HA* 535a16; Xenocrates *T* 106; Pliny *NH* 32.151; Galen *AF* 6.734; Oppian *H* 1.316; Athenaeus *D* 86d–90f *passim* quoting Sophron 24 Kaibel and Hicesius; Hesychius *s.v. solen*.

- Greek *onyx* was 'the female *solen*' according to Xenocrates and Pliny; the female razor-shells are sweeter to the taste, says Diphilus. These might possibly be references to the slightly smaller, straighter species *Solen Vagina*.

Xenocrates *T* 106; Pliny *NH* 32.103, 32.134; Athenaeus *D* 90d quoting Diphilus of Siphnos.

Recipes are found in ancient COOKERY BOOKS, in dietary writings by physicians, and in farming manuals. For examples of surviving sources see entries for ANTHIMUS; APICIUS (4); CATO; COLUMELLA; GALEN; HEIDELBERG PAPYRUS; ORIBASIUS; PALLADIUS. As a rule recipes for prepared dishes are much briefer than their usual modern equivalents: it seems likely that they functioned rather as aids to the memory than as a way of learning a new skill. Recipes for conserved foods tend to provide fuller detail, for the good reason that errors in these processes may render a large quantity of food inedible and deprive a household of essential winter supplies.

The following are among modern books whose aim is to reinterpret ancient recipes. Since a few ancient ingredients are now extinct or unidentifiable, some are difficult to obtain, and some are now usually avoided, it will be found that interpretations differ wildly and the results achieved will also differ. How near any of them may be to the tastes experienced by classical eaters is a hard question.

Flower and Rosenbaum 1961; John Edwards, *The Roman Cookery of Apicius* (London: Hutchinson, 1985); Nico Valerio, *La tavola degli antichi* (Milan: Mondadori, 1989); Eugenia Salza Prina Ricotti, *Dining as a Roman Emperor: how to cook ancient Roman recipes today* (Rome: L'Erma di Bretschneider, 1995); Dalby and Grainger 1996 (see the review by John Wilkins in *Journal of Hellenic Studies* vol. 121 (2001) pp. 203–4); Junkelmann 1997; Günther E. Thüry and Johannes Walter, *Condimenta: Gewürzpflanzen in Koch- und Backrezepten aus der römischen Antike* (Vienna: Institut für Botanik und Botanischer Garten der Universität Wien, 1997); Grant 1999.

Red mullet, a pair of Mediterranean fish species much prized by gourmets ancient and modern. They were good at Thasos and Teos but finest of all at the harbour of Teichiussa near Miletus, says Archestratus. They were best in winter or early spring, and were to be grilled on the coals. Young red mullet made a good *aphye* or dish of small fry, called in Greek *triglitis*. Romans kept red mullet in pools, as mentioned in an aside by Cicero, and paid extremely high prices for these pretty but not very big fish: they scarcely grow bigger than two pounds, unless artificially fattened, according to Pliny. It was a reported price paid for three red mullet – 30,000 *sestertii* – that impelled Tiberius to legislate against luxury.

The gourmet APICIUS (2) stated (again according to Pliny) that red mullet were best to eat if they had been drowned in *garum sociorum*. Their fine flavour and high gastronomic reputation encouraged the attribution to red mullet of unexpected nutritional powers. It was this, perhaps, that allowed an unnamed early Greek physician to characterise them as among the 'most deadly' of foods (in a view cited in Hippocrates, *Sacred Disease* 2). They were sometimes considered aphrodisiac; one notes also Pliny's statement, not wholly incredible, that drinking wine in which a red mullet has died and been left to decompose will put you off wine.

The red mullet or surmullet (*Mullus barbatus* and the larger *Mullus Surmuletus*) is Greek *trigle*, Latin *mullus*.

Epicharmus 124 Kaibel; Archestratus *H* 41–2 Brandt with Olson and Sens *ad l.*; Sotades Comicus 1 Kassel; Cicero, *Letters to Atticus* 2.1.7 (*mullus barbatus*); Varro *RR* 3.17.6–8; Horace, *Satires* 2.2.34; Columella *DA* 8.17.7; Seneca, *Letters* 95, *Natural Questions* 3.18; Xenocrates *T* 8, 41, 147; Pliny *NH* 9.64–7, *al.*; Martial 3.45, 10.31, 11.49, 13.79; Juvenal 4.15, 5.92, 11.37; Suetonius, *Tiberius* 34, 60; Galen *AF* 6.715–17; Athenaeus *D* 324c–325f, also 285a citing Dorion, also 355e citing Diphilus of Siphnos; Macrobius *S* 3.16.9; *Apicius* 4.2.22, 10.1.11–12; Vinidarius *BC* 14–15.

Thompson 1947 pp. 264–8; A.C. Andrews, 'The Roman craze for surmullets' in *Classical World* vol. 42 (1949) pp. 186–8; Davidson 1981 pp. 92–5; Dalby 1996 p. 117; Higginbotham 1997 pp. 48–50.

Refrigeration *see* SNOW; WATER

Regimen *see* DIET

Resinated wine. The presence of pitch, pine resin, terebinth resin or mastic in a bouquet during fermentation resulted in a stabilised and flavoured wine comparable with modern retsina; but the flavour was probably perceptible in many ancient wines, since the *dolia* or vats in which they usually matured were waterproofed with pitch or resin. Resinated wine (Latin *resinatum*; Greek *retinites*) is medicinally an astringent, and it is less likely to spoil on contact with air. According to Plutarch, resinated wine was a speciality of the island of Euboea and also of the Po valley; Pliny agrees on the latter and adds Liguria. You could certainly find resinated wine at Rome, since Martial accuses one of his grosser addressees of liking it.

Celsus *DM* 2.30.3; Dioscorides *MM* 4.150, 5.34–5; Pliny *NH* 14.17–18, 14.120, 14.124–5, 16.54; Martial 3.77; Plutarch *QC* 5.3.

F.N. Howes, 'Age old resins of the Mediterranean regions and their uses' in *Economic Botany* vol. 4 (1950) pp. 307–16; Jacques André, 'La résine et la poix dans l'antiquité' in

L'Antiquité classique vol. 33 (1964) pp. 86–97; Patrick E. McGovern and others, 'Neolithic resinated wine' in *Nature* vol. 381 (1996) pp. 480–1.

Rhegium *see* MESSANA

Rhodes, large island of the southeastern Aegean. LYNCEUS of Samos, in a *Letter to Diagoras*, wrote an extended comparison of Rhodian with Athenian culinary delicacies; fragments are preserved by Athenaeus. He singled out its figs, grapes, bread, cakes and seafood. Small fry, Greek *aphye*, was said to be at its best at Athens but pretty good at Rhodes. Archestratus agreed with Lynceus on the excellence of the thresher shark of Rhodes. A saffron perfume was made there, according to Pliny. A breed of CHICKENS was named for the island.

Archestratus *H* 9, 21 Brandt with Olson and Sens *ad ll.*; Lynceus *F* 6–16; Pliny *NH* 13.5, 13.59, 15.70, 21.117, 24.112.

Rhodian wine (Greek *Rodios*; Latin *Rhodium*), from Rhodes in the southeastern Aegean. Rhodian appears in history (or legend) at the deathbed of Aristotle. On this occasion Aristotle preferred Lesbian to Rhodian, but that was his way of recommending as his successor Theophrastus of Eresus on Lesbos over Eudemus of Rhodes: the story is told by Aulus Gellius. The popularity of Rhodian parallels that of COAN WINE; imports of Rhodian to Italy are easily recognisable in the second and first centuries BC because the amphorae are stamped. Rhodian was salted, like Coan, but less heavily; dieticians were equally dismissive of it, and few other sources mention it at all, in spite of its archaeological ubiquity. In fact, 'Rhodian amphora stamps are by far the most numerous class known to modern study ... The wine concerned [so V.R. Grace conjectures] was of ordinary grade, consumed in bulk ... Perhaps not much of it was made in Rhodes.'

Vergil, *Georgics* 2.101–2; Pliny *NH* 14.42, 14.79; Aulus Gellius 13.5; Athenaeus *E* 32e.

Tchernia 1986 pp. 102, 105; François Salviat, 'Le vin de Rhodes et les plantations du Dème d'Amos' in *La Production du vin et de l'huile en Méditerranée* ed. M.-C. Amouretti and J.-P. Brun (Athens: Ecole Française d'Athènes, 1993) pp. 151–61; V.R. Grace in *OCD* 1996 *s.v.* Amphoras and amphora stamps, Greek.

- There is epigraphic evidence for a raisin wine, *passum Rhodium*, possibly the same as the sweet wine *hypokhytos* mentioned by Timachidas of Rhodes.

Athenaeus *E* 31d citing Timachidas of Rhodes; *CIL* 4.9327.

Rice, grain crop native to southern or southeastern Asia. Rice was grown in the middle Ganges valley, according to recent reports, well before 4000 BC, and in the Indus valley (Harappan) culture before 2000.

Rice is first mentioned in Greek texts at the time of Alexander. Aristobulus described wet rice farming, and Megasthenes explains how rice was used as the staple food in Indian meals. Transplanted westwards, presumably by the Persians, rice was already plentiful in Susiana (western Iran) by the time of Alexander's death; after a further spread in the Hellenistic period it was a familiar crop in Babylonia and lower Syria by the first century BC. Not long afterwards rice was being exported from India to Somalia.

Rice was not a common food to Greeks or Romans. Rice gruels and rice cakes are mentioned by medical authors, and Anthimus gives a recipe for a rice pudding made with goat's milk (see Grant 1999 p. 154 for a modern interpretation).

Rice (*Oryza sativa*) is *oryza* in Greek and Latin. This is a loanword originating in a language of ancient northwestern India (cf. Sanskrit *vrīhi*, modern Pashto *vriže*).

Theophrastus *HP* 4.4.10 (*oryzon*); Strabo 15.1.18 citing Aristobulus, also 15.1.53–60 citing Megasthenes, also 17.3.23; Diodorus Siculus 2.36, 19.13; *Periplus Maris Erythraei*

14, 41; Dioscorides *MM* 2.95; Galen *AF* 6.525, 6.687, *SF* 12.92; Athenaeus *D* 153d citing Megasthenes; Anthimus *OC* 70 with Grant *ad l.*

Laufer 1919 pp. 372–3; Y. Feliks, 'Rice in Rabbinic literature' [in Hebrew with English summary] in *Bar-Ilan* vol. 1 (1963) pp. 177–89, xxxix–xli; Nino Marinone, *Il riso nell' antichità greca* (Bologna: Patron, 1992); Zohary and Hopf 1993 pp. 84–5; Waruno Mahdi, 'Linguistic data on transmission of Southeast Asian cultigens to India and Sri Lanka' in *Archaeology and Language* ed. Roger Blench and Matthew Spriggs (London: Routledge, 1997–9) vol. 2 pp. 390–415; Te-Tzu Chang, 'Rice' in *CWHF* 2000 vol. 1 pp. 132–49.

Rich and poor *see* POOR

Rocket, salad vegetable, one of the best native Mediterranean species. Rocket was grown in classical Greek kitchen gardens and was equally familiar to Romans. Apart from the use of the leaf, rocket seed is called for as a culinary spice in *Apicius*.

Rocket had an enduring reputation among APHRODISIACS. Its description by Dioscorides emphasises this point: 'Rocket, eaten in rather large quantity, arouses to intercourse; its seed has the same effect. It is diuretic, digestive and good for the bowel. They also use the seed as a flavouring in cooked dishes.' Pliny's notice (*NH* 20.126) is more redolent of the superstitions of the 'root-cutters': 'If three leaves of wild rocket, picked with the left hand, are pounded and drunk in honey water, they serve as aphrodisiac.' Because of this reputation rocket was often served at dinners mixed with lettuce, an antaphrodisiac, so that their qualities would counteract one another. In other circumstances it was taken with the equally stimulating grape-hyacinth bulbs and pepper to make sure of the desired result: Varro, quoted in *Apicius*, provides an example.

Rocket (*Eruca sativa*) is Greek *euzomon*, Latin *eruca*.

Hippocrates *R* 54; Theophrastus *CP* 2.5.3; Hippolochus *D* [Athenaeus *D* 130d]; *Moretum* 84; Ovid, *Cure for Love* 799; Columella *DA* 10.109, 12.59.1; Dioscorides *MM* 2.140; Pliny *NH* 10.182, 19.154–5, 20.125–6; Martial 3.75; *Priapeia* 46.8, 51.20; Galen *AF* 6.639; *Apicius* 1.27, also 7.12 quoting Varro (see translation at BULBS), also 9.10.7; Vinidarius *BP* 6.

Roman wines, grown in the neighbourhood of Rome and sold there as table wine. For the higher quality wines of this region see ALBAN WINE; MARSIAN WINE; SABINE WINE; SETINE WINE; SIGNINE WINE; SPOLETINE WINE; TIBURTINE WINE; TUSCAN WINE. Information on the following comes largely from the first century AD.

- Caeretan wine (Latin *Caeretanum*) came from Caere in southwestern Etruria. Columella suggests that here, as at Nomentum, growers like himself aimed at high yield.

  Columella *DA* 3.3.3 with Ash (vol. 1 p. xv) *ad l.*; Martial 13.124.

- Labican wine (Greek *Labikanos*), from the hill town of Labicum east of Rome. In the first century Labican was pleasant and 'oily'; it was ready for drinking in ten years.

  Athenaeus *E* 26f.

- Nomentan wine (Latin *Nomentanum*, Greek *Noumentanos*), from due north of Rome, was made on vineyards famous for their extremely high productivity (which is generally a sign of poor quality). They were vineyards that fetched a high price: both Columella and Pliny mention the property owned here by Seneca. Nomentan aged quickly: ready after five years, according to the *Epitome of Athenaeus*; but not particularly pleasant to the taste and not light. Martial (who had a house at Nomentum) also has something to say of the ageing of Nomentan wine. The *nomentana* vines (see GRAPE VARIETIES) are named after this district.

  Columella *DA* 3.3.3; Pliny *NH* 14.48–52; Martial 1.105, 13.119; Athenaeus *E* 27b.

  Dalby 2000a pp. 36–7.

- Praenestine wine (Greek *Prainestinos*), from vineyards east of Rome. Athenaeus's source places it alongside the neighbouring Tiburtine wine and judges it less 'oily' than Gauran wine from Campania.

  Athenaeus *E* 26f.

- Privernan wine (Latin *Privernas*, Greek *Priouernos*), from the vineyards of Privernum (modern Piperno), is spoken of in the first century AD. It was best after fifteen years' storage and lighter and less heady than Regian. By Pliny's time its reputation was in decline.

  Pliny *NH* 14.65; Athenaeus E 26e.

- Vatican wine (Latin *Vaticanum*) from the right bank of the Tiber, very close to Rome, was disliked by Martial at the end of the first century AD.

  Martial 1.18, 6.92, 10.45, 12.48.

  Dalby 2000a p. 38.

- Veientan wine (Latin *Veientanum*), from Veii, northwest of Rome. The 'thick lees of brown Veientan' (in Martial's uninviting phrase) are never praised. The word here translated 'brown', *rubellum*, is reminiscent of the name of a grape variety grown at Nomentum.

  Horace, *Satires* 2.3.143; Persius 5.147; Martial 1.103, 2.53, 3.49; *CIL* 15.4595.

- Veliternan wine (Latin *Veliternum*; Greek *Oueliternos*) was from Velitrae (modern Velletri). It was pleasant and wholesome but 'has the peculiarity of appearing to have another kind mixed with it', according to the *Epitome of Athenaeus*. By Pliny's time its reputation was in decline.

  Pliny *NH* 14.65; Athenaeus E 27a.

Rome, central Italian city, eventually capital of the Roman Empire. The traditional lifestyle of republican Rome, with its staple food of *puls* or EMMER porridge, with its beans and bacon, was looked back upon with nostalgia by moralists of the Roman Empire (Garnsey 1999 pp. 77–81). In those days, it was said, wives sat demurely on their husbands' couches and drank no wine. In fact little was understood later of the Roman way of life before the second century BC; in particular, the extent of Etruscan and Greek influences was unclear.

At the centre of a vast and rapidly growing empire, Rome in the first century BC and later was a place where much of the LUXURY of the ancient world could be tasted. The old market sites near the Tiber landing – the *Forum Boarium* 'cattle market' and *Forum Holitorium* 'vegetable market' – were possibly in due course superseded, as was the *Macellum* 'covered market for meat' at the centre of the city. Under the early Empire there were certainly food and spice shops in and near the Velabrum district: Horace talks of 'the fishmonger, the fruiterer, the poulterer, the perfumier and all the unholy crowd from the Vicus Tuscus', the street which bordered the Velabrum to the southeast. There were shops selling luxury goods, but perhaps not food, in the Saepta Iulia in the Campus Martius near the Tiber bend. There were market stalls selling fresh fruit, wine and no doubt much other produce in the Subura, just north of the city centre. There was hot street food; there were taverns and hot food shops (*thermopolia*) at which many must have habitually eaten who were unable to cook safely in their crowded apartment blocks; there were bars and restaurants at the big public baths, common meeting places for those with leisure.

One of the largest cities in the world in its time, imperial Rome exerted a powerful economic influence on its immediate neighbourhood. As early as the mid second century BC Cato, in his farming manual, advises on a special range of produce to be grown at a *suburbanum*, a property near the city. In due course specialisation is evident from the list of market products attributed to each locality. From Alba came smoked raisins; from Amyclae mackerel (Athenaeus D 121a); from Anagnia grain; from Aricia cabbages and leeks (Pliny *NH* 19.110, 19.140–1; Marcus Aurelius, *Letters* [Fronto vol. 1 p. 116 Haines]); from CASINUM 'green oil' (Cato *DA* 145): there was also a recognised grade or style called 'Roman oil'; from Circeii beet and aromatic herbs, and also oysters: there were none sweeter or more tender, according to Pliny (Horace, *Satires* 2.4.30–4; Pliny *NH* 19.134,

32.62–3); from Crustumeria pears; from Falerii little sausages and also the white oxen that were favoured for sacrifice; from Lanuvium pears; from the Laurentian marshes wild boar; from the Marsian hills came broad beans, figs and onions, the kind that locals called *unio* 'pearl' (Columella *DA* 2.9.8, 12.10.1; Macrobius *S* 3.20.1 citing Cloatius Verus); from Praeneste hazelnuts and roses (Cato *DA* 8; Pliny *NH* 13.5, 21.16); from the Sabine hills olive oil, recommended by Galen as least astringent (Galen *ST* 6.196); from Signia pears (Celsus 2.24.2, 4.26.5); from Tibur apples; from Tusculum roses, violets and figs (Varro quoted by Macrobius *S* 3.16.12). For additional references on these specialities see Dalby (below) pp. 30–46. For the wines of Rome's neighbourhood see ROMAN WINES.

For the food of the various regions of the Roman Empire see AFRICA; ANATOLIA; ARABIA; BALKAN PROVINCES; BRITAIN; CYRENAICA; DACIA; EGYPT; GAUL; GERMANY; GREECE (with further cross-references there); HELLESPONT; ITALY (with further cross-references there); MACEDONIA; PONTUS; SARDINIA; SICILY; SPAIN; SYRIA; THRACE. For wines of the Roman Empire see cross-references at ANATOLIA; GREECE; ITALY; see also EGYPTIAN WINES; NARBONENSIAN WINES; PHOENICIAN WINE; SPANISH WINES.

Cato *DA* 7–8 with Dalby *ad l.*; Horace, *Satires* 2.3.227–8; Athenaeus 153c–154c quoting Poseidonius and others.

André 1981; Corbier 1989, 1996; Dalby 2000a pp. 30–46, 209–42; David Downie, *Cooking the Roman Way* (New York: Harper Collins, 2002) [on modern Rome].

Rose, garden flower. The matchless aroma of roses was employed in various ways in Greek and Roman festivity. They were used in WREATHS and in a rose perfume. Rose petals served occasionally as a flavouring for food, such as the rich *rodonia lopas* 'rose casserole' with which a fictional cook, in Athenaeus's dialogue, impresses his audience; he supplies a recipe. Confections included a rose wine (Greek *rosatos*; Latin *rhosatum*), for which Pliny (*NH* 14.106) and Palladius give brief recipes: this was of sufficiently general importance to be given a fixed maximum price in *Diocletian's Price Edict*. There was also a rose jam or syrup (Greek *rodomeli*) for which recipes are supplied by Philagrius and in the *Geoponica*: see Grant 1999 p. 43 for a modern interpretation. A rose medicine, *to aleuron to syn toi rodinoi*, is used in the Hippocratic text *Epidemics*.

Cultivated roses were a prized garden plant in classical Athens, but roses were also gathered from the wild and sold at street stalls. Rome's roses grew at neighbouring Praeneste and, far to the south, at Paestum; there was also a Tarentine variety. However, the best rose perfume came to classical Rome from Cyrene.

The rose (*Rosa damascena* and other species) is Greek *rodon*, Latin *rosa*.

Hippocrates, *Epidemics* 7.64; Theophrastus *HP* 6.6.4–6, 6.8.5; Dioscorides *MM* 5.27; Pliny *NH* 14.106, 21.14–21, 21.121–5; Marcus Aurelius, *Letters* [Fronto vol. 1 p. 116 Haines]; Athenaeus *D* 403d, 406a–b; Palladius *OA* 6.13; *Diocletian's Price Edict* 2.19; Oribasius *CM* 5.17.5 quoting Philagrius; *Geoponica* 8.29.

W.L. Carter, 'Roses in antiquity' in *Antiquity* vol. 14 (1940) pp. 250–6.

Rosemary, medicinal herb. Rosemary was said to be good for the digestion and had other medicinal uses. It was not used as a culinary herb in classical times.

Rosemary (*Rosmarinus officinalis*) was known to Greeks as *libanotis*, to Romans as *rosmarinum*.

Dioscorides *MM* 3.75; Pliny *NH* 19.187, 24.99–100; Pseudo-Apuleius, *Herbarius* 80.

Rue, one of the most important culinary herbs in the Greek and Roman repertoire. The bittersweet flavour and aroma of rue are called for about a hundred times in the recipes of *Apicius*. Rue was also an

Map 2 Food specialities of the neighbourhood of Rome

important medicinal plant. It was considered to be antaphrodisiac, and was prescribed to prevent nocturnal emission of semen. It was regarded as harmful to pregnant women.

Rue grows wild in the eastern Mediterranean; it was often taken into garden cultivation, but 'was all the better if it was stolen', according to Pliny. A hardy shrub which thrives in most parts of Europe, rue is now practically a forgotten flavour.

Rue (*Ruta graveolens*) is Greek *peganon*, Latin *ruta*.

Aristophanes, *Wasps* 480 with scholia; Hippocrates *R* 54; Aristotle, *Problems* 867b8, 924b35; Theophrastus *HP* 1.3.4; Strabo 6.2.3; Pliny *NH* 19.123, 19.156–7, 20.131–43; Luke, *Gospel* 11.42; Plutarch *QC* 3.1 [647b]; Galen *SF* 12.100–1; Palladius *OA* 4.9.13–14; Pseudo-Apuleius, *Herbarius* 90.

A.C. Andrews, 'The use of rue as a spice by the Greeks and Romans' in *Classical Journal* vol. 43 (1948) pp. 371–3.

Rye, a cereal crop of central Europe, unfamiliar in Greece and Italy but significant in the Roman northern provinces.

Galen describes without enthusiasm the black bread that was baked from rye.

Rye (*Secale cereale*) is *briza* in Greek, *secale* and *centenum* in Latin.

Pliny *NH* 18.141; Galen *AF* 6.514; *Diocletian's Price Edict* 1.3.

Buck 1949 p. 517; Zohary and Hopf 1993 pp. 64–73; Hansjörg Küster, 'Rye' in *CWHF* 2000 vol. 1 pp. 149–52.

S

Sabine wine (Latin *Sabinum*), from the Sabine hills north of Rome. The local *vinaciola* grape variety, and the more widely known *visulla*, were among those grown here.

Sabine was an easy wine, good for drinking between seven and fifteen years of age, according to the *Epitome of Athenaeus*, which represents a view from the first century AD. A little earlier, Horace had talked of *vile Sabinum* (meaning 'cheap', not 'vile'), but also calls for a better, four-year-old amphora of Sabine to be served to him on a winter day when the snow stands deep on Mount Soracte. Horace's own country property being in Sabine territory, the wine he made himself was Sabine, so he is entitled to hold complex views on it; but, later at any rate, there really were two kinds of Sabine (and we may decide that it was the cheap kind that Martial disliked). According to Galen there were both fine or 'noble' and light Sabine wines (all were white, incidentally). The fine Sabine was moderately astringent, not especially austere and not especially 'winy'. The other was less astringent, and was light enough to be drunk young. In spite of the strong pull of the markets of Rome, growers appear to have concentrated on quality, to judge by the fact that at the end of the third century Sabine was one of only seven named wines of the Empire allowed a special high price in *Diocletian's Price Edict*.

Sabine wine with parsley (no alternatives are suggested for either ingredient) was a good medicine for the arthritic, according to Galen.

Strabo 5.3.1; Horace, *Odes* 1.9, 1.20; Pliny *NH* 14.28, 14.38; Martial 4.4, 10.49; Galen *ST* 6.275, 6.334–8, *BM* 6.806–7, *SF* 11.648, 11.837, *On Therapeutic Method* 10.483–5, 10.831–3, *On Compounding* 12.517, *DA* 14.15–16, *al.*; Athenaeus E 27b; *Diocletian's Price Edict* 2.3; *Expositio Totius Mundi* 55; Cassiodorus, *Variae* 12.12.3.

Tchernia 1986 pp. 206–7, 344.

Sacrifice, a regular practice in Greek and Roman and also in Near Eastern religions. The Babylonian gods are imagined as 'gathering like flies over the offering' (*Atrahasis* tablet 3). In some of the earliest Greek references to the subject it is by the smoke of sacrifice that the gods are nourished.

In Greek mythology it was Prometheus who offered the first sacrifice. His act can be seen as marking the end of the GOLDEN AGE; before him, humans did not kill or eat animals. Whatever its origin and logic, Greek practice in the classical period is clear. Sacrificial animals and domesticated animals destined for food were coterminous categories (the sense of Greek *hiereion* covers both). The impulse to offer a sacrifice came from a state or religious calendar, from a family event, from individual piety, or from the wish to eat fresh meat. The animal was killed at an altar; a share was offered to a god; the SPLANKHNA were tasted; a share (Greek *hierosyna*) was reserved to the *mageiros* (cook–sacrificer) or priest if officiating; the offal was retained, in due course to be cooked or conserved (and often sold); the rest of the muscle meat was shared equally among the participants, but 'after sacrificing at Delphi you must buy your own meat for dinner' (according to a proverb quoted by Plutarch), meaning that at this busy shrine the priests and chance arrivals got nearly all of your sacrifice. By domesticated animals is meant oxen, sheep, goats, pigs, pigeons, geese and chickens. Birds which were trapped in the wild and reared (such as quails) are not normally included; fish are not normally included; animals which were hunted are not included: with the exception of a few atypical traditional practices, these were all killed and eaten without any religious formality. The practice of sacrifice is fully described in passages of the *Iliad* and *Odyssey*; later descriptions include two scenes by Aristophanes and a play by Menander, and in due course Homeric sacrifice is well reimagined by Nonnus, in his early Byzantine mythological epic. The term *theoxenia* is used for rituals in which a whole meal is set out for a god, or to be shared by god and worshippers.

Roman sacrificial practice is in many ways different from Greek and is far less closely linked with the everyday diet. There was less sacrificial meat, and humans eventually ate a smaller proportion of it. It was the large domesticated animals that were normally sacrificed. However, most such animals were killed for the food trade without any religious ceremony. Sacrifices were made for two principal reasons, to observe a public religious calendar and to ascertain the will of the gods concerning a crucial decision: skilled seers (*haruspices*) did this

by examining the animal's liver and other vital organs after sacrifice. The sharing of the remaining meat among the participants is, as in Greek sacrifice, an important matter.

The problem for Greek and Roman gastronomes was that meat is not at its best for eating immediately after slaughter. Plutarch discusses how this problem might be alleviated by hanging the meat briefly in a fig tree before cooking.

Sacrifice was not confined to meat. Offerings of cakes were common in Greek and Roman practice. A character in Menander's *Dyscolus* (449–51) observes that cakes (*popana*) and incense are the truly holy offerings to the gods, because the gods get all of them once they are put on the fire, which is not the case with animal sacrifice. If not burnt, sacrificial cakes were left on the altar.

Sacrifice redistributed. We have already seen that officiators and other participants had their shares of meat. At a family sacrifice this included family slaves: sacrificial ritual did not distinguish slave from free. We have seen that passers-by (so frequent at Delphi) were invited to partake. In Greece and Rome, sacrifices of meat or cakes at crossroad shrines of Hecate were, as everyone knew, eaten by the poor. If the priests did not want the cakes from Roman altars, they went to feed the priests' assistants and slaves.

Homer, *Iliad* 1.458–74, *Odyssey* 3.404–73, cf. Nonnus, *Dionysiaca* 5.1–34; Aristophanes, *Peace* 923–1126, *Wealth* 672–87; Menander, *Dyscolus passim*; *Deuteronomy* 14.23–7; Cato *DA* 132, 134, 139–41; Terence, *Eunuchus* 491; Catullus 59.2–3; Plutarch *QC* 6.10, 7.6; Longus, *Daphnis and Chloe* 2.30–2; Porphyry *DA* book 2, *Life of Pythagoras* 36; Arnobius, *Against the Gentiles* 7.25; Julian, *Hymn to the Mother* 14–18.

W. Burkert, 'Greek tragedy and sacrificial ritual' in *Greek, Roman and Byzantine Studies* vol. 7 (1966) pp. 87–121; J. Casabona, *Recherches sur le vocabulaire des sacrifices en grec* (Aix-en-Provence, 1966); R.M. Ogilvie, *The Romans and their Gods in the Age of Augustus* (London: Chatto and Windus, 1969); D. Gill, 'Trapezomata: a neglected aspect of

Greek sacrifice' in *Harvard Theological Review* vol. 67 (1974) pp. 117–37; E. Will, 'Banquets et salles de banquet dans les cultes de la Grèce et de l'Empire Romain' in *Mélanges d'histoire ancienne et d'archéologie offerts à Paul Collart* ed. P. Ducrey (Lausanne, 1976) pp. 353–62; Jean-Pierre Vernant, 'Sacrifice et alimentation humaine à propos du Prométhée d'Hésiode' in *Annali della Scuola Normale di Pisa* vol. 7 (1977) pp. 905–40, translation: 'The myth of Prometheus in Hesiod' in *Myth, Religion and Society* ed. R.L. Gordon (Cambridge, 1981) pp. 57–79; also included in *La Cuisine du sacrifice en pays grec* ed. Marcel Detienne and Jean-Pierre Vernant (Paris: Gallimard, 1979), translation: *The Cuisine of Sacrifice among the Greeks* (Chicago: Chicago University Press, 1989); Jean-Pierre Vernant and others, *Le Sacrifice dans l'antiquité* (Geneva: Fondation Hardt, 1981) (*Entretiens sur l'antiquité classique*, 27); N. Loraux, 'La cité comme cuisine et comme partage' in *Annales: économies, sociétés, civilisations* vol. 36 (1981) pp. 614–22; G.J. Baudy, 'Hierarchie oder die Verteilung des Fleisches' in *Neue Ansätze in der Religionswissenschaft* ed. B. Gladigow and H.G. Kippenberg (Munich, 1983) pp. 131–74; W. Burkert, *Homo Necans: the anthropology of ancient Greek sacrificial ritual and myth* (Berkeley: University of California Press, 1983); J. Scheid, 'Les Romains au partage' in *Studi storici* vol. 25 (1984) pp. 945–56; J. Scheid, 'Sacrifice et banquet à Rome: quelques problèmes' in *Mélanges de l'Ecole Française de Rome. Antiquité* vol. 97 no. 1 (1985) pp. 193–206; J.-L. Durand, *Sacrifice et labour en Grèce ancienne* (Paris, 1986); *Sacrificio e società nel mondo antico* ed. C. Grottanelli and N.F. Parise (Rome, 1988); *Early Greek Cult Practice* ed. R. Hägg, N. Marinatos and G.C. Nordquist (Stockholm, 1988); M.H. Jameson, 'Sacrifice and animal husbandry in classical Greece' in *Pastoral Economies in Classical Antiquity* ed. C.R. Whittaker (Cambridge, 1988); Corbier 1989; Louise Bruit, 'The meal at the Hyakinthia: ritual consumption and offering' in *Sympotica: a symposium on the symposion* ed. Oswyn Murray (Oxford: Oxford University Press, 1990) pp. 162–74; G. Nagy, 'On the symbolism of apportioning meat in archaic Greek elegiac poetry' [revised version] in G. Nagy, *Greek Mythology and Poetics* (Ithaca: Cornell University Press, 1990) pp. 269–76; Pauline Schmitt-Pantel, 'Sacrificial meal and symposion: two models of civic institutions in the archaic city?' in *Sympotica: a symposium on the symposion* ed. Oswyn Murray (Oxford: Oxford University Press, 1990) pp. 14–33; R. Osborne, 'Women and sacrifice in ancient Greece' in *Classical Quarterly* vol. 43 (1993) pp. 392–405; F.T. van Straten, *Hiera Kala:*

images of animal sacrifice in archaic and classical Greece (Leiden, 1995); Matthew P.J. Dillon, 'The ecology of the Greek sanctuary' in *Zeitschrift für Papyrologie und Epigraphik* vol. 118 (1997) pp. 113–27; N. Bookidis and others, 'Dining in the sanctuary of Demeter and Kore at Corinth' in *Hesperia* vol. 68 (1999) pp. 1–54.

Safflower, a dye and oil plant probably domesticated in southwestern Asia. Safflower was in use in the Near East and in Egypt in the second millennium BC. It produces a pure yellow dye and thus rivals saffron as a colouring agent, though it lacks aroma. The plant was used medicinally as a laxative. Its reddish yellow edible oil had additional medicinal uses, described by Dioscorides, and was one of five oils taxed under Ptolemy II (see EGYPT).

Safflower (*Carthamus tinctorius*) is Greek *knekos*, Latin *cnecos*.

Hippocrates *R* 54, *RA* 64, *Epidemics* 7.118; Theophrastus *HP* 6.4.3–5; Dioscorides *MM* 4.188; Pliny *NH* 21.90 (confused).

Laufer 1919 pp. 323–8; Darby and others 1977 p. 805; Zohary and Hopf 1993 pp. 193–4; Brewer and others 1995 p. 45.

• The distaff-thistle (*Carthamus lanatus*), *atraktylis* in Greek, noted for its red juice, is listed as a potherb by Galen.

Epicharmus 161 Kaibel; Theophrastus *HP* 6.4.6, 9.1.1; Pliny *NH* 21.95; Galen *AF* 6.623, 6.636.

Saffron, spice and dye consisting of the flower stamens of the saffron crocus. The plant is known only in cultivation: it is believed to be native to southern Turkey or Iran.

Saffron produces a yellow to red dye (depending on its age) and gives a yellow colour and distinctive aroma to food. It is an ancient Mediterranean commodity: Pliny observes that it is one of the flowers named in the *Iliad*, while Minoan frescoes from Knossos and Akrotiri show the picking of saffron (by monkeys and by beautiful women respectively). In Roman times the best saffron grew in coastal

Cilicia at the Corycian cavern, a vast cauldron-like limestone depression.

By Romans saffron was burnt in sacrifice. It was also mixed with sweet wine and the resulting sticky yellow mixture was sprayed liberally into the air at theatres and circuses, a custom alluded to by Martial and others. Was the fictional Trimalchio (in Petronius's *Satyricon*) the only host to think of serving fruit that would squirt saffron when squeezed?

Saffron was used in an aromatic hair oil, *crocinum*. This was made at Soli near Corycus, and also on Rhodes. Typical additives included wine and two other plant dyes, *cinnabaris* (dragon's blood, *Dracaena Cinnabari*) and *anchusa* (see ALKANET), to adjust the colour.

Saffron (*Crocus sativus*) is Greek *krokos*, Latin *crocus*.

Homer *Iliad* 14.348; Theophrastus *HP* 6.6.10, 6.8.3, 7.7.4; Plautus, *Curculio* 103; Vergil, *Georgics* 1.56 with Servius *ad loc.*; Horace, *Satires* 2.4.68; Propertius, *Elegies* 3.10.22, 4.6.74; Ovid, *Fasti* 1.76; *Elegies for Maecenas* 1.123; Strabo 14.5.5; Mela 1.71–5; Petronius *S* 60; Pliny *NH* 21.31–4, 21.137–9; Martial 3.65, *al.*, *Spectacula* 3; *Apicius* 1.1, 1.3, *al.*

Laufer 1919 pp. 309–23; Darby and others 1977 pp. 805–6; Zohary and Hopf 1993 pp. 189–90; Jacqueline Manessy-Guitton, 'Le nom grec du crocus' in *Actes du colloque international 'Les phytonymes grecs et latins' tenu à Nice les 14–16 mai 1992* (Nice: Université de Nice-Sophia Antipolis [1993?]) pp. 223–44; R. Goubeau, 'De quelques usages médicaux du crocus dans l'antiquité' in *Des hommes et des plantes: plantes méditerranéennes, vocabulaire et usages anciennes* ed. M.-C. Amouretti and G. Comet (Aix-en-Provence, 1993) pp. 23–6; Lambraki 1997 pp. 54–64; Alice Lindsell, 'A note on Greek crocus' in J.E. Raven and others, *Plants and Plant Lore in Ancient Greece* (Oxford: Leopard's Head Press, 2000) pp. 49–54.

Sage, an aromatic herb of which several species grow wild in Mediterranean lands. These were well known to Greeks and Romans and were valued for medicinal purposes but were not normally used in food. Dioscorides gives a recipe for a medicinal wine incorporating sage.

The Greek names *sphakos* and *elelisphakos* and the Latin *salvia* were applied to typical species such as *Salvia triloba* and *S. grandiflora*. Clary (*S. Sclarea*) is *horminon* in Greek, *horminum* in Latin.

Hippocrates *R* 54; Theophrastus *HP* 6.2.5, 8.7.3; Dioscorides *MM* 3.33, 5.61; Pliny *NH* 22.146–7; Pseudo-Apuleius, *Herbarius* 102.

Saguntine wine *see* SPANISH WINES

Salep *see* SATYRION

Salmon (*Salmo Salar*), a fish of northern European rivers. The salmon is scarcely mentioned by classical Greek authors. Latin writers name it – under several different names – and praise it. According to Pliny, the *salmo* (of the Garonne) is considered in Aquitania to be better than any sea fish; he also mentions the *esox* [*s.v.l.*] of the Rhine. Ausonius is enthusiastic concerning the salmon of the Moselle, pink-fleshed centrepiece of any banquet. Cassiodorus recommends the *ancorago*, salmon of the Rhine, to the table of Theodoric the Ostrogothic king of Italy. Anthimus, addressing another Germanic monarch, suggests young salmon, *teccones*, fried in oil with salt.

Pliny *NH* 9.44, 9.68; Ausonius, *Mosella* 97–105; Cassiodorus, *Variae* 12.4; Hesychius, *Lexicon s.v. isox*; Anthimus *OC* 41, 45 with Grant *ad l.*

Thompson 1947 *s.vv.*; A.C. Andrews, 'Greek and Latin terms for salmon and trout' in *Transactions and Proceedings of the American Philological Association* vol. 86 (1955) pp. 308–18.

Salsify *see* GOLDEN THISTLE

Salt, known in classical times in the forms both of sea salt and of rock salt. There were salt mines; under the Roman Empire there was also a considerable industry of salt production.

Salt was extremely important for conserving food; large quantities are called for, for example, in the instructions for conserving ham (see PORK). Salt was also in regular use in cooking; we hear of it sprinkled on roasting meat and of its use to flavour fish. Dry salt seems to be used as a table condiment in a satirical dig by Aristophanes. The information on salt as culinary flavouring and table condiment is, however, not plentiful. Instead, we are told of various combined forms in which salt was used (Athenaeus D 366b): in Greek there are *hales thymitides* 'thyme salt' (Aristophanes, *Acharnians* 772, 1099); *hales kyminotriboi* 'cumin salt' (Archestratus H 13 Brandt); *halme* 'brine', sea water or water to which salt has been added, and various further combinations such as *oxalme* 'vinegar brine' (see SAUCE) and *halmyris*. The last of these is the name for a liquor both salty and fishy. In Latin we hear of *muria*, the equivalent to *halmyris*. But in both languages, by far the commonest salt compound is fermented fish sauce or *garum* (Greek usually *garos*; Latin also *liquamen*). It seems clear that the usual way to incorporate salt in all kinds of dishes was in the form of *garum*.

'We shared salt' serves in Greek as shorthand implying the sharing of a meal and the establishment of friendship and mutual obligation.

For *halme, halmyris, muria* and *garum* see GARUM. For salted wine see ANTHOSMIAS.

Herodotus 4.185; Aristophanes fragment 158 [*s.v.l.*]; Antiphanes 221 Kassel; Pliny *NH* 31.73–92; Plutarch *QC* 4.4, 4.5, 5.10, 8.8; Heliodorus, *Ethiopian Story* 4.16, 6.2; *Lucius or the Ass* 1.

M. Besnier, 'Sal' in *DAGR* 1877–1919; Buck 1949 p. 382; J. Nenquin, *Salt* (Bruges, 1961); Forbes 1964–72 vol. 3 pp. 164–81; *Salt: the study of an ancient industry* ed. K.W. de Brisay and K.A. Evans (Colchester, 1975); Jean Claude Hocquet and Jacqueline Hocquet, 'The history of a food product: salt in Europe. A bibliographic review' in *Food and Foodways* vol. 1 (1985–7) pp. 425–47; *Iron Age and Roman Salt Production and the Medieval Town of Droitwich: excavations at the Old Bowling Green and Friar Street* ed. S. Woodiwiss (London, 1992); Christiane Perrichet-Thomas, 'Le symbolique du sel dans les textes anciens' in

Mélanges Pierre Lévêque ed. Marie-Madeleine Mactoux and Evelyne Geny (Paris: Les Belles Lettres, 1993) vol. 7 pp. 287–96; Grant 1999 pp. 19, 28; Olson and Sens 2000 p. 73.

Samos, island in the eastern Aegean. Samos emerges into history in the mid sixth century BC under the rule of POLYCRATES. At the same period, and for many centuries after, the precinct of the temple of Hera at Samos was a place where exotic animals and plants could be found in a kind of botanical–zoological garden. These included specimens of food species.

Samos was good for tunny, according to Archestratus; it produced bad wine, Strabo tells us. The modern Samian wine co-operative maintains the ancient tradition.

Archestratus H 34 Brandt; Menodotus [Athenaeus D 655a]; Varro *RR* 3.6.2; Strabo 14.1.15; Athenaeus D 525e–f.

J. Boessneck and A. von den Driesch, 'Reste exotischer Tiere aus dem Heraion auf Samos' in *Mitteilungen des Deutschen Archäologischen Instituts: Athenische Abteilung* vols 96 (1981) and 98 (1983); L. Soverini, 'Il commercio nel tempio: osservazioni sul regolamento dei kápeloi a Samo (*SEG* XXVIII, 545)' in *Opus* vol. 9/10 (1990/1) pp. 59–121; Dušanka Kučan, 'Zur Ernährung und dem Gebrauch von Pflanzen im Heraion von Samos im 7. Jahrhundert v. Chr.' in *Jahresbericht des Deutschen Archäologischen Instituts* vol. 110 (1995) pp. 1–64; Dušanka Kučan, 'Rapport synthétique sur les recherches archéobotaniques dans le sanctuaire d'Héra de l'île de Samos' in *Paysage et alimentation dans le monde grec* ed. Jean-Marc Luce (Toulouse, 2000) pp. 99–108.

Samphire, a plant of seaside rocks. Samphire was eaten raw, boiled or (as now) conserved in brine. It was said to be good for bladder diseases. As a typically rustic food it was served to Theseus by Hecale in Callimachus's poem *Hecale*.

Samphire (*Crithmum maritimum*) is Greek *krethmon*, Latin *crethmum* and *batis marina* or *batis sativa*.

Dioscorides *MM* 2.129; Columella *DA* 12.13; Pliny *NH* 21.86, also 26.82 citing Callimachus fragment 249 Pfeiffer.

Saperdes *see* CASTAGNOLE

Sarabus or Sarambus, Plataean in origin, a tavern-keeper who made a noticeable contribution to the gastronomy of Athens around 400 BC, assuming that all three of these glancing references are to the same person.

Plato, *Gorgias* 518d; Achaeus 20 F 13 Snell; Poseidippus 31 Kassel.

Sardinia, Roman province. Sardinia, formerly a Carthaginian possession, was acquired by Rome around 240 BC. In the first century it was one of Rome's three 'granaries' according to Cicero.

Cicero, *De Lege Manilia* 34.

P. Bartoloni, 'Tracce di coltura della vite nella Sardegna fenicia' in *Stato, economia, lavoro nel Vicino Oriente antico* (Milan, 1988) pp. 410–12.

- What salt fish was *sarda*? It was similar in size to the *kolias* 'Spanish mackerel', appetising, with something of the sourness of *kybion* 'salted tunny'. It was big enough to stuff, as in a recipe in *Apicius*. It may have been named originally after Sardinia (this is not clear). By Galen's time the conserved fish of this type from the Black Sea and Spain as well as from Sardinia, perhaps originating only from bonito (see TUNNY) but perhaps also from other species, was generally called *sarda* in Greek and Latin.

Pliny *NH* 32.151; Xenocrates *T* 142; Galen *AF* 6.728, 6.745; Athenaeus *D* 120f citing Diphilus of Siphnos; *Diocletian's Price Edict* 5.12; *Apicius* 9.10.1–4, *al.*; Vinidarius *BC* 12.

A.C. Andrews, 'The Sardinian fish of the Greeks and Romans' in *American Journal of Philology* vol. 70 (1949) pp. 171–85.

- Greek *sardine*, *sardinos*, Latin *sardina* is the pilchard or sardine (*Sardina Pilchardus*), a much smaller fish than the *sarda*. It was given this name because it could be, and often was, conserved in the style of *sarda*. The species belongs to the western Mediterranean; never very familiar in Greece, it was sometimes equated there with *khalkis* (see under APHYE).

Columella *DA* 8.17.12 (*sardina*); Galen *AF* 6.745 (*sardene*); Athenaeus *D* 328f–329a citing Aristotle fragment 329 Rose and

Epaenetus (*sardinos*); *Diocletian's Price Edict* 5.12 (*sardeine?*).

Saturnalia, Roman winter festival. The *Saturnalia* were held on 17 December and eventually extended over several days. 'Our custom is that slaves dine together with their masters,' says Accius, and they had plenty to drink, too (three litres per person, according to Cato). At a later period the *Saturnalia* extended to several days of carnival, and slaves and their masters exchanged roles. See also APOPHORETA.

Cato *DA* 57; Accius, *Annales* 3 Dangel; Athenaeus *D* 639b–640a; Martial 4.46; Macrobius *S* 1.7–10, *al.*.

Satyrion, best known nowadays as salep, the twin bulbs of certain orchid species. Salep was one of the more reliable APHRODISIACS in the classical repertoire, and to some extent retains this reputation in modern Greece and neighbouring countries. In ancient times the bulb was 'given in the milk of a mountain goat', according to Theophrastus; or in a honeyed spiced wine, according to the *Herbarius* ascribed to Apuleius. In modern use powdered salep is taken as a hot milky drink, and is also used as a flavouring for ice cream.

Salep (*Orchis mascula* and similar species) is Greek *satyrion* and *orkhis*, Latin *satyrion*, *satureum*, *priapiscus*.

Theophrastus *HP* 9.18.3 (text, *Theophrasti Eresii opera* ed. F. Wimmer [Paris: Didot, 1866] p. 159; translation and notes, Andrew Dalby in *Petits Propos culinaires* no. 64 [2000] pp. 9–15); Ovid, *Art of Love* 2.415; Dioscorides *MM* 3.126–8; Pliny *NH* 26.95–8, 27.65; Martial 3.75; Galen *SF* 12.92–3; Pseudo-Apuleius, *Herbarius* 15.3.

Yule and Burnell 1903 p. 784; John Scarborough, 'The pharmacology of sacred plants, herbs and roots' in *Magika Hiera: ancient Greek magic and religion* (New York: Oxford University Press, 1991) pp. 148–9; Dalby 1996 pp. 86, 202, 237; Lambraki 1997 pp. 76–7.

Satyrs, in Greek mythology the companions of Silenus. He and his crew were the

male attendants on DIONYSUS, often en-
tangled with the Maenads who were his
female attendants. Satyrs are frequently
depicted in archaic and early classical
Athenian vase paintings, sometimes engaged in harvesting grapes and making
wine, sometimes enjoying the results and
participating in divine analogues of the
symposion (see SYMPOSION (1) and KOMOS.
Conventionally bull-necked, snub-nosed
and ithyphallic, sometimes tailed, a satyr
(Greek *satyros*) is slightly uglier and less
inhibited than a drunken human male.

K. Schauenburg, 'Silene beim Symposion' in
*Jahrbuch des Deutschen Archäologischen Insti-
tuts* vol. 88 (1973) pp. 1–26; François Lissarrague, 'The sexual life of satyrs' in *Before
Sexuality: the construction of erotic experience
in the ancient Greek world* ed. D.M. Halperin
and others (Princeton: Princeton University
Press, 1990); François Lissarrague, 'Le vin des
satyres' in G. Garrier and others, *Le Vin des
Historiens* (Suze-la-Rousse: Université du Vin,
1990) pp. 49–63; Alexander A.J. Heinemann,
'Bilderspiele beim Gelage: Symposiast und Satyr im Athen des 5. Jahrhunderts' in *Gegenwelten zu den Kulturen Griechenlands und Roms
in der Antike* ed. Tonio Hölscher (Munich:
Saur, 2000) pp. 321–49.

Sauce, liquid prepared separately to be
served as part of a cooked dish. Sauces
were already a significant feature of classical as they are of modern European
cookery.

Detailed information on the named
sauces of Greek cuisine (see below; for
halme and *muria* see under GARUM)
comes largely from Byzantine scholia and
lexica. Roman cuisine dealt differently
with sauces: there are few distinctive
names but (it appears from *Apicius*)
sauces were separately adjusted to each
dish with which they were served.

- The general Latin term for sauce is *ius*.
  Distinctions are occasionally made by colour: *ius candidum* 'white sauce', *ius viride*
  'green sauce' (e.g. *Apicius* 6.5.3–5). Hundreds of the recipes in *Apicius* are wholly or
  principally for sauces.

- Greek *abyrtake* is described by Photius as 'a
  hypotrimma [sauce] made from sour things,
  cress, garlic, mustard, raisins, serving as an

aperient'. Other lists of ingredients suggest
leeks and pomegranate seeds. It was a
foreign fashion in fourth century BC Athens,
linked by the comic playwright Theopompus
with Persia in particular. Polyaenus confirms
that *abyrtake* was prepared for the Persian
King's Dinner, a main ingredient being capers.

- Antiphanes 140 Kassel; Alexis *F* 145 Kassel
  with Arnott *ad l.*; Aelius Dionysius, *Attic
  Words s.v. abyrtake* quoting Theopompus
  Comicus 18 Kassel; Lucian, *Lexiphanes* 6
  with scholia; Polyaenus 4.3.32; Hesychius,
  *Lexicon s.vv. abyrtakopoiou, neodartes,
  parthenias*; Photius, *Lexicon s.v. abyrtake*.

- Greek *embamma* is a dip. The one recommended by Archestratus is of hyssop in
  vinegar, thus resembling modern English
  mint sauce. This term, like *bamma*, is used
  also for liquid mixtures and dips used in
  non-food contexts, such as dyes and lotions.

  Xenophon, *Cyropaedia* 1.3.4; Archestratus
  H 22 Brandt with Olson and Sens *ad l.*;
  Dioscorides *MM* 2.159, 3.80; Oribasius *CM*
  8.47.9.

- For Greek *hyposphagma* see the recipes
  quoted at ERASISTRATUS and GLAUCUS of
  Locri.

  Athenaeus 324a citing Erasistratus and
  Glaucus of Locri.

- Greek *hypotrimma* is a general term for a
  sauce. It is also sometimes a specific sauce,
  and one that was adopted into Roman
  cuisine.

  Hippocrates *R* 2.56; Antiphanes 221 Kassel;
  Apicius 1.33; *Etymologicum Magnum*
  492.49, 784.9.

  Dalby 1996 pp. 245–6.

- Greek *karyke* is a spicy and perhaps a fairly
  thick sauce, if a physician can describe loose
  stools as *karykoeidea* 'sauce-like'. It is at
  any rate a typical sauce of fourth-century
  Greek cuisine: the men of Delphi, where
  plenty of cooking went on, were called
  karykkopoioi 'sauce-makers' in an Athenian
  satyr play. An aside in a play by Menander
  suggests some ingredients.

  Hippocrates, *Epidemics* 4.25; Menander
  fragment 451 Körte; Athenaeus *D* 173c
  quoting Achaeus.

  Dalby 1996 pp. 106–7 and note 44.

- Greek *katakhysma* is a dressing or sauce to
  be poured over a dish when served. It is also
  the Greek term for the shower of walnuts
  and figs with which a newly married woman

and a newly acquired slave were welcomed to their new home.

Aristophanes, *Birds* 535, 1637; Plato Comicus *F* 189 Kassel; Plutarch, *Amatorius* 753d.

- Greek *oxalme* is a cooking liquor of vinegar and brine, used hot. In the passage by Cratinus, the Cyclops promises to dip Odysseus' sailors in *halme*, *oxalme* and hot *skorodalme* 'garlic brine', in that order, before eating whichever is tenderest. The *gliskhre halme* 'greasy brine' forbidden by Archestratus is evidently a brine with oil. Greek *oxelaion* is a sauce or dressing based on vinegar and olive oil.

Aristophanes, *Wasps* 331; Archestratus *H* 45 Brandt; Galen *AF* 6.616; Athenaeus *D* 385b–d quoting Cratinus 150 Kassel.

- Greek *trimmation, trimma* are mixtures of ground fresh herbs either added during cooking or served, moistened with olive oil and maybe vinegar, in a side-dish.

Archestratus *H* 11, 23, 33 Brandt with Olson and Sens *ad ll.*; Alexis *F* 193 Kassel with Arnott *ad l.*

Sausage, minced meat (usually offal, and most often pork) stuffed into a casing before being cooked. Traditionally the usual casing is the stretched lining of the intestine (Greek *entera*). This is carried as part of his equipment by the sausage-seller in Aristophanes's *Knights*. Some sausages are made from fresh minced meat and are to be cooked and eaten quickly, but many – and probably the great majority in the ancient world – were cured, initially with salt, and could then be kept for a long time. Some cured sausages are eaten raw; some are cooked.

Greek *allas*, Latin *botulus*, *botellus* are the usual words for sausage: 'pig intestine stuffed with meat, fat, and a variety of more dubious substances', to quote Frost's enticing definition. From its shape it is not surprising that, as far back as the sixth century BC, *allas* is likened to the penis. Latin *botulus* is characterised as a vulgar word by Gellius, who prefers the vaguer *farcimen*. Seneca lists a *botularius* 'sausage-seller' (compare Greek *allantopoles*)

as a contributor to the street cries of Rome.

Hipponax 84.17 West; Aristophanes, *Knights* 161, 1183, *al.*; Eubulus *F* 14 Kassel; Seneca, *Letters* 56.2; Petronius *S* 49, 66; Martial 5.78, 11.31, 14.72; Gellius 16.7.11; Pollux *O* 6.52–54; *Apicius* 2.3–5.

Buck 1949 pp. 366–7; R. Laur-Belart, 'Gallische Schinken und Würste' in *Suisse primitive* vol. 17 (1953) pp. 33–40; Frank Frost, 'Sausage and meat preservation in antiquity' in *Greek, Roman and Byzantine Studies* vol. 40 (1999) pp. 241–52.

- Latin *isicium* and Greek *isikion, isikos* are names for minced or ground meat (the meat of any animal, including chicken and peafowl). The Latin term *salsa isicia*, literally 'salted minced meat', is not attested, but its abridged form *salsicia* is the origin of modern words in many languages, including French *saucisse* and English *sausage*. Minced meat is the most desirable ingredient in sausages as we know them, accompanied by a preservative such as salt and a casing such as intestine. A string of sausages, *seira salsikion*, though surely a common sight in the ancient market, does not occur in Greek or Latin literature before the Byzantine *Life of St Simeon Salos*. The saint wore them like a wreath.

Varro, *On the Latin Language* 5.110; Athenaeus *D* 376b citing Paxamus; Macrobius *S* 7.8.1; Anthimus *OC* 33; Leontius of Naples, *Life of St Simeon Salos* 8.52 [*Patrologia Graecolatina*, ed. Migne, vol. 93 col. 1733].

- Greek *gaster* is an animal's stomach. As a food term it means a stomach used as a casing, such as the one described as 'full of fat and blood' in the *Odyssey*, evidently an equivalent of the modern black pudding. It was typically cooked by boiling, then sliced and grilled.

Homer, *Odyssey* 18.44–5, 18.118–19, 20.25–7; Aristophanes, *Clouds* 409, *Knights* 1179; Archestratus *H* 62 Brandt; Eubulus *F* 14 Kassel.

- Greek *khorde, kholix* and *physke* are all names for large sausages that are served in slices. The *khorde haimatitis* is a blood sausage. Latin *tomaculum* may belong in this category.

Aristophanes, *Knights* 1179 with scholia, cf. 214, 315; Theophrastus, *Characters* 9.4; Athenaeus *D* 94f–95f, 125e; Petronius *S* 31, 49; Juvenal 10.355.

- Latin *lucanica*, Greek *loukánika* has the distinction of being one of the oldest specific recipes whose name is still in use – a recipe for smoked sausage that Roman soldiers of the third century BC brought home from service in Lucania, in southern Italy. This is still the modern Greek name for a cured, dry sausage; the same term, in different forms, is used from end to end of the Mediterranean and even beyond. The first detailed recipe is in *Apicius*; Frost (above) has tested it.

  Varro, *On the Latin Language* 5.111; Cicero, *Letters to Friends* 9.16.8; Martial 13.35; *Philogelos* 237; *Apicius* 2.4, cf. 4.2.13, 5.4.2.

  Johan Mathiesen, 'The children of Lucanica' in *Petits Propos culinaires* no. 43 (1993) pp. 62–3.

Savory, genus of culinary herbs. Of these the best known in the classical world is the species now called Roman hyssop; it is mentioned in literary texts, is called for in recipes (such as Epaenetus's recipe for MYMA) and is found in archaeological contexts such as the latrine deposits at Cologne in Roman Germany.

Savory or Roman hyssop (*Satureja Thymbra*) is Greek *thymbra*, Latin *satureia*. The Latin name is not always distinguished from that of the aphrodisiac SATYRION. For this reason 'savory' (French *sarriette*) sometimes occurs in translations in contexts where an aphrodisiac is required: *satyrion* or 'salep' should be substituted.

Aristophanes, *Acharnians* 254, *Clouds* 421; Hippocrates *R* 54, *Nature of Woman* 32; Theophrastus *HP* 7.6.1, *CP* 3.1.4; Nicander *T* 531, 628; Dioscorides *MM* 3.37; Pliny *NH* 19.165; Galen *AF* 6.527, 6.572, *al.*; Athenaeus *D* 187d, also 215c, also 662e quoting Epaenetus (see translation at MYMA).

- Summer savory (*S. hortensis*) is Latin *cunila*. Winter savory (*S. montana*) is probably Latin *cunilago*.

  Columella *DA* 9.4.2; Pliny *NH* 20.168–73, *al.*

Scad, sea fish superficially resembling mackerel. Its flesh is rather dry, according to Diocles; palatable, but not nutritious,

says Xenocrates. In a lost play by Alexis a cook appears to be testing a slave's knowledge of cookery, using scad as an example:

> 'Do you know how to cook *sauros*?'
> 'I will when you've told me.'
> 'Take out the gills, rinse, cut off the spines all round, split neatly and spread it out flat, whip it good and sound with silphium and cover with cheese, salt and oregano.'

Scad or horse-mackerel (*Trachurus Trachurus* and other species) is Greek *sauros* and *trakhouros*, Latin *saurus*. Some Greek sources distinguish the two names; others, including Xenocrates, treat them as synonymous.

Xenocrates *T* 17; Pliny *NH* 32.89; Galen *AF* 6.720–7 citing Phylotimus; Oppian *H* 3.398–400; Athenaeus *D* 322c–e quoting Alexis *F* 138 Kassel, also 326a citing Diocles of Carystus; Marcellus, *On Medicaments* 29.45; Cassiodorus, *Variae* 11.40.

Thompson 1947 pp. 230, 263; Davidson 1981 p. 101.

Scallop, group of bivalve shellfish. They are among the best of shellfish gastronomically; their flavour is finest in spring when they spawn, as observed by Aristotle. They were cooked as a separate dish; 'grilled and served with vinegar and silphium they tend to loosen the bowels owing to their excessive sweetness; they are juicier and easier to digest if they are baked,' according to Xenocrates. They were also used as an ingredient, for example, in the soufflé-like dish *spumeum* for which Anthimus gives a recipe.

Scallops (Greek *kteis*, Latin *pecten*) belong to the family *Pectinidae*. Several species are common in the Mediterranean, and Xenocrates goes into some detail on their qualities. Other ancient authors focus on two kinds, each of which was at its best in a specified locality (see below).

Hippocrates *R* 48; Aristotle *HA* 607b2; Theocritus 14.17; Xenocrates *T* 56–71; Athenaeus 86b–92d *passim* quoting Archestratus *H* 56 Brandt; *Apicius* 1.29.1; Anthimus *OC* 34, 48 with Grant *ad l.*

Thompson 1947 pp. 133–4; Davidson 1981 pp. 200–1; Dalby 2000a pp. 65, 150.

- 'Soft Tarentum boasts its saucer-like scallops' in Horace's gastronomic satire. The pilgrim scallop or coquille Saint-Jacques (*Pecten Jacobaeus*) was said to be wholesome, easily digested and good for the bowels. 'Take with cumin and pepper,' advised Diphilus. Earlier gastronomes had already signalled the big scallops to be found at Ambracia, just across the straits from Tarentum.

Archestratus *H* 56 Brandt; Ennius *H* 3; Horace, *Satires* 2.4.34; Athenaeus 90f quoting Diphilus of Siphnos.

- Methymna and Mitylene were proud of the scallop (perhaps *Proteoplecten glaber*) that was caught in the straits between Lesbos and the Anatolian coast. It had once been wiped out locally by a combination of over-fishing and drought, but had returned by Roman times. These shellfish are smaller than the coquille Saint-Jacques but just as good in flavour. They were conserved in brine and exported.

Philyllius 12 Kassel; Aristotle *HA* 603a21–3.

Scybelite wine (Greek *Skybelites*; Latin *Scybelites*), from Galatia in central Asia Minor. This sweet *protropos* wine had a flavour like *mulsum* or honey-wine, according to Pliny. Quite 'thick', very sweet and black, according to Galen, it formed the basis of a medicinal wine flavoured with liquorice. It surely shared an origin with the big, sweet *skybelitides* raisins named by Galen.

Pliny *NH* 14.80; Galen *ST* 6.337, *AF* 6.582, *BM* 6.800, 6.804, *On Diagnosis by Pulse* 8.775, *On Compounding* 13.85.

Sea anemone, a creature that clings to undersea rocks. Some species are edible, but they are painful to collect 'unless one first smears one's skin with oil', Diphilus advises. 'In winter time,' according to Aristotle, 'their flesh is firm and accordingly they are sought after as articles of food, but in summer weather they are worthless.' Archestratus recommends frying sea anemone tentacles with *aphyai*, small fry. The flavour of sweet wine and honeyed wine went well with sea anemone, Xenocrates suggests. The Pythagoreans, according to Plutarch, avoided sea anemone.

The sea anemone (*Anemonia sulcata*) and the larger and not-so-good tomate de mer (*Actinia equina*) are Greek *akalephe* and *knide*, Latin *urtica*, homonymous in both languages with the nettle.

Aristophanes, *Lysistrata* 549 with scholia; Archestratus *H* 9 Brandt with Olson and Sens *ad l.*; Aristotle *HA* 531a31–b17; Xenocrates *T* 46–9; Plutarch *QC* 4.5; Athenaeus *D* 89f–90b quoting Diphilus of Siphnos, also 92c.

Thompson 1947 pp. 5, 118; Davidson 1981 p. 218.

Sea squirt, sea creature (actually a colony or microcosm rather than a creature), one of the more unusual of Mediterranean delicacies. According to Alan Davidson, 'the yellow part inside, which is what you eat, looks like scrambled egg and is considered to be a delicacy in Provence'.

The sea squirt breaks into literature in the *Iliad*, and is carefully described by Aristotle in an interesting passage of his *History of Animals*. Its earliest gastronomic success comes with Archestratus's recommendation to buy sea-squirts at Calchedon. Xenocrates advises on a method of cooking: 'It is cut and rinsed and seasoned with Cyrenaic silphium and rue and brine and vinegar, or with fresh mint in vinegar and sweet wine.'

The sea squirt or ascidian, called *violet* or *figue de mer* in French (*Microcosmus sulcatus*) is Greek *tethyon*. Translators of the *Iliad* traditionally pretend that in this one text *tethyon* means an oyster.

Homer, *Iliad* 16.747; Archestratus *H* 56 Brandt; Aristotle *HA* 531a8–30; Xenocrates *T* 110–15; Pliny *NH* 32.99, *al.* (*tethea*).

Thompson 1947 p. 261; Davidson 1981 p. 216.

Sea urchin, spiny, hard-shelled sea creature of which only the five ovaries are eaten. These tiny, often coral-coloured sacs are a prized delicacy in modern as they were in ancient times, but puzzling to those unfamiliar with them. The story was told by Demetrius of Scepsis of a Spartan who was faced with a sea urchin for the first time at a banquet and tried to eat it whole. The ovaries were called in Greek *oa*, 'eggs'; in Latin *carnes*, 'flesh'. They were said to swell when the moon was full. They were salted in December, according to Palladius. Galen recommends them eaten with *mulsum* or with *garum*; *Apicius* provides recipes for sea urchin both fresh and salted. The shell had medicinal uses.

The sea urchin (notably *Echinus esculentus* and *Paracentrotus lividus*) is Greek *ekhinos*, homonymous with the hedgehog; Latin *echinus*.

Hipponax 70 West; Aristophanes, *Lysistrata* 1169; Hippocrates *R* 48; Alexis 115 Kassel; Aristotle *HA* 530a32–531a7, 544a16–22; Ennius *H* 11; Dioscorides *MM* 2.1; Martial 13.86; Aulus Gellius 20.8 quoting Lucilius 1201 Marx; Galen *AF* 6.738; Athenaeus *D* 91b–d quoting Aristophanes fragment 425 Kassel and Demetrius of Scepsis; Palladius *OA* 2.16, 13.6; *Apicius* 9.8; Photius, *Lexicon s.v. ambrytoi*.

Thompson 1947 *s.vv. ekhinos, spatanges, bryssos*.

- Greek words denoting other similar species – not edible, according to Aristotle – are *bryssos* and *spatanges*. All three Greek terms are also used metaphorically for women's pubic hair. Thompson's view that the *spatanges* of Aristophanes fragment 425 must be 'an edible species', because the speaker associates with it the verbs *dardapto, mistyllo, dialeikho* 'munch', 'divide', 'lick', has amused more than one student of classical indecency.

Sebesten or gunda (*Cordia Myxa*), small olive-like tree fruit now grown in southern India and east Africa. Remains of sebesten fruits have been found in Egyptian tombs. The species is identified with a fruit described as 'Egyptian plum' by Theophrastus and under the Latin name *myxa* by Pliny.

Theophrastus *HP* 4.2.10 (*kokkymelea he Aigyptia*); Diodorus Siculus 1.34.9 (*myxaria, s.v.l.*); Pliny *NH* 13.51, 15.45–6 (*myxa*), cf. 13.64 (*prunus Aegyptia*); Palladius *OA* 3.25.32.

Darby and others 1977 pp. 705–8; S. Facciola, *Cornucopia: a source book of edible plants* (Vista: Kampong Publications, 1990) p. 81.

Sesame, an oil plant apparently native to India and domesticated there probably in the second millennium BC. Historians used to believe that sesame was the everyday oil of the ancient Near East, serving as food and medicine and as a base for perfumes. Ancient terms obviously connected with classical Greek *sesamon* (Akkadian *šamaššammu*; Egyptian *smsmt*; Mycenaean Greek *sa-sa-ma*) were translated 'sesame'. All this is now in doubt because of the entire absence of archaeobotanical evidence for sesame in the ancient Near East before the end of the second millennium BC. Pending earlier finds of sesame seeds, it is now often concluded that LINSEED was the common oil of ancient Mesopotamia and Egypt and bore these names. On this assumption, whenever sesame was introduced from India, possibly shortly before 1000 BC, it will rapidly have displaced linseed as a food oil – since it is much more easily kept fresh – and the names formerly applied to linseed oil must henceforth have been used for sesame oil.

At the Persian King's Dinner (see PERSIANS) sesame oil was used both in the cooking process and as a seasoning (Polyaenus). It remained rather unfamiliar in classical Greece and Rome, but was observed in use in contemporary Mesopotamia and Egypt (Herodotus; Pliny). It was one of five oils taxed under Ptolemy II (see EGYPT).

Sesame grew in Egypt, Syria and Babylonia in large quantities by Hellenistic times (Raschke p. 651 and nn. 1014–21), and was familiar as a summer crop in Greece by that time (Theophrastus). The seed was a popular ingredient in CAKES, particularly wedding cakes, to judge by Greek literary sources; one such cake was known as *sesamous*.

Sesame (*Sesamum indicum*) is Greek *sesamon*, Latin *sesamum*.

Hipponax 26a West; Solon 40 West; Herodotus 1.193, 3.48, 3.117; Aristophanes, *Acharnians* 1092, *Birds* 159, *Wasps* 676, *Thesmophoriazusae* 570, *Peace* 869 with scholia; Hippocrates *R* 45, *Epidemics* 7.68; Xenophon, *Anabasis* 1.2.22, 4.4.13; Philoxenus *D* e.16–19 Page; Alexis *F* 132 Kassel with Arnott *ad l.*; Theophrastus *HP* 8.1.2, 8.3.1–4; Dioscorides *MM* 1.34, 2.99; Pliny *NH* 15.28, 15.30, 18.96; Polyaenus 4.3.32; *Scholia on Aristophanes, Knights* 277.

Laufer 1919 pp. 288–96; Miller 1969 p. 87; M.G. Raschke, 'New studies in Roman commerce with the East' in *Aufstieg und Niedergang der römischen Welt* part 2 vol. 9 section 2 (Berlin, 1978) pp. 650–81; J.N. Postgate, 'The oil plant in Assyria' in *Bulletin on Sumerian Agriculture* vol. 2 (1985) pp. 145–52; Dorothea Bedigian, 'Is se-gis-i sesame or flax?' in *Bulletin on Sumerian Agriculture* no. 2 (1985) p. 159–78; Dorothea Bedigian and J.R. Harlan, 'Evidence for cultivation of sesame in the ancient world' in *Economic Botany* vol. 40 (1986) pp. 137–54; Zohary and Hopf 1993 pp. 132–3; Brewer and others 1995 pp. 43–5; Simoons 1998 pp. 174–80; Dorothea Bedigian, 'Sesame' in *CWHF* 2000 vol. 1 pp. 411–21.

- Greek *kopte* (*sesamis*), Latin *gelonianum* was a sweetmeat of Hellenistic and Roman times, made of pounded sesame, perhaps not unlike halva.

  Pollux *KH* 21; Alexander of Tralles, *Medicine* 1.15.

Setine wine (Latin *Setinum*), from Setia in the hills above Forum Appi in Latium. Setine was the favourite of the emperor Augustus and some of his successors.

Strabo 5.3.6; Pliny *NH* 3.60, 14.52, 14.61, 23.36; Martial 4.69, 13.112, *al.*; Juvenal 5.33–5, 10.27.

Tchernia 1986 pp. 204, 345–7; Dalby 2000a p. 34.

Shad, a small, rather dry and bony fish, migrating from sea to rivers. This was the nearest relative to the herring known in the ancient Mediterranean. It is specially listed among fish of the Nile, though also well known in Greece and in European rivers. Young shad counted among the fish that Greek cooks might include in aphye. The boniness of this species makes full-grown specimens tiresome to eat, but the shad as fished in the Moselle, 'sizzling on the fire, [is] a food for the people' according to Ausonius. Shad appears in Columella's farming manual as food for larger fish.

Greek *thrissa*, and perhaps also *thraitta*, are general names for the shad (the commonest species being *Alosa Alosa* and *A. fallax*). Latin names are *alecula* (or *hallecula*) and *alausa*, perhaps also *clupea*. There is a link between the first two of these Latin names and that of ALLEC, fermented fish paste, for which shad made a good ingredient. Diphilus considered *thrissa* to be 'of the same race' as *khalkis* and *eritimos*: for these Greek terms see APHYE.

Acraephia Price List (*thraitt.*); Columella *DA* 8.15.6, 8.17.12–14; Athenaeus *D* 328c–329b, also 355f citing Diphilus of Siphnos; Ausonius, *Mosella* 127.

Thompson 1947 *s.vv.*

Shark, group of large sea fish, fiercer relatives of the DOGFISH. The Greek word *kyon*, literally 'dog', refers in general to fish of these two groups, comprising the scientific order *Squaliformes* (this name is a direct translation of Aristotle's *galeoeideis* 'of the dogfish kind'), sometimes also including the SWORDFISH. A term meaning 'dog' serves in many languages as a metaphor for the fish of these groups. The dogfish were distinguished under such names as *kyon pion* 'fat dog' and *galeos*; thus, when it is being used more specifically, in opposition to these names, *kyon* on its own designates a shark. Shark was not good to eat – its meat was coarse and productive of bad humours – but it made a good table display, Xenocrates observes.

Homer, *Odyssey* 12.96; Epicharmus 47–8 Kaibel; Cratinus 171.50 Kassel; Aristotle *HA* 566a31, *al.*; Xenocrates *T* 21; Pausanias 4.34.3; Galen *AF* 6.727; Aelian, *Nature of Animals* 1.55; Oppian *H* 1.373–82, 5.365–75.

- Greek *elakaten*, said to be a big fish whose meat was salted, is possibly a shark but is unidentified. The name was not in current use in later Greek.

Acraephia Price List (*alak...o*); Columella *DA* 8.17.12 (*elacata*); Athenaeus *D* 301d citing Menander, *Kolax* fragment 7 Sandbach.

- Greek (*kyon*) *karkharias* is possibly the porbeagle (*Lamna Nasus*). Archestratus, dismissing as illogical the objections of those who preferred not to eat a man-eating fish, suggests an excellent recipe, for which see the modern interpretation by Dalby and Grainger 1996 pp. 33–4.

Plato Comicus *F* 189 Kassel; Archestratus *H* 23 Brandt; *Acraephia Price List* (*kouon karkharias*); Columella *DA* 8.17.12 (*carcharus*); Athenaeus *D* 306d.

- Greek *lamia*, *lamna* may be the big shark *Carcharodon Carcharias*. It is indigestible and productive of salty humours, according to Phylotimus.

Aristotle *HA* 540b17; Oppian *H* 1.370, 5.358–64; Galen *AF* 6.727 quoting Phylotimus.

- Greek *zygaina* is the hammerhead shark (*Sphyrna Zygaena*). Its meat was tough and hard to digest, but was much more palatable when it had been salted.

Epicharmus 59 Kaibel; Galen *AF* 6.727 citing Phylotimus, also 6.738.

Sheatfish, very large river fish. The sheatfish has been common in the Danube and other big rivers of southeastern Europe. Pliny knew of it in the Main, and Ausonius in the Moselle. The female was better eating than the male, said Aristotle. It was available salted: *Apicius* provides a recipe.

The sheatfish (*Silurus Glanis*) is Greek *glanis* and *silouros*, Latin *silurus*.

Aristotle *HA* 608a2–5, *al.*; Pliny *NH* 9.45, *al.*; Ausonius, *Mosella* 135; *Apicius* 9.10.8.

Thompson 1947 pp. 43–8, 233–7.

- In some of its details Aristotle's description of *glanis* applies not to the big sheatfish but

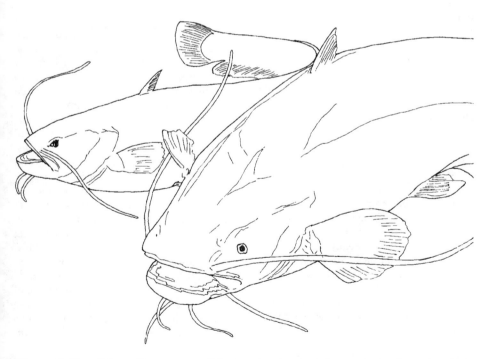

Figure 13 Sheatfish or European catfish, Greek *silouros, glanis*, Latin *silurus*. Top left: Aristotle's catfish (*Silurus Aristotelis*). Bottom right: sheatfish or Wels catfish (*Silurus Glanis*).

to a smaller river fish of the Greek rivers Achelous and Peneius. This species was rediscovered on the basis of his description and named in his honour *Silurus Aristotelis*. Thompson hypothesises that this same species may also be the otherwise unidentified *kapros*, literally 'boar', a noisy fish of the Achelous, said by Archestratus to be one of the delicacies of Ambracia and linked by Philemon with Argos, presumably Amphilochian Argos.

Aristotle *HA* 535b16–18 (*kapros*), also 568a21–568b17 (*glanis*) with Thompson *ad ll.*; Athenaeus *D* 305d–f quoting Archestratus *H* 15 Brandt (see Olson and Sens *ad l.*) (*kapros*); Philemon 82 Kassel (*kapros*); Pausanias 4.34.2 (*glanis*).

Thompson 1947 pp. 101–2; Andrews 1948 pp. 244–6.

Sheep, animal domesticated in the Near East, perhaps in western Iran, where domesticated sheep existed as early as 9000 BC. This versatile creature is a source of wool, of milk (which makes fine cheese) and of the meat which in modern English is called pejoratively mutton and approvingly lamb. In southern Europe much sheep-farming has been migratory, from summer pastures in the mountains to winter pastures in the lowlands among olive groves and orchards.

In Greece and Rome the sheep was a common sacrificial animal, and in consequence a common centrepiece for a feast. Menander's *Dyscolus* depicts the events surrounding a family sacrifice of this kind. The clear implication of some literary sources, including the *Dyscolus*, is that a sheep for slaughter was an old animal which had already given generously of wool and milk. Spring lamb was, however, favoured by those who could afford this luxury (see also SUCKLING ANIMALS). A spring lamb is the PASSOVER sacrifice in Jewish custom, whence it became the usual Easter meal among Christians.

The sheep (*Ovis Aries*) is *probaton* in Greek (also *krios* 'ram', *ois* 'ewe', *aren* 'lamb'; *arneion* 'lamb meat'), *ovis* in Latin (also *aries* 'ram', *agnus* 'lamb'; *agnina* 'lamb meat'). The wild sheep, not commonly mentioned in ancient texts, is said by Oppian to be hunted in Crete.

Menander, *Dyscolus passim*; Cato *DA* 149–50 with Dalby *ad loc.*; Mark, *Gospel* 14.12; Oppian, *Cynegetica* 2.377–81; Anthimus *OC* 4–5 with Grant *ad l.*

Buck 1949 pp. 143–60; Liliane Bodson, 'Le mouton dans l'antiquité gréco-romaine' in *Ethnozootechnie* vol. 21 (1977) pp. 107–21; Darby and others 1977 pp. 212–21; P. Halstead, 'Counting sheep in Neolithic and Bronze Age Greece' in *Patterns of the Past: studies in honour of David Clarke* ed. I. Hodder and others (Cambridge, 1981) pp. 307–39; Joan M. Frayn, *Sheep-rearing and the Wool Trade in Italy during the Roman Period* (Liverpool: Cairns, 1984); S. Bökönyi, 'Horses and sheep in East Europe in the Copper and Bronze Ages' in *Proto-Indo-European: the archaeology of a linguistic problem. Studies in honor of Marija Gimbutas* ed. S.N. Skomal and E.C. Polomé (Washington: Institute for the Study of Man, 1987) pp. 136–44; Brewer and others 1995 pp. 90–3; Toynbee 1996.

Shellfish, a rich source of food in the Mediterranean, exploited since prehistoric times. Species collected at FRANCHTHI Cave, the fullest recorded sequence so far, included *Monodonta* spp., *Gibbula* spp. and *Patella* spp. 'limpet' from *c*.9000 to 7500 BC; then *Cerithium vulgatum* was popular till about 5000; then *Cerastoderma glaucum*, *Tapes decussatus*, *Donax trunculus*, *Donacilla cornea* and others till 3000 BC. For species that were of importance in the classical period see LIMPET; MUSSEL; OYSTER; PINNA; PURPLE-SHELL; RAZOR-SHELL; SCALLOP; TOP-SHELL; VENUS CLAM; WEDGE-SHELL; WHELK. Useful surveys are given by Pliny, Xenocrates, Galen and Athenaeus.

Shellfish were regarded as generally aphrodisiac according to Mnesitheus and other dietary sources, some species more so than others. The general view explains Horace's choice of adjective, *lubrica conchylia* 'sexy shellfish'.

Aristotle *HA* 527b35–529b19; Horace, *Satires* 2.4.30; Pliny *NH* 9.101–42; Xenocrates *T* 50–132; Galen *AF* 6.733–5; Athenaeus *D* 85c–94b.

Liliane Karali, *Shells in Aegean Prehistory* (Oxford: Archaeopress, 1999) (*BAR International Series*, 761); Liliane Karali, 'La malacofaune à l'âge du bronze et à la période géométrique' in *Paysage et alimentation dans le monde grec* ed. Jean-Marc Luce (Toulouse, 2000) pp. 115–31; María José García Soler, 'Nombres de moluscos en la obra de Ateneo de Náucratis' in *Veleia* vol. 11 (1994) pp. 197–235.

Shrimp and prawn, group of small river and sea creatures. The larger species are easily cooked and very easily eaten. The smaller and less attractive kinds were used by fishermen as bait.

Shrimps were best and biggest at Iasus in Caria, according to Archestratus; he adds that there were plenty of them in Macedonia (for these see below) and in Ambracia. In Italy, if Martial is to be believed, the shrimp was at its best in the tidal reaches of the River Liris in southern Latium. This river reached the sea at Minturnae. Now it was at Minturnae, according to legend, that Apicius lived – eighty years before Martial's time – and enjoyed the local 'magnificent shrimps, which grow bigger than the shrimps at Smyrna, bigger indeed than the lobsters at Alexandria' to quote Athenaeus (for the dénouement to this story see APICIUS (2)). Pliny the Younger boasted of good shrimps a little further north, at his Laurentan villa.

Shrimps danced when roasted on the coals, Ophelion tells us; they also turned red when cooked, hence the no doubt proverbial expression 'redder than a roasted shrimp' which Athenaeus quotes from the comic playwright Anaxandrides. In a very early poem, by Ananius, the 'best of all good dishes' is said to be shrimp in fig-leaf, the leaf perhaps being used as a plate rather than eaten with the shrimps. They were served honey-glazed at the dinner described or imagined by Philoxenus, and in general in ancient cuisine they were roasted, or fried in a skillet, rather than boiled. A shrimp sauce serves to garnish a moray or lamprey in the satirical 'dinner of Nasidienus' narrated by Horace.

Shrimps or prawns in general are Greek *karis* (occasionally *koris*), Latin *squilla*. Latin *cammarus*, originally the term for a freshwater CRAYFISH, eventually came to mean shrimp as well.

Ananius 5 West; Philoxenus *D* b.17 Page; Aristotle *HA* 525b1–33, 591b15; Lucilius 1240 Marx; Horace, *Satires* 2.4.58, 2.8.42; Pliny *NH* 11.152; Martial 13.83; Juvenal 5.81; Pliny the Younger, *Letters* 2.17; Galen *AF* 6.735; Oppian *H* 3.177, 3.184, 4.221; Athenaeus *E* 7a–b, also *D* 104c–106e quoting Archestratus *H* 25 Brandt, Ophelion 1 Kassel and Anaxandrides; *Historia Augusta, Heliogabalus* 19.7; *Apicius* 2.1.3 (*scilla*); Vinidarius *BC* 17.

Thompson 1947 p. 103; Davidson 1981 pp. 170–6.

- In specifying the larger species, those most commonly caught and eaten, in distinction to the rest, Aristotle calls them *karides hai kyphai*, literally 'hunchbacked shrimps'. This adjective and other similar ones are also used as poetic epithets for shrimps; examples are gathered by Athenaeus. If the designation is to be linked with any particular species, one would suggest those larger kinds more commonly called *garida* in modern Greek, such as *Aristeus antennatus* and *Aristeomorpha foliacea*.

Philoxenus *D* b.17 Page; Aristotle *HA* 525b1; Athenaeus *D* 105e–106e quoting Araros, Anaxandrides, Eubulus, Ophelion and Epicharmus; Ovid, *Halieutica* 130.

- Aristotle's second group is of *karidon to mikron genos* 'the family of little shrimps'. With this designation one might link those now grouped as *garidaki* in modern Greek, such as the common prawn (*Palaemon serratus*).

Aristotle *HA* 525b1.

- Aristotle's third group, *krangon*, is much more distinct. This is the mantis shrimp or squilla (*Squilla Mantis*). It is about the same size as the largest shrimps, but does not resemble them in detail.

Thompson 1947 p. 132.

- A species of large marine shrimp well known in Macedonia (*Penaeus Kerathurus*, French *grosse crevette*) is probably the kind that Archestratus refers to in the passage cited below. It is apparently the same kind that was locally called *kommara, komara*, a variant of the usual Greek name for freshwater crayfish. It still has this name; the forms in the modern Greek of Macedonia are *gammaras, gambaros*.

Archestratus *H* 25 Brandt; Hesychius, *Lexicon s.v. kommarai, komarai*.

Thompson 1947 p. 100; Davidson 1981 p. 176.

Sicily, land of plenty to archaic Greeks and Carthaginians, who planted colonies in Sicily in the eighth and seventh centuries BC. It was universally believed that the land of the CYCLOPS, visited by Odysseus in the Homeric *Odyssey*, was Sicily. It was therefore appropriate that CHEESE, made of sheep's milk mixed with goat's milk just as the Cyclops might have made it, was a Sicilian speciality in classical Greece. Sicily was also good for TUNNY, notably the promontories of Cephaloedium and Tyndaris on the north coast (Archestratus *H* 34, 38 Brandt with Olson and Sens *ad l.*); and there was salted tunny (Athenaeus *D* 116a–117b quoting Euthydemus of Athens). The *elops* – a STURGEON, apparently – was best at Syracuse (Archestratus *H* 11 Brandt). Cape Pelorus, at the northeast corner of the island, was good for SWORDFISH (Archestratus *H* 40 Brandt with Olson and Sens *ad l.*) and a good place for hunting too. The wines of Sicily known in Roman times included MAMERTINE WINE, one of the great names; there was also wine of Tauromenium (Pliny *NH* 14.66) and the sweet wine called *Alintium* (Pliny *NH* 14.80).

In the fifth century BC Sicilian luxuries were famous in Greece, a stereotype that made 'Sicilian tables' a synonym for gastronomic pleasures. Alongside the rumours, Sicilian cooks and Sicilian cookbooks came to Greece. There were allusions to them in many Athenian comedies. They were personified by MITHAECUS, first named author of a Greek cookbook, and by ARCHESTRATUS,

who spurned Sicilian cooks yet in some sense was a Sicilian cook himself.

The court of the kings of Syracuse was celebrated for its pleasures. It is possible, but unverifiable, that the *Dinner* of Philoxenus describes a dinner at that court, of which PHILOXENUS ((1) and ARISTIPPUS were habitués and at which Plato was an occasional visitor.

Aristophanes fragment 225 Kassel; Plato, *Letter 7* 326b, *Republic* 404d; Cratinus Junior 1 Kassel; Antiphanes 90 Kassel; Archestratus *H* 45 Brandt, *al.*; Aristotle *HA* 522a23; Athenaeus *D* 527c–e, 541c–e.

V.M. Scramuzza in Frank 1933–40 vol. 3 pp. 225–378; Dalby 1996 pp. 108–21; Sophie Collin-Bouffier, 'La cuisine des Grecs d'Occident, symbole d'une vie de tryphè?' in *Paysage et alimentation dans le monde grec* ed. Jean-Marc Luce (Toulouse: Presses Universitaires du Mirail, 2000) pp. 195–208; Wilkins 2000 pp. 312–68; Dalby 2000a pp. 113–17.

Sicon, a common fictional name (and probably a common real name) for a cook in Athens of the fifth and fourth centuries BC. Literary examples include Aristophanes's lost play entitled *Aeolosicon* 'Aeolus as Cook', the cook named Sicon in Menander's *Dyscolus*, and the character Sicon in Alexis's play *Asotodidaskalos* 'Teacher of Profligacy'. In a play by Sosipater a cook claims to be one of three faithful disciples who have preserved 'the teaching of Sicon … the founder of the art' (see also COOKERY AS ART AND SCIENCE).

Sosipater 1 Kassel [Athenaeus *D* 377f].

Sicyon, Greek city of the northern Peloponnese. Sicyon was a good place for fish, especially conger eels; it was from here that Poseidon brought them to the dinners of Mount Olympus.

Antiphanes 233 Kassel; Pausanias 2.13; Athenaeus *D* 288c–294c quoting Philemon 82 Kassel, Archestratus *H* 18 Brandt (see Olson and Sens *ad l.*) and Eudoxus.

Sieges *see* FAMINE

Signine wine (Latin *Signinum*), from Signia in central Latium. Signine wine was recommended for its medicinal effects. It was good after six years but 'more useful after longer ageing' according to the *Epitome of Athenaeus*. The emperor Marcus Aurelius insists, in a jocular letter, that he would rather drink the wine than the fresh must, such is its bitterness.

Strabo 5.3.10; Celsus 4.12.8, 4.26.9; Scribonius Largus 112, 113; Dioscorides *MM* 5.6.11; Pliny *NH* 14.65, 23.36; Martial 13.116; Silius Italicus 8.378; Marcus Aurelius, *Letters* [Fronto vol. 1 p. 176 Haines]; Galen *ST* 6.334–7, *DA* 14.15, *On Therapeutic Method* 10.831, *On Compounding* 13.659; Athenaeus *E* 27b.

Tchernia 1986 pp. 205–6.

Silenus *see* SATYRS

Silphium, a spice that was much prized in classical Greece and in republican Rome. Silphium was the resin tapped from the root and stem of a fennel-like plant that grew in the hinterland of Cyrene in Libya. The stem itself was also a delicacy for those who could get it. Never cultivated, silphium became extinct in the first century AD: but meanwhile an alternative had been found in central Asia, the aromatic resin now known as ASAFOETIDA.

First mentioned in Greek in the poems of Solon in the sixth century BC, silphium was to be present as a flavouring in almost every banquet narrated in the literature of the centuries that followed. Its role in cuisine was not unlike that of garlic in French or of onion in English cooking. It was also important in medicine: doctors recommended its use in the diet, and it was a frequent constituent of compound drugs. The best description of the plant and the harvest is given by Theophrastus:

> the harvesters cut in accordance with a sort of mining-concession, a ration that they may take based on what has been cut and what remains, and it is not permitted to cut at random; nor indeed to cut more than the ration, because the resin spoils and decays with age. When exporting it to Piraeus they put it in jars, mix flour with it and shake it: thus treated it remains stable.

The Libyan harvesters were contracted to sell all their silphium to the Greek-speaking kingdom of Cyrene, which grew rich in the trade. The silphium plant, a sturdy umbellifer, was a regular Cyrenaic coin type for hundreds of years. A sixth-century BC vase painting shows the king of Cyrene supervising the weighing and storage of what are apparently sacks of silphium. Plautus alludes to the trade in *sirpe* and *laserpicium* between Cyrene and Capua, nexus of the Italian spice trade. Some of the harvest was, however, smuggled to Carthage.

In Greek sources *silphion* (sometimes *opos*) and *kaulos* are often specified separately. *Kaulos* in these cases is the preserved stem; *silphion* is the resin, the usual commodity of trade, prepared for export as described by Theophrastus above, stabilised with beanmeal or a similar additive, just as asafoetida is prepared in modern times.

Mismanagement and overtapping led to a catastrophic decline in the silphium supply in the first century BC. In the 70s AD, Pliny tells us, silphium was 'worth its weight in silver ... For many years now it has not been seen in the region ... The single stem found within living memory was sent to the emperor Nero.' The recipes of *Apicius* often call for *silphium*: 'Median silphium', or asafoetida, is what was used.

Silphium is Greek *silphion* (see above), Latin *sirpe*, *laserpicium*, *laser*. The pseudo-scientific name 'Ferula tingitana' has no authority, since no remains of the plant have yet been found.

Solon 39 West; Aristophanes, *Knights* 895–6, *Birds* 534, 1579; Hippocrates *RA* 18; Antiphanes 216 Kassel; Alexis *F* 132, 138, 191, 193

Kassel with Arnott *ad ll.*; Theophrastus *HP* 6.3 with Amigues *ad l.*, also 9.1.7; Plautus, *Rudens* 629–34; Dioscorides *MM* 3.80; Strabo 17.3.20–2; Pliny *NH* 19.38–45, 22.100–6; Polyaenus 4.3.32.

A.C. Andrews, 'The silphium of the ancients: a lesson in crop control' in *Isis* vol. 33 (1941) pp. 232–6; V. Vikentiev, 'Le silphium et le rite du renouvellement de la vigueur' in *Bulletin de l'Institut d'Egypte* vol. 37 (1954) pp. 123–50; F. Chamoux, 'Du silphion' in *Cyrenaica in Antiquity* ed. G. Barker and others (Oxford, 1985); Alice Arndt, 'Silphium' in *Spicing up the Palate: proceedings of the Oxford Symposium on Food and Cookery 1992* (Totnes: Prospect Books, 1993) pp. 28–35; Andrew Dalby, 'Silphium and asafoetida: evidence from Greek and Roman writers' in *Spicing up the Palate: proceedings of the Oxford Symposium on Food and Cookery 1992* (Totnes: Prospect Books, 1993) pp. 67–72; D. Roques, 'Médecine et botanique: le silphion dans l'oeuvre d'Oribase' in *Revue des études grecques* vol. 106 (1993) pp. 380–99.

Sitos *see* MEALS

Skate or ray, a group of fish belonging to the family *Rajidae*. There are several Greek names (fewer Latin ones), and they are not easily assigned to the modern species, but in any case the species change in appearance with age. All have coarse flesh, according to Galen, and there is something in this. The best was said to be the *batis*.

Galen *AF* 6.737.

Thompson 1947 *s.vv.*; Davidson 1979 pp. 172–5; Davidson 1981 pp. 33–6.

- Greek *aetos*, literally 'eagle', may have been the eagle ray (*Myliobatis Aquila*) as suggested by Thompson. It made tough eating.

  Aristotle *HA* 540b18; Pliny *NH* 9.78; Galen *AF* 6.729.

- Greek *batis* is the most general term. When used specifically it may be identified with the thornback ray (*Raja clavata*). It was to be found at its best in midwinter, and was to be eaten, according to Archestratus, with cheese and silphium, his general strategy for dealing with a coarse-fleshed fish. It was as good eating as an old cloak, according to 'Dorion the flute-player' in an anecdote told by Lynceus.

Aristophanes, *Wasps* 510; Aristotle *HA* 565a22–9, *al.*; *Acraephia Price List*; Athenaeus *D* 286b–e quoting Archestratus *H* 49 Brandt (see Olson and Sens *ad l.*) and Epicharmus 59 and 90 Kaibel, also 337d quoting Lynceus *F* 32.

- Greek *batos* was somehow different from *batis*, as Epicharmus makes clear. The difference might be sexual (*batos* male, *batis* female), since the thornback ray tends to migrate in unisexual shoals; or it might be a species distinction, in which case *batos* could be the very large *Raja alba*, French *raie blanche*.

  Epicharmus 59, 90 Kaibel; Aristotle *HA* 566a26–566b2, *al.*, *Parts of Animals* 697a6; Hesychius, *Lexicon s.v. batis*.

- Greek *bous*, literally 'ox', and Latin *cornuta*, literally 'horned', may both be names for the very large fish *Mobula Mobular*. The *bous* is classed by Diphilus as 'fleshy' from the nutritional point of view.

  Pliny *NH* 9.78, 32.145; Oppian *H* 1.103, 2.141–66; Athenaeus *D* 356c citing Diphilus of Siphnos; Apicius 10.1.10.

  Thompson 1947 p. 34.

- Greek *rinobatos* is the strangely-shaped guitar fish, *Rhinobatus Rhinobatus*; the Greek name arises not just because this is a kind of *batis* with the shape of the *rine* or monkfish (see DOGFISH), but also because it was thought to be a cross between the two. The term occurs only in Aristotle's works and in the list of fish sold at Acraephia in Boeotia.

  Aristotle *HA* 566a30; *Acraephia Price List*.

  Thompson 1947 p. 222.

- Greek *leiobatos* was a smooth-skinned species, perhaps the skate, *Raja Batis*. It was white-fleshed, according to the culinary author Epaenetus; Archestratus, thinking perhaps of the coarse texture, would just as soon eat a lizard.

  Archestratus *H* 46 Brandt; Galen *AF* 6.737; Athenaeus *D* 312b quoting Plato Comicus *F* 146 Kassel and Epaenetus.

- Latin *raia* is a general term equating to Greek *batis*.

  Pliny *NH* 9.78, 9.144.

Skirret, root vegetable of central and southern Europe. Skirret (*Sium Sisarum*) is apparently Greek *sisaron*, Latin *siser*.

This food is rarely spoken of with enthusiasm in classical sources; however, the emperor Tiberius liked *siser* enough to send for some from Germany every year. The best came from around the fort of Gelduba (Gelb) on the Rhine. Columella gives instructions for conserving *siser*. Its bitterness was complemented by cooking in MULSUM.

Hippocrates, *Nature of Woman* 34; Horace, *Satires* 2.8.9; *Moretum* 73; Columella *DA* 10.114, 11.3.35, 12.58; Dioscorides *MM* 2.113; Pliny *NH* 19.90–2, 20.34–5; Galen *SF* 12.124; Athenaeus *D* 120d.

- The identification is very doubtful. According to Davidson skirret was unknown in Europe before the sixteenth century, when it was introduced from China. The *Oxford English Dictionary* provides evidence for a different history in which the modern European names such as English 'skirret' have a medieval Arabic origin.

  Oxford English Dictionary (Oxford, 1989) 2nd edn, *s.v. skirret*; Davidson 1999 p. 725.

Snail, group of terrestrial molluscs. Numerous species are native to Europe, some much bigger and better to eat than others. An early sign of their use for human food is the pile of discarded snail shells at FRANCHTHI, dated around 10,700 BC. Snails were also eaten at Minoan AKROTIRI, perhaps imported there from Crete as a luxury item.

Romans took snails seriously; theirs was probably the first civilisation in which snails were kept and fattened for the table. They made a suitable *gustus* or appetiser, as *Apicius* shows. Snails were also a common food among Greeks of the Roman period, according to Galen; however, Greeks rather seldom wrote about eating snails, except when listing them among aphrodisiac foods, as in the text by Alexis. In Latin texts, too, snails belong in the category of aphrodisiacs, as shown by Petronius.

Snails were fattened on emmer meal mixed with grape syrup. Varro, in his dialogue on farming, explains the business of making a *coclearium* or enclosure for

keeping snails, while Pliny gives a brief history of snail-keeping at Rome: 'Fulvius Lupinus, shortly before the civil war against Pompey, was the first to set up *coclearia*. He kept the different kinds separate.' I add Pliny's suggested recipe for snails as a food for invalids (*NH* 30.44): 'Simmer, whole, in water, then, without flavouring, roast on hot coals. Take with wine and fish sauce.' *Apicius* gives instructions for fattening snails on milk.

The edible snails of Europe (Greek *kokhlias*, Latin *cochlea*) belong mostly to genus *Helix*. Arnott lists the edible Greek species.

Alexis *F* 281 Kassel with Arnott *ad l.*; Theocritus 14.17 with Gow *ad l.*; Varro *RR* 3.14; Horace, *Satires* 2.4.58–9; Dioscorides *MM* 2.9; Petronius *S* 130; Pliny *NH* 8.139–40, 9.173–4, 30.44–6; Galen *AF* 6.669 (for translation see Dalby 1996 p. 62); Athenaeus *E* 63a–d; *Apicius* 4.5.1, 7.16.1–4.

Thompson 1947 pp. 129–31; Dalby 1996 p. 38.

- Varro lists the types of snails that were farmed in Italy: *albulae*, little white ones from the Reate district; very big ones from Illyricum; moderately large, from Africa; and the extremely large *solitannae*, also from Africa. Thompson discusses the identification of these types, suggesting *Helix lucorum* for the Illyrian species and *H. carsoliana* for that of Reate.

Snow, used in ancient gastronomy as a cooling agent, as a mixer for wine, and as a garnish. In the circumstances of a Mediterranean summer, if one wanted to lower the temperature of food or drink to near freezing point, there was no other method than the use of snow: this could be gathered in high mountain regions until late spring and was transported to cities (where lived the gastronomes who could pay for this). Alexander the Great's use of deep pits to conserve snow is reported by Chares: it was therefore perhaps new to Greeks at that time, and might have been introduced under the Persian or some earlier empire. This remained the usual method (Greek *or-*

ygma psykheion, Latin *cisterna frigidaria* 'freezing pit') until the spread of mechanical refrigeration in the twentieth century.

Snow was used directly as an additive to wine; it was also placed above a wine cup, either in a filter bag (Latin *saccus nivarius*) from which it gradually melted into the cup, or in a colander (Latin *colum nivarium*) through which the wine could be poured. The safety of these methods depended on the cleanness of the snow, which there was no way of assuring; hence the importance of Nero's method for producing *decocta*, ice-cold WATER, as a mixer for wine.

Pliny describes the use of snow as a garnish when serving food; *Apicius* calls for this in the recipe for *sala cattabia Apiciana*.

Xenophon, *Memorabilia* 2.1.30; Martial 5.64, 14.103–4; Pliny the Younger, *Letters* 1.15; Plutarch *QC* 6.6; Dio Cassius 63.28.5; Athenaeus *D* 123f–124d citing Chares; *Apicius* 4.1.2.

Russel M. Geer, 'On the use of ice and snow for cooling drinks' in *Classical Weekly* vol. 29 no. 8 (16 December 1935) pp. 61–2; Dalby 2000a p. 248.

Socrates *see* PLATO

Soda *see* NITRON

Sorb, domesticated tree fruit of southeastern Europe. The sorb is a slow-growing tree. Its fruit ripens late in the season and is never very good to eat fresh. In these various ways the sorb resembles the olive; in addition it fruits only after many years' growth. In the classical Mediterranean sorbs were an important winter fruit: they were halved and sun-dried or else conserved in *sapa*, light grape syrup. They were also, so Palladius had heard, made into a kind of cider (which is called *cormé* in modern French).

The sorb or service-apple (*Sorbus domestica*) is Greek *oon*, *ouon*, Latin *sorbum*. Latin *sorbum torminale* is the fruit of a related species, probably the che-

quers-tree (*S. torminalis*); Pliny is aware of two other kinds, presumably the whitebeam (*S. Aria*) and the rowan (*S. aucuparia*).

Plato, *Symposium* 190d; Hippocrates *R* 55; Theophrastus *HP* 3.2.1, *CP* 3.1.4; Cato *DA* 7.4, 143.3; Varro *RR* 1.68.1; Celsus, *Medicine* 2.24.2; Dioscorides *MM* 1.120; Columella *DA* 8.17.13; Pliny *NH* 15.85, 16.74, 17.221; *Priapeia* 51.10; Dio of Prusa, *Orations* 7.75; Galen *SF* 12.87; Palladius *OA* 2.15.1–5.

Sorghum or durra (*Sorghum bicolor*), a cereal crop of arid climates. Sorghum was domesticated in the savanna region south of the Sahara, perhaps as early as 6000 BC. Sorghum was grown in Oman (southern Arabia) by *c.*2500 BC and in western India soon after 2000 BC. Unfamiliar in Pharaonic Egypt, sorghum was known as a southern exotic to some in the classical Mediterranean. Theophrastus, relying on a report from India, describes it as a 'kind of wild barley'. Pliny characterises sorghum as 'a millet' and reports its experimental introduction to Italy.

Theophrastus *HP* 4.4.9; Pliny *NH* 18.55.

Peter Rowley-Conwy, 'Sorghum from Qasr Ibrim, Egyptian Nubia, *c.*800 BC–AD 1811: a preliminary study' in *New Light on Early Farming: recent developments in palaeoethnobotany* ed. Jane M. Renfrew (Edinburgh: Edinburgh University Press, 1991) p. 191 ff.; Zohary and Hopf 1993 p. 84; Brewer and others 1995 p. 31; Randi Haaland, 'The puzzle of the late emergence of domesticated sorghum in the Nile valley' in *The Prehistory of Food: appetites for change* ed. Chris Gosden and Jon Hather (London: Routledge, 1999) pp. 397–418; J.M.J. de Wet, 'Sorghum' in *CWHF* 2000 vol. 1 pp. 152–8.

Sorrel, salad vegetable and medicinal plant. Sorrel is a laxative, as we are told by many authors both Greek and Latin, both medical and non-medical. As such it was appropriately one of the ingredients in the Egyptian purge KYPHI.

Sorrel (*Rumex* spp.) is Greek *lapathon*, Latin *lapathum*. At least one species was regularly cultivated, but leaves gathered from the wild were also used.

Epicharmus 161 Kaibel; Hippocrates *R* 54, *On*

Affections 55; Theophrastus *HP* 7.6.1, *CP* 3.1.4; Horace, *Epodes* 2.57, *Satires* 2.4.29; Dioscorides *MM* 2.114–15; Columella *DA* 10.373; Pliny *NH* 19.98, 19.184, 20.231–5; Plutarch, *On Isis and Osiris* 383e–384b; Galen *AF* 6.634, *SF* 12.56.

- The larger-leaved species known as dock (*R. Patientia*) was used medicinally but not usually in food: it is called *hippolapathon* in Greek, *rumex* in Latin.

  Moretum 72.

Soup in general, meaning a liquid food preparation, is Greek *rophema* or *ryphema*, Latin *sorbitio*. The term is regularly distinguished from *potos* 'drink' and has its own proper verbs, Greek *rophein*, *ryphanein*, Latin *sorbere* 'sup' (Hippocrates *RA* 12, *Epidemics* 7.2, *al.*).

This category included liquid foods for invalids, such as beaten EGG, barley and emmer gruel (see under BARLEY) and the water from boiling pulses, vegetables or other foods (Greek *khylos*, Latin *tisana*); it included soups or purées made from vegetables or fruits (Greek *hepsema*, Latin *pulmentarium*, *pulmentum*: *II Kings* 4.39; Plato, *Republic* 372c; Pliny *NH* 15.58); it included broth made with meal of legumes or cereals with added animal fat (Greek *lekithos*) and it included soup in the usual modern English sense, based on meat and vegetables (Greek *zomos*): these last were not common items in Roman cuisine, but Latin *ius* and *puls* served as equivalents (Ausonius, *Epigrams* 86–8; Apicius 5.1.1–4). A recipe for *zomos* is given in the *Heidelberg Papyrus*; see the modern version by Grant 1999 pp. 131–2. Medicinal spices and herbs might be added to these various soups, especially if they were intended for invalids as part of a prescribed diet.

Buck 1949 pp. 368–9.

Sow-thistle, potherb of Mediterranean lands. Sow-thistle was served by Hecale to Theseus in Callimachus's poetic narrative (see HOSPITALITY), an indication of its status as a rustic standby.

Sow-thistle (*Sonchus arvensis* and *S. oleraceus*) is Greek *sonkos*, Latin *soncos*.

Theophrastus *HP* 6.4.3; Nicander *F* 71 Schneider; Dioscorides *MM* 2.131; Pliny *NH* 22.88–90 citing Callimachus fragment 250 Pfeiffer; Athenaeus *D* 250e citing Hegesander, also *E* 64c quoting Matron *AD*; Oribasius *CM* 15.1.18.47.

Laufer 1919 pp. 400–2.

Spain, region of western Europe which was gradually incorporated into the Roman Empire between the third and first centuries BC. Southern and eastern Spain had previously been under Carthaginian influence, a legacy of early Phoenician links with the kingdom of Tartessus via the ancient seaport of Gades (Cadiz).

The native fertility of Lusitania (modern Portugal) before the Roman conquest was engagingly described by Polybius in a passage quoted by Athenaeus. In this text the *medimnos* is a dry measure of 52 litres, the amphora (see AMPHORAE) a liquid measure of 26 litres.

Because of the temperate quality of the air, animals and human beings alike are very prolific, and the fruits of the country never fail. The roses in that country, the stocks, the asparagus, and similar plants are dormant only for three months or less, while sea-food, in point of abundance, excellence, and beauty, far exceeds that found in Our Sea [the Mediterranean]. Sicilian barley fetches only a drachma the *medimnos*, and wheat nine Alexandrian obols. Wine costs a drachma the *amphora*; a kid of moderate size, one obol; so also a hare. The price of lambs is three or four obols; a fattened pig weighing a hundred pounds is five drachmae, a sheep two; sixty pounds of figs may be bought for three obols, a calf for five drachmae, a yoke ox for ten. They would not price the meat of wild animals at all: they make it a good-will gift, expecting the like in return.

In classical times Gades was well

known for its production of salted tunny, a business at first operated (according to Aristotle) 'by the Phoenicians' for export to Carthage (see under TUNNY). Other salt fish products of southern Spain included John Dories, conger eels and moray eels (all from Gades) and the Saxitan or Hexitan salteries for tunny and mackerel (near Malaga) described by Strabo.

Large quantities of wine were produced in Spain. For fine wines noticed in literature see SPANISH WINES. Roman Spain was also noted for its production of olive oil and of GARUM or fish sauce. Several Roman authors frequently cited in this book were of Spanish origin, notably Martial and the farming author COLUMELLA, whose uncle had been a farmer and an innovative stock-breeder in southern Spain.

Aristotle, *On Marvellous Things Heard* 844a24–34; Strabo 3.2.7; Columella *DA* 8.16.9; Pliny *NH* 9.68; Athenaeus *D* 116a–d quoting Euthydemus of Athens, also 118d–e, also 330f quoting Polybius 34.8.4 Büttner-Wobst; Ausonius, *Epistles* 9.32, cf. Pliny *NH* 32.60.

J.J. van Nostrand in Frank 1933–40 vol. 3 pp. 119–224; J.C. Edmondson, *Two Industries in Roman Lusitania: mining and garum production* (Oxford: BAR, 1987) (*BAR International Series*, 362), review by K. Greene in *Classical Review* vol. 42 (1992) pp. 407–9; A. González Blanco, 'Pressoirs à huile d'époque romaine dans la péninsule ibérique' in *La Production du vin et de l'huile en Méditerranée* ed. M.-C. Amouretti and J.-P. Brun (Athens: Ecole Française d'Athènes, 1993) pp. 397–412; Maria Salete da Ponte and others, 'La production de l'huile et du vin au Portugal durant l'antiquité' *ib.* pp. 413–22; J.S. Richardson, *The Romans in Spain* (Oxford: Blackwell, 1996).

Spanish wines, prolific and widespread production as is clear both from literature and from archaeological finds. Spanish vineyards were presumably first developed under Phoenician influence. Four names of fine wines are mentioned in literary sources (see below).

Carlos Gómez Bellard and others, 'Témoignage d'une production de vin dans l'Espagne préromaine' in *La Production du vin et de l'huile*

en Méditerranée ed. M.-C. Amouretti and J.-P. Brun (Athens: Ecole Française d'Athènes, 1993) pp. 379–96; Maria Salete da Ponte and others, 'La production de l'huile et du vin au Portugal durant l'antiquité' in *La Production du vin et de l'huile en Méditerranée* ed. M.-C. Amouretti and J.-P. Brun (Athens: Ecole Française d'Athènes, 1993) pp. 413–22; *El vino en la antigüedad romana (Jerez, 2–4 de Octubre, 1996)* ed. Sebastián Celestino Pérez (Madrid: Dipto. de Prehistoria y Arqueología, Facultad de Filosofía y Letras, Universidad Autonoma de Madrid, 1999).

- Laeetan wine (Latin *Laeetanum, Laletanum*) was exported in quantity to Rome in the first century AD.

  Pliny *NH* 14.71; Martial 1.26, 7.53.

- Lauran wine (Latin *Lauronense*), like Tarraconensian, was comparable with the best Italian vintages according to Pliny.

  Pliny *NH* 14.71, cf. *CIL* 4.5558, 15.4577–9.

- Saguntine wine (Latin *Saguntinum*) was a second-rate wine imported to Rome from the Spanish Mediterranean coast.

  Juvenal 5.29; Fronto, *Letters* vol. 2 p. 50 Haines; *CIL* 15.2632.

- Tarraconensian wine (Latin *Tarraconense*) from the neighbourhood of Tarraco in northeastern Spain, was in competition with the best Italian vintages according to Pliny. It reached a somewhat lower rank (comparable with Etruscan wine) according to Martial.

  Pliny *NH* 14.71; Silius Italicus 3.369, 15.177; Martial 13.118.

Sparta, city in southern Greece. To classical Greeks Sparta seemed unique for its communal lifestyle and its abjuring of luxury. The city's discipline and the bravery of its men and women were legendary, as was the pitiless subjection of its serf class, the Helots. There was regular communal dining, regulated to ensure equality: see especially Xenophon and Athenaeus (*D* 138b–143a).

In archaic times Sparta had been very different, a place of music, dancing and cheerful festivity, the latter hinted at in several fragments of the Spartan poet Alcman. Some descriptions even of later Sparta fit with difficulty into the usual stereotype. Seasonal festivals persisted, and some of the kings of Sparta set an example of luxury living rather than of Spartan simplicity.

After the wines enjoyed by Alcman (92 Davies), no local food specialities are noted in later Sparta. The cook MITHAECUS was said in later legend to have been expelled from here as a threat to the moral order.

Alcman 17, 19, 56, 92, 96, 98 Davies; Xenophon, *Spartan Constitution*; Theopompus 115 F 22 Jacoby [Athenaeus *D* 657b–c]; Plutarch *EC* 995b–c; Athenaeus *D* 91c–d, 138b–143a, 432d–433b, 535e–536e, 550c–e.

A.J. Holladay, 'Spartan austerity' in *Classical Quarterly* vol. 27 (1977) pp. 111–26; E. David, 'The Spartan syssitia in Plato's *Laws*' in *American Journal of Philology* vol. 99 (1978) pp. 486–95; S. Hodkinson, 'Social order and the conflict of values in classical Sparta' in *Chiron* vol. 13 (1983) pp. 239–81; T.J. Figueira, 'Mess contributions and subsistence at Sparta' in *Transactions of the American Philological Association* vol. 114 (1984) pp. 87–109; N.R.E. Fisher, 'Drink, hybris and the promotion of harmony' in *Classical Sparta: techniques behind her success* ed. A. Powell (London, 1989) pp. 26–50; Louise Bruit, 'The meal at the Hyakinthia: ritual consumption and offering' in *Sympotica: a symposium on the symposion* ed. Oswyn Murray (Oxford: Oxford University Press, 1990) pp. 162–74; Tyler Jo Smith, 'Dances, drinks and dedications: the archaic komos in Laconia' in *Sparta in Laconia: the archaeology of a city and its countryside* ed. W.G. Cavanagh and S.E.C. Walker (London, 1998) pp. 75–81; Andrew Dalby, 'The vineyards of Laconia' in *Classica* (Sao Paulo) vol. 11/12 (1998–9) pp. 281–8.

Spelt, subspecies of wheat typical of central and eastern Europe. Spelt was never economically important in the classical Mediterranean but was familiar in the northern provinces of the Roman Empire.

Spelt (*Triticum aestivum* subsp. *Spelta*) is Greek *skandoula*, *pistikion*, Latin *scandala*, *spelta*. In English translations of classical texts 'spelt' often stands for EMMER.

Pliny *NH* 18.62; *Diocletian's Price Edict* 1.7–8.

Speusippus, Greek philosopher, nephew of Plato. His work *Similars*, perhaps an attempt to classify the natural world, is often cited by Athenaeus in discussing the names of fish. Speusippus was also the author of a *Symposium*, of which no identified fragments survive, and of a *Funeral Feast for Plato*, cited once by Diogenes Laertius.

Diogenes Laertius 3.2, 4.1–5; Plutarch *QC* 1.preface.

Leonardo Tarán, *Speusippus of Athens: a critical study with a collection of the related texts and commentary* (Leiden: Brill, 1981).

Spices, defined in modern usage as exotic aromatics used in food. There is no precisely equivalent word in classical Greek or Latin. The term is often extended to AROMATICS that had medicinal, cosmetic, festive and religious uses: the 'spice trade' (see TRADE) dealt, and still deals, in all these without discrimination. Most such aromatics are of vegetable origin, consisting of dried saps and resins, barks, seeds and dried fruits.

Few spices were used in classical Greek cuisine (but see MASTIC; POPPY; SAFFRON; SILPHIUM; SUMACH). Theophrastus considered that most such aromas would ruin food, though they might be acceptable in wine. Greek cooks, however, made much use of freshly grown local aromatics, including ANISE, CORIANDER and CUMIN, often now classed as spices.

Spices became an important element in Roman cuisine, to judge by available sources, including the recipes in *Apicius*. Why? Their aroma, with accompanying non-food aromas such as perfumes, incenses and wreaths, promoted festivity and sensuality. Their use demonstrated wealth and generosity, since exotic aromatics were extremely expensive. To those who could afford them they had become a crucial element in nutrition, being sufficiently powerful in terms of humoral theory to permit radical adjustments to the diet (see also FLAVOUR): for this purpose they were used in cooked dishes, in spiced wines such as CONDI-TUM, and in DIGESTIVES. An additional use of spices, in conserving food, is seldom mentioned in ancient sources (but RESINATED WINE is an example of this use); recipes for spiced conserves become more widespread in medieval Europe. Major food spices under the Roman Empire were PEPPER, GINGER, ASAFOETIDA and again anise, coriander and cumin. COSTUS, MYRRH and spikenard (see NARD), now very little used in food, were ingredients in spiced wines. Some now-familiar spices, including CARDAMOM, CINNAMON, CLOVES and SUGAR, were less used in food than might be expected, perhaps largely because of their cost.

Theophrastus, *On Odours* 10; *Periplus Maris Erythraei* 6, 49, 56 and *passim*; Pliny *NH* book 12; Galen *SF passim*; *Apicius passim*.

Miller 1969; M. Loewe, 'Spices and silks: aspects of world trade in the first seven centuries of the Christian era' in *Journal of the Royal Asiatic Society* (1971) pp. 166–79; Dalby 2000b.

- It is sometimes asserted that spices are or were used to mask the taste of rotting food. This supposed use has not so far been demonstrated in any culture. As regards Greece and Rome the idea is demonstrably false, and no ancient source supports it.

  Gillian Riley, ' "Tainted meat" ' in *Spicing up the Palate: proceedings of the Oxford Symposium on Food and Cookery 1992* (Totnes: Prospect Books, 1993) pp. 1–6.

Spikenard *see* NARD

Splankhna, the 'vital organs' in the terms of Greek sacrifice. These organs were roasted, tasted by participants in the sacrifice and shared with the god. Those usually eaten were LIVER and HEART. Lungs and spleen (and, according to some classifications, kidneys) are also included. An approximate Latin equivalent is *exta*, denoting the organs which in Roman sacrifice were used in making predictions.

Homer, *Odyssey* 3.9, 3.461, *al.*; Aristophanes, *Birds* 518–19, *Peace* 1040–111; Philoxenus *D* b.27 Page; Cato *DA* 134; Galen *AF* 6.679–80.

Spoletine wine (Latin *Spoletinum*; Greek *Spoletinos*), mentioned in the first century AD, was pleasant to the taste and of a golden colour.

Martial 6.89, 13.120, 14.116; Athenaeus *E* 27b.

Spoon (Greek *mystron*; Latin *ligula, lingula*), a utensil mentioned occasionally at ancient meals, sometimes without undertone (Cato *DA* 84), sometimes in contexts of lavish display (Hippolochus *D* [Athenaeus *D* 129c]), and also known in kitchen use (Columella *DA* 9.5). Perhaps more commonly the Greek word denotes a hollow piece of bread in the shape of a spoon; this was served with stews and soups. Alternative terms for such bread spoons in Greek were *mystile* and the Latin loanword *ligla* (Pollux *O* 6.87 citing King Alexander; Athenaeus *D* 126a–f citing Nicander *F* 68 Schneider).

Sportula (Greek *spyris*), a gift (literally a 'basket') from patron or benefactor. The *sportula*, which might consist of food but more usually of money, may be regarded as an impersonal alternative or substitute to the provision of a meal (see also CHARITY; COMMENSALITY).

Squid, marine cephalopod, good to eat whatever its size. Little ones could be fried, and could be part of a mixed fry-up or *hepsetos*, as Dorion says. Philoxenus writes with enthusiasm of a dish of *epipastai teuthides*, squid with something – perhaps breadcrumbs – sprinkled over. A character in a play by Sotades talks of *teuthis onthyleumene*, a stuffed squid, and a cook in Alexis explains in more detail: 'As for the squids, I cut up their fins, mixed in a little fat, sprinkled a few fresh herbs and stuffed them.' They were to be found at Dium, the Macedonian ceremonial centre, and also at Ambracia in northwestern Greece, according to Archestratus; but indeed they are widespread in the Mediterranean.

The general Greek term for squid is

teuthis; the Latin equivalent is *loligo, lolligo*.

Philoxenus *D* b.16 Page; Aristotle *HA* 524a20–32 with Thompson *ad l.*; Sotades Comicus 1 Kassel; Plautus, *Casina* 493 (*lolliguncula*); Athenaeus *D* 326b–e quoting Archestratus *H* 54 Brandt and Alexis *F* 84 Kassel, also 300f citing Dorion; *Apicius* 9.3.

Thompson 1947 p. 260; Davidson 1981 pp. 211–12.

- When used specifically, Greek *teuthis* is the name for the small *Loligo vulgaris* and related species.
- Greek *teuthos* is the name for full-grown specimens of the much larger species *Todarodes sagittatus* and its relatives. This is the squid that can fly, though it does not fly far.

Squill, a large bulb whose pungent juice was used to treat coughs and was widely credited in antiquity with averting poisons and supernatural dangers. Squill was used in scapegoat rituals and was planted and hung at entrances to houses (see Theophrastus and Pliny). In the form of squill-flavoured wine and vinegar it was a regular constituent of many prescribed diets. The recipes given by Palladius may be compared with the instructions of the *Geoponica*, which include a recipe for squill vinegar attributed to Pythagoras.

Squill (*Urginea maritima*) is Greek *skilla*, Latin *scilla*.

Theophrastus *HP* 7.12–13, *Characters* 16.13; Dioscorides *MM* 2.171; Pliny *NH* 19.93–4 citing Pythagoras, also 20.97–101, 23.59; Galen *VA* 112; Pseudo-Apuleius, *Herbarius* 42; *Geoponica* 2.47, 8.42; Tzetzes, *Chiliades* 5.726–61, citing Hipponax 6 West.

Jerry Stannard, 'Squill in ancient and medieval materia medica, with special reference to its employment for dropsy' in *Bulletin of the New York Academy of Medicine* vol. 50 (1974) pp. 684–713; John Scarborough, 'The pharmacology of sacred plants, herbs and roots' in *Magika Hiera: ancient Greek magic and religion* (New York: Oxford University Press, 1991) pp. 146–8.

- A related plant, *Scilla bifolia* (Latin *hyacinthus*), was said to delay the signs of puberty in boys and was used by slave dealers to produce this effect.

Pliny *NH* 21.170.

- Also related, the star of Bethlehem (*Ornithogalum umbellatum*) is the edible root known in Greek as *ornithos gala*, literally 'bird's milk', or *ornithogalon*.

Nicander *F* 71 Schneider with Gow *ad l.*; Dioscorides *MM* 2.44; Pliny *NH* 21.102.

Lambraki 1997 pp. 154–6.

Staple foods of the classical world were GRAIN and LEGUMES. Greek *sitos*, a term whose range of meanings comes closest to English 'staple food', normally implies wheat or barley: for this term, and its nearest Latin equivalents, see MEALS.

Statan wine (Greek *Statanos*), named alongside Falernian and Calene by Strabo, named again in his list of fine wines from along the Latin and Campanian coast. It is also named in the *Epitome of Athenaeus*: 'one of the prime wines, resembling Falernian, but lighter and not so intoxicating'. The wine had fallen in esteem by Pliny's time.

Strabo 5.3.6, 5.4.3; Pliny *NH* 14.65, 23.36; Athenaeus *E* 26e.

Tchernia 1986 p. 160.

Stibas *see* OPEN-AIR DINING; TRICLINIUM

Storage. Ever since the development of farming, food storage has been crucial to survival; somehow, each harvest has to last till the next. The same was surely true with the catch of tunny and the trapping of wild goats which contributed to the diet of Mediterranean peoples before farming began.

Ancient houses were intended partly as food stores. What was stored? In a big Homeric house it was wine and olive oil, according to the *Odyssey*. But in houses of the prehistoric Mediterranean grain, pulses and other seeds were stored, while from classical Athens Xenophon's dialogue on household management emphasises the importance of making the supply of food stretch through the year. This implies, once more, the correct preparation and bulk storage of grain and pulses. Writing under the early Roman Empire, Columella provides a large collection of recipes for the domestic conserving and storage of many other foods. Ancient governments also found it necessary to store food, from the grain warehouses of Egypt (of which, according to *Genesis*, Joseph was put in charge) to the PEPPER warehouses of classical Rome.

'Why is it that in wine the middle part is best, in olive oil the top, and in honey the bottom?' asks a speaker in Plutarch's dialogue. These questions arise from accurate observation of foods stored in AMPHORAE; the answers demand lateral thinking.

Homer, *Odyssey* 2.337–48; Hesiod *OD* 368; *Genesis* 39–47; Xenophon, *Oeconomicus* 7–9; Columella *DA* book 12; Plutarch *QC* 7.3; Macrobius *S* 7.12.

G.E. Rickman, *Roman Granaries and Store Buildings* (Cambridge, 1971); P.B. Adamson, 'Problems over storing food in the ancient Near East' in *Die Welt des Orients* vol. 16 (1985) pp. 5–15; G. Jones and others, 'Crop storage at Assiros' in *Scientific American* vol. 254 no. 3 (1986) pp. 96–103; O. Soffer, 'Storage, sedentism and the European palaeolithic record' in *Antiquity* vol. 63 (1989) pp. 719–32; M.E. Kislev, 'Archaeobotany and storage archaeoentomology' in *New Light on Early Farming: recent developments in palaeoethnobotany* ed. Jane M. Renfrew (Edinburgh: Edinburgh University Press, 1991) pp. 121–36; Hamish Forbes and Lin Foxhall, 'Ethnoarchaeology and storage in the ancient Mediterranean: beyond risk and survival' in *Food in Antiquity* ed. John Wilkins and others (Exeter: Exeter University Press, 1995) pp. 69–86; Kostas S. Christakis, 'Pithoi and food storage in neopalatial Crete: a domestic perspective' in *World Archaeology* vol. 31 (1999) pp. 1–20.

Stork, large migratory marsh bird. The meat of the stork was briefly and undeservedly fashionable in early imperial Rome.

The stork (*Ciconia Ciconia*) is Greek *pelargos*, Latin *ciconia*.

Horace, *Satires* 2.2.49–50; Petronius *S* 55 quoting Publilius Syrus; Pliny *NH* 10.60.

Thompson 1936 p. 221; Toynbee 1996.

Strawberry, woodland fruit. Strawberries were gathered from the wild in prehistoric Italy (before 6000 BC at Grotta dell'Uzzo, Sicily) and in classical Italy. The tiny fruits are described as resembling the fruit of the arbutus. They are now called 'wild strawberry' or 'Alpine strawberry' to distinguish them from the large hybrid strawberry of modern cultivation.

The strawberry (*Fragaria vesca*) is Latin *fragum*.

Vergil *E* 3.92; Pliny *NH* 15.98; Pseudo-Apuleius, *Herbarius* 37.

Zohary and Hopf 1993 p. 200.

Structuralism *see* ANTHROPOLOGY

Sturgeon, large and relatively rare fish of Europe and northern Asia. The sturgeon has an impressive, armoured appearance. Several species provide good meat. Sturgeons are now also the source of caviar, but there is no evidence that this delicacy was known to Greeks or Romans. The five Greek and Latin names can be linked with the three best-known species of the Mediterranean, the Black Sea and the Caspian, to which, no doubt, others such as *Acipenser Gueldenstaedtii* and *A. ruthenus* were assimilated.

Thompson 1947 pp. 7, 16, 19, 62, 184; E.D. Carney in *Phoenix* vol. 21 (1967) pp. 202–20; D.J. Georgacas, *Ichthyological Terms for the Sturgeon and Etymology of the International Terms Botargo, Caviar and Congeners* (Athens, 1978); Davidson 1981 pp. 37–40.

- Latin *acipenser* (*akkipensios* as a loanword in Greek) is the Mediterranean sturgeon (*Acipenser Sturio*). Pliny, bored by sturgeons, says merely that it had lost all its former popularity in his time. Macrobius provides good evidence of the value formerly placed on this rarely taken fish, quoting Plautus's lost play *Baccaria*, Cicero's *On Fate*, Pliny himself, and finally the dietary writer Sammonicus Serenus, who shows that by about AD 200 the sturgeon was in gastronomic favour once more. As Aelian describes the rejoicing in Pamphylia when an *elops* is caught (see below), so Athenaeus describes the flutes and wreaths that celebrated the arrival of an *acipenser* at a Roman banquet.

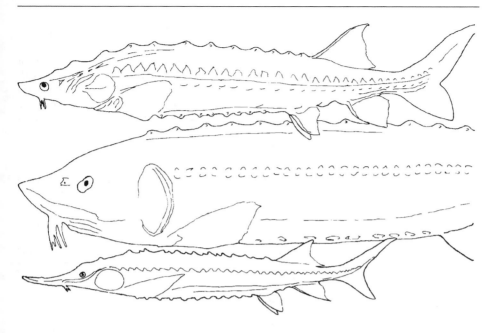

Figure 14 Sturgeons. Top: Atlantic or Mediterranean sturgeon (*Acipenser Sturio*), Greek *elops*, Latin *acipenser*. Middle: Beluga sturgeon (*Huso Huso*), Greek *oxyrynkhos*, Latin *attilus*. Bottom: stellate sturgeon (*Acipenser stellatus*), Greek *antakaios*.

Cicero, *Tusculan Disputations* 3.43, *De Finibus* 2.24–25 quoting Lucilius 1240 Marx, also 2.91; Horace, *Satires* 2.2.47; Ovid, *Halieutica* 134; Pliny *NH* 9.60; Athenaeus *D* 294e–f; Macrobius *S* 3.16.1–8 quoting Cicero, *On Fate* fragment 5 Müller.

- Greek *antakaios* is the sturgeon of the Dnieper, the Danube, and other rivers that flow into the Black Sea (*Acipenser stellatus* and other species). 'Nursling of the mighty Danube', 'delight of the Bosporus', 'joy of the Scythians', its belly flesh came to classical Greece in squares, salted, as *tarikhos antakaion*, and was served hot.

  Herodotus 4.53; Lynceus *F* 1 [Athenaeus *D* 132a]; Aelian, *Nature of Animals* 14.23, 14.26; Athenaeus *D* 116a–d quoting Euthydemus of Athens, also 118d–119a quoting Sopater 12 Kaibel and others, also 284e quoting Archestratus *H* 39 Brandt.

- Latin *attilus* is the beluga (*Huso Huso*) as found in the River Po and the Adriatic. It can grow up to six metres according to Alan Davidson (above), and up to a thousand pounds weight according to Pliny, at which size, though it can be caught with a hook, it needs a team of oxen to pull it out of the water.

  Pliny *NH* 9.44.

- Greek *elops* (or *ellops*; as a Latin loanword *elops*, *helops*) is an obscure word, at first an epic formulaic adjective (of forgotten meaning) qualifying *ikhthys* 'fish'. In late archaic and classical Greek it serves as a name for a particular fish, but which fish? The one that was selected by Zeus for himself and Hera, said Epicharmus; it is worth its weight in bronze. According to Archestratus the *elops* will be best at Syracuse; in the Aegean, off the Asiatic coast, or off Crete, it will be tough and wave-beaten. According to Lynceus – followed faithfully by Varro – it is good at Rhodes; Aelian and Columella say that its capture is fêted in neighbouring Pamphylia. But while Lynceus knew Rhodes, Varro and the others probably did not, and no authors of Varro's date or later (except Xenocrates) appear to know what the *elops* really was. Ovid carefully describes it as 'costly *helops*, unknown in our seas', and is followed by Quintilian; yet Ennius, long before, had claimed to find it no further away than Surrentum. Apion and Pliny (doubtfully) identify it with Latin *acipenser*; modern scholars, too, have been doubtful. There may be texts which demand a different interpretation, but in general *elops* is certainly the Mediterranean sturgeon (*Acipenser Sturio*).

Archestratus *H* 11 Brandt; Aristotle *HA* 505a15, 506b15; Matron *AD* 69; Ennius *H* 6; Varro *RR* 2.6.2; Ovid, *Halieutica* 96; Quintilian, *Education* 5.10.21; Columella *DA* 8.16.9; Xenocrates *T* 26; Pliny *NH* 9.60, cf. 32.153; Aelian, *Nature of Animals* 8.28; Athenaeus *D* 277c–e, also 282c–e quoting Epicharmus 71 Kaibel, also 285e quoting Lynceus *F* 8, also 294f quoting Apion, also 308b–c.

- Greek *oxyrynkhos* is the beluga (*Huso Huso*) as found in the Black Sea and the Caspian, a rare intruder into classical texts. Verses quoted by Euthydemus, probably of the fourth century BC, show that the Black Sea fish was known to Greeks 'either whole or sliced, adorned with rough salt'. Aelian describes how the *oxyrynkhos* of the Caspian was salted and dried and sent by camel caravan to the Iranian metropolis of Ecbatana. For another fish also called *oxyrynkhos* see NILE FISH.

Aelian, *Nature of Animals* 17.32; Athenaeus *D* 116a–d quoting Euthydemus of Athens.

Suckling animals, a luxury food because economically the best return for effort is gained by slaughtering animals when they have reached their full size. Suckling animals are costly in terms of effort; in a monetary economy they are likely to be costly in money terms also. The cost gives them their attraction: in general their meat, though tender, is less flavoursome than that of fully grown animals.

Those in the ancient world who aspired to luxury aspired to feast on them. Already, in the Persian Empire before Alexander's conquest, lambs and goose chicks were supplied in large quantity to the King's Dinner (see PERSIANS). In descriptions of Greek banquets, such as that by Philoxenus, milk-fed kids form a fitting centrepiece. In Italy in the mid second century BC shepherds brought their flocks close to Rome in early spring so that spring lambs (and sucking-pigs fed on

sheep's milk) would be available to city markets.

The lost treatise of Aristophanes of Byzantium *Peri Helikion* 'On Ages' dealt with the stages of life of animals and their technical names, a matter of importance to farmers whether or not the animals were about to be slaughtered.

Philoxenus *D* b.29; Cato *DA* 150 with Dalby *ad l.*; Polyaenus 4.3.32; Athenaeus *D* 396b–f.

Joan M. Frayn, *Sheep-rearing and the Wool Trade in Italy during the Roman Period* (Liverpool: Cairns, 1984) p. 3; Stella Georgoudi, 'Galathena: sacrifice et consommation de jeunes animaux en Grèce ancienne' in *L'Animal dans l'alimentation humaine: les critères de choix: actes du colloque international de Liège 26–29 nov. 1986* ed. Liliane Bodson (Liège, 1988) pp. 75–82.

Sugar, crystallised sap of the sugar cane. This plant appears to be a hybrid, first grown in New Guinea several thousand years ago. By the first millennium BC it was familiar in southern China, southeast Asia and India. It was in India that Europeans first heard of it, during or soon after the expedition of ALEXANDER THE GREAT; Eratosthenes wrote of sugar as the product of reeds that were 'sweet by nature and from the sun's heat'.

The invention of granulated sugar had taken place, in north India, some time before Dioscorides, who is the first datable author to mention this product, wrote of 'a sort of crystallised honey, found in India and Arabia ... not unlike salt in its texture, and it can be crunched between the teeth like salt'. Dioscorides is also the first to give a Greek name for sugar. In the classical Mediterranean this costly spice, 'good to drink dissolved in water', was hardly used except in medicine. It was said to be laxative, beneficial in bladder disorders and good for the kidneys.

Cane sugar (*Saccharum officinarum*) is Greek *sakkhar* (variously spelt). The word is borrowed from Pali or Prakrit *sakkhara*.

Strabo 15.1.20 citing Eratosthenes; Dioscorides *E* 2.112, *MM* 2.82 (*sakkharon*); *Periplus Maris*

Erythraei 14 (*sakkhari*); Lucan 3.237; Seneca, *Letters* 84.4; Pliny *NH* 12.32 (*saccoron?*); Galen *SF* 12.71 (*sakkhar*); Oribasius *CM* 15.1.12.15; Alexander of Aphrodisias, *Problems* 3.2.

Yule and Burnell 1903 pp. 862–4; Laufer 1919 pp. 376–7; Buck 1949 pp. 384–5; Casson 1989 p. 133; K.T. Achaya, *Indian Food: a historical companion* (Delhi: Oxford University Press, 1994) pp. 112–14, 215–17; Dalby 2000b pp. 26–9.

Sumach, one of the first exotic spices to find a use in Greek cuisine. Sumach is the ground fruit of a tree native to the Near East. The fruit grows in tight clusters and is only good to eat in this dried form. It was exported to Greece (and in due course to Roman Italy) from Syria. Sumach is still familiar as a condiment in Middle Eastern cuisine; it gives a red colour and a sour, fruity aroma. 'It has astringent and cooling properties,' says Pliny; 'it is sprinkled on food instead of salt if the bowels are loose; alongside silphium, it improves the flavour of all meats ... it checks excessive menstruation.' Anthimus recommends it to season lentils.

Sumach (*Rhus coriaria*) is Greek *rous*, Latin *rhus*. The same species provided a juice that was used in tanning leather, as observed by Dioscorides and Pliny. Other trees of the genus are now familiar as rhus in Britain, as poison ivy in North America.

Solon 41 West; Hippocrates, *Nature of Woman* 32, 34; Antiphanes 140 Kassel; Alexis *F* 132 Kassel; Theophrastus *HP* 3.18.1, 3.18.5; Scribonius Largus 111, 113; Dioscorides *MM* 1.108; Pliny *NH* 13.55, 24.91–3; Galen *SF* 12.353, *On Compounding* 12.922, *On Substitutes* 19.741; Anthimus OC 67.

Dalby 1996 pp. 86, 238.

Sumptuary law *see* LUXURY

Surmullet *see* RED MULLET

Surprise dishes, those which contain an unexpected ingredient or do not contain the expected one. These parallel ideas had a long vogue in classical gastronomy, for the poet Philoxenus must have had them in mind when he said, as quoted by Plutarch, 'The best meats are those that are not meats; the best fish are those that are not fish.' The *Apicius* cookery book evokes the same culinary philosophy, seven hundred years later, with the concluding words of one recipe, 'No one at table will know what he is eating.'

Typical examples of the first idea are the eggs that turn out, when dismantled by the eater, to contain something other than egg. Encolpius, hero of Petronius's *Satyricon*, encountered what he thought was an addled egg at Trimalchio's dinner. 'But then I heard a habitual guest say, "There'll be something good inside this!" So I broke the pastry shell, and found a fat little beccafico, with peppered yolk for sauce.' This was a traditional recipe known in Greek as THRYMMATIS (but making it in the shape of an egg may have been a new idea). Another possibility, described by Juvenal, was to substitute minced crayfish for the yolk of a hard-boiled egg, thus creating surprise both at the colour and at the flavour. Several other surprise dishes are described in the *Satyricon*, including fruits that unexpectedly squirt saffron: the inventive cook, significantly, is named Daedalus.

The classic surprise dish of the second kind – one that lacks the expected major ingredient – was whitebait without whitebait. The idea is first heard of when, in the third century BC, King Nicomedes I of Bithynia demanded APHYE, whitebait, when he was twelve days' journey from the sea and in the depths of winter. His cook, Soterides, cleverly served him an imitation based on turnip, salt and poppy seeds, without any fish. So the story was told in an Athenian comedy by Euphron, by a stage cook who claims to be pupil of Soterides. Many centuries later the Roman cookbook *Apicius* gives a recipe for *patina de apua sine apua* 'whitebait tart without whitebait'; also three recipes for *salsum sine salso* 'salt fish without salt fish'.

Petronius *S* 33, 60, 68, 70; Juvenal 5.84; Plutarch, *Listening to Poets* 14e citing Philoxenus *D* f.1 Page; Athenaeus *E* 7d–f quoting Euphron 10 Kassel; *Apicius* 4.2.12, 9.10.10–12; *Suda s.v. aphya es pyr.*

Surrentine wine (Latin *Surrentinum*; Greek *Syrentinos*), from the promontory south of the Bay of Naples such wine was rated fairly high in the first century AD after earlier obscurity: it had newly been recognised that Surrentine improved with age. Being not 'oily' but very 'grainy' it was best kept for twenty or even twenty-five years before drinking, and even then (adds the *Epitome of Athenaeus*) it was only suited to those who drank it regularly. Tiberius called it *generosum acetum* 'high-class vinegar', attributing its vogue to the physicians; *nobilis vappa* 'noble plonk', said Caligula. It was described in the second century as strong (the grapes were especially sweet), 'winy', thin, rather austere, white or amber in colour. It continued to be a first-class wine until Diocletian's time, when it was one of the seven named wines of the Empire allowed a special high price. The *aminnia gemina minor* grape variety was widely grown here.

Horace, *Satires* 2.4.55; Strabo 5.4.3; Ovid, *Metamorphoses* 15.710; Dioscorides *MM* 5.6.7–11; Scribonius Largus 115; Columella *DA* 3.2.10, 3.8.5; Persius 3.93; Pliny *NH* 14.39, 14.64, *al.*; Statius, *Silvae* 2.2.82, 3.5.102, 4.8.9; Martial 13.110; Juvenal 6.15; Galen *ST* 6.334–5, *On Therapeutic Method* 10.831–3, *SF* 11.604, *DA* 14.15; Athenaeus *E* 26d; *Diocletian's Price Edict* 2.6; Justinian, *Digest* 33.6.16 quoting Labeo.

Tchernia 1986 pp. 344–7; Dalby 2000a p. 56.

Swan, large, majestic water bird. The swan is scarcely ever mentioned as food in classical sources. Plutarch, however, asserts that some farmers kept swans to fatten for the table: the practice was to sew up their eyes because they would feed and fatten better 'in darkness'.

The swan (*Cygnus Olor* and *C. Cygnus*) is Greek *kyknos*, Latin *cygnus, olor*.

Anaxandrides 42 Kassel; Plutarch *EC* 997a [*s.v.l.*]; Athenaeus 393c–e.

Thompson 1936 p. 179; J. Witteveen, 'On swans, cranes and herons' in *Petits Propos culinaires* nos 24–6 (1986–7); Toynbee 1996.

Sweet reed, sweet rush, sweet cane, conventional translations of Greek *skhoinos euodes, kalamos euodes*, Latin *calamus* (*odoratus*), *calamus olens, iuncus odoratus*. These are the ancient terms for certain aromatic roots used in perfumery and occasionally in drinks and food. The plants concerned were perhaps *Cymbopogon citratus* lemon grass, *C. Nardus* citronella grass, *C. Schoenanthus* gingergrass, and related species.

Isaiah 43.24 [Vulgate version]; *Jeremiah* 6.20 [Vulgate version]; *Exodus* 30.23; Theophrastus *O* 25, 33, *al.*; Pliny *NH* 12.104–7, 21.120; Oribasius *CM* 5.33.11 (*skhoinanthos*).

I.H. Burkill, *A Dictionary of the Economic Products of the Malay Peninsula* (London: Crown Agents for the Colonies, 1935) pp. 724–8; Miller 1969 pp. 94–6; Nigel Groom, *The New Perfume Handbook* (London: Blackie Professional, 1995) p. 67.

Sweeteners in classical cuisine were HONEY, grape syrup (grape juice concentrated by boiling), date syrup, dried dates and dried figs. Cane SUGAR was a rarity, an import from India, sufficiently costly to be reserved for medicinal rather than culinary use.

Sweets *see* CAKES

Swine *see* PORK

Swordfish, large, sharp-snouted sea fish. They were good at Byzantium and at Cape Pelorus at the northeastern point of Sicily, according to Archestratus, who recommends his reader to choose a slice from the tail. Xenocrates would eat it with mustard. Oppian tells how swordfish of enormous size were caught by the

Gauls of Massilia (modern Marseille); Polybius describes the harpooning of swordfish off Cape Scyllaeum by the Sicilians. These fisheries were perhaps of some economic importance locally, but swordfish is mentioned relatively seldom as an article of diet.

The swordfish (*Xiphias Gladius*) is Greek *xiphias* or *thranis*, Latin *gladius* or *xiphias*.

Epicharmus 58 Kaibel (*skiphias*); Anaxippus fragment 2 Kassel (*xiphias kyon*); Xenocrates *T* 19; Strabo 1.2.15–16 citing Polybius 34.2.12–34.3.9 Büttner-Wobst (*galeotes*); Pliny *NH* 32.151; Aelian, *Nature of Animals* 14.23; Oppian *H* 2.462–9, 3.529–75; Athenaeus *D* 314e–f quoting Archestratus *H* 40 Brandt (see Olson and Sens *ad l.*).

Sybaris, Greek colony in southern Italy whose lifestyle was (and has remained) synonymous with free-spending luxury. This lifestyle is described by Athenaeus with a special focus on food. It is asserted that at Sybaris cooks who had devised a new dish were given exclusive rights to the recipe for a year, the earliest recorded form of patent protection. Sybaris flourished in the sixth century BC until destroyed by its neighbour and rival, Croton, in 510. Croton itself, and TARENTUM, and in due course the fifth-century colony Thurii established near the site of Sybaris, inherited something of its sybaritic reputation.

Aelian, *Varia Historia* 12.24; Athenaeus *D* 269f, 273b–c, 518c–522c, 541a–c.

Sophie Collin-Bouffier, 'La cuisine des Grecs d'Occident, symbole d'une vie de tryphè?' in *Paysage et alimentation dans le monde grec* ed. Jean-Marc Luce (Toulouse: Presses Universitaires du Mirail, 2000) pp. 195–208.

Sycamore fig, fruit native to Egypt. This unusual fruit is rather fully described by Theophrastus: it grows directly on the trunk of the tree; it will not ripen unless scratched, and then ripens within a few days. If it is picked, another fruit grows in the same spot.

Remains of sycamore figs have been found in Egypt in pre-dynastic contexts as well as from the Pharaonic and Graeco-Roman periods. It was also cultivated in Palestine: the Jewish prophet Amos was once employed as a sycamore-scratcher. The fruit was important locally in the diet, particularly because it ripened before the fig. It had many medicinal uses, specified both in Egyptian texts (see Darby and others) and by classical authors including Dioscorides and Athenaeus.

The sycamore fig or Egyptian fig (*Ficus Sycomorus*) is Greek *sykomoron*. In Latin it is *sycomorum* or *morum Aegyptium*. The tree is called *sykomorea* or *sykaminos he Aigyptia* in Greek, *ficus Aegyptia* in Latin. The tree now called sycamore in Britain and North America has no connection with the sycamore fig.

Amos 7.14 (Septuagint: *sykaminon*; Vulgate: *sycomorum*); Theophrastus *HP* 4.2.1–3; Diodorus Siculus 1.34.8; Strabo 17.2.4; Dioscorides *MM* 1.127, 5.33; Pliny *NH* 13.56–8, 23.134; Luke, *Gospel* 19.4; Galen *AF* 6.616–17; Athenaeus *E* 51b–c; Heliodorus, *Ethiopian Story* 8.14.3; *Suda s.v. sykomorrea*.

Darby and others 1977 pp. 744–8; Zohary and Hopf 1993 pp. 156–7; Brewer and others 1995 pp. 52–4.

Symbola, mechanisms of classical Greek exchange of hospitality. *Symbola*, as explained by Gow, are either 'contributions in kind of wine or food' or else 'in the nature of tokens, [i.e.] pledges that when the cost of the meal is reckoned up by the host the contributor will pay his scot or forfeit the pledge'. In Athens, therefore, one dined *apo symbolon* if on an agreed basis of equal shares; one dined *asymbolos* if one was not contributing. Too much dining under the latter arrangement caused observers to wonder if the host was expecting some other form of recompense from his guest – who incurred the name of *kolax* 'flatterer', or the imputation of passive homosexuality, or, eventually, the name of PARASITOS.

Games and competitions, in which the penalty for losing was to pay for or contribute to a dinner, were not unknown in ancient as in later times: see Aulus Gellius.

Machon C 5.44 [Athenaeus D 244d], 16.266 [Athenaeus D 579e] with Gow *ad ll.*; Aulus Gellius 18.13; Athenaeus D 572c citing Ephippus 20 Kassel and Aeschines, *Against Timarchus* 75.

Symposion (1). A drinking party. But it's more than that. In many cities of classical Greece, and notably Athens, the *symposion* was an important focus of men's social life.

It was an after-dinner and often an overnight event, typically held in a private house. Wine was consumed in large quantities, after first having been mixed with water in a *krater* according to proportions which were agreed by the drinkers on each occasion (see WINE-MIXING). Drinkers reclined on couches which were designed for one, but might have to hold two or three. Most were invited; some turned up unexpectedly; some came because they made a profession of attending *symposia* (see PARASITOS). Many, depending on how much everybody drank, how much an individual could avoid drinking, and how susceptible one was to alcohol, would eventually be very drunk. At the end of an all-night *symposion* many participants might be asleep.

See COMPORTMENT for the ways in which participants entertained themselves – sometimes taking turns, led by the MYRTLE branch. The idea of taking turns is well exemplified in Plato's *Symposium*, in which each symposiast in turn discourses in his own chosen fashion on the nature of love. This dialogue also shows, and Xenophon's *Symposium* shows in another style, how a formally set topic such as this might be interwoven with other themes and thus continue to animate a long *symposion*. In the literary sources there is much discussion and exemplification of appropriate and inappropriate topics of conversation, particularly in Plutarch's *Symposium Questions*

and in Athenaeus's *Deipnosophists*, but also in the literary symposia (see SYMPOSION (2)). Philosophy is an appropriate topic from Plato's *Symposium* onwards; homosexual flirtation, courtship and seduction were already conducted at *symposia* in Plato's time, though to the disapproval of some; politics was also a frequent subject of discussion, though it was felt by many that decisions should not be made amid drinking (Plutarch QC 7.9–10); indeed, it was proverbial that the best guest was one who forgot what had been said, a proverb which, if observed, would have made the writing of literary symposia difficult (Plutarch QC 1.preface; see the paper by Romeri).

See ENTERTAINMENT for hired and professional entertainment. This included the hire of slave musicians, dancers and acrobats, both male and female, whose range of duties partly coincided with those of prostitutes; it is clear from texts as well as vase paintings that sexual acts were part of the later stages of some Greek *symposia*.

Equality among the participants is to be noted. Events were controlled not by the host, it seems, but by democratic consensus: we hear occasionally of a *symposiarkhos*, a 'king of the *symposion*' chosen by vote (Plutarch QC 1.4). We should also note the limits on equality. One might turn out be the 'butt' of the party on some occasion. The professional joker and *parasitos* earned their share of wine and company by attracting laughter. Slave waiters and entertainers do not speak and are not spoken to in the literary symposia.

The *symposion* was not a Greek invention and in its origin had nothing to do with classical democracy. For information on Near Eastern antecedents and analogues see under COMPORTMENT.

Pindar, *Isthmians* 6.1; Plato, *Symposium*; Xenophon, *Symposium*.

W.J. Slater, 'Symposion at sea' in *Harvard Studies in Classical Philology* vol. 80 (1976) pp. 161–70; M. Davies, 'Sailing, rowing and

Figure 15 The pleasures of the symposium. The pleasures of the symposium are exemplified on five couches: the wine, the game of *kottabos*, the music and the sexual pleasures. On the sixth couch (as is clear although the vase is damaged at this point) a diner vomits: an attendant steadies his head while turning away. Redrawn from an Athenian *kylix* by Macron, about 480 BC.

sporting in one's cup on the wine-dark sea' in *Athens Comes of Age. From Solon to Salamis* (Princeton, 1978) pp. 72–90; W.J. Slater, 'Peace, the symposium and the poet' in *Illinois Classical Studies* vol. 6 (1981) pp. 206–14; Oswyn Murray, 'Symposion and Männerbund' in *Concilium Eirene* vol. 16 (1982) part 1 pp. 47–52; Oswyn Murray, 'The Greek symposion in history' in *Tria corda. Scritti in onore di Arnaldo Momigliano* ed. E. Gabba (Como:

New Press, 1983) pp. 257–72; Oswyn Murray, 'The symposion as social organisation' in *The Greek Renaissance of the Eighth Century B.C. Tradition and innovation* ed. R. Hägg (Stockholm, 1983) pp. 195–99; D.B. Levine, 'Symposium and the polis' in *Theognis of Megara: poetry and the polis* ed. T. Figueira and G. Nagy (Baltimore, 1985) pp. 176–96; François Lissarrague, *Un Flot d'images: une esthétique du banquet grec* (Paris: Biro, 1987), translation:

The Aesthetics of the Greek Banquet: images of wine and ritual (Princeton: Princeton University Press, 1990); Oswyn Murray, 'Death and the symposion' in *Annali dell'Instituto Universitario Orientale di Napoli. Sezione di Archeologia e Storia Antica* vol. 10 (1988) pp. 239–55; Murray 1990; M. Miller, 'Foreigners at the Greek symposium?' in *Dining in a Classical Context* ed. W.J. Slater (Ann Arbor: University of Michigan Press, 1991) pp. 59–81; Oswyn Murray, 'War and the symposium' in *Dining in a Classical Context* ed. W.J. Slater (Ann Arbor: University of Michigan Press, 1991) pp. 83–103; Oswyn Murray, 'Nestor's cup and the origin of the Greek symposion' in *Apoikia* ed. B. D'Agostino and D. Ridgway (*Aion*, n.s. vol. 1: Naples, 1994) pp. 47–54; Murray and Tecuşan 1995; Oswyn Murray, 'Hellenistic royal symposia' in *Aspects of Hellenistic Kingship* ed. P. Bilde and others (Aarhus, 1996) pp. 15–27; Davidson 1997; Luciana Romeri, 'Food and forgetfulness at Socratic symposia' in *Food and the Memory: papers of the Oxford Symposium on Food and Cookery 2000* ed. Harlan Walker (Totnes: Prospect Books, 2001) pp. 199–204.

Symposion (2). A literary form, the framework of which is conversation over food and wine. A philosophical essay in this form permitted the author to be more playful in topic and treatment than would be appropriate to other forms of philosophical writing, because the literary *symposion* must to some extent imitate real conversation. This involves disagreement, argument and change of mind; it includes humorous statements, irrelevant asides and impertinent interruptions.

Literary *Symposia* were written, says Plutarch, by 'Plato, Xenophon, Aristotle, Speusippus, Epicurus, Prytanis, Hieronymus and Dio of the Academy: these considered it was worth the effort to record conversations over wine'. Two quite different examples exist among the works of Plutarch himself. Others who wrote symposia or similar dialogues under the Roman Empire include Lucian, Athenaeus, Macrobius and Methodius.

Later in the work already quoted, Plutarch observes that Plato and Xenophon recorded only the conversations, not 'the savoury dishes, the sweets and the desserts that were served at Callias's and

at Agathon's'. The literary *Symposia* were in fact paralleled by a more earthy genre, that of the *Deipna* or *Dinners*, several of which survive more or less complete: they describe foods, wines, entertainment of all kinds, but scarcely a word of conversation. Authors include Philoxenus, Matron, Lynceus and Hippolochus.

Plutarch himself does something towards conflating the two forms. Although he records no menus, his conversations deal extensively with food and the mechanics of conviviality. Athenaeus goes further in the same direction. His conversations are supposed to be held over dinner (and not a classical *symposion*); there is repeated mention of foods that were served; these foods link with and sometimes redirect the conversation; and, more singlemindedly than Plutarch, Athenaeus makes his conversations focus on food, dining and entertainment.

The classical symposia, particularly the ones by Plato and Xenophon which remained well known and frequently read while the rest were forgotten, were destined to be held up as models for appropriate behaviour and appropriate conversation at later dinner parties.

For another literary form similar in conception if not in atmosphere see FUNERAL FEAST. For further information on the works listed in this entry see their authors' names – with the exception of Prytanis, Hieronymus and Dio, of whose *Symposia* nothing is known. A quotation by Athenaeus from 'Dio of the Academy', concerning wine and beer in Egypt, may be an extract from his *Symposium*.

Plutarch *QC* especially 1.preface, 3.6, 6.preface; Athenaeus *E* 1a–2b, also 34b citing Dio of the Academy.

J. Martin, *Symposion: die Geschichte einer literarischen Form* (Paderborn: Schöningh, 1931) (*Studien zur Geschichte und Kultur des Altertums*, 17); M.D. Gallardo, 'Estado actual de los estudios sobre los simposios de Platón, Jenofonte y Plutarco' in *Cuadernos de filología clásica* vol. 3 (1971) pp. 127–91; M.D. Gallardo, 'Los simposios de Luciano, Ateneo, Metodio y Juliano' in *Cuadernos de filología clásica* vol. 4 (1972) pp. 239–96; J.B. Burton, 'The symposium theme in Theocritus' Idyll 14' in *Greek, Roman and Byzantine Studies* vol. 33 (1992) pp. 227–45; Joel C. Relihan, 'Rethinking the history of the literary symposium' in *Illinois Classical Studies* vol. 17 no. 2 (1992) pp. 213–44; Judith Mossman, 'Plutarch's Dinner of the Seven Wise Men and its place in symposion literature' in *Plutarch and his Intellectual World* ed. J. Mossman (London: Duckworth, 1997) pp. 119–40.

Sympotic poetry *see* ENTERTAINMENT

Syracuse *see* SICILY

Syria, region at the eastern end of the Mediterranean. Syria was the location of very early developments in domestication and farming. In classical times Syria belonged successively to the Assyrian, Persian, Seleucid and Roman Empires. Its principal cities were Damascus, whose origins lie far back in the prehistoric period, and Antioch, which was for a while the Seleucid capital and afterwards one of the greatest cities of the Roman Empire.

Although bordering on the arid Arabian desert Syria was a fertile country, rich in wheat and olive oil, productive of dates and other fruits, a source of aromatics. Among these were storax, galbanum (see under ASAFOETIDA) and BALSAM; the latter came from plantations in Palestine at the southern extremity of Syria. Syria also commanded a major trade route, which ran from the ports at the head of the Persian Gulf, and from inland Mesopotamia, up the lower Euphrates and then due west across Syria to the Mediterranean coast. Its wealth helps to explain the conspicuous consumption evidenced at banquets of the Seleucid kings of Syria, lovingly described by Athenaeus, who quotes Poseidonius and other sources.

Syria was known for distinct varieties of several domesticated plants; the *nicolaos* date and the *damascenum* plum (whose name is at the origin of English 'damson') are named in sources of Roman date. Ascalon in Palestine was noted as the origin of a species or variety of ONION; in late Roman and Byzantine times Ascalon and Gaza were major producers of wine.

Strabo 16.2.29; Athenaeus *D* 193c–196a, 210c–211e, 438c–439f, 527e quoting Poseidonius *F* 10 Jacoby, also 540a quoting Poseidonius *F* 21 Jacoby; Oribasus *CM* 5.33.7.

F.M. Heichelheim in Frank 1933–40 vol. 4 pp. 121–258; L. Milano, 'Alimentazione e regime alimentari nella Siria preclassica' in *Dialoghi di archeologia* n.s. no. 3 (1981) pp. 85–120; M. Broshi, 'Wine in ancient Palestine: introductory notes' in *Israel Museum Journal* vol. 3 (1984) pp. 21–40; M. Broshi, 'The diet of Palestine in the Roman period: introductory notes' in *Israel Museum Journal* vol. 5 (1986) pp. 41–56; Michael Heltzer, 'Olive oil and wine production in Phoenicia and in the Mediterranean trade' in *La Production du vin et de l'huile en Méditerranée* ed. M.-C. Amouretti and J.-P. Brun (Athens: Ecole Française d'Athènes, 1993) pp. 49–54; A. Kloner and N. Sagiv, 'The olive presses of Hellenistic Maresha, Israel' in *La Production du vin et de l'huile en Méditerranée* ed. M.-C. Amouretti and J.-P. Brun (Athens: Ecole Française d'Athènes, 1993) pp. 119–36; P. Mayerson, 'The use of Ascalon wine in the medical writers of the fourth to the seventh centuries' in *Israel Exploration Journal* vol. 43 (1993) pp. 169–73; S. Dar, 'Food and archaeology in Romano-Byzantine Palestine' in *Food in Antiquity* ed. John Wilkins and others (Exeter: Exeter University Press, 1995) pp. 326–35; *Olive Oil in Antiquity: Israel and neighbouring countries from the Neolithic to the early Arab period. Proceedings of the conference held in Haifa, Israel, 1995* ed. David Eitam and Michael Heltzer (Padova: Sargon, 1996) (*History of the Ancient Near East: studies*, 7); Dalby 2000a pp. 168–71.

Syssition *see* COMMENSALITY

T

Tables and tableware *see* DINING AND
DRINKING UTENSILS

Tamarisk, feathery-leaved tree, the most
usual source of MANNA in the ancient
world. The leaves and bark were used in
medicine.

The tamarisk (*Tamarix canariensis*) is
Greek *myrike*, Latin *tamarix*, *tamarice*.

Herodotus 7.31; Dioscorides *MM* 1.87; Galen
SF 12.80.

Tarentine wine (Greek *Tarantinos*; Latin
Tarentinum), from the territory of Tarentum in southeastern Italy. Tarentine is
taken by both the *Epitome of Athenaeus*
and Pliny as the pattern for wines of deep
southern Italy: they are all 'simple', not
intoxicating, not forceful, pleasant, easy
on the stomach.

Horace, *Odes* 2.6.19–20; Pliny *NH* 14.69;
Statius, *Silvae* 2.2.111; Martial 13.125; Juvenal
6.297; Athenaeus *E* 27c.

Tarentum (Greek *Taras*: modern Taranto),
Greek colony in southern Italy. Tarentum
was known for its salt; for its figs, grapes,
chestnuts and walnuts; also for its pears
(but this may be an error: some call them
Tarentini, others *Terentiani*, a name
which would have no connection with
Tarentum); and for its salted tunny, according to Euthydemus of Athens.

Pliny *NH* 15.61, 15.71, 15.90, 15.94, 31.84–6;
Athenaeus *D* 116a–d quoting Euthydemus of

Athens, also 522d–523b.

Tarikhos *see* CONSERVING

Taro or dasheen, a tropical root of which
one variety, now called eddoe, was grown
in ancient Egypt. It resembles ARUM root
and was, like arum, regarded as an
aphrodisiac.

The eddoe or qolqas (*Colocasia escu-
lenta* var. *antiquorum*) is Greek *koloka-
sion*, Latin *colocasia*. A recurrent
confusion between the taro root and the
root of the pink lotus or Egyptian bean
(see LOTUS (1)) is found in classical
authors who had not visited Egypt, including Diphilus of Siphnos (cited by
Athenaeus *E* 73a), Dioscorides (*MM*
2.106) and Pliny (*NH* 21.87).

Theophrastus *HP* 1.1.7, 1.6.11 (*ouingon*);
Claudius Iolaus 1 Müller; Columella *DA*
8.15.4; Pliny *NH* 19.96 (*aron*), 21.174; Martial
13.57; Galen *AF* 6.623; Athenaeus *E* 72a–b
quoting Nicander *F* 81–2 Schneider (in Nicander 82 read *kyamous*); Aetius, *Medicine* 1.210,
11.35.

Darby and others 1977 pp. 638–40, 655–6.

Tarraconensian wine *see* SPANISH WINES

Taverns in classical Greek are not distinguished from retail shops, *kapeleia*. These
were places where you bought, haggled
and talked; if wine and food were for sale,
you drank and ate. Isocrates and his

audience would despise any who did, but the female speaker in a fragment by Eubulus would explain in justification that the barman mixed the wine just right. These were not luxurious places, but, as Davidson shows, they were much more significant in daily life than has usually been admitted.

However, when Strabo has to describe the pleasure resorts beside the canal at Canobus in Egypt, where men and women went to eat and drink together, he has no Greek word for them: he uses *diaita* 'rooms', *katagoge* 'hostel'.

In Italy, too, such places existed; there is an engaging description of one, to be imagined somewhere in rural central Italy, in the *Copa*. The functions of an innkeeper in Italy included stating a menu, fixing the price and reckoning what a guest had spent (although at inns in Cisalpine Gaul in the second century BC, according to Polybius, you paid a fixed price for a day's stay). Plutarch, evidently familiar with these establishments from his own time in Italy, is able to describe the kings who preside over dinner in HOMERIC SOCIETY as 'more dreadful than Italian innkeepers: while in battle, in hand-to-hand combat, they can still remember precisely how much each man who dined with them had to drink'.

See also TRAVELLER'S FOOD

Lysias 1.24; Aristophanes, *Thesmophoriazusae* 347, *Assemblywomen* 153–7; Eubulus F 75 Kassel [Athenaeus D 108b]; Isocrates 7.49; Polybius 2.15.5; Strabo 17.1.16–17; *Copa*; Juvenal 8.158–80; Plutarch *QC* 2.10; *Philogelos* 227, 230.

T. Kleberg, *Hôtels, restaurants et cabarets dans l'antiquité romaine* (Uppsala, 1957); G. Hermansen, 'The Roman inns and the law: the inns of Ostia' in *Polis and Imperium: studies in honour of Edward Togo Salmon* ed. J.A.S. Evans (Toronto, 1974) pp. 167–81; J. Packer, 'Inns at Pompeii' in *Cronache pompeiane* vol. 4 (1978) pp. 12–24; Davidson 1997 pp. 53–60; Grant 1999 pp. 84–92.

Teasel (*Dipsacus fullonum*), meadow plant with a familiar prickly seed-head

and with spiny but edible leaves for which it is listed among potherbs by Galen (*AF* 6.623, 6.636). It is *dipsakos* in Greek.

Tejpat *see* CINNAMON

Terebinth (turpentine tree: *Pistacia atlantica*), widespread wild tree whose range extands from the Maghreb eastwards to the Hindu Kush. This species assisted the westward spread of the PISTACHIO in Hellenistic times and after, because it provided, as it still does, rootstocks on which pistachio may be grafted. Old terebinths – big, slow-growing trees – have often served as landmarks in the Near East: one near Hebron was said to have grown there since the creation of the world.

The tiny oil-rich fruits of the terebinth can be eaten and are sometimes pressed for oil, as they were in Achaemenid Persia, according to Xenophon, Ctesias and Polyaenus. Famously, they were a major item in the traditional diet of young PERSIANS. They cured headaches and were mildly laxative and aphrodisiac, according to Dioscorides and Pliny. Fruits of the related shrubby trees *P. Terebinthus* and *P. Lentiscus* have had similar uses. Such fruits are frequently reported from archaeological sites in the region, from Mesolithic times onwards (e.g. *c.*10,000 BC at Franchthi; *c.*7000 BC in southern France), usually as '*Pistacia* sp.' but also, erroneously, as 'pistachio'. The lentisk fruited three times a year, warning the farmer of the dates on which three different groups of crops were to be sown (see Theophrastus and Aratus). Palladius gives instructions for making lentisk oil.

Terebinth resin comes mainly from *P. atlantica*: the other two species produce little resin, except trees of *P. Lentiscus* var. *Chia*, for which see MASTIC. The many modern names of terebinth resin include Chios balsam, Cyprus turpentine and Bombay mastic. The ancient method of tapping is described by Pliny (*NH* 16.58). The resulting resin was chewed as gum and was used in perfumes; it served to give a waterproof inner surface to the DOLIUM, earthenware vat, in which wine would mature; it was sometimes added to wine itself to stabilise it, and for flavour. Nearly half a ton of terebinth resin went down in the shipwreck dated c.1200 BC excavated off the Turkish coast at Ulu Burun (see Mills and White).

The terebinth tree and its fruit are *terminthos* in Greek, *terebinthus* in Latin. The lentisk tree is Greek *skhinos*, Latin *lentiscus*. Terebinth resin (Greek *retine terminthine*, Latin *resina terebinthina*) may have been the *ki-ta-no* of Linear B tablets.

Xenophon, *Anabasis* 4.4.13; Ctesias 688 F 17 Jacoby; Theophrastus *HP* 3.15.3–4, 9.2.1–2, 9.4.7–8, *CP* 6.14.4, *On Weather Signs* 55; Aratus, *Phenomena* 1051–9; Dioscorides *MM* 1.71, *E* 2.101, 2.127; Pliny *NH* 12.72, 13.54, 24.27–43; Josephus, *Jewish War* 4.533; Plutarch, *Life of Artoxerxes* 3.2, *On Isis and Osiris* 383e–384b; Julius Africanus, *Cesti* 1.19; Polyaenus 4.3.32; Palladius *OA* 2.20.

V. Loret, *La résine de térébinthe (sonter) chez les anciens Egyptiens Recherches d'archéologie, de philologie et d'histoire*, (Cairo: Institut Français d'Archéologie Orientale, 1949); M. Zohary, 'A monographical study of the genus *Pistacia*' in *Palestine Journal of Botany. Jericho series* vol. 5 (1952) pp. 187–228; J. Melena, '*ki-ta-no* en las tabillas de Cnoso' in *Durius* vol. 2 (1974) pp. 45–55; J. Mills and R. White, 'The identity of the resins from the Late Bronze Age shipwreck at Ulu Burun (Kas)' in *Archaeometry* vol. 31 (1989) pp. 37–44; H.H. Hairfield and E.M. Hairfield, 'Identification of a Late Bronze Age resin' in *Analytical Chemistry* vol. 62 (1990) pp. 41–5; Zohary and Hopf 1993 p. 197 ('wild pistachio'); Sancisi-Weerdenburg 1995.

- The *mastiche nigra* of Pliny and the *mastikhe Aigyptia* of Galen may both be Bombay mastic, that is, terebinth resin from the Indian trees sometimes identified as *Pistacia mutica*.

Pliny *NH* 14.128; Galen, *To Glaucon on Therapeutic Method* 11.106.

Terpsion, said by Athenaeus (*D* 337b) on the authority of Clearchus of Soli to have been the forerunner of ARCHESTRATUS as gastronomic preceptor. 'Eat up, or don't eat, the tortoise's meat,' is Terpsion's only recorded maxim.

Tertullian (Quintus Septimius Florens Tertullianus), Latin Christian author, c.AD 155–222. Tertullian wrote a good deal on the subject of religious fasting, which he was the first Christian author to recommend wholeheartedly. Grimm gives a summary and analysis of his short work *On Fasting*, which was written after he had given his adherence to the controversial Montanist sect.

Grimm 1996 pp. 114–39.

Testicles (Greek *orkheis*; Latin *testiculi*) were food of special value in ancient dietary thinking. Cock's testicles are frequently recommended. They were called *parastatai* in Greek, *testes* in Latin, as a euphemism (the words mean 'witnesses'); they were sometimes called 'kidneys' for the same reason (similarly they can be called *rognons blancs* 'white kidneys' in modern French).

Galen *AF* 6.675–6; Athenaeus *D* 384e quoting Philippides 5 Kassel, with Gulick *ad l.*; Apicius 4.3.3.

Tetrafarmacum, 'a mess of four kinds of food' as Lewis and Short succinctly put it. It contained sow's udder, pheasant, ham in pastry, and wild boar. The *Historia Augusta* states that the luxury-loving Caesar, Aelius Verus (died AD 138), an admirer of Apicius, invented the dish, that his senior colleague, the emperor Hadrian, liked it, and that a century later Alexander Severus liked it too. All of this information is credited to Marius Maximus's biography of Hadrian. The dish appears to have been named after a standard medicinal compound (Greek *tetrapharmakon* 'fourfold drug') on which see Galen.

Galen *SF* 12.328, *al.*; *Historia Augusta, Hadrian* 21, *Aelius Verus* 5, *Alexander Severus* 30, all citing Marius Maximus.

Charlton T. Lewis and Charles Short, *A Latin Dictionary* (1879) *s.v. tetrapharmacum*; Ignazio Cazzaniga, 'Il tetrapharmacum cibo adrianeo' in *Poesia latina in frammenti: miscellanea filologica* (Genoa: Instituto di Filologia Classica e Medievale, 1974) pp. 359–66.

Thasian wine, one of the best-known of classical Greek appellations. It was a 'black' wine and is frequently praised in sources of the fourth century BC. Its fame was maintained later, as is evident from the wide distribution of Thasian amphorae, from which the regular patterns of trade to the Black Sea coasts, to Greece and into the wider Mediterranean can be reconstructed. Florentinus, writing in Roman imperial times, gives a recipe for imitating Thasian wine.

Unusually, an inscription survives laying down rules by which the trade in Thasian wine was regulated in the Hellenistic period: for studies of this text see Mantzoufas and Salviat. It begins with the memorable words *Gleukos mede oinos* . . . : 'Must nor wine, the fruit on the vine shall not be bought before the New Moon of Plynteria: any offending buyer shall pay a fine, stater for stater.'

Later in the same text the landing of non-Thasian wine on the southern coast of Thrace is regulated. It is probable that some wine called 'Thasian' was produced on this mainland coast, along which the Thasians maintained a string of coastal settlements.

Aristophanes, *Assemblywomen* 1119–39, also fragment 364 Kassel; Baton 3 Kassel; Hippolochus D; Florentinus [*Geoponica* 8.23]; Athenaeus E 28d–29e quoting Hermippus 77 Kassel and Archestratus H 59–60 Brandt (see Olson and Sens *ad l.*); *Inscriptiones Graecae* vol. 12 suppl. no. 347.

A.-M. Bon and A. Bon, *Les Timbres amphoriques de Thasos* (Paris, 1957) (*Études thasiennes* vol. 4); G. Mantzoufas, *La Loi thasienne Gleukos mede* oinos *sur le commerce du vin* (Athens, 1967); François Salviat, 'Le vin de Thasos: amphores, vin et sources écrites' in *Recherches sur les amphores grecques* ed. Jean-Yves Empereur and Yvon Garlan (Athens, 1986) (*Bulletin de correspondance hellénique* suppl. 13) pp. 145–96; Dalby 2000c.

Thasos, northern Aegean island. Apart from its wine (see THASIAN WINE), Thasos was a good place for rascasse, red mullet and octopus; also for *alphita* or barley meal. The sweet almond was sometimes called *karyon Thasion* 'Thasian nut' in Greek.

Archestratus H 4, 29, 41–2, 53 Brandt; Athenaeus E 54b citing Diphilus of Siphnos.

Thearion, Athenian baker of the late fifth century BC. Thearion is credited with inventing an oven for mass-producing bread – or at any rate with introducing it to Athens, where the bread sold on the market became renowned in Greece. The statement in the *Scholia on Aristides* that Thearion wrote a book on cookery is an error.

Plato, *Gorgias* 518d; Athenaeus D 112c–e quoting Antiphanes and Aristophanes; *Scholia on Aristides, On the Four* 122.9.

Theophrastus of Eresus (*c.*370–287 BC), successor to Aristotle as head of the Peripatetic school of philosophy. Few of his many writings survive. Of those that do, the most important are two botanical treatises, 'Study of Plants' and 'Plant Physiology', which give a great deal of information about farming, gardening and wild plants, and thus about plant foods. They record the results of direct research, but also of wide-ranging enquiries made among farmers, 'root-cutters' (herbalists) and others with specialised knowledge: for herbal lore see especially *HP* book 9. These researches extended as far as Alexander the Great's Persian expedition, from which information was sent back on the trees and the food plants of Persia, Afghanistan and India: thus Theophrastus's writings contain the earliest reports in Europe of citrons, bananas, mangoes, jackfruits, pistachios, jujubes and tamarinds (*HP* 4.4.2, 4.4.5, 4.7.8). They also provide evidence that gardeners in the fourth century BC were already selecting and developing varieties of fruits and vegetables with attention to soil and climate requirements, yield and flavour.

The researches of Theophrastus were excerpted by PLINY the Elder in his *Natural History*. They were also incorporated in Greek and Roman dietary and pharmacological writings. His classification of plants was not significantly improved on until it was finally superseded by the entirely different system of Linnaeus in the eighteenth century.

H. Bretzl, *Botanische Forschungen des Alexanderzuges* (Leipzig, 1903); Robert W. Sharples, 'Theophrastus on tastes and smells' in *Theophrastus of Eresus: on his life and work* ed. William W. Fortenbaugh and others (New Brunswick: Transaction Books, 1985) pp. 183–207; John Scarborough, 'Theophrastus on herbals and herbal remedies' in *Journal of the History of Biology* vol. 11 (1978) pp. 353–85; *OCD* 1996 *s.vv.* Botany, Theophrastus; Suzanne Amigues, 'Les traités botaniques de Théophraste' in *Geschichte der Mathematik und der Naturwissenschaften in der Antike. 1, Biologie* ed. Georg Wöhrle (Stuttgart: Steiner, 1999) pp. 124–54.

Theophrastus CP: *De Causis Plantarum* 'On Plant Physiology'. Text and English translation: Theophrastus, *De Causis Plantarum* ed. and tr. B. Einarson and G.K.K. Link, 3 vols (1976–90, LCL).

—— **HP**: *Historia Plantarum* 'Study of Plants'. Text and English translation: Theophrastus, *Enquiry into Plants* ed. and tr. Sir Arthur Hort, 2 vols (1916–26, LCL); with index of plant names (on which see John Scarborough, 'The pharmacology of sacred plants, herbs and roots' in *Magika Hiera: ancient Greek magic and religion* [New York: Oxford University Press, 1991] pp. 163–4). Text, French translation and commentary: Théophraste, *Recherches sur les plantes* ed. and tr. Suzanne Amigues (Paris, 1988– , CUF). Hort's edition omits a section on sexual drugs, and Amigues's edition has not reached that point. For the missing text see *Theophrasti Eresii opera* ed. F. Wimmer (Paris: Didot, 1866) p. 159; for a translation and notes see Andrew Dalby in *Petits Propos culinaires* no. 64 (2000) pp. 9–15.

—— **O**: *On Odours*, included in Hort's edition of *HP*, vol. 2 pp. 326–89.

Theoxenia *see* SACRIFICE

Theran wine *see* CRETAN WINE

Thessaly, region of northern Greece. Central Thessaly is a rich alluvial plain – as such unusual in Greece. The introduction of farming took place here in the course of the seventh millennium BC. In the Neolithic period Thessalian farmers kept all the major farm animals and grew and gathered a range of plant foods, but principally they kept cattle and grew wheat. So did the Greeks of Thessaly in classical times. Fairly or unfairly, Thessalians were notorious in Athens for their heavy meals, rich in beef, and their unabashed pursuit of luxury.

Theopompus 115 F 49 [Athenaeus *D* 527a]; Athenaeus *D* 418b–e.

H. Kroll, 'Thessalische Kulturpflanzen' in *Zeitschrift für Archäologie* vol. 15 (1982) pp. 97–103.

Tholos *see* ARCHITECTURE

Thrace, region of the southern Balkans. The Thracian coast of the Aegean was known for its seafood. Abdera was a good place to find the *kestreus* grey mullet; Abdera and Maronea offered good cuttlefish. The Thracians, unlike their Greek neighbours, hunted dolphins. Southern Thrace was also famous for wine – ever since Odysseus, in Homer's *Odyssey*, told of the strong wine he was given by the priest Maron. In classical times some wine from here was probably sold as THASIAN WINE.

Thracians are characterised by classical Greeks as butter-eaters and as drinkers of unmixed wine. The system of gift-exchange through which the Thracian court maintained its power was not understood by Greeks. The finest description of a meal in Thrace is by XENOPHON, who recounts a dinner at which Seuthes, king of Thrace, entertained him and the other leaders of the Ten Thousand in 400 BC.

Xenophon, *Anabasis* 3.21; Anaxandrides 42 Kassel; Archestratus *H* 55 Brandt; Oppian *H* 5.519–88; Athenaeus *D* 118b–c citing Dorion, also 155e, also 307b, also 534b citing Satyrus.

Susanne Ebbinghaus, 'Between Greece and

Persia: rhyta in Thrace from the late 5th to the early 3rd centuries BC' in *Ancient Greeks West and East* ed. G.R. Tsetskhladze (Leiden, 1999) pp. 385–425.

Thrush, plump wild bird, a well-known classical delicacy. According to legend a gift of thrushes was Homer's payment for composing a minor epic – which was named, as a result of the incident, *Epikikhlides* ('For the Thrushes'). Thrushes were sometimes prescribed by physicians, as once, famously, to Pompey. Since it was summer and they were out of season, they could only be found in LUCULLUS's aviaries. Pompey replied, 'So Pompey would die if Lucullus were not a gastronome?' He took some other food instead, and recovered.

Thrushes were trapped from the wild with nets and were hung on a hoop (Latin *corona*, literally 'crown') to be sold at market; the astute salesman would blow air into his thrushes' stomachs before selling them to make them look fatter. In Roman Italy thrushes were trapped from the wild and fattened in aviaries for the luxury table. Typically they were spitted, roasted and glazed with honey. They are assessed at the luxury price of sixty denarii for ten in *Diocletian's Price Edict*.

The thrush (*Turdus* spp.) is Greek *kikhle*, Latin *turdus*.

Aristophanes, *Clouds* 339, *Acharnians* 961, 1007; Alexis *F* 168 Kassel with Arnott *ad l.*; Menander fragment 451 Körte; Horace, *Satires* 1.5.72; Varro *RR* 3.5.7; Columella *DA* 8.10; Martial 3.47, 13.51; Plutarch, *Life of Lucullus* 40.2, *Life of Pompey* 2.6; Athenaeus *E* 64f–65b, *D* 639a; Palladius *OA* 1.26, 13.6; *Diocletian's Price Edict* 4.27.

Thompson 1936 p. 148; J. Oroz Reta, 'Nil melius turdo. Gastronomía clásica y moderna' in *Helmantica* vol. 28 (1977) pp. 403–16.

- Greek *kopsikhos, kossyphos*, Latin *merula* is the blackbird (*Turdus Merula*), which would be seen at market hanging from a feather threaded through its nostrils. It was a winter food, says Oribasius.

  Aristophanes, *Acharnians* 970, *Birds* 1081 with scholia; Rhianus [*Anthologia Palatina* 12.142]; Horace, *Satires* 2.8.91; Dionysius,

On Bird-Catching 3.13; Athenaeus *E* 65d–e; Oribasius *CM* 1.3.4 with Grant *ad l.*

Thompson 1936 p. 174; Toynbee 1996.

Thrymmatis, a surprise dish. *Thrymmatis* (a Greek name) was a kind of cake or pastry, a costly hors d'oeuvre, which, when broken open, revealed a small roasted bird such as a beccafico.

In Petronius's *Satyricon* the narrator is surprised by an egg which turns out to be made of pastry and to contain a beccafico; this is a description of the same or a similar dish. No name is given.

Philoxenus *D* b.18 Page with Dalby *ad l.*; Anaxandrides 42 Kassel (*enthrymmatis*); Lynceus *F* 1 [Athenaeus *D* 131f]; Petronius *S* 33 (see quotation at SURPRISE DISHES); Pollux *O* 6.77; Photius, *Lexicon s.v. thrymmatis*.

Thurine wine (Latin *Thurinum*; Greek *Thourinos*), from the territory of Thurii in Lucania, was well regarded in the first centuries BC and AD. Certain local grape varieties on these hills were not harvested till the first frost, which must have resulted in a sweet and very strong wine. The wine of adjacent Lagaria (Greek *Lagaritanos*, Latin *Lagarinum*) had a special reputation as a medicinal wine.

Strabo 6.1.14; Pliny *NH* 14.39, 14.69.

Thyme, the name in English of two aromatics. One, the thyme that is known as *thym* in French, *Thymian* in German, is a culinary herb and potherb. It is frequently called for as a flavouring in *Apicius*, was an ingredient in compound medicines, and according to Columella might serve as a rennet in cheese-making. It lent its aroma (and still does) to Attic honey; also to that of Hybla in Sicily, or so the poets say.

In the classical world this thyme was typical of Greece, and within Greece typical of the country round Athens, and in Athens typical of an old-fashioned life of poverty. Hence MACHON's writing is politely said by the poet Dioscorides to be redolent of thyme, meaning that, though not Athenian, he had hit off the style and atmosphere of Athenian comedy perfectly. How did these Athenians eat their thyme? Freshly picked, and perhaps simply with bread and salt, like za'tar (see under HYSSOP). The view stated in Liddell and Scott, that the word *thymon* may denote 'a mixture of thyme with honey and vinegar', is not well-supported.

Thyme (including *Thymus vulgaris, T. capitatus* or Cretan thyme, and other species) is Greek *thymon*, Latin *thymum*.

Aristophanes, *Wealth* 253, 283; Hippocrates *R* 54; Antiphanes 166 Kassel [Athenaeus *D* 108f]; Eubulus *F* 18 Kassel; Theophrastus *HP* 1.12.2, *Characters* 4.1; Hippolochus *D* [Athenaeus *D* 130d]; Dioscorides 24 Gow [*Anthologia Palatina* 7.708]; Vergil, *Eclogues* 5.77, *Georgics* 4.169, 4.181; Columella *DA* 7.8.7, 9.4.2, *al.*; Dioscorides *MM* 3.36; Pliny *NH* 20.245–6; Martial 5.39, 11.42; Lucian, *Saturnalia* 21; Pseudo-Apuleius, *Herbarius* 100.

Liddell and Scott 1925–40 *s.v. thymon*; A.C. Andrews, 'Thyme as a condiment in the Graeco-Roman era' in *Osiris* vol. 13 (1958) pp. 127–56; Valérie Bonet, 'Le thym médicinal antique, un cadeau divin' in *Des hommes et des plantes: plantes méditerranéennes, vocabulaire et usages anciennes* ed. M.-C. Amouretti and G. Comet (Aix-en-Provence, 1993) pp. 11–21.

• Thyme of the second kind, the aromatic herb called creeping thyme or mother-of-thyme in English, *serpolet* in French, *Quendel* in German (*Thymus atticus* and similar species) is *herpyllos* in Greek, *serpyllum, serpullum* in Latin. It was suitable for wreaths; good to plant near beehives; useful in medicine; scarcely ever used in cookery. It was brought from the mountains where it grew, such as Hymettus, to be replanted in city gardens.

Aristophanes, *Peace* 168; Hippocrates, *Affections of Women* 194; Aristotle *HA* 627b18; Theophrastus *HP* 6.7.2–6, *CP* 6.20.1–3; Nicander *F* 74.40 Schneider; Cato *DA* 73; Varro *RR* 3.16.13; Dioscorides *MM* 3.38; Pliny *NH* 21.59; Galen *AF* 6.657, *SF* 11.877, *On Compounding* 12.512; Apicius 10.1.15.

Tiburtine wine (Latin *Tiburtinum*; Greek *Tibourtinos*), from the hill town of Tibur near Rome. In the first century Tiburtine was light, good after ten years, even better if kept longer. In the second century there were both fine and light Tiburtine wines; both were white. The fine Tiburtine was fairly astringent, fairly austere, not especially 'winy'. Tiburtine was still familiar at the end of the third century, and is one of the seven named wines of the Empire that are allowed a special high price in *Diocletian's Price Edict*.

Galen *ST* 6.334–7, *DA* 14.15, *On Therapeutic Method* 10.831, *On Compounding* 13.659; Athenaeus *E* 26e; *Diocletian's Price Edict* 2.2.

Tchernia 1986 pp. 206–7, 344.

Timachidas of Rhodes, Greek philologist of about 100 BC. One of his works (which appears to have been as much concerned with Greek lexicography and grammar as all his others) was called *Deipna* 'Dinners'. Timachidas is quoted fourteen times by Athenaeus (once on Rhodian wine), and occasionally in other scholarly sources.

Athenaeus *D* 82d, *E* 5a (cf. *Suda s.v. Timakhidas*), 31d.

Konrat Ziegler, 'Timachidas' in *RE* 1893–1972.

Tmolite wine *see* ASIAN WINES

Tongue The tongue of sacrificial animals is said to have been the prerogative of the officiator. 'Those leaving a dinner pour a libation to Hermes over the tongues,' according to the *Epitome of Athenaeus*.

Tongue is not frequently mentioned among gastronomic delicacies, though one may think it deserves to have been. However, flamingoes' tongues and nightingales' tongues are costly delicacies served to gourmandising Roman emperors. For so-called 'carp's tongue' see under CARP.

Aristophanes, *Peace* 1109; Menander, *Kolax* fragment 1 Sandbach [Athenaeus *D* 659d]; Pliny *NH* 10.133; Suetonius, *Vitellius* 13; Galen *AF* 6.672–3; Athenaeus *E* 16b; *Historia Augusta, Heliogabalus* 20.

Top-shell, group of univalve spiral shellfish (*Monodonta turbinata* and other species). The top-shell is possibly to be identified with Greek *nerites*, *anarites*, which is appropriately described as 'like a snail' and 'very beautiful'. These shell-fish shared with limpets the reputation for clinging tightly to the rocks, as in a simile employed by Herodas.

Aristotle *HA* 530a12–25; Aelian, *Nature of Animals* 14.28; Athenaeus *D* 85d–92d *passim* quoting Herodas fragment 2 Bergk; Hesychius, *Lexicon s.v. neriton.*

Thompson 1947 p. 176; Davidson 1981 p. 191.

Tortoise and turtle, hard-shelled reptiles, potentially a food source but one that is avoided by many peoples. The uncertain taboo is reflected in a proverbial hexameter line attributed to TERPSION on the authority of Clearchus of Soli: 'Eat up, or don't eat, the tortoise's meat.' Derivatives such as tortoise liver and turtle brain are called for in a few of the most magical of Hippocratic remedies; Galen has uses for tortoise blood and turtle bile. In general, these sources say little or nothing of tortoises and turtles as normal food, which helps to explain why the Lydian king Croesus, on the occasion when he tested the Greek oracles (in the story told by Herodotus), thought they would be unlikely to guess that he was cooking tortoise stew and was correspondingly impressed when the Delphic Oracle got it right.

In Greek, the tortoise (*Testudo graeca* and other species) is *khelone*; the turtle (*Thalassochelys corticata*) is *khelone he thalassia*. In Latin the tortoise is *testudo*, the turtle *testudo marina*.

Herodotus 1.47–8; Hippocrates, *Affections of Women* 78.1, 78.151, 203.7; Dioscorides *MM* 2.78–9; Galen *SF* 12.310, *al.*; Athenaeus *D* 337b quoting Clearchus of Soli.

Dalby 1996 p. 21 and note 71.

Trade, links between producer and consumer lubricated by a conventional exchange mechanism such as money. It makes sense in the ancient context to distinguish local trade, in which the relationships might be informal and the medium of exchange might exist only in the imagination, from long-distance trade, which required the trader to make an investment and to take a risk.

In the eastern Mediterranean in the second millennium BC there was already some long-distance trade in spices (for example, in MYRRH and in TEREBINTH resin) and other luxuries. In archaic and classical Greece, and in the contemporary Mediterranean more widely, long-distance trade had developed in wine and some other durable foods such as DATES; more aromatics, including SILPHIUM and SUMACH, were traded over long distances; speculative investment in long-distance trade became common practice. In Hellenistic times and under the Roman Empire such products regularly traversed the whole Mediterranean; Tchernia (1983 pp. 100–7) provides a series of significant incidents and dates concerning imports of Greek wine to Rome, beginning in 161 BC. Mediterranean trade routes were connected with others running further east. Mediterranean wines were in demand in India: the PEPPER, CARDAMOM, COSTUS and NARD of India, and CINNAMON and MALABATHRON from beyond India, fetched high prices in Rome. By the second and third centuries some foods (including spices) and some potential foods (such as sheep and oxen) were traded at fairs associated with religious festivals, usually repeating annually, but the volume of this trade is unknown.

Locally, certainly by Hellenistic times, there were periodic MARKETS in several Mediterranean regions. Already in classical Greece large cities such as Athens had had daily food markets. There were permanent retail stores (see also TAVERNS). The relative importance in the ancient context of these three types of retail trade is, again, unknown, as is the absolute volume of trade involved.

The trade in Mediterranean wine contributed to the changes in central

European society that led to and accompanied Roman conquest. One of these changes was the growth of slave-raiding. Illyrians exchanged cattle, skins and slaves for wine in wooden barrels; in Gaul, it was said, an amphora of wine was worth a slave.

Strabo 5.1.8 and *passim*; *Periplus Maris Erythraei* 6, 49, 56 and *passim*; Pliny *NH* book 12 and *passim*.

M.P. Charlesworth, *Trade Routes and Commerce in the Roman Empire* (Cambridge, 1924); J. Rougé, *Recherches sur l'organisation du commerce maritime en Méditerranée dans l'Empire romain* (Paris, 1966); Miller 1969; M. Loewe, 'Spices and silks: aspects of world trade in the first seven centuries of the Christian era' in *Journal of the Royal Asiatic Society* (1971) pp. 166–79; J. Rougé, *Ships and Fleets of the Ancient Mediterranean* (Middletown, 1981); R.P. Duncan-Jones, *The Economy of the Roman Empire: quantitative studies* (Cambridge, 1982), 2nd edn; John Scarborough, 'Roman pharmacy and the Eastern drug trade' in *Pharmacy in History* vol. 24 (1982) pp. 135–43; *Trade in the Ancient Economy* ed. Peter Garnsey, K. Hopkins and C.R. Whittaker (London, 1983); A. Tchernia, 'Italian wine in Gaul at the end of the Republic' in *Trade in the Ancient Economy* ed. Peter Garnsey and others (London, 1983) pp. 87–104; V. Nutton, 'The drug trade in antiquity' in *Journal of the Royal Society of Medicine* vol. 78 (1985) pp. 138–45; D.P.S. Peacock and D.F. Williams, *Amphorae and the Roman Economy: an introductory guide* (London: Longman, 1986); Tchernia 1986; Jean-François Salles, 'Du blé, de l'huile et du vin: notes sur les échanges commerciaux en Méditerranée orientale vers le milieu du 1er millénaire av. J. C.' in *Achaemenid History* vol. 5 (1991) pp. 207–36; Albert Leonard, '"Canaanite jars" and the late Bronze Age Aegeo-Levantine wine trade' in *The Origins and Ancient History of Wine* ed. Patrick E. McGovern, Stuart J. Fleming and Solomon H. Katz (London: Gordon and Breach, 1995) pp. 233–54; Lin Foxhall, 'Cargoes of the heart's desire: the character of trade in the archaic Mediterranean world' in *Archaic Greece: new approaches and new evidence* ed. Nick Fisher and Hans van Wees (London: Duckworth, 1998) pp. 295–309; Fergus Millar, 'Caravan cities: the Roman Near East and long-distance trade by land' in *Modus Operandi: essays in honour of Geoffrey Rickman* ed. M. Austin and others (London: Institute of Classical Studies, 1998).

Tragemata, the foods that accompanied wine at a Greek *symposion* (see SYMPOSION (1)) or in the final stage of a dinner. The Homeric epics give no sign of such usages; the earliest mention of them comes in a seventh-century BC poem by Xenophanes, who suggests bread, cheese and honey. The bread drops out of the picture in later descriptions: cheese, with honey as sauce, remains. Around 350 Archestratus suggests cakes from Athens drenched in Attic honey; he condemns boiled chickpeas, beans, apples and dried figs, but these were all commonly served by others. Ephippus lists 'after dinner pomegranate seed, chickpea, bean, porridge, cheese, honey, sesame sweets … pyramid cakes, apple, walnut, milk, cannabis seeds' and in another fragment 'walnuts, pomegranates, dates, the rest of the *nogala*, and small jars of Phoenician wine'.

Nogala, *nogaleumata*, *nogalismata* and *trogalia* are synonyms used by Ephippus, Aristotle and others, but *tragemata* 'things to chew' is the standard term. It was in due course borrowed into Latin and is the origin of modern French *dragée* 'sugared almond'.

Xenophanes 1.9–10 West; Aristophanes, *Peace* 1127–39; Ephippus 8, 13, 24 Kassel; Plato, *Republic* 372c; Archestratus *H* 62 Brandt; Pliny *NH* 13.38; Athenaeus *E* 54f, also 641a–643e quoting Aristotle fragment 104 Rose and Philoxenus *D* e.1–23 Page.

Travellers' food In a useful short text Diocles of Carystus, Greek dietary author of the fourth century BC, discusses the health of those setting out on a land journey – which means walking. In summer it is advisable to pause for lunch, *ariston*, and to take a siesta before continuing; if this is impossible, Diocles advises a midday drink of water mixed with barley meal and salt to help the traveller to keep going. In winter it is preferable to keep moving, and one should not eat or drink if breaking the journey at midday. Dieuches, a slightly later author, gave advice on diet for those liable to sea-sickness.

Travellers must often carry supplies with them. What to carry depended on the route: it might be water; it might be bread. Useful alternatives to bread were the BARLEY meal, *alphita*, recommended by Diocles above (because it was more compact); a prepared form of EMMER meal, *tragos* (compact and highly nourishing); and the various forms of BISCUIT including *paximadia* (because they were lighter). *Conditum viatorium*, 'traveller's spiced wine', for which *Apicius* gives a recipe, takes the form of a concentrate to be added to whatever beverage might be available. The need for such a product is evidence of the important health benefits expected from adding spices and herbs to wine in correct proportions.

If stopping at an inn (see also HOSPI-TALITY; TAVERNS) you bought food and gave it to the innkeeper to cook. Some of this food, but not necessarily all of it, would be on sale at the inn. Some said that women innkeepers mixed drugs with the cheese they supplied to guests, to change them temporarily into beasts of burden (Augustine, *City of God* 18.18). Some said that innkeepers killed their guests and served their flesh as pork (see CANNIBALISM).

Diocles of Carystus *RV*; Horace, *Satires* 1.5; Plutarch *EC* 995b–c; Oribasius *CM* 5.33 quoting Dieuches; *Apicius* 1.1.2; Anthimus *OC* preface.

A. Hug, 'Pandokeîon' in *RE* 1893–1972; W.C. Firebaugh, *The Inns of Greece and Rome, and a History of Hospitality from the Dawn of Time to the Middle Ages* (Chicago, 1928); T. Kleberg, *Hôtels, restaurants et cabarets dans l'antiquité romaine* (Uppsala, 1957); E. Kislinger, 'Kaiser Julian und die (christlichen) Xenodocheia' in *Byzantios. Festschrift für Herbert Hunger zum 70. Geburtstag* ed. W. Hörandner and others (Vienna: Ernst Becvar, 1984) pp. 171–84; V. Nutton, 'Galen and the traveller's fare' in *Food in Antiquity* ed. John Wilkins and others (Exeter: Exeter University Press, 1995) pp. 359–70.

Triclinium, the classic three-couch arrangement in Roman dining of the late Republic and early Empire. *Triclinium* is also the name for a room set aside for dining on this pattern, but a permanent *triclinium* might equally be set up in a domestic garden (see OPEN-AIR DINING) with solid, sloping stone couches. Both indoors and outdoors care was taken that the surroundings of the *triclinium* and the view from it should be as attractive as possible.

The three couches were arranged in a U shape. Each was intended for three diners. Each couch and each place had its name. The guest of honour was customarily placed *imus in medio* and the host customarily took the adjacent place *summus in imo*, an ideal location to converse with the guest of honour and to ensure that he is well provided with food and wine. We know this, paradoxically, because, in two of the most informative narratives, those of Horace and Petronius, the host takes a different place, demonstrating that custom could be set aside.

At his fictional dinner, Nasidienus (Horace, *Satires* 2.8) wants a tame gastronome to tell the guest of honour all about the food: this expert is therefore placed *summus in imo* and Nasidienus relegates himself to the ineffective place *medius in imo*. At his fictional dinner, Trimalchio (Petronius, *Satyricon* 31) takes the commanding position *summus in summo*.

The guest of honour's *umbrae* or 'shadows' lie directly behind him (as shadows do, especially if the lamp is placed in the corner between the host and the guest of honour).

Those to your left are always 'above' you; those to your right are always 'below' you. At large banquets the emperor Caligula liked to place his wife above him and his three sisters below him (according to Suetonius, *Caligula* 24). If he took the place *summus in imo*, as seems likely, his sisters were crowded cosily beside him; his wife observed their

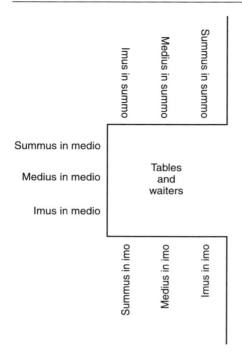

Figure 16 The nine reclining places at dinner in a classical *triclinium*. Each place has its advantages and disadvantages. The logic of the names becomes clearer if one realises that the diner who reclines *summus in summo* 'highest on the highest couch' looks at everybody – nobody looks at him. The diner who reclines *imus in imo* 'lowest on the lowest couch' is looked at by everybody – he looks at nobody.

behaviour from the strategic position *imus in medio*.

The word *triclinium* is of Greek origin (*triklin(i)on* 'three-couch room') but the pattern described was never typically Greek. The word continued to be used for a dining room even when, under the later Empire, the three-couch arrangement ceased to be fashionable, replaced by a

dais or *stibadium* on which diners reclined in a semicircle.

Horace, *Satires* 2.8; Petronius *S* 31.

I. Lavin, 'The house of the lord: aspects of the role of palace triclinia in the architecture of late antiquity and the early middle ages' in *Art Bulletin* vol. 44 (1962) pp. 1–27; D. Hemsoll, 'Reconstructing the octagonal dining room of Nero's Golden House' in *Architectural History* vol. 32 (1989) pp. 1–17; Roger Ling, 'The decoration of Roman triclinia' in *In Vino Veritas* ed. Oswyn Murray and Manuela Tecuşan (London: British School at Rome, 1995) pp. 239–51; E.S.P. Ricotti, 'Forme speciali di triclini' in *Cronache pompeiane* vol. 5 (1979) pp. 104–30; Katherine M.D. Dunbabin, 'Triclinium and stibadium' in *Dining in a Classical Context* ed. W.J. Slater (Ann Arbor: University of Michigan Press, 1991) pp. 121–48.

Trifoline wine (Latin *Trifolinum*; Greek *Triphylinos*, *Tripholinos*), from Campania. Trifoline was newly celebrated in Pliny's time; it held the seventh place among Italian wines according to Martial. It was more 'earthy' than Surrentine and was likewise slow to mature.

Pliny *NH* 14.69; Martial 13.114; Juvenal 9.56; Caelius Aurelianus, *Acute Diseases* 2.37, 2.212; Galen *ST* 6.334, *DA* 14.19; Athenaeus *E* 26e; *CIL* 4.5518.

Trigger-fish, sea fish of unusual ellipsoidal shape, good to eat when skinned and well prepared. The trigger-fish or file-fish (*Balistes Capriscus*) is possibly to be identified with Greek *hys* (meaning literally 'pig') and *kapriskos* (meaning 'little boar'), Latin *sus*. The *hys* is said by Archestratus to be good at Aenus and in the Pontus.

Ovid, *Halieutica* 131; Athenaeus *D* 326e–327a quoting Archestratus *H* 22 Brandt (see Olson and Sens *ad l.*) and Numenius *H* 575, also 305d quoting Aristotle fragment 294 Rose (*kapros*).

Andrews 1948.

• Archestratus gives this fish the alternative name or epithet of *psammitis oryktes* 'burrower in sand', for which compare Aristotle's report of an unidentified fish that does exactly that. Athenaeus links the *hys* with the equally unidentified *psamathis* mentioned by Numenius.

Aristotle, *On Marvellous Things Heard* 835b15–23.

Tripe, an animal's stomach – and especially a pig's stomach – considered as food. Tripe requires long boiling (enough to remove all of its native flavour, some would say) after which treatment it is of unusual but palatable texture and is good to eat. Tripe is Greek *enystron* and *takon*. A more general Greek word, *koilia* 'intestines' perhaps, as Frost suggests, covered tripe as well as chitterlings when used as the name of a food. For stomach and intestine considered not as substantive foods but as casings for meat see SAUSAGE.

Aristophanes, *Knights* 143–222, al.; Pollux O 6.53; Anthimus OC 17, 20 with Grant *ad l.*

Frank Frost, 'Sausage and meat preservation in antiquity' in *Greek, Roman and Byzantine Studies* vol. 40 (1999) pp. 241–52.

Trout, fish of northern European waters. The trout is never mentioned by classical Greek authors, but surfaces under various names in later Latin texts from the western Empire. Ausonius describes the trout of the Moselle in a line of verse, and addresses the salmon trout as 'intermediate between salmon and trout'. Anthimus recommends both the full-grown salmon trout and its young (*trucanti*, a Celtic word), the latter either baked or fried.

The trout (*Salmo Fario*) is Latin *salar*; the brown trout or salmon trout (*Salmo Trutta*) is Latin *fario* and later *tructa*.

Ausonius, *Mosella* 88, 128–30; Anthimus OC 39 with Grant *ad l.*, 44; Isidore of Seville, *Origins* 12.6 (on which see Thompson 1947 p. 73).

A.C. Andrews, 'Greek and Latin terms for salmon and trout' in *Transactions and Proceedings of the American Philological Association* vol. 86 (1955) pp. 308–18.

Truffle, edible fungus growing underground on the roots of oak trees. Edible is an understatement: truffle-hunters expend great efforts on finding them and gastronomes pay very high prices for them.

It was thought by some in classical Greece that truffles resulted from thunderbolts; Theophrastus (if the quotation by Athenaeus is really from his work) took the idea seriously, while Plutarch's symposiasts discuss it sceptically. Greeks ate them both raw and cooked, and in the same quotation Theophrastus lists the districts in Greece where they were most often found. Among Romans there were truffle enthusiasts: six recipes are given in *Apicius*. Pliny tells the story of the praetorian Licinius Lartius who, serving in Spain, bit into a truffle and twisted his teeth on a denarius inside it.

The truffle (*Tuber melanosporum*) is Greek *hydnon*, Latin *tuber*. The variant form *tufera*, used by Anthimus, is of interest as the direct ancestor of French *truffe*, whence English *truffle*.

Theophrastus *HP* 1.6.5, 1.6.9; Dioscorides *MM* 2.145; Pliny *NH* 19.33–7; Plutarch *QC* 4.2; Galen *AF* 6.655, *SF* 12.147; Athenaeus *E* 62a–d citing Theophrastus fragment 167 Wimmer; *Apicius* 7.14.1–6; Anthimus OC 38 with Grant *ad l.*

Anne Helttula, 'Truffles in ancient Greece and Rome' in *Arctos* vol. 30 (1996) pp. 33–47.

Trumpet-shell *see* WHELK

Tunny and bonito, group of large, fierce, migratory fish. Fish of the tunny group provide excellent, firm meat and were important in the ancient as in the modern Mediterranean diet.

Because of their patterns of migration tunny and bonito can be caught in large numbers, quite predictably, at certain times of year. The value of the potential catch makes elaborate preparations worthwhile. Hence, along certain coasts such as the west coast of Italy, watchtowers (*thynnoskopeia*) were built to give warning of the approach of the migratory shoal, and strong nets were built out into the sea to channel and trap the fish. Their strength and desperation is such that the conclusion of the 'hunt', *thera*, when the fish were speared with tridents, was and is a bloody business. It is described by Manilius, Aelian, Philostratus and Oppian.

Aristotle, Dorion, Hicesius and Strabo (quoted here) speak in some detail of the migration of bonito and tunny.

> The *pelamydes* originate in the marshes of Maeotis [Sea of Azov]. Getting a little bigger, they escape through its mouth [the Straits of Kerch] in shoals, and are swept along the Asian coast to Trapezus and Pharnacia. That is where the hunting of them begins, though it is not a major activity, because they have not yet reached full size. As they pass Sinope they are riper [*horaiotera*] for catching and for salting. When they have reached the Cyaneae and entered the strait, a certain white rock on the Calchedonian side so frightens them that they cross to the opposite side, and there the current takes them: and the geography at that point is such as to steer the current towards Byzantium and its Horn, and so they are naturally

driven there, providing the Byzantians and the Roman people with a considerable income.

It is difficult – and was even more difficult in ancient times, when no human could travel as fast as the tunny – to determine how far any particular shoal might migrate. Aristotle believed in a single long migration in which the fish travelled from the Black Sea to the Atlantic and back. This view is no longer held; however, ancient observations and deductions regarding shorter migrations, through the Black Sea and Bosporus, or through the Straits of Gibraltar, are in general accurate.

The various species in the tunny and bonito group are not always distinguished in everyday language, since what is important to fishermen and cooks is not the species but the size, which depends chiefly on the age of the fish. In general, classical Greek texts have most to say about the bonito, mainstay of the fishery of Byzantium, where excellent salted bonito (*tarikhos horaion*) was prepared; later, more is heard about the tunnies of the western Mediterranean and the Atlantic, and

Figure 17 Tunnies, Greek *pelamys*, *thynnos*, Latin *tunnus*. Top left: bonito (*Sarda Sarda*), Greek *pelamys*, *amia*. Top right: albacore or longfin tuna (*Thunnus Alalonga*), Greek *aulopias*, *thynnis*. Bottom: tunny or bluefin tuna (*Thunnus Thynnus*), Greek *thynnos*, *orkynos*.

about the fine salted tunny that was prepared at Gades (Cadiz) and was exported to Italy and Greece. Sicily and Tarentum were also sources of salted tunny or bonito. At Antipolis (Antibes), according to Martial, *muria* or fish brine was made from tunnies, and it was good (see GARUM).

Indeed, without full knowledge of the migrations, ancient observers simply had insufficient information to distinguish between differences of species and differences of age. According to Sostratus, whose views agree to some extent with several other authors, there was essentially one species (his generic term for it is *pelamys*) of which *thynnis* is the smallest form, *thynnos* the next, *orkynos* next, *ketos* the biggest of all. Pliny makes the sequence even more complicated, inserting *pelamys* and *apolectus* as additional growth stages.

Thynneion is the general term for the meat of these fish. Because of the migration pattern, few Greeks or Romans tasted it fresh, unless they were at the right place at the right time. The fresh meat of the larger specimens is in fact hard to eat – as Galen rightly says – unless prepared in the right way; perhaps with the sauce called MYTTOTOS, as we are told by the early Greek poets Hipponax and Ananius; perhaps following Archestratus's recipe for *amia*, quoted below; perhaps preferring the head, as suggested by Alexis and (obscurely as always) Lycophron. The best bit of tunny or bonito, sufficiently juicy or oily to be extremely palatable, was the 'underbelly' cut, *hypogastrion*, known to Romans as *abdomen* and similarly in modern Italian as *ventresco*. There was also the tail cut, *ouraion*, and the shoulder, *aukhen* and perhaps *kleidion*, Latin *cervix*, a speciality of Gades, but drier and not so digestible. From the biggest tunnies came the oily meat, disliked by Aristotle and Martial, that was conserved under the name *melandrya*.

Hipponax 26 West; Ananius 5 West; Herodotus 1.62; Aristotle *HA* 537a19–23 with Thompson *ad l.*, also 543b2–6, also 571a7–22, also 607b28; Lycophron, *Alexandra* 381–3; Lucilius 49–50 Marx; Strabo 7.6.2; Pliny *NH* 9.44–9; Xenocrates *T* 20; Manilius, *Astronomica* 4.657–93; Martial 3.77, 13.103; Aelian, *Nature of Animals* 15.5–6; Philostratus, *Pictures* 1.13; Oppian *H* 3.620–48; Athenaeus *D* 116a–120b quoting Archestratus *H* 38 Brandt and Euthydemus of Athens, also 301e–304b quoting Archestratus *H* 34 and 37 Brandt (see Olson and Sens *ad ll.*), Alexis *F* 159 Kassel (see Arnott *ad l.*) and Sostratus, also 315c–e quoting Dorion and Hicesius, also 356f–357a quoting Diphilus of Siphnos.

Thompson 1947 pp. 79–90, 197–99, *al.*; J. Dumont, 'La pêche du thon à Byzance à l'époque hellénistique' in *Revue des études anciennes* vol. 78/9 (1976/7) pp. 96–119; Davidson 1981 p. 123; B.A. Sparkes, 'A pretty kettle of fish' in *Food in Antiquity* ed. John Wilkins and others (Exeter: Exeter University Press, 1995) pp. 150–61; Grant 1999 pp. 130–1.

- Greek *amia* was a full-grown bonito (*Sarda Sarda*). This is the commonest of the species that migrate from the Black Sea to the Aegean in autumn and back in spring, though it is also found elsewhere and is now called, in full, Atlantic bonito. It was at its best in autumn, while en route; it was to be bought at Byzantium and along the Hellespont, Archestratus advises. He also provides a recipe:

  > Use fig leaves and season with oregano, but not very much of it, no cheese, no nonsense: just do it up nicely in fig leaves fastened above with string, then hide it under hot ashes, keeping a watch on the time when it will be baked, and don't overcook it.

  A modern version of this recipe is suggested by Grant. An alternative method for smaller fish, to split them down the middle and grill them, is outlined in a fragment by Epicharmus, a description of the good life in the mythical land of the Sirens.

  Aristotle *HA* 571a22, *al.*; Matron *AD* 61–2 [Athenaeus *D* 135f] (*amias*); *Acraephia Price List*; Juvenal 4.41–4; Athenaeus *D* 276f–278e quoting Archestratus *H* 35 Brandt and Epicharmus 124 Kaibel.

  Thompson 1947 p. 13; Grant 1999 pp. 130–1.

- Greek *aulopias* may have been, as suggested by Thompson following Cuvier, a smaller tunny such as the albacore (*Thunnus Alalunga*). Caught off the Lipari islands, it was a fish well worth eating. Buy the head, said Archestratus, in summer, and serve with a sauce; roast the belly meat on a spit. The forms *allopies* and *aulopos* also occur, but none was in current use in later Greek. The *anthias* (see BARBIER) is identified with the *aulopias* by Aristotle and Oppian.

Archestratus *H* 33 Brandt with Olson and Sens *ad l.*; Aristotle *HA* 570b20; Numenius *H* 579 [Athenaeus *D* 326a] (*allopies*); Acraephia Price List; Aelian, *Nature of Animals* 13.17; Oppian *H* 1.255–7 (*aulopos*).

Thompson 1947 p. 20 with references; Davidson 1981 p. 128.

- The salted tunny from Gades, already known to Antiphanes, emerges into the fuller light of history in the writings of Aristotle, in whose time the business was operated 'by the Phoenicians' and the barrels of salted tunny were exported to Carthage. Hicesius, not long afterwards, commends the *Gadeirikon*, the tunny of Gades, with particular praise for the dietary qualities of the shoulders or *kleidia* 'keys'. Galen says that the 'Spanish' supply of salted tunny is second only in quality to the Byzantian. For the products of the Saxitan or Exitan salteries in southeastern Spain see MACKEREL.

Aristotle, *On Marvellous Things Heard* 844a24–34; Galen *AF* 6.728; Athenaeus *D* 116a–120b quoting Euthydemus of Athens, Antiphanes and Nicostratus, also 315c–e quoting Hicesius.

- Greek *horaion* means 'ripe, at its peak'. This – in full *tarikhos horaion*, ripe salt fish – was the name for the finest salted bonito, produced at Byzantium from the one-year-old fish (*pelamys*) caught in autumn in the course of its migration from the Black Sea to the Aegean, when, as Strabo explains in the quotation above, the shoals were naturally steered into the Golden Horn and there easily caught. Slices of *horaion* might sometimes be the most expensive and the most honoured item at a classical Greek dinner, to judge from the literary menus. *Horaion* is evidently the ancestor of the product now called *lakerda*, which is bonito, caught at Istanbul or in the Aegean, cut in slices and salted in barrels. Other ancient forms of salted bonito, apparently also originating at Byzantium, are *omotarikhos*, *kybion*, the latter with a sour flavour; there were many others, less frequently mentioned.

Xenocrates *T* 142; Pliny *NH* 32.146; Athenaeus *D* 116a–120b quoting Archestratus *H* 38 Brandt and Euthydemus of Athens.

Thompson 1947 pp. 89, 134 with references.

- Greek *orkynos* was the mature tunny (*Thunnus Thynnus*). Sostratus (summarised above) gives a list of size names of which *orkynos* and *ketos* are the two largest (but *ketos* is a general term meaning 'monstrous sea creature'); Archestratus advises his audience to buy this fish in Samos and asserts that it was called *orkys* at Samos and *ketos* elsewhere. Dorion traces its migration from 'beyond the Pillars of Heracles', that is, from the Atlantic, into the Mediterranean as far as the west coast of Italy. For the salted tunny of Gades, which belonged to this species, see *Gadeirikon* above.

Aristotle *HA* 543b5 (*orkys*); Xenocrates *T* 20 (*orkyinos*); Athenaeus *D* 301e–304b quoting Archestratus *H* 34 Brandt and Sostratus, also 315c–e quoting Dorion.

Thompson 1947 p. 185; Davidson 1981 p. 127.

- Greek *pelamys* is sometimes used (as by Sostratus, summarised above) as a general term for the tunnies and bonitos. When it has a specific meaning, as it usually has, it means a one-year-old bonito (*Sarda Sarda*). 'Here the immigrant *pelamys* spends the winter,' wrote Sophocles in a lost play set somewhere in the north Aegean, 'our Hellespontine visitor, the Bosporans' midsummer luxury.' Aristotle reports, but does not accept, the view of 'the fishermen' that a *pelamys* was a tunny one year younger than a *thynnus*. By the better-informed authors *pelamys* is described as the best or most nourishing food of all this group – and by this they mean that *pelamys* was the fish that was salted at Byzantium to make the famous *horaion*. For the *pelamys* and smaller fish salted in Sardinia, or in sardine style, see SARDINIA.

Aristotle *HA* 571a10–18, *al.*; Strabo 7.6.2 (quoted above); Oppian *H* 4.503–92; Xenocrates *T* 20; Galen *AF* 6.728–9, 6.769; Athenaeus 319b quoting Sophocles fragment 503 Radt.

- Greek *skordyle*, regional Greek *auxis*, and Latin *cordyla* were names for the young bonitos in the Black Sea, at the beginning of their migration, and sometimes caught and salted (and called *tarikhe kordyleia*) at this stage. They were also the names for a fish of the tunny kind, large enough to be eaten in steaks, and larger than a mere mackerel. This was perhaps *Auxis Rochei*, the bullet mackerel or frigate mackerel.

Aristotle *HA* 571a17; Diphilus of Siphnos [Athenaeus *D* 120e] (*tarikhe kordyleia*); Strabo 12.3.19; Pliny *NH* 32.146; Martial 3.2, 11.52, 13.1; *Apicius* 9.10.5 (*cordula*).

Thompson 1947 p. 245; Davidson 1981 p. 130.

- Greek *thynnis* is Archestratus's name for a tunny 'whose mother-city is Byzantium', and of which he recommends a tail cut. Aristotle and others treat *thynnis* as the name for a one-year-old tunny (*Thunnus Thynnus*).

Archestratus *H* 37 Brandt; Aristotle *HA* 571a10, *al.*; *Acraephia Price List*; Xenocrates *T* 20.

- Greek *thynnos* is the most general term of all of these; references are given at the end of the main article above. It may also be a scientist's name for the tunny (*Thunnus Thynnus*) of whatever age; this is Aristotle's and Galen's usage. When *thynnos* is given its most specific meaning, it means a two-year-old tunny; whether this was the *thynnos* that Hipponax imagined being eaten by a eunuch at Lampsacus will remain uncertain. The largest tunnies are *thynnokeitos* 'monster tunny' in the *Acraephia Price List*. The *thynnos*, says Archestratus, was best bought at Cephaloedium in Sicily and at Hipponium in south Italy. Pollux, some centuries later, had heard that the *thynnos* of Tyre was the best. This is an interesting opinion because *thynnos* is believed to be a loanword from a Semitic language.

Hipponax 26 West; Archestratus *H* 34 Brandt; Aristotle *HA* 571a10–18, *al.*; *Acraephia Price List*; Xenocrates *T* 20; Galen *AF* 6.769; Pollux *O* 6.63.

Turmeric, south Asian spice and dye from the ground root of *Curcuma domestica*, unknown or little known in the ancient Mediterranean. Turmeric has been identified with Akkadian *kurkanû* (very unlikely), Greek *khroma* (Theophrastus, *On Odours* 33: possible but unverifiable), Latin *cancamum* (impossible: see under MYRRH) and Latin *cypira*, which Pliny describes as an Indian plant with the shape of ginger and the effect, when chewed, of saffron. This is true, in a sense, of turmeric (Pliny *NH* 21.117, cf. Dioscorides *MM* 1.5).

Turnip, root vegetable. In modern Europe the turnip has, one may say, lost ground to the potato; in the ancient world it was an important food item. 'Its usefulness surpasses that of any other plant,' says Pliny enthusiastically; 'it serves as fodder for all animals,' yet (like most other vegetables) it was not a food of which humans boasted. When fresh it needs to be prepared by boiling; it is most likely, perhaps, to be an ingredient in stews with meat or ham, as suggested, for example, by Anthimus. Its pure white colour was a temptation to Roman cooks, who (according to Pliny again) stained it in six different colours: the only correct colour, Pliny adds, was purple. Nicander gives instructions for conserving turnip, as do Columella and Palladius (see the modern interpretation of Columella's recipe by Grant 1999 pp. 75–6).

The turnip (*Brassica campestris*) and similar roots are Greek *gongylis*, *bounias*, *raphys*. The Latin word for turnip is *rapa*, *rapum*. Latin *napus* is the name for rape or colza (*B. Napus*).

Aristophanes fragment 581 Kassel; Hippocrates *R* 54; Theophrastus *HP* 7.2.5; Dioscorides *MM* 2.110; Columella *DA* 12.57; Pliny *NH* 18.125–32, 19.75–7, 20.18–21; Athenaeus *D* 369a–e and 133d quoting Nicander *F* 70 Schneider; Palladius *OA* 8.2, 13.5; Anthimus *OC* 52 with Grant *ad l.*

A.C. Andrews, 'The turnip as food in the classical era' in *Classical Philology* vol. 53 (1958) pp. 131–52; André 1981 pp. 15–16; Zohary and Hopf 1993 p. 132.

- A method of cooking or presenting meat, coating it with grated turnip, was called *rapatum* or *rapulatum* or *ex rapis* in Latin, translated into Greek by Pollux as *gongyloton*. Apicius suggests one recipe of this type, for crane or goose.

Pollux *KH* 83; *Apicius* 6.2.3; Vinidarius *BC* 7.

Turnsole, a blue dye plant native to the Maghreb. It was employed medicinally and in colouring foods and drinks.

Turnsole (*Chrozophora tinctoria*) is Latin *heliotropium* (*tricoccum*).

Pliny *NH* 22.57–61; Fronto, *Letters* vol. 2 pp. 28–30 Haines.

Tuscan wine (Greek *Thouskos*), one of the secondary wines of Italy. Some Tuscan was light enough to be drunk young, according to Galen. Galen also recommends (to older men with strong heads) an AMINNIAN WINE from Etruria.

Martial 13.118; Galen *ST* 6.335, *BM* 6.806; Athenaeus *D* 702b quoting Sopater 196 Kaibel.

• Pliny lists *Latiniense*, *Graviscanum*, *Statoniense* among Tuscan wines, and gives first place to those from Luna. For vineyards in the neighbourhood of Rome see under ROMAN WINES.

Pliny *NH* 14.67–8.

Tutankhamun, Egyptian monarch (died 1327 BC) whose tomb is of special interest in food history. A great variety of foods was buried beside his mummified body. Jars of fine wine from several named locations in Egypt, dated with vintage years, were also present.

L.H. Lesko, *King Tut's Wine Cellar* (Berkeley, 1977); R. Germer, *Die Pflanzenmaterialien aus dem Grab des Tutanchamun* (Hildesheim: Gerstenberg, 1989); Hepper 1990.

U

Udder (Greek *outhar*; Latin *sumen*), usually sow's udder, a luxury food in ancient cuisine; served, for example, at the dinner of the high priests hosted by CAESAR (see quotation there). See WOMB for the cruel practice described by Plutarch by which udder and womb were obtained in their best gastronomic condition.

Philodemus 23 Gow [*Anthologia Palatina* 11.44] with Gow *ad l.*; Plutarch *EC* 997a, *Precepts on Health* 124f; Galen *AF* 6.673–5; Athenaeus *D* 399c; Alciphron 3.37.1; Macrobius *S* 3.13.12 citing Metellus Pius; Anthimus

OC 19 with Grant *ad loc.*

Umami *see* GARUM

Urd or green gram (*Vigna Mungo*), encountered and used by Alexander's troops in their march through India. Theophrastus describes it briefly as a 'lentil'.

Theophrastus *HP* 4.4.9–10.

Utensils *see* COOKING UTENSILS; DINING AND DRINKING UTENSILS

V

Varro, M(arcus) Terentius, Roman writer and polymath (116–27 BC). Varro took some part in politics, taking the side of Pompey against Caesar. Nonetheless he was eventually commissioned by Caesar to gather and arrange Greek and Latin books to form a public library. Varro himself wrote on many subjects, in prose and verse, but little of his work survives complete. The text that is important in the present context is *Farming*, a readable introduction to the subject, written at the age of 80 and dedicated to Varro's wife Fundania, who is said to have just inherited a farm. *Farming* takes the form of a fictional dialogue in which both real Roman landowners and some imaginary characters take part. In spite of its dialogue format Varro's *Farming* is much more systematic than Cato's earlier *On Agriculture*, and was a major source for Columella's even more comprehensive work *On Agriculture*. It is particularly informative on the keeping of wild mammals, birds and fish and the fattening of animals for the table.

Quintilian, *Education in Rhetoric* 10.1.95; Suetonius, *Julius* 44.

K.D. White, 'Roman agricultural writers I' in *Aufstieg und Niedergang der römischen Welt* ed. H. Temporini, part 1 vol. 4 (Berlin: De Gruyter, 1973).

Varro RR: *Res Rusticae* 'Farming'. Text, German translation and commentary: Marcus Terentius Varro, *Gespräche über die Land-wirtschaft* ed. Dieter Flach (Darmstadt: Wissenschäftliche Buchgesellschaft, 1996–2002), 3 vols. Text and English translation in *Marcus Porcius Cato On Agriculture; Marcus Terentius Varro On Agriculture* ed. and tr. William Davis Hooper and Harrison Boyd Ash (1934, LCL) pp. 160–529.

Vases *see* DINING AND DRINKING UTENSILS

Vegetables, less commonly mentioned in literature than meat, fish, bread and wine as constituents of the ancient diet. Among ordinary people, nonetheless, vegetables were surely more frequently consumed than meat or fish. Many species were cultivated by classical times and were grown in gardens. Those gathered as WILD FOODS were probably also significant in the diet. Vegetables counted as an *opson* 'relish' in Greek MEALS; they were taken alongside bread, no doubt helped by olive oil. They were also constituents of stews. *Apicius* includes a whole book of recipes for preparing vegetables as the main constituents of a dish, most of them probably to serve as side dishes rather than as a main course.

The general terms are Greek *lakhanon* (cf. *lakhaino* 'dig'), Latin *holus*.

Theophrastus *HP* 1.6.6, 7.7.1–2, *al.*; Galen *AF* 6.624–59; *Apicius* book 3.

Buck 1949 pp. 369–70.

Vegetarianism, the conscious exclusion of animal foods from one's diet. Even the poorest are likely to have eaten animal foods occasionally; no one (since the GOLDEN AGE, or in Christian terms since the Flood) will have been vegetarian by default. Why, then, was vegetarianism chosen? Not generally for physical health; in very few cases do dieticians recommend a vegetarian diet. Not generally for taste; no writer hints at a simple preference for vegetable foods or a simple dislike of animal ones. Three groups of arguments remain.

One focuses on the eater, who will (it was widely thought) be duller, more brutal, less civilised, less spiritual and more libidinous as a result of eating meat. A second focuses on the act of slaughter (and, in classical terms, of sacrifice) which was argued by some to be cruel, not pleasing to the gods (contrary to the common assumption) and unnecessary to humans; it was, after all, noted by dietary authors that a vegetarian diet did no harm. A third, identified with PYTHAGORAS, focuses on the souls of animals, which may have been, and may be in the future, the souls of human beings.

'Socrates', in sketching a diet for Plato's utopian Republic, makes it vegetarian; he does not say clearly why (Strabo takes it that it is because meat is unnecessary). However, in 'Socrates' and later in Clement of Alexandria there is a suggestion that reducing meat reduces the sex drive. Diogenes, philosopher of the CYNICS, recommended vegetarianism for this reason, says Strabo; so, much later, did some Christian thinkers.

Explicit arguments for vegetarianism are made by Plutarch (in what appears to be a youthful, unfinished work); by the Neoplatonist philosopher Porphyry; and by the early Christian authors Clement of Alexandria and Tertullian.

There is very little discussion in any ancient source of the practical difficulties in observing vegetarianism scrupulously. Two points will have caused difficulty. CHEESE was most often made with animal rennet; various vegetarian rennets were available but nothing suggests that the buyer of cheese could normally find out which rennet had been used. GARUM, the usual way to add salt in ancient cooking, was made from fish: a *liquamen ex piris*, made from pears instead of fish, is specifically recommended to vegetarians by Palladius (3.25.12) but wherever one dined out most dishes would probably incorporate *garum*. A practical difficulty of a different kind was caused to some by the fact that vegetarianism, like ASCETICISM, was associated in the popular mind with strange Eastern cults. Seneca, in his youth, became a vegetarian for philosophical reasons, but abandoned the practice at his father's request, because it was unsafe in Rome under the early Empire to be conspicuously identified with such cults.

Plato, *Republic* 372c; Archestratus *H* 23 Brandt with Olson and Sens *ad l.*; *Daniel* 1.8–18; Strabo 15.1.65; Seneca, *Letters* 108.22; Plutarch *EC*; Clement of Alexandria, *Stromateis* 7.6, *Paidagogos* 2.1.15; Tertullian *On Fasting* 4; Heliodorus, *Ethiopian Story* 2.22–3, 3.11; Porphyry *DA*.

S.H. Lonsdale, 'Attitudes towards animals in ancient Greece' in *Greece and Rome* vol. 26 (1979) pp. 146–59; Liliane Bodson, 'Quelques critères antiques du choix et de l'exclusion de l'animal dans l'alimentation humaine' in *L'Animal dans l'alimentation humaine: les critères de choix: actes du colloque international de Liège 26–29 nov. 1986* ed. Liliane Bodson (Liège, 1988) pp. 229–34; Catherine Osborne, 'Boundaries in nature; eating with animals in the fifth century B.C.' in *Bulletin of the Institute of Classical Studies* vol. 37 (1990) pp. 15–29; Colin Spencer, *The Heretic's Feast: a history of vegetarianism* (London: Fourth Estate, 1993), reprinted as *Vegetarianism: a history* (London: Grub Street, 2000); Catherine Osborne, 'Ancient vegetarianism' in *Food in Antiquity* ed. John Wilkins and others (Exeter: Exeter University Press, 1995) pp. 214–24; *OCD* 1996 *s.v.* Animals, Attitudes to; Grimm 1996 pp. 58–9, 103–4, 167–8, *al.*; Grant 1999 pp. 19–23; Garnsey 1999 pp. 85–91.

Venafrum, modern Venafro, central Italian town where CATO farmed. Venafrum was renowned in literature for its olive oil, the best in Italy. Its wine (Greek *Benefranos*) was easy drinking and easy on the stomach, according to the *Epitome of Athenaeus*.

Varro *RR* 1.2.6; Horace *Odes* 2.6, *Satires* 2.4; Pliny *NH* 15.7; Martial 12.63; Juvenal 5.86; Athenaeus *E* 27c.

Venus clam, group of shellfish species. The venus clams are collectively named *kheme* in Greek. Several species were distinguished by name, and there were others, not separately named in Greek but very good, around the island of Pharos at Alexandria.

Xenocrates *T* 52–5, 122–9; Pliny *NH* 32.147 (*chema*); Aelian, *Nature of Animals* 15.12; Athenaeus 92f.

Thompson 1947 pp. 49, 194, 288.

- Greek *glykymaris* was an alternative name for *kheme trakheia* (see below), but it was also a distinct kind. There were good ones in the lagoon at Alexandria. Linnaeus's identification for this was the dog-cockle (*Glycymeris Glycymeris*); there is insufficient evidence to allow a confident identification.

  Xenocrates *T* 52–3, 128–9; Pliny *NH* 32.147 (*glycymeris*); Galen, *On Compounding* 13.174 citing Archigenes [*s.v.l.*]; Macrobius *S* 3.13.12 quoting Metellus Pius (*glycomaris*).

- Greek (*kheme*) *leia*, literally 'smooth clam', was surely the smooth venus (*Callista Chione*). It was good at Ephesus, according to Archestratus; sweet, digestible and nourishing, according to Xenocrates. You ate it with silphium and mustard.

  Archestratus *H* 56 Brandt; Xenocrates *T* 126–7.

- Greek *kheme trakheia*, literally 'rough clam', had a rough shell like that of an acorn. They tasted of the sea; their tough but nutritious flesh made them good eating for delicate constitutions. Thompson suggests an identification with the warty venus (*Venus verrucosa*).

  Xenocrates *T* 122–5; Athenaeus 87f citing Hicesius.

- Greek *peloris, pelorias* was said to be named after Cape Pelorus, north of Messana in Sicily; Archestratus says that they were good there. One might identify them with the typical *vongola* of Italy, *palourde* of France (*Tapes decussatus*).

Archestratus *H* 56 Brandt with Olson and Sens *ad l.*; Martial 10.37; Pollux *O* 6.63 (quoted at LOCAL SPECIALITIES); Macrobius *S* 3.13.12.

- Romans liked the *Lucrina peloris*, the specimens that were farmed, or at any rate encouraged, in the Lucrine lake near Puteoli; these were sweet and productive of good humours, says Xenocrates.

  Horace, *Satires* 2.4.32; Xenocrates *T* 54; Martial 6.11.

- The smaller *aquosa peloris*, served up to a client while the patron gets the *Lucrina peloris*, might be a smaller specimen of the same species; or it might be the clovisse (*Venerupis aurea*), only half the size.

  Martial 6.11.

  Dalby 2000a p. 53.

Vervain, medicinal herb. Its leaves and twigs, Latin *verbena*, were used in purifying and scenting rooms. A decoction of vervain perfumed the floor and couches of a dining room before a party, with the aim of increasing the gaiety of the participants.

Vervain (*Verbena officinalis*) is Greek *aristereon, peristereon, hiera botane*, Latin *verbenaca*.

Dioscorides *MM* 4.59–60; Pliny *NH* 25.105–7, *al.*; Plutarch *QC* 1.1; Pseudo-Apuleius, *Herbarius* 3.

Vetch, legume of the Mediterranean. Not familiar in early Greece, vetch was well known in Roman Italy and the western Mediterranean, but was more used as animal fodder than as human food.

Vetch (*Vicia sativa*) is Latin *vicia*, Greek *bikos*. The botanical genus includes also the species listed below and the broad BEAN or fava bean, *Vicia Faba*.

Cato *DA* 35; Varro *RR* 1.31; Pliny *NH* 18.137–9; Galen *AF* 6.551; *Diocletian's Price Edict* 17.6; Oribasius *CM* 1.34.

F. Kupicha, 'The infrageneric structure of *Vicia*' in *Royal Botanic Garden Edinburgh: notes* vol. 34 (1976) pp. 287–326; John Scarborough, 'The pharmacology of sacred plants, herbs and roots' in *Magika Hiera: ancient Greek magic and religion* (New York: Oxford University

Press, 1991) p. 158; Zohary and Hopf 1993 pp. 110–14.

- Bitter vetch (*V. Ervilia*) is Greek *orobos*, Latin *ervum*. This species is perhaps native to inland Anatolia. It was being gathered there by about 8000 BC and spread in cultivation to the Balkans and Greece in early Neolithic times. It is an even less attractive staple than vetch: it was known to have toxic properties (and was used as what would now be called a disinfectant in the treatment of skin diseases). It is more often used as animal fodder, but in classical Greece it certainly did serve for human food.

Hippocrates *R 45, Epidemics* 2.4.3=6.4.11; Demosthenes, *Against Androtion* 15; Theophrastus *HP* 8.5.1; Dioscorides *MM* 2.108; Pliny *NH* 22.151–3; Plutarch, *Roman and Greek Questions* 302a–b; Galen *AF* 6.546; Oppian, *Halieutica* 3.401; Oribasius *CM* 4.8.7–18.

Jean-Marc Luce, 'De l'ers ou du bonheur chez les boeufs' in *Paysage et alimentation dans le monde grec* ed. Jean-Marc Luce (Toulouse, 2000) pp. 109–14.

- Cow vetch or bird vetch (*V. cracca*) or a similar species was being gathered at Franchthi Cave by 10,000 BC. It was still familiar in classical times, known in Greek as *arakos*, in Latin as *cracca*. It was regarded as very poor food for humans, likely to be used only by the destitute or in times of famine. Soup made from it, *to ek ton arakon etnos*, was also very bad according to Oribasius (above).

Vinalia, festival celebrated in Rome on 23 April on the occasion when new wines were tasted. The *Vinalia Rustica* were celebrated on 19 August.

Varro, *On the Latin Language* 6.16; Ovid, *Fasti* 4.877–900; Pliny *NH* 18.287–9.

Olivier de Cazanove, 'Rituels romains dans les vignobles' in *In Vino Veritas* ed. Oswyn Murray and Manuela Tecuşan (London: British School at Rome, 1995) pp. 214–23.

Vindolanda, Roman fort just south of Hadrian's Wall in Britain. Vindolanda is important as the source of a large collection of Latin letters and documents, written on sheets of alder wood, providing evidence of the daily life of the soldiers and the attached community.

Alan K. Bowman and J. David Thomas, *The Vindolanda Writing-tablets: Tabulae Vindolandenses II* (London: British Museum Press, 1994).

Vine *see* GRAPE

Vinegar, product of a secondary fermentation of wine (or other alcohol). In the ancient Mediterranean vinegar was practically always made from wine, hence the epic epithet *oininon oxos* 'winy vinegar' employed by Archestratus. Although by no means as desirable as fine wine, vinegar has important food uses and has been purposefully made ever since ancient times: instructions are given by Columella.

Vinegar is most often used as a culinary ingredient and as a preservative. Numerous medicinal uses are listed by ancient physicians. A vinegar and water mixture, known in Greek as *oxykraton*, was also used medicinally. A very similar mixture, flavoured with herbs, formed a popular cheap drink (Latin *posca*, Greek *oxos* and later *phouska*): see POSCA.

Vinegar is Greek *oxos*, Latin *acetum*. These terms are often used metaphorically for 'bad wine' in comic contexts, by Eubulus in Greek and by Martial in Latin with reference to the *Vaticanum* that he claims to despise so much. A cool satirist might even use phrases meaning 'noble vinegar', Greek *oxos gnesion* (so Eubulus) and Latin *generosum acetum* (so the emperor Tiberius), for wine that is not so bad.

Eubulus *F* 65, 136 Kassel with Hunter *ad ll.*; Archestratus *H* 23 Brandt; Columella *DA* 12.5; Pliny *NH* 14.64 citing Tiberius, 23.54–8; Martial 10.45; Athenaeus *E* 67c–f.

Buck 1949 p. 383; Tchernia 1986 pp. 11–13.

Vinidarius, unknown compiler of late Roman or early medieval times. To 'the illustrious Vinidarius' is attributed a brief list of kitchen supplies, 'Memo on spices that should be in the house so that no flavourings will be lacking', followed by a collection of thirty-one recipes headed 'Memo on foods'. A phrase in the text has been taken as an overall title: *Apici Excerpta* 'Abridged Apicius'. The compilation is found in an eighth-century manuscript now in Paris. It has nothing to do with the *Apicius* cookery book, but is sometimes edited alongside it.

John Edwards provides modern interpretations of the recipes alongside his translation.

Vinidarius BC: *Brevis Ciborum* 'Memo on Foods'. Critical text in *Apicii decem libri qui dicuntur De re coquinaria* ed. M.E. Milham (Leipzig, 1969, *BT*), pp. 87–94. English translation in John Edwards, *The Roman Cookery of Apicius* (London: Hutchinson, 1985) pp. 291–302.

—— **BP**: *Brevis Pimentorum* 'Memo on Spices'. Critical text and translation as above.

Vintage, the grape harvest and the first step in the manufacture of wine. Ancient winemakers harvested relatively late by comparison with modern practice – resulting in a stronger wine which was more likely to keep. Typically the grapes were gathered in pitched baskets. They were first trodden and then pressed. If a press was lacking – particularly in earlier times and on smaller farms – it was necessary to extract all the available MUST by treading. However, treading remained important even when pressing was to follow: treading breaks up the grapes so that the must will flow more easily. It was typically gathered in a tank, *lacus*, from which it was transferred to a deep fermenting vat or DOLIUM. The interior surface of the vat would have been previously fumigated, sealed and aromatised with pitch or resin. For subsequent processes see WINE-MAKING. For vintage years see WINE STORAGE AND AGEING. Greek vase paintings and Roman reliefs often depict the treading, the pressing and associated festivity.

Varro *RR* 1.54; Pliny *NH* 18.315–16.

Olivier de Cazanove, 'Rituels romains dans les vignobles' in *In Vino Veritas* ed. Oswyn Murray and Manuela Tecuşan (London: British School at Rome, 1995) pp. 214–23.

Vitellius, briefly Roman emperor in AD 69. In his earlier life Vitellius is said to have been the first to plant pistachio trees in Italy; he also brought some new varieties of figs from Syria to his Alban estate after serving as *legatus* in Syria. He used to play dice with the emperor Claudius, from whom, perhaps, he learnt the trick of VOMITING to make room for a further intake of food. His dining habits are described by Suetonius, who focuses on his vast and shameless greed and the enormous distances from which delicacies were brought to him in ships of the Roman navy. They may even have delivered British oysters to his table.

'Even now, some cakes and other dishes are called Vitellian after him,' writes Dio at the end of the second century. Three recipes in *Apicius* are named after Vitellius, whether in honour of a famous gourmet or with the implication that they were invented by or for him. A dish, perhaps rather two dishes invented by Vitellius are actually described. Suetonius writes of the so-called 'Shield of All-Protecting Minerva' which incorporated parrot-wrasse livers, pheasant and peacock brains, flamingoes' tongues and *murenarum lactes* 'milk of moray eels', whatever that may be. Pliny knew of a huge *patina* or quiche, cooked in a specially built oven in the Campus Martius: the reliable Mucianus afterwards called this dish *palus Vitellii*, 'the swamp of Vitellius'. The silver vessel in which some such dish had been cooked for Vitellius was eventually, according to Dio, shown in the imperial kitchen to the emperor Hadrian, who had it melted down.

Pliny *NH* 15.83, 15.91, 35.163–4 citing Mucianus ter consul; Tacitus, *Histories* 2.95; Suetonius, *Vitellius* 4, 13 with Murison *ad l.*, 16; Dio Cassius 64.2.2–64.3.3; *Apicius* 5.3.5, 5.3.9, 8.7.7.

Dalby 2001.

Vomiting was, according to some Roman gluttons in the first century AD, the way to empty the stomach of excess contents to

Figure 18 Satyrs performing the work of the vintage, picking, tasting, gathering, treading and pressing the grapes. They are observed by Dionysus on horseback. Redrawn from an Athenian *kylix* of about 500 BC.

leave room for more. The practice is recorded of the emperors Claudius and Vitellius. Seneca roundly criticises his whole generation for indulging in it: 'They vomit in order to eat, they eat in order to vomit: the whole earth supplies them their meals, and they do not even bother to digest them.'

However, since both Seneca and Vitellius were courtiers of Claudius, the total number of vomiting Roman gluttons may be no more than two. It is true that Nero (Seneca's pupil) also habitually vomited, not out of gluttony but because he was an obsessive weight-watcher.

Seneca, *Consolation to Helvia* 10.3; Suetonius, *Claudius* 33, *Nero* 20, *Vitellius* 13.

W

Walnut, oil-rich nut. The walnut was a rare tree in southern Europe and the eastern Mediterranean in Neolithic times, but was found in the southern Caucasus and in parts of the Balkans. It spread rapidly in human cultivation from soon after 1200 BC (see also POLLEN ANALYSIS).

In classical Greece walnuts grew locally but they, or perhaps a favoured variety, were regarded as 'royal' or 'Persian'. They were among the typical desserts at Greek and Roman dinners. As such, walnuts were present (presumably thrown?) in company with the Fescennine songs that were sung at Roman weddings; in Greece, too, a shower of walnuts and dried figs welcomed home both a new bride and a new slave.

Walnut oil was used medicinally: Dioscorides provides details. The heady and soporific aroma of a walnut tree was regarded as harmful, according to Plutarch.

The walnut (*Juglans regia*) is Greek *karyon* (*basilikon*, *Persikon*), Latin *iuglans*, *nux*.

Batrachomyomachia 31; Theophrastus *HP* 4.5.4, *al.*; Cato *DA* 8 (*nux calva*); Dioscorides *MM* 1.34, 1.125; Pliny *NH* 15.86–91, 23.147–9; Plutarch *QC* 3.1; Athenaeus *E* 52a–54d; Macrobius *S* 3.18.1–4; Palladius *OA* 2.15.14–19.

Laufer 1919 pp. 254–75; Darby and others 1977 pp. 753–4; Zohary and Hopf 1993 pp. 177–8; Patrice Josset and Christine Couzeli, 'Mythes et usages thérapeutiques du noyer' in *Des hommes et des plantes: plantes méditerranéennes, vocabulaire et usages anciennes* ed. M.-C. Amouretti and G. Comet (Aix-en-Provence, 1993) pp. 149–61; S. Bottema, 'The Holocene history of walnut, sweet chestnut, manna-ash and plane tree in the Eastern Mediterranean' in *Paysage et alimentation dans le monde grec* ed. Jean-Marc Luce (Toulouse, 2000) pp. 35–59.

Warbler *see* BECCAFICO

Water is best, said Pindar. Water was a significant article of the ancient diet, used alone, as a mixer in wine (see WINE-MIXING) and as an ingredient in food production and cuisine. In the two former cases it was often boiled before use. Ancient peoples did not understand the nature of microbial contamination of fresh water, but had found by experience that boiled water was safer.

The water supply varied from place to place. Sources including Plutarch, Athenaeus and the Hippocratic text *Airs Waters Places* discuss the supposed properties (some of them highly imaginative) of local drinking waters.

In Greece water was taken from streams, wells and fountains, the latter often outside city walls (since cities were often built on a high elevation). Fetching water, for drinking and other household uses, was a task for women: in the secluded society of classical Greece this was one occasion on which they were seen in public (and might be accosted by strangers). In the Roman Empire a growing number of cities had aqueducts, sometimes bringing water from many miles away. Aqueduct channels were lined with LEAD.

Pindar, *Olympian Odes* 1.1; Hippocrates, *Airs Waters Places* 7–9, *RA* 62–3; Plutarch *QC* 6.3–4, 8.5; Athenaeus *E* 40f–46e, *D* 122e–125a.

- The emperor Nero is said to have invented a system for boiling water, then immediately chilling it in snow. The result was ice-cold water (Latin *decocta*) which was more or less sterilised and therefore safe to mix with wine, but so costly that to add it to any but the finest wine was wasteful.

  Pliny *NH* 31.40; Suetonius, *Nero* 48; Martial 14.116; Juvenal 5.49–50; Athenaeus *D* 121e; Dio Cassius 63.28.5.

  Emily Gowers, 'Persius and the decoction of Nero' in *Reflections of Nero: culture, history and representation* ed. Jas Elsner and Jamie Masters (London, 1994) pp. 131–50; Dalby 2001.

- Water itself served as a refrigerating agent when wine was plunged into deep wells to chill it in preparation for serving. Later, and perhaps in classical times also, fresh fruit was kept and chilled in the same way.

  Athenaeus *D* 124c–d.

Water buffalo, domesticated animal native to southern Asia. Greeks observed the buffalo in Afghanistan at the period of Alexander's expedition. It was introduced to eastern Europe, perhaps by a route north of the Black Sea, in later Roman times. Its meat was like beef, says Anthimus; that of young animals was better boiled or steamed than roasted.

The water buffalo (*Bubalus Bubalis*) is late Greek *boubalos*, Latin *bubalus, bufalus*.

Aristotle *HA* 499a4–8 (*bous ho agrios*); Agathias, *History* 1.4 (*boubalos*); Anthimus *OC* 11 (*bualis [s.v.l.]*); Venantius Fortunatus, *Poems* 7.4.21 (*bufalus*).

Robert Hoffpauir, 'Water buffalo' in *CWHF* 2000 vol. 1 pp. 583–607.

Watercress (Latin *sium*: *Rorippa Nasturtium-aquaticum*) a salad vegetable and medicinal plant growing in running water (Pliny *NH* 22.84). Elsewhere (*NH* 20.247) Pliny describes watercress without naming it as a 'kind of mint growing in watercourses and resembling cress'.

Watermelon, fruit domesticated in prehistoric times in the deserts of northern Africa or southwestern Asia. Watermelons were cultivated in Egypt by 2000 BC and were known in the Aegean region by around 1000 BC: their seeds have been found at sites including KASTANAS. They are not commonly mentioned in classical literature but are familiar from dietary texts. Andrews (below), not yet aware of archaeobotanical finds, was able to show from the texts, against doubts of earlier scholars, that watermelons and melons were familiar in the classical world. Watermelons are to be eaten with vinegar and pennyroyal, according to Anthimus.

The watermelon (*Citrullus lanatus*) is Greek *melopepon*, Latin *melopepo, melo*.

Hippocrates *R* 55, *Epidemics* 5.71, 7.115, *al.*; Pliny *NH* 19.67–8, 20.11–12; Apicius 3.7; Anthimus *OC* 58.

Laufer 1919 pp. 438–45; A.C. Andrews, 'Melons and watermelons in the classical period' in *Osiris* vol. 12 (1956) pp. 368–75; M. Stol, 'The cucurbitaceae in the cuneiform texts' in *Bulletin on Sumerian Agriculture* no. 3 (1987) pp. 57–92; Zohary and Hopf 1993 pp. 181–2; David Maynard and Donald N. Maynard, 'Cucumbers, melons and watermelons' in *CWHF* 2000 vol. 1 pp. 298–313.

Wedding and betrothal feasts, frequently portrayed or hinted at in classical Greek literature. Literary materials include several fragments from Athenian comedy quoted by Athenaeus. The sacrifice depicted in Menander's *Dyscolus* has turned into a betrothal feast by the end of the play (a reminder that comedy plots, and therefore comedy portrayals of social events, are not guaranteed to be realistic). Roman sources give us little information on feasts celebrating weddings and betrothals.

Homer, *Odyssey* 4.1–624; Sappho 44 Lobel; Menander, *Dyscolus* 784–969; Euangelus 1 Kassel; Dio of Prusa, *Orations* 7.65–79; Plutarch *QC* 4.3 citing Hecataeus of Abdera A 5 Diels; Xenophon of Ephesus, *Ephesian Tale* 1.7–9; Athenaeus 128a–130d quoting Hippolochus *D*, also 131a–f quoting Anaxandrides, also 150a, also 245a–c.

N. Robertson, 'The betrothal symposium in early Greece' in *Dining in a Classical Context* ed. W.J. Slater (Ann Arbor: University of Michigan Press, 1991) pp. 25–57.

Wedge-shell, small bivalve shellfish. Wedge-shells are common in the Mediterranean and especially around the mouth of the Nile, where they were and still are popular. They are found at Canobus in large numbers, says Diphilus, especially at the time when the Nile waters are rising.

You could get pickled wedge-shells, according to Galen, who supplies several medicinal uses for the pickled product. Epicharmus had said, long before, that wedge-shells were sweet to eat fresh and sharp when in pickle.

The wedge-shell (*Donax Trunculus*) is Greek *telline* or *xiphydrion*.

Hippocrates *R* 48; Dioscorides *MM* 2.6; Xenocrates *T* 116–21; Galen *SF* 12.362; Athenaeus *D* 85e–86b quoting Epicharmus 42 Kaibel (*skiphydrion*), Aristophanes of Byzantium 367 Slater, and Diphilus of Siphnos.

Thompson 1947 p. 259; Davidson 1981 p. 206.

Weever, small sea fish with a dangerous sting. The fish was familiar in the ancient Mediterranean; it was eaten, though its flesh was coarse, according to the Hippocratic *Regimen* and to Galen. Numerous cures were prescribed for the sting.

The weever (*Trachinus Draco* and other species) is Greek *drakon*, *drakainis*, literally 'snake'; Latin *araneus*, literally 'spider'. The French name *vive* and English *weever* derive from Latin *vipera*, literally 'adder', but this does not occur as a fish name in classical texts.

Epicharmus 60 Kaibel; Hippocrates *R* 48; Pliny *NH* 9.155 (*araneus*), 32.145 (*draco, dracunculus*); Galen *AF* 6.727.

Thompson 1947 p. 56; Davidson 1981 pp. 113–15.

- Greek *kallionymos*, occasionally said to be identical with the *anthias* (see BARBIER) is more often something quite different, and can be tentatively identified with the stargazer (*Uranoscopus scaber*), a small fish distantly related to the weevers but with a distinctive physiognomy and a very large gall bladder. Its eyes point upwards (hence its scientific name).

  Hippocrates *R* 2.48; Aristotle *HA* 506b10, al.; *Acraephia Price List*; Aelian, *Nature of Animals* 13.4 quoting Menander fragment 270 Körte; Athenaeus *D* 282c–e.

  Thompson 1947 p. 98; Davidson 1981 p. 116.

Wet-nursing *see* BABIES

Wheat, in this article, means club wheat, durum wheat and bread wheat (see separate entries for EINKORN; EMMER; SPELT). These are 'naked' or free-threshing wheats, not requiring to be parched before threshing and therefore demanding less time and trouble in preparation than emmer.

Club wheat developed from emmer in cultivation. The earliest evidence for it comes in Syria and Turkey, not long after 8000 BC. It spread very rapidly in cultivation, as far east as Baluchistan by 6000 BC, and as far west as southern France by 5500. In western Europe, emmer and einkorn arrived on the scene later than club wheat. There is little evidence of club wheat in Pharaonic Egypt. Turning to Greece, club wheat was being grown in Crete and in Thessaly soon after 6000 BC. At some time in the later prehistoric period durum wheat begins to be distinguishable as a separate variety or group of varieties.

Bread wheat is a new species that arose in cultivation. Its appearance on the scene is much later than that of club wheat: it seems to have originated in northwestern

Iran, not far south of the Caspian, in the late second millennium BC.

Wheat was the preferred staple food of the classical world; club wheat and durum wheat for flat cakes, flat breads and eventually for PASTA; bread wheat for raised bread. The two obvious alternative cereals, barley and emmer, were suitable for some types of cakes and biscuits, and made a better basis for broths and gruels than does wheat, but they were little use for bread. However, wheat did not grow well in central and southern Greece, nor in most of central Italy. As cities grew and demand for bread wheat grew, Greek cities, if they did not make do with barley, imported their wheat from north or south. Rome's wheat arrived in big grain ships, much of it from Egypt.

The three groups of varieties dealt with in this article are *Triticum aestivum* subsp. *compactum*, club wheat; *T. turgidum* conv. *durum*, durum wheat; and *T. aestivum*, bread wheat. Greek *pyros* is the term for wheat, and for the *T. turgidum* varieties in particular; the Latin equivalent is *frumentum*. *Setanias pyros*, *semidalites pyros* and *silignion* were varieties recognised in Greek nomenclature, the first approximating to club wheat, the second to durum wheat (thus *semidalis* 'durum wheat flour'), the third to bread wheat. Latin *siligo* denotes bread wheat.

Hermippus 63 Kassel; Hippocrates *R* 42–4; Theophrastus *HP* 8.4.1–5; Pliny *NH* 18.63–70, 18.85–95; Oribasius *CM* 1.2 with Grant *ad l.*; Anthimus *OC* 82.

N. Jasny, *The Wheats of Classical Antiquity* (Baltimore, 1944); Buck 1949 pp. 515–16; L.A. Moritz, *Grain-mills and Flour in Classical Antiquity* (Oxford, 1958); J.K. Evans, 'Wheat production and its social consequences in the Roman world' in *Classical Quarterly* vol. 31 (1981) pp. 428–42; C.N. Runnels and P.M. Murray, 'Milling in ancient Greece' in *Archaeology* vol. 36 (1983) pp. 62–3, 75; Zohary and Hopf 1993 pp. 39–53; Joy McCorriston, 'Wheat' in *CWHF* 2000 vol. 1 pp. 158–74.

- Greek *aleuron* and Latin *farina* mean flour, and unless otherwise specified they nearly always mean wheat flour. Diphilus of Siphnos is among authors who use the term specifically for club wheat flour. Greek *krimnon* is a coarser wheatmeal. *Krimnites* is a name for cakes made from wheatmeal, *krimmatias* for bread; while a Hippocratic text mentions *ta apo krimnou* as a drink, a gruel on the basis of wheatmeal.

  Hippocrates, *Epidemics* 7.80; Archestratus *H* 4 Brandt; Nicander *F* 68 Schneider; Athenaeus *D* 115c citing Diphilus of Siphnos.

- Latin *granea triticea* is a porridge made from durum or bread wheat, described by Cato. Evidently it was comparable to PULS, which was made from emmer. A similar porridge is described by Galen under the name *hephthoi pyroi*: he tried it after seeing poor people in Asia Minor eat it, but found it very disturbing to the stomach. Other Greek equivalents are *alphita pyrina* and *poltos*. Grant 1999 p. 40 gives a modern recipe based on Cato.

  Hippocrates *RA* 53; Cato *DA* 86; Galen *AF* 6.498–500.

- Greek *amylos*, Latin *amylum* denoted boiled wheat and its eventual product, starch. In gastronomy *amylos* was a frumenty or boiled wheat pudding, made from white *semidalis*, and attaining the consistency of a *hypostasis* or jelly. Frumenty was a confection popular in the fifth and fourth centuries BC, sometimes as dessert, sometimes providing a bed on which meat delicacies such as thrushes or hare were served. In due course *amylum* featured at CAESAR's dinner for the high priests. Oribasius provides a recipe.

  Aristophanes, *Acharnians* 1092, *Peace* 1195; Pherecrates 113 Kassel; Telecleides 34 Kassel; Philoxenus *D* e.10, e.18 Page; Euangelus 1 Kassel (*amylion*); Theocritus 10.21; Cato *DA* 87; Dioscorides *MM* 2.101; Pliny *NH* 18.76–7; Pollux *O* 6.59–72; Oribasius *CM* 4.8.

Whelk, group of spiral univalve shellfish. 'Trumpet-shell, nursling of the sea, child of purple-shell,' so the comic poet Archippus once addressed them; they are indeed similar to the PURPLE-SHELL but have tougher flesh, according to Xenocrates and Galen. Others considered them aphrodisiac, but not Galen; the gastronome Archestratus dismisses them. Big ones were found at Carteia near modern Gibraltar, says Strabo.

Mediterranean whelks (including those sometimes called horn-shell and trumpet-shell) belong to the genera *Charonia*, *Ranella* and *Cymatium*. The general names for them are Greek *strombos* and *strabelos*, Latin *turbo*.

Xenocrates *T* 105.

Thompson 1947 pp. 251, 252; Davidson 1981 p. 194.

- Greek *keryx* (which also means 'herald') may be the name of the large species called trumpet-shell or triton (*Charonia Tritonis*); at any rate it is the name of a species often used for food. A Latin equivalent is *bucinum* (which also means 'trumpet'). *Kerykes* are all the better, says Xenocrates, if cooked with nettles.

Alexis *F* 175, 281 Kassel with Arnott *ad l.*; Aristotle *HA* 528a10 with Thompson *ad l.*; Strabo 3.2.7; Dioscorides *MM* 2.4; Xenocrates *T* 72–7; Galen *AF* 6.734, *SF* 12.344, *al.*; Athenaeus 86c–92e *passim* citing Archippus 23 Kassel, Archestratus *H* 56 Brandt and Diphilus of Siphnos; Alciphron 4.13.16.

Thompson 1947 p. 113.

Wild foods, source of subsistence to hunters and gatherers. After the spread of farming in the Neolithic period, from 8000 BC in the Near East, somewhat later in the central and western Mediterranean, relatively few people relied on foods gathered from the wild for daily survival.

Even in the classical period, however, and especially in times of famine and food shortage, the contribution made by wild foods to the diet, especially that of poorer people, was significant. In the following list, spoken by an old woman in a classical Athenian comedy, at least four, perhaps as many as eight, of the foods named would be gathered from the wild:

My man is a beggar, I am a poor old woman: our daughter, our son a mere child, and this good girl here, make five in all. There are three to dinner and two to share the little barley-cake with them ... The parts and the whole of our life are bean, lupin, potherb,

turnip, black-eyed pea, grass pea, acorn, bulb, cicada, chickpea, wild pear, and the divinely roasted heritage that I love so dearly, dried fig, invention of a Phrygian fig tree.

Information on the subject is scattered. Athenaeus gathers a few additional references to subsistence foods in classical Greek literature. Dioscorides and Pliny mention in passing that various medicinal plants gathered from the wild are also used as salad vegetables, root vegetables or potherbs. Galen in *On the Properties of Foods* gives generous space to wild fruits and vegetables. Finally, as if to show that others as well as the poor gained nourishment from the wild, *Apicius* gives a recipe for dressing *herbae rusticae*, wild greens, for the table: Junkelmann 1997 p. 202 provides a modern interpretation. See also FISH; HUNTING.

Alexis *F* 167 Kassel with Arnott *ad l.*; Cato *DA* 149; Galen *AF* 6.619; *Apicius* 3.16.

Joan M. Frayn, 'Wild and cultivated plants' in *Journal of Roman Studies* vol. 65 (1975) pp. 32–9, reprinted in Joan M. Frayn, *Subsistence Farming in Roman Italy* (London, 1979) pp. 57–72; Mary Clark Forbes, 'The pursuit of wild edibles, present and past' in *Expedition* vol. 19 (1976) pp. 12–18; Mary Clark Forbes, 'Farming and foraging in prehistoric Greece: a cultural ecological perspective' in *Regional Variation in Modern Greece and Cyprus* (New York: New York Academy of Sciences, 1976) pp. 127–42.

Wine, the most prestigious of drinks in Greek and Roman culture. Was it the commonest? Our information is incomplete: its rivals for this title were WATER, POSCA and (in the Roman northern provinces) BEER.

If reasons need be given for the popularity of wine, here are some: it is easy to make (though not so easy to make well); if made well, it keeps (but proper storage is needed); like other ALCOHOLIC DRINKS, it makes the drinker happy (if used in moderation: see DRUNKENNESS); it is safe (if used in moderation), safer than fresh water because less susceptible to bacterial pollution. Moderation was promoted by the almost universal Greek and Roman habit of drinking wine mixed with water. Abstinence from wine was a serious matter in the ancient Mediterranean, where wine was probably the most easily available drink and in some ways the safest. However, abstinence from wine was sometimes enjoined, particularly on CHILDREN and WOMEN.

The sources suggest that Greeks did not customarily drink (wine or anything else) while eating the 'main course' of their MEALS, the staple and accompanying relish. At dinner, after the first tables were cleared away, a libation of unmixed wine was poured and tasted. With the second tables came more wine, mixed with water (see also WINE-MIXING). Some, including Archestratus, thought that to take wine without eating anything alongside it was uncivilised; the proper accompaniments included both savoury foods and TRAGEMATA. Among savouries Archestratus suggests a stomach (see SAUSAGE), a sow's womb, and small birds roasted. The dinner-party thus became a drinking-party or *symposion* (see SYMPOSION (1)).

Roman drinking habits were different; they took honeyed or spiced wine (see CONDITUM; MULSUM) before a dinner party (CONVIVIUM) and drank wine, usually mixed with water, with the main course. In Roman practice wine was sometimes poured through a *saccus* to strain and at the same time flavour it. In the *saccus* might be placed aromatics such as bitter almonds and anise seeds; or, in a *saccus nivarius*, SNOW. Some, however, as Plutarch shows, disapproved of any straining of wine, considering it a sophistication that reduced the wine's natural flavour and nutritional quality.

In spite of the usual practice of drinking wine mixed with water, it was recognised that unmixed wine correctly prescribed by physicians might be salutary. Wine was an important element in the prescriber's armoury, part of the regimen prescribed for many patients.

As the custom of LIBATION shows, wine was of great symbolic importance in classical thinking. It was the gift to humanity of the god DIONYSUS in Greece, of Father Liber in Rome. Among Christians, following its use in the narratives of the LAST SUPPER, it came to play a role in the EUCHARIST.

Wine is Greek *oinos*, Latin *vinum*. The word, like the substance, is of Near Eastern origin, cf. Hittite *wijana*, Armenian *gini*, Akkadian *inu*, Hebrew *yayin*, Arabic *wayn*.

Hippocrates *R* 52, *RA* 50–2, *Epidemics* 2.6.30, *al.*; Archestratus *H* 62 Brandt; Pliny *NH* 14.53–150, 23.31–51; Plutarch *QC* 6.7; Athenaeus *E* 25f–40f.

J. Bottéro, 'Getränke' ['Les boissons': the article is in French] in *RA* 1928 vol. 3 pp. 302–6; A. Aymard, 'L'interdiction de plantations de vignes en Gaule transalpine sous la République romaine' in *Mélanges Faucher* (Toulouse, 1948) pp. 27–47, reprinted in *Etudes d'histoire ancienne* (Paris, 1968) pp. 409–17; Buck 1949 p. 389; C. Seltman, *Wine in the Ancient World* (London, 1957); D. Stanislawski, 'Dionysus westward: early religion and the economic geography of wine' in *Geographical Review* vol. 65 (1975) pp. 427–41; G. Hagenow, *Aus dem Weingarten der Antike* (Mainz, 1982); Tchernia 1986; V.R. Badler, M.E. McGovern and R.H. Michel, 'Drink and be merry! Infrared spectroscopy and ancient Near Eastern wine' in *Organic Contents of Ancient Vessels* ed. W.R. Biers and P.E. McGovern (Philadelphia, 1990) pp. 25–36; Milano 1994; Brewer and others (1995 ?) pp. 55–60; B. Bouloumié, 'Le vin étrusque' in *Quaderni della Scuola di Specializzazione in Viticoltura e Enologia* vol. 7 (1983) pp. 165–88; N. Purcell, 'Wine and wealth in ancient Italy' in *Journal of Roman Studies* vol. 75 (1985) pp. 1–19; Michèle Brunet, 'Vin local et vin de cru: les exemples de Délos et de Thasos' in *La Production du vin et de l'huile en Méditerranée* ed. M.-C. Amouretti and J.-P. Brun (Athens: Ecole Française d'Athènes, 1993) pp. 201–12; Nicolas Savvonidi, 'Wine-making on the northern coast of the Black Sea' in *La Production du vin et de l'huile en Méditerranée* ed. M.-C. Amouretti and J.-P. Brun (Athens: Ecole Française d'Athènes, 1993) pp. 227–36; André Tchernia, 'Le vignoble italien du 1er siècle avant notre ère au 3e siècle de notre ère' in *La Production du vin et de l'huile en Méditerranée* ed. M.-C. Amouretti and J.-P. Brun (Athens: Ecole Française d'Athènes, 1993) pp. 283–96; Roger Brock, 'Greece:

ancient Greece' in *The Oxford Companion to Wine* ed. Jancis Robinson (Oxford: Oxford University Press, 1994) pp. 464–8; Jeremy Paterson, 'Rome, Classical' *ib.* pp. 818–20; Jean Bottéro, 'Le vin dans une civilisation de la bière: la Mésopotamie' in *In Vino Veritas* ed. Oswyn Murray and Manuela Tecuşan (London: British School at Rome, 1995) pp. 21–34; McGovern and others 1995; J. Jouanna, 'Le vin et la médecine dans la Grèce ancienne' in *Revue des études grecques* vol. 109 (1996); Yannis Hamilakis, 'Wine, oil and the dialectics of power in Bronze Age Crete: a review of the evidence' in *Oxford Journal of Archaeology* vol. 15 (1996) pp. 1–32; Alexander H. Joffe, 'Alcohol and social complexity in ancient western Asia' in *Current Anthropology* vol. 39 (1998) pp. 297–322; Patrick E. McGovern, 'Wine for eternity' in *Archaeology* vol. 51 no. 4 (1998) pp. 28–34; André Tchernia and Jean-Pierre Brun, *Le Vin romain antique* (Grenoble: Glénat, 1999); Yannis Hamilakis, 'Food technologies, technologies of the body: the social context of wine and oil production and consumption in Bronze Age Crete' in *World Archaeology* vol. 31 (1999) pp. 38–54; *El vino en la antigüedad romana (Jerez, 2–4 de Octubre, 1996)* ed. Sebastián Celestino Pérez (Madrid: Dipto. de Prehistoria y Arqueología, Facultad de Filosofía y Letras, Universidad Autonoma de Madrid, 1999); Fleming 2001.

Wine-making. The processes described under VINTAGE resulted in MUST or grape juice, the raw material for wine – and also in a by-product, the freshly pressed grape-skins and pips, known in French as *marc* (Latin *vinacei*, Greek *stemphyla*). Vigorous fermentation in the vat (see DOLIUM) would be completed about a month after the vintage, and this process also had a by-product, the solid sediment known in French as *lie* (Latin *faex*). Both of these by-products had their uses (see below).

The *dolium* now contained drinkable but yeasty and cloudy new wine (Greek *tryx, trygias*: Aristophanes, *Peace* 576; Plutarch, *Greek Questions* 19 quoting Aristotle fragments 596–7 Rose; *Geoponica* 6.13), which might be encouraged to clear by adding gypsum or other minerals (Cato *DA* 23; Pliny *NH* 14.129). At this point it was sealed and left, perhaps for four months. During this period the wine might produce a surface fungus known in

French as *fleur* (Latin *flori*, Greek *anthos*: Cato *DA* 11.2; Ovid, *Fasti* 5.269–270). In spring the mature wine was drawn off, some into skins (see CULLEUS) for distribution, some into jars (see AMPHORAE) either for distribution or for further maturing. This is the point at which the wine is said to be 'born', French *né* (Latin *natus*: Horace, *Odes* 3.21).

Once the rapid fermentation is completed, wine must be protected from contact with air or it will turn vinegary. Greek *oxines oinos* and Latin *vappa* mean, technically, wine that has begun this secondary fermentation (Pliny *NH* 14.125; Plutarch *QC* 8.9; Amouretti 1986; Tchernia 1986 p. 35). When the secondary fermentation is completed, the result is VINEGAR, a non-alcoholic product which has its own uses.

Wine is credited with a range of colours in ancient sources, all the way to Greek *melas*, meaning literally 'black'. How this range of colours related to the modern distinction between red and white wines is not an easy question. The sources strongly suggest, and evidence from iconography, archaeology and archaeochemistry confirms, that some ancient wine was red and some was white. If it were not so, Galen could not have observed, as he does, that after very long storage the colours of originally red and white wines tend eventually almost to coincide. Yet no ancient author refers to maceration of red grapes after the pressing (except to produce a cheap secondary wine), while it is through this maceration after pressing that modern red wine acquires its pigment. This suggests that a deep red pigment would have been rare in classical wines, though a light red, acquired from brief contact of the must with strongly pigmented skins, could have been common. Setting this aside, ancient perceptions of wine colour were affected by the fact that wine was normally seen in red or black earthenware vessels, and very rarely in glass. Finally, then, the term *melas* might apply to a young wine pigmented like a modern red, or to an originally white wine which, in the course of long storage, had developed through maderisation a brown colour tending towards black.

Galen notes that wines which were light and required little admixture of water would be ready for drinking young and also did not travel well: there were such wines in all regions, but you would only get to know them on the spot. The best-made wines of the heavier, slow-maturing type needed no sophistication or additions (Galen BM 6.804–5). Particular care went into the production of two special wine types, PROTROPOS and PASSUM.

Some of those that would not have turned out quite so well were, instead, destined to become the principal ingredients in flavoured and cooked wines (Palladius OA 11.14). These processes were particularly important for wines which needed stabilisation for long-distance travel – hence, in the West, the use of the term vinum Graecum, literally 'Greek wine', to mean a flavoured and cooked wine (Cato DA 105; Geoponica 7.17). To the must might be added defrutum (see MUST), various aromatics, resin or pitch, and salt or sea water. On salted wines see ANTHOSMIAS. On pitched and resinated wines see RESINATED WINE. On smoked wines see KAPNIAS. It was also possible to mix good old wines, in small quantity, with poorer new ones to give the latter a better aroma and flavour; this was the remaining use for wines of the Opimian vintage, said Pliny, since they were now too old to be truly drinkable (Pliny NH 14.55; Galen BM 6.805).

Six kinds of flavoured wines are mentioned in general literary sources: salted wine, to which the flavouring was added before fermentation; pitched, resinated and smoked wines, which picked up the flavour in the course of fermentation and maturing; and MULSUM and CONDITUM, which were flavoured afterwards. Excepting these six types, other flavoured wines are generally mentioned only in pharmaceutical and dietetic texts, suggesting that

their chief use was medicinal. Recipes are to be found in works by Dioscorides, Galen, Oribasius and several later dietary authors; also in the Byzantine farming manual Geoponica (8.1–21).

A.D. Fitton Brown, 'Black wine' in Classical Review vol. 12 (1962) pp. 192–5; B.A. Sparkes, 'Treading the grapes' in Bulletin antieke beschaving vol. 51 (1976) pp. 47–64; J.J. Rossiter, 'Wine and oil processing on Roman farms in Italy' in Phoenix vol. 35 (1981) pp. 345–61; Amouretti 1986; Tchernia 1986; André Tchernia, 'La vinification des Romains' in G. Garrier and others, Le Vin des historiens (Suze-la-Rousse: Université du Vin, 1990) pp. 65–74; Lambert-Gócs 1990; Jean-Pierre Brun, 'L'oléi-culture et la viticulture antiques en Gaule d'après les vestiges d'installations' in La Production du vin et de l'huile en Méditerranée ed. M.-C. Amouretti and J.-P. Brun (Athens: Ecole Française d'Athènes, 1993) pp. 307–41; Milano 1994; Roger Brock, 'Greece: ancient Greece' in The Oxford Companion to Wine ed. Jancis Robinson (Oxford: Oxford University Press, 1994) pp. 464–8; Jeremy Paterson, 'Rome, Classical' in The Oxford Companion to Wine ed. Jancis Robinson (Oxford: Oxford University Press, 1994) pp. 818–20; McGovern and others 1995; M.A. Murray, N. Boulton and C. Heron, 'Viticulture and wine production' in Ancient Egyptian Materials and Technology ed. P.T. Nicholson and I. Shaw (Cambridge: Cambridge University Press, 2000) pp. 577–608; Fleming 2001.

- Cheap wines, typically for farm workers, were made in several ways. Latin vinum praeliganeum was made rapidly from the early-ripe grapes for the vintagers to drink (Cato DA 23). Latin lora, lorea, Greek thamna was a secondary wine made from the maceration of newly pressed marc (Cato DA 7, 25, 57; Columella DA 12.40; Pliny NH 14.86; Geoponica 6.13). Greek deuterias was made by diluting the must and then cooking it (Dioscorides MM 5.6.15). A similar vinum familiae, fermented and flavoured with vinegar and brine, is described by Cato (DA 104). Latin vinum faecatum was made from the lees or sediment from the fermentation of wine (Cato DA 153; Pliny NH 18.318; Vindolanda Tablets 2.185).

Pliny NH 14.86.

Amouretti 1986.

Wine-mixing. In Greece, even down to medieval times, it was the received wisdom that wine must be mixed with water, and that excessive drinking of unmixed wine would lead to madness and death. Peoples of the north, such as Macedonians, Thracians and Scythians, were known to drink wine this way, and no further proof was needed. It was said by some that the Spartan king Cleomenes, and also ALEXANDER THE GREAT, had died from over-indulgence in unmixed wine.

The discussion in Greece was over the proportion of water to be added to the wine. Plutarch, in Symposium Questions, reverts to the issue several times, quoting the proverb 'Drink five or three but never four', which appears to be a recommendation for a less than half-and-half mixture, either two of wine to three of water or one of wine to two of water. Old men were supposed to like (and to need) stronger wine than others. Women, with their 'cold' and 'wet' constitutions, were also believed to need stronger wine.

Romans, like classical Greeks, customarily drank wine mixed with water, yet Roman authors show no interest in the question of the strength of the wine–water mixture. The reason, as argued by Dunbabin, is that Romans did not mix wine for a whole party in a *krater*: each drinker added water to wine as needed. The proportion was therefore a matter of individual choice, not an issue for debate. Lynceus, in early Hellenistic times, is the first author to argue the benefits of this civilised practice.

In ancient conditions the water to be added to wine should, for safety, be recently boiled and therefore warm or hot. The temptation to add cold water or SNOW was not always resisted, but these might easily be polluted and therefore dangerous to health: see also under WATER.

Homer, *Iliad* 9.203–4; Hesiod *OD* 591–6 with scholia; Herodotus 6.84, cf. Pausanias 3.4.5; Hippocrates, *Epidemics* 4.15; Lynceus *F* 6 [Athenaeus *D* 499c]; Satyrus [Athenaeus *D* 534b]; Plutarch *QC* 1.7, also 3.3 citing Aristotle *S* 108 Rose, also 3.9, also 5.4; Athenaeus *D* 423c–432a.

P. Villard, 'Le mélange et ses problèmes' in *Revue des études anciennes* vol. 90 (1988) pp. 19–33; Andrew Dalby, 'Food and sexuality in classical Greece' in *Food, Culture and History* vol. 1 (1993) pp. 165–90; Katherine M.D. Dunbabin, 'Scenes from the Roman convivium: frigida non derit, non derit calda petenti (Martial xiv.105)' in *In Vino Veritas* ed. Oswyn Murray and Manuela Tecuşan (London: British School at Rome, 1995) pp. 252–65; Dalby 1996 pp. 102–3 and note 33.

Wine regions. Wine was made in every region surrounding the Mediterranean and in many more distant localities. As now, only a minority of wine-producing regions were represented by fine wines sold under a regional name and famed under that regional name in literature. Others produced generic, usually cheaper, wines (notably the COAN WINE style). But much of the wine of the ancient world was made by farmers for their own use or for local consumption, even though some of it may have been well made and worth keeping for years.

Each category is represented differently in the sources. Fine wines are prominent in literature but relatively rare in archaeological finds. Generic wines, much less prominent in literature, are sometimes heavily represented by remains of amphorae and sometimes not, since they might also be distributed in wooden barrels or in ox skins. Local wines are often hinted at in literary sources but the economic historian can do little with these hints.

In Roman gastronomy the most general geographical distinction among wines divided the *transmarina* 'overseas' from the *cis mare nata* 'laid down on this side of the sea'. The sea in question was the strait separating southern Italy from Greece: even if they reached Rome by sea the wines of Spain and Gaul were not classed as *transmarina*. Other general classes appear occasionally in discussions of wine: in Greece, for example, we find *nesiotai* or 'island wines' from the islands of the Aegean.

Choices among Greek wines are

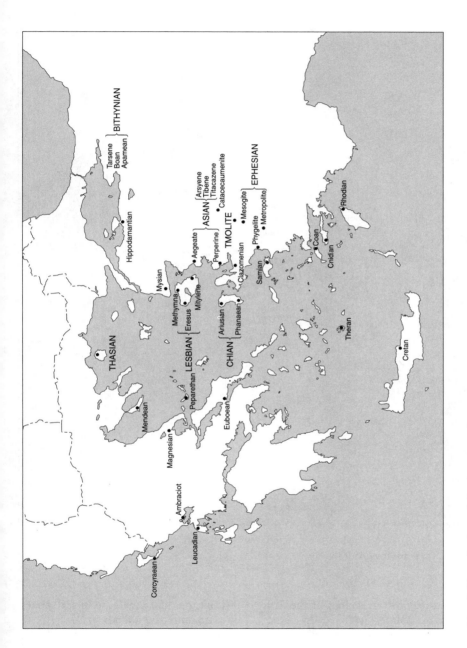

Map 3 Named wines of the Aegean region

Map 4 Named wines of Italy

suggested in informal listings of the fifth and fourth century gathered by Athenaeus. Fuller than these is a listing by APOLLODORUS, presumably to be dated around 300 BC, quoted by Pliny: this is difficult to evaluate because several names in it are otherwise unknown.

For Roman Italy, Pliny provides a ranking of the recent past – Tchernia shows that it originates around the time of Augustus – which places Caecuban first, Falernian second, Alban and Surrentine in a third class, and Mamertine fourth (Pliny *NH* 14.61–6; see Tchernia 1986 pp. 345–7 and Tchernia 1997). A long and interesting list of Italian wines in the *Epitome of Athenaeus*, confusingly attributed to 'the Galen of our author' (the real source attribution is lost), belongs, I estimate, not later than the first half of the first century AD (others have assumed that it is much later, representing the views of Galen or of Athenaeus himself). It begins with wines that age well, and indicates in each case how many years they take to reach their prime. The list contained about twelve of these wines, and about twelve others that did not benefit from long maturing. The text has suffered in transmission.

In the course of his survey just cited, and elsewhere in book 14, Pliny mentions many other Italian wine districts, most of them apparently from his own knowledge and therefore active in the mid first century AD. Another, later list of Italian wine districts could be assembled from numerous remarks by Galen on flavour, quality and medicinal uses, based on his own observations in the late second century.

Pliny *NH* book 14; Athenaeus *E* 26c–27d adducing 'Galen', also 28d–33c quoting Archestratus *H* 59–60 Brandt and others.

Tchernia 1986; André Tchernia, 'Le cercle de L. Licinius Crassus et la naissance de la hiérarchie des vins à Rome' in *Comptes-rendus de l'Académie des Inscriptions et Belles-Lettres* (1997) pp. 1247–59.

- The following wine districts have alphabetical entries: ABATE WINE; ALBAN WINE; ANCONITAN WINE; ASIAN WINES; BABBIAN WINE; BIBLINE WINE; BITHYNIAN WINE; CAECUBAN WINE; CALENE WINE; CHALYBONIAN WINE; CHIAN WINE; CNIDIAN WINE; COAN WINE; CORCYRAEAN WINE; CRETAN WINE; EGYPTIAN WINES; EPHESIAN WINES; EUBOEAN WINE; FALERNIAN WINE; FORMIAN WINE; FUNDAN WINE; GAURAN WINE; HADRIAN WINE; HIPPODAMANTIAN WINE; LESBIAN WINE; LEUCADIAN WINE; MAMERTINE WINE; MARSIAN WINE; MASSIC WINE; MENDAEAN WINE; MY-

SIAN WINE; NARBONENSIAN WINES; NEAPOLITAN WINES; PEPARETHAN WINE; PHOENICIAN WINE; PRAMNIAN WINE; PUCINE WINE; RAETIAN WINE; RAVENNA WINE; RHODIAN WINE; ROMAN WINES; SABINE WINE; SCYBELITE WINE; SETINE WINE; SIGNINE WINE; SPANISH WINES; SPOLETINE WINE; STATAN WINE; SURRENTINE WINE; TARENTINE WINE; THASIAN WINE; THURINE WINE; TIBURTINE WINE; TRIFOLINE WINE; TUSCAN WINE.

- In addition to these, the following named wines are mentioned each by a single ancient author: *Africum* (Pliny *NH* 14.81), *Akanthios* (Athenaeus *E* 30e citing Amphis, cf. Thucydides 4.88), *Alintium, s.v.l.* (Pliny *NH* 14.80), *Ambraciotes* (Pliny *NH* 14.76), *Aphrodisiaios, Aphrodisieus* (Galen, *On Therapeutic Method* 10.835, *On Compounding* 13.659), *Baliaricum* (Pliny *NH* 14.71), *Byxentinos* (Athenaeus *E* 27a), *Caesenas* (Pliny *NH* 14.67), *Cantharites* (Pliny *NH* 14.75), *Caulinum* (Pliny *NH* 14.69), *Cyprium* (Pliny *NH* 14.74), *Erboulos* (Athenaeus *E* 27c), *Erythraias* (Theophrastus *O* 48, 52), *Herakleotes* (Theophrastus *O* 52), *Ikarios* (Athenaeus *E* 30b–d), *Lucanum* (Pliny *NH* 14.69), *Maecenatianum* (Pliny *NH* 14.67), *Magnes* (Hermippus 77 Kassel), *Myconium* (Pliny *NH* 14.75), *Mysticum* (Pliny *NH* 14.75), *Naspercenites* (Pliny *NH* 14.76), *Oeneates* (Pliny *NH* 14.76), *Oreticum* (Pliny *NH* 14.76), *Oulbanos, s.v.l.* (Athenaeus *E* 26f), *Petrites* (Pliny *NH* 14.75), *Phorineum* (Pliny *NH* 14.79), *Pompeianum* (Pliny *NH* 14.70), *Pteleatikos* (Theocritus 7.65 [see Gow *ad l.*]), *Reginos* (Athenaeus *E* 26e), *Servitianum* (Pliny *NH* 14.69), *Sicyonium* (Pliny *NH* 14.74), *Skiathios* (Strattis 64 Kassel), *Telmesicum* (Pliny *NH* 14.74), *Tigrinum, s.v.l.* (Philumenus, *Latin Fragments* 114), *Trebulanum* (Pliny *NH* 14.69), *Zakynthios* (Athenaeus *E* 33b).

- Place-names that happen to be mentioned in literary sources alongside a hint that wine was made there – but without any indication that it was a fine wine or well-known – are not listed in this book. For further references on places in Italy that produced wines see Tchernia 1986 esp. pp. 322–41. On places in Anatolia see T.R.S. Broughton in Frank 1933–40 vol. 4 pp. 609–11. On places in Greece see V. Chapot in *DAGR* 1877–1919 *s.v.* 'Vinum'.

Wine storage and ageing. Modern oenologists doubt that ordinary ancient wine can have lasted well, since the conditions of manufacture and storage were far from what would now be considered ideal. However, literary evidence is that fine wines were often aged over many years. In the society imagined by Homer, wine could be kept for eleven years and be appreciated all the more for it. The same was clearly true in classical Athens, and later in classical Rome, though a host who over-emphasised the vintage invited a put-down, whether 'It's small for its age!' (attributed to Gnathaena by Lynceus) or 'It bears old age well ...' (attributed to Cicero by a speaker in Macrobius).

There is no information that classical Greeks labelled their wines with vintage years. Romans sometimes did, as is clear from surviving inscriptions on amphorae. The outstanding vintages of the late republican period in Rome are listed below from literary evidence. One might have expected Pliny and Martial to name some later vintages, fine wines still at their peak in the later first century AD: I don't know why they don't.

Homer, *Odyssey* 2.337–48, 3.388–96; Archestratus *H* 59–60 Brandt with Olson and Sens *ad l.*; Lynceus *F* 24 [Athenaeus *D* 584b]; Horace, *Odes* 3.8.11–12, 3.14.18, 3.21.1; Pliny *NH* 14.55–7, 14.94; Macrobius *S* 2.3.2; Palladius *OA* 1.18.

B. Baldwin, 'Opimian wine' in *American Journal of Philology* vol. 88 (1967) pp. 173–5.

- According to Cicero, writing in 55 BC, a Falernian wine of the Anician vintage (160 BC) might still be found, but would hardly still be drinkable.

  Cicero, *Brutus* 287.

- Pliny's benchmark for the development of the Italian wine business was the Opimian vintage, the consulship of L. Opimius in 121 BC. In that year the weather was ideal, and wines of extraordinary quality had been made. Opimian wines were served, already 160 years old, at the banquet given by the *vates* Pomponius Secundus for the emperor Caligula in AD 39. When Pliny wrote, perhaps thirty years later still, Opimian wines were no longer really drinkable, he said: they were used in tiny quantities to give age to younger wines. The 'Opimian Falernian' served by Trimalchio in Petro-

nius's *Satyricon* has been seen as a joke – intended to demonstrate Trimalchio's ignorant vulgarity – and the same might be said of the Opimian Fundan of Martial, since (apart from the question of drinkability) at the date of Opimius, according to Pliny, Italian wines were not yet labelled with their origins but only their dates. Against that, labelling is not everything: one might acquire a farm in the *ager Falernus* or *ager Fundanus* whose cellar was still stocked with its own antique wines.

  Pliny *NH* 14.55–6, 14.94; Petronius *S* 34; Martial 1.26, 3.82, 9.87, 10.49, 13.113.

- Later vintages mentioned by Horace are dated by the consulships of Tullus in 66 BC, of Manlius Torquatus in 65 BC (the year of Horace's own birth), and the second consulship of Taurus in 26 BC.

  Horace, *Odes* 3.8, 3.21; *Epodes* 13.6, *Epistles* 1.5.

Wine tasting, a necessary procedure both for commercial buyers and for the eventual consumers of wine. As a natural product of fermentation, wine is dependent both on good management and on chance for its quality; it is dependent on the grape variety and growing conditions for its flavour. Finally only the taster can judge its value, and the judgment becomes a matter of taste.

The business of wine tasting is hardly mentioned in classical Greek sources. It is hinted at by Cato in a model contract for the speculative sale of wine: the buyer is allowed a fixed period during which he is accorded facilities to visit the producing farm and taste the product. It must be assumed that he is free to cancel the purchase if the wine is of unacceptable quality. Finally Florentinus, who farmed in Bithynia in the imperial period, gives some indication of how such a tasting might be conducted.

Flavour is described in Greek and Latin in terms that do not match modern English terms one-to-one; some of them are difficult to translate at all (see also FLAVOUR). They are tied in, as modern terms are not, with dietary effects and in particular with humoral theory. If no

English equivalent is available I have chosen in this book to give a literal rendering in single quotes, thus 'austere' for *austeros*.

Several ancient sources offer judgments on a range of wines. From these judgments it becomes clear that some tasting terms are frequently correlated and some are mutually exclusive. The major sources are the *Epitome of Athenaeus*, Pliny and Galen; the last is by far the most discursive (indeed repetitive) and for this reason is the most informative on the implications of tasting terms. They make use of touchstone wines, likely to be familiar to contemporary readers, in evaluating the flavour and quality of others. The *Epitome* relies on Surrentine and Alban for this purpose, and takes Tarentine as the pattern for wines of deep southern Italy. Galen uses Falernian, Surrentine, Signine, Tiburtine more than others; he also finds parallels between Italian wines, well known in the Empire generally, and those of the province of Asia, his birthplace.

Some tasting terms are listed below. All of these are applied to good wines. It is true that some qualities tend to correlate with high price, low yield and slow maturing, while others go with modest price, high yield and rapid maturing; for all that, none of these words means 'bad' (unlike such terms as *skleros* 'rough' and *drimys* 'sour', which are only used of unpleasant wine). Satisfactory definitions require much more discussion than there is room for below, and satisfactory translations into English are in many cases not to be found.

Hippocrates *RA* 50–2; Aristotle, *On Marvellous Things Heard* 832a10, *Problems* 872b35, 934a34; Theophrastus *CP* 6.14; Cato *DA* 148; Galen *AF* 6.484–5, 6.578, *BM* 6.806–7, *On Therapeutic Method* 10.831, *DA* 14.14–15; Athenaeus *E* 26c–27d; *Geoponica* 7.7 citing Florentinus (for translation see Dalby 1996 p. 150).

W.G. Arnott, 'Toothless wine' in *Greek, Roman and Byzantine Studies* vol. 11 (1970) pp. 43–7; Lambert-Gócs 1990; Vernon L. Singleton, 'An enologist's commentary on ancient wines' in *The Origins and Ancient History of Wine* ed. Patrick E. McGovern, Stuart J. Fleming and Solomon H. Katz (London: Gordon and Breach, 1995) pp. 67–77; Dalby 2000c.

- Greek *austeros*, Latin *austerus* 'austere'. The term does not correspond to 'dry' (although often so translated): a wine can be both *glykys* and *austeros*. One of the two styles of Falernian is highly 'austere', and many other wines are so described.
- Greek *styphizon* 'astringent' describes Signine and (to a lower degree) Sabine and Surrentine.
- Greek *iskhyros*, Latin *fortis* 'strong' is a quality attributed to Falernian and Surrentine. Greek *plektikos* 'intoxicating' has a different nuance. Greek *eutonos* 'forceful' is different again: Caecuban, Fundan and Mamertine are high on this scale.
- Greek *oinodes*, Latin *vinosus*, *vinolentus* 'winy'. Surrentine is highly 'winy'; so are the austere style of Tmolite and the Ariusian wine of Chios. Falernian is 'winy'; Sabine is not. This term was also applied to the flavour of fruits, notably grapes.
- Greek *hydatodes* 'watery', *sarkodes* 'fleshy', *psapharos* 'grainy', *geodes* 'earthy', *polytrophos* 'nourishing', *trypheros* 'rich', are used to define the flavour of particular wines.
- Greek *glykys* probably corresponds closely to English 'sweet' and therefore falls between French *doux* and *sucré*. Greek *hedys* is to be distinguished absolutely from *glykys*; it can be translated 'pleasant', 'palatable' (or maybe even 'gluggable'?). Greek *glykys* is to be distinguished absolutely from *glykys*; it can be translated 'pleasant', 'palatable' (or maybe even 'gluggable'?). Nomentan, a cheap wine of Rome, is not *hedys*, but some other cheap wines, Labican and Veliternan among the table wines of Rome, Tarentine and others from the far south, are *hedys*. In non-specialist sources, by contrast, *hedys* is a very general term of approval for 'good' or 'nice' wine. Latin *dulcis* seems to fall between the two Greek terms *glykys* and *hedys* and is probably close to its etymological offspring, French *doux*. Alban wine in the first century is *praedulce*, extremely high in this taste grade.
- Greek *eugenes*, Latin *nobilis* 'noble' are terms that belong to Caecuban wine. Greek *kalos* 'fine' seems to correlate with low production; Gauran is an example.
- Greek *leptos* 'light' is a quality applied to Falernian, Ariusian and Lesbian; Nomentan lacks it. This term correlates with translucence. Greek *kouphos* 'easy' is applied especially to Sabine; unlike *leptos* this term has no correlation with the appearance of the wine. Greek *eustomakhos* 'drinkable' is applied to Calene and Tarentine. Greek *hapalos* 'simple' is applied to wines of

Tarentum and the Italian south. Latin *tenuis* 'thin' is applied to Surrentine.

- Greek *liparos* 'oily' correlates with rapid maturing. Formian is very high in this quality; Surrentine is low in it.

Womb, a favourite dish in ancient cuisine and a taste which few now share. The typical preparation was sow's womb, stuffed, boiled and presented in slices, served with a sauce of vinegar and silphium. Plutarch seems to regard the taste for womb as something new in his time (the second century AD), but this is not supported by other sources.

It is also Plutarch who explains how the *vulva eiectitia* 'miscarried womb', a special delicacy in Roman gastronomy, was obtained, by jumping on the sow when she was heavily pregnant in order to force a miscarriage. The UDDER, too, was at its best after this revolting treatment, according to Plutarch.

Womb is Greek *metra*, Latin *vulva*.

Archestratus *H* 62 Brandt with Olson and Sens *ad l.*; Lynceus *F* 5 [Athenaeus *D* 100e]; Pliny *NH* 11.210–11; Martial 13.56; Plutarch *QC* 8.9, *EC* 997a; Galen *AF* 6.680; Athenaeus *D* 96e, 101a; Anthimus *OC* 18 with Grant *ad l.*

Women, in ancient societies, were distinct from men in their social and household status. Their nutritional status, too, was probably sharply different, but, as in the case of CHILDREN, it is difficult to know for certain because literary sources are nearly all written by men: what they say of women's lifestyles is not necessarily well observed. Other sources, too, give partial rather than complete information. It seems a fair generalisation that in typical households it was a wife's duty to control household supplies and the preparation of food, giving her and other household women some independence of male opinions; on the other hand, the husband's status as head of the household, in overall command, was guaranteed by custom and law.

Ancient physicians considered that women's constitutions were typically 'cold' and 'wet': they should therefore eat rather dry foods and less-diluted wine. The last detail correlates, curiously enough, with the frequent assertion in Greek literary sources that women drank wine relatively undiluted and in excessive quantities (however, this is probably a salvo in a sex war rather than an objective statement). By contrast, Romans believed that 'in the old days' Roman women had not drunk wine at all. In the later Roman period Christian thinkers, such as Clement, came to believe that women should not drink wine.

Clement and others added that women's natural gluttony should be strictly controlled; by contrast, neither Greek nor Roman sources of earlier periods had suggested that women typically over-ate.

In classical Greek society, because of the imbalance of the sources, we know relatively little of how and when women ate. When men dined with strangers, women of the household were not normally present. At family parties and festivals men and women dined in separate circles (see Menander with Dalby's comments: but the evidence is weak). Women who dined with male strangers were regarded as, and often were, prostitutes or entertainers and in either case sexually available: in other words, mixed dining and drinking equated with promiscuity in common belief.

At Etruscan and Roman meals husbands and wives ate in public together, a practice that shocked early Greek observers. There was in general less segregation of the sexes than is apparent in classical Greek dining. Hence at Roman dinners, by contrast with Greek, there were real opportunities for courtship and seduction among people of equal social status. However, in Rome, too, separate circles might be the rule on formal occasions; in Rome, too, some women found it slightly improper to eat with their menfolk (see Petronius: once more, the evidence is weak).

Hippocrates *RS* 6, *R* 34; Menander, *Dyscolus* 568–949 (see Dalby 1996 pp. 2–6); Petronius *S* 66–7; Clement of Alexandria, *Paidagogos* 1.3, 2.1–3; Athenaeus *D* 440d–442b, also 517d–518b citing Timaeus and Theopompus; Oribasius, *Liber Incertus* 18–22 (for summary translation see Garnsey 1999 pp. 101–2).

M. Durry, 'Les femmes et le vin' in *Revue des études latines* vol. 33 (1955) pp. 108–13; *Images of Women in Antiquity* ed. A. Cameron and A. Kuhrt (London, 1983); P. Villard, 'Femmes au symposion' in *Sociabilité, pouvoir et société: actes du colloque de Rouen, 24–26 novembre 1983* ed. F. Thelamon (Rouen, 1987) pp. 106–10; Andrew Dalby, 'Food and sexuality in classical Greece' in *Food, Culture and History* vol. 1 (1993) pp. 165–90; N. Purcell, 'Women and wine in ancient Rome' in *Gender, Drink and Drugs* ed. M. McDonald (Oxford, 1994) p. 191ff.; Davidson 1997; Ann Ellis Hanson, 'Talking recipes in the gynaecological texts of the Hippocratic corpus' in *Parchments of Gender: deciphering the bodies of antiquity* ed. Maria Wyke (Oxford: Clarendon Press, 1998) pp. 71–94; K. Bradley, 'The Roman family at dinner' in *Meals in a Social Context: aspects of the communal meal in the Hellenistic and Roman world* ed. Inge Nielsen and Hanne Sigismund Nielsen (Aarhus: Aarhus University Press, 1998) pp. 36–55; Garnsey 1999 pp. 97–112, *al.* ; Wilkins 2000 pp. 36–8, 58–62.

Woodcock, game bird, never domesticated. Woodcock are treated as a wild variety of chicken by Varro and, following him, Columella. From the eater's point of view they tasted the same as partridge, said Martial.

The woodcock (*Scolopax Rusticola*) is usually *skolopax* in Greek. There is no widely used Latin name.

Aristotle *HA* 614a33 (*skolopax*), 617b23–6 (*askalopas*); Varro *RR* 3.9.2, 3.9.16 (*gallina rustica*); Columella *DA* 8.12 (*gallina rustica*); Pliny *NH* 10.111 (*rusticula*); Martial 13.76 (*rusticula*); Nemesianus, *On Bird-Catching* (*scolopax*).

Thompson 1936 p. 56.

Wormwood, source of the bitter flavouring absinthe, used in medicines and in a very popular medicinal wine (Latin *apsinthium*; Greek *apsinthatos*) for which Oribasius supplies a recipe. Ancient absinthe wine was evidently comparable to modern vermouth (modern absinthe has a much higher alcohol content).

Wormwood or absinthe (*Artemisia Absinthium*) is Greek *apsinthion*, Latin *apsinthium*.

Theophrastus *HP* 7.9.5; Dioscorides *MM* 3.23; Pliny *NH* 14.109, 21.160–2, 27.45–52; *Diocletian's Price Edict* 2.18; Oribasius *CM* 5.33; Pseudo-Apuleius, *Herbarius* 101; Anthimus *OC* 15 (*aloxinum*).

Wrasse, family of Mediterranean fish. If there is a collective Greek name for the family it is *petraia* 'rock fish', a category in which those listed below are often grouped, though not exclusively. Wrasses are smallish fish of only moderate gastronomic interest. They are light to eat, said Hippocrates; tender, said Xenocrates; healthy, said Galen.

Many are prettily coloured. It is generally supposed (because no one has yet thought of any other reason) that the parrot wrasse, Latin *scarus*, was so keenly sought after by Roman fish farmers and gourmets not because of its flavour but for its rainbow colouring, which made it at the least a conversation piece when served at dinner.

Hippocrates *R* 48; Aristotle *HA* 607b15–18; *Acraephia Price List* (*ithoulis, ikhla, kottouphos*); Xenocrates *T* 2; Aelian, *Nature of Animals* 12.28; Galen *VA* 59, *AF* 6.718–20; Athenaeus *D* 305a–d quoting Diocles of Carystus.

Thompson 1947 pp. 10, 91, 116, 128, 272, 276; Davidson 1981 pp. 109–12.

- Greek *ioulis*, said by the literary scholar Hermippus to be identical with *hyke*, is the rainbow wrasse (*Coris Iulis*). Dorion instructed that it was to be fried in a skillet or cooked in brine.

  Galen *VA* 59, *AF* 6.718–20; Athenaeus *D* 304f quoting Dorion, also 327a–c citing Hermippus of Smyrna.

- Greek *kikhle* and Latin *turdus*, homonymous in both languages with the thrush, is perhaps *Labrus viridis*. Greek *kossyphos* and Latin *merula*, homonymous with the blackbird, may be *Labrus Merula*. These two are often listed together, as by Aristotle, Ennius and Athenaeus. Both could be kept in fishponds, according to Columella, and repaid the cost of doing so. The *kossyphos* was fished using shrimp for bait.

Hippocrates *R* 48; Ennius *H* 9; Columella *DA* 8.17.8; Xenocrates *T* 2; Galen *VA* 59, *AF* 6.718–20; Oppian *H* 4.221; Athenaeus *D* 305a–d quoting Aristotle fragment 299 Rose.

- Greek *phykis*, Latin *phycis* may be *Crenilabrus Tinca*. Little is said of eating it, but it was certainly fished, with shrimp as bait.

Hippocrates *R* 48; Aristotle *HA* 591b15, 607b18–20; Asclepiades 26 Gow [*Anthologia Palatina* 5.185]; Ovid, *Halieutica* 122 [*s.v.l.*]; Apollonides 1, 12 Gow [*Anthologia Palatina* 6.105, 7.702]; Pliny *NH* 9.81, 32.150; Xenocrates *T* 2; Galen *VA* 59, *AF* 6.718–20.

Andrews 1949 pp. 12–14.

- Greek *skaros*, Latin *scarus* is the parrot wrasse (*Sparisoma cretense*). This fish 'is purple on the back and rose-red on the sides, and its tail is violet with an edge of white,' according to Thompson; you caught it with a bait of coriander seed, says Aelian. The *skaren* of the *Acraephia Price List*, if this is the same fish, is priced low. The flesh was easily digestible, according to Phylotimus, and the *skaros* was said by Archestratus to be good eating at Ephesus, Byzantium and Carthage [*s.v.l.*: the alternative reading 'Calchedon' is preferred by editors]. Not in fact found in the Black Sea or Sea of Marmara, the species was abundant in the southern Aegean (as it still is) and the middle Mediterranean as far east as Cilicia and as far west as Sicily. It was unknown in Italian waters, until, while Claudius was emperor, the Roman admiral Ti. Julius Optatus Pontianus gathered a huge number of parrot wrasses into tanks in the ships of his fleet, brought them to Italy, and released them into the sea along the coast of Latium and northern Campania. For five years thereafter Italian fishermen were instructed to return to the sea any parrot wrasses that they had inadvertently taken. The result was that a new species was introduced to the Tyrrhenian Sea, and a new flavour to the palates of Roman gourmets – according to Pliny and Macrobius, who both tell the story, and Quintilian and Petronius, who allude to it

disapprovingly. The fashion eventually passed: Martial feels able to say that only the innards of *scarus* taste good, while the rest is worthless. The stock artificially transferred to Italian waters eventually disappeared.

Aristotle *HA* 508b11, *al.*; *Acraephia Price List*; Ennius *H* 7–8; Horace, *Epodes* 2.50; Columella *DA* 8.16.1 [*s.v.l.*]; Petronius *S* 119.32; Quintilian, *Education* 5.10.21; Pliny *NH* 9.62–3, 32.151; Suetonius, *Vitellius* 13; Martial 13.84; Galen *VA* 59, *AF* 6.718; Oppian *H* 4.40–126; Aelian, *Nature of Animals* 12.42; Aulus Gellius 6.16 citing Varro (see translation at LOCAL SPECIALITIES); Athenaeus *D* 319e–320c quoting Archestratus *H* 13, 41 Brandt (see Olson and Sens *ad l.*); Macrobius *S* 3.16.10.

Thompson 1947 pp. 238–41; Higginbotham 1997 pp. 51–2.

- Greek *alphestes* is possibly an alternate name for one of the species already listed. The *alphestai* were wrasses, and were yellow. They were said to follow one another about like homosexual lovers, a habit that gave rise to numerous derogatory nicknames for the fish, and, in return, to the proverbial description for homosexuals, *katapygoteros alphestân* 'more arse-chasing than a wrasse', quoted indirectly by Athenaeus from the satirist Sophron. Unlike the five terms listed above, *alphestes* was no longer in everyday use in Roman times.

Acraephia Price List; Pliny *NH* 32.146; Athenaeus *D* 281e–282a.

Wreaths were an essential part of ancient Greek and Roman festivity, ceremony and sacrifice. Their importance was not only, and probably not mainly, visual. Wreaths were chosen and used for their aroma. Careful and very detailed rules were stated for their choice at dinners and drinking parties, a choice that would depend on the circumstances and on the wearer's health and constitution.

Archestratus *H* 62 Brandt with Olson and Sens *ad l.*; Pliny *NH* 20.1–69; Plutarch *QC* 3.1; Athenaeus *D* 668f–686c.

X

Xenia *see* APOPHORETA

Xenocrates, dietary author. Xenocrates, born at Aphrodisias in Caria, probably wrote in the late first century AD. Clement of Alexandria quotes him for the view that pork is an inappropriate food; Galen reproduces his version of the famous *Mithridateion* (see under MITHRIDATES) and criticises him for reporting therapeutic effects from eating human body parts (see CANNIBALISM). Xenocrates's work *On Food from the Waters*, apparently a part of a longer book *On Animal Foods*, is reproduced or summarised at length by Oribasius. The section on shellfish is particularly detailed and useful.

Clement of Alexandria, *Stromateis* 7.6.32; Galen *SF* 12.248–51, *DA* 14.164, *al.*

Xenocrates T: *On Food from the Waters*. Critical text: in Raeder's edition of *Oribasius, Medical Collections* book 2 section 58. Text with commentary in modern Greek: *Xenokratous kai Galenou peri tis apo ton enidrion trofis* ed. Adamantios Korais (Paris: Eberhard, 1814). Reprint with introduction by G.A. Christodoulou (Chios, 1998).

Xenophon, Athenian soldier and writer on history, philosophy and other topics. His *Anabasis*, a memoir of the Greek mercenary troops who fought with the Persian usurper Cyrus and were left to return home as best they could, is important as a depiction of the social behaviour and food behaviour of Greeks under arms. His *Symposium* is one of several works aiming to show Socrates at work; as such it is an instructive foil to Plato's *Symposium*, which describes a quite different occasion. It gives a convincing picture of classical Athenian drinking parties. Both texts are available in many editions and translations.

Andrew Dalby, 'Greeks abroad: social organization and food among the Ten Thousand' in *Journal of Hellenic Studies* vol. 112 (1992) pp. 16–30; Suzanne Amigues, 'Végétation et cultures du Proche-Orient dans l'Anabase' in *Pallas* no. 43 (1995) pp. 61–78.

Z

General bibliography

Encyclopaedias

CWHF 2000: *The Cambridge World History of Food* ed. Kenneth F. Kiple and Kriemhild Coneè Ornelas (Cambridge: Cambridge University Press, 2000).

DAGR 1877–1919: *Dictionnaire des antiquités grecques et romaines* ed. C. Daremberg and E. Saglio (Paris, 1877–1919).

KP 1975: *Der kleine Pauly* ed. Konrat Ziegler and Walther Sontheimer (Munich: Artemis, 1975).

LA 1975–92: *Lexikon der Ägyptologie* ed. Wolfgang Helck and Eberhard Otto (Wiesbaden: Harrassowitz, 1975–92).

OCD 1996: *Oxford Classical Dictionary* (Oxford: Oxford University Press, 1996), 3rd edn by Simon Hornblower and Anthony Spawforth.

RA 1928– : *Reallexikon der Assyriologie* ed. Erich Ebeling, Bruno Meissner [and others] (Berlin: De Gruyter, 1928–).

RAC 1950– : *Reallexikon für Antike und Christentum* ed. T. Klauser (Stuttgart, 1950–).

RE 1893–1972: *Paulys Real-Enzyklopädie der classischen Altertumswissenschaft* (Stuttgart: Metzler, 1893–1972), new edn by Georg Wissowa, W. Kroll and Konrat Ziegler.

RGA 1973– : *Reallexikon der germanischen Altertumskunde* ed. Herbert Jankuhn, Hans Kuhn, Kurt Ranke and Reinhard Wenskus (Berlin: De Gruyter, 1968–), 2nd edn.

Series and periodicals

BT: *Bibliotheca Teubneriana*, formerly published by Teubner, Leipzig and Stuttgart; now by Saur, Munich.

CIL: *Corpus inscriptionum Latinarum* (Berlin, 1863–).

CUF: *Collection des universités de France*, known as 'Budé series', published by Les Belles Lettres, Paris.

Food and Foodways (London: Harwood Publishers, 1986–).

Gastronomica (Berkeley, Ca.: University of California Press, 2000–).

LCL: *Loeb Classical Library*, formerly published by Heinemann, London, and Putnam, New York; now by Harvard University Press, Cambridge, Mass.

Petits Propos culinaires (London, Totnes, Devon: Prospect Books, 1979–).

Collected editions of fragmentary authors

Blockley: *The Fragmentary Classicising Historians of the Later Roman Empire* ed. and tr. R.C. Blockley (Liverpool: Francis Cairns, 1981–3).

Davies: *Poetarum melicorum Graecorum fragmenta* post D.L. Page ed. Malcolm Davies (Oxford: Clarendon Press, 1991–). [Generally retains the fragment numbering of Page's edition.]

Diehl: *Anthologia lyrica* ed. E. Diehl (Leipzig: Teubner, 1923–52), 6 parts, 3rd edn of parts 1–3 under title *Anthologia lyrica graeca*.

Gow: *The Greek Anthology: Hellenistic epigrams* ed. A.S.F. Gow and D.L. Page (Cambridge: Cambridge University Press, 1965).

Jacoby: *F. Gr. Hist.: die Fragmente der griechischen Historiker* ed. F. Jacoby (Berlin, 1923–58).

Kaibel: *Comicorum Graecorum fragmenta* ed. G. Kaibel, vol. 1 pt 1: *Doriensium comoedia, mimi, phlyaces* (Berlin, 1899).

Kassel: *PCG: Poetae comici Graeci* ed. R. Kassel and C. Austin (Berlin: De Gruyter, 1983–).

Lobel: *Poetarum Lesbiorum fragmenta* ed. E. Lobel and D.L. Page (Oxford: Clarendon Press, 1968), 2nd edn.

Müller: *Fragmenta historicorum Graecorum* ed. C. Müllerus (Paris: Didot, 1841–83).

Nauck: *Tragicorum Graecorum fragmenta* ed. A. Nauck (Leipzig, 1889), 2nd edn.

Page: *Poetae melici Graeci* ed. D.L. Page (Oxford: Clarendon Press, 1962).

PG: *Patrologia Graecolatina* (Paris: J.-P. Migne).

Powell: *Collectanea Alexandrina* ed. J.U. Powell (Oxford: Clarendon Press, 1925).

Snell, Radt: *Tragicorum Graecorum fragmenta* ed. B. Snell, S. Radt and R. Kannicht (Göttingen: Vandenhoeck & Ruprecht, 1977–86). Vol. 1 (2nd edn): Minor poets, by B. Snell, revised by R. Kannicht (1986). Vol. 2: Minor poets, by R. Kannicht (1981). Vol. 3: Aeschylus, by S. Radt (1985). Vol. 4: Sophocles, by S. Radt (1977).

West: *Iambi et elegi Graeci* ed. M.L. West (Oxford: Clarendon Press, 1989–92), 2nd edn.

Works frequently cited and widely relevant

Amouretti, M.-C. (1986) *Le Pain et l'huile dans la Grèce antique: de l'araire au moulin* (Paris: Les Belles Lettres) (*Annales littéraires de l'Université de Besançon*, 328; Centre de Recherche d'Histoire Ancienne, 67).

Amouretti, M.-C. and Brun, J.-P. (eds) (1993) *La Production du vin et de l'huile en Méditerranée* (Athens: Ecole Française d'Athènes) (*Bulletin de correspondance hellénique*, supplement 26).

André, Jacques (1967) *Les Noms d'oiseaux en latin* (Paris: Klincksieck).

—— (1981) *L'Alimentation et la cuisine à Rome* (Paris: Les Belles Lettres), 2nd edn.

—— (1985) *Les Noms de plantes dans la Rome antique* (Paris).

Andrews, A.C. (1948) 'Greek and Latin mouse-fishes and pig-fishes' in *Transactions and Proceedings of the American Philological Association* vol. 79 pp. 232–53.

—— (1949) 'The codfishes of the Greeks and Romans' in *Journal of the Washington Academy of Sciences* vol. 39 pp. 1–20.

Arnott, W.G. (1996) *Alexis: the fragments. A commentary* (Cambridge: Cambridge University Press).

Berthiaume, G. (1982) *Les rôles du mágeiros: étude sur la boucherie, la cuisine et le sacrifice dans la Grèce ancienne* (Leiden: Brill).

Bilabel, F. (1921) 'Kochbücher' in *Paulys Real-Enzyklopädie der classischen Altertumswissenschaft* (Stuttgart: Metzler, 1893–1972). New edn by Georg Wissowa, W. Kroll and Konrat Ziegler.

Bökönyi, S. (1974) *History of Domestic Mammals in Central and Eastern Europe* (Budapest: Akadémiai Kiadó).

Braund, David and Wilkins, John (eds) (2000) *Athenaeus and his World: reading Greek culture in the Roman Empire* (Exeter: University of Exeter Press).

Brewer, Douglas, Redford, Donald B. and Redford, Susan (1995?) *Domestic Plants and Animals: the Egyptian origins* (Warminster: Aris and Phillips).

Brothwell, Don and Brothwell, Patricia (1969) *Food in Antiquity: a survey of the diet of early peoples* (London: Thames and Hudson).

Buck, Carl Darling (1949) *A Dictionary of Selected Synonyms in the Principal Indo-European Languages* (Chicago: University of Chicago Press).

Carcopino, Jérôme (1940) *Daily Life in Ancient Rome* (New Haven: Yale University Press). English translation by E.O. Lorimer.

Casson, Lionel (ed.) (1989) *The Periplus of the Erythraean Sea* (Princeton: Princeton University Press).

Corbier, Mireille (1989) 'The ambiguous status of meat in ancient Rome' in *Food and Foodways* vol. 3 (1988–9) pp. 223–64.

—— (1996) 'La fève et la murène: hiérarchies sociales des nourritures à Rome' in *Histoire de l'alimentation* ed. Jean-Louis Flandrin and Massimo Montanari (Paris) pp. 215–36.

Curtis, Robert I. (ed.) (1989) *Studia pompeiana et classica in honor of Wilhelmina F. Jashemski* (New Rochelle: Caratzas).

—— (2001) *Ancient Food Technology* (Leiden: Brill).

Dalby, Andrew (1995) 'Archestratos: where and when?' in *Food in Antiquity* ed. John Wilkins, David Harvey and Mike Dobson (Exeter: Exeter University Press) pp. 400–12.

—— (1996) *Siren Feasts: a history of food and gastronomy in Greece* (London: Routledge).

—— (2000a) *Empire of Pleasures: luxury and indulgence in the Roman Empire* (London: Routledge).

—— (2000b) *Dangerous Tastes: the story of spices* (London: British Museum Press).

—— (2000c) 'Topikos oinos: the named wines of Old Comedy' in *The Rivals of Aristophanes: studies in Athenian Old Comedy* ed. David Harvey and John Wilkins (London: Duckworth) pp. 397–405.

—— (2001) 'Dining with the Caesars' in *Food and the Memory: papers of the Oxford Symposium on Food and Cookery 2000* ed. Harlan Walker (Totnes: Prospect Books) pp. 62–88.

Dalby, Andrew and Grainger, Sally (1996) *The Classical Cookbook* (London: British Museum Press).

Darby, William J., Ghalioungui, Paul and Grivetti, Louis (1977) *Food: the gift of Osiris* (London: Academic Press), 2 vols.

D'Arms, John H. (1970) *Romans on the Bay of Naples* (Cambridge: Harvard University Press).

Davidson, Alan (1979) *North Atlantic Seafood* (London: Macmillan).

—— (1981) *Mediterranean Seafood* (Harmondsworth: Penguin), 2nd edn.

—— (1999) *The Oxford Companion to Food* (Oxford: Oxford University Press).

Davidson, James (1997) *Courtesans and Fishcakes: the consuming passions of classical Athens* (London: Harper Collins).

Dosi, Antonietta and Schnell, François (1984) *A tavola con i Romani antichi* (Rome: Quasar).

Fenton, A. and Owen, T.M. (eds) (1981) *Food in Perspective. Proceedings of the Third International Conference on Ethnological Food Research, Cardiff, 1977* (Edinburgh).

Flandrin, Jean-Louis and Montanari, Massimo (eds) (1996) *Histoire de l'alimentation* (Paris). Abridged English translation, *Food: a culinary history from antiquity to the present* tr. Clarissa Botsford and others, ed. Albert Sonnenfeld (New York: Columbia University Press, 1999).

Fleming, Stuart J. (2001) *Vinum: the story of Roman wine* (Glen Mills, Pa.: Art Flair).

Flower, Barbara and Rosenbaum, Elisabeth (tr.) (1961) *Apicius, The Roman Cookery Book* (London: Harrap).

Forbes, R.J. (1964–72) *Studies in Ancient Technology* (Leiden: Brill), 2nd edn, 9 vols.

Fournier, Dominique and D'Onofrio, Salvatore (eds) (1991) *Le Ferment divin* (Paris: Maison des Sciences de l'Homme).

Frank, Tenney (ed.) (1933–40) *An Economic Survey of Ancient Rome* (Baltimore: Johns Hopkins University Press), 6 vols.

Gamkrelidze, T.V. and Ivanov, V.V. (1995) *Indo-European and the Indo-Europeans: a reconstruction and historical analysis of a proto-language and a proto-culture.* English version compiled by Richard A. Rhodes, translated by Johanna Nichols (Berlin: Mouton De Gruyter), 2 vols.

Garnsey, Peter (1988) *Famine and Food Supply in the Graeco-Roman World* (Cambridge: Cambridge University Press).

—— (1998) *Cities, Peasants and Food in Classical Antiquity: essays in social and economic history* ed. W. Scheidel (Cambridge, 1998).

—— (1999) *Food and Society in Classical Antiquity* (Cambridge: Cambridge University Press).

Garnsey, Peter and Saller, R. (1987) *The Roman Empire: economy, society and culture* (London).

Garnsey, Peter and Whittaker, C.R. (eds) (1983) *Trade and Famine in Classical Antiquity* (Cambridge).

Garrier, G. and others (1990) *Le Vin des historiens* (Suze-la-Rousse: Université du Vin).

Germer, R. (1985) *Flora des pharaonischen Ägypten* (Mainz: Philipp von Zabern).

Gowers, Emily (1993) *The Loaded Table* (Oxford: Oxford University Press).

Grant, Mark (1997) *Dieting for an Emperor: a translation of books 1 and 4 of Oribasius' Medical Compilations with an introduction and commentary* (Leiden: Brill).

—— (1999) *Roman Cookery: ancient recipes for modern kitchens* (London: Serif).

Griffin, Jasper (1985) *Latin Poets and Roman Life* (London: Duckworth).

Grimm, Veronika E. (1996) *From Feasting to Fasting: the evolution of a sin* (London: Routledge).

Henderson, Jeffrey (1991) *The Maculate Muse* (New York: Oxford University Press), 2nd edn.

Hepper, F. Nigel (1987) 'Trees and shrubs yielding gums and resins in the ancient Near East' in *Bulletin on Sumerian Agriculture* vol. 3 pp. 107–14.

—— (1990) *Pharaoh's Flowers* (London: HMSO).

Higginbotham, James (1997) *Piscinae: artificial fishponds in Roman Italy* (Chapel Hill: University of North Carolina Press).

Jacob, Irene and Jacob, Walter (eds) (1993) *The Healing Past: pharmaceuticals in the biblical and rabbinic world* (Leiden: Brill) (*Studies in Ancient Medicine*, 7).

Jashemski, Wilhelmina Feemster (1979–93) *The Gardens of Pompeii, Herculaneum and the Villas Destroyed by Vesuvius* (New Rochelle: Caratzas), 2 vols.

—— (1999) *A Pompeiian Herbal* (Austin: University of Texas Press).

Junkelmann, Marcus (1997) *Panis militaris: die Ernährung des römischen Soldaten oder der Grundstoff der Macht* (Mainz: Philipp von Zabern).

Krauss, Samuel (1910–12) *Talmudische Archäologie* (Leipzig: Fock), 3 vols.

Lambert-Gócs, Miles (1990) *The Wines of Greece* (London: Faber).

Lambraki, Mirsini (1997) *Ta khorta* (Khania: Trokhalia). An English edition is said to be available.

Laufer, Berthold (1919) *Sino-Iranica: Chinese contributions to the history of civilization in ancient Iran with special reference to the history of cultivated plants and products* (Chicago: Field Museum of Natural History) (*Field Museum of Natural History publication*, 201).

Leon, E.F. (1943) 'Cato's cakes' in *Classical Journal* vol. 38 pp. 213–21.

Liddell, Henry George and Scott, Robert (1925–40) *A Greek–English Lexicon* (Oxford: Clarendon Press), 9th edn by Henry Stuart Jones and Roderick McKenzie.

Longo, Oddone and Scarpi, P. (eds) (1989) *Homo edens: regime, rite e pratiche dell' alimentazione nella civiltà del Mediterraneo* (Milan: Diapress).

—— (1995) *Homo edens IV: regimi, miti e pratiche dell' alimentazione nella civiltà del Mediterraneo. Atti del Convegno 'Nel nome de pane', Bolzano, giugno 1993* (Bolzano).

Luce, Jean-Marc (ed.) (2000) *Paysage et alimentation dans le monde grec* (Toulouse: Presses Universitaires du Mirail) (*Pallas*, 52).

McGovern, Patrick, Fleming, Stuart J. and Katz, Solomon H. (eds) (1995) *The Origins and Ancient History of Wine* (London: Gordon and Breach).

Milano, Lucio (ed.) (1994) *Drinking in Ancient Societies: history and culture of drinks in the ancient Near East. Papers of a symposium held in Rome, May 17–19, 1990* (Padova: Sargon).

Miller, J. Innes (1969) *The Spice Trade of the Roman Empire* (Oxford: Clarendon Press). Note the reviews by E.W. Gray in *Journal of Roman Studies* vol. 60 (1970) pp. 322–4; by J. Rougé in *Latomus* vol. 29 (1970) pp. 536–40; by P. Grimal in *Revue des études latines* vol. 47 (1969) pp. 665–7.

Murray, Oswyn (ed.) (1990) *Sympotica: a symposium on the symposion* (Oxford: Oxford University Press).

Murray, Oswyn and Tecuşan, Manuela (eds) (1995) *In Vino Veritas* (London: British School at Rome).

Nielsen, Inge and Nielsen, Hanne Sigismund (eds) (1998) *Meals in a Social Context:*

aspects of the communal meal in the Hellenistic and Roman world (Aarhus: Aarhus University Press).

Olson, S. Douglas and Sens, Alexander (2000) *Archestratos of Gela; Greek culture and cuisine in the fourth century BCE: text, translation and commentary* (Oxford: Oxford University Press).

Pritchard, James B. (1969) *Ancient Near Eastern Texts Relating to the Old Testament* (Princeton: Princeton University Press), 3rd edn.

Renfrew, Jane M. (1973) *Palaeoethnobotany: the prehistoric food plants of the Near East and Europe* (London: Methuen).

—— (ed.) (1991) *New Light on Early Farming: recent developments in palaeoethnobotany* (Edinburgh: Edinburgh University Press).

Ricotti, Eugenia Salza Prina (1983) *L'arte del convito nella Roma antica* (Rome: L'Erma di Bretschneider).

Rotberg, R.I. and Rabb, T.K. (eds) (1983) *Hunger and History: the impact of changing food production and consumption patterns on society* (Cambridge: Cambridge University Press).

Sancisi-Weerdenburg, Heleen (1995) 'Persian food: stereotypes and political identity' in *Food in Antiquity* ed. John Wilkins, David Harvey and Mike Dobson (Exeter: Exeter University Press) pp. 286–302.

Scarborough, John (1985) *Pharmacy's Ancient Heritage: Theophrastus, Nicander and Dioscorides* (Lexington).

Scarpi, P. (ed.) (1991) *Homo edens II. Storie del vino* (Milan).

Schäfer, Alfred (1997) *Unterhaltung beim griechischen Symposion: Darbietung, Spiele und Wettkämpfe von homerischer bis in spätklassische Zeit* (Mainz: Philipp von Zabern).

Simoons, Frederick J. (1994) *Eat Not This Flesh: food avoidances in the Old World* (Madison: University of Wisconsin Press), 2nd edn.

—— (1998) *Plants of Life, Plants of Death* (Madison: University of Wisconsin Press).

Slater, William J. (ed.) (1991) *Dining in a Classical Context* (Ann Arbor: University of Michigan Press). Note the review by E. Steinholkeskamp in *Gnomon* vol. 66 (1994) pp. 423–31.

Soler, María José García (2001) *El arte de comer en la antigua Grecia* (Madrid: Biblioteca Nueva).

Sparkes, Brian (1962–5) 'The Greek kitchen' in *Journal of Hellenic Studies* vol. 82 (1962) pp. 121–37 and plates IV–VIII, with 'The Greek kitchen: addenda' in *Journal of Hellenic Studies* vol. 85 (1965) pp. 162–3 and plates XXIX–XXX.

Tannahill, Reay (1988) *Food in History* (Harmondsworth: Penguin), 2nd edn.

Tchernia, André (1986) *Le Vin de l'Italie romaine: essai d'histoire économique d'après les amphores* (Rome: Ecole Française de Rome).

Thompson, D'Arcy W. (1936) *A Glossary of Greek Birds* (London: Oxford University Press), 2nd edn.

—— (1947) *A Glossary of Greek Fishes* (London: Oxford University Press).

Toynbee, Jocelyn M.C. (1996) *Animals in Roman Life and Art* (Baltimore: Johns Hopkins University Press).

White, K.D. (1970) *Roman Farming* (London: Thames and Hudson).

Wilkins, John (2000) *The Boastful Chef: the discourse of food in ancient Greek comedy* (Oxford: Oxford University Press).

Wilkins, John, Harvey, David and Dobson, Mike (eds) (1995) *Food in Antiquity* (Exeter: Exeter University Press).

Yule, Henry and Burnell, A.C. (1903) *Hobson-jobson: a glossary of colloquial Anglo-Indian words and phrases* (London: Murray), 2nd edn.

Zohary, Daniel and Hopf, Maria (1993) *Domestication of Plants in the Old World: the origin and spread of cultivated plants in West Asia, Europe and the Nile Valley* (Oxford: Oxford University Press), 2nd edn.

Zohary, Michael (1982) *Plants of the Bible* (Cambridge: Cambridge University Press).

INDEX OF SCIENTIFIC NAMES

Authorities are cited in the preferred styles for zoological names (original author, unabridged, with date) and botanical names (authors of original and revised name, abridged in standard form).

LATIN INDEX

GREEK INDEX